D0850601

AENEAS TACTICUS
ASCLEPIODOTUS
ONASANDER

LCL 156

AENEAS TACTICUS
ASCLEPIODOTUS
ONASANDER

WITH AN ENGLISH TRANSLATION

BY MEMBERS OF

THE ILLINOIS GREEK CLUB

HARVARD UNIVERSITY PRESS

CAMBRIDGE, MASSACHUSETTS

LONDON, ENGLAND

First published 1928

LOEB CLASSICAL LIBRARY® is a registered trademark
of the President and Fellows of Harvard College

ISBN 978-0-674-99172-9

*Printed on acid-free paper and bound by
The Maple-Vail Book Manufacturing Group*

CONTENTS

AENEAS TACTICUS

PREFACE

EARLY in 1917, *Marte iam diu furente*, the attention of the Faculty Greek Club of the University of Illinois was turned toward the art of war, in which, as in so many other fields of scientific and humanistic interest, the Greeks achieved results of more than transitory value. The military manual of Aeneas, styled the Tactician, suggested itself as a monograph in this field well suited for discussion by such a club, and portions of this treatise were accordingly translated by the following members : J. C. Austin, E. C. Baldwin, H. J. Barton, L. Bloomfield, H. V. Canter, M. J. Curl, F. K. W. Drury, S. Engel, H. S. V. Jones, J. W. McKinley, C. M. Moss, W. A. Oldfather, A. F. Pauli, A. S. Pease, R. P. Robinson, C. A. Williams, and J. Zeitlin. Of the versions thus produced a number were discussed and criticized at a series of meetings, and all were subsequently revised and edited by Messrs. W. A. Oldfather, A. S. Pease, C. M. Moss, and H. V. Canter. An introduction, critical apparatus, notes, and index have been added to make the work conform to the general plan of the Loeb Classical Library.[1]

[1] The introduction, the preparation of the text, and the notes have been the work of W. A. Oldfather ; the text and translation of the excerpts from Julius Africanus have been made jointly by Messrs. Oldfather and Pease.

INTRODUCTION

OF Aeneas, commonly known, since Casaubon's time, as the Tactician, little is recorded, and not much more may be with a fair degree of probability inferred from the treatise before us. Mr. T. Hudson Williams very properly insists upon the scantiness of our direct evidence that Aeneas was actually the name of the author of this military handbook, and upon the necessary uncertainty that attaches to all arguments based upon conjecture only. But after all, the evidence, though not amounting to demonstration, has unusual cogency, and little of our knowledge regarding the minor authors of antiquity can be regarded as resting upon a firmer basis of attestation and inference. The case for Aeneas may be put thus.

It is true that the MS. superscription runs Αἰλιανοῦ τακτικὸν ὑπόμνημα περὶ τοῦ πῶς χρὴ πολιορκουμένους ἀντέχειν, 'Aelian's tactical treatise on how men in a state of siege should resist'; but the ascription to Aelian is absurd, partly because of the utmost difference in style between this tractate and Aelian's other work, but more especially because it contains not a single historical reference to an event that occurred within four centuries of Aelian's time.

Again, τακτικὸν ὑπόμνημα is an impossible designation for the work of Aeneas, if for no other reason, because it contradicts his own definition of tactics, quoted by Aelian iii. 4, as ἐπιστήμην πολεμικῶν κινήσεων 'science of military movements,' of which there is hardly a trace in the present work. The length of the remainder of the title, furthermore, when compared with the brief designations by which the author refers to his other works, shows clearly that this latter part does not belong to the original superscription. If we bear in mind, finally, that in the sole authoritative MS.[1] this treatise follows the work of Aelian, the conclusion is unavoidable that the superscription derives from a misapplied subscription to Aelian, to whose treatise the words τακτικὸν ὑπόμνημα exactly apply. The subscription to our work runs Aἰνείου πολιορκητικά· ἢ Aἰλιανοῦ καθὼς ἡ ἀρχή (followed by an erasure of thirteen letters), ' Aeneas on Siege Operations ; or Aelian as at the beginning.' Here we clearly have to do with a bit of genuine tradition, followed by a corrective note intended to bring the conjectural superscription and the traditional subscription into harmony. Direct MS. evidence, accordingly, where it possesses any substantial authority, assigns our treatise to an Aeneas. Whether, however, πολιορκητικά was the author's own designation for his book may be doubted, partly because, in referring to his other works, he generally uses an adjective with the word βίβλος, and partly because this manual contains almost no advice about how to besiege a town,

---

[1] And so probably in the collection of military writers dating from early Byzantine times, for M seems to have been copied from an uncial MS.

which is the only meaning of πολιορκέω and related words.

Accepting the unimpeachable MS. testimony to authorship by Aeneas, we may now compare the internal evidence offered by the work itself with what is known from other sources about the military writer Aeneas.

Beginning with the latest and the least specific, Johannes Lydus, De magistratibus, i. 47, in the sixth century of our era,[1] mentions along with five others an Aeneas as an authority upon πολιορκητικά or 'Siege Operations.' Aelian, Tactica, i. 2, in the second century after Christ, mentions Aeneas as the first military writer (after Homer, to be sure) who composed στρατηγικὰ βιβλία ἱκανά, 'a considerable number of military manuals,' which Cineas the Thessalian (an associate of Pyrrhus of Epirus) epitomized ; and in iii. 4, Aelian quotes his definition of tactics as ἐπιστήμην . . . πολεμικῶν κινήσεων, 'the science of military movements.' Polybius, x. 44, inveighs in a characteristic vein against the recommendation of an Aeneas, ὁ τὰ περὶ στρατηγικῶν ὑπομνήματα συντεταγμένος, 'who composed treatises on military science,' with regard to signal fires.[2]

The conclusion from this evidence is that an Aeneas, living before the time of King Pyrrhus, composed a number of treatises on military science, among them works on tactics and siege operations, and discussed signal fires. All this agrees perfectly with the internal evidence of the treatise itself,

---

[1] For some reason omitted by Schöne in his testimonia.

[2] The brief note in the lexicon of Suidas (tenth century), under the lemma Αἰνείας, seems to be taken entire from Polybius.

which deals with siege operations, particularly from
the side of the defence, and which several times
mentions signal fires, the very passage of which
Polybius speaks being cited from another work in
ch. 7. 4. Furthermore, the author frequently refers
to other writings of his on military science, and the
first sentence of a book on naval operations is contained in the MS. at the end of the present treatise,
so that, even without the evidence of the subscription, there can hardly be a justifiable doubt that
ours is the work of the Aeneas whom Polybius,
Aelian, and Johannes Lydus mention. The argu-
ment derives additional support from Fr. Haase's
happy emendation in 31. 18, where the author, as
would be not unnatural, chooses his own name as a
sample with which to illustrate a system of crypto-
gramic writing. To be sure, the account of the
operation breaks off after spelling out αινε, but one
can hardly avoid the conclusion that Αἰνείαν or
Αἰνέαν (for the accusative is required) originally
stood in the text. Mr. Williams, indeed, pronounces
the verdict ' not proven,' but he seems to demand
a completeness of demonstration which can seldom
be secured in things philological, and with this single
exception Haase's emendation has been generally
approved.

Aeneas gives abundant evidence of first - hand
acquaintance with his subject and an experience
in military operations which, though extensive, is
almost wholly confined to the geographical limits of
the Peloponnesus and the western coast of Asia
Minor (with the adjacent islands). He seems, accordingly, to have served in these two fields, and as
few Asiatic Greeks were drawn to the Peloponnesus,

while thousands of Peloponnesians, and especially Arcadians, served as *condottieri* in the East, it can hardly be doubted that Aeneas was a Peloponnesian who had seen service in the Aegean and in Asia Minor.[1]

Regarding the period in which Aeneas wrote, it has been observed that more than half his historical examples fall within the years 400–360 B.C., and that their number becomes greater as one approaches the latter date. Thus incidents are cited for 397, 382, 379, 370, 369, 368, 363, 362, 361, and close with the capture of Ilium by Charidemus in 360. On the other hand the book was written before 346, because it represents the Locrians as still sending maidens to Ilium, a custom which Timaeus[2] tells us ended at that time. We can, therefore, with a high degree of certainty place the composition in the years just following 360, because neither Philip of Macedon nor the stirring events of the Phocian war (356–346) are mentioned. Indeed it is extremely probable that Aeneas composed his manual in 357–356. Alfred von Gutschmid has pointed out Aeneas's habit of illustrating his point by the most recent events, and with that in mind the two specimens of secret messages Διονύσιος καλός· Ἡρακλείδας ἡκέτω (as given by M). 'Dionysius is fair; let Heracleides come,' in 31. 31, can hardly refer to anything but the war between Dionysius II of Syracuse and Dio and Heracleides operating from the Peloponnesus in

---

[1] The utter neglect of Athens as well as the employment of occasional non-Attic idiom and vocabulary make it almost certain that he was not an Athenian.

[2] Preserved in the scholia to Lycophron v. 1144 (Scheer's edition).

5

AENEAS TACTICUS

357.[1] Heracleides, it may be noted, remained behind for a while and came on after Dio with a few warships and a considerable force of men. Now the use of the singular form τόδε in the text and the absence of a connective between the first two and the last two words make it evident that we have here to do with a single message, whereas no one who ordered Heracleides to follow could possibly be speaking in a favourable manner of Dionysius. A further touch of verisimilitude is furnished by the use of the Syracusan (Doric) dialectal form Ἡρακλείδας, the very way in which Dio would have addressed Heracleides, although Aeneas himself is writing in Attic-Ionic, and consistently avoids Doricisms. καλός accordingly must be changed to agree with the remainder of the message, and here Hermann Schöne's emendation κόλος, ‘docked’ or ‘de-horned,’ used of an ox or goat which had been rendered harmless, is an apt expression, equivalent to our English phrase ‘with one's wings clipped,’ or ‘shorn of one's locks.’ Considering also that κόλος was actually used in military parlance of an indecisive or interrupted engagement, witness the κόλος μάχη of the *Iliad*, Book viii, and that the corruption to καλός is easy in view of the commonness of this formula in dedications and inscriptions of many kinds, it may be accepted as highly probable that Aeneas is here giving an actual or supposititious message, very likely from Dio himself, to Heracleides in Greece, ordering him to follow, since Dionysius had lost his power and was no longer dangerous.[2] This message

[1] For the details of which one may refer to A. Holm, *Geschichte Siziliens*, ii. 177 ff.

[2] This corresponds exactly with the facts. Dio set out

6

was sent in the fall of 357, very shortly after which the present treatise was probably written.

Casaubon thought that our Aeneas might be identical with the Aeneas of Stymphalus in Arcadia, who, as general of the Arcadian League, in 367 B.C. drove out Euphron the tyrant of Sicyon with the help of Sicyonian exiles (Xenophon, *Hellenica*, vii. 3. 1). This suggestion, which has been elaborated by Hug, has been very widely, although not universally, accepted, and in view of the converging lines of evidence from several different quarters, the discussion of which here, however, would take us too far afield, may be regarded as probably correct, although it is perhaps unwise to call our author outright ' Aeneas of Stymphalus ' as does Hug.

In its general literary setting the work of Aeneas belongs to the type of the didactic handbook which began to appear toward the end of the fifth century, under the influence of the Sophists and Socrates.[1]

---

against Dionysius II with scarcely eight hundred men, a ridiculously small number in comparison with the enemy. " But Dio was justified in his belief that the ruler's power was crumbling and that he had completely undermined it," as Eduard Meyer, *Geschichte des Altertums*, v. 513, expresses it.

Hermann Diels and, independently, Herbert Fischer, conjecture κακῶς, which requires something more of a change than κόλος, for M, and probably its predecessor, had only ΚΛΣ. Diels speaks of a telegram of the younger Dionysius to Heracleides, but it seems more reasonable to suppose that Dio sent the message, because, although Dio and Heracleides eventually fell out, they were both in exile in Greece in 357 B.C., and it was Heracleides' victory over Philistus in the sea-fight the next year which finally compelled Dionysius to flee.

[1] Examples of which from this same period we have in Xenophon's essays *On Horsemanship* and *On the Duties of a Cavalry Commander*.

His literary work, which Polybius sums up under the general title στρατηγικὰ βιβλία, 'Works on military Science,' was divided into a series of special monographs. Aeneas himself refers to five : (1) ἡ παρασκευαστικὴ βίβλος (7. 4, etc.), 'Treatise on military Preparations'; (2) ἡ ποριστικὴ βίβλος (14. 2), 'On (War-)Finance'; (3) ἡ στρατοπεδευτικὴ βίβλος (21. 2), 'On Encampments'; (4) <ἐπιβουλῶν?> βίβλος, 'On Plots' (11. 2, see the apparatus criticus at this point); and (5) ἀκούσματα (38. 5). This last title has been variously understood, either as 'Historical Illustrations' (Casaubon, Mahlstedt), 'Lectures' (Christ-Schmid), or 'Admonitions' (Köchly, Hug, and others), of which the last suits the context best, besides being supported to some extent by Isocrates' use of the word (*Ad Demonicum*, 12 and 17), which he paraphrases by σπουδαῖοι λόγοι and σοφία. Besides these the MS. contains at the end a fragment of what Aeneas himself calls (6) a ναυτικὴ τάξις, or a work 'On naval Tactics.' That this was an independent monograph has been doubted by Hug, but upon insufficient grounds. Such a treatise was essential to a well rounded scheme of manuals on military science, since nowhere in the world has so large a part of warfare been necessarily waged upon the water as in Greece. We must also assume the existence of a special treatise (7) 'On the Conduct of Siege Operations,' a πολιορκητικὴ βίβλος, partly because Aeneas was subsequently listed among the poliorcetic writers, whereas the present treatise deals exclusively with the defence of fortifications, but especially because the introduction to the present monograph, when considered as but a chapter in a comprehensive treatise on military science, by its

8

emphatic contrast of the relative positions of the attacker and the defender, clearly indicates that the conduct of siege operations had already been treated.[1] Last is (8) a τακτικὴ βίβλος, or τακτικά, 'On Tactics,' to which Aelian refers, and from which he quotes the definition of tactics as given above. Into this general scheme of military manuals the present treatise would fall most naturally as a counterpart to the πολιορκητικὴ βίβλος, if it be not actually the second half of that work, to which the introductory sentence makes such direct reference. This supposition would also relieve us of the necessity of restoring by conjecture an otherwise unknown adjective to agree with βίβλος as a title for this treatise. A general work treating of both the offensive and the defensive in time of siege might, without too great impropriety, be called a πολιορκητικὴ βίβλος 'On the Conduct of Siege Operations,' but the second part alone could not be designated by that title. As regards chronological order, it is obvious that Nos. 1, 2, 4, and 5 preceded the present treatise because they are referred to as already written. Also, according to our hypothesis, No. 7 immediately preceded, just as No. 6 followed. No. 8 is in no place referred to, even where, as in 1. 2, such a reference would have been most appropriate. It was probably, therefore, planned and composed after this book was written. No. 3, on the other hand, although not yet written, was clearly planned, and, as is natural, the author is more ready to introduce a few topics from it into his present work

[1] The parallel with the ναυτικὴ τάξις which is bipartite also suggests that the present treatise was cast in the same form, as Fischer suggests.

9

than from a treatise which had been published and was already known.

Literary sources of a direct kind did not exist for Aeneas, and his account is mainly drawn from experience and from oral tradition. Herodotus is occasionally used for illustrations, Thucydides once only (for the siege of Plataea); but Aeneas was under the influence of the latter's vocabulary and style. Xenophon's *Anabasis* may have been drawn upon for the anecdote of how a panic was stopped by a clever joke (27. 11), but there is a marked variation in detail and the same anecdote is elsewhere ascribed to Iphicrates. Von Gutschmid thought that Ephorus was used occasionally, but that is doubtful.

The title of the present treatise, as already noted, has probably been lost; the latter part of the superscription, however, we retain, enclosing it in brackets, as the best designation that has come down, and use as a translation of it the somewhat conventionalized title, ' On the Defence of fortified Positions,' the equivalent of which in Latin, German, or French has become sanctioned by general usage and is essentially correct.

Our treatise shows evidence of systematic planning, and although certain paragraphs, or even chapters, might appear somewhat more logically in a different connexion, and some of the transitions are not well marked, Kirchhoff's theory of wholesale displacement is certainly wrong.[1] The following are the general divisions of the subject :

[1] Fischer's recently proposed explanation, namely that Aeneas was engaged upon this from 379 to 356 B.C., constantly revising his lecture notes and adding references to the most

INTRODUCTION

I. On selecting and disposing troops and on preparing positions in and about the city for facilitating the defence (1-10.24).

II. On maintaining morale and discipline and general measures for thwarting treachery and revolution (10.25-14; phases of this latter topic are considered in a number of other chapters).

III. On repelling sudden forays (15-16.15).

IV. On checking, at a distance from the walls, the advance of a foe, and on taking special precautions in regard to religious processions outside the city walls and treachery at the gates of the city (16.16-20 : 21 is transitional).

V. On guarding the walls by night and by day and preventing smuggling of arms to revolutionary factions and their direct communication with the foe (22-31).

VI. On means to meet the actual assault of the foe upon the fortifications (32-40).

It may be said of the measures recommended by Aeneas that many of them seem to us simple, a few almost trivial. But the same is true of the elements of all great inventions which have become part of our thought and action. Even the somewhat naïve

---

recent happenings as illustrative material, is not likely to win general assent. The case of Aristotle's *Metaphysics* is very different. There is nothing to show that Aeneas was a school lecturer and it is difficult to picture him in that capacity.

cryptogram in 31. 31 which called forth von Gut-schmid's scorn, though hardly likely to deceive any military censor today, might well have imposed upon a simple-minded gateman or upon barbarian police, at a time when all reading was uncommon, writing none too easily legible, and tricks with vowels and consonants well-nigh unheard of even among the learned.[1]   Military science in the hands of its great masters is still a simple thing.   Battles and campaigns are won and lost, as the annals of the great strategists show, by the observance or neglect of such elementary considerations as rapidity of motion, concealment of purpose, concentration of a superior force at the point of impact, and the like,[2] which anyone can appreciate and which seem almost too trivial for formal statement. Ἁπλοῦς ὁ μῦθος τῆς ἀληθείας ἔφυ — " Truth's story is by nature plain."

One ought rather to note the large number of devices which, although war has taken on such a different external aspect, even yet apply, such as censorship of letters, police prohibition of gatherings, putting out of lights, passports, exclusion or intern-ment of suspicious aliens, special regulations for the surveillance of lodging-houses, interest moratoria and

---

[1] In this connexion it might be noted that precisely this very cryptogram was employed for the title of a mediaeval MS. in Rome, Cod. Roman. Bibl. Vitt. Em. 1369 (Sesso-rianus 43), s. xiii.   L ∴ c ∴ br · t ⋮ ∴ nc ∴ l ∷ g ⋮ d ∷, that is *Lucubratiuncule Egidii*.   (From Herr Sechel as reported by Diels, p. 29, note 4.)

[2] Thus it is reported of the Confederate General Forrest, that he summed up his military science in a single phrase in response to the question, how he won his successes : " I get there first with the most men."

supertaxes on wealth, bonuses for importers of food and munitions, signals, trenches, mining and countermining, masks for protection against smoke and fire, secret methods of communication, and the employment of dogs. As the first writer upon military science Aeneas should always command the attention of students of that subject, so long at least as the necessity of defence against aggression devolves upon a watchful citizenship.

That the works of Aeneas were highly regarded is shown by the fact that early in the next century Cineas, the friend of King Pyrrhus, prepared an epitome of them, a thing that he would hardly have done except at the suggestion or with the approval of that great commander, who himself wrote a treatise upon the art of war. The true worth of Aeneas is better appreciated by the admiration of Pyrrhus, one of the world's half-dozen greatest captains, than by the strictures of any closet philologist. In the second half of the second century B.C. the fifth book of Philo the Mechanician upon the attack and defence of fortifications makes use of Aeneas. Polybius used his treatise on *Military Preparations*. Onasander towards the middle of the first century after Christ, Aelian early in the second century, and Polyaenus shortly after the middle of the same century, knew and made use of this work. Early in the third century Sextus Julius Africanus transferred bodily large portions of the present treatise to his Κεστοί.[1] Traces of Aeneas's influence appear also in an anonymous Byzantine military writer of the sixth century, and possibly elsewhere.

[1] These excerpts will be found at the end of the present translation.

Probably about this time was composed the corpus of Greek military writers as represented in the Laurentian MS. at Florence, a MS. which alone saved to the modern world Aeneas and several other authors of this group.

In the nineteenth century the text of Aeneas passed through singular vicissitudes. Almost rediscovered for scholarship by Haase, Köchly and Rüstow, it was inevitable that a certain *furor philologicus* then raging should fall foul of it. The earliest editors had followed the MS. tradition wherever it could be understood, and had not attempted to prescribe how Aeneas ought to have expressed himself. With the greater refinement in the study of style and syntax which the nineteenth century achieved, but while the historical attitude had not gained the ascendancy, it happened more than once that a text was practically rewritten by a courageous but over-zealous philologist. Thus Rudolph Hercher in the early 'seventies, misapprehending the numerous non-Attic forms, strange syntax, and loose or redundant expressions in Aeneas, conceived the idea that a pure and succinct Attic text had been disfigured by an interpolator, and accordingly discarded about one-twelfth of the book. Arnold Hug went further in this direction, eliminating about one-fourth in order to secure a correct and elegant literary form, and even Adolph Lange, though defending the text with great acumen against many changes of interpolation, himself rejected approximately one-tenth of the whole. This was of course to reduce the process of emendation to the point of absurdity and a reaction inevitably followed. A theory of wholesale displacement of paragraphs and

14

chapters, first suggested by Adolf Kirchhoff, had but a short vogue. No motive or occasion for such transpositions is conceivable, and the order of topics, although not in every instance the most logical, is on the whole satisfactory when one bears in mind that the author was neither a scientist nor an accomplished man of letters.

The increase in our knowledge of the changes in syntax, forms, and vocabulary brought about by the inscriptions and papyri discovered in the last few decades, and the greater attention paid to the language of others than the Atticists, has enabled us to form a truer judgement of the κοινή, or common Greek idiom, which was the universal means of literary communication in the Hellenistic period. The formation of this common idiom has now been traced back with certainty to the Delian league of the fifth century, and its basis is recognized to be a mixture of Attic and Ionic with elements, in greater or less proportion, from other dialects. As a fully developed literary style it makes its appearance shortly after the age of Alexander, but we now recognize that Aeneas is one of the very earliest documents preserved from the period of transition and development, and our duty is not to reduce his work to the standards of the strictest Attic prose of the fourth century, but to accept it as it has come down to us, emending only what is impossible in form and syntax, and endeavouring to understand rather than to transform the document. Mahlstedt's exhaustive lexicographical study of the vocabulary of Aeneas, and the more general treatment of his style by Behrendt, both appearing in 1910, reached the certain conclusion that Aeneas is a forerunner of the κοινή. This sober historical point of view is also characteristic of Schöne's elaborate recension, which is the basis of the present text. Much remains yet to be cleared up in the interpretation of the subject matter, but the essential character of the language and style can now be regarded as finally determined.

In yet another aspect Aeneas supplies us with a valuable historical document, and that is in the light he throws upon the chaotic conditions that obtained in Greece during the severe social revolutions of the fourth century, which contributed perhaps more than any other single cause to the destruction of the fabric of early Hellenic civilization. The history of the time is full of the records of brutal revolution and bloody revenge. Plato has drastically characterized the oligarchic state as " not one but two States, the one of the poor, the other of the rich men ; and they are living on the same spot and always conspiring against one another." [1] Again he depicts Greece as he knew it in a prophecy of what would happen should his ideal guardians " acquire houses and lands and moneys of their own. . . . Hating and being hated, plotting and being plotted against, they will pass their whole life in much greater fear of internal than of external enemies, and the hour of ruin, both to themselves and to the rest of the State, will be at hand." [2]

We have at times in this treatise what seems almost a commentary upon these passages from Plato in the matter-of-fact words of Aeneas, who like a professional soldier seems to have held aloof

[1] *Republic*, 551 E (Jowett).
[2] *Republic*, 417 A, B (Jowett).

16

from the partisanships of politics, so that some who
have failed to grasp his true attitude have regarded
him as a moderate democrat and others as a supporter
of oligarchy. More than half his military admonitions are directed towards preventing treachery and
forestalling revolution. The men for whom he wrote
his manual were clearly in constant danger of the
enemy within their own gates, a peril which became
more rather than less acute when armed foes without
were threatening the very existence of the state.
Upon one memorable occasion at Argos the revolutionary assassins carrying concealed daggers mingled
with the officials and leading citizens at a religious
festival outside the walls, and struck them down,
each one his man, at the very moment of their
devotions about the altar (17. 2 ff.). Paralysing
indeed must have been the terror in many a community in Greece when such occurrences were felt
to be not merely possible but perhaps actually
impending.

Manuscripts

Aeneas survived the Middle Ages in but a single MS., now preserved in Florence and the parent of all others known to exist. This is the famous Laurentianus Graecus LV 4, commonly called M (*i.e. Mediceus*, described by Bandini, *Catal. Codd. MSS. Bibl. Laurent.* t. ii., 1768, 218-38). It contains the corpus of Greek military writers, a collection which no doubt dates from early Byzantine times. The three descendants of M are all in Paris, known respectively as A (Parisinus Graecus 2435), B (Parisinus Graecus 2522), and C (Parisinus Graecus 2443). Of these C, although the only MS. known to Casaubon, and hence the source of the *editio princeps*, is worthless, being descended from B or a copy of B, except in so far as some corrections of corrupt passages, introduced by its copyist, Angelus Bergelius, possess independent value as emendations. A and B, however, are not without critical worth, because M suffered somewhat from dampness after they were written and is in consequence quite illegible in places, besides containing a few lacunae which did not exist when the copies were made. They are cited only where the text of M is lost. Fortunately they were copied with unusual fidelity, so that almost nothing of the text of M, as it existed in the fifteenth century, is lost to us.

INTRODUCTION

For a considerable portion of Aeneas the excerpts included by Julius Africanus in his Κεστοί furnish an excellent check upon M, since they represent a tradition of Aeneas—rather seriously disfigured to be sure—which is seven or eight centuries older than that MS. A text of these portions of Africanus is furnished by R. Schöne in his edition of Aeneas, based in part upon materials collected by Fr. Haase and K. K. Müller, and in part upon his own collations. The most important readings in which Africanus differs from the tradition in M are given in our apparatus criticus as MS. readings.

Jacob Gronov was the first to use M as an aid in constituting the text of Aeneas. The peculiarities and characteristic faults of this MS. are best set forth in A. C. Lange, *De Aeneae Commentario Poliorcetico*, 58-65, and R. Schöne's edition, x f. Despite the bad state of the tradition and the abysmal ignorance of the scribe, the comparatively large number of places where a critical mark was written above words which were thought to be corrupt, and the blank spaces left where the original was illegible or defective, are evidence of the faithfulness with which the copy was prepared.

The chapter headings, although older than the third century of our era, because known to Africanus, can hardly have come from Aeneas himself. In deference to custom, and for the sake of convenience, they are retained, but enclosed in brackets, to indicate their later origin.

19

AENEAS TACTICUS

EDITIONS

Is. Casaubonus : Αἰνείου τακτικόν τε καὶ πολιορκητικὸν
ὑπόμνημα περὶ τοῦ πῶς χρὴ πολιορκούμενον ἀντέχειν.
Paris, 1609. Text, notes, and Latin translation.
This is the *editio princeps*, appended to
Casaubon's edition of Polybius, and the whole
republished by Jacob Gronov and by J. A.
Ernesti in their editions of Polybius published
at Amsterdam in 1670 and at Leipzig in 1763-64,
respectively. Gronov later published from M
(see below) *Supplementa Lacunarum in Aenea
Tactico*, etc. Leyden, 1675.

Jo. Conradus Orellius : *Aeneae Tactici Commentarius
de toleranda Obsidione*, etc. Leipzig, 1818. This
edition contains Casaubon's translation, together
with notes of Casaubon, Gronov, Koës, Caspar
Orelli, Conrad Orelli, and others. It appeared
as a supplement to Schweighäuser's Polybius.

H. Köchly und W. Rüstow : *Aeneas von Verteidigung
der Städte*. Leipzig, 1853. Aeneas occupies a
part of vol. i of the editors' well-known *Griechische Kriegsschriftsteller, Griechisch und Deutsch*.
A supplement in vol. ii. 2, contains readings
from B (see above). This edition is particularly
valuable because of the introduction, the schol-
arly translation, the notes, and the illustrative
diagrams.

R. Hercher : *Aeneae Commentarius poliorceticus*.
Berlin, 1870. *Editio maior*. An *editio minor*,
later in the same year, corrected a number of
errors that appeared in the former edition.

A. Hug : *Aeneae Commentarius poliorceticus*. Leipzig,
1874.

INTRODUCTION

R. Schöne : *Aeneae Tactici de Obsidione toleranda Commentarius.* Leipzig, 1911. This admirable work, based upon new collations of M, A, and B (see above) and prepared with the utmost accuracy and acumen, completely supplants all previous editions, and is the basis of the text as printed in this volume. An *index verborum* (which is in large part actually a concordance), composed with the assistance of Ferdinand Koester, adds materially to the value of the work.[1]

Translations

In addition to the translations, listed above, by Casaubon, and by Köchly and Rüstow, the following should be mentioned :

M. le Comte de Beausobre : *Commentaires sur la Défense des Places d'Aeneas le Tacticien, avec quelques Notes,* etc. Amsterdam, 1757, 2 vols.

A. de Rochas d'Aiglun : *Traité de Fortification, d'Attaque et de Défense des Places par Philon de Bysance.* Paris, 1872. This is vol. vi of series iv of the *Mém. de la Soc. d'Emulation du Doubs,* 1870–1871 (Besançon, 1872), and contains a translation, with notes, of Aeneas, chapters 8, 16, 21, 22, 24-26, 31-35, 37, 39, 40, in whole or in part. Chapter 31 is taken from the translation of Beausobre. See R. Schöne, *Rhein. Mus.* lxvii. (1912) 303.

[1] An edition announced by L. W. Hunter in 1913 is awaited with interest because of the promise to explain much of the corruption in M stichometrically, *i.e.*, by the falling out of an entire line at points where a group of similar letters appears either at the beginning or at the end of successive lines.

AENEAS TACTICUS

No translation of Aeneas has previously appeared in English.

CRITICAL WORKS

Beside the editions and translations enumerated above, the following monographs have contributed much to the understanding of Aeneas :

C. Behrendt : *De Aeneae Tactici Commentario poliorcetico Quaestiones selectae* Diss., Königsberg, 1910. Behrendt's commentary as published covers only the first seven chapters. It is to be hoped that the remainder may soon appear.

Fr. Blass : *Literarisches Zentralblatt*, 1879, 1261 f.

Hermann Diels : Die Entdeckung des Alkohols. *Abhandl. der Königl. Preuss. Akad. der Wiss.*, Berlin, 1913, No. 3, 19.

Herbert Fischer : *Quaestiones Aeneanae.* Pars I. Giessen Diss., Dresden, 1914.

A. von Gutschmid : *Kleine Schriften*, vol. iv. 218-21 ; v. 191 ff. ; 214 ff.

Fr. Haase : *Neue Jahrbücher*, xiv. (1835) 93 ff. ; xvii. (1836) 206 ff.

F. C. Hertlein : *Symbolae criticae ad Aeneam Tacticum.* Wertheim, 1859.

A. Hug : (1) *Prolegomena critica ad Aeneae Editionem.* Zürich, 1874. (2) *Aeneas von Stymphalos*, etc. Zürich, 1877. (3) *Neue Jahrbücher*, cxix. (1879) 241 ff., 639 ff.

L. W. Hunter : Aeneas Tacticus and Stichometry *Classical Quarterly*, vii. (1913) 256-64.

A. Kirchhoff : *Hermes*, i. (1866) 448 ff. and in the preface to Hug's edition, vii ff

INTRODUCTION

G. H. Koës : *Epistolae Parisienses*, ed. Bredow, 1812, 110 ff. (dealing with MSS. ABC).

A. C. Lange : (1) *De Aeneae Commentario poliorcetico*. Berlin, 1879. (2) *Neue Jahrbücher*, cxix. (1879) 461 ff. (3) *Animadversiones criticae in Aeneae Commentarium poliorceticum*. Cassel, 1883.

Chr. Mahlstedt : *Über den Wortschatz des Aeneias Taktikus*. Kiel Diss., Jena, 1910.

M. E. E. Meier : *Opuscula academica*, vol. ii., Halle 1863, 292-306.

A. Mosbach : *De Aeneae Tactici Commentario poliorcetico*. Diss., Berlin, 1880.

R. Pöhlmann : *Geschichte des antiken Kommunismus und Sozialismus*. Munich, 1901, vol. ii. 346-8 (= *Geschichte der sozialen Frage und des Sozialismus in der antiken Welt*. Munich, 1912, i. 421-24).

J. J. Reiske : *Animadversiones ad Aeneam Tacticum*, published by R. Hercher in his *editio maior*, 128-33.

J. Ries : *De Aeneae Tactici Commentario poliorcetico*. Diss., Halle, 1890.

W. Rüstow und H. Köchly : *Geschichte des griechischen Kriegswesens*. Aarau, 1852, 196 ff.

H. Sauppe : *Ausgewählte Schriften*. Berlin, 1896, 631-645.

K. Schenkl : *Bursian's Jahresberichte*, xxxviii. (1884) 261-270.

E. Schwartz : *Aineias*, in Pauly-Wissowa's *Realencyklopädie*, i. (1897) 1019-1021.

T. Hudson Williams : The Authorship of the Greek military Manual attributed to 'Aeneas Tacticus.' *Amer. Journ. of Philol.* xxv. (1904) 390-405.

AENEAS TACTICUS

Symbols

A = *Codex Parisinus Graecus* 2435, s. xvi ; the more careful copy of M.

B = *Codex Parisinus Graecus* 2522, s. xv.

C = *Codex Parisinus Graecus* 2443, a. 1549.

M = *Codex Laurentianus Graecus* LV, 4, s. x.

J. Afr. = Excerpts from the Κεστοί of Sextus Julius Africanus, an author of the third century.

Note on Julius Africanus

As a necessary supplement to Aeneas we have included a text and translation of those portions of the Κεστοί of Sextus Julius Africanus which are clearly derived from the treatise before us. In so doing we have been compelled to emend the MS. tradition of Africanus in a much more drastic way than we should consider justified in a critical edition. Schöne, following Hercher's example, very properly left the MS. tradition as it stood, so as not to disguise any variants which might possibly throw light upon the present state of M. But to translate it is necessary to have a text which makes tolerable sense, which in this case necessitates liberal emendation. As in Aeneas, however, every real departure from the MS. tradition is noted in the apparatus. The references to MSS. are taken from Schöne's edition and represent his selection of the critical materials gathered for a recension of Africanus by Fr Haase and K. K. Müller, with his own collation

24

of the Barberini ms. in the Vatican (see the preface
to his edition of Aeneas, ix). We have also made
use of the text of the Κεστοί in Thevenot's edition of
the *Veteres Mathematici*, Paris, 1693, 275-316, with
Boivin's notes, 339-60.

ΑΙΝΕΙΟΥ

ΠΕΡΙ ΤΟΥ

ΠΩΣ ΧΡΗ ΠΟΛΙΟΡΚΟΥΜΕΝΟΥΣ ΑΝΤΕΧΕΙΝ[1]

Ὅσοις τῶν ἀνθρώπων ἐκ τῆς αὐτῶν[2] ὁρμωμένοις χώρας ὑπερόριοί τε ἀγῶνες καὶ κίνδυνοι συμβαίνουσιν, ἄν τι σφάλμα γένηται κατὰ γῆν ἢ κατὰ θάλασσαν, ὑπολείπεται τοῖς περιγιγνομένοις αὐτῶν οἰκεία τε χώρα καὶ πόλις καὶ πατρίς, ὥστε οὐκ ἂν 2 ἄρδην πάντες ἀναιρεθείησαν· τοῖς δὲ ὑπὲρ τῶν μεγίστων μέλλουσι κινδυνεύειν, ἱερῶν καὶ πατρίδος καὶ γονέων καὶ τέκνων καὶ τῶν ἄλλων, οὐκ ἴσος οὐδὲ ὅμοιος ἀγών ἐστιν, ἀλλὰ σωθεῖσι μὲν καὶ καλῶς ἀμυναμένοις τοὺς πολεμίους φοβεροὺς τοῖς ἐναντίοις καὶ δυσεπιθέτους εἰς τὸν λοιπὸν χρόνον εἶναι, κακῶς δὲ προσενεχθεῖσι πρὸς τοὺς κινδύνους 3 οὐδεμία ἐλπὶς σωτηρίας ὑπάρξει. τοὺς οὖν ὑπὲρ τοσούτων καὶ τοιούτων μέλλοντας ἀγωνίζεσθαι οὐδεμιᾶς παρασκευῆς καὶ προθυμίας ἐλλιπεῖς εἶναι δεῖ, ἀλλὰ πολλῶν καὶ παντοίων ἔργων πρόνοιαν ἐκτέον, ὅπως διά γε αὐτοὺς[3] μηδὲν φανῶσι 4 σφαλέντες· ἂν δὲ ἄρα τι σύμπτωμα γένηται, ἀλλ᾽ οἵ γε λοιποὶ τὰ ὑπάρχοντα εἰς ταυτό ποτε κατα-

AENEAS

ON THE DEFENCE OF FORTIFIED
POSITIONS

WHEN men set out from their own country to encounter strife and perils in foreign lands and some
disaster befalls them by land or sea, the survivors
still have left their native soil, their city, and their
fatherland, so that they are not all utterly destroyed
But for those who are to incur peril in defence of
what they most prize, shrines and country, parents
and children, and all else, the struggle is not the
same nor even similar. For if they save themselves
by a stout defence against the foe, their enemies
will be intimidated and disinclined to attack them
in the future, but if they make a poor showing in the
face of danger, no hope of safety will be left. Those,
therefore, who are to contend for all these precious
stakes must fail in no preparation and no effort,
but must take thought for many and varied activi-
ties, so that a failure may at least not seem due to
their own fault. But if after all a reverse should
befall them, yet at all events the survivors may

---

[1] Αἰλιανοῦ τακτικὸν ὑπόμνημα περὶ τοῦ κτλ. M. *Cf.* Introduction, 2 ff.
[2] Hertlein : αὐτῶν M.   [3] Köchly and Rüstow : αὐτοὺς M.

στήσαιεν ἄν,[1] καθάπερ τινὲς τῶν Ἑλλήνων εἰς τὸ
ἔσχατον ἀφικόμενοι πάλιν ἀνέλαβον ἑαυτούς.

I.

Τὴν οὖν τῶν σωμάτων σύνταξιν σκεψαμένους
πρὸς τὸ μέγεθος τῆς πόλεως καὶ τὴν διάθεσιν τοῦ
ἄστεος καὶ τῶν φυλάκων τὰς καταστάσεις καὶ
περιοδίας, καὶ ὅσα ἄλλα σώμασι κατὰ τὴν πόλιν
χρηστέον, πρὸς ταῦτα τοὺς μερισμοὺς ποιητέον.
2 τοὺς μὲν γὰρ ἐκπορευομένους δεῖ συντετάχθαι
πρὸς τοὺς ἐν τῇ πορείᾳ τόπους, ὡς χρὴ πορεύεσθαι
παρά τε τὰ ἐπικίνδυνα χωρία καὶ ἐρυμνὰ καὶ
στενόπορα καὶ πεδινὰ καὶ ὑπερδέξια καὶ ἐνεδρευτικά,
καὶ τὰς τῶν ποταμῶν[2] διαβάσεις καὶ τὰς ἐκ τῶν
3 τοιούτων παρατάξεις· τὰ δὲ τειχήρη καὶ πολιτο-
φυλακήσοντα[3] πρὸς μὲν τὰ τοιαῦτα οὐδὲν δεῖ
συντετάχθαι, πρὸς δὲ τοὺς ἐν τῇ πόλει τόπους καὶ
4 τὸν παρόντα κίνδυνον. πρῶτον μὲν οὖν αὐτῶν[4]
ἀπονεῖμαι δεῖ τοὺς φρονιμωτάτους τε καὶ ἐμ-
πείρους μάλιστα πολέμου, οἳ περὶ τοὺς ἄρχοντας

---

[1] Added by Hertlein.　　[2] L. Dindorf: πολεμίων M.
[3] Meier : πολιτοφυλακῆσ ὄντα M, Haase.
[4] Casaubon : αὐτὸν M.

---

[1] Because this was the side unprotected by their shields.
Approaches to city gates in particular were frequently so
constructed as to compel assailants to expose their right
sides to missiles hurled by the defenders, for example, the
main entrances at Tiryns and at Mycenae.　Such also was
undoubtedly the character of the famous " Scaean (i.e. left-
hand) Gate" of Troy.

[2] See below § 6, and especially ch. 10.

[3] These men constitute a staff of military advisers, the
remote prototype of the modern General Staff.　Köchly and

some time restore their affairs to their former condition, like certain Greek peoples who, after being reduced to extremes, have re-established themselves.

I.

Now the disposition of the troops is to be made with reference to the size of the state and the topography of the town, its sentries and patrols, and any other service for which troops are required in the city,—in view of all this the assignments are to be made. So men who are going to fight outside the walls must be drawn up in a manner suitable to the country along their line of march, according as they are to march past dangerous or fortified places, through narrow passes or across plains, past higher ground upon the right [1] and points exposed to ambush, with reference also to the river-crossings and the formation of a line of battle under such conditions. But the forces which are to defend the walls and keep watch over the citizens [2] need not be so arranged, but rather with reference to the positions within the city and to the immediate danger. First, then, it is necessary to select the most prudent citizens and those most experienced in war for attendance upon the civil authorities.[3]

Rüstow seem to be in error in identifying these men with the body of troops mentioned in 16. 7 ; 17. 6 ; 26. 10 ; 38. 2, for these latter are selected for some particular purpose, or else are the same as the reserves mentioned in §§ 6 and 7 below. In some of the more highly organized Greek states military control was vested in a permanent board of Generals, ten in number (as at Athens), elected directly by the citizens. Livy xxiv. 28 gives an example of how this precept of Aeneas was put into practice during the confusion at Syracuse in 214 B.C.

5 ἔσονται· ἔπειτα λοιπὸν ἀπολέγειν σώματα τὰ[1]
δυνησόμενα μάλιστα πονεῖν, καὶ μερίσαντα[2]
λοχίσαι, ἵνα εἴς τε τὰς ἐξόδους καὶ τὰς κατὰ πόλιν
περιοδίας καὶ τὰς τῶν πονουμένων βοηθείας ἢ
εἴς τινα ἄλλην ὁμότροπον ταύταις λειτουργίαν
ὑπάρχωσιν οὗτοι προτεταγμένοι τε καὶ δυνατοὶ
6 ὄντες ὑπηρετεῖν. εἶναι δὲ αὐτοὺς εὔνους τε καὶ
τοῖς καθεστηκόσι πράγμασιν ἀρεσκομένους· μέγα
γὰρ πρὸς τὰς τῶν ἄλλων ἐπιβουλὰς τοιοῦτο[3]
ἀθρόον ὑπάρχον ἀντ' ἀκροπόλεως· φόβος γὰρ ἂν
7 εἴη τοῖς ἐναντία θέλουσιν ἐν τῇ πόλει. ἡγεμὼν
δὲ καὶ[4] ἐπιμελητὴς αὐτῶν ἔστω τά τε ἄλλα
φρόνιμος καὶ εὔρωστος, καὶ ᾧ ἂν πλεῖστοι κίνδυνοι
8 εἶεν μεταβολῆς γενομένης. τῶν δὲ λοιπῶν τοὺς
ῥωμαλεωτάτους ἡλικίᾳ καὶ νεότητι ἐκλέξαντα
ἐπὶ τὰς φυλακὰς καθιστάναι καὶ τὰ τείχη, τὸ δὲ
περιὸν πλῆθος μερίσαντα πρὸς τὸ μῆκος τῶν
νυκτῶν καὶ τῶν φυλάκων τὸ πλῆθος κατανεῖμαι,
9 τῶν δὲ ὄχλων τοὺς μὲν εἰς τὴν ἀγοράν, τοὺς δὲ εἰς
τὸ θέατρον, τοὺς δὲ ἄλλους εἰς τὰς οὔσας[5] ἐν τῇ
πόλει εὐρυχωρίας, ἵνα μηδὲν ἔρημον ᾖ εἰς δύναμιν
τῆς πόλεως.

II.

Ἄριστον[6] δὲ τὰς ἀχρείους οὔσας εὐρυχωρίας
ἐν τῇ πόλει, ἵνα μὴ σωμάτων εἰς αὐτὰς δέῃ,
τυφλοῦν ταφρεύοντα καὶ ὡς μάλιστα ἀβάτους

[1] Added by Köchly and Rüstow.
[2] Casaubon : μετρίσαντα M.
[3] Hertlein (τοιοῦτον): τοῦτο M.　　[4] Hertlein : καὶ ὁ M.
[5] δυσιασ M (ι deleted ? οὔσας A, οὔσας B).
[6] Casp. Orelli : εὔχρηστον? R. Schöne : ἀχρηστον M (retained by Casaubon, defended by Fischer).

Next one must pick out men capable of the greatest physical exertion and divide them into companies, that there may be ready for sallies, for patrolling the city, for the relief of those hard pressed, or for any other similar service, these who are picked men and able to give assistance.[1] They must be both loyal and satisfied with the existing order, since it is a great thing to have such a group acting like a fortress against the revolutionary designs of the other party, for it would be a terror to the opposition inside the city.[2] And let the man who is to lead and have charge of them be not merely prudent and vigorous, but also one who would run the greatest risks from a change of government. From the rest the strongest, in the prime of manhood, should be chosen for the watches and the walls, while the remainder should be divided and apportioned according to the length of the nights and the number of the watches. Of the common soldiers some should be stationed in the market-place, some in the theatre, and the rest in the open places in the city, so that as far as the city's power permits no part may be unguarded.

II.

And that there may be no need of troops to guard them, it is best to block up the useless open places in the city by digging ditches[3] and by

---

[1] Compare the modern equivalent in the shape of *Arditi*, *Stoss-Truppen*, and Battalions of Death.
[2] See ch. 10 for a detailed treatment of this topic.
[3] That is, across the entrances to them.

ποιοῦντα τοῖς νεωτερίζειν βουλομένοις καὶ προ-
2 καταλαμβάνειν αὐτάς. Λακεδαιμόνιοι δὴ[1] Θηβαίων ἐμβαλόντων ἔκ τε τῶν ἐγγυτάτω οἰκιῶν
διαλύοντες καὶ ἐκ τῶν αἰμασιῶν καὶ τειχίων[2]
ἄλλοι κατ' ἄλλους τόπους φορμοὺς γῆς καὶ λίθων
πληροῦντες, φασὶν δὲ καὶ τοῖς ἐκ τῶν ἱερῶν χαλκοῖς
τρίποσιν, ὄντων πολλῶν καὶ μεγάλων, χρησάμενοι
καὶ τούτοις προαποπληρώσαντες τάς τε εἰσβολὰς
καὶ τὰς διόδους καὶ τὰ εὐρύχωρα τοῦ πολίσματος
ἐκώλυσαν τοὺς εἰσβάλλειν ἐπιχειροῦντας εἰς αὐτὸ
τὸ πόλισμα.

3 Πλαταιεῖς δὲ ἐπεὶ ᾔσθοντο νυκτὸς ἐν τῇ πόλει
Θηβαίους ὄντας, κατανοήσαντες οὐ πολλοὺς αὐτοὺς
ὄντας οὐδὲ ἔργων τῶν προσηκόντων ἁπτομένους,
οἰομένους γε μέντοι κατέχειν τὴν πόλιν, ἐνόμισαν
ἐπιθέμενοι ῥᾳδίως κρατήσειν. τεχνάζουσιν οὖν
4 εὐθέως τοιόνδε. τῶν ἀρχόντων οἱ μὲν ὁμολογίας
ἐποιοῦντο τοῖς Θηβαίοις ἐν τῇ ἀγορᾷ, οἱ δὲ παρήγ-
γελλον κρύφα τοῖς ἄλλοις πολίταις σποράδην μὲν
ἐκ τῶν οἰκιῶν μὴ ἐξιέναι, καθ' ἕνα δὲ καὶ δύο
τοὺς κοινοὺς τοίχους διορύττοντας λαθραίως παρ'
5 ἀλλήλους ἀθροίζεσθαι. ἑτοιμασθέντος δὲ πλήθους
ἀξιομάχου τὰς[3] μὲν διόδους καὶ τὰς ῥύμας
ἐτύφλωσαν ἁμάξαις ἄνευ ὑποζυγίων, ἀπὸ[4] δὲ

---

[1] Sauppe : δὲ M.
[2] Meineke : τειχῶν M.
[3] A corrector in C : τοὺς M.
[4] Hertlein : ὑπὸ M.

making them as inaccessible as possible to any who might wish to start a revolt and begin by taking possession of them. So, when the Thebans had broken in, the Lacedaemonians, some here and others there, filled baskets with earth and stones from the nearest houses, which they tore down, and from fences and walls, making use also, it is said, of the many massive bronze tripods from the temples, and with these they managed, in advance of the Thebans, to block up the entrances and passages and open places and kept them out when they tried to break into the city proper.[1]

On another occasion, when the Plataeans became aware during the night that the Thebans were in the city, they perceived that there were not many of them and that they were taking none of the proper precautions because they fancied that they were in possession of the town.[2] The Plataeans concluded, therefore, that they could easily defeat them by an attack, and so promptly devised the following scheme. Some of the authorities engaged the Thebans in the market-place in a discussion of terms, while others were secretly passing the word around to the rest of the citizens not to go out of their houses singly, but one or two at a time to break through the party-walls and assemble stealthily in one another's houses. When a sufficient fighting force was ready, they blocked up the streets and alleys, using wagons without the draft-

---

[1] This occurred in the summer of 362 B.C., shortly before the battle of Mantinea, in which Epaminondas lost his life.

[2] This was the famous night attack upon Plataea in the spring of 431 B.C. which opened the Peloponnesian war. It is described in detail by Thucydides ii. 2 ff., whose account is closely followed by Aeneas.

σημείου ἀθροισθέντες ἐφέροντο ἐπὶ τοὺς Θηβαίους.
6 ἅμα δὲ τούτοις τὰ γύναια καὶ οἱ οἰκέται ἦσαν
ἐπὶ τοῖς κεράμοις, ὥστε βουλομένων τῶν Θηβαίων
πράσσειν καὶ ἀμύνεσθαι ἐν σκότει, οὐκ ἐλάττω ὑπὸ
τῶν ἁμαξῶν βλάβην ἢ ὑπὸ τῶν προσκειμένων
αὐτοῖς ἀνθρώπων γενέσθαι. οἱ μὲν γὰρ ἔφευγον[1]
ἄπειροι ὄντες ᾗ χρὴ σωθῆναι διὰ τὰς φράξεις τῶν
ἁμαξῶν, οἱ δὲ ἐμπείρως διώκοντες ταχὺ πολλοὺς
ἔφθειραν.
7 Ἐξοιστέον δὲ καὶ τὰ ὑπεναντία τούτοις, ὡς μιᾶς
μὲν οὔσης εὐρυχωρίας κίνδυνον εἶναι τοῖς ἐν τῇ
πόλει, ἂν προκαταλαμβάνωσιν οἱ ἐπιβουλεύοντες·
κοινοῦ γὰρ καὶ ἑνὸς ὄντος τόπου τοιούτου τῶν
φθασάντων ἂν εἴη τὸ ἔργον. δύο δὲ ἢ τριῶν ὄντων
8 τοιῶνδε τόπων, τάδε ἂν εἴη τὰ ἀγαθά· εἰ μὲν
ἕνα ἢ δύο καταλαμβάνοιεν τόπους, τὸν λοιπὸν ἂν
τοῖς ἐναντίοις ὑπάρχειν· εἰ δὲ πάντας, χωρισθέντες
ἂν καὶ μερισθέντες ἀσθενεστέρως διακέοιντο πρὸς
τοὺς ὑπεναντίους ἀθρόους ὄντας, εἰ μὴ ἑκάστῳ
μέρει ὑπερέχοιεν τῶν ἐν τῇ πόλει. ὡς δὲ αὕτως
καὶ κατὰ τῶν ἄλλων πάντων θελημάτων χρὴ τὰ
ἐνόντα ὑπεναντία τοῖς προγεγραμμένοις ὑπονοεῖν,
ἵνα μὴ ἀπερισκέπτως τι ἕτερον αἱρῇ.[2]

III. [Ἄλλη πολιτοφυλάκων σύνταξις]

Ἐκ προσφάτου δὲ ἐγγιγνομένου φόβου ἀσυν-
τάκτῳ πόλει, τάχιστα ἄν τις εἰς σύνταξιν καὶ
φυλακὴν τῆς πόλεως τοὺς πολίτας καταστήσαι,[3]

[1] ἔφυγον Kirchhoff, from Thucydides ii. 4. The better
reading ἔφευγον was restored in Thucydides by Hude.
[2] R. Schöne : αἱρῆσαι M.
[3] Köchly and Rüstow : καταστήσοι M.

animals, and rushing together at a given signal, fell upon the Thebans. At the same time the women-folk and the house-slaves were on the tile-roofs.[1] The result was that when the Thebans wished to act and to defend themselves in the darkness they suffered no less harm from the wagons than from their assailants, since they fled without knowing which way to turn for safety because of the barricades of wagons, while their pursuers, being acquainted with the ground, soon killed many of them.

Yet it is necessary to set forth also the reasons which make against this practice, such as the great danger to the besieged if there is only one open place and the conspirators are the first to seize it. For when there is only one such common spot, the advantage would lie with those who first take it. But if there are two or three such places, there would be these advantages : If the conspirators should seize one or two there would still be one left for their opponents ; and if they should seize them all, by separation and division they would be weaker in the face of their united opponents, unless indeed each division were numerically superior to the defenders of the city. In the same way in all other decisions one should consider the inherent objections to the prescribed rules, that one may not inadvisedly adopt another course.

III. [*Another Organization of City Guards*]

When sudden fear falls upon a city without military organization, one could most speedily organize the citizens for its defence by allotting

---

[1] From this vantage-point they joined in the outcry and hurled tiles upon the enemy in the streets below.

AENEAS TACTICUS

εἰ ἑκάστῃ φυλῇ μέρος τι τοῦ τείχους κλήρῳ
ἀποδείξειεν, ἐφ᾽ ᾧ ἐλθοῦσαι εὐθὺς αἱ φυλαὶ φυλά-
ξουσιν. κατὰ πολυπλήθειαν[1] δὲ φυλῆς ἑκάστης
2 τὸ μέγεθος τοῦ τείχους φυλαττόντων. ἔπειτα
οὕτως ἀφ᾽[2] ἑκάστης φυλῆς τοὺς δυναμένους τοῖς
σώμασι πονέσαι ἀπολέγειν εἴς τε τὴν ἀγορὰν καὶ
τὰς περιοδίας, καὶ εἴ τι ἄλλο δεῖ χρῆσθαι τοῖς
3 τοιούτοις ἀνθρώποις.[3] ὁμοτρόπως δὲ καὶ φρουρίου
ὑπὸ συμμάχων φρουρουμένου μέρος τι τοῦ τείχους
τῶν συμμάχων ἑκάστοις ἀποδιδόσθω φυλάττειν.
ἐὰν δὲ πολῖται ἐν ὑποψίᾳ πρὸς ἀλλήλους[4] ὦσιν,
κατὰ ἀνάβασιν ἑκάστην τοῦ τείχους δεῖ ἐπιστῆσαι
ἄνδρας πιστούς, οἳ κωλυταὶ ἔσονται, ἄν τις ἐπι-
4 χειρῇ ἄλλος ἀναβαίνειν. ἐν εἰρήνῃ δὲ καὶ ὧδε
χρὴ συντετάχθαι τοὺς πολίτας. πρῶτον μὲν ῥύμης
ἑκάστης ἀποδεῖξαι ῥυμάρχην ἄνδρα τὸν ἐπιει-
κέστατόν τε καὶ φρονιμώτατον, πρὸς ὅν, ἐάν τι
ἀπροσδοκήτως νυκτὸς γένηται, συναθροισθήσονται.
5 χρὴ δὲ τὰς ἐγγυτάτας[5] ῥύμας τῆς ἀγορᾶς εἰς τὴν
ἀγορὰν ἄγειν τοὺς ῥυμάρχας, τοῦ δὲ θεάτρου τὰς
ἐγγυτάτω ῥύμας εἰς τὸ θέατρον, εἴς τε τὰς ἄλλας
ἕκαστον ἐγγύτατα εὐρυχωρίας ἀθροίζεσθαι τοὺς
ῥυμάρχας μετὰ τῶν ἐξενεγκαμένων παρ᾽ αὑτοὺς
6 τὰ ὅπλα· οὕτω γὰρ ἂν τάχιστα ἔς τε τοὺς προσ-
ήκοντας ἕκαστοι τόπους ἀφίκοιντο καὶ ἐγγυτάτω
τῶν σφετέρων οἴκων εἶεν, διαπέμποιέν τε ἂν
οἰκονομοῦντες πρὸς τοὺς κατ᾽ οἶκον, τέκνα καὶ
γυναῖκας, οὐ πρόσω αὐτῶν διατελοῦντες. τῶν
τε ἀρχόντων δεῖ προκεκληρῶσθαι εἰς ὃν ἕκαστοι

---

[1] Hercher: καταπολυπληθίαν M. [2] Reiske: ἐφ᾽ M.
[3] Casaubon: ἄνθρωπος M. [4] Casaubon: ἄλλους M.
[5] ἐγγύτατα R. Schöne: ἐγγυτάτω Hercher.

to each ward a section of the wall to which it is
to hurry and mount guard, letting the number of
the inhabitants of the ward determine the extent
of that section of the wall to whose defence it
is appointed. The next step is to assign the
able-bodied men from each ward to duty at the
market-place, upon patrols, and wherever else such
men may be needed. Similarly when a stronghold
is occupied by allies, let a section of the wall be
given to each contingent of the allies to defend.
Should the citizens, however, suspect one another,
trustworthy men should be stationed at the several
places for ascending the wall, who, if anyone else
attempts to mount, will prevent him from doing so.
In peace, also, the citizens ought to be organized
in the following manner. First of all one should
appoint as captain of each precinct the most capable
and prudent man, to whom the citizens are to rally
if anything unexpected occurs at night. The precinct captains should muster at the market-place
the men of those precincts nearest the market-
place, at the theatre the men of those precincts
nearest the theatre, and so for the other open
places the precinct captains with the armed men
who have reported to them should gather, each
in the one that lies nearest to him. For this is the
quickest way by which each group would both
reach their stations and be near their own homes,
and so, as heads of families, could communicate with
their households, that is, with their children and
wives, because stationed not far from them. And
it should be determined beforehand by lot to which

37

τόπον ἐλθόντες τῶν συλλεγέντων ἐπὶ τὰ χείλη
ἀποστελοῦσι· καὶ τῶν λοιπῶν ἕνεκα ἐπιμελείας
ἡγεμόνες ἔσονται, ἅνπερ εὐθὺς ἡγεμονεύσωσιν
ὧδε.

IV. [Περὶ συσσήμων]

Εὐθύτατα δεῖ[1] αὐτοῖς πεποιῆσθαι σύσσημα,
ἀφ᾽ ὧν μὴ ἀγνοήσουσι τοὺς προσιόντας αὐτοῖς·
ἤδη γὰρ τοιόνδε συνέβη. Χαλκὶς ἡ ἐν Εὐρίπῳ
κατελήφθη ὑπὸ φυγάδος ὁρμωμένου ἐξ Ἐρετρίας,[2]
τῶν ἐν τῇ πόλει τινὸς τεχνασαμένου τοιόνδε.
2 κατὰ τὸ ἐρημότατον τῆς πόλεως καὶ πύλας οὐκ
ἀνοιγομένας ἔχων[3] ἔφερεν πυργάστρην, ἣν[4] φυλάσ-
σων τὰς ἡμέρας καὶ τὰς νύκτας ἔλαθεν νυκτὸς
τὸν μοχλὸν διαπρήσας καὶ δεξάμενος ταύτῃ[5]
3 στρατιώτας. ἀθροισθέντων δὲ ἐν τῇ ἀγορᾷ ὡς
δισχιλίων ἀνδρῶν ἐσημάνθη τὸ πολεμικὸν σπουδῇ.
πολλοὶ δὲ τῶν Χαλκιδέων δι᾽ ἄγνοιαν ἀπόλλυνται·
οἱ γὰρ ἐκφοβηθέντες ἐτίθεντο φέροντες τὰ ὅπλα
πρὸς τοὺς πολεμίους ὡς πρὸς φιλίους,[6] αὐτὸς
4 ἕκαστος δοκῶν ὕστερος[7] παραγίνεσθαι. οὕτως
οὖν καθ᾽ ἕνα καὶ δύο οἱ πλεῖστοι ἀπώλλυντο,[8]
μέχρι χρόνῳ ὕστερον ἔγνωσαν τὸ συμβαῖνον, τῆς
5 πόλεως ἤδη κατεχομένης. πολεμοῦντα οὖν χρὴ

---

[1] Sauppe : δὲ M. [2] Hertlein : ἐρετρείας M.
[3] ἔχον C, adopted by Casaubon and Hercher.
[4] R. Wünsch : πυργαστρήνην M : πῦρ ἐν γάστρῃ L. Dindorf : πῦρ ἐν γάστρῃ καὶ Jacoby.
[5] Orelli (after Casaubon) : ταῦτα ἢ M.
[6] Hercher : φίλους M. [7] Hertlein : ὕστερον M.
[8] Casaubon : ἀπώλλοιντο M.

---

[1] This incident probably took place during the war over
the Lelantine plain in the latter part of the seventh
century B.C.

quarter each of the authorities should go and send detachments of troops to the battlements. Moreover, there will be leaders to look after everything else, provided that they thus assume immediate command.

IV. [*On pre-arranged Signals*]

As quickly as possible the besieged must be provided with signals, so that they will not fail to recognize those who approach them. For this is the sort of thing that has happened : Chalcis on the Euripus [1] was captured by a fugitive operating from Eretria, aided by one of the inhabitants of the town who practised a stratagem of the following description. To the most deserted part of the city, where the gate was regularly closed, he kept bringing a firepot, and by keeping the fire going day and night he secretly one night burned through the bar of the gate and admitted soldiers at that point.[2] When about two thousand men had gathered in the market-place, the alarm was hastily sounded and many of the Chalcidians were killed because they were not recognized, for in their panic they aligned themselves with their enemies as though they were their friends, each thinking that he was late in coming up. In this way, then, most of them perished by ones and twos, and the city had been in the hands of the enemy for some time before the citizens knew what was happening. It is necessary,

---

[2] In this difficult passage we follow Wünsch and Behrendt (see the latter's dissertation, pp. 78 ff.). The word translated " firepot " occurs nowhere else in Greek, but there are close parallels and the general sense of the passage is clear.

καὶ ἐγγὺς ὄντων τῶν πολεμίων, πρῶτον μὲν τὰ
ἀποστελλόμενα ἐκ τῆς πόλεως κατὰ γῆν ἢ κατὰ
θάλατταν ἐπί τινα πρᾶξιν πρὸς τοὺς ὑπομένοντας
μετὰ συσσήμων ἀποστέλλεσθαι καὶ ἡμερινῶν καὶ
νυκτερινῶν, ἵνα μὴ ἀγνοῶσι πολεμίων αὐτοῖς
6 ἐπιφαινομένων, εἰ[1] φίλιοι ἢ πολέμιοί εἰσιν· ἐπὶ
δὲ πρᾶξιν πορευθέντων καὶ πέμπειν τινὰς γνωσο-
μένους, ἵνα καὶ τὰ τοιαῦτα ὡς ἐκ πλείστου τῶν
ἀπόντων οἱ ὑπομένοντες εἰδῶσιν·[2] μέγα γὰρ ἂν
φέροι πρὸς τὸ μέλλον ἐκ πλείονος παρασκευάζεσθαι.
7 τοῖς δὲ μὴ οὕτω πράττουσιν ἃ συμβέβηκεν ἐμφανι-
σθήσεται τινῶν[3] ἤδη γενομένων, ἃ[4] ἐπὶ παραδείγματος καὶ μαρτυρίου καθαροῦ παραλέγηται.
8 Πεισιστράτῳ γὰρ Ἀθηναίων στρατηγοῦντι ἐξηγ-
γέλθη ὅτι οἱ ἐκ Μεγάρων οἱ ἐπιχειροῖεν ἀφικόμενοι πλοίοις ἐπιθέσθαι νυκτὸς ταῖς τῶν Ἀθηναίων
γυναιξὶν θεσμοφόρια ἀγούσαις ἐν Ἐλευσῖνι· ὁ δὲ
9 Πεισίστρατος ἀκούσας προενήδρευσεν.[5] ἐπεὶ δὲ
οἱ ἐκ τῶν Μεγάρων ὡς λεληθότες ἀπέβησαν καὶ
ἀπὸ τῆς θαλάττης ἐγένοντο, ἐξαναστὰς ὁ Πεισίστρατος τῶν ἐνεδρευθέντων[6] τε ἀνδρῶν ἐκράτησεν
καὶ διέφθειρεν τοὺς πλείστους, καὶ τῶν πλοίων
10 οἷς ἀφίκοντο ἐγκρατὴς ἐγένετο. ἔπειτα παραχρῆμα τοῖς ἑαυτοῦ στρατιώταις πληρώσας τὰ
πλοῖα ἔλαβε τῶν γυναικῶν τὰς ἐπιτηδειοτάτας

---

[1] Added by Casaubon.
[2] Reiske: ἴδωσιν M.   [3] Wünsch: τῶν M.
[4] Wünsch (cf. Goodwin, *Moods and Tenses*, § 258; Kühner-
Gerth, i. 220, n. 2; perhaps the least unsatisfactory restoration of a serious corruption): ἵνα M: R. Schöne indicates a
lacuna after γενομένων.
[5] Casaubon: προσενέδρευσεν M.
[6] Meineke: ἐνεδρευόντων M.

then, in time of war, especially when the enemy is near at hand, first, that the forces which are being sent from the city on some enterprise by land or sea should be furnished with signals for use both by day and by night to those who remain, in order that the latter, if the enemy appear in the meantime, may not be unable to tell friend from foe. And, secondly, after their departure upon the enterprise, persons who will recognize the signals should be sent to watch, so that the men at home may get information of this kind while those returning are still a great way off   For it would be a great advantage to make preparations long beforehand for what is impending. What has befallen those who did not take such precautions will be clear from some actual incidents which may be told in passing as illustration and definite evidence. Word was brought to Peisistratus, when he was general at Athens,[1] that the Megarians would come in ships, and attempt a night attack upon the Athenian women while they were celebrating at Eleusis the festival of Demeter. On hearing this Peisistratus set an ambush ahead of them, and when the Megarians disembarked, in secrecy as they supposed, and were some distance from the sea, he rose up and overcame those who had been trapped, killed most of them, and captured the ships in which they had come. Then after quickly filling the ships with his own soldiers, he took from among the women those best fitted to

---

[1] This incident occurred during the long series of wars with Megara in which Salamis was first lost by Athens and then recovered for her by Solon, and Peisistratus captured Nisaea, the haven of Megara. As Peisistratus at the time of the adventure here described was not yet tyrant, it must have occurred prior to 561-60 B.C.

make the voyage, and late in the day landed at Megara at some distance from the city. Now many of the Megarians, officials and others, when they caught sight of the ships sailing into the harbour, went out to meet them, wishing, no doubt, to see as many women as possible brought in as captives. [Then the Athenians were ordered to attack the enemy], and disembarking with daggers in their hands to strike down some of the Megarians, but to bring back to the ships as many as possible of the most prominent men ; and this they did. From what has been said, then, it is clear that for the conduct of musters and expeditions it is necessary to have prearranged signals, and those of a kind that cannot be misunderstood.

V. [*On Gate-keepers*]

In the next place, no chance persons should be appointed keepers of the gates, but only discreet and sagacious men always capable of suspecting anything brought into the city ; and besides they should be well-to-do and men who have something at stake in the city, that is to say, wife and children ; but not men who, because of poverty, or the pressure of some agreement, or from other stress of circumstances, might either be persuaded by anyone or of themselves incite others to revolt. Leuco, the tyrant of Bosporus,[1] used to discharge even those among his guards who were in debt as a result of dice-playing or other excesses.

[1] This was the region about the Cimmerian Bosporus (the entrance to the Sea of Azov) over which Leuco, an able and honourable man, ruled from 393 to 353 B.C.

VI. ['Ημεροσκοπία]

Χρὴ δὲ καὶ ἡμεροσκόπους πρὸ τῆς πόλεως
καθιστάναι ἐπὶ τόπῳ ὑψηλῷ καὶ ὡς ἐκ πλείστου
φαινομένῳ· ἡμεροσκοπεῖν δὲ ἐφ᾽ ἑκάστῳ χωρίῳ
τρεῖς τοὐλάχιστον, μὴ τοὺς τυχόντας, ἀλλ᾽ ἐμπεί-
ρους πολέμου, ὅπως μὴ δι᾽ ἄγνοιαν δοξάζων[1] τι
ὁ σκοπὸς σημάνῃ ἢ διαγγείλῃ εἰς τὴν πόλιν καὶ
2 ματαίως ὀχλῇ τοῖς ἀνθρώποις. πάσχουσι δὲ ταῦτα
οἱ ἄπειροι τάξεων καὶ πολέμου, ἀγνοοῦντες τὰς
τῶν πολεμίων ἐργασίας καὶ πράξεις, εἴτε ἐκ
παρασκευῆς πράσσεται, εἴτε καὶ παρὰ ταὐτομάτου.
3 ὁ δὲ ἔμπειρος, γνοὺς τὴν τῶν πολεμίων παρασκευὴν
καὶ πλῆθος καὶ πορείας καὶ τὴν ἄλλην κίνησιν
τοῦ στρατεύματος, οὕτω τὴν ἀλήθειαν ἐμφανιεῖ.
4 Ἐὰν δὲ μὴ ὑπάρχωσιν τοιοίδε τόποι, ὥστε καὶ
εἰς τὴν πόλιν ἀπ᾽ αὐτῶν[2] φαίνεσθαι τὰ σημεῖα,
ἄλλους ἐπ᾽ ἄλλοις τόποις διαδεκτῆρας εἶναι τῶν
ἀειρομένων σημείων, οἳ σημανοῦσιν[3] εἰς τὴν
5 πόλιν. εἶναι δὲ τοὺς ἡμεροσκόπους καὶ ποδώκεις,
οἳ ὅσα μὴ οἷά τε διὰ[4] τῶν σημείων δηλοῦν, ἀλλ᾽
αὐτῶν τινα δέῃ ἐξ ἀνάγκης ἀγγέλλειν, δύνωνται[5]
ταχὺ ἀφικνεῖσθαι, καὶ[6] ὡς ἐκ πλείστου ἀγγέλλωσιν.
6 Ἄριστον δὲ ἱππασίμων ὄντων τόπων καὶ ὑπαρχόντων ἵππων[7] ἱππέας συνείρειν,[8] ἵνα διὰ τῶνδε
θᾶσσον ἀγγέλληται. πέμπειν δὲ ἐκ τῆς πόλεως
τοὺς ἡμεροσκόπους ὄρθρου ἢ ἔτι νυκτός, ἵνα τοῖς
τῶν πολεμίων σκοποῖς μὴ κατάδηλοι ὦσιν ἡμέρας
7 πορευόμενοι ἐπὶ τὰ[9] ἡμεροσκοπεῖα.[10] σύνθημα

---

[1] Casaubon: δοξάζον M.   [2] ἀπαντῶν M.
[3] Köchly and Rüstow: σημαίνουσιν M.
[4] Added in B (C).   [5] δυνήσονται R. Schöne.

VI. [*Scouting by Day*]

Day scouts also must be stationed before the city
on a high place visible for as long a distance as
possible. At least three scouts should be at each
place, not chosen at random, but men skilled in
warfare, so that a single scout may not ignorantly
form an opinion and signal or announce it to the city
and trouble the inhabitants to no purpose. Persons
inexperienced in military formations are likely to
do this through not knowing whether the enemy's
acts and deeds are intentional or only accidental,
but the experienced man, understanding the preparations of the enemy, his numbers, line of march,
and other movements, will report the truth.

If there are no such places from which the signals
may be given to the city, there must be relays of
persons at different points to receive the signals as
they are raised and pass them on to the city. The
day scouts must also be swift of foot so that they
can come quickly and report, even from great dis-
tances, matters which cannot be signalled but must
by all means be reported by one of them.

If there are at hand horses and places fit for the use
of horses, it is best to employ relays of horsemen so
that messages may be conveyed more quickly. The
day scouts must be sent from the city at dawn or while
it is still night, lest they be seen by the scouts of
the enemy as they go by daylight to their posts.

---

⁶ κἂν Hercher. ⁷ C: ἱππέων M.

⁸ A correction in B (C): συνιμείρειν M: συνεργεῖν Hercher:
συναίρειν Meineke: συνημερεύειν Bursian: συναγείρειν Old-
.father.

⁹ B in margin (C): ἔπειτα M.

¹⁰ Casaubon: ἡμεροσκοπία M.

δὲ μὴ[1] ἔχειν αὐτοὺς ἓν καὶ τὸ αὐτὸ . . .,[2] ὅπως μήτε
ἑκόντες μήτε ἄκοντες, ἐὰν συλληφθῶσιν ὑπὸ τῶν
πολεμίων, εἰπεῖν ἔχωσι τὸ τῶν ἐν τῇ πόλει σύνθημα.
παραγγέλλεσθαι δὲ τοῖς ἡμεροσκόποις αἴρειν τὰ
σύσσημα[3] ἐνίοτε, καθάπερ οἱ πυρσευταὶ τοὺς
πυρσούς.

VII.

Ὅταν δὲ ἡ χώρα ἐγκάρπως[4] διακέηται[5] μὴ
πόρρω ὄντων πολεμίων, εἰκὸς πολλοὺς τῶν ἐν τῇ
πόλει περὶ τοὺς ἐγγὺς χώρους διατελεῖν, γλιχο-
2 μένους τοῦ καρποῦ. τούτους δ᾽ οὖν εἰς τὴν πόλιν
ἀθροίζειν ὧδε χρή. πρῶτον μὲν τοῖς ἔξω ἅμα
ἡλίῳ δύνοντι σημαίνειν ἀπιέναι εἰς τὴν πόλιν·
ἐὰν δὲ καὶ ἐπὶ πλέον τῆς χώρας ἐσκεδασμένοι
ὦσιν, ὑπὸ διαδεκτήρων σημαίνεσθαι, ὅπως πάντες
3 ἢ οἱ πλεῖστοι παραγίγνωνται εἰς πόλιν. ἐπειδὰν
δὲ τούτοις σημανθῇ ἀπιέναι, οὕτως τοῖς ἐν τῇ
πόλει δειπνοποιεῖσθαι· τὸ δὲ τρίτον σημαίνειν εἰς
4 φυλακὴν ἰέναι καὶ καθιστάναι. ὡς δὲ δεῖ τοῦτο[6]
γίγνεσθαι καὶ ὡς αἴρειν τοὺς φρυκτούς, ἐν τῇ
Παρασκευαστικῇ βίβλῳ πλειόνως εἴρηται. ὅθεν
δεῖ τὴν μάθησιν λαμβάνειν, ἵνα μὴ δὶς[7] περὶ τῶν
αὐτῶν γράφειν συμβῇ.

---

[1] Added by Köchly and Rüstow.
[2] A lacuna of five letters is indicated here in M.
[3] σύσσιμα M.   [4] Reiske: ἔγκαρπος M.
[5] W. Dindorf: διάκειται M.
[6] Casaubon: τούτους M.   [7] Casaubon: μηδεὶς M.

---

[1] For one of the recommendations of Aeneas upon this·
point see the long quotation from Polybius given as Frag. 3
at the end of this text. This, the earliest form of telegraphy,

They must not have the same watchword . . . so that
if they are captured by the enemy they may be able
neither willingly nor unwillingly to reveal the watchword of those in the city. The day scouts should
be told to raise their signals now and then just as the
night scouts raise their torches.

VII.

Whenever it is harvest time in the country and
the enemy is not far away, many of those in the city
are likely to tarry in near-by places, eager to save
the crops. These persons must be gathered into
the city thus. First, they must be signalled to
come into the city by sunset, but if they are scattered
over too much territory signals must be given by
relays, so that all, or most of them, may reach the
city. When the signal is given for them to leave
the fields, one must also be given to those in the
city to prepare the evening meal. Third, the guard
must be signalled to go and take their posts. How
this is to be done and how they are to raise the
signal fires [1] is treated more fully in the book on
Military Preparations. One must get his information from that, so that I may not have to write twice
about the same matters.

seems to have been employed first by the Persians in 490
B.C. (Ephorus, Frag. 107 in *Fragm. Hist. Graec.*), then by
the Greeks at Artemisium in 480 B.C. (Herodotus vii. 182),
and became a common thing in the Peloponnesian war.
Readers will be reminded of the brilliant description of such
a beacon signal given by Aeschylus in the *Agam.* vv. 281-
316. Compare in general A. C. Merriam, "Telegraphing
among the Ancients"; Papers of the Archaeolog. Inst. of
America, iii. 1, 1890.

VIII.

Μετὰ δὲ ταῦτα εἰς τὴν χώραν προσδεχόμενον πλείω καὶ μείζω δύναμιν πολεμίων πρῶτον μὲν τὴν χώραν δυσεπίβολον εἶναι τοῖς πολεμίοις καὶ δυσστρατοπέδευτον καὶ δυσπροσπόριστον κατασκευάζειν καὶ τοὺς ποταμοὺς δυσδιαβάτους καὶ πλείους.[1]

2 Πρός τε τὰς ἀποβάσεις τῶν πολεμίων εἰς τὰ ψαμμώδη καὶ στερεὰ ὅσα καὶ οἷα χρὴ κατασκευάζεσθαι δολώματα τοῖς ἀποβαίνουσι, τοῖς τε ἐν τῇ χώρᾳ καὶ τῇ πόλει λιμέσιν οἷα εἰς τούτους δεῖ φράγματα παρασκευάζεσθαι πρὸς τὸ μὴ εἰσπλεῖν ἢ τὰ εἰσπλεύσαντα μὴ δύνασθαι ἐκπλεῦσαι, 3 τά τε καταλιμπανόμενα ἐν τῇ χώρᾳ ἑκουσίως, εἰς χρείαν δὲ φέροντα τοῖς ἐναντίοις, οἷον πρὸς[2] τειχοποιίαν ἢ σκηνοποιίαν ἢ ἄλλην τινὰ πρᾶξιν ὡς 4 δεῖ[3] ἀχρεῖα ποιεῖν ἢ μή[4] φθείροντα ἀφανίζειν τά τε βρωτὰ καὶ ποτὰ καὶ τὰ κατ' ἀγροὺς ἔγκαρπα[5] καὶ τὰ ἄλλα[6] κατὰ τὴν χώραν, καὶ τὰ[7] στάσιμα ὕδατα ὡς ἄποτα δεῖ ποιεῖν, τά τε ἱππάσιμα τῆς 5 χώρας ὡς δεῖ ἄνιππα ποιεῖν, περὶ μὲν οὖν τούτων πάντων ὧδε μὲν νῦν παραλείπεται, ὡς δεῖ ἕκαστον τούτων γίγνεσθαι, ἵνα μὴ καὶ ταύτῃ, λίαν πολλά, δηλῶται·[8] γέγραπται δὲ τελέως περὶ αὐτῶν ἐν τῇ Παρασκευαστικῇ βίβλῳ.

---

[1] ἀπλεύστους Orelli: ἀπλοίους Meineke (ἀπλόους Koester): ἐλαίους Haupt: δύσπλους Hercher.
[2] Hertlein: πρόσ τε M.   [3] Casaubon: ὡσδὴ M.
[4] Added by Haase; cf. ch. 21.
[5] R. Schöne indicates a lacuna here.
[6] πάντα R. Schöne.
[7] καὶ τὰ added by Meineke.
[8] Orelli: δηλοῦται M.

VIII.

Next, if the invasion of a more numerous and larger force of the enemy is expected, first, the region must be made difficult for the enemy to attack, to encamp in, and to forage in, and the rivers must be made hard to ford and swollen.[1]

The number and kinds of stratagems to be employed against enemies disembarking on sandy and rocky shores ; what kind of barriers must be ready against them at the harbour of the country or of the city so that vessels cannot enter, or, if they do, cannot sail out ; how to make useless the material voluntarily left in the country which might be useful to the foe, for example, that for building walls or huts, or any other enterprise ; or, if it is not destroyed, how to conceal both food and drink, the products of the fields and other things in the country ; and how one must make standing[2] waters undrinkable, and places fit for cavalry movements unfit for them,—the particular treatment of all these subjects is for the present omitted, to avoid explaining them at this point, since they are too numerous. They have been fully treated in the book on *Military Preparations*.

[1] For this idiomatic use of πολύς for a thing in violent motion compare especially Demosthenes, *De corona*, 136 πολλῷ ῥέοντι, and Plutarch, *Agesilaus*, 32 ἐρρύη δὲ πλεῖστος . . . ὁ Εὐρώτας. The manœuvres intended are probably damming up stream courses or breaking dikes, so that the rivers would occupy more beds, channels, or depressions, and thus become literally 'larger.' Notable examples of the same thing in the recent war have occurred on the Yser, the Piave, and the Scarpe.

[2] That is lakes, pools, wells, and cisterns ; not 'stagnant' water.

IX.

Ἂν δὲ θρασύνεσθαί τι ἐπιχειρῶσιν οἱ ἐπιόντες
πρός σε, τάδε ποιητέον. πρῶτον μὲν χρὴ σώμασι
τόπους τινὰς τῆς οἰκείας χώρας καταλαβεῖν,
ἔπειτα ἐκκλησιάσαντα τοὺς αὐτοῦ[1] στρατιώτας
ἢ πολίτας ἄλλα τε προειπεῖν αὐτοῖς, ὡς ὑπαρχούσης τινὸς αὐτοῖς πράξεως εἰς τοὺς πολεμίους,
καὶ ὅταν νυκτὸς σημάνῃ τῇ σάλπιγγι, ἑτοίμους
εἶναι τοὺς ἐν τῇ ἡλικίᾳ, ἀναλαβόντας τὰ ὅπλα καὶ
ἀθροισθέντας εἰς χωρίον ῥητὸν ἕπεσθαι τῷ ἡγου-
2 μένῳ. διαγγελθέντων οὖν τούτων εἰς τὸ στρατόπεδον τῶν πολεμίων ἢ τὴν πόλιν, δύνασαι[2] ἀπο-
3 τρέψαι ὧν ἐπιχειρῶσι πράσσειν. τούτων δὲ
οὕτω πραχθέντων τοῖς μὲν φίλοις θάρσος ἐμποιή-
σεις[3] ἐπιχειρῶν τι ἀλλ' οὐ[4] δεδιώς, τοῖς δὲ
πολεμίοις φόβον ἐμπαρασκευάσεις, ὥστε[5] ἐπὶ
τῆς αὐτῶν[6] ἠρεμεῖν.

X.

Δεῖ δὲ καὶ τάδε παρηγγέλθαι τῶν πολιτῶν τοῖς
κεκτημένοις ζεύγη ἢ ἀνδράποδα ὑπεκτίθεσθαι εἰς
τοὺς προσοίκους, ὡς οὐκ εἰσαξόντων[7] εἰς τὴν
2 πόλιν. οἷς δ' ἂν μὴ ὑπάρξῃ ξενία παρ' οὓς θήσονται,
τοὺς[8] ἄρχοντας δημοσίᾳ παρατίθεσθαι τοῖς προσ-
οίκοις, παρασκευάζοντας δι' ὧν σωθήσεται τὰ
ὑπεκτιθέμενα.

---

[1] Casaubon : αὐτοῦ M.
[2] Casaubon : δύνανται M : δύναται Herm. Schöne.
[3] Meier : ἐμποιήσειας M.
[4] Casaubon : ἐπιχειρῶντι ἄλλου M.

IX.

If the invaders try to overawe you, your first action must be to occupy certain places in your own country with men, and calling an assembly of your own soldiers or citizens, explain the situation to them, telling them that there is some operation on hand for them against the enemy and that when a signal is given by trumpet at night those of military age are to be ready to take arms, gather in an appointed place, and follow their leader. So when this is reported to the camp of the enemy, or to their city, you can divert them from what they are attempting to do. If these things are so done you will inspire your friends with courage by your initiative and fearlessness and arouse fear in your enemies so that they will remain quietly at home.

X.

One must also notify those citizens who own cattle or slaves to place them in safety among neighbours, since they cannot bring them into the city. The authorities at public expense must place such property with neighbouring peoples and provide means for its support if the owners have no friends to whom they may entrust it.

---

[5] Added by Casaubon.
[6] Hertlein: ἀντῶν M.
[7] Casaubon: εἰσαξιόντων M.
[8] Hertlein: πρὸσ τοὺς M.

[Κηρύγματα]

3 Ἔπειτα κηρύγματα ποιεῖσθαι τοιάδε διά τινος χρόνου, φόβου καὶ ἀποτροπῆς τῶν ἐπιβουλευόντων ἕνεκεν. κατακομίζειν τὰ ἐλεύθερα σώματα καὶ τοὺς καρποὺς ἐν τῇ πόλει, τοῦ δὲ ἀνηκουστοῦντος ἐξουσίαν εἶναι τῷ βουλομένῳ ἀζήμια ἄγειν καὶ 4 φέρειν τὰ ἐκ τῆς χώρας. τάς τε ἑορτὰς κατὰ πόλιν ἄγειν, συλλόγους τε ἰδίους μηδαμοῦ μήτε ἡμέρας μήτε νυκτὸς γίγνεσθαι, τοὺς δὲ ἀναγκαίους ἢ ἐν πρυτανείῳ[1] ἢ ἐν βουλῇ ἢ ἐν ἄλλῳ φανερῷ τόπῳ. μηδὲ θύεσθαι μάντιν ἰδίᾳ ἄνευ 5 τοῦ ἄρχοντος. μηδὲ δειπνεῖν κατὰ συσσιτίαν ἀλλ' ἐν ταῖς αὐτῶν[2] οἰκίαις ἑκάστους, ἔξω γάμου καὶ περιδείπνου, καὶ ταῦτα προαπαγγείλαντας τοῖς ἄρχουσιν.

Ἐὰν δὲ ὦσιν φυγάδες, ἐπικηρύσσειν, ὃς ἂν ἀστῶν ἢ ξένων ἢ δούλων ἀποκινῇ, ἃ ἑκάστῳ 6 τούτων ἔσται. καὶ ἐάν τίς τινι τῶν φυγάδων συγγένηται ἢ παρ' ἐκείνων τισὶν ἢ ἐπιστολὰς πέμψῃ ἢ δέξηται, εἶναί τινα κίνδυνον ἢ ἐπιτίμιον

---

[1] Casaubon: πυρσανείῳ M.
[2] Köchly and Rüstow: αὐτῶν M.

---

[1] That is, within the walls, since many Greek festivals, then, as now, were held at sacred spots in the countryside.

[2] So as to avoid unauthorized efforts to foretell the future. The unwelcome prophecies of those who did not represent the 'patriotic' point of view, might be very disconcerting, as well-known instances from the Old Testament show. Similarly under the Roman Empire the charge of merely having had a horoscope prepared was sometimes regarded as sufficient warrant for putting a prominent and ambitious man out of the way.

[3] The exception made is due to the marked religious character of these particular feasts. The meal, attended by

[*Proclamations*]

Furthermore, proclamations such as these are to issued from time to time to frighten and deter conspirators : The free population and the ripe crops are to be brought into the city, authority being given to anyone so disposed to lead away or carry off from the country, without fear of punishment, the possessions of anyone who disobeys this regulation. The usual festivals are to be celebrated in the city,[1] and private gatherings shall not take place, either by day or by night, but those which are really necessary may be held in the town-hall, the council-chamber, or other public place. A soothsayer shall not make sacrifice on his own account without the presence of a magistrate.[2] Men shall not dine in common but each in his own house, except in the case of a wedding or a funeral feast,[3] and then only upon previous notice to the authorities.

If there are any citizens in exile, announcement is to be made what is to be done with each citizen, stranger, or slave who may try to leave.[4] And if any person associate with any of the exiles, or in dealing with any of them send or receive letters, there is to be a definite risk or even a penalty awaiting him. Out-

---

large numbers of guests, was an essential feature, serving originally, no doubt, to secure as many competent witnesses as possible to the fact and the good faith of the transaction. Even after a battle the funeral meal might be held in the house of some private person very closely associated in some responsible way with the enterprise. Thus after the battle of Chaeronea in 338 B.C. the funeral feast was held in the house of Demosthenes (*De corona*, 288).

[4] For the purpose namely of getting in touch with those exiles, the most dangerous class of enemies to the established government.

αὐτῷ. τῶν δὲ ἐκπεμπομένων καὶ εἰσαγομένων
ἐπιστολῶν εἶναι ἐπισκόπησιν, πρὸς[1] οὓς οἰσθή-
7 σεται πρότερον. ὅπλα οἷς ἐστιν ἑνὸς πλείω
ἀπογράφεσθαι, καὶ ἐξάγειν μηδένα μηδὲν ὅπλον,
μηδὲ ἐνέχυρον δέχεσθαι. στρατιώτας μὴ μισθοῦ-
σθαι μηδὲ ἑαυτὸν μισθοῦν ἄνευ τῶν ἀρχόντων.
8 ἐκπλεῖν μηδένα ἀστῶν μηδὲ μέτοικον ἄνευ συμ-
βόλου, τά τε πλοῖα προπαρηγγέλθαι[2] ὁρμίζεσθαι
9 καθ' ἃς πύλας ἐν τοῖς ἐχομένοις ῥηθήσεται. ξένους
τοὺς ἀφικνουμένους τὰ ὅπλα ἐμφανῆ καὶ πρόχειρα
φέρειν, καὶ εὐθὺς[3] αὐτῶν παραιρεῖσθαι,[4] καὶ
αὐτοὺς μηδένα ὑποδέχεσθαι, μηδὲ τοὺς πανδοκέας,[5]
ἄνευ τῶν ἀρχόντων, τοὺς δὲ ἄρχοντας ἀπογράφεσθαι καὶ παρ' ᾧ τίνες,[6] ὅταν[7] κατάγωνται.
10 τὰς δὲ νύκτας ὑπὸ τῶν ἀρχόντων τὰ πανδοκεῖα[8]
ἔξωθεν κλείεσθαι. διὰ χρόνου δέ τινος, ὅσοι ἂν
ταλαπείριοι αὐτῶν ὦσιν,[9] ἐκκηρύττεσθαι. ὁμόρους
δὲ ἢ κατὰ παίδευσιν ἢ κατ' ἄλλην τινὰ χρείαν
11 ἐπιδημοῦντας ἀπογράφεσθαι. ταῖς δὲ δημοσίαις
ἀφικνουμέναις πρεσβείαις ἀπὸ πόλεων ἢ τυράννων
ἢ στρατοπέδων οὐ χρὴ ἐν αὐτοῖς[10] τὸν ἐθέλοντα
διαλέγεσθαι, ἀλλ' ἀεὶ παρεῖναί[11] τινας τῶν πολιτῶν
τοὺς πιστοτάτους, οἳ μετ' αὐτῶν συνδιατελοῦσιν[12]

---

[1] C: πρὸς M.   [2] Hertlein: προσηγγέλθαι M.
[3] Hercher: εὐθὺ M.   [4] Reiske: παρῆσθαι M (cf. 30. 2).
[5] Hertlein: πανδοχέας M.   [6] Herm. Schöne: ὦτινεσ M.
[7] Köchly and Rüstow: ὅτ' ἂν M.
[8] Hertlein: πανδοχεῖα M.   [9] B: ὡσεὶ M.
[10] Herm. Schöne: αὐτοῖς M.
[11] Suggested by R. Schöne.   [12] Reiske: συντελοῦσιν M.

going and incoming letters shall be brought to censors before being sent out or delivered.[1] Men who have more than one equipment of arms shall return a list of them, and no one shall send any weapon out of the city or receive such as security. Soldiers may not be hired nor may one serve for hire without the permission of the authorities. No citizen or resident alien shall take passage on a ship without a passport,[2] and orders shall be given that ships shall anchor near gates designated in what follows. Strangers arriving shall carry their weapons unconcealed and ready at hand, and immediately upon arrival shall be disarmed, while no one, not even the innkeepers, shall receive them without permission from the authorities, who shall record also in whose house any persons are, when they take lodging; and at night inns must be locked from the outside by the authorities. From time to time vagrants among these strangers shall be publicly expelled. Citizens of neighbouring states, however, residing in the city for the sake of education[3] or for some other special purpose, shall be registered. Not everyone who wishes may converse with public embassies representing cities, princes, or armies, but there must always be present certain of the most trusted citizens who shall stay with the ambas-

---

[1] Plautus in the *Trinummus* (from Philemon †c. 263 B.C.), vv. 793-5 makes mention of *portitores* who even in time of peace might break the seals and inspect letters.

[2] The first mention of such a passport is in the *Birds* of Aristophanes (414 B.C.), vv. 1212-15, where it would seem that a σφραγίς or visé by an officer was also required.

[3] That is, in the larger places mainly students, but in the ordinary cities for which Aeneas wrote more likely visiting sophists, philosophers, music teachers, and the like.

12 μέχρις ἂν ἐνδημῶσιν οἱ πρέσβεις. καὶ ὧν ἂν
σπανίζῃ ἡ πόλις, σίτου ἢ ἐλαίου ἢ ἄλλου τινός,
τῷ εἰσάγοντι κατὰ πλῆθος τῶν εἰσαγομένων
τόκους προκεῖσθαι καὶ στέφανον δίδοσθαι εἰς
τιμήν, τῷ δὲ ναυκλήρῳ ἀνολκὴν καὶ καθολκήν.[1]

13 ἐξοπλισίας τε πυκνὰς ποιεῖσθαι, καὶ ξένους τοὺς
ἐνδήμους τὸν καιρὸν τούτου μεθίστασθαι εἰς
χωρίον ῥητὸν ἢ κατ' οἶκον διατελεῖν· ἧ δὲ ἂν
ἄλλῃ[2] φαίνηται, ζημίαν προκεῖσθαι ὡς ἀδικοῦντι.

14 ὅταν τε σημήνῃ, τούτοις τὰ[3] ἐμπόρια καὶ πρατήρια
κλείεσθαι, καὶ τὰ λύχνα κατασβέννυσθαι, καὶ τῶν

15 ἄλλων μηδένα ἔτι παρεῖναι·[4] ὅταν δέ τινι ἀναγ-
καῖόν τι συμβῇ, μετὰ λαμπτῆρος βαδίζειν, ἕως ἂν
ἀντιπαραγγελθῇ.[5] καὶ ὃς ἂν καταμηνύσῃ τινὰ
ἐπιβουλεύοντα τῇ πόλει, ἢ ὅ τι ἂν τῶν προγεγραμμένων τις πραττόμενον ἐξαγγείλῃ, ἀνηγγέλθαι τε
αὐτῷ ἀργύριον καὶ τὸ ἀγγελθὲν ἐμφανῶς προκεῖσθαι ἐν ἀγορᾷ ἢ ἐπὶ βωμοῦ ἢ ἐν ἱερῷ, ἵνα
προχειρότερόν τις τολμήσῃ μηνύειν τι τῶν προγεγραμμένων.

16 Ἐπὶ δὲ μονάρχῳ ἢ στρατηγῷ ἢ φυγάδι δυνα-
στεύοντι χρὴ καὶ τάδε προκηρύττεσθαι . . . . .[6]

---

[1] Casaubon: καθολικὴν M.
[2] Casaubon, Behrendt: ἧι δε, αν ἀλλη M.
[3] Meineke, Schenkl: τὰ τόυτοισ M.
[4] παριέναι Meineke: προϊέναι Hercher.
[5] R. Schöne: παραγγελθῇ M.
[6] Köchly and Rüstow indicated the lacuna.

---

[1] This seems to be the earliest instance of profit-fixing
(and hence price-fixing) as a special war measure. Casaubon
thought that the purpose was to prevent profiteering;
Köchly and Rüstow on the other hand, that it was to

sadors so long as they remain. For the importer of whatever the city lacks, grain or oil or anything else, profits shall be specified in proportion to the amount of his importations,[1] and he shall be honoured with a crown, and the shipmaster shall be granted allowance for the hauling up and down of his vessel.[2] Frequent calls to arms shall be given and all strangers in the town shall at this time assemble in a specified place or remain indoors ; if, however, one of them shall appear elsewhere, a penalty shall be prescribed for him as a malefactor. At a given signal their stores and shops shall be closed and their lights extinguished, and no one else shall come in. Whenever it is necessary for anyone, he may go out with a lantern, until orders are issued to the contrary. For whoever points out anyone conspiring against the city, or reports anyone as doing any of the things above-mentioned, a reward in money shall be announced, and the reward shall be displayed openly in the market-place or on an altar or in a temple, in order that men may the more readily venture to report any violation of the provisions mentioned.

Concerning a sovereign, a general, or a fugitive ruler one should make also the following proclama-

encourage capitalists to undertake the serious risks involved in supplying a city during war–time. It seems most reasonable to suppose that the setting of a fixed percentage of profit which must have been guaranteed by the state would act both to " encourage production," that is, in this case, importation, and to keep down prices as well.

[2] In ancient times, as now, the bulk of the foodstuffs transported in Greece was carried in light coasting vessels which were pulled up on shore when not in use. Aeneas probably has in mind the charges for this hauling up and down, and not ordinary harbour tolls, as is generally assumed.

ἐὰν δέ τι καὶ αὐτὸς πάθῃ ὁ ἀποκτείνας, τοῖς τέκνοις αὐτοῦ ἀποδίδοσθαι τὸ ἀγγελθὲν ἀργύριον·

17 ἐὰν δὲ μὴ ᾖ τέκνα, τῷ ἐγγυτάτω γενομένῳ.[1] καὶ ἐάν τις τῶν συνόντων τῷ φυγάδι ἢ μονάρχῳ ἢ στρατηγῷ πράξῃ τι . . .[2] τῶν προκειμένων ἀποδίδοσθαι καὶ κάθοδον αὐτῷ εἶναι· διὰ γὰρ ταῦτα

18 προχειροτέρως ἂν ἐγχειροῖεν. ἐν[3] δὲ ξενικῷ στρατοπέδῳ τοιάδ', ἀναγγείλαντα[4] σιγήν, πάντων

19 ἀκουόντων κηρῦξαι. εἴ τις βούλεται ἀπιέναι, μὴ ἀρεσκόμενοι[5] τοῖς παροῦσιν, ἐξεῖναι ἀπαλλάττεσθαι· ἀλλ' ὕστερον[6] . . .[7] πεπωλήσεται· τὰ δ' ἐλάσσω τούτων ἀδικήματα, κατὰ τὸν νόμον τὸν προκείμενον δεσμὸς ἢ[8] ζημία. ἐὰν δέ τις φαίνηται βλάπτων τι τὸ στράτευμα, διαλύων τὸ στρατό-

20 πεδον, θάνατος ἔστω ἡ[9] ζημία. μετὰ δὲ ταῦτα τῶν ἄλλων τάξεων ἐπιμέλειαν ποιητέον. καὶ πρῶτον ἐπισκεπτέον εἰ ὁμονοοῦσιν οἱ πολῖται, ὡς ἂν ὄντος μεγίστου τούτου ἀγαθοῦ ἐν πολιορκίᾳ· εἰ δὲ μή, τῶν τὰ ἐναντία φρονούντων τοῖς παροῦσι

---

[1] γένει Reiske: γένει or γένους Kirchhoff: γένους Hercher.

[2] Hercher indicated the lacuna: R. Schöne suggests very plausibly τὸ ἥμισυ, which the translation follows.

[3] Orelli: ἐὰν M.   [4] Meier: ἀναγγείλαντι M.

[5] ἀρεσκόμενος Casaubon.   [6] ὑστερῶν Wünsch.

[7] R. Schöne indicated the lacuna.

[8] Orelli: ἢ M.   [9] AC: ἢ M.

---

[1] Obviously the reward of the assassin has been lost here, the general character of which can be learned from other sources. Thus in the decree of Demophantus at Athens, in 410-9 B.C., the assassin was to be regarded innocent of all crimes or guilt and to receive one-half of the confiscated estate of the tyrant, while if he perished in the attempt his children were to be treated like the descendants of Harmodius and Aristogeiton, that is, maintained and honoured at the public expense (Andocides, De mysteriis, 93 ff.; Demo-

tions[1]: If the tyrannicide himself come to grief, the reward announced shall be paid to his children, and if he have none, to his next of kin. And if anyone of the associates of the exile or sovereign or general do some [service to the state, one-half of] the reward shall be paid him and a return to his home shall be granted, for because of these considerations he would the more readily make the attempt. In a mercenary force, after a call for silence, the following shall be proclaimed in the hearing of all : If anyone is displeased with the existing conditions, and wishes to withdraw, he may do so, but afterwards . . . he will be sold into slavery. For offences less than these imprisonment shall be the penalty, according to the existing law. If anyone be shown to be injuring the army or demoralizing the camp, death shall be the penalty. Then attention shall be given to the other classes. First, one must note whether the citizens are of one mind, since that would be of greatest advantage during a siege. If not, one must, without arousing suspicion, remove [the most

sthenes xx. 159). At Ilium, early in the third century, the rewards are most detailed and explicit. The tyrannicide is to receive a talent of silver and have a bronze statue erected in his honour ; he shall be kept at the public expense ; at contests called to the front seat by name ; and receive a pension of two drachmas a day as long as he lives. A foreigner is to receive citizenship in addition to these rewards, while a slave is given his freedom, one half talent of silver, and (probably) one drachma a day as pension (Inscr. in Dittenberger's *Orientis Graeci Inscr. Sel.* no. 218, ll. 19 ff.). Fragments of a similar decree from Eretria at about the middle of the fourth century B.C. have also been published (see A. Wilhelm, *Jahresh. d. österr. arch. Inst.* 8 (1905), pp. 13 ff.), and for Erythrae, in the age of Cimon (*I.G.* i. 9). For a general discussion of such legislation see *Recueil des inscr. jurid. grecques* ii. (1898), pp. 25-57.

influential of] those out of sympathy with the existing
order of things, especially those who might become
leaders and responsible for action in the city, sending
them away somewhere on a plausible pretext, as
ambassadors or on other public business. For instance, Dionysius did this in the case of his brother
Leptines, when he saw that he was popular with the
people of Syracuse and in many ways influential.
Becoming suspicious of him and desiring to get rid of
him, he did not openly attempt to expel him, for he
knew that he would have great support and favour
and that a revolution might ensue, so he devised this
scheme. He sent him with a few mercenaries to a
city named Himera, directing him to bring back part
of its garrison and reorganize the rest. When he
arrived at Himera, Dionysius sent him word to stay
there until he sent for him.[1]

When a city has given hostages and a campaign
is made against it, the parents and next of kin of
the hostages should depart from the place until
the siege is over, in order that they may not, in the
assaults by the enemy, see their own sons brought
forward and meeting a cruel end. For it is possible
that these people, if they were in the city, might go

---

[1] The Dionysius mentioned here is the first of that name
(405–367). The event mentioned occurred probably in 397 B.C.,
the year in which Himera came over to Dionysius (Diodorus,
xiv. 47. 6), or soon thereafter, at all events before the battle
of Cronium, in 383 B.C., in which Leptines lost his life
(Diodorus xv. 17. 1). From the phrase used by Diodorus,
μεθ' οὓς Ἱμεραίους μετεπέμψατο (xiv. 47. 6), it would seem
that this might be the very occasion referred to by Aeneas,
although it is possible that the year 386 B.C. is meant, at
which time Dionysius I sent Leptines and Philistus into
exile (Diodorus xv. 7. 3).

24 ὑπεναντίον τι πρᾶξαι. ἐὰν δὲ ἄρα δυσχερὲς[1] ᾖ[2]
μετὰ τῶνδε τῶν προφάσεων ἐκπέμπειν, συνδιάγειν
αὐτοὺς ὡς ἐλαχίστων μετέχοντας ἔργων καὶ
πράξεων καὶ μήτε ὅπου ἔσονται μήτε ὅ τι πρά-
ξουσιν προειδέναι, καὶ ὡς ἥκιστα ἐπὶ σφῶν αὐτῶν
διατηροῦντας καὶ νύκτα καὶ ἡμέραν· καὶ ἄλλας
ἐπ᾽ ἄλλαις[3] πράξεις καὶ λειτουργίας αὐτοῖς τὸ
πλῆθος ἐπιρρεῖν ἀνυπόπτως, μεθ᾽ ὧν ὄντες ἐν
25 φυλακῇ μᾶλλον ἔσονται ἢ φυλάξουσί τι. ἔστωσαν
δὲ διειλημμένοι ὡς εἰς παρατήρησιν·[4] οὕτως γὰρ
ἂν διακείμενοι ἥκιστα ἂν δύναιντο νεωτερίσαι.

Ἔτι τοίνυν μηδὲ εἰς τὰς κοίτας λαμπτῆρας
φέρεσθαι μηδὲ ἄλλο νυκτερινὸν φέγγος· ἤδη γάρ
τινες, ἐπεὶ πάντῃ[5] ἐξείργονται μηδὲν[6] νεωτερίσαι,
θέλοντες, μηδὲ πρὸς τοὺς πολεμίους τι πρᾶξαι,
26 τοιόνδε τεχνάζουσι. σὺν γὰρ τοῖς καλάθοις[7] καὶ
στρώμασι φερόμενοι[8] εἰς τὰς φυλακὰς λύχνα οἱ
δὲ δᾷδας οἱ δὲ λαμπτῆρας, ἵνα δὴ[9] πρός τι κοιτα-
σθῶσιν, διὰ[10] τούτων τῶν φεγγέων[11] σύσσημον
ἐποιήσαντο· διὸ δεῖ πάντα τὰ τοιαῦτα ὑποπτεύειν.

XI. [Ἐπιβουλαί]

Ἔτι δὲ καὶ τῶν πολιτῶν δεῖ τοῖς[12] ἀντιπρο-
θυμουμένοις προσέχειν τὸν νοῦν καὶ μηδὲν εὐθέως[13]
2 ἀποδέχεσθαι διὰ τάδε. ῥηθήσονται δὲ ἑξῆς αἱ

---

[1] Casaubon : δυσχερὴς M.
[2] Added by Köchly and Rüstow.
[3] Reiske : ἐπάλλας M.
[4] Köchly and Rüstow : ὡσεὶ παρὰ τρισίν M.
[5] Casaubon : ἐπὶ πάντη M.   [6] Casaubon : μηδὲ M.
[7] Orelli : ἀκολούθοις M.   [8] Haase : φερομένοις M.
[9] Casaubon : δὲ M.   [10] Added by Hercher.

so far as to engage in some act of opposition. If, however, it prove difficult to send such persons out on these pretexts, they must continue in the city but share in only the fewest possible works and undertakings, and they must not know in advance where they are to be or what they are to do, being as little as possible their own masters by night and day. And on one duty and special service after another, without raising suspicion, many persons should keep coming and going about them, in whose company they will be under guard rather than on guard. But let them be divided, so that they may be kept under watch, for in this manner they would be least able to begin a revolution.

Again, citizens are not to go to bed with lamps or any light at night, for in some instances persons who have been thwarted in every way from beginning a revolution (which was what they wished), and from entering into negotiations with the enemy, have contrived thus : carrying lights to their positions on guard-duty, along with their baskets and bedding — sometimes taking torches, sometimes lamps — ostensibly in order to have some light to go to bed by, they have by these lights given a pre-arranged signal. Accordingly, all such matters must be regarded with suspicion.

XI. [Plots]

One must, further, keep an eye on those of the citizens who are disaffected and not be too ready to accept their advice. To show this, I shall here

---

[11] Hercher (φεγγῶν : φεγγέων Behrendt): τοῦτον τὸν φεγγαῖον M.

[12] R. Schöne: τοῖσ δει (with indication of wrong order) M.

[13] εὐήθως (cf. xxviii. 7) Herm. Schöne.

ἐπιβουλαὶ ἐκ τῆς βίβλου[1] παραδείγματος ἕνεκεν,
ὅσαι κατὰ πόλιν ἐξ ἀρχόντων ἢ ἰδιωτῶν γεγόνασιν
καὶ ὡς ἔνιαι αὐτῶν κωλυθεῖσαι διελύθησαν.

3 Χίου γὰρ μελλούσης προδίδοσθαι, τῶν ἀρχόντων
τις, συμπροδιδοὺς καὶ ἀπατῶν τοὺς συνάρχοντας[2]
ἔπεισε λέγων, ὡς, ἐπειδὴ εἰρήνη εἴη, τοῦ τε
λιμένος τὸ κλεῖθρον εἰς γῆν ἀνασπάσαντας ξηρᾶναι
δεῖ καὶ πισσαλοιφῆσαι καὶ τὰ παλαιὰ τῶν νεῶν
ἄρμενα ἀποδόσθαι, τῶν τε νεωρίων ἐπεσκευάσθαι
τὰ στάζοντα καὶ τὴν ἐχομένην αὐτῶν στοὰν καὶ
τὸν πύργον, ἐν ᾧ διῃτῶντο οἱ ἄρχοντες, ἐχόμενον
τῆς στοᾶς, ἵνα ἐκ προφάσεως κλίμακες προ-
πορισθῶσιν[3] τοῖς μέλλουσι καταλαμβάνειν τὰ
4 νεώρια καὶ τὴν στοὰν καὶ τὸν πύργον. ἔτι δὲ
συνεβούλευε καὶ τὸ πλῆθος τῶν τὴν πόλιν φυλασσόντων ἀπόμισθον ποιῆσαι, ἵν' ὡς ἐλάχιστον
5 δῆθεν ἀνάλωμα τῇ πόλει ᾖ.[4] καὶ ἄλλα τούτοις
ὁμότροπα λέγων ἔπεισε τοὺς συνάρχοντας ἅπερ
ἔμελλεν[5] τοῖς προδιδοῦσι καὶ ἐπιτιθεμένοις[6] συνοίσειν πρὸς τὴν κατάληψιν· ὥστε ἀεὶ δεῖ προσέχειν τοῖς τὰ τοιαῦτα τελειοῦν[7] σπουδάζουσιν.
6 ἅμα δὲ τοῦ τείχους ἐκδήσας[8] κατεκρέμασε δίκτυα
ἐλάφεια καὶ σύεια, ὡσεὶ ξηρᾶναι θέλων, καὶ ἄλλῃ
ἱστία[9] ἔξω τοὺς κάλους ἔχοντα· καθ' ἅπερ ἐν
νυκτὶ ἀνέβησαν στρατιῶται.

---

[1] ποριστικῆς βίβλου Hercher : πολιτικῆς Köchly and
Rüstow : Casaubon thought of the ἀκούσματα : R. Schöne
with great probability suggests an ἐπιβουλῶν βίβλος.
[2] Casaubon : ἄρχοντας M.
[3] R. Schöne : προσπορισθῶσιν M.
[4] Casaubon : ἢ M.   [5] Meineke : ἔμελλον M.
[6] Köchly and Rüstow : ἐπιθεμένοις M.
[7] B²C : λειοῦν M.
[8] Haupt : ἐπιδήσας M.   [9] Orelli : σύεια M.

note in order and by way of example, from the book on this subject, how many plots have been made within various cities by officials or by private citizens, and how some of these have been completely frustrated.

Just before the betrayal of Chios,[1] one of the officials, who was a party to the act of treason, deceitfully persuaded his colleagues, that, since the state was at peace, they ought to draw the barrier of the harbour up on land for drying and caulking, to sell the old rigging of the ships, and to repair the leaky roofs of the ship-houses as well as of the adjoining arsenal and of the tower next to this arsenal, in which the magistrates took their meals—all as a pretext, so that ladders might be at hand for those who were to seize ship-houses, arsenal, and tower. He further advised that the majority of the men who were doing guard-duty in the city should be paid off, on the pretext that the expense to the state might be as small as possible. With these and similar arguments he won over his colleagues to every measure that would contribute to the victory of the conspirators when they made this seizure. Accordingly, one must always keep an eye on those who are too eager to effect matters of this kind. At the same time he fastened to the wall and hung out, as if for drying, deer nets and boar nets, and in other places sails with the ropes hanging, and it was by these that the soldiers climbed up at night.

[1] Nothing is known further about this event. Chios had tyrants (Athen. vi. 259 A, B), and was the scene of frequent and fierce struggles between oligarchs and democrats (Aristotle, *Pol.* 1306 b 3 ff.; Aelian, *Var. Hist.* xiv. 25).

7 Πρὸς δὲ ἀντιστασιώτας τοιόνδε ἐπράχθη ἐν Ἄργει. μελλόντων γὰρ τῶν πλουσίων τὴν δευτέραν ἐπίθεσιν ἐπιτίθεσθαι τῷ δήμῳ καὶ ξένους ἐπαγομένων, ὁ τοῦ δήμου προστάτης, προαισθόμενος τὸ μέλλον, τῶν ἐπιθησομένων τινὰς τῶν ὑπεναντίων ὄντων τῷ δήμῳ ἄνδρας δύο προσποιησάμενος φίλους εἶναι ἀπορρήτους, πολεμίους αὐτῷ[1] καθίστησιν αὐτοὺς καὶ ἐποίει κακῶς ἐν τῷ φανερῷ, σιγῇ δὲ τὰ[2] ἐκ τῶν ἐναντίων βουλεύματα ἤκουεν παρ' αὐτῶν.

8 ἐπεὶ δ' ἐν τῷ εἰσάγεσθαι τοὺς ξένους ἦσαν οἱ πλούσιοι, ἅμα δὲ καὶ τῶν ἐν τῇ πόλει τινὲς ἦσαν ἕτοιμοι, καὶ εἰς τὴν ἐπιοῦσαν νύκτα ἔμελλεν τὸ ἔργον ἔσεσθαι, ἔδοξε τῷ τοῦ δήμου προστάτῃ τὴν[3] ταχίστην ἐκκλησίαν συναγαγεῖν καὶ τὸ μέλλον μὴ προειπεῖν, ἵνα μὴ πᾶσα ἡ πόλις ταραχθῇ, εἰπόντα[4] δὲ ἄλλα τε καὶ ὅτι συμφέρον εἴη ἐν τῇ ἐπιούσῃ νυκτὶ σὺν τοῖς ὅπλοις πάντας Ἀργείους[5] παρεῖναι

9 ἐν τῇ αὐτοῦ[6] φυλῇ ὄντας ἕκαστον.[7] ἐὰν δέ τις ἄλλως[8] ἐκθῆται τὰ ὅπλα ἢ ἄλλῃ ἐξενεγκάμενος φανῇ, ὡς προδότης καὶ ἐπιβουλεύων τῷ δήμῳ

10 πασχέτω τι. τοῦτο δὴ αὐτὸ ἵνα κατὰ τὰς φυλὰς ὄντες οἱ πλούσιοι μὴ δύνωνται εἰς ταὐτὸ ἀθροισθέντες μετὰ τῶν ξένων ἐπιθέσθαι, ἀλλ' ἐν ταῖς φυλαῖς ὄντες διακεχωρισμένοι ὦσιν ἐν πολλοῖς ὀλίγοι φυλέταις. καλῶς δὲ δοκεῖ καὶ ἀγχινόως μετ' ἀσφαλείας διαλῦσαι τὸ μέλλον.

---

[1] Orelli : αὐτῷ M.

[2] Casaubon : τὸ M.　　　　　　[3] Added by Schenkl.

[4] εἰπεῖν Köchly and Rüstow : εἶπεν Herm. Schöne.

[5] Schöne : M, now illegible, formerly reported to have μὲν οὖσ(?) : ἄγει οὖς A : ἔχει οὖς B.

[6] Köchly and Rüstow : αὐτοῦ M.　　　[7] Meier : ἑκατὸν M.

[8] ἄλλοσε Reiske (ἄλλοσ' R. Schöne).

Against revolutionists the following plan was carried out in Argos. When the rich men's party was about to launch the second attack [1] against the people and was bringing up mercenaries, the leader of the people's party, who had found out what was about to happen, just before the attack won over two men of the party hostile to the people, to be his secret accomplices, and while publicly treating them as his enemies and abusing them he heard from them in private the plans of the opposing party. Then, when the rich men were in the act of bringing in their mercenaries, and others of their party were at the same time ready within the city, and the deed was to take place the next night, he decided to call an immediate assembly of the people, without announcing what was to come, that the city might not be thrown into utter confusion, and told them, among other things, that it was desirable for all Argives to stand at arms during the coming night, each man with his own tribe. Further, that if anyone should follow a different course in arming himself or should appear elsewhere and out of his proper station, he should be punished as a traitor and conspirator against the people. The purpose of this was that the rich men, scattered among the various tribes, should not be able to assemble at one point and attack with the mercenaries, but should be distributed in the several tribes as a small minority among their fellow-tribesmen. And he seems to have dealt skilfully, cleverly, and safely with the impending danger.

[1] This is probably to be referred (with Hug, *Aeneas von Stymphalus*, p. 6, n. 6) to the revolutions of 370 B.C., that finally ended in the notorious σκυταλισμός, in which the people clubbed to death more than a thousand of the oligarchs. See Ed. Meyer, *Gesch. d. Alt.* v. § 948.

10ª   Παραπλησίως δὲ ἐν Ἡρακλείᾳ τῇ ἐν τῷ Πόντῳ,
οὔσης δημοκρατίας καὶ ἐπιβουλευόντων τῶν
πλουσίων τῷ δήμῳ καὶ μελλόντων ἐπιτίθεσθαι,
προγνόντες οἱ προστάται τοῦ δήμου τὸ μέλλον, οὐσῶν
αὐτοῖς τριῶν φυλῶν καὶ τεσσάρων ἑκατοστύων,
ἔπεισαν τὸ πλῆθος ἑξήκοντα εἶναι ἑκατοστύας, ἵνα
ἐν ταύταις καὶ εἰς τὰς φυλακὰς καὶ εἰς τὰς ἄλλας
11 λειτουργίας φοιτῶσιν οἱ πλούσιοι. συνέβαινεν
καὶ ἐνταῦθα διεσκεδασμένους εἶναι τοὺς πλουσίους
καὶ ἐν ταῖς ἑκατοστύσιν ὀλίγους[1] ἑκάστοθι παρα-
12 γίγνεσθαι ἐν πολλοῖς δημόταις· ὁμότροπον δέ τι
τούτῳ καὶ πάλαι[2] ἐν Λακεδαίμονι γενέσθαι.[3]
μηνυθείσης γὰρ ἐπιβουλῆς τοῖς ἄρχουσιν ὅτι ὅταν
ὁ πῖλος[4] ἀρθῇ ἐπιθήσονται, ἔπαυσαν τοὺς ἐγ-
χειροῦντας ἐπιθέσθαι, κήρυγμα ἀναγγείλαντες τοὺς
τὸν πῖλον[5] μέλλοντας ἆραι μὴ ἆραι.
13   Ἐν Κορκύρᾳ δὲ ἐπανάστασιν δέον γενέσθαι ἐκ τῶν
πλουσίων καὶ ὀλιγαρχικῶν τῷ δήμῳ (ἐπεδήμει[6] δὲ
καὶ Χάρης Ἀθηναῖος φρουρὰν ἔχων, ὅσπερ[7] συν-
14 ήθελεν τῇ ἐπαναστάσει) ἐτεχνάσθη τοιόνδε. τῶν
τῆς φρουρᾶς τινες ἄρχοντες σικύας προσβαλόμενοι[8]

---

[1] Casaubon: ὀλίγοις M.
[2] Köchly and Rüstow: παλαιὸν M.
[3] C: γίνεσθαι M.   [4] Casaubon: ὅτ' ἂν ὁ πηλὸς M.
[5] Casaubon: πηλὸν M.   [6] Casaubon: ἐπιδημεῖ M.
[7] Casaubon: ὥσπερ M.   [8] Casaubon: προβαλλόμενοι M.

---

[1] Some details of the party strife are given in Aristotle,
Pol. 1305 b 2 ff. The date of this particular occurrence is
not known. For further experiences of the city see below,
xii. 5.
[2] That is, each of the three tribes (a characteristic of Doric
social structure) had four ' hundreds,' or twelve ' hundreds '
in all, as in old Athens each of the four tribes was divided
into three trittyes or ' thirds.'

Similarly, in Heracleia Pontica,[1] when the democracy was in power and the rich were conspiring against it and about to make an attack, the leaders of the popular party, who knew what was imminent, persuaded the people to establish a division into sixty 'hundreds' in place of their former three tribes and four 'hundreds,'[2] so that, in the new divisions, the rich should do both guard-duty and the other services. The result was that here, too, the rich were scattered, and were, in each 'hundred,' few among many of the popular party. And a similar thing took place long ago in Lacedaemon.[3] When the authorities were informed of a conspiracy to attack at the moment when the felt cap[4] was raised, they thwarted those who planned the attack by giving the men who were about to raise the felt cap the order not to raise it.

In Corcyra a rebellion of the wealthy oligarchic party against the rule of the people (the Athenian Chares, who at that time lived there and commanded the guard, helped in this rebellion) was contrived in the following manner.[5] Some of the captains of the guard drew blood from themselves

---

[3] This was the dangerous revolution of the Parthenii, or 'half-breeds,' as they might be called, which finally ended in the peaceful colonization of Tarentum, about 708 B.C., according to an untrustworthy legend. See Ed. Meyer, *Gesch. d. Alt.* ii. § 306 A.

[4] The felt cap had probably a symbolic meaning here. It was the headdress of the ordinary free man as such, and seems never to have been worn by slaves, so that its elevation symbolized the assumption of the status of free men. Among the Romans, indeed, one of the formal symbolic acts of manumission was the bestowal of a *pileus*, the Italic equivalent of the Greek πῖλος.

[5] This is set in 361 B.C. by Diodorus xv. 95. 3.

69

καὶ τομὰς ἐν τῷ σώματι ποιησάμενοι καὶ αἱμα-
τωθέντες ἐξέδραμον εἰς τὴν ἀγορὰν ὡς πληγὰς
ἔχοντες, ἅμα δ' αὐτοῖς εὐθὺς προπαρεσκευασμέ-
νοι οἵ τε ἄλλοι στρατιῶται τὰ ὅπλα ἐξηνέγκαντο
15 καὶ τῶν Κορκυραίων οἱ ἐπιβουλεύοντες. τῶν
δ'[1] ἄλλων ἀγνοούντων τὸ πρᾶγμα καὶ εἰς ἐκκλησίαν
παρακληθέντων συνελαμβάνοντο οἱ προστάται τοῦ
δήμου, ὡς ἐπαναστάσεως γενομένης[2] ἐξ αὐτῶν,
καὶ τὰ ἄλλα μεθίστασαν πρὸς τὸ συμφέρον αὐτοῖς.[3]

XII. [Περὶ συμμάχων ἃ δεῖ προνοεῖν]

Χρὴ δὲ καὶ συμμάχων εἰς τὴν πόλιν . . .[4] μήποτε
ἅμα διατελεῖν τοὺς συμμάχους, ἀλλὰ διεσκεδάσθαι
ὁμοτρόπως τῶν αὐτῶν ἕνεκεν τοῖς προειρημένοις.
2 τὸ δὲ αὐτὸ καὶ μετὰ ξένων μισθοφόρων μέλλοντάς
τι πράσσειν ἀεὶ χρὴ ὑπερέχειν πλήθει καὶ δυνάμει
τοὺς ἐπαγομένους πολίτας τῶν ξένων· εἰ δὲ μή,
3 ἐπ' ἐκείνοις γίγνονται αὐτοί τε καὶ ἡ πόλις. οἷον
Χαλκηδονίοις πολιορκουμένοις παρόντες σύμμαχοι
. . .[5] ἔπεμψαν φρουρὰν αὐτοῖς οἱ τῶν Χαλκη-
δονίων[6] σύμμαχοι. βουλευομένων τὰ αὐτοῖς[7]
συμφέροντα οὐκ ἔφασαν[8] οἱ φρουροὶ ἐπιτρέψειν,
ἐὰν μὴ καὶ Κυζικηνοῖς δοκῇ[9] εἶναι συμφέροντα,
ὥστε τοῖς Χαλκηδονίοις[10] τὴν φρουρὰν ἔσω οὖσαν[11]

---

[1] Added by Casaubon.   [2] Meineke: γινομένης M.
[3] Hercher: αὐτοῖς M.
[4] Casaubon indicated the lacuna: Reiske suggested ἐπηγ-
μένων, which is followed in the translation.
[5] Sauppe indicated the lacuna: R. Schöne suggests that
an expression like κίνδυνον παρεσκεύασαν and some mention
of the Cyzicenes have fallen out.
[6] καλχιδονίων M.   [7] Köchly and Rüstow: αὐτοῖς M.

with cupping-glasses, and made cuts on their bodies and ran out bleeding into the market-place, as though they had been wounded. At the same time the other soldiers, who had been prepared for this, speedily took up their arms, and with them the Corcyreans who were in the conspiracy ; and while the others had no notion of what was happening, and had, indeed, been summoned to an assembly, the leaders of the people's party were seized, as if they had been the ones who made the uprising. The rest of the affair, also, the conspirators arranged to their own advantage.

XII. [*Precautions with regard to allied Forces*]

If allied forces [are admitted] into the city they should never be stationed together, but should be separated in the manner already suggested and for the same reasons. In the same way those who are to make use of mercenary troops should always have citizens under arms surpassing these mercenaries in number and power, otherwise both the citizens and the state are at their mercy. [A danger] of this sort [befell] the Chalcedonians [1] while in a state of siege, due to the presence of allied forces sent by [the people of Cyzicus], their allies. When the Chalcedonians were deliberating upon measures affecting their interest, the troops of the garrison said that they would not consent unless it seemed advantageous to the people of Cyzicus as well, so that the garrison within the walls was much more

---

[1] Nothing further is known about this event.

8 Casaubon : ἔφησαν M.   9 Casaubon : δοκεῖ M.
10 καλχιδονίοισ M.   11 Casaubon : ἔσω ὁρᾶν M.

71

πολὺ φοβερωτέραν εἶναι τῶν προκαθημένων πο-
4 λεμίων. δεῖ οὖν μήποτε εἰς πόλιν οἰκείαν μείζω
δύναμιν ἐπακτὸν[1] δέχεσθαι τῆς ὑπαρχούσης τοῖς
πολίταις, ξένοις τε χρωμένην[2] ἀεὶ δεῖ τὴν πόλιν
πολλῷ ὑπερέχειν τῆς τῶν ξένων δυνάμεως· οὐ
γὰρ ἀσφαλὲς ξενοκρατεῖσθαι καὶ ἐπὶ[3] μισθο-
5 φόροις γίγνεσθαι. οἷον καὶ Ἡρακλεώταις τοῖς
ἐν τῷ Πόντῳ συνέβη. ἐπαγόμενοι γὰρ ξένους
πλείονας τοῦ προσήκοντος, πρῶτον μὲν τοὺς
ἀντιστασιώτας ἀνεῖλον, ἔπειτα αὐτούς[4] καὶ τὴν
πόλιν ἀπώλεσαν, τυραννευθέντες ὑπὸ τοῦ εἰσ-
άγοντος τοὺς ξένους.

XIII. [Ξενοτροφία[5]]

Ἂν δὲ δέῃ ξενοτροφεῖν, ὧδε ἂν ἀσφαλέστατα[6]
γίγνοιτο. χρὴ τοῖς ἐν τῇ πόλει εὐπορωτάτοις
προστάξαι κατὰ δύναμιν ἑκάστῳ παρασχεῖν ξένους
ἕκαστον, τοὺς μὲν τρεῖς, τοὺς δὲ δύο, τινὰς δὲ
ἕνα· ἀθροισθέντων δὲ ὅσων ἂν δέοιο,[7] διελεῖν
2 αὐτούς[8] εἰς λόχους, καταστήσαντας ἐπ' αὐτοὺς
τῶν πολιτῶν τοὺς πιστοτάτους λοχαγούς. τὸν
δὲ μισθὸν καὶ τὴν τροφὴν οἱ ξένοι παρὰ τῶν
μισθωσαμένων λαμβανόντων, τὸ μέν τι παρ'
3 αὐτῶν, τὸ δὲ καὶ τῆς πόλεως συμβαλλομένης.
καὶ διαιτάσθωσαν ἕκαστοι ἐν ταῖς τῶν μισθωσαμένων οἰκίαις, οἱ δὲ τὰς λειτουργίας καὶ τὰς

---

[1] Casaubon : ἐπ' αὐτὸν M.
[2] Köchly and Rüstow : χρώμενον M.
[3] Casaubon : ἔτι M.   [4] R. Schöne : αὐτοὺς M.
[5] In M this word follows the next sentence.
[6] Hercher : ἀσφαλέστατοι M.   [7] R. Schöne : ὅσων δέοιτο M.
[8] C (?), Casaubon : ἑαυτοὺς M.

---

[1] This is clearly a reference to the career of Clearchus, a

terrible to the Chalcedonians than was the besieging enemy. One must, therefore, never admit into a city an alien force greater than that already available to the citizens, and the state employing mercenaries must always be much superior to them in strength, since it is not safe to be outnumbered by aliens nor to be in the power of mercenaries, as actually happened to the inhabitants of Heracleia Pontica; for, by bringing in more hired troops than they should, they first made away with those of the opposing faction, but later brought destruction to themselves and the state, being forced into subjection to the man who introduced the mercenaries.[1]

XIII. [*Maintenance of Mercenaries*]

If, however, it is necessary to maintain mercenaries it may be most safely done as follows. The wealthiest citizens should be required to provide mercenaries, each according to his means, some three, some two, others one. When as many as you need are assembled, they should be divided into companies, and the most trustworthy of the citizens placed over them as captains. Pay and maintenance the mercenaries should receive from their employers, partly at the private expense of the latter, partly from funds contributed by the state. And each group of them should board in the houses of their employers, but they should be

former pupil of Plato and Isocrates, who entered the city with a force of mercenaries in 364-3 (Diodorus xv. 81. 5) and ruled for twelve years. His régime was marked by much violence, not all due to his fault, and he enjoys the distinction of being the first prince of whom it is recorded that he founded a library. See Ed. Meyer, *Gesch. d. Alt.* v. § 980.

ἐκκοιτίας καὶ τὰ ἄλλα ἐπιτάγματα ἐκ τῶν ἀρχόντων
ἀθροιζόμενοι ὑπὸ τῶν λοχαγῶν ὑπηρετούντων.
4 κομιδῇ δὲ τοῖς προαναλίσκουσιν εἰς τοὺς ξένους
χρόνῳ τινὶ γενέσθω ὑπολογιζομένων[1] τῶν εἰς τὴν
πόλιν εἰσφερομένων παρὰ ἑκάστου τελῶν· οὕτω
γὰρ ἂν τάχιστά τε καὶ ἀσφαλέστατα καὶ εὐτελέ-
στατα ξενοτροφηθείη.

XIV. [Ὑπόδειξις εἰς ὁμόνοιαν[2]]

Τοῖς μὲν οὖν ἐν τῇ πόλει ὑπεναντία θέλουσιν
τοῖς καθεστηκόσι προσφέρεσθαι ὡς προγέγραπται.
τὸ δὲ πλῆθος τῶν πολιτῶν εἰς ὁμόνοιαν τέως
μάλιστα χρὴ προάγειν, ἄλλοις τε ὑπαγόμενον
αὐτοὺς καὶ τοὺς χρεωφειλέτας[3] κουφίζοντα τόκων
βραχύτητι ἢ ὅλως ἀφαιροῦντα, ἐν δὲ τοῖς λίαν
ἐπικινδύνοις καὶ τῶν ὀφειλημάτων τι μέρος, καὶ
πάντα ὅταν δέῃ,[4] ὡς πολύ γε φοβερώτατοι ἔφεδροί
εἰσιν οἱ τοιοίδε ἄνθρωποι, τούς τε ἐν ἀπορίᾳ ὄντας
2 τῶν ἀναγκαίων εἰς εὐπορίαν καθιστάναι. καὶ
ὅπως ἴσως καὶ ἀλύπως τοῖς πλουσίοις ταῦτ' ἂν[5]
γιγνόμενα πράττοιτο καὶ ἐξ οἵων πόρων[6] πορί-
ζοιτο, καὶ περὶ τούτων ἐν τῇ Ποριστικῇ βίβλῳ
δηλωτικῶς γέγραπται.

XV.

Κατασκευασθέντων δὲ τούτων, ἄν τι ἀγγελθῇ[7]
ἢ πυρσευθῇ βοηθείας δεόμενον, ἐξιέναι ἐπὶ τὰ

---

[1] Haase: ὑπολογιζομένοις ὑπὸ M.
[2] In M these words follow the next sentence.
[3] Casaubon: χρεοφειλέτας M.   [4] Haase: ὅτ' ἂν δὲ M.

74

assembled by their captains for the performance
of public services, night watches, and other tasks
assigned by the authorities. Reimbursement should
be made in due time to those who have incurred
expense for the mercenaries, after deducting the
taxes due the state from each individual. For in
this way maintenance may be provided for mercenaries most quickly, safely, and cheaply.

XIV. [*Suggestions for securing Loyalty*]

With those, then, in the city who are opposed to the
existing order one may deal in the manner already
prescribed. In the meantime it is of primary importance to win over the mass of the citizens to a spirit of
loyalty, both by other influences and in the case of the
debtors by the reduction or complete cancellation of
interest, and, in cases of especial danger, of some
part of the principal, or even all of it when necessary ;
for such men as these are the most formidable of
adversaries. Adequate provision must also be made
for those who are in want of the necessities of life.
How these measures may be taken fairly and without
offence to the wealthy, and from what revenues the
expenses may be met, has also been clearly explained in the book on *Finance*.[1]

XV.

After the foregoing matters have been arranged,
if a call for help come, either by messenger or by
signal-fire, troops must be sent out to the parts of

[1] See Introd. p. 8.

---

[5] Hertlein : ταῦτα M.   [6] Casaubon : πόνων M.
[7] Casaubon : ἀγγελθὲν M (ἀγγελθὲν ᾗ Oldfather).

2 κακούμενα τῆς χώρας. τοὺς δὲ στρατηγοὺς τούς[1] παρόντας εὐθὺς συντάττειν,[2] ἵνα μὴ σποράδην καὶ κατ' ὀλίγους ἐξιόντες ἐπὶ τὰ αὐτῶν[3] ἀπολλύωνται[4] δι' ἀταξίαν καὶ κόπον ἄκαιρον, ἐνεδρευόμενοί τε ὑπὸ τῶν πολεμίων καὶ κακὰ πάσχοντες.
3 ἀλλὰ χρὴ τούς τε παραγιγνομένους ἐπὶ τὰς πύλας ἀθροίζεσθαι μέχρι τινὸς πλήθους, ὡς λόχου[5] ἢ διλοχίας, εἶτα συνταχθέντας καὶ ἡγεμόνος αὐτοῖς φρονίμου δοθέντος, οὕτως ἐκπέμπεσθαι καὶ σπεύδειν ἰόντας[6] ἐν τάξει ὡς μάλιστα. ἔπειτα ἄλλο
4 καὶ[7] ἄλλο πλῆθος[8] οὕτως ἐκπέμπειν καὶ ἐν τάχει μέχρις οὗ ἱκανοὶ δοκοῦσιν ἐκβεβοηθηκέναι, ἵνα καὶ ἐν τῇ πορείᾳ ἐχόμενα ᾖ τὰ μέρη, καὶ ἐάν τε[9] μέρει[10] μέρος δέῃ βοηθῆσαι ἐάν τε ἅμα πάντα δέῃ, ῥαδίως ὑπάρχῃ[11] συμμίσγειν ἀλλήλοις καὶ
5 μὴ δρόμῳ πόρρωθεν παραγίγνωνται.[12] πρὸ δὲ αὐτῶν δεῖ πρώτους τοὺς ὑπάρχοντας ἱππέας καὶ κούφους ἐξιέναι, μηδὲ τούτους ἀτάκτους,[13] προεξερευνῶντάς τε καὶ προκαταλαμβάνοντας τὰ ὑψηλὰ τῶν χωρίων, ἵν' ὡς ἐκ πλείστου προείδωσιν οἱ ὁπλῖται[14] τὰ τῶν πολεμίων καὶ μηδὲν ἐξαίφνης
6 αὐτοῖς προσπέσῃ.[15] περί τε τὰς καμπὰς τῶν χωρίων καὶ τὰς βάσεις τῶν ἀκρολοφιῶν καὶ τὰς ἐκτροπὰς τῶν ὁδῶν, ὅπου ἂν τρίοδοι ὦσιν, εἶναι σημεῖα, ἵνα μὴ περὶ ταῦτα σχίζωνται ἀπ' ἀλλήλων
7 οἱ ὑπολελειμμένοι δι' ἄγνοιαν τῆς ὁδοῦ. ἀπιόντα[16]

---

[1] Added by Hercher.   [2] Casaubon: συντάττει M.
[3] Hertlein: αὐτῶν M.   [4] Casaubon: ἀπολλύονται M.
[5] Casaubon: λόχῳ M.   [6] Reiske: ὄντασ M.
[7] Meineke: καὶ κατὰ M.   [8] Casaubon: πάθος M.
[9] Casaubon: τὰ M.   [10] Reiske: μέρη M.
[11] Casaubon: ὑπάρχειν M.
[12] Casaubon: παραγίγνονται M.
[13] Suggested by R. Schöne.

the country that are being devastated. The generals must immediately marshal such men as are at hand, in order that they may not go forth in small and scattered groups, each bent upon saving his own property, and ruin themselves from lack of discipline and premature exertion, meeting disaster through ambuscades of the enemy. Those who report for duty must assemble, up to a certain number, at the gates, for instance, the quota of one or two companies, and only after they have been marshalled and a capable leader has been assigned them must they be dispatched from the town, and then they must hasten as fast as military order will allow. Then other groups in succession must be speedily dispatched in the same fashion until enough seem to have been sent forth to render the assistance needed. This must be done in order that the divisions may be close together on the march, and, if it is necessary for one division to assist another, or for all to act together, they may easily be united and those in the rear may not have to come from a distance on the run. The available cavalry and light-armed troops, however, also in good order, should go ahead of the others and should reconnoitre and preoccupy the elevated positions, that the heavy-armed troops may be aware as early as possible of the movements of the enemy and may not be surprised by any sudden attack. At places where there are turning-points, bases of the ridges, and forks in the roads, that is, wherever there are diverging ways, signs should be placed, lest at these points the stragglers, through ignorance of the road, be separated from their fellows.

---

[14] Köchly and Rüstow : πολῖται M.
[15] Reiske : προσπέσοι M.   [16] Hertlein : ἀπιόντας M.

Likewise when the bands return to the city they
should employ caution, for many reasons, but chiefly
for fear of the enemy's ambuscades. For this sort of
thing has been known to happen to incautious relief
parties. When the Triballi were invading the country
of the Abderites,[1] the latter sallied forth against
them, formed in battle array, and carried out a
brilliant operation ; for joining battle they killed
many and defeated a large and powerful force.
Now the Triballi, enraged at the occurrence, with-
drew and reorganized, and making another inroad
into the country set ambuscades and started to lay
waste the land of the Abderites not far from the
city. The Abderites held them in contempt because
of the previous achievement and made a hasty attack
against them with great force and eagerness, but
the Triballi drew them into their ambuscades. On
that particular occasion it is said that more men
perished in a shorter time than had ever been the
case, at least from a single city of similar size.
For the others, not having learned of the destruction
of those who had gone out first, did not pause in
their rush to the rescue, but cheering one another
on, hurried away to render assistance to those who
had already sallied forth, until the city was bereft
of men.

XVI. [Other Kinds of Relief]

Still another kind of relief would be more effective
against the invaders. In the first place one should

of Thracians who turned upon the Abderites in the course
of the battle.

οὐ χρὴ εὐθὺς[1] βοηθεῖν, εἰδότα ὅτι ἀτακτότατοι ἂν
καὶ ἀπαράσκευοι πρὸ τῆς ἕω[2] εἶεν οἱ ἄνθρωποι,
τῶν μὲν ἐπειγομένων τὰ οἰκεῖα σῴζειν ὡς τάχιστα
ἐκ τῶν ἀγρῶν, ἑτέρων δὲ πεφοβημένων εἰς τοὺς
κινδύνους προϊέναι, οἷα[3] εἰκὸς προσφάτως ἀγγελ-
μένων,[4] ἄλλων δὲ πάμπαν ἀπαρασκεύων ὄντων.
3 χρὴ οὖν τὴν μὲν βοήθειαν εὐτρεπίζειν ἀθροίζοντα ὅτι
τάχος, ἅμα τῶν μὲν τὸ δεῖμα ἀφαιροῦντα, τοῖς δὲ
4 θάρσος ἐμποιοῦντα[5] τοὺς δὲ ὁπλίζοντα.[6] δεῖ γάρ
σε εἰδέναι ὅτι τῶν πολεμίων οἱ μετὰ ξυνέσεως καὶ
ἐπιστήμης γιγνόμενοι ἐν πολεμίᾳ,[7] κατ' ἀρχὰς μὲν
τὸ ἰσχυρότατον αὐτῶν[8] ἐν τάξει ἄγουσι προσδεχό-
μενοί τινας ἐφ' ἑαυτοὺς ἰέναι[9] καὶ ἑτοίμως ἔχοντες
ἀμύνεσθαι· τινὲς δὲ διασπαρέντες αὐτῶν κατὰ τὴν
χώραν ἀδικοῦσιν, ἄλλοι δ' ἂν ἐνεδρεύοιεν προσδεχό-
μενοί τινας βοηθοῦντας ὑμῶν[10] ἄτακτον βοήθησιν.
5 δεῖ οὖν μὴ εὐθὺς αὐτοὺς προσκείμενον ἐνοχλεῖν, ἀλλ'
ἐᾶσαι τούτους πρότερον θαρσῆσαι καὶ καταφρονή-
σαντάς σου ἐπὶ λεηλάτησιν καὶ πλεονεξίαν ὁρμῆσαι·
ἅμα δ' ἂν οὗτοι σιτίων καὶ πόσεως πληρούμενοι καὶ
οἰνωθέντες ἀμελεῖς[11] καὶ ἀπειθεῖς τοῖς ἄρχουσι
6 γίγνοιντο. ἐκ δὲ τούτων εἰκὸς μοχθηροὺς αὐτῶν
τοὺς ἀγῶνας καὶ τὴν ἀποχώρησιν συμβαίνειν,
7 ἐάνπερ γε σὺ αὐτοῖς εὐκαίρως ἐπιθῇ.[12] ἡτοιμα-
σμένης γάρ σοι τῆς βοηθείας εἰς τὸν παρηγγελμένον
τόπον καὶ ἐσπαρμένων ἤδη τῶν πολεμίων πρὸς
ἁρπαγήν, οὕτω χρὴ αὐτοῖς προσκεῖσθαι τοῖς μὲν

---

[1] Hercher : εὐθὺ M.
[2] προθέσεως Wünsch (accepted by Behrendt and Fischer).
[3] Casaubon : οἱ δ' M.
[4] Defended by Behrendt from usage of Herodotus : ἠγγελμένων Casaubon.
[5] Casaubon : ἐμποιοῦντασ M.

not in the night-time go straight out to give assistance, seeing that before dawn the inhabitants would
be in very great disorder and also unprepared, some
hurrying with all speed to save their property on the
farms, others dreading to face danger, as is natural
when the alarm is sudden, while still others are
wholly unready. It is necessary, therefore, to
assemble and prepare the rescue force with all
speed, at the same time freeing some from their
fear, inspiring others with confidence, and arming
still others. For you must know that when an
enemy goes to war with judgement and understanding, he at first advances the strongest of his
forces in military order, expecting a counter-attack
and ready to defend himself. Meanwhile a part of
these invaders separate and devastate the country,
while others would lie in ambush expecting some
of your forces to come in disorder to lend assistance.
It is not best, therefore, to disturb them by an
immediate attack, but to allow them first to become
bold, and in their contempt of you to start off
pillaging and satisfying their greed. At the same
time these men when sated with food and drink
and heavy with wine would become careless and
disobedient to their leaders; and as a result of this
they will be likely to put up a poor fight, and
will retreat, at least if you fall upon them oppor-
tunely. For, when your supporting force is ready at
the appointed place, and the enemy has already
scattered for plunder, then and then only you should

---

6 Casaubon: ὁπλίζοντασ M.   7 Casaubon: ἐν πόλει μιᾷ M.
    8 Hercher: αὑτῶν M.   9 Added by R. Schöne.
10 Casaubon: ἡμῶν M.   11 Casaubon: ἀμελλεῖς M.
              12 Haase: ἐπιθῇσῃ M.

81

ἱππεῦσιν προκαταλαμβάνοντα τὰς ἀποχωρήσεις,
τοῖς δ' ἐπιλέκτοις ἐνέδρας ποιούμενον, τοῖς δ'
ἄλλοις κούφοις[1] ἐπιφαινόμενον αὐτοῖς, τοὺς δ'
ὁπλίτας ἀθρόους ἐν τάξει ἄγοντα,[2] μὴ πόρρω δὲ τῶν
προπεμφθέντων[3] μερῶν.

Ἐπιτίθεσο δὲ τοῖς πολεμίοις ἐν οἷς ἄκων μὲν μὴ[4]
μαχήσῃ, μαχόμενος δὲ μὴ ἔλασσον ἕξεις τῶν πολε-
8 μίων. διὰ οὖν τὰ πρότερα[5] εἰρημένα λυσιτελεῖ
ποτε ἐφεῖναι καὶ ἐᾶσαι τοὺς πολεμίους ὡς πλείστην
κατασῦραι τῆς χώρας, ἵνα δὴ[6] λεηλατοῦντες καὶ
διαπεπληρωμένοι λαφύρων ῥᾳδίως σοι τὴν δίκην
δώσουσιν· τά τε γὰρ ληφθέντα πάντ' ἂν[7] σῴζοιτο,[8]
οἵ τ' ἀδικήσαντες κατ' ἀξίαν λάβοιεν τὰ ἐπιτίμια.
9 ὀξέως δ' ἂν βοηθήσας τοῖς μὲν σαυτοῦ ἀπαρασκεύοις
τε καὶ οὐ[9] τεταγμένοις κινδυνεύοις, οἵ τε πολέμιοι
μικρὰ μὲν ἂν φθάσαιεν κακουργήσαντες, ἐν τάξει δ'
10 ἂν ἔτι ὄντες ἀτιμώρητοι ἂν ἀπέλθοιεν. πολὺ δὲ
κρεῖσσον, ὡς γέγραπται, ἐνδόντα ἀφυλάκτως διακει-
11 μένοις αὐτοῖς ἐπιθέσθαι. ἐὰν δέ σε λάθῃ ἢ φθάσῃ
τὰ ἐκ τῆς χώρας λεηλατηθέντα, οὐ χρὴ τὴν δίωξιν
αὐτῶν ποιεῖσθαι τὰς αὐτὰς ὁδοὺς καὶ τοὺς αὐτοὺς
χώρους, ἀλλὰ τῇδε[10] μὲν ὀλίγους ἐπιφαίνεσθαι καὶ
διώκοντας μὴ ἐπικαταλαμβάνειν ἑκουσίως καὶ
ἀνυπόπτως, ἄλλο δὲ πλῆθος μετὰ ἀξιοχρέου δυνάμεως σπεύδειν κατ' ἄλλας ὁδοὺς ὅτι τάχιστα
πορευόμενον, καὶ φθάσαντας[11] ἐν τῇ τῶν ἀγόντων

---

[1] Casaubon : κούφως M.   [2] Casaubon : ἄγοντασ M.
    [3] Casaubon : προοφθέντων M.
[4] Added by Casaubon.   [5] πρότερον Casaubon.
[6] Reiske : ἢ M.   [7] Hertlein : πάντα M.
              [8] Orelli : σώζοιντο M.
[9] Added by Casaubon.   [10] Casaubon : τῆσδε M.

attack them, cut off their retreat with your cavalry, set ambuscades of picked men, and, engaging them with your other light-armed forces, bring up your heavy-armed troops in close formation not far behind the divisions already sent forward.

Attack the enemy where you are not unwilling to do battle, and where you will not be at a disadvantage in the fight. Hence, for the reasons already stated, it is sometimes to your interest to give the enemy rein, and to allow him to lay waste as much of the land as he wishes, where, while plundering and laden with spoil, he will easily suffer punishment at your hands. For in this way all that has been taken would be recovered, and those who had done the damage would receive their just deserts. On the other hand, if you should hastily send out relief forces, you might endanger your own men, unprepared and not yet in order, while the enemy, although they would already have done a little harm, yet, because they were still in order, would get away unpunished. But it is much better, as I have written,[1] to give way to them, and then attack them when off their guard. But if the plundering of the country has escaped your notice or has occurred before you could prevent it, you should not make your pursuit of the enemy along the same roads nor in the same places, but should cause only a few to make a demonstration there, and, in their pursuit, intentionally but without arousing suspicion, refrain from overtaking them, while the army as a whole, in considerable strength, should hasten as quickly as possible by other roads, and,

---

[1] The reference is to §§ 5, 6, and 7 of this same chapter.

---

11 Haase : φθάσαντος M.

12 χώρᾳ περὶ τὰ ὅρια ἐνεδρεῦσαι (φθάσαι δέ σε εἰκός ἐστι, πρότερον εἰς τὴν ἐκείνων ἀφικόμενον, διὰ τὸ λείαν[1] ἄγοντας αὐτοὺς βραδυτέρως πορεύεσθαι), τὴν δ᾽ ἐπίθεσιν αὐτοῖς ποιεῖσθαι δειπνοποιουμένοις· οἱ γὰρ λεηλατήσαντες, ἔν τε τῇ αὐτῶν[2] ἤδη γεγονότες καὶ ἐν ἀσφαλεῖ ὄντες, πρὸς ῥᾳθυμίαν τρε-

13 πόμενοι ἀφυλακτοτέρως ἂν διακέοιντο. ἄριστον δ᾽,[3] ἵνα νεοκμῆσιν[4] τοῖς στρατιώταις χρήσῃ, ὑπαρχόντων γε[5] πλοίων, κατὰ θάλατταν τὴν δίωξιν ποιεῖσθαι· τό τε γὰρ φθάσαι καὶ τὰ ἄλλα εἰς τὸ δέον σοι συμβήσεται, ἐὰν μὴ κατοφθῇς πλέων ὑπ᾽

14 αὐτῶν. Κυρηναίους δὲ[6] καὶ Βαρκαίους λέγεται καὶ ἄλλας τινὰς πόλεις τὰς ἁμαξηλάτους τε ὁδοὺς καὶ μακρὰς βοηθείας ἐπὶ συνωρίδων καὶ ζευγῶν βοηθεῖν· κομισθέντων δὲ εἰς τὸ προσῆκον καὶ ἑξῆς τῶν ζευγέων παραταχθέντων, ἀποβάντες οἱ ὁπλῖται καὶ ἐν τάξει γενόμενοι εὐθὺς νεοκμῆτες προσ-

15 εφέροντο τοῖς πολεμίοις. οἷς οὖν εὐπορία ζευγῶν, καλὸν τὸ πλεονέκτημα, ταχύ τε καὶ νεοκμῆτας τοὺς στρατιώτας εἰς τὸ δέον ἐλθεῖν· εἴησαν δὲ ἂν αἱ ἅμαξαι εὐθὺς καὶ ἔρυμα ταῖς στρατοπεδείαις· οἱ τραυματίαι καὶ εἴ τι ἄλλο γένοιτο σύμπτωμα τοῖς στρατιώταις, ἐπὶ τούτοις ἀπάγοιντ᾽ ἂν εἰς τὴν πόλιν.

16 Καὶ ἐὰν μὲν ᾖ ἡ χώρα μὴ εὐείσβολος, ἀλλ᾽ ὀλίγαι ὦσιν αἱ εἰσβολαὶ καὶ στεναί, προκατασκευάσαντας[7]

---

[1] Casaubon: λίαν M.   [2] Hercher: αὐτῶν M.
[3] Added by Casaubon.   [4] Casaubon: ἰνανεομησσιν M.
[5] Casaubon: δὲ M.   [6] Casaubon: κρηναίους καὶ M.
[7] Köchly and Rüstow: προκατασκευάσαντα M.

---

[1] This region was widely celebrated for its horses and cars, and according to one account the Libyans were the first to yoke horses to a chariot, a tradition which would

anticipating the enemy, should lie in ambush in the land of the invaders, near the border. You may reasonably expect to reach their land first, since because of driving their booty they must advance more slowly. And you should make your attack upon them while they are at the evening meal; for when the marauders are already within their own border and feel themselves secure they would be inclined to carelessness and be more off their guard. The best plan of all, however, in order to have your soldiers fresh for battle, provided boats are at hand, is to make the pursuit by sea; for you will thus outstrip the enemy, and the other conditions necessary for success will favour you, provided you are not detected by them on your voyage. Of the people of Cyrene and Barca and certain other cities the story runs that they made their rescue expeditions over long wagon-roads in four- and in two-horse vehicles;[1] and when they had reached the appointed place, and the vehicles had been arranged in order, the heavy-armed troops alighted, and, forming at once in ranks, attacked the enemy with unimpaired strength. Hence, for those who have a ready supply of vehicles, it is a great advantage to have their soldiers arrive quickly where they are needed and with fresh strength; further, the wagons would be a ready defence for the camp, while soldiers who were wounded or suffering from any other mishap could be conveyed in them back to the city.

And if the country be not easy to invade but have few and narrow approaches, you should prepare

be very natural if the suggestion that Libya was the original home of the ancestors of the thorough-bred horse be correct.

αὐτάς,[1] ὡς προγέγραπται οὕτω μερισθέντας,[2] ἐπὶ
ταῖς εἰσβολαῖς[3] ἐναντιοῦσθαι τοῖς ἐπιχειροῦσι καὶ
βουλομένοις πρὸς τὴν πόλιν προσιέναι, προδιατάξα-
μένους[4] καὶ τοὺς[5] φρυκτοῖς γνωρίζοντας τὰ ἀλλήλων
πάθη, ὅπως τὰ μέρη βοηθῇ, ἄν τι δέωνται ἀλλήλων.
17 ἂν δὲ μὴ δυσείσβολος ᾖ ἡ χώρα, ᾗ δὲ[6] πολλαχῇ
πολλοὺς εἰσβάλλειν, χρησίμους[7] καταλαβεῖν τῆς
χώρας τόπους, ὥστε τοῖς πολεμίοις χαλεπὴν εἶναι
18 τὴν πάροδον ἐπὶ τὴν πόλιν. ἂν δὲ μηδὲ ταῦτα
ὑπάρχῃ, τῶν λοιπῶν καταλαβεῖν ἐγγὺς τῆς πόλεως
χωρία σύμμαχα πρὸς τὸ μάχεσθαί τε[8] πλεονεκτικῶς
καὶ εὐαπαλλάκτως ἔχειν τοῦ χωρίου[9] ὅταν βούλῃ[10]
ἀπιέναι πρὸς τὴν πόλιν· κἂν[11] οὕτως ἐμβαλόντες οἱ
πολέμιοι εἰς τὴν χώραν πρὸς τὴν πόλιν πορεύωνται,
κατάρχειν[12] ὑμᾶς τῆς μάχης ἐκ τῶν χωρίων τούτων
19 ὁρμωμένους. τὰς δ' ἐπιθέσεις αὐτοῖς ποιεῖσθαι
ἀεὶ πλεονεκτοῦντα ἐκ τῆς χώρας τῇ συνηθείᾳ· πολὺ
γὰρ προέξεις[13] προειδὼς τὰ χωρία καὶ προάγων εἰς
τόπους οἵους ἂν σὺ βούλῃ,[14] σοὶ μὲν γνωστοὺς[15] καὶ
ἐπιτηδείους καὶ φυλάξασθαι καὶ διῶξαι καὶ φυγεῖν
καὶ ἀπιέναι εἰς τὴν πόλιν λαθραίως καὶ φανερῶς—
ἔτι δὲ καὶ τὰ ἐπιτήδεια προειδότα ὅπου ἂν τῆς
χώρας ὑπάρχῃ ὑμῖν —, τοῖς δὲ πολεμίοις ἀσυνήθεις[16]
καὶ ἀγνῶτας καὶ λελειμμένους πάντων τούτων.

[1] Orelli : αὐτὰ M : αὐταῖς Capps.
[2] Casaubon : μερισθέντα M : μέρη μερισθέντα Capps.
[3] Köchly and Rüstow ; τῆς εἰσβολῆσ M.
[4] Casaubon : προσδιαταξαμένουσ M.
[5] Added by Hercher.   [6] Hertlein : ἤδη M.
[7] Herm. Schöne : χρὴ ὑμᾶς M.
[8] Casaubon : τι M.
[9] Herm. Schöne : ἔχων τὸ χωρίον M.
[10] Hertlein : ὅτ' ἂν βούλει M.
[11] Herm. Schöne : καὶ M.

these in advance by such a distribution of forces as has just been described, placing soldiers at the approaches to oppose those who are attacking and wish to march upon the city, having stationed in advance other troops who are made aware by signal-fires of the fortunes of the several divisions, in order that these may bring support, if in any way they need one another's help. If, on the other hand, the land is not difficult to invade, but it is possible for large forces to attack at many points, the strategic positions of the country should be seized, so that the approach to the city may be difficult for the enemy. Again, if such places do not exist, it is necessary to occupy near the city other points of support, so that you may both fight to good advantage and also be able easily to withdraw from the place whenever you wish to retreat to the city. And then if the enemy break into the country and make for the city, you must begin the fighting, setting out from these places. You must always, in making your attacks upon the enemy, strive to profit from your acquaintance with the terrain; for you will have a great advantage from previous knowledge of the country and by leading the enemy into such places as you may wish, which are known to you and suitable, whether for defence, or pursuit, or flight, or withdrawal into the city either secretly or openly. Moreover, you will also know in advance what part of the country will supply you with provisions, whereas the enemy will be unacquainted, ignorant, and embarrassed in all these particulars.

[12] Herm. Schöne: πορεύονται καὶ ἄρχειν M.
[13] Reiske: προήξεις M.   [14] Hertlein: βούλει M.
[15] Casaubon: γνωτοὺς M.   [16] Casaubon: συνήθεις M.

The enemy, moreover, knowing that if one is unfamiliar with the country, not only is he unable to accomplish anything that he wishes, but it is also difficult for him to get away in safety, at least if the inhabitants wish to attack him, would come to grief from their spiritless and timid disposition towards everything, because they are unable to conjecture anything of the sort. For there would be as great a difference between the two parties as if it were the lot of the one to fight by night and the other by day, if this could in any way happen at the same time. If you have a naval force the ships must be manned, for the marines will annoy the enemy as much as the infantry if your fleet sails by the coasts and the roads along the shore, so that the enemy will be embarrassed both by you and by the men from the ships who disembark in their rear. By your doing so the enemy would be most unprepared for your attack, and they would be surprised by the outcome of your manœuvre.

XVII.

In a city in which harmony is wanting and where the citizens are mutually distrustful, you must exercise foresight and caution about the crowds that go out to see a torch-race,[1] horse-racing, or other

[1] A characteristic form of sport among the Greeks, in which not merely speed and endurance were tested, but especially the skill with which a lighted torch could be carried a considerable distance. It was most famous at Athens, but also is attested for a number of other communities.

---

[11] Casaubon : πράττων M. [12] Casaubon : ἐὰν M.
[13] Casaubon : τοὺσ M.

ἱεροποιίαι πανδημεὶ ἐκτὸς τῆς πόλεως καὶ σὺν
ὅπλοις πομπαὶ ἐκπέμπονται, ἔτι καὶ περὶ τὰς
πανδήμους νεωλκίας[1] καὶ τὰς συνεκφορὰς τῶν
τελευτησάντων· ἔνι γὰρ καὶ ἐν τοιῷδε καιρῷ
2 σφαλῆναι τοὺς ἑτέρους.[2] παράδειγμα δὲ ἐξοίσω
γενόμενον πάθος. ἑορτῆς γὰρ πανδήμου ἔξω τῆς
πόλεως Ἀργείων γενομένης ἐξῆγον[3] πομπὴν σὺν
ὅπλοις τῶν ἐν τῇ ἡλικίᾳ· συχνοὶ δὲ τῶν ἐπιβουλευόντων καὶ αὐτοὶ παρεσκευάζοντο καὶ αὐτοῖς
3 συνείποντο ἔνοπλοι εἰς τὴν πομπήν, καὶ ὡς[4] ἐγένετο
πρὸς τῷ ναῷ τε καὶ τῷ βωμῷ, οἱ μὲν πολλοὶ τὰ
ὅπλα θέμενοι ἀπωτέρω τοῦ ναοῦ πρὸς τὰς εὐχάς τε
καὶ τὸν βωμὸν ὥρμησαν. τῶν δὲ ἐπιβουλευόντων
οἱ μὲν ἐπὶ τῶν ὅπλων ὑπέμειναν, οἱ δὲ ταῖς ἀρχαῖς
τε καὶ τῶν πολιτῶν τοῖς προέχουσι παρέστησαν ἐν
4 ταῖς εὐχαῖς, ἀνὴρ ἀνδρί, ἔχοντες ἐγχειρίδια· καὶ
τοὺς μὲν κατεβεβλήκεσαν,[5] οἱ δὲ αὐτῶν εἰς τὴν
πόλιν σὺν τοῖς ὅπλοις ἔσπευσαν. ἕτεροι δὲ τῶν
συνεπιβουλευόντων ὑπομείναντες ἐν τῇ πόλει μετὰ
τῶν προαλισθέντων[6] ὁπλιτῶν[7] προκατέλαβον οὓς
προσῆκε τόπους τῆς πόλεως, ὥστε δέξασθαι τῶν
ἔξω οὓς ἐβούλοντο.[8] διὸ δεῖ[9] τὰς τοιαύτας
ἐπιβουλὰς ἐν οὐδενὶ καιρῷ ἀφυλάκτως διακεῖσθαι.
5 Χῖοι δὲ ἄγοντες τὰ Διονύσια καὶ πέμποντες πομπὰς
λαμπρὰς πρὸς τοῦ Διονύσου τὸν βωμόν, προκατα-

---

[1] Casaubon : νεολκίασ M.
[2] Casaubon : ἑταίρους M.   [3] Casaubon : ἐξείργων M.
[4] συχνοὶ (Meier) δὲ τῶν (Köchly and Rüstow) . . . παρεσκευάζοντο (Meier) . . . συνείποντο ἔνοπλοι (Hercher) . . . ὡς
(added by Orelli) : συχνῶν τῶν δὲ κτλ. . . . παρεσκεύαζον κτλ.
. . . συνηττοῦντο ὅπλα M.
[5] Hertlein : κατεβεβλήκεισαν M.
[6] W. Dindorf : προσαλισθέντων M.   [7] Meineke : ὅπλων M.
[8] Casaubon : ἐβουλεύοντο M.   [9] Casaubon : δὴ M.

contests—whenever, that is, there are sacred rites in which the entire people engage outside the city, and processions that issue from the city under arms—; also about the public hauling up of ships and the obsequies of the dead. For it is possible on such an occasion for one faction to be overthrown, and as an example I will cite an actual instance. A public festival of the Argives[1] took place outside the city, and the citizens formed an armed procession of men of military age. Meanwhile many conspirators also got ready, equipped themselves with arms, joined the procession, and when it came to the temple and the altar the majority set down their weapons at a distance from the temple and went to pray at the altar. Of the conspirators, however, some remained with their arms, and others took their stand beside the magistrates and leading men of the city while they were at prayer, each beside his man, with dagger in hand. These men some of the conspirators struck down, while others with their arms hastened into the city, and still others of the conspirators, who had remained in the town with the hoplites who had been previously collected, captured those quarters which were necessary for their purpose, and so admitted only those whom they wished. Accordingly, against such treachery one must at no time be off his guard. The people of Chios, when they celebrate the festival of Dionysus and send brilliant processions to his altar, first with

---

[1] This was on the occasion of the short-lived oligarchic revolution after the battle of Mantinea in 418 B.C. The "hoplites who had been previously collected," of whom Aeneas speaks below, were clearly the thousand Lacedaemonians who helped the oligarchs, according to Thucydides v. 81 (*cf.* Plutarch, *Alcib.* 15).

λαμβάνουσι τὰς εἰς τὴν ἀγορὰν φερούσας ὁδοὺς
φυλακαῖς καὶ δυνάμεσι πολλαῖς, κώλυμα γοῦν[1] οὐ
6 μικρὸν τοῖς βουλομένοις νεωτερίζειν. ἄριστον δὲ
τὰς ἀρχὰς πρῶτον μετὰ τῆς προῃρημένης[2] δυνάμεως ἱεροποιῆσαι, τούτων δὲ ἐκ τοῦ ὄχλου ἀπαλλα-
γέντων, οὕτω τοὺς ἄλλους συνιέναι.

XVIII.

῞Οταν δὲ οἱ ἐκπορευθέντες[3] παραγένωνται καὶ
δείλη γίγνηται, σημαίνειν[4] δειπνοποιεῖσθαι καὶ
εἰς φυλακὴν ἰέναι. ἐν ᾧ οἱ φύλακες εὐτρεπίζονται,
ἐν τούτῳ περὶ τῶν πυλῶν ἐπιμελητέον ὅπως
καλῶς κλείωνται· καὶ γὰρ[5] περὶ τὰς βαλάνους
πολλὰ σφάλματα γίγνεται διὰ τὰς τῶν ἀρχόντων
2 μαλακίας. ὅταν γὰρ ἐπὶ τὰς πύλας τις αὐτῶν
ἐλθὼν κλεῖσαι μὴ αὐτουργὸς γίγνηται, ἀλλὰ
παραδοὺς τὴν βάλανον τῷ πυλωρῷ κλεῖσαι κελεύῃ,
τάδε κακουργεῖται ὑπὸ πυλωρῶν βουλομένων
3 νυκτὸς δέξασθαι τοὺς πολεμίους. ὁ μέν· τις

---

[1] Köchly and Rüstow: οὖν M.
[2] Meier: προειρημένης M.
[3] Meineke: εἰσπορευθέντας M.
[4] Casaubon: σημαίνει M.
[5] Oldfather (cf. xxiii. 2): κλείωνται (space of 5 letters) περὶ
πέρτασ M: γὰρ B in margin (for πέρτασ): περὶ γὰρ τὰς
Casaubon.

---

[1] For understanding the following passage it is perhaps
necessary to observe that ancient city gates, which were
regularly two-valved and opened inward, were locked by
passing a long bar from jamb to jamb. In the upper
surface of the opening into one of the jambs in which the
bar rested, a deep socket was cut and a hole bored through
the bar at the point which overlay this socket. Through
this hole and into this socket was then dropped the bolt-pin,

guards and numerous forces take possession of the roads leading to the market-place—truly no slight hindrance to those who wish to begin a revolution. It is best for the officials to begin the celebration accompanied by the previously selected force, and only after these have been separated from the populace to allow the others to come.

XVIII.

And whenever those who have gone out return and it is late afternoon, one should give the signal for the evening meal and for mounting guard; and while the guards are making ready care must be taken that the gates are well locked, since many mistakes are made about the bolt-pins as the result of slackness on the part of the authorities. For when any of them goes to lock the gate, yet does not do so with his own hands, but gives the bolt-pin over to the gate-keeper and orders him to lock it, the following sorts of mischief are done by gate-keepers who wish to admit the enemy by night.[1]

a metal cylinder, in such a way that approximately one half of it would be in the socket, the other half in the hole in the bar, but that its top should be below the upper surface of the bar, so that it could not be pulled out by any chance comer. In order to extract the bolt-pin it was necessary, therefore, to have a key so shaped as to reach down into the hole, while the bolt-pin and the key had to be fitted to one another by hooks or catches, so that the key could take firm hold of the pin and draw it out.—The above note follows the results of Köchly and Rüstow's elaborate discussion of the passage. For modern survivals in Greece and elsewhere of this general method of locking by means of a bar and a bolt-pin see H. Diels, *Antike Technik* (1920), 40 ff., and the literature cited there.

ἡμέρας εἰς τὴν βαλανοδόκην τῶν πυλῶν ἄμμον προενέβαλεν, ὅπως ἡ βάλανος ἔξω μένῃ καὶ μὴ[1] ἐμβάλληται εἰς τὸ τρύπημα. φασὶ δὲ καὶ ἐμ-

4 βεβλημένας[2] βαλάνους ὧδε ἐξαιρεθῆναι. ἐμβαλλομένης κατ᾽ ὀλίγον ἄμμου εἰς τὴν βαλανοδόκην σείεσθαι ἀψοφητί, ἵνα μηδεὶς αἴσθηται. μετέωρος οὖν ἡ βάλανος ἐγίγνετο προσπιπτούσης τῆς ψάμμου, ὥστε ῥᾳδίως αὐτὴν ἐξαιρεθῆναι.

5 Ἤδη δὲ πυλωρὸς δεξάμενος τὴν βάλανον παρὰ στρατηγοῦ ἐμβαλεῖν, ἐντεμὼν λάθρα σμίλῃ[3] ἢ ῥίνῃ τὴν βάλανον, βρόχον λίνου περιβαλὼν ἐνέβαλεν, εἶτα μετ᾽ ὀλίγον τῷ λίνῳ ἀνέσπασεν.

6 ἄλλος δὲ προετοιμάσας ἐν γυργάθῳ λεπτῷ ἐνέβαλεν[4] προσημμένου λίνου, καὶ ὕστερον ἀνέσπασεν. ἐξῃρέθη δὲ καὶ ἀνακρουσθεῖσα ἡ βάλανος. ἔτι δὲ καὶ θερμαστίῳ λεπτῷ ἐξῃρέθη· χρὴ δὲ τοῦ θερμαστίου τὸ μὲν ἓν μέρος εἶναι οἷον σωλῆνα, τὸ δὲ ἕτερον πλατύ, ὥστε τῷ μὲν σωληνοειδεῖ ὑπολαμβάνειν τὴν βάλανον, τῷ δὲ ἐπιλαμβάνειν.

7 ἕτερος δὲ ἔλαθεν τρέψας τὸν μοχλὸν μέλλων ἐμβάλλειν, ἵνα μὴ κατέλθῃ εἰς τὸ τρύπημα ἡ βάλανος καὶ ὕστερον ὠσθεῖσα[5] ἀνοιχθῇ ἡ πύλη.[6]

8 Περὶ Ἀχαΐαν δὲ ἐν πόλει[7] . . . ἐπιχειροῦντες κρυφαίως δέξασθαι ξένους πρῶτον μὲν τῆς βαλάνου

---

[1] Casaubon : ἐζομένη μὴ M.
[2] ἐμβεβλημμένας M.   [3] Casaubon : σμηλη M.
[4] Köchly and Rüstow : ἔβαλεν M.
[5] Hertlein : ἐωσθεῖσα M.
[6] Added by Köchly and Rüstow : space of four letters vacant in M.
[7] Casaubon added Ἡραιέων from Polyaenus ii. 36, but that is more than doubtful.

---

[1] That is, so as to fit about the cylindrical pin.
[2] A similar story is told about Heraea in Polyaenus ii.

Some one during the day has poured sand into the bolt-socket of the gate, so that the bolt may stick outside and not drop into the hole. They say, too, that bolt-pins already dropped into place have been extracted in the following manner. While sand was poured into the socket a few grains at a time, the bolt-pin was shaken noiselessly so that no one would notice it. Accordingly, as the sand worked down, the bolt-pin came to the top, so that it was easily taken out.

It has also happened that a keeper of the gate, on receiving from the general the bolt-pin to put in place, with a chisel or file surreptitiously made a groove in the pin, looped a linen thread about it, and inserted it, and then after a little drew it out by the thread. Yet another prepared a net of fine meshes to which was attached a linen thread, put the pin in that, and afterwards drew it out. The bolt-pin has also been removed by driving it up out of the socket with blows from beneath. Again, it has been removed by means of delicate pincers; and for this one part of the pincers must be grooved,[1] the other flat, so as to get an under-hold on the bolt-pin with the grooved part and an over-hold with the other. And still another, just as he was to drop the bolt-pin in place, secretly turned the bar in order that the pin might not fall into the hole and that afterwards the gate might be forced open.

In the city of . . . near the border of Achaea [2] certain men who were endeavouring to smuggle in mercenaries began by getting the dimensions of

36, but Heraea is an Arcadian city at a considerable distance from Achaea, and the event described by Polyaenus took place between 240–235 b.c., more than a century later than the time of Aeneas.

9 ἔλαβον τὰ μέτρα τρόπῳ τοιῷδε. προκαθέντες ἐν τῇ ἡμέρᾳ εἰς τὴν βαλανοδόκην λίνου λεπτοῦ καὶ ἰσχυροῦ βρόχον καὶ τὰς ἀρχὰς ἔξω οὔσας ἀφανεῖς, ὡς ἐν τῇ νυκτὶ ἐνεβλήθη ἡ βάλανος, ἀνέσπασαν[1] ταῖς ἀρχαῖς[2] τοῦ λίνου τὸν βρόχον καὶ τὴν βάλανον, λαβόντες δὲ τὰ μέτρα αὐτῆς πάλιν καθῆκαν. ἔπειτα πρὸς μέτρα οὕτω τῆς βαλάνου βαλανάγραν
10 ἐποιήσαντο τρόπῳ τοιῷδε. ἐχαλκεύσαντο σί- φωνά τε καὶ φορμορραφίδα.[3] ἦν δὲ ὁ μὲν σίφων ἐργασθεὶς καθάπερ εἴωθε γίγνεσθαι· τῆς δὲ[4] φορμορραφίδος τὸ μὲν ὀξὺ καὶ πολὺ μέρος εἴργαστο καθάπερ ταῖς ἄλλαις φορμορραφίσιν, ἡ δὲ λαβὴ ἦν κοίλη ὥσπερ στυρακίου ᾗ τὸ στελεὸν[5] ἐμ-
11 βάλλεται. καὶ παρὰ μὲν τῷ χαλκεῖ ἐνεβλήθη στελεόν, ἀπενεχθέντος δὲ ἐξῃρέθη, ὥστε πρὸς τὴν βάλανον[6] προσαχθεῖσαν ἁρμόσαι. προνοητικῶς δὴ δοκεῖ ποιηθῆναι πρὸς τὸ[7] τὸν χαλκέα μηδὲν ὑποπτεῦσαι ὅ τε σίφων οὗ ἕνεκα ἐργασθεὶς εἴη καὶ ἡ φορμορραφίς, καὶ τὰ ἄρμενα γίγνεσθαι.
12 Ἤδη δέ τινες ἐν τῇ βαλανοδόκῃ οὔσης βαλάνου τὸ περίμετρον ὧδε ἔλαβον. πηλὸν κεραμικὸν περιελίξαντες ὀθονίῳ λεπτῷ καθῆκαν, ἁρμένῳ πιέζοντες περὶ τὴν βάλανον τὸν πηλόν· ἔπειτα ἀνέσπασαν τὸν πηλὸν καὶ ἔλαβον τὸν τύπον τῆς βαλάνου, πρὸς ὃν τὴν βαλανάγραν ἐποιήσαντο.
13 Συμβάλλεται[8] γενέσθαι Τημένῳ Ῥοδίῳ ἐν Ἰωνίᾳ

---

[1] Orelli: ἀνέσπασεν M.   [2] Lange: τὰς ἀρχὰς M.
[3] L. Dindorf: φορμοροφίδα M (and so below where M has only one ρ).
[4] Köchly and Rüstow: τε M.
[5] R. Schöne: ἦ· (lacuna of thirty letters) στελέα M.
[6] σίφωνα Köchly.
[7] Köchly and Rüstow: πρὸς τῷ Behrendt: πρόστε M.

the bolt-pin in the following manner. During the day they let down into the socket a loop of fine and strong linen thread, the ends of which were outside but not in sight, and when at night the bolt-pin was put in place, with the ends of the thread they pulled up the loop and the pin, took its dimensions, and replaced it. Next they made a pin-hook to fit the dimensions of the pin thus taken, in the following manner. They had a tube made and a needle for sewing rush-mats. Now the tube was made in the usual fashion, but the mat-needle had the point and the longer end made like other such needles, while the head was hollow like that of a spike at the butt of a spear into which the shaft is fitted ; and at the blacksmith's shop a shaft was fitted into it, but when they took it home this was removed, so that the head fitted the bolt-pin when they were put together. Now that seems a very shrewd device to prevent the blacksmith from suspecting the purpose for which the tube and the mat-needle were made and the fittings devised.

Some other men once, while the bolt-pin was in the socket, got its measurements in the following manner. They wrapped a lump of potter's clay in a fine linen cloth and let it down into the socket, pressing the clay about the bolt-pin with a tool : then they drew up the clay, took a cast of the pin, and made the key to fit.

The great city of Teos in Ionia once came very near

---

[8] Herm. Schöne suggests παρ' ἐλάχιστον ἦλθεν ὑποχείριος in place of συμβάλλεται, because it appears that the town was not actually captured ; the end of the narrative, however, § 19, is suspiciously abrupt.

AENEAS TACTICUS

Τέως πόλις εὐμεγέθης πρόδοτος[1] ὑπὸ τοῦ πυλωροῦ.
ἄλλα τε οὖν προσυνέθεντο καὶ νύκτα ἀσέληνον καὶ
σκοτεινήν, ἐν ᾗ ἔδει τὸν μὲν ἀνοῖξαι, τὸν δὲ μετὰ
14 ξένων εἰσελθεῖν. ἐπεὶ δ' ἔδει[2] εἰς τὴν ἐπιοῦσαν
νύκτα πραχθῆναι, παρῆν τῷ πυλωρῷ ἀνὴρ ὅστις
ἐπεὶ ὀψὲ ἦν καὶ φυλακαί τε ἐπὶ τοῦ τείχεος καθ-
ίσταντο καὶ αἱ πύλαι ἔμελλον κλείεσθαι, σκότους
οὖν ἤδη ὄντος, ἀπηλλάσσετο, ἐκδήσας ἀρχὴν
ἀγαθίδος[3] λίνου κλωστοῦ, ὅπερ οὐκ ἔμελλεν
15 ῥαδίως διαρραγῆναι. τὴν δὲ ἀγαθίδα ἐπορεύθη[4]
ἀπελίσσων[5] ἀπὸ τῆς πόλεως πέντε στάδια, ὅπη
16 ἔμελλον οἱ εἰσπορευσόμενοι[6] ἥξειν. ἐπεὶ δὲ
παρῆν ὁ στρατηγὸς κλεῖσαι τὰς πύλας, καὶ ἔδωκε
κατὰ τὸ ἔθος τῷ πυλωρῷ ἐμβαλεῖν τὴν βάλανον,
δεξάμενος ἐνέτεμεν λαθραίως ἀψοφητὶ ῥίνῃ ἢ
σμίλῃ[7] τὴν βάλανον, ὥστε ἐνέχεσθαι λίνον. εἶτα
βρόχον περιθεὶς καθῆκε τὴν βάλανον ἐχομένην
ὑπὸ τοῦ λίνου· μετὰ δὲ ταῦτα κινήσας τὸν μοχλὸν
καὶ ἐπιδείξας τῷ στρατηγῷ κεκλεισμένην τὴν
17 πύλην εἶχεν ἡσυχίαν. χρόνου δὲ προϊόντος ἀνα-
σπάσας τὴν βάλανον, τὴν ἀρχὴν τοῦ σπάρτου
πρὸς αὑτὸν[8] ἔδησεν τοῦδε ἕνεκεν, ὅπως,[9] εἰ
καθυπνώσας τύχοι,[10] ἐγερθείη σπώμενος ὑπὸ τοῦ
18 λίνου. ὁ δὲ Τήμενος παρῆν διεσκευασμένος μεθ'
ὧν ἔμελλεν εἰσπορεύεσθαι εἰς χωρίον ῥητὸν πρὸς
τὸν τὴν ἀγαθίδα ἔχοντα. ἦν δὲ προσυγκείμενον

---

[1] Schenkl: προειδότοσ M (defended by Hunter who follows Hug placing ὑπό before Τημένῳ).
[2] Haase: δὲ M.
[3] Casaubon: ἀκανθίδος M (and similarly below).
[4] Casaubon: ἐπορεύθην M.   [5] Hertlein: ἀπιλάσσων M.
[6] Hertlein: εἰσπορευόμενοι M.   [7] Casaubon: σμήλη M.
[8] Hercher: αὐτὸν M.   [9] Hercher: ὅτι M.

falling into the hands of Temenus the Rhodian
through the treachery of the gate-keeper.[1] Among
other things they agreed upon a dark, moonless
night, on which one was to open the gate and the
other to enter with mercenaries. Now when the
plan was to be put into execution the following
night, a man came up to the gate-keeper late in the
evening, when the guards were stationed on the
wall and the gates were about to be locked, as it
was already dark, and then disappeared, after first
making fast the end of a ball of twisted linen cord,
which was not likely to be easily broken. He went
away, unrolling the ball as he went, until he reached
a spot five stadia [2] from the city, where the troops
which were to enter would come. Then, when the
general came to lock the gates, and as usual gave
the gate-keeper the bolt-pin to put in place, the
latter took it, and with a file or a chisel, noiselessly and without attracting attention, cut a groove
in it so that a thread would catch it. He then
slipped a loop over the pin and let it down with
the thread attached to it. After that he shook
the bar, showing the general that the gate was
locked, and held his peace. Some time after he
drew up the pin and tied the end of the cord to
himself, so that if he should happen to fall asleep
he would be awakened by a pull at the cord. Now
Temenus, provided with the forces which were to
enter with him, came near to a place agreed upon
with the man who had the ball of cord. And a

[1] Nothing further is known about the incident described
here.
[2] Approximately one-half mile.

---

[10] L. Dindorf: τύχη M.

τῷ Τημένῳ πρὸς τὸν πυλωρὸν ἐλθόντι¹ εἰς τὸν
19 χῶρον σπᾶν τὸ² σπάρτον. καὶ εἰ μὲν ἦν ἕτοιμα
τῷ πυλωρῷ ἅπερ ἤθελε, προσεπιδῆσαι³ πρὸς τὴν
ἀρχὴν τοῦ λίνου μαλλὸν ἐρίου καὶ ἀφεῖναι, ὅπερ
ἰδὼν ὁ Τήμενος ἔμελλε σπεύδειν πρὸς τὰς πύλας·
εἰ δ' ἀπετύγχανεν ὁ πυλωρὸς τοῦ θελήματος . . .⁴
οὐδὲν προσάψας ἀφῆκεν τὸ λίνον,⁵ ὥστε τὸν
Τήμενον ἐκ πολλοῦ φθάσαι τε καὶ λαθεῖν ἀπαλ-
λαγέντα.⁶ ἠσθάνοντο οὖν ἐν τῇ νυκτὶ τὸ σπάρτον
ὑπάρχον . . .⁷ ἐν τῇ πόλει, οὐχ οἷόν τε ἦν προϊέναι.
20 Τρόπον δὲ κατὰ τόνδε προεδόθη πόλις ὑπὸ
πυλωροῦ. σύνηθες ἐποιήσατο, ἐπεὶ μέλλοιεν αἱ
πύλαι κλείεσθαι, ὑδρίον ἔχων ἐξιέναι⁸ ὡς ἐφ' ὕδωρ.
ἀφικνούμενος δὲ ἐπὶ τὴν κρήνην⁹ λίθους ἐτίθει εἰς
τόπον γνωστὸν τοῖς πολεμίοις, ἐφ' οὗ φοιτῶντες
εὕρισκον διὰ τῶν τιθεμένων λίθων ἅπερ θέλοι
21 δηλοῦν ὁ τῆς πόλεως φύλαξ. εἰ μὲν γὰρ πρώτην
φυλάσσοι,¹⁰ ἕνα λίθον¹¹ ἐτίθει πρὸς τὸν συγκείμενον τόπον, εἰ δὲ δευτέραν, δύο, εἰ δὲ τρίτην,
τρεῖς,¹² εἰ δὲ τετάρτην, τέτταρας. ἔτι δὲ καὶ ᾗ¹³
τοῦ τείχους καὶ κατὰ τί¹⁴ τῶν φυλακῶν¹⁵ λελόγχοι,
τούτῳ δοῦν¹⁶ τῷ τρόπῳ σημαίνων ἐνέδωκεν.
ταῦτα δεῖ οὖν συμβαλλόμενον πάντα φυλάττεσθαι

¹ Hertlein: ἐλθὼν M.
² Köchly and Rüstow: τὸν M.
³ Casaubon: προσπηδῆσαι M.
⁴ Capps and Rouse indicate a lacuna.
⁵ Hertlein: τὸν λίνον M.
⁶ Casaubon: ἀπαλλαγέντασ M.
⁷ R. Schöne suggests ἄνευ μαλλοῦ and an indication that
from this Temenus concluded that conditions were unfavourable for his attempt.
⁸ Casaubon: εἰσιέναι M.
⁹ Casaubon: κλίνην M.

previous arrangement had been made with the gate-keeper that Temenus was to pull the cord when he reached the spot, and if the keeper had things ready as he wished, he was to tie a flock of wool to the end of the cord and let it go, and, when Temenus saw that, he was to hurry to the gate. But in case of failure to secure what he wished [he was to let the cord go without anything tied to it. Accordingly] he let the cord go without anything tied to it, so that Temenus with a long start got away without being discovered. They found out accordingly in the night that the cord was [. . . so because the situation was unfavourable] in the city it was impossible to proceed.

Here is also another way in which a city was betrayed by a gate-keeper. He made it his custom to go out with a water-jug, as though for water, when the gates were about to be locked. On arriving at the spring he would put stones in a spot known to the enemy, who, when reaching the place, found out by means of the stones just what the city watchman wished to reveal. For if he was to keep the first watch, he would place one stone at the prearranged spot, if the second, two, if the third, three, if the fourth, four. Furthermore, by giving signals in this fashion, he furnished information both as to what position on the wall and to which detachment of the guards he had been assigned by lot. Accordingly, with all this in mind, the officer should be on

[10] Köchly and Rüstow: φυλάσσοιεν AB.
[11] Casaubon: ἀνθ' ὧν AC (ἀνθῶν B).
[12] Casaubon: τρίτησ M.   [13] Casaubon: ἡ ABC.
[14] Orelli: τι M.   [15] Köchly and Rüstow: φυλάκων M.
[16] R. Schöne (sc. δὴ οὖν): δ' οὖν ABC.

καὶ τὰς πύλας αὐτὸν τὸν ἄρχοντα κλείειν καὶ μὴ
ἄλλῳ διδόναι τὴν βάλανον.

22 . . .[1] πράσσοντα δέ τι τοιοῦτον τὸν μοχλὸν
ἀφανίζειν· ἤδη γάρ τινες ἐπιφανέντες ὑπεναντίοι
ἐβιάσαντο πάλιν κλεῖσαι, τοῦ μοχλοῦ παρόντος.
διὸ δεῖ πάντα τὰ τοιαῦτα προνοεῖν.

XIX. [Μοχλοῦ πρίσις]

Διαπρίοντα δὲ μοχλὸν ἔλαιον ἐπιχεῖν· θᾶσσον
γὰρ καὶ ἀψοφητὶ μᾶλλον πρισθήσεται. ἐὰν δὲ
καὶ σπόγγος ἐπί τε τὸν πρίονα καὶ τὸν μοχλὸν
ἐπιδεθῇ, πολλῷ κωφότερος ὁ ψόφος[2] ἔσται.
πολλὰ δ' ἄν τις καὶ ἄλλα ὁμότροπα τούτοις γράψαι.
ἀλλὰ ταῦτα μὲν παρετέον.

XX. [Κώλυμα τῶν περὶ μοχλοὺς καὶ βαλάνους
κακουργημάτων]

Εἰς δὲ τὸ τούτων μηδὲν κακουργεῖσθαι χρὴ
πρῶτον μὲν στρατηγὸν μὴ δεδειπνηκότα δι'
αὐτοῦ[3] τὴν κλεῖσιν καὶ τὴν ἐπιμέλειαν ποιεῖσθαι,
μηδὲ ἄλλῳ πιστεύειν ῥαθύμως διακείμενον· ἐν
δὲ τοῖς[4] ἐπικινδύνοις καὶ πάμπαν σύννουν δεῖ
2 περὶ ταύτην εἶναι. ἔπειτα τὸν μοχλὸν σεσιδηρῶσθαι διὰ μήκους τριχῇ ἢ τετραχῇ· ἄπριστος
γὰρ ἔσται. ἔπειτα βαλάνους ἐμβάλλεσθαι τρεῖς
μὴ ὁμοτρόπους, τούτων δὲ ἕκαστον φυλάττειν

---

[1] Hercher indicated the lacuna : a short space in M.
[2] Haupt : κουφότερος ὁ μοχλὸς M.
[3] Hertlein : αὑτοῦ M.
[4] Added by Hertlein.

his guard, should lock the gate himself, and should not give the bolt-pin to anyone else.

. . . When engaged in any such enterprise one ought to conceal the bar; for it has happened that opponents have appeared and locked the gate again by force because the bar was still there. And so one should make provision for all such contingencies.

XIX. [*Sawing through a Bar*]

In sawing through a bar pour on oil; for thus the sawing will go faster and with less noise. And if a sponge [1] be tied to the saw and to the bar, the noise will be much less distinct. One might write down many other similar suggestions, but we may let them pass.

XX. [*Prevention of Tampering with Bars and Bolt-pins*]

To prevent deception of the kinds just mentioned, in the first place the general ought before dining to give personal attention to the locking of the gate, and not carelessly to trust to anyone else, while in dangerous situations he must be extremely vigilant about this. Next, the bar should have three or four strips of iron from end to end, for thus it cannot be sawed through. Then, three dissimilar bolt-pins should be put in, and each general is to have one of

[1] He probably means that the sponge should have been first soaked in oil. In that way it would feed oil steadily and uniformly. This is one of the very few suggestions for the assailants of a beleaguered city rather than its defenders. It is clearly an afterthought on his part, and would have been relegated to a footnote were he writing under modern conditions.

ἀνὰ μίαν[1] τῶν στρατηγῶν· εἰ δὲ πλείονες εἴησαν,
3 πάλῳ καθ' ἡμέραν τοὺς λαχόντας. ἄριστον δὲ
τὰς βαλάνους μὴ ἐξαιρετὰς εἶναι, ὑπὸ δὲ λοπίδος
σιδηρᾶς κατέχεσθαι, ἵνα μὴ πλέον ἐξαιρομένη
μετεωρίζηται τῷ καρκίνῳ ἢ ὥστε τὸν μοχλὸν
ὑποθεῖσθαι[2] ἐπικλειομένων τῶν πυλῶν καὶ ἀνοι-
γομένων· τὸν δὲ καρκίνον ἐσκευάσθαι, ὅπως ὑπὸ
τὴν λοπίδα καθίηται[3] καὶ ῥαδίως τὴν βάλανον
4 μετεωρίζῃ. Ἀπολλωνιᾶται δὲ οἱ ἐν τῷ Πόντῳ
παθόντες τι τῶν προγεγραμμένων κατεσκεύασαν
τὰς πύλας κλείεσθαι ὑπὸ σφύρας τε μεγάλης καὶ
κτύπου παμμεγέθους γιγνομένου, ὡς σχεδὸν κατὰ
πᾶσαν τὴν πόλιν ἀκούεσθαι ὅταν κλείωνται ἢ
ἀνοίγωνται αἱ πύλαι· οὕτω μεγάλα τε καὶ σε-
5 σιδηρωμένα ἦν τὰ[4] κλεῖθρα. τὸ δὲ αὐτὸ καὶ ἐν
Αἰγίνῃ. ὅταν δὲ αἱ πύλαι κλεισθῶσιν, τοῖς φύλαξι
σύνθημα καὶ παρασύνθημα δόντας ἐπὶ τὰ φυλάκια
διαπέμψαι.

XXI.

Περὶ δὲ ἁρμένων ἑτοιμασίας καὶ ὅσα χρὴ[5] περὶ
χώραν φιλίαν προκατασκευάζειν[6] καὶ[7] τὰ ἐν
τῇ χώρᾳ ὡς δεῖ ἀφανίζειν ἢ ἀχρεῖα[8] ποιεῖν τοῖς
ἐναντίοις ὧδε μὲν[9] παραλείπεται· ἐν δὲ τῷ
Παρασκευαστικῷ περὶ τούτων τελείως δηλοῦται.
2 περὶ δὲ φυλάκων καταστάσεως καὶ περιοδειῶν[10]
καὶ πανείων καὶ συνθημάτων καὶ παρασυνθη-

---

[1] R. Schöne: ἄνδρα M.
[2] Eberhard: ὥστε μοχλῷ ὑποθεῖσθαι M.
[3] " Nescio quis " in Hercher's ed. : κάθηται M.
[4] R. Schöne: πάντα M.
[5] Added by Hercher.
[6] Casaubon (C ?): προκατασκεύαζε AB.

these in his keeping ; if, however, there should be more than three generals, then the custody of the bolt-pins must be determined each day by lot. But the best thing is to have the bolt-pins so that they cannot be removed but are held in place by an iron plate, so that when it is raised up the pin cannot be lifted higher by the pincers than just enough to slip the bar under when the gate is closed and opened, while the pincers must be so made that they can pass under the plate and easily lift the bolt-pin. The citizens of Apollonia Pontica, after having had one of the experiences already described, provided that the gates should be locked with a great hammer and the making of a tremendous noise, so that the locking or opening of the gates could be heard over almost the entire city, so ponderous were the fastenings and so strengthened with iron ; and the same thing was done in Aegina also. When the gates are locked, give the guards password and answer and send them to their posts.

XXI.

Provision of tools, and all suitable preparations on friendly soil, and the methods necessary for concealing the property in the land or for rendering it useless to one's opponents, are here omitted, but these have been fully set forth in the book on *Military Preparations*. About the disposition of guards and patrols, however, and panics, and watch-words, and countersigns, the greater part will have

---

[7] Oldfather: καὶ εἰ A καὶ ἡ B : καὶ δὴ R. Schöne.
[8] Casaubon: ἠχρεία M.
[9] Herm. Schöne: με AB (μοι B in margin).
[10] Hertlein: περιοδιῶν M.

μάτων τὰ μὲν πολλὰ ἐν τῇ Στρατοπεδευτικῇ
βίβλῳ γραπτέον ὃν τρόπον δεῖ γενέσθαι, ὀλίγα δὲ
αὐτῶν καὶ νῦν δηλώσομεν.

XXII. [Φυλακαί]

Νυκτοφυλακεῖσθαι ἐν μὲν τοῖς κινδύνοις καὶ
προσκαθημένων[1] ἤδη ἐγγὺς πολεμίων πόλει ἢ
2 στρατοπέδῳ ὧδε.[2] τὸν μὲν στρατηγὸν[3] τὸν τοῦ
ὅλου ἡγεμόνα καὶ τοὺς μετ᾽ αὐτοῦ τετάχθαι
κατὰ[4] τὰ περιαρχεῖα καὶ τὴν ἀγοράν, ἐὰν ὀχυρό-
τητος μετέχῃ· εἰ δὲ μή, προκατειληφέναι τόπον
τῆς πόλεως ἐρυμνότατόν τε καὶ ἐπὶ πλεῖστον ἀπ᾽
3 αὐτοῦ τῆς πόλεως ὁρώμενον. περὶ δὲ τὸ στρα-
τήγιον σκηνοῦν καὶ διατελεῖν ἀεὶ τὸν σαλπιγκτὴν
καὶ τοὺς δρομοκήρυκας, ἵν᾽,[5] ἐάν τι δέῃ σημῆναι
ἢ παραγγεῖλαι, ἐξ ἑτοίμου ὑπάρχωσι, καὶ οἵ τε[6]
ἄλλοι φύλακες τὸ μέλλον αἴσθωνται καὶ οἱ περίοδοι
ὅπου ἂν[7] ὄντες τύχωσι κατὰ περιοδίαν τῆς πόλεως.
4 ἔπειτα τούς τε ἐπὶ τῷ τείχει φύλακας καὶ τοὺς ἐν
τῇ ἀγορᾷ καὶ ἐπὶ τῶν ἀρχείων καὶ τῶν εἰς τὴν
ἀγορὰν εἰσβολῶν καὶ τοῦ θεάτρου καὶ τῶν ἄλλων
κατεχομένων χωρίων διὰ βραχέων τε φυλάσσειν,
καὶ πολλὰς εἶναι τὰς φυλακὰς καὶ ἅμα πολλοὺς
5 ἀνθρώπους. ἐν γὰρ τῷ δι᾽ ὀλίγου φυλάσσειν
οὔτ᾽ ἂν[8] κατὰ μῆκος χρόνου δύναιτό τις πρᾶξαί
τι πρὸς τοὺς πολεμίους καὶ νεωτερίσαι φθάσας,
ἧττόν τ᾽ ἂν ὕπνοι ἐγγίγνοιντο διὰ βραχέος φυλασσόντων, τῷ[9] τε πολλοὺς ἅμα φυλάσσειν μᾶλλον
δύναιτο ἐκφερομυθεῖσθαί τι τῶν πρασσομένων.

---

[1] Meier: προκαθημένων M.　　　　　[2] Added by Meier.
[3] Köchly and Rüstow add ἢ after στρατηγόν.
[4] R. Schöne: καὶ M.　　　　[5] Added by Casaubon.

to be written in the book on *Encampments*, but a few of these points we shall now also set forth.

XXII. [*Guards*]

To keep guard by night when danger threatens, and the enemy are already lying near the city or camp, it is necessary for the general in command of the entire force and his staff to take their post at the city-hall and the market-place, provided these be defensible ; but if not, the strongest place in the whole city and the most conspicuous should have been previously occupied. Close by the general's quarters the trumpeter and the dispatch-bearers should encamp, and remain there, so that if a signal or a dispatch be needed, they may be ready at hand, and the other watchmen and the patrols wherever they may happen to be in their circuit of the city may be aware of what is to occur. Moreover, the guards upon the wall and in the market-place, and those at the municipal buildings and entrances to the market-place and at the theatre, and other occupied points, should keep guard in short watches ; and there should be many guard shifts, and many men together in each. For in guarding by short watches, no one would be able, through the length of time he was on guard, to have any dealings with the enemy, or to gain headway in starting a revolution. And in short watches sleep would be less likely to steal upon the guards. Moreover, with many men on guard at once, some rumour of what is being done would be more likely to leak out. It is

---

[6] Casaubon : εἴτε οἱ ABC.   [7] Orelli : ἐὰν AB.
[8] Sauppe : ὅτ' ἂν M.   [9] Casaubon : τό M.

5ª ἐγρηγορέναι τε ὡς πλείστους ἄμεινον ἐν τοῖς
κινδύνοις καὶ πάντας[1] φυλάξαι ἐν τῇ νυκτί, ἵν᾽
ὡς πλεῖστοι καθ᾽ ἑκάστην φυλακὴν προφυλάσ-
6 σωσιν. ἐὰν δὲ ὀλίγοι τε καὶ μακρὰς φυλάσσωσιν,
ὕπνος τ᾽ ἂν ἐγγίγνοιτο διὰ τὸ μῆκος τῶν φυλακῶν, καὶ εἴ τινές τι ἐγχειροῖεν νεωτερίσαι, ὑπάρχοι
ἂν αὐτοῖς τοῦ χρόνου τὸ μῆκος καὶ φθάσαι καὶ
λαθεῖν πράξαντάς τι πρὸς τοὺς πολεμίους· διὸ
7 δεῖ τὰ τοιαῦτα μὴ ἀγνοεῖν. ἔτι δὲ χρὴ ἐν τοῖς
κινδύνοις καὶ τάδε προνοεῖν. τῶν φυλάκων
μηδένα προγιγνώσκειν μήτε ὁπόστην[2] μήτε[3]
ὅπου φυλάξει τῆς πόλεως· μηδὲ τῶν αὐτῶν ἀεὶ
τοὺς αὐτοὺς ἡγεῖσθαι, ἀλλ᾽ ὡς πυκνότατα πάντα
μεθιστάναι τὰ περὶ τὴν πολιτοφυλακίαν· οὕτω
γὰρ ἂν ἥκιστά τις δύναιτο τοῖς ἔξω προδιδοὺς
δηλοῦν τι ἢ προσδέξασθαι παρὰ τῶν πολεμίων,
8 μὴ προειδότες[4] ὅπου τοῦ τείχους τὴν νύκτα ἔσονται
μηδὲ μεθ᾽ ὧν, ἀλλ᾽ ἀγνοοῦντες τὸ μέλλον. καὶ
τοὺς ἡμέρας φυλάξαντας μὴ φυλάσσειν νυκτός·
οὐ γὰρ ἐπιτήδειον[5] προειδέναι ἃ μέλλει ἕκαστος
πράσσειν.

9 Προφυλάσσοιέν τ᾽ ἂν ἐκ τῶν ἐπὶ τῷ τείχει
φυλακίων[6] προφύλακες ὧδε. ἐξ ἑκάστου γὰρ
φυλακίου καθ᾽ ἑκάστην φυλακὴν[7] προφυλασσόντων εἷς ἀνὴρ ἐπὶ τὸ ἐχόμενον φυλάκιον,
καὶ ἀπ᾽ ἐκείνου ἄλλος εἷς τὸ ἐχόμενον, καὶ ἀπὸ

---

[1] R. Schöne : πάντα M.
[2] Mor. Schmidt : ὁπουστῆναι M.
[3] Meineke : μηδὲ M.
[4] Behrendt : προειδότων M : προειδόντων R. Schöne.
[5] R. Schöne suggests that μηδὲ belongs after ἐπιτήδειον :
Herm. Schöne thinks of a lacuna. Ought not the clauses
καὶ . . . νυκτός and οὐ . . . πράσσειν to appear in reverse
order? (Oldfather).

better for as many as possible to be on watch in
time of peril, and for all to do guard-duty during
the night, so that as many as possible may be keeping
guard at each watch. But if few are on guard, and
for long watches, sleep would steal upon them
because of the length of the watches, and if any men
should attempt a revolution, the length of the time
of duty would favour them both in getting a start
and in escaping detection in any dealings with the
enemy. Such considerations, then, ought not to
be ignored ; but in times of peril one must keep
still other things in mind. Thus, no one of the
guards should have any previous knowledge either
of the number of his watch, or where in the city
he is to be on guard. Nor should the same officers
always command the same men ; but as frequently
as possible all the regulations concerning the watching of the citizens should be changed, for thus would
a traitor be least able to betray anything to outsiders,
or to receive anything from the enemy, not knowing
beforehand on what part of the wall he would be
in the night, nor with whom, but being ignorant of
what was to occur. And those who guard by day
should not be employed at night, for it is not
fitting that they should know beforehand what
each is to do.

Guards from the stations on the wall should keep
watch as follows. From each of the stations, at
each change of the watch, one of the guards should
go to the nearest station, and from this another to
the next, and from the other stations still others

---

⁶ Köchly and Rüstow : φυλάκων M.
⁷ Casaubon : φυλακὴν τῶν M.

τῶν ἄλλων ἄλλοι[1] εἰς τὰ ἄλλα· παρηγγέλθω δὲ
10 ποιεῖν ἀπαξάπαντας[2] τοῦτο ἀπὸ συσσήμων. καὶ
οὕτω πολλοί τε καὶ ἅμα περιοδεύσουσιν[3] καὶ
μικρὸν ἕκαστος[4] χωρίον κινηθήσεται, καὶ οὐ
θαμὰ[5] οἱ αὐτοὶ παρὰ τοῖς αὐτοῖς διατελοῦσι,
πυκνὰ ἄλλων φυλάκων παρ' ἄλλοις γιγνομένων
φύλαξιν.[6] τούτου δὲ οὕτω πρασσομένου οὐκ
ἄν τι[7] ἐκ τῶν φυλάκων νεωτερισθείη.

11 Τοὺς δὲ προφυλάσσοντας[8] ἀντιπροσώπους ἀλλήλοις
ἑστάναι· οὕτως γὰρ ἂν πάντη ἀπ' αὐτῶν βλέποιντο,
καὶ ἥκιστα ὑπό τινων ἀγρευθεῖεν λάθρα προσελ-
θόντων,[9] ἅπερ ἤδη γεγονότα περὶ τὰ ἡμεροσκόπια
12 δεδήλωται. ἐν δὲ ταῖς χειμεριναῖς καὶ σκοτειναῖς
νυξὶν ἄλλην καὶ[10] ἄλλην αὐτοὺς λίθους βάλλειν
εἰς τὸ ἔξω μέρος τοῦ τείχους, καὶ ὡς δὴ ὁρωμένους
τινὰς ὑπ' αὐτῶν ἐρωτώντων τίνες εἶεν·[11] ἀπὸ
ταὐτομάτου γὰρ ἂν γνωσθεῖέν τινες προσπελάζοντες.
13 ἂν δὲ δοκῇ, καὶ εἰς τὸ ἔσω μέρος τῆς πόλεως τὸ αὐτὸ
ποιεῖν. οἱ δέ τινες τοῦτό φασιν βλαβερὸν εἶναι·
τοὺς γὰρ προσιόντας τῶν πολεμίων ἐν τῷ σκότει
προαισθάνεσθαι ὅτι ἐνταῦθα οὐ προσιτητέον[12] ἐστὶ
διὰ τὴν φωνήν τε τῶν περιόδων καὶ τὸ βάλλειν,
14 ἀλλὰ μᾶλλον εἰς τὸν σιγώμενον τόπον. ἄριστον
δ' ἐν τοιαύταις νυξὶν ἔξω τοῦ τείχεος κύνας[13]

---

[1] Added by Köchly and Rüstow.
[2] Herm. Schöne: ἄπα πάντας M.
[3] Meier: περιοδεύουσιν M.
[4] Casaubon: ἕκαστον M.   [5] Hertlein: ὀνδ' ἅμα M.
[6] Casaubon: προσφύλαξιν M.   [7] Sauppe: ὅτἄντι M.
[8] Kirchhoff: προφυλάσσωσιν M.
[9] Köchly and Rüstow: προελθόντων M.
[10] ἄλλην καὶ added by Casaubon.   [11] εἰσίν Hercher.
[12] Mor. Haupt: προαισθάνεσθαι (space of 3-4 letters) οὐ
προσπήγαιον M.   [13] Casaubon: κύνα M.

to the remaining ones. Let everyone be ordered to do this at given signals. In this way many will make their way around the walls at the same time, and each will move but a short distance, and the same men will not often remain together, since different guards will be constantly coming in contact with one another. If this be done no act of treachery could be performed by the guards.

The guards should stand facing one another, for in this way they can see in all directions and they will rarely be caught by any foe coming secretly against them, a thing that I have noted [1] as having actually happened to day-watches. During the dark winter nights stone after stone should be thrown over the walls, and, as if persons were seen, let the guard ask, "Who goes there?", for any who might be approaching would thus be recognized without more ado. If it should seem best, this could be done also inside the city. Some, however, say this is dangerous, for a party of the enemy which might be approaching in the darkness are made aware in advance that they must not attack at this point, by the noise of the patrols and the throwing of stones, but rather at the point where there is no noise. The best plan, however, on such nights is to have dogs tied outside the wall to keep watch.[2] For

---

[1] The reference may be to Ch. vi. 6, but this precise detail is not in the form in which the treatise has come down to us, very likely as a fault of the tradition rather than an oversight on the part of the author.

[2] Dogs were used by the Spartan Agesipolis at the siege of Mantinea in 385 B.C. (Polyaenus ii. 25); by Philip of Macedon for tracking down his foes in the Balkan mountains (*ibid.* iv. 2. 16); by Aratus for guarding the key fortress of Acrocorinth after its capture in 243 B.C. (Plutarch, *Aratus*, 24); and Vegetius iv. 26 recommends that they be used

they will detect at a greater distance the presence of a hostile spy, a deserter who is stealthily approaching the city, or one who is somewhere making his way out to desert ; they will also by their barking rouse the sentinel if he happens to be asleep.

If any part of the city is easily accessible and exposed to the attacks of the enemy, the sentinels stationed there should be the wealthiest and most highly respected citizens and those who hold the most important offices in the city. For it would be in the highest degree to the interest of such men not to turn aside to pleasures, but rather, bearing in mind their position, to maintain a vigilant watch. At the time of the public festivals those of the city guards who are greatly suspected and distrusted by their own comrades should be sent away from their posts to celebrate the festival at home. For they will think that they are being honoured and at the same time would have no opportunity to carry out any plot. And in their places more trustworthy men should be assigned to guard duty ; for during the festivals and on such occasions revolutionists are extremely likely to venture on some enterprise. An account of the disturbances which have arisen on such occasions has been given elsewhere.

It is better, moreover, that the ramps leading to the top of the wall should not be open, but rather be kept closed, thus rendering it impossible for anyone desirous of betraying the city to the

for guarding the walls at night, along with geese, which made themselves famous by saving the Capitol from the Gauls. See also below, § 20, for the use of dogs by Nicocles.

AENEAS TACTICUS

μένῳ ἐνδοῦναι τοῖς πολεμίοις, ἀλλ' ὦσιν οἱ[1] φύλακες
οὓς ἂν σὺ βούλῃ[2] ἐξ ἀνάγκης ἐπὶ τοῦ τείχους διατελοῦντες καὶ μὴ καταβαίνοντες, ἄν τέ τινες
ἔξωθεν τῆς πόλεως λάθωσιν ὑπερβάντες, μὴ ῥᾳδίως
διὰ ταχέων καταβαίνωσιν[3] ἀπὸ τοῦ τείχους εἰς
τὴν πόλιν, ἐὰν μὴ θέλωσιν ἀφ' ὑψηλῶν[4] κατα-
πηδῶντες κινδυνεύειν καὶ μήτε λαθεῖν μήτε φθάσαι.
πρέποι[5] δ' ἂν τὸ παρασκεύασμα τοῦτο περὶ τὰς
20 ἀναβάσεις καὶ ἐν τυράννου ἀκροπόλει.   μετὰ δὲ
τὴν ἐν Νάξῳ[6] ναυμαχίαν ἐπιβουλευόμενος[7] ὁ
φρούραρχος Νικοκλῆς ἀναβάσεις κλειστὰς ποιήσας
κατέστησε φύλακας[8] ἐπὶ τῷ τείχει, ἔξω δὲ τῆς
πόλεως περιοδίας ἐποιεῖτο μετὰ κυνῶν· προσεδέχοντο γὰρ ἔξωθέν τινα ἐπιβουλήν.

21   Ἐν ὁμονοοῦσι δὲ καὶ μηδενὸς ὑποπτεύοντος ἐν τῇ
πόλει ἐν τοῖς ἐπὶ[9] τῷ τείχει φυλακείοις δεῖ τὰς
νύκτας λύχνα καίεσθαι ἐν[10] λαμπτῆρσιν, ἵνα καθ' οὓς
ἄν τι προσπελάζῃ πολέμιον, ἄρωσι τῷ στρατηγῷ
22 τὸν λαμπτῆρα.   ἐὰν δὲ[10] μὴ φαίνηται πρὸς τὸν
στρατηγὸν ὁ λαμπτὴρ τόπου κωλύοντος, ἄλλος
διαδεκτὴρ ὑπολαμβάνων λαμπτῆρι φαινέτω τῷ
στρατηγῷ, ὁ δὲ στρατηγὸς τὸ ἐμφανιζόμενον
αὐτῷ τοῖς ἄλλοις φύλαξι δηλούτω σάλπιγγι ἤ[10]

---

[1] Added by Capps.   [2] Hertlein: βούλει M.
[3] Casaubon: καταβαίνουσιν AB.
[4] Hertlein: ἀπαλλήλων M.
[5] Casaubon: προτρέποι M (ABC).
[6] Casaubon: τὴν ἔξω M: ἐν Κιτίῳ Köchly and Rüstow.
[7] Casaubon: ἐπιβουλευομένοις M.
[8] φυλακὰς Behrendt.
[9] τοῖς ἐπὶ added by Köchly and Rüstow.
[10] Added by Casaubon.

---

[1] If Casaubon's conjecture be right we have a reference

enemy to seize part of the wall in advance, and that
the sentinels, men of your choice, may be obliged
to remain constantly on the wall and not come down.
Then if any enemy, attacking the city from the outside, should succeed in scaling the wall by surprise,
they could not easily and quickly descend from the
wall into the city, unless they were willing to take
the risk of leaping down from high places and to
forgo the advantages of surprise and initiative.
This method of guarding the ramps would be suitable also for the citadel of a prince. After the naval
battle off Naxos,[1] Nicocles, the commander of the
garrison, inasmuch as plots were being formed
against him, closed the ramps, posted sentinels on
the walls, and kept up a patrol with dogs outside the
city; for the people were expecting a treacherous
attack from without.

When the people are united and no one in the
city cherishes suspicions, lamps set in lanterns should
be kept burning throughout the night at the posts
of the sentinels on the wall, so that if a hostile
movement should be directed against any of them,
they may raise the lantern as a signal to the commander. If the nature of the ground prevents the
light from reaching the commander, another guard,
as a relay, should with his lantern give the signal
to the commander, who, either with the bugle or
by means of dispatch-bearers, as the circumstances
may demand, should transmit to the rest of the

to the famous battle off Naxos in 376 B.C., in which Athens
won back her supremacy at sea. On the other hand, if
Köchly and Rüstow's suggestion ἐν Κιτίῳ be followed,
the great defeat of Evagoras of Cyprus by the Persians in
380 B.C. is meant. The latter had a son Nicocles, well
known from the works which Isocrates addressed to him.

23 τοῖς δρομοκήρυξιν, ὁποτέρως¹ ἂν συμφέρῃ. κατὰ
δὲ τοὺς καιροὺς τούτους καὶ οὕτω περὶ τὰς φυλακὰς διατελούντων παραγγελλέσθω τῷ ἄλλῳ
ὄχλῳ, ὅταν σημανθῇ,² μηδένα ἐξιέναι· ἐὰν δέ
τις ἐξίῃ ἐπί τινα πρᾶξιν ἀναγκαῖον, μετὰ λαμπτῆρος πορεύεσθαι, ἵνα πόρρωθεν κατάδηλος ᾖ
24 τοῖς περιοδεύουσι. μηδ' ἐργάζεσθαι μηδένα
δημιουργὸν ἢ³ χειροτέχνην, ἵνα μὴ ψόφοι ἀπό
τινων γίγνωνται τοῖς φύλαξιν.

Ὃν δ' ἂν τρόπον ἴσως καὶ κοινῶς μακροτέρων ἢ
βραχυτέρων νυκτῶν γιγνομένων καὶ πᾶσιν αἱ
φυλακαὶ γίγνοιντο, . . .⁴ πρὸς κλεψύδραν χρὴ φυλάσσειν, ταύτην δὲ συμμεταβάλλειν διὰ δεχημερίδος.⁵
25 μᾶλλον δὲ αὐτῆς κεκηρῶσθαι τὰ ἔσωθεν, καὶ μακροτέρων μὲν γιγνομένων τῶν νυκτῶν ἀφαιρεῖσθαι τοῦ
κηροῦ, ἵνα πλέον ὕδωρ χωρῇ, βραχυτέρων δὲ
προσπλάσσεσθαι,⁶ ἵνα ἔλασσον δέχηται. περὶ
μὲν οὖν φυλακῶν ἰσότητος ἱκανῶς⁷ μοι δεδηλώσθω.

26 Ἐν δὲ τοῖς ἀκινδυνοτέροις τοὺς ἡμίσεας τῶν προγεγραμμένων εἰς τὰς φυλακὰς καὶ περιοδίας χρὴ
τετάχθαι, καὶ οὕτω τὸ ἥμισυ τῆς στρατιᾶς νύκτα
ἑκάστην φυλάξει· ἀκινδύνων δὲ καὶ εἰρηναίων ὄντων
ἐλάχιστά τε καὶ ἐλαχίστους τῶν ἀνθρώπων ὀχλεῖν.
27 καὶ ἐάν τε περιοδείας χρὴ τῷ στρατηγῷ,⁸ σκυ-

¹ Köchly and Rüstow : ἢ ὁποτέρως M.
² Kirchhoff : σημειωθῆ M.
³ Added by Meineke.
⁴ The lacuna determined by Herm. Schöne : πάντως suggested by R. Schöne.
⁵ Diels (Antike Technik², 1920, 195. 1) : συμβάλλειν διαδοχῇ
μερίδος M.
⁶ J. Afr. : προπελάσσεσθαι M.
⁷ Casaubon : ἱκανόσ M.
⁸ Capps : τῶν στρατηγῶν M.

sentinels the warning he has received. On such occasions, while the sentinels are thus engaged, the rest of the inhabitants should be notified that after a given signal no one is to leave his house. If, however, one should go out on some necessary errand, he should take a lantern with him in order to be visible to the patrols at a distance. Moreover, no workman or artisan should work at his trade lest noises made by any persons reach the sentinels.

A plan by which the watches may be apportioned fairly and equally to all the sentinels, according as the nights become longer or shorter [has been explained . . .[1], where it was stated that the watches] should be measured by the water-clock, and this should be reset every ten days. But a better plan is to smear the interior of the clock with wax and then to remove some of the wax when the nights grow longer, so that the clock may contain more water. When, on the other hand, the nights grow shorter, more wax should be added in order that the clock's capacity may be less. Let this, then, be sufficient explanation about the equalization of the watches.

At times of less imminent peril half the men enrolled in the army should be detailed for guard or patrol duty, and in this way half the army will be on guard every night. In times of peace and security the smallest possible number of the troops should be subjected to inconvenience, and to as little as possible. And if the commander needs some

---

[1] A reference to some other work by the author has fallen out here, as H. Schöne saw. It was probably the Στρατο-πεδευτικὴ βίβλος which treated of closely related topics, as one can see from Ch. xxi. 2 above.

ταλίδα ἔχουσαν σημεῖον παρὰ τοῦ στρατηγοῦ[1]
παραδίδοσθαι τῷ πρώτῳ φύλακι, τοῦτον δὲ τῷ
ἐχομένῳ καὶ ἕτερον ἑτέρῳ, μέχρι ἂν[2] περιενεχθῇ
ἡ σκυταλὶς κύκλῳ τὴν πόλιν καὶ κομισθῇ παρὰ
τὸν στρατηγόν· προειρῆσθαι δὲ τοῖς προφύλαξιν μὴ
πορρωτέρω προενεγκεῖν τὴν σκυταλίδα τοῦ ἐχομέ-
28 νου φύλακος. ἐὰν δ' ὁ[3] ἐλθὼν καταλάβῃ τόπον
ἔρημον φύλακος, πάλιν[4] ἀντιδιδόναι παρ' οὗ ἔλαβεν
τὴν σκυταλίδα, ἵν'[5] αἴσθηται ὁ στρατηγὸς καὶ γνῷ
τὸν μὴ παραδεξάμενον ἀλλ' ἐκλείποντα φυλακήν.
29 ὃς δ' ἂν φυλακῆς αὐτῷ οὔσης μὴ παρῇ εἰς τὸ
τεταγμένον, ὁ λοχαγὸς αὐτοῦ παραχρῆμα τὴν
φυλακὴν ἀποδόσθω, ὁπόσον[6] δἂν[7] εὑρίσκῃ, καὶ
καταστησάτω ὅστις ὑπὲρ αὐτοῦ φυλάξει. ἔπειτα
ὁ[8] πρόξενος ἐξ αὐτῆς[9] ἀποδιδότω τῷ πριαμένῳ τὴν
φυλακήν, ὁ δὲ ταξίαρχος αὐτὸν τῇ ὑστεραίᾳ ζημιούτω
τῇ νομιζομένῃ ζημίᾳ.

XXIII. [Ἐπέξοδος λαθραία ἐν νυκτί]

Ἐπεξόδους δὲ ποιούμενον λαθραίως ἐν νυκτὶ τοῖς
προσκαθημένοις πολεμίοις τάδε προνοεῖν.   πρῶτον

---

[1] The words παρὰ τοῦ στρατηγοῦ after σημεῖον in M seem
to be a gloss (Oldfather).   [2] Added by Meineke.
[3] Hercher: δὲ M.   [4] Orelli: πάντ' M.
[5] Added by Casaubon.   [6] Hertlein: πόσον M.
[7] Herm. Schöne (= δὴ ἂν): δ' ἂν M.
[8] Added by Köchly and Rüstow.
[9] Herm. Schöne: αὐτοῦ M.

---

[1] This passage is obscure because almost nothing is
known of the method by which mercenaries were hired,
but it seems most probable that agents contracted with a
state to furnish a certain number, and that the agent continued to represent these men, i.e., be their πρόξενος, since

patrol-work, a marked baton should be handed by him to the first sentinel ; he in turn must pass it on to the next man, and one to another, until it has made the round of the city and has been returned to the commander. And previous instructions should have been given to the watchmen not to carry the baton beyond the position of the next man. If, however, a sentinel, on his arrival at a post, should find it deserted, he should return the baton to the man from whom he received it, so that the commander may be aware and may investigate which of the sentinels has failed to take the baton and has deserted his post. Whenever a man who has a turn at the watch does not report for duty, his company-commander should at once sell his position for whatever it may bring, and should put another man on guard to take his place. Then the contractor of mercenaries, the same day, should pay the money to the man who has purchased the post, and on the following day the taxiarch should impose on the contractor the customary fine.[1]

XXIII. [*Secret Sallies by Night*]

One who is making secret sallies by night upon an enemy encamped outside must use caution in

they would not be citizens of the city which hired them. In this case it would appear that the contractor or agent whose man had failed to do his guaranteed duty would have to pay back the fee to the one who bought the vacant position, as well as pay a fine for the failure of his man to be at his post. Where the risks of the contractor were as high as this would indicate, we may be certain that he must have counted on making a large gross profit on his original contract. The closest parallel to such a person nowadays would perhaps be the *padrone*.

119

μὲν φυλάξαι ὅπως μή τις ἐξαυτομολήσῃ.[1] ἔπειτα φῶς ὑπαίθριον μηδὲν εἶναι, ἵνα μὴ ὁ[2] ὑπὲρ τῆς πόλεως ἀὴρ πυρωδέστερος ὢν τοῦ ἄλλου ἐκφήνῃ τὸ
2 μέλλον. τούς τε τῶν κυνῶν ὑλαγμοὺς καὶ τῶν ἀλεκτρυόνων τὰς φωνὰς ἀφανίζειν ἄφωνα ποιοῦντα τόνδε τὸν καιρόν, ἐπικαύσαντά τι[3] τοῦ σώματος· καὶ γὰρ αἱ τούτων φωναὶ πρὸ[4] ὄρθρου φθεγγόμεναι
3 ἐκφαίνουσι τὸ μέλλον. ἐποιήσαντο δέ τινες καὶ τοιόνδε τεχνάσαντες. στασιασμοῦ προσποιητοῦ μετὰ προφάσεως εὐλόγου γενομένου[5] παρ' αὐτοῖς, καιρὸν τηρήσαντες καὶ ἐπεξελθόντες ἐπέθεντο παρ'
4 ἐλπίδα τοῖς πολεμίοις καὶ κατώρθωσαν. ἤδη δέ τινες τειχήρεις ὄντες καὶ ὧδε ἔλαθον ἐπεξελθόντες.[6] τὰς μὲν πύλας ἀπέδειμαν[7] ὁρατῶς τοῖς πολεμίοις· ᾗ δὲ μάλιστα εὐεπιθέτως εἶχον οἱ ἐναντίοι,[8] ταύτῃ κατεπέτασαν ἀκάτειον[9] καὶ ἀνῆραν διὰ χρόνου τινός, ὥστε κατ'[10] ἀρχὰς μὲν θαυμάσαι τοὺς πολεμίους, ὕστερον δὲ καὶ πολλάκις γιγνομένου ἀμέλειαν εἶχον.
5 οἱ δὲ ἐν τῇ πόλει ἐν νυκτὶ διελόντες τοῦ τείχους ὅσον ἤθελον, καὶ ἀντιδομὴν παρασκευασάμενοι κατεπέτασαν τὸ ἱστίον. τηρήσαντες δὲ καιρὸν ἐπεξελθόντες ἐπέθεντο παραδόξως τοῖς πολεμίοις· ποιοῦντες δὲ ταῦτα ἐφύλασσον μή τις αὐτομολήσῃ. διὸ δεῖ μηδὲν τῶν τοιούτων παρορᾶν.
6 Οὐ μὴν οὐδ' ἐν ταῖς νυξὶν ἀσκέπτως μετ' ὄχλου

---

[1] Casaubon: μὴ ἐξαυτομολήσῃ M: μὴ ἐξαυτομοληθῇ Herm. Schöne.   [2] Köchly and Rüstow: μήθ' ὑπὲρ M.
[3] C: τε M.   [4] Added by Lange.
[5] Casaubon: γενομένης M.
[6] Köchly and Rüstow: ὧδε ἐλθόντες M.
[7] Hertlein: ἀνέδειμαν M.
[8] Hercher: εἶχεν τοῖσ ἐναντίοισ M.
[9] Kirchhoff: ἀγγεῖον M.   [10] Casaubon: καὶ M.

these matters : first, to see that no one deserts, and then that there is no light burning out-of-doors, lest the air above the city, becoming more luminous than the rest, should disclose his purpose. He must suppress the howling of dogs and the crowing of cocks, making them mute for this occasion, by cautery of some part of their bodies, because their cries, uttered before daybreak, reveal what is on foot.[1] Some have used the following devices in making sallies : a pretended sedition arising among them on some specious pretext, watching an opportune moment and sallying forth they have attacked their enemies unexpectedly, and have succeeded. Others who were besieged have secretly gone out thus : They walled up the gates in sight of the enemy, but where he was most open to attack they let down a sail, which they raised after a time, so that the enemy was at first surprised, but later, when it was done many times, became indifferent. Then the residents at night broke down as much of the wall as they desired and built a false structure in its place and let the sail down over it. Then, watching the favourable moment, they sallied forth and attacked the enemy unexpectedly. But while they were doing all this they took good care to prevent any desertions. Accordingly, one must overlook none of these considerations.

Nor again should a leader inconsiderately go out

[1] Similarly Julius Africanus, Κεστοί, 9, tells how the Parthians kept their horses from neighing by so tightly binding their tails as to rob them of their spirit by the pain which the cord inflicted. It is reported that the mules belonging to the American army in France were prevented from braying by a simple surgical operation.

ἐκπορευτέον,[1] οἷα καὶ ἐν τοῖς καιροῖς τῶν ἐπιβουλευόντων τινὲς τεχνάζουσιν, οἱ μὲν ἔσω τῆς
πόλεως οἱ δὲ καὶ ἔξωθεν, προσάγεσθαι βουλόμενοι
τοιοῖσδε ἀπατήμασι, πυρσεύσαντές τι ἢ ἐμπρή-
σαντες νεώριον ἢ γυμνάσιον ἢ[2] ἱερὸν πάνδημον ἢ
δι᾽ ὅπερ ἂν ἔξοδος γένοιτο πλήθους ἀνθρώπων
καὶ οὐ τῶν τυχόντων. προνοοῦντα οὖν καὶ τὰ
7 τοιαῦτα μὴ ἑτοίμως ἀποδέχεσθαι.   πρᾶξις δὲ
καὶ ἥδ᾽ ἐξοισθήσεται ἐξ ἀρχόντων.[3] προετοιμά-
σαντες κατὰ τὴν χώραν θόρυβον γενέσθαι καὶ ἐκ
τῶν ἀγρῶν εἰς τὴν πόλιν ἀγγελθῆναι κλωπῶν
ἐπιβουλήν, δι᾽ ὅπερ ἔμελλον οἱ πολῖται σπεύσειν εἰς
8 βοήθειαν, γενομένου δὲ τούτου οἵ τε[4] ἄρχοντες καὶ
οἱ συνεθέλοντες[5] τοὺς πολίτας[6] παρεκάλουν εἰς
βοήθειαν. ἐπειδὴ δ᾽[7] ἠθροίσθη τὸ πλῆθος τῶν
πολιτῶν πρὸς τὰς πύλας σὺν ὅπλοις, τοιόνδε
9 ἐτεχνάσαντο. προεῖπον οἱ ἄρχοντες τοῖς ἠθροισμέ-
νοις ὅτι τρία μέρη αὐτοὺς γενομένους δεῖ ἐνεδρεῦσαι μικρὸν ἀπωτέρω τῆς πόλεως, παραγγείλαντες
ἃ προσῆκεν πρὸς τὰ μέλλοντα, τοῖς δὲ ἀκούουσιν ἦν
10 ἀνύποπτα.   καὶ τοὺς μὲν ἐξαγαγόντες ἐκάθισαν εἰς
χωρία ἐπιτήδεια ὡς ἐνεδρεύσοντας τοῖς ἐμβεβληκόσι
πολεμίοις· αὐτοὶ δὲ λαβόντες σώματα αὐτοῖς
συνίστορα τῆς πράξεως προεπορεύοντο ὡς κατα-
σκεψόμενοι[8] τε τὰ ἀγγελλόμενα καὶ προκινδυ-
νεύσοντες[9] τῶν ἄλλων, ἵνα δῆθεν προαγάγοιεν τοὺς
πολεμίους εἰς τὰς ἐνέδρας ὡς ὑποφεύγοντες.
11 πορευθέντες δὲ εἰς τόπον ὅπου ἦν αὐτοῖς ξενικὸν

---

[1] Casaubon : ἐκπορευταῖον M.   [2] Added by Orelli.
[3] Köchly and Rüstow : πράξεις . . . ὧδε ξοισθήσεται ἐξ-
αρχόντων M.
[4] Köchly and Rüstow : γε M.

at night with a crowd, because at such times some of the conspirators are forming plots, some within, some without the city, wishing to lure one out with deceptions such as beacon-torches, setting fire to a dockyard, or a gymnasium, or a public temple, or some building on account of which a crowd of men —and influential men too—might rush out. A leader should, therefore, use foresight, and not readily accept at their face value even such incidents. I shall relate also the following sharp practice on the part of officials. It was arranged that a disturbance should arise in the country, and that word should be brought from the fields to the city of a robbers' plot, of the very kind at which the citizens were sure to hurry to the rescue. And when this occurred, the magistrates and their supporters summoned the citizens to the rescue, and when the full number of the townsmen was gathered at the gates under arms, they contrived as follows. The magistrates told the crowd that they must divide into three parts and lay an ambush a little distance from the city, and explained what they must do, the hearers having no suspicion of the truth. They then led the people forth and stationed them in suitable places as though to ambush the invading enemy, while they them-selves, taking troops who were accomplices in the matter, went ahead as though to inquire into the report and meet the danger first, ostensibly in order to entice the enemy into the ambuscades by pretend-ing to flee. But going to a place where they had a

---

[5] Köchly and Rüstow: συνελθοντεσ M.
[6] Casaubon: πολεμίουσ M. [7] Added by Herm. Schöne.
[8] Casaubon: κατακοψόμενοί τε M.
[9] Hertlein: προκινδυνεύοντεσ M.

123

προητοιμασμένον κρυφαίως[1] κομισθέντες[2] κατὰ
θάλατταν, ἀναλαβόντες ἔφθασαν καὶ ἔλαθον εἰσαγα-
γόντες εἰς τὴν πόλιν κατ' ἄλλας ὁδούς, ὡς τοὺς
ἐπεξελθόντας πολίτας πάλιν ἀπαγαγόντες· τὴν δὲ
πόλιν καταλαβόντες τοῖς ξένοις τῶν ἐν ταῖς
ἐνέδραις ὄντων τοὺς μὲν ἐφυγάδευον, τοὺς δὲ ἐδέ-
χοντο. διὸ δεῖ πάντα τὰ τοιαῦτα ὑποπτεύειν καὶ
μὴ ἀλογίστως νύκτωρ εἰς πολεμίους ἔξοδον πλήθους
ποιεῖσθαι.

XXIV. [Συνθημάτων[3]]

Παραδιδόντα δὲ συνθήματα δεῖ προνοεῖν, ἐὰν
τύχῃ τὸ στράτευμα μιγάδες ὄντες ἀπὸ πόλεων ἢ
ἐθνῶν, ὅπως μή, ἂν παρέχῃ τὸ ἓν εἶδος δύο ὀνόματα,
ἀμφιβόλως παραδοθήσεται, οἷον τάδε, Διόσκουροι
Τυνδαρίδαι, περὶ ἑνὸς εἴδεος δύο ὀνόματα οὐ τὰ
2 αὐτά· καὶ ἄλλοτε δὲ Ἄρης Ἐννάλιος, Ἀθηνᾶ
Παλλάς, ξίφος ἐγχειρίδιον, λαμπὰς φῶς, καὶ ἄλλα
ὁμότροπα τούτοις, ἅπερ δυσμνημόνευτά ἐστιν παρὰ
τὰ νομιζόμενα ἑκάστῳ ἔθνει[4] τῶν ἀνθρώπων καὶ
βλάβην φέρει, ἐὰν κατὰ γλῶσσάν τις παραγγέλλῃ
3 μᾶλλον[5] ἢ κοινόν τι ἅπασιν. ἐν μιγάσι δ' οὖν
ξένοις οὐ δεῖ τὰ τοιαῦτα παραγγέλλειν, οὐδὲ ἐν
ἔθνεσι συμμάχοις. οἷον Χαριδήμῳ Ὠρείτῃ περὶ
τὴν Αἰολίδα συνέβη, καταλαβόντι Ἴλιον τρόπῳ
4 τοιῷδε. τῷ ἄρχοντι τοῦ Ἰλίου ἦν οἰκέτης ἐκπο-
ρευόμενος ἐπὶ λείαν ἀεί, καὶ μάλιστα ἐν ταῖς νυξὶν

---

[1] Casaubon: κρύψαι ὡσ M.   [2] C (AB?): κονισθέντεσ M.
[3] περὶ σ. suggested by R. Schöne: σ. παράδοσις by Herm.
Schöne.
[4] Casaubon: ἔθει M: ἔθη Hercher.
[5] Added by R. Schöne after Haase.

mercenary force, previously arranged and secretly brought in by sea, they picked them up before anyone knew of it, and secretly entered the city by other roads, as though returning with the citizens who had gone out for the attack. Then, with the mercenary force, they occupied the city, and of those in the ambuscades they banished some and admitted others. Accordingly, one must be suspicious of such acts and not inconsiderately make a sally in force at night against an enemy.

XXIV. [*Of Watchwords*]

In giving out watchwords it is needful to provide, if the army happen to be a mixture from different cities or tribes, that the word shall not be given out in an ambiguous way, in case one concept may have two different names, as for example, *Dioscuri* and *Tyndaridae*, two dissimilar words for one concept; or, again, *Ares*, *Enyalius*; *Athena*, *Pallas*; *sword*, *dagger*; *torch*, *light*; and others like these; for they are hard to remember if contrary to the custom of the several tribes, and they cause harm if one issues a password in dialect instead of in language common to all. One should not, then, issue such words to mixed mercenaries nor to allies of different tribes. Such a thing happened to Charidemus of Oreus in Aeolis when he had taken Ilium [1] as follows. A slave of the commander of Ilium went out for booty from time to time, and particularly at night

---

[1] This happened in 360 B.C. and is the latest event to which Aeneas makes reference. An account varying in some minor details is given by Polyaenus iii. 14. Thus, for a second time, as Polyaenus remarks, was Ilium captured by the use of a horse.

ἐξεπορεύετο καὶ εἰσεπορεύετο εἰσάγων¹ τὰ ἀγρευ-
5 θέντα ἑκάστοτε. ἐν δὲ τῷ χρόνῳ τούτῳ κατα-
μαθὼν ὁ Χαρίδημος ταῦτα πράσσοντα οἰκειοῦται,
καὶ εἰς λόγους κρυφαίους ἀφικόμενος διομολογεῖται,
καὶ ἔπεισεν αὐτὸν ἐκπορευθῆναι ἐν ῥητῇ νυκτὶ ὡς
ἐπὶ λείαν· μεθ' ἵππου δὲ ἐκέλευσεν αὐτὸν ἐξελθεῖν
ἐν τῇ νυκτί, ἵνα αἱ πύλαι αὐτῷ ἀνοιχθεῖεν, ἀλλὰ μὴ
κατὰ τὴν διάδυσιν² ἢ τὴν ἐκτομάδα πυλίδα ὥσπερ
6 εἰώθει,³ εἰσέλθοι.   γενόμενος δ' ἔξω καὶ διαλεχ-
θεὶς τῷ Χαριδήμῳ ἔλαβεν παρ' αὐτῶν ξένους ὡς
τριάκοντα τεθωρακισμένους καὶ ἔχοντας ἐγχειρίδια
7 καὶ ὅπλα καὶ περικεφαλαίας κρυφαίας.⁴ ὡς
ἀπήγαγέν τε οὖν αὐτοὺς ἐν τῇ νυκτὶ ἐν ἐσθῆτι
φαύλῃ καὶ ἔκρυψε τὰ ὅπλα, καὶ ὁμοιώσας αἰχμαλώ-
τοις, μετ' ἄλλων γυναικῶν καὶ παιδαρίων, καὶ
τούτων ὡς αἰχμαλώτων, εἰσεπορεύετο ἀνοιχθεισῶν
8 αὐτῷ τῶν πυλῶν διὰ τὸν ἵππον.   ὅπου δὴ εὐθὺς οἱ
εἰσελθόντες ἔργου εἴχοντο τόν τε πυλωρὸν ἀποκτεί-
ναντες καὶ εἰς ἄλλας ξένας πράξεις ὁρμήσαντες, καὶ
τῶν πυλῶν ἐγκρατεῖς ὄντες, ἐφ' ἃς εὐθύς, οὐ πόρρω
ὄντος τοῦ Χαριδήμου, παρῆσαν τάξεις καὶ κατ-
9 έλαβον τὸ πόλισμα.   μετὰ δὲ ταῦτα καὶ αὐτὸς
εἰσεπορεύθη μετὰ πάσης τῆς δυνάμεως.   ἅμα δὲ
10 τούτοις καὶ τοιόνδ' ἔπραξεν.   τοῦ στρατεύματός
τινι μέρει ἐνέδρας ἐποιήσατο, προνοήσας ὅτι
παρέσοιτο βοήθεια ἐπὶ τὸ χωρίον.   ὅπερ συνέβη·
εὐθὺς γὰρ αἰσθόμενος Ἀθηνόδωρος Ἴμβριος, ὢν οὐ
πόρρω μετὰ στρατεύματος, ἐπειρᾶτο βοηθεῖν ἐπὶ τὸ
11 χωρίον.   ἔτυχε δὲ καὶ αὐτὸς ἀγχίνως⁵ πάλιν ἀνθ-
υποπτεύσας,⁶ καὶ οὐ τὰς ἐνεδρευομένας ὁδοὺς
ἐπορεύθη πρὸς τὸ Ἴλιον, ἀλλὰ ἄλλας πορευθεὶς

¹ Casaubon : εἰσάγρὸν M.   ² Hertlein : διάλυσιν M.

used to go out and come in with what he had on each
occasion taken. At this time Charidemus learned
that he was engaged in this business and made a
friend of him. At a secret conference an agreement
was made, and Charidemus induced him to go out on
a given night as though for booty, bidding him leave
on horseback, after nightfall, that the gates might
be opened for him, but not to re-enter by the passage
or the wicket-gate as he was accustomed. When
he was outside and talking with Charidemus he
received from him about thirty mercenaries secretly
provided with breastplates, swords, weapons, and
helmets. So he led them off in the dark, in mean
garb and with arms concealed, disguising them as
captives, in company with others, women and
children, these too apparently captives, and entered
the city through the gate which was opened for him
because of his horse. There, immediately upon their
entrance, they set to work, killing the gate-keeper
and doing other barbarous acts. Charidemus was near
the gates of which they kept control, and his troops
immediately went in and took the town. Then he
entered in person with all his forces. At the same
time he carried out such a scheme as this, also:
He laid an ambush with a part of his army, foreseeing
that aid would come to the place, as actually happened. For Athenodorus, the Imbrian, who was not
far away with his army, as soon as he learned the
news, set out to succour the place. He too seems
shrewdly to have had his suspicions and marched
unobserved during the night to Ilium, not by the

---

³ Casaubon: εἰώθη M.   ⁴ Casaubon: κορυφαίας M.
⁵ C?: βαγχίνως MAB.
⁶ Casaubon: πάλιν ἀν (space) ὑποπτεύσας M.

roads which were ambushed but by other routes, and came to the gates. In the confusion, some of his troops went into the city with the others without being noticed, as though they belonged to the army of Charidemus. Then before many of them had entered they were detected by their countersign, and some were expelled and some killed at the gates, for their countersign was *Tyndaridae* while that of Charidemus was *Dioscuri*. By so narrow a margin it was that the city was not recaptured at once, that same night, by Athenodorus. So it is important to issue watchwords easily remembered and as nearly related as possible to the intended operations. For instance, when going for game, *Artemis the Huntress*; for some stealthy enterprise, *Hermes the Trickster*; for some deed of violence, *Heracles*; for open undertakings, *Sun* and *Moon*; and others as similar as possible to these and quite comprehensible to all. Iphicrates [1] would not allow the same watchword to be issued to the patrol and the guard, but employed a different word for each, that the one first questioned might reply, *Zeus the Saviour*, if he happened to have this one, and the other *Poseidon*. For in this manner they would be least

---

[1] Probably the greatest tactician whom Greece produced. He was active from about 395 to 355 b.c. Numerous stratagems are ascribed to him, and a large number of new weapons and pieces of equipment, the best known being, perhaps, the *Iphicratides*, or marching shoes. He developed the use of light-armed men, the peltasts, and was the first to introduce the constantly fortified camp. It was to these two features of their tactics that the Romans owed most of their military supremacy, and as the development of their military organization followed soon after the time of Iphicrates, it is tempting to think that they took these two epoch-making ideas from him.

likely to be deceived by the enemy, and the watchword to be betrayed. If the guards become separated from one another they should give a whistle agreed upon beforehand to call one another. For, except to the man who already knows it, this signal will be unfamiliar, as well to Greeks as to barbarians. One should watch the dogs lest on account of the whistling there be some trouble from them. This method was used at Thebes when the Cadmea was captured: the forces were scattered in the darkness and unable to recognize one another, but were collected by whistling.[1] The watchwords should be asked by the men on patrol and the advanced pickets, each from the other, for there is no propriety in having only the one do the asking, since in the guise of a patrol even an enemy might do that.

XXV. [*Additional Tokens of Recognition*]

Some employ an additional token of recognition, both to prevent panics and the better to recognize their friends. Additional tokens of recognition must be as distinctive and as difficult as possible for the enemy to understand. They may be as follows. On dark nights ask the watchword and say something else, or rather also make a noise, and the one questioned must in reply give the watchword and utter some other word or make a noise, according to previous agreement. Again, when it

---

[1] This was probably the recapture of the Cadmea from the oligarchs and the Spartans in 379 B.C., rather than the original capture in 383. The reference in Ch. xxxi. 34 doubtless points to the former.

φαεινοῖς χρόνοις τὸν μὲν ἐρωτῶντα τὸ σύνθημα τὸν
πῖλον ἀφελέσθαι ἢ ἐν τῇ χειρὶ ἔχοντα ἐπιθέσθαι,
3 ἔστι δὲ καὶ ἐπαγαγέσθαι τὸν πῖλον ἐπὶ τὸ πρόσω-
4 πον καὶ ἀπαγαγέσθαι ἀπὸ τοῦ προσώπου, ἔτι δὲ
καὶ τὸ δόρυ καταπῆξαι προσιόντα ἢ εἰς τὴν ἀριστερὰν
παραλαβεῖν, ἢ[1] ἔχειν ἐν τῇ χειρὶ ἄραντα ἢ ἀνελέσθαι,
τὸν δὲ ἐρωτώμενον τό τε σύνθημα ἀποκρίνασθαι
καὶ τούτων τι προσυγκείμενον ποιῆσαι.

XXVI. [Περιοδεῖαι]

Περιοδεύειν μὲν[2] ἐν τοῖς κινδύνοις πρῶτον[3] τῶν
ἐν τῇ ἀγορᾷ ἠθροισμένων λόχων δύο ὑπὸ τὸ τεῖχος
ἐναλλὰξ ἀλλήλοις, διεσκευασμένους τοῖς ὑπάρχουσιν
ὅπλοις καὶ παρασυνθήμασιν,[4] ὡς ἀκριβῶς ἐκ
2 πλείονος διαγνῶναι ἑαυτούς. τοὺς δὲ τὴν πρώτην
φυλακὴν περιοδεύοντας ἀδείπνους χρὴ περιοδεύειν·
τυγχάνουσι γὰρ οἱ τὴν πρώτην προφυλάσσοντες ἀπὸ
δείπνου ὄντες[5] ῥαθυμοτέρως τε καὶ ἀκολαστοτέρως
3 διακείμενοι. περιοδεύειν δὲ ἄνευ λαμπτῆρος, ἂν
μὴ λίαν χειμὼν ᾖ[6] καὶ σκότος· εἰ δὲ μή, οὕτω ὁ
λαμπτὴρ φεγγέτω, εἰς ὕψος μὲν μηδέν (κεκαλύφθω
γάρ τινι), ἐπὶ δὲ τὴν γῆν καὶ τὰ πρὸ τῶν ποδῶν[7]
4 μόνον φεγγέτω. ἐν ἱπποτροφούσῃ δὲ πόλει καὶ ἐν
ἱππασίμῳ χειμῶνος ἱππεῦσι περιοδεύειν· ἐν γὰρ
τοῖς ψύχεσιν καὶ πηλοῖς[8] καὶ μήκεσι τῶν νυκτῶν
5 θᾶσσον ἀνύοιτ᾽ ἂν ἡ περιοδεία. ἐὰν δὲ ἅμα τούτοις

---

[1] Herm. Schöne suggests λίθον after ἤ, comparing xxvi. 6.
[2] Added by Herm. Schöne.
[3] Herm. Schöne: πρῶτον δὲ M.
[4] Casaubon: παρασύνθημα M.
  Casaubon: οτιοδειπνουοντοσ M.

is light, the person asking the watchword may remove his cap, or, if he holds it in his hand, may put it on, or he may also bring his cap to his face and take it away from his face, or, further, may advance and fix his spear, or transfer it to his left hand, or hold it aloft in his hand, or merely raise it ; and the person who is asked for the watchword must both reply and do whichever of these actions has been agreed upon.

XXVI. [Patrols]

In times of danger the first thing is for two of the companies assembled in the market-place to patrol alternately at the base of the wall, provided with the arms available and with tokens of recognition so as to recognize one another with certainty from a considerable distance. And those who patrol during the first watch must do so before they have had their supper, for those who are on guard during the first watch, if they have just eaten, are more careless and undisciplined. And they should patrol without a light, unless it be very stormy and dark. But if they have a light it must not shine upward (for it must be covered with something), but merely upon the ground and in front of their feet. In a town in which horses can be kept and on ground passable for them patrolling can be done in winter by horsemen, for in the cold and mud and long nights the patrolling would thus be more quickly accomplished.

---

⁶ Casaubon : ἤ M.
⁷ Casaubon : διπων M (with indication of corruption over π).
⁸ Orelli : δηλοισ M.

καὶ ἐπὶ τοῦ τείχους περιοδεύωσιν, . . .[1] ὥστε τινὰς
μὲν τὰ[2] ἔξω τοῦ τείχους ἐπισκοπεῖσθαι, τινὰς δὲ
6 τὰ ἔσω· ἔχειν δὲ καὶ περιοδεύοντας λίθους ἐν ταῖς
σκοτειναῖς νυξὶ καὶ βάλλειν ἄλλην καὶ ἄλλην εἰς τὸ
ἔξω μέρος τοῦ τείχους. οἱ δὲ οὐκ ἐπαινοῦσι τοῦτο
7 διὰ τὰ προγεγραμμένα. ἐν ὑποψίᾳ ὄντων ἀλλήλοις . . .[3] χρὴ δὲ τὰς περιοδείας εἶναι κάτω τοῦ
τείχους, καὶ μὴ ἀναβαίνειν τοὺς[4] περιόδους πλὴν
τῶν φυλάκων.

Καὶ ἐὰν στράτευμα κεκακοπαθήκῃ[5] μάχῃ λειφθέν,[6]
ἢ διὰ τὸ πλῆθος ἀποβαλεῖν νεκρῶν ἢ τραυμα-
τιῶν,[7] ἢ συμμάχων ἀποστάσει ἢ δι᾽ ἄλλο τι
σύμπτωμα ἀθυμῇ[8] καὶ τεταπεινωμένον ᾖ,[9] ἐπικίν-
δυνά τε ᾖ[10] πολεμίων ἐγγὺς ὄντων, χρὴ τὰ προγε-
8 γραμμένα κατὰ τὰς φυλακὰς πράσσειν. καὶ τὰς
περιόδους ἐν τοῖς τοιούτοις καιροῖς πυκνάς τε χρὴ
περιοδεύειν καὶ οὐ δεῖ προθυμεῖσθαι ἐν ταῖς
περιοδείαις εὑρίσκειν τινὰς τῶν προφυλασσόντων
ἀμελεστέρως διακειμένους διὰ ὕπνον ἢ κάματον·
οὐ γὰρ συμφέρει οὕτω διακείμενον τὸ στράτευμα ἔτι
ἀθυμότερον καθιστάναι (εἰκὸς δὲ ὅταν εὑρεθῇ
αἰσχρόν τι ποιῶν ἀθυμεῖν), ἀλλὰ μᾶλλον πρὸς
9 θεραπείαν τε καὶ ἀνάληψιν αὐτῶν[11] τραπέσθαι. καὶ
περιόδους ἐν τοῖς τοιούτοις καιροῖς ἐκ πλείονος
χωρίου καταδήλους εἶναι προσιόντας τοῖς φύλαξι

---

[1] R. Schöne places a lacuna here for which he suggests
τούτους οὕτω τετάχθαι.　　　　　　[2] Hercher: εἰς τὰ M.
[3] R. Schöne places a lacuna here (space of three letters
in M) in which he supposes that some prescription beginning
χρὴ μὲν . . . to balance χρὴ δὲ stood.
[4] Casaubon: τὰσ M.
[5] Köchly and Rüstow: κεκακοπάθηκεν M.
[6] Casaubon: ληφθέν M.

And if together with these some men also patrol
upon the walls [they should be so placed] that some
may watch the outside of the wall and some the
inside. They should also on dark nights as they
make their rounds have stones and throw them now
and then outside the wall. Some, however, do not
approve this custom for the reasons already mentioned.[1] In case they are suspicious of one another
. . . the patrolling should be done at the base of the
wall and no patrol except the watchmen should go
up on the wall.

Now if an army has suffered in morale because of
defeat in battle, or from the size of their losses in
dead and wounded, or from desertion by allies, or
through any other misfortune it loses heart and has
become discouraged, and if there is danger because
of the nearness of the enemy, the directions already
given in regard to the watchmen are to be carried
out. At such times frequent rounds are necessary,
but the patrol must not be too eager on his rounds
to find members of the outposts in a rather careless
condition from sleep or weariness. For it is not
expedient to make the army, when in this state,
still more disheartened—and a man is naturally discouraged if he is found behaving basely—but rather
to turn one's attention to the care and recovery of
one's troops. And at such times the approach of
the patrols should be evident to the guards from

---

[1] The reference is to Ch. xxii. 13.

[7] R. Schöne: ἀποβαλεῖν ἢ τραυμάτων M.
[8] Casaubon: ἀθυμεῖ M.   [9] Casaubon: ἢ M.
[10] Casaubon: ἢ M.   [11] R. Schöne: αὐτῶν M.

φωνοῦντάς τι πόρρωθεν, ὅπως ἀνεγερθῇ[1] ἐὰν
καθεύδη ὁ προφύλαξ καὶ παρασκευάσηται ἀπο-
10 κρίνεσθαι τὸ ἐρωτώμενον. ἄριστον δὲ αὐτὸν τὸν
στρατηγὸν ἐν τοῖς τοιούτοις καιροῖς ἐπιμελῶς
ἑκάστην[2] περιοδεύειν μετὰ τῶν αὐτῶν ἀπολέκτων[3]
ἀνδρῶν. ὑπεναντίως[4] δὲ τούτοις διακειμένου
στρατεύματος ἐπισπερχεστέρως τοὺς φύλακας ἐξετά-
11 ζειν. ἐφοδεύειν τε τὸν στρατηγὸν μηδέποτε τὴν
αὐτὴν ὥραν ἀλλ᾽ ἀεὶ διαλλάσσοντα,[5] ἵνα μὴ προειδότες[6] σαφῶς ἐκ πολλοῦ χρόνου τὴν ἄφιξιν τοῦ
στρατηγοῦ οἱ στρατιῶται ταύτην[7] μάλιστα τὴν
ὥραν φυλάσσωσιν.
12 Ἀποδέχονται δέ τινες καὶ τόδε ἐπαγγελλομένων
τινῶν καὶ κελευόντων. τὸν πολίταρχον, ἐὰν μὴ
θέλη περιοδεύειν διὰ κόπον[8] τινὰ ἢ ἀρρωστίαν,
θέλη δὲ εἰδέναι τὸν μὴ φυλάσσοντα καθ᾽ ἑκάστην
13 φυλακήν, τάδε ποιεῖν χρή· λαμπτῆρας εἶναι προσυγκείμενον ἔστω[9] πᾶσι τοῖς ἐπὶ τῷ τείχει
φύλαξιν καὶ ἕνα[10] πρὸς ὃν πάντες ἀνταροῦσιν[11] οἱ
προφύλακες· ἀειρέσθω δὲ ἐκ τόπου ὅθεν πάντες
14 ὄψονται οἱ ἐπὶ τοῦ τείχους φύλακες. ἐὰν δὲ μὴ
ὑπάρχῃ ὁ τοιοῦτος τόπος, παρασκευασθήτω ἔκ
τινων ὕψος ὡς μέγιστον. ἔπειτα ἀπὸ τούτου
αἱρέσθω λαμπτήρ, καὶ πρὸς τοῦτον ἀνταίρεσθαι
τοὺς ἄλλους καθ᾽ ἕνα ἕκαστον ἀφ᾽ ἑκάστου φυλα-

[1] Meineke: ἂν ἐγερθῇ M.   [2] Herm. Schöne: ἕκαστον M.
[3] Casaubon: ἀποδεκτων M.   [4] Casaubon: ὑπεναντίοισ M.
[5] Mor. Haupt: ἀλλὰ ἰδία λαμβάνοντα M.
[6] Köchly and Rüstow: προϊδόντεσ M.
ταύτην Ταύτην M.   [8] Meineke: φόβον M.
[9] Added by Meineke.
[10] Added by Köchly and Rüstow (εἰς Casaubon).
[11] Meineke: ἀνταίρουσιν M.

a long way off by their uttering some sound from a distance, so that the guard may be wakened if he is sleeping, and may be prepared to answer whatever is asked. It is best of all at such times for the general himself carefully to make each circuit with the same picked men. But when the army is in the opposite mood it is well to inspect the guards much more energetically. The general must never make his round at a fixed hour, but must constantly shift it, lest the soldiers, knowing definitely long beforehand the coming of the general, may watch with especial care during that time.

At the advice and bidding of certain persons, however, some men adopt the following plan. If the commander of the city,[1] on account of some weariness or ill-health, does not wish to go on patrols, yet desires to know who, in each watch, fails to keep guard, he should act as follows. Let it be previously arranged that all the watchmen at the wall shall be supplied with lanterns, and that there shall be a particular one at the appearance of which all the watchmen shall raise theirs. This one should be raised from a place at which all the watchmen on the wall will see it, but if there be no such place ready, let one be built somehow, as high as possible. Then from the top of this let a lantern be raised and at its appearance let the others be raised, one by one, from each several post. Then

---

[1] The rare word πολίταρχος occurs elsewhere (e.g., Acts of the Apostles xvii. 6 and 8, in the form πολιτάρχης ; CIG. ii. 1967 ; Dittenberger, Sylloge³ 700. 2 and 48, cf. note 3) almost exclusively at Thessalonica (Saloniki) and the vicinity. It is not improbable that Aeneas got the term from there, as it appears that he saw military service at one time or another in the north Aegean.

κείου. ἔπειτα ἀριθμεῖσθαι, καὶ οὕτως εἰδέναι εἰ
πάντες ἦραν οἱ προφύλακες ἢ ἐκλείπει τις τῶν
φυλάκων.

XXVII. [Πανείων[1]]

Τοὺς δὲ περὶ πόλιν ἢ στρατόπεδα ἐξαίφνης
θορύβους καὶ φόβους γενομένους νυκτὸς ἢ μεθ'
ἡμέραν, ἅπερ ὑπό τινων καλεῖται πάνεια (ἔστιν
δὲ τὸ ὄνομα Πελοποννήσιον[2] καὶ μάλιστα Ἀρκα-
2 δικόν), πρὸς[3] ταῦτ' οὖν τινες κελεύουσι, κατα-
παύειν[4] θέλοντες αὐτά, προσυγκεῖσθαι τοῖς ἐν
τῇ πόλει σημεῖα, ἃ[5] ἰδόντες γνώσονται· γνώ-
σονται[6] δὲ ὅτι ἔστιν πάνειον ὧδε· αἰσθήσονται
διὰ[7] πυρός τι προσυγκείμενον ἐπὶ χώρου εὐκατό-
3 πτου[8] πᾶσιν εἰς δύναμιν τοῖς ἐν τῇ πόλει. ἄριστον
δὲ προπαρηγγέλθαι, καθ' οὓς ἂν τῶν στρατιωτῶν
γένηται φόβος, κατὰ χώραν τε ἠρεμεῖν καὶ ἀναβοᾶν
παιᾶνα, ἢ λέγειν ὅτι εἴη πάνειον[9] καὶ τὸν ἀκούοντα
4 ἀεὶ τῷ πλησίον[10] παραγγέλλειν. καθ' οὓς ἂν
τοῦ στρατεύματος μὴ ἀντιπαιανίζωσιν,[11] εἰδέναι

[1] περὶ πανείων or πανείων κατάπαυσις suggested by R.
Schöne.   [2] Casaubon: πελοποννήσιον M.
[3] Added by Herm. Schöne.   [4] C: καταπάνειν M.
[5] Haase: ὃ' M.   [6] αἰσθήσονται Hunter.
[7] Herm. Schöne: πάνειον· ἔστω δὲ αἰσθήσονται πυρός M:
ἔστω δὲ πυρός Hunter.
[8] Köchly and Rüstow: ἐκκατόπτου M.
[9] λέγειν τὸ ἰὴ ἰὴ παιῆον Herm. Schöne.
[10] C: τὸν πλησίον M.   [11] Meier: ἀντιπαιανίζουσιν M.

---

[1] Groundless fear, called ' panic ' fear, was ascribed to
the mysterious Arcadian mountain god, Pan. Greek armies
seem to have been peculiarly subject to these panics, due,
doubtless, to the rather indifferent discipline which generally
prevailed.

they should be counted, and thus it may be known whether all the watchmen have raised them, or if any one of the guards is missing.

XXVII. [*Of Panics*]

The confusions and terrors that suddenly arise in a city or a camp, by night or by day, are by some called *panics*—the word is a Peloponnesian, particularly an Arcadian one.[1] Accordingly, against these some who wish to stop them advise that signals be appointed in advance for all the inhabitants of the town, which they will see and recognize, and in the following way they will know that there is a panic, namely, by noticing a previously arranged signal-fire at a place as conspicuous as may be to all those in the city. And it is best to announce beforehand that, wherever panic occurs among the soldiers, they should stand in their places and shout ' Paean,' [2] or say that it is a mere panic, and that every one who hears it should pass the word along to his neighbour. Now wherever in the army they do not answer the paean, it will be known that there the terror pre-

---

[2] Paean was a very ancient god of healing among the Greeks, who later came to be identified with Apollo, Asclepius, and others. He was called upon with the cry ἰὴ Παιῆον or ἰήιε Παιάν to cure an evil or avert a misfortune. Out of this custom developed a song in honour generally of Apollo as god of healing, with the refrain ἰὴ Παιάν. A paean, or solemn hymn with the refrain ἰὴ Παιάν, was commonly sung before entering battle, but it is likely that a mere invocation of the god is here intended. (A. Fairbanks, in his exhaustive work on the Greek Paean, *Cornell Studies in Class. Philol.* xii, seems to have overlooked this passage in Aeneas.)

κατὰ τούτους τὸν φόβον ὄντα. ἐὰν δέ τι ὁ
στρατηγὸς φοβερὸν αἴσθηται, τῇ σάλπιγγι ση-
μαίνειν· τοῦτο δ' ἔστω γνωστὸν ὅτι εἴη τὸ πολέμιον.
μάχης δὲ γενομένης καὶ νικηθέντων ὡς τὰ πολλὰ
γίγνονται φόβοι, ἐνίοτε μὲν καὶ ἡμέρας, καὶ
5 νυκτὸς δὲ καὶ πάνυ. ὡς δὲ[1] οὖν ἧσσόν τι[2]
τοιοῦτον γενέσθαι, χρὴ εἰς τὴν νύκτα παρηγγέλθαι
τοῖς στρατιώταις πᾶσι κατὰ τὰ ὅπλα εἶναι ὡς
6 μάλιστα, ὡς ἐσόμενόν τι περὶ αὐτούς. προειδότας οὖν εἰκός ἐστιν,[3] ἐάν τι γίγνηται, μὴ
ἀπροσδοκήτους[4] προσπεσεῖν, μηδὲ ὑπὸ φόβων
ἐξαπιναίων ταράσσεσθαι καὶ ἀπόλλυσθαι.

7 Εὐφράτας δέ, ὁ Λακώνων ἁρμοστὴς ἐπὶ Θρᾴκης,
ἐπεὶ αὐτῷ πυκνὰ ἐγίγνοντο ἐν τῷ στρατεύματι
τὰς νύκτας φόβοι, καὶ οὐκ ἠδύναντο ἄλλῳ τρόπῳ
8 παῦσαι, τοιόνδε παρήγγειλεν εἰς νύκτα. ὅταν
τις θόρυβος γίγνηται, ἀνακαθίζειν αὐτοὺς εὐθὺς
πρὸς τὰ ὅπλα ἐν τῇ εὐνῇ, ἀνίστασθαι δὲ μηδένα
ὀρθόν· ἂν δέ τις ἴδῃ τινὰ ὀρθόν, παρήγγειλεν ἐν
πᾶσιν, ὥσπερ πολεμίῳ τῷ ἐπαναστάντι[5] χρῆσθαι.
9 διὰ γὰρ τὸν φόβον τοῦ παραγγελθέντος οὐδένα
ᾤετο[6] ἀμνημονήσειν. πρὸς δὲ τούτοις, ὅπως
ἀληθῶς[7] τὸ παράγγελμα μετὰ φόβου ᾖ, γενομένου[8]
τινὸς θορύβου ἐπλήγη τις τῶν σπουδαιοτέρων
ἀνδρῶν οὐχὶ θανατηφόρον, τῶν δὲ φαύλων τινὰ
10 ὥστε καὶ ἀποθανεῖν. συμβάντος δὲ τούτου
ὑπήκουσάν τε οἱ ἄνθρωποι καὶ εὐλαβούμενοι[9]

---

[1] Hertlein: ὥστε M.
[2] C: ησσοντισ M (with some unknown mark over σσ).
[3] ἐστι M. [4] Herm. Schöne: ἀπροσδοκήτοις M.
[5] ἐξαναστάντι Meier (cf. § 10). [6] Hertlein: ᾤετο ἂν M.
[7] Hercher: ἀληθὲσ M. [8] Köchly and Rüstow: ἡγεμόνος M.
[9] Casaubon: εὐλαβουμένου M (εὐλαβουμένοι B).

140

vails. But if the commander sees any reason for fear, he must give warning by the trumpet, and this is to be understood as a call to arms. It is after a defeat in battle that such fears are most likely to arise, sometimes by day but especially by night. But that this may be less likely to happen, orders for the night should be given to all the soldiers to keep under arms as much as possible, as though something might happen where they are. Thus, if they are forewarned, it is not likely that, in case anything happens, they will be taken by surprise on colliding with the enemy, or that they will be disturbed because of sudden terror and perish.

Euphratas,[1] the Laconian governor in Thrace, since panics occurred in his army frequently at night and could not be quieted in any other way, used to give orders of this sort for the night : that if any confusion should arise, his men should immediately sit up in their beds with their arms at hand, but that no one should stand upright, and if anyone saw a man standing up, Euphratas gave orders in the hearing of all to treat him as an enemy. For he thought that through the fear which this command would inspire none would forget it. Moreover, that the command should actually inspire fear, on one occasion when a panic arose, one of the more respectable soldiers was wounded, though not mortally, while one of the baser sort was fatally injured. As a result of this, the men obeyed and, paying close attention, refrained from panics and from

---

[1] Nothing further is known of him, and his name is not mentioned in Porolla's *Prosopographie der Lakedaimonier,* Breslau, 1913. Some have thought that Eudamidas (Porolla, No. 295), who was campaigning in Thrace in 362 B.C., may have been meant.

rising from their beds in terror. And panics have
been stopped in this way also : when confusion arose
in camp at night, the herald commanded silence and
announced that the man who reported the one who
had turned loose the horse which had caused the
commotion would receive a present of silver.[1] It is
necessary, too, if an army has this sort of experience
by night, to station men in each watch of the night
over every company or band, both on the flanks and
in the centre, to take special care that, if they
should perceive any disturbance coming on because
of sleep or anything else, whoever of them is at
hand may check it immediately. And of the rest
of the troops, there should stand on guard one
men from each mess, so that if any fear should arise,
they, knowing what fears are groundless, may each
calm the men at his own post.

But the commander should himself throw the
army of the enemy into confusion at night by driving
into their camp a herd of cows wearing bells, or other
animals, having first made them drunk with wine.[2]

[Reveille]

At daybreak one must not permit the guards
to leave their posts at once until the neighbourhood

---

[1] Much the same story is told by Xenophon of Clearchus
on the retreat after the battle of Cunaxa (*Anab.* ii. 2. 20),
and by Polyaenus iii. 9. 4, of Iphicrates. The idea was a
good one and was probably employed more than once.

[2] The use of a similar device, *i.e.*, oxen with lighted faggots
tied to their horns, enabled Hannibal to escape with his
booty through the mountain passes of Campania (Polybius
iii. 93. 10 ff. ; Livy ii. 16. 5 ff.).

---

[11] Köchly and Rüstow: ποτίσασ M.
[12] Added by R. Schöne (after χρὴ Meier).

προερευνηθέντα ἐμφανισθῇ καὶ καθαρὰ εἶναι πο-
λεμίων· καὶ οὕτω ἀπιέναι τοὺς ἀπὸ τῶν φυλακῶν
μὴ ἅμα πάντας[1] ἀλλὰ κατὰ μέρη, ὅπως ἀεί τινες
ἐπὶ τοῖς φυλακείοις διατελῶσιν.

XXVIII. [Πυλωρικά]

Προνοεῖσθαι δὲ καὶ τάδε ἐν φόβῳ οὔσης πόλεως.
πύλας τὰς μὲν ἄλλας κεκλεῖσθαι, μίαν δὲ ἀνεῷχθαι ᾗ ἂν δυσπροσοδώτατον ᾖ τῆς πόλεως καὶ
ἐπὶ πλεῖστον ἀπ’ αὐτῆς[2] μέλλωσιν ὁρᾶσθαι οἱ
2 προσιόντες, καὶ ἐν ταύτῃ ἐκτομάδα, ἵνα σώματα
μὲν ἀνθρώπων κατὰ τὴν ἐκτομάδα πυλίδα ἐξίῃ
καὶ εἰσίῃ καθ’ ἕνα.[3] οὕτω γὰρ ἂν ἥκιστά τις
λανθάνοι[4] αὐτομολῶν ἢ κατάσκοπος εἰσιών,
3 ἐάνπερ γε ᾖ ὁ πυλωρὸς νοηρός.[5] πᾶσαν[6] δὲ
ἀνοίγεσθαι ὑποζυγίων ἕνεκεν καὶ ἁμαξῶν καὶ
ἀγωγίμων ἐπισφαλές.[7] καὶ[8] ἐάν τι δέῃ εἰσενέγ-
κασθαι σίτου ἢ ἐλαίου ἢ οἴνου ἐν τάχει ἢ τῶν
ὁμοτρόπων τούτοις, ἁμάξαις ἢ σωμάτων πλήθει,[9]
ταῦτα δὲ χρὴ κατὰ τὰς ἐγγύτατα[10] πύλας κομίζειν,[11]
. . .[12] καὶ οὕτως ἂν[13] τάχιστα καὶ ῥᾷστα εἰσκομισθείη.
4 τὸ δ’ ὅλον[14] μὴ ἀνοίγεσθαι πρωὶ πύλας ἀπροσκέ-
πτως ἀλλ’ ὀψιαίτερον, ἔξω τε μηδένα[15] ἀφίεσθαι
πρὶν ἢ[16] ἐξερευνῆσαι[17] τὰ περὶ τὴν πόλιν· ἔτι τε
μηδὲ[18] πλοῖα κατὰ ταύτας[19] ὁρμίζεσθαι ἀλλ’

---

[1] Meineke: ἅπαντασ M.   [2] Boivin: αὐτῶν M, J. Afr.
[3] ἐν καθ’ ἕν J. Afr.   [4] Meier: λανθάνῃ M.
[5] M, J. Afr.: defended by Mahlstedt.
[6] Added by Hercher: πᾶν J. Afr.
[7] Casaubon: ἐπισφασ (?) M: ἐπίσφὰς AB.
[8] εἰ δέ τι τούτων ἀναγκαίως δεήσει J. Afr.
[9] J. Afr.: πάθη M.   [10] Cf. note on iii. 5.

has been carefully reconnoitred and shown to be clear of the enemy. Even then they must not all leave their posts at once, but in detachments, so that some shall always continue on guard.

XXVIII. [On Gates]

When a city is in fear precautions must also be taken as follows. Close the other gates but leave one open where access to the city is most difficult, and where those who approach are going to be in plain sight for the longest distance. In this there should be a wicket gate so that through it men may go and come singly, for in this way a deserter or spy would be least able to escape notice if he should enter, that is, if the gate-keeper is discreet. But it is unsafe to open the entire gate for beasts of burden, wagons, and loads. And if there be any need of importing quickly food or oil or wine or similar supplies, either by wagons or by a squad of men, these should be brought in by the nearest gates, . . . as that would be quickest and easiest. In general, the gates must not be opened incautiously early in the day, but later, and no one should be let out until the region around the city has been reconnoitred. Again, boats are not to be moored

---

[11] C: κοιμίζειν M.
[12] Hercher placed a lacuna here, comparing J. Afr. προεξιόντος στρατεύματος.
[13] Hercher: καὶ ἐὰν M.   [14] ὅλον πρᾶγμα J. Afr.
[15] B (second hand) C: μηθέντα M: ὀψίτερόν τι μηθένα ἔξω J. Afr.   [16] ἂν J. Afr.
[17] ἐξερευνήσῃ J. Afr.   [18] Hercher: μήτε M, J. Afr.
[19] κατ' αὐτὰς J. Afr.

AENEAS TACTICUS

ἀπωτέρω, ὡς ἤδη γε καὶ ἡμέρας[1] πολλαὶ πράξεις
ἀνοιχθεισῶν ἀμφοτέρων πυλῶν γεγόνασιν ἐπὶ
τεχνασμάτων καὶ προφάσεων τοιῶνδε· γνωσθήσεται δὲ[2] ἐφ᾽ ἑνὸς ἔργου πολλὰ παραπλησίως
τούτῳ πραχθέντα. Πύθων μὲν ὁ Κλαζομένιος,
καὶ τῶν ἐν τῇ πόλει τινῶν συνεθελόντων, τηρήσας
τελέως τὸ ἡσυχαίτατον[3] τῆς ἡμέρας, ἁμάξαις ἐκ
παρασκευῆς πίθους εἰσαγούσαις κατέλαβε Κλαζο-
μενάς· μενουσῶν[4] ἐν ταῖς πύλαις τῶν ἁμαξῶν,
καθ᾽ ἅς, ξένων προϋπαρχόντων κρυφαίως οὐ
πόρρω τῆς πόλεως, τοὺς μὲν τῶν πολιτῶν λαθόντες,
τοὺς δὲ φθάσαντες, τινὰς δὲ τῶν ἔσω συνεργοὺς
ἔχοντες κατέσχον τὴν πόλιν. Ἰφιάδης τε Ἀβυ-
δηνὸς κατὰ Ἑλλήσποντον καταλαμβάνων Πάριον
ἄλλα τε περὶ τὴν ἀνάβασιν νυκτὸς ἐπὶ τοῦ τείχους
λάθρᾳ παρεσκευάσατο[5] καὶ ἁμάξας πληρώσας
φρυγάνων καὶ βάτων παρέπεμψεν πρὸς τὸ τεῖχος,
ἤδη τῶν πυλῶν κεκλεισμένων, ὡς τῶν Παριανῶν
οὔσας τὰς ἁμάξας, αἵτινες[6] ἐλθοῦσαι πρὸς τὰς
πύλας ηὐλίζοντο, ὡς φοβούμεναι πολεμίους. ἃς
ἔδει ἐν καιρῷ τινι ὑφαφθῆναι, ἵνα αἱ πύλαι ἐμ-
πρησθῶσι καὶ πρὸς τὸ σβεννύειν τῶν Παριανῶν
ὁρμησάντων αὐτὸς κατὰ ἄλλον τόπον εἰσέλθῃ.

Δοκεῖ δέ μοι συναγαγόντι[7] δηλωτέον τίνα δεῖ
φυλάσσεσθαι[8] καὶ ἐν οἷς καιροῖς ἕκαστα, ἵνα
τις μηδὲν εὐήθως ἀποδέχηται.

[1] Gronov: ἡμέραι M.
[2] Suggested by Herm. Schöne: τοιῶνδε ἐφ᾽ M.
[3] Hercher: ἡσυχότατον M.
[4] Added by Casaubon: R. Schöne suggests plausibly
κατάξας τινὰ or μίαν (sc. ἅμαξαν).   [5] παρεσκευάσατο M.
[6] Herm. Schöne: ἔτι ἐγγὺς M.   [7] Casaubon: συναγαγόντα M.
[8] Haase, Kirchhoff: ἵνα δὴ φυλάσσησθε M.

at the gates, but at a distance, since in time past, even in the daytime, when both gates have been open at once, many things have happened by tricks and pretexts such as the following—and from a single occurrence many cases similar to it will be understood. Pytho of Clazomenae,[1] having also some confederates in the city, watched carefully for the most quiet hour of the day, and captured Clazomenae by means of wagons, which, in accordance with his plan, were bringing in wine-jars. While the wagons were stopping in the gates (for there were mercenaries ready in concealment not far from the city near the gates), his men, eluding some of the citizens and outstripping the others, with the aid of some persons inside got possession of the city. And Iphiades of Abydus[2] on the Hellespont. in his capture of Parium, among other preparations for scaling the wall by night, secretly prepared wagons filled with brush and brambles and sent them to the wall (the gates being already closed), as though they were wagons of the Parians, which after their arrival were parked near the gates from fear of the enemy. At a suitable moment they were to set fire to the wagons, so that the gates might catch fire, and when the citizens of Parium had gone to put out the flames he himself might enter at another point.

It seems to me that I must show, by a collection of instances, against what things one must guard and on what occasions, so that one may not be so simple as to take anything for granted.

---

[1] Otherwise entirely unknown.

[2] He is known merely as a tyrant of Abydus at the time of Aeneas (Aristotle, *Politics*, 1306 a 30; Demosthenes xxiii. 176 f.).

AENEAS TACTICUS

XXIX. ['Όπλων λάθρα εἰσκομιδή]

Περὶ δὲ τῶν εἰσκομιζομένων εἰς τὴν πόλιν
ἀγγείων τε καὶ φορημάτων, ἐν οἷς ἄν τι κρυφαῖον
ἐνείη, οἷς[1] ἤδη πόλις καὶ ἡ ἀκρόπολις κατελήφθη,
2 νῦν δηλωθήσεται. ἅπερ εὐλαβεῖσθαι δεῖ καὶ
μὴ ἀφροντίστως αὐτῶν ἔχειν, καὶ μάλιστα τὸν
πυλωρὸν ἔν τισι καιροῖς, ὅταν ἔξωθέν τι ἢ ἔσωθεν
φοβερὸν ᾖ. ἔστιν δέ οἱ προσεκτέον εἰσκομιζο-
μένοις. ἐξοίσω δὲ καὶ παραδείγματος ἕνεκεν
3 ἐπὶ πράξει γεγενημένα. κατελήφθη γὰρ πόλις,[2]
ἔσωθέν τινων συνθελόντων, ἐν ἑορτῇ πανδήμῳ
4 τρόπῳ τοιῷδε. πρῶτον μὲν τοῖς προενδημήσασι
ξένοις ἐπὶ τὸ μέλλον[3] καὶ πολιτῶν τοῖς ἀνόπλοις
τε καὶ συνεργοῖς ἐσομένοις εἰσεκομίσθησαν θώρακες
λίνεοι[4] καὶ στολίδια[5] καὶ περικεφαλαῖα[6] ὅπλα
κνημίδες μάχαιραι τόξα τοξεύματα ἐν κιβωτοῖς[7] ὡς
φορταγωγοῖς κατεσκευασμένα,[8] ὡς ἱματίων ἐνόν-
5 των καὶ ἄλλων ἀγωγίμων· ἅπερ οἱ ἐλλιμενισταὶ
ἀνοίξαντες καὶ ἰδόντες ὡς ἱμάτια μόνον κατ-
εσημήναντο, μέχρι τιμήσονται οἱ εἰσαγόντες.
6 καὶ ταῦτα μὲν ἐτέθη ἐγγὺς τῆς ἀγορᾶς, ὅπου
ἔδει· ἐν δὲ ταρσοῖς καὶ ῥίποις καὶ ἱστίοις[9] ἡμι-

[1] Casaubon : αντικρυφαιον ἐνίοις M.
[2] Meineke conjectured here Ἀμφίπολις and for ἐπὶ πράξει
either ἐπὶ Θρᾳξὶ or ἐν τοῖς ἐπὶ Θρᾴκης (see explanatory note).
[3] Hunter places these words after συνεργοῖς.
[4] Behrendt (λινέους J. Afr.) : λιναῖοι M.
[5] στολίδας J. Afr.
[6] Defended by Mahlstedt : περικεφαλαίας J. Afr.
[7] κιβωτίοις J. Afr.
[8] This reading of M and J. Afr. is retained by Casaubon
and Behrendt ; it is generally changed to κατασκευασμένοις
(or -αις).
[9] Köchly and Rüstow : ἰστοῖσ M.

XXIX. [*Importation of Arms by Stealth*]

I shall now discuss the smuggling into the city
of jars and packages, in which there may be something hidden by means of which a city with its
acropolis has in past instances been seized. These
matters must be attended to and not disregarded,
particularly by the gate-keeper, at certain times, when
there is reason to fear any disturbance from without
or within; and he should look to it when things
are being brought in. I shall relate likewise, as
illustration, some things that have actually happened.
A city was captured, with the complicity of some
within it, upon a public holiday, in some such manner
as this.[1] First of all, to the aliens who had established
themselves there in anticipation of what was to take
place, and to the unarmed citizens who were to be
accomplices there were brought in linen corslets,
cloaks, helmets, shields, greaves, short swords, bows,
arrows, stowed away in chests like those of merchants,
with the statement that clothing and other merchandise were in them. The revenue officers, opening
these, and seeing what they thought was only clothing,
affixed their seals until the importers should put a
value upon them. These cases were then stored in a
convenient spot near the market-place. In crates
also and wicker frames and wrapped up in half-woven

---

[1] Meineke, by clever emendations, made it out that the
city was Amphipolis, and the occasion the capture by
Brasidas in 424-3 B.C., which caused Thucydides to be
exiled. But a careful comparison with the conditions
described by Thucydides iv. 103 ff. makes it clear that that
occurrence is not the one referred to here.

ὑφάντοις[1] δοράτια καὶ ἀκόντια ἐνειλημένα εἰσηνέχθη, καὶ ἐτέθη ὅπου ἕκαστα συνέφερεν ἀνυπόπτως· ἐν δ' ἄγγεσιν ἀχύρων καὶ ἐρίων πέλται καὶ μικρὰ ἀσπίδια[2] ἐν τοῖς ἐρίοις καὶ ἀχύροις[3] κεκρυμμένα, καὶ ἄλλα εὐογκότερα ἐν σαργάναις ἀσταφίδος καὶ σύκων πλήρεσιν, ἐγχειρίδια δὲ ἐν

7 ἀμφορεῦσι πυρῶν καὶ ἰσχάδων καὶ ἐλαιῶν. εἰσηνέχθη δὲ ἐγχειρίδια καὶ ἐν σικυοῖς πέποσι γυμνά, ἀπεωσμένα[4] κατὰ τοὺς πυθμένας εἰς τὸ σπέρμα τῶν σικυῶν. ὁ δ' ἐπιβουλεύων τε καὶ ἡγεμὼν

8 ἔξωθεν εἰσηνέχθη ἐν φρυγάνων φορήματι. νυκτὸς δὲ γενομένης καὶ ἀθροισθέντων τῶν ἐπιθησομένων, ἕκαστος ὃν ἔδει τηρήσαντες καιρόν, ἐν ᾧ μάλιστα οἰνωμένοι ἦσαν οἱ ἄλλοι κατὰ τὴν πόλιν οἷα δὴ[5] ἐν ἑορτῇ, πρῶτον μὲν τὸ φόρημα ἐλύθη, καὶ ἐξ αὐτοῦ[6] ὁ ἡγεμὼν ἕτοιμος ἦν· ἔπειτα ἄλλοι μὲν αὐτῶν τοὺς ταρσοὺς ἐξείλισσον[7] πρὸς τὰς λήψεις τῶν δοράτων καὶ ἀκοντίων, ἕτεροι[8] δὲ τὰ ἄγγη τῶν ἀχύρων καὶ ἐρίων ἐξεκένουν,[9] οἱ δὲ τὰς σαργάνας ἀνέτεμνον,[10] ἄλλοι δὲ τὰς κιβωτοὺς ἀνοίγοντες τὰ ὅπλα ἐξῄρουν, οἱ δὲ τοὺς ἀμφορέας συνέτριβον, ἵνα ταχεῖα ἡ λῆψις τῶν ἐγχειριδίων

9 γένοιτο. ἅμα δὲ ταῦτα καὶ οὐ πόρρω ὄντα ἀλλήλων ἐπορσύνετο ἀπὸ σημείου τοῦ ἐν τῇ πόλει

10 καὶ ὡς φάλαγγι γενομένου.[11] ὁπλισθέντες[12] δ' ἕκαστοι τοῖς προσήκουσιν ὅπλοις οἱ μέν τινες αὐτῶν ἐπὶ πύργους ὥρμησαν καταλαβεῖν καὶ

---

[1] ἡμιυφαντιαίοις J. Afr. [2] ἀσπιδίσκια J. Afr.
[3] Casaubon : ἀχύρεσ M.
[4] Casaubon : απεω ω ενα M (with mark of corruption over second ω). [5] Schenkl : οἱ δὲ M.
[6] ἐξ αὐτῆς (' forthwith ') Eberhard, Mor. Schmidt.
[7] Meineke : ἐξέλισσον M. [8] Meineke : ἕτερυς M.

sail-cloth, spears and javelins were brought in, and, without arousing suspicion, placed where each would be serviceable. And in baskets of chaff and of wool, bucklers and small shields were concealed in the wool and chaff; and others still smaller in baskets full of raisins and figs, as well as daggers concealed in jars of wheat and dried figs and olives. And daggers were likewise carried in unsheathed in ripe gourds, pushed down along the stems among the seeds of the gourd. Likewise the deviser and leader of the plot was carried in from without hidden in a load of faggots. And when night was come, and those who were to make the attack were assembled, and each one was looking out for the opportune time, at which all the rest of the citizens were completely intoxicated (as would be likely on a festival day), first of all the load was loosened and out of it came the leader ready prepared. Then some of them unrolled the crates to seize the spears and javelins, others emptied the baskets of chaff and wool, others cut open the hampers, others, opening the chests, took out the arms, and still others smashed the jars so as to lay hands upon the daggers as quickly as possible. All these things took place at the same time and not far away from each other, at a signal given in the city as if for battle array. And when each one had equipped himself with arms suited to him, some of them rushed to seize the towers and the gates, through which they

---

⁹ Added by Hercher (very uncertain).
¹⁰ Hercher: ἀνέτεμον M.
¹¹ R. Schöne: γινόμενον M: καὶ ὡς φάλαγξ ἦν τὸ γινόμενον Meineke: ταῖς ἔξω φάλαγξι γενομένου Hug.
¹² B (second hand) C: ὁπλισθέντας M.

πύλας, καθ' ἃς καὶ τοὺς[1] ἄλλους προσεδέχοντο,
οἱ δὲ ἐπὶ τὰ ἀρχεῖα καὶ τὰς ἐναντίας[2] οἰκίας, οἱ
δέ, ἄλλοι[3] ἄλλων τόπων εἴχοντο.

11 Εἰς δὲ ὁμοίας πράξεις τῶν εἰρημένων δεόμενοί
τινες ἀσπίδων ἐπεὶ οὐδενὶ ἄλλῳ τρόπῳ ἐδύναντο
ἑτοιμάσασθαι οὐδὲ εἰσαγαγέσθαι, πλῆθος οἰσυῶν[4]
12 καὶ ἐργάτας ἅμα τούτων[5] εἰσηγάγοντο. καὶ ἐν
μὲν τῷ φανερῷ ἄλλα ἀγγεῖα ἔπλεκον, ἐν δὲ ταῖς
νυξὶν ὅπλα, περικεφαλαίας καὶ ἀσπίδας, ἔπλεκον,
αἷς ὄχανα περιετίθεσαν[6] σκύτινα[7] καὶ ξύλινα.
ἀλλὰ μὴν οὐδὲ τῶν κατὰ θάλατταν προσορμιζο-
μένων πλοίων νυκτὸς καὶ ἡμέρας οὔτε μεγάλων
οὔτε μικρῶν ἀδιασκέπτως[8] ἔχειν, ἀλλὰ ἐμβαίνοντας τ ὺς λιμενοφύλακάς τε καὶ ἀποστολέας ἰδεῖν
αὐτοῦ[9] τὰ ἀγώγιμα, ἐνθυμουμένους[10] ὅτι καὶ
Σικυωνιοι ἀμελήσαντες τῶν τοιούτων μεγάλα
ἐσφάλησαν.

XXX. [Περὶ ὅπλων εἰσαγωγῆς]

Προνοεῖν δὲ καὶ τὰ ἐπὶ πράσει εἰσαγόμενα καὶ
εἰς τὴν ἀγορὰν ἐκτιθέμενα ὅπλα τά τε ἐπὶ τῶν
καπηλείων καὶ παντοπωλείων, ὧν[11] ἀθροισθέντων
πλῆθός τι γένοιτ' ἄν,[12] ὅπως μηδενὶ ἕτοιμα ᾖ
2 τῶν βουλομένων νεωτερίζειν· εὔηθες γὰρ τῶν μὲν

---

[1] Köchly and Rüstow, and Hercher from J. Afr.

[2] ἐναντίων Casaubon: τῶν ἐ. Köchly and Rüstow (cf.
J. Afr. τὰς πολέμου [for πολεμίων] οἰκίας).

[3] Herm. Schöne: οἱ δὲ ἄλλοι M.

[4] Oldfather: ὅπλα οισυων M (with mark of corruption over
ω): ὅπλα suspected by Hercher: οἰσύας Casaubon: οἰσυνον
R. Schöne: ὅπλα, πλῆθος οἰσύων Hunter.

[5] Hertlein: οὕτωσ M.   [6] προσετίθεσαν Meineke.

152

admitted the rest also; others fell upon the city-hall and the houses opposite; some took one place and some another.

In an enterprise similar to the kind already described, certain persons were without shields, and when in no other manner were they able to provide or import them, they brought in quantities of osiers and also workmen to handle them. And by day they wove other kinds of basketry, but by night they wove armour, such as helmets and shields, to which they attached leathern and wooden handles. Furthermore, it is necessary to be watchful not only of vessels which come in by sea to anchor near by, night or day, whether great or small, but also it is necessary for the inspectors of the port and the supervisors to go on board and personally to see the wares, having in mind that the Sicyonians also, forgetting such precautions, suffered a serious disaster.

XXX. [*On the Introduction of Arms*]

One ought also to take precautions in regard to the arms imported for sale and displayed in the market-place, likewise those in the small shops and the bazaars (since these, if gathered together, would make a considerable number), to prevent them from being ready at hand for anyone of those who desire to start a revolution. For it is silly to take

---

[7] Casaubon: συκινα M.
[8] J. Afr. διασκέπτως M : δεῖ ἀσκέπτως Köchly and Rüstow.
[9] J. Afr. : εἰδέναι ἀυτοῖσ M.
[10] J. Afr.: εὐθυμουμένουσ M.
[11] Added by Casaubon.   [12] Schenkl: γένοιτο M.

ἀφικνουμένων ἀνδρῶν παραιρεῖσθαι τὰ ὅπλα, ἐν
δὲ τῇ ἀγορᾷ καὶ ταῖς συνοικίαις ἀθρόα ὑπάρχειν
σωράκους[1] τε ἀσπιδίων καὶ ἐγχειριδίων κιβώτια.
διὸ δεῖ τὰ εἰσαφικνούμενά τε καὶ ἠθροισμένα
ὅπλα μὴ ἐκφέρεσθαί τε εἰς τὴν ἀγορὰν καὶ νυκ-
τερεύειν ὅπου ἂν τύχῃ, ἀλλὰ πλὴν δείγματος τὸ
ἄλλο πλῆθος πρὶν[2] ἐκτίθοιτό τις, εἶναι δημοσίᾳ[3]
κρίνειν.

XXXI. [Περὶ ἐπιστολῶν κρυφαίων]

Περὶ δὲ ἐπιστολῶν κρυφαίων παντοῖαι μέν
εἰσιν αἱ πέμψεις, προσυγκεῖσθαι δὲ δεῖ[4] τῷ
πέμψαντι καὶ δεχομένῳ ἰδίᾳ· αἱ δὲ λανθάνουσαι
μάλιστα τοιαίδε ἂν εἶεν. ἐπέμφθη ἐπιστολὴ
2 ὧδε. εἰς φορτία ἢ ἄλλα σκεύη ἐνεβλήθη βυβλίον
ἢ ἄλλο τι γράμμα[5] τὸ τυχὸν καὶ μεγέθει καὶ
παλαιότητι. ἐν τούτῳ δὲ γέγραπται[6] ἡ ἐπιστολὴ
ἐπιστιζομένων γραμμάτων τοῦ πρώτου στίχου[7]
ἢ δευτέρου ἢ τρίτου, ἐπιστιγμαῖς δὲ ἐλαχίσταις
καὶ ἀδηλοτάταις πλὴν τῷ πεμπομένῳ. εἶτα
ἀφικομένου τοῦ βυβλίου παρ᾽ ὃν δεῖ,[8] ἐξεγράφετο
καὶ τὰ ἐπισεσημασμένα γράμματα τιθεὶς ἐφεξῆς
τὰ ἐκ τοῦ πρώτου στίχου καὶ δευτέρου καὶ τὰ
3 ἄλλα ὡσαύτως, ἐγνώριζε τὰ ἐπισταλέντα. ὀλίγα
δ᾽ ἄν τις θέλων ἐπιστεῖλαι καὶ ὧδε ποιῆσαι,

---

[1] Casaubon: συρακους M.
[2] Added by Herm. Schöne.
[3] Schenkl: δημοσία M (δημόσια generally).
[4] Added by Casaubon.   [5] Meineke: δράμα M.
[6] δ᾽ ἐγέγραπτο Hertlein.
[7] Added by Hug: γραμμάτων ἢ M. It would seem, however, that something more has fallen out.
[8] ἔδει Hertlein.

away the weapons from men who are entering the town [1] while there are assembled in the market-place and the lodging-houses boxes of small shields and chests of daggers. Accordingly the imported and collected arms ought not to be exposed in the market-place and be left overnight in any chance spot, but, with the exception of a sample, official permission may be required before anyone exhibits them in bulk.

XXXI. [*On secret Messages*]

In regard to secret messages, there are all sorts of ways of sending them, but a private arrangement must be previously made between the sender and the receiver. Especially secret messages might take the following forms. In one case a message was sent in this way : in with merchandise or other baggage there was inserted a book, or some other chance document, of any size or age, and in this the message had been written by marking the letters of the first, second, or third line with dots, very small and discernible only to the recipient. Then, when the person intended received the book, he made a transcript, and by setting down in order the marked letters from the first line and the second and the others in the same way he discovered the message.[2] But should anyone wish to send a brief

---

[1] See Chap. x. 9.
[2] The following instance from recent events may be of interest in this connexion : " Chandra (that is, Ram Chandra, the editor of a Hindoo revolutionary paper in San Francisco) got all the news he wanted for his paper from India, and said he did it through copies of the Koran, marked peculiarly " (*The Washington Post*, April 24, 1918, p. 1, col. 6).

155

παρόμοιον τούτῳ. ἐπιστολὴν γράψαντα[1] περὶ
τινων φανερῶς ἐν πλείοσιν, ἐν ταύτῃ τῇ ἐπιστολῇ
τὸ αὐτὸ ποιεῖν ἐπισημαινόμενον γράμματα, δι᾽
ὅτων[2] ἐμφανιεῖς ἅπερ ἂν βούλῃ.[3] τὴν δὲ ἐπι-
σημασίαν εἶναι ὡς ἀδηλοτάτην ἐπιστιγμαῖς διὰ
πολλοῦ ἢ γραμμαῖς παραμήκεσιν. ἃ τοῖς μὲν
ἄλλοις μηδεμίαν ὑπόνοιαν ἕξει, τῷ δὲ πεμπομένῳ
4 γνωστὴ ἔσται ἡ ἐπιστολή. . . .[4] πεμπέσθω ἀνὴρ
ἀγγελίαν φέρων τινὰ ἢ καὶ ἐπιστολὴν περὶ ἄλλων
φανερῶν· τοῦ δὲ μέλλοντος πορεύεσθαι κρυφαίως
αὐτοῦ εἰς τὸ τῶν ὑποδημάτων πέλμα ἐντεθήτω
εἰς τὸ μεταξὺ βυβλίον καὶ καταρραπτέσθω, πρὸς
δὲ τοὺς πηλοὺς καὶ τὰ ὕδατα εἰς κασσίτερον
ἐληλασμένον[5] λεπτὸν γραφέσθω πρὸς τὸ μὴ
ἀφανίζεσθαι ὑπὸ τῶν ὑδάτων τὰ γράμματα.
4a ἀφικομένου δὲ παρ᾽ ὃν δεῖ, καὶ ἀναπαυομένου ἐν
τῇ νυκτί, ἀναλυέτω τὰς ῥαφὰς τῶν ὑποδημάτων,
καὶ ἐξελὼν καὶ ἀναγνούς, ἄλλα γράψας λάθρᾳ ἔτι
καθεύδοντος καὶ ἐγκαταρράψας ἀποστελλέτω τὸν
ἄνδρα, ἀνταγγείλας ἤ[6] καὶ δούς τι[7] φέρειν φανερῶς.
5 οὕτως οὖν οὔτε ἄλλος οὔτε ὁ φέρων εἰδήσει· χρὴ δὲ
τὰς ῥαφὰς τῶν ὑποδημάτων ὡς ἀδηλοτάτας ποιεῖν.
6 Εἰς Ἔφεσον δ᾽ εἰσεκομίσθη γράμματα τρόπῳ
τοιῷδε. ἄνθρωπος ἐπέμφθη ἐπιστολὴν ἔχων
φύλλοις ἐγγεγραμμένην,[8] τὰ δὲ φύλλα ἐφ᾽ ἕλκει

[1] Köchly and Rüstow: γράψασ M.
[2] Herm. Schöne: δὲ ὅτε M.
[3] Kirchhoff: ἐμφανῆ ὥσπερ ἐν βούλλῃ M.
[4] Hercher placed a lacuna here.
[5] Meineke: ἡλασμένον M.
[6] Herm. Schöne (partly after Hercher): ἀποστείλας καὶ M
(defended by Behrendt and Mahlstedt): ἀνταποστείλας J.
Afr.: ἀντεπιστείλας Köchly and Rüstow.

message, he might use also the following method,
which is similar to the preceding. Writing in detail
and undisguisedly on some subject, in this message
you may reach the same result by marking letters
by which you will indicate whatever you may wish.
And the marking must be made as inconspicuous as
possible, by dots placed far apart or by rather long
dashes. These will arouse no suspicion whatsoever
in others, but the letter will be clear to the
recipient. . . . Let a man be sent bearing some
message or even a letter ostensibly about general
matters, not secret, and, just before he starts,
without his knowledge let a letter be inserted in
the sole of his sandals and be sewed in,[1] and, to
guard against mud and water, have it written on a
piece of thin-beaten tin, so that the writing will
not be effaced by the water. And when he reaches
the one intended and goes to rest for the night, this
person should pull out the stitchings of the sandals,
take out and read the letter, and, writing another
secretly while the man is still asleep, sew it in and
send him back, having given him some message in
reply or even something to carry openly. In this
way, then, neither the messenger nor anyone else
will know the message. It is necessary, however,
to make the sewings of the sandals as inconspicuous
as possible.

Again, a letter was brought to Ephesus in some
such manner as this. A man was sent with a
message written on leaves which were bound to a

[1] This particular device is mentioned by Ovid in the *Ars
amat.* iii. 621 ff.

---

[7] Köchly and Rüstow: τε M, J. Afr.
[8] Meineke: γεγραμμένην M.

7 καταδεδεμένα ἦν ἐπὶ κνήμην. εἰσενεχθείη δ'
ἂν γραφὴ καὶ ἐν τοῖς τῶν γυναικῶν ὠσὶν ἔχουσιν[1]
ἀντ' ἐνωτίων ἐλασμοὺς ἐνειλημένους λεπτοὺς μολι-
8 βδίνους.[2] ἐκομίσθη δὲ ἐπιστολὴ περὶ προδοσίας[3]
εἰς στρατόπεδον ἀντικαθημένων πολεμίων[4] ὑπὸ
τοῦ προδιδόντος ὧδε. τῶν ἐξιόντων ἱππέων ἐκ
τῆς πόλεως εἰς προνομὴν τῶν πολεμίων ἑνὶ ἐγ-
κατερράφη ὑπὸ τὰ πτερύγια τοῦ θώρακος βιβλίον·
ᾧ[5] ἐντέταλτο, ἐάν τις ἐπιφάνεια τῶν πολεμίων
γένηται, πεσεῖν ἀπὸ τοῦ ἵππου ὡς ἄκοντα καὶ
ζωγρηθῆναι. καὶ γενομένου δ' ἐν τῷ στρατοπέδῳ
ἀποδοθῆναι[6] τὸ βυβλίον ᾧ ἔδει.[7] ὑπηρέτησεν
9 δ' ὁ[8] ἱππεὺς ἀδελφὸς ἀδελφῷ.[9] ἄλλος δὲ ἱππέα
ἐκπέμπων εἰς τὴν ἡνίαν τοῦ χαλινοῦ βυβλίον
ἐνέρραψεν.[10] ἐγένετο δὲ περὶ ἐπιστολὴν τοιόνδε.
πόλεως γὰρ πολιορκουμένης ἐπεὶ παρῆλθεν ἔσω
τῆς πόλεως ὁ κομίζων τὰς ἐπιστολὰς τῷ μὲν
προδιδόντι καὶ τοῖς ἄλλοις οἷς ἔφερεν[11] οὐκ ἀπο-
δίδωσιν, πρὸς δὲ τὸν ἄρχοντα τῆς πόλεως ἦλθεν
9ª μηνύων καὶ τὰς ἐπιστολὰς ἐδίδου. ὁ δ' ἀκούσας ἐκέλευεν ταύτας μὲν τὰς ἐπιστολὰς οἷς ἔφερεν[12]
ἀποδοῦναι, τὰ[13] δὲ παρ' ἐκείνων, εἰ ἀληθές τι
μηνύει, παρ' αὐτὸν ἐνεγκεῖν· καὶ ὁ μηνύων ταῦτα
ἔπραξεν. ὁ δὲ ἄρχων λαβὼν τὰς ἐπιστολὰς καὶ
ἀνακαλεσάμενος τοὺς ἀνθρώπους τὰ σημεῖά τε

---

[1] Köchly and Rüstow: ἐχούσαις M.
[2] Köchly and Rüstow: ἐνωτίων ἐνειλημένοις λεπτοῖς μολι-
βδίνοις M.
[3] Casaubon: προσοδίας M.
[4] Casaubon: ἀντικαθήμενον πολέμιον M.
[5] Casaubon: ἐν ᾧ M.
[6] Hercher suggested plausibly ἀπεδόθη.
[7] Hertlein (Hercher?): ὡσ δεῖ M.   [8] Capps: δὲ M.

158

wound on his leg. Writing could be brought in also on thin pieces of beaten lead rolled up and worn in women's ears in place of ear-rings. A letter having to do with betrayal was once conveyed by the traitor to the camp of the beleaguering enemy in this way. As the horsemen were going out of the city for a raid upon the enemy one of them had a sheet of papyrus sewn under the flaps of his breast-plate, and he was instructed, if the enemy should appear, to fall from his horse as though by accident, and to be captured alive; and when he was taken into camp he was to give the sheet of writing to the proper person. The horseman assisted as a brother would a brother.[1] Another man, when sending out a horseman, sewed a sheet of papyrus to the bridle-rein. And the following incident happened about a letter. During the siege of a city, when the man carrying the message entered the town, he did not give the letters to the traitor and to the others to whom he was bringing it, but went to the command-ing officer of the city, disclosed the matter, and handed over the letters. When the officer heard it he ordered him to deliver these letters to those to whom he was bringing them, but to bring to him their answer as evidence that he was telling the truth. The informer did so, and the officer, taking the letters, called the men to him, showed them the

---

[1] A proverbial expression; *cf.* Plato, *Rep.* ii. p. 362 D ἀδελφὸς ἀνδρὶ παρείη.

---

[9] Kirchhoff: ὑπηρετησ εν . . . ἀδελφὸν M.
[10] Casaubon: ἐνέγραψεν M.
[11] R. Schöne: καὶ προσέφερεν M (with mark of corruption over o).　　　[12] Casaubon: ἔφερον M.
[13] *sc.* γράμματα (R. Schöne): τὰς Casaubon.

ἐδείκνυεν τῶν δακτυλίων, ἅπερ ὡμολόγουν αὐτῶν[1]
εἶναι, καὶ λύων τὰ βιβλία ἐδήλου τὸ πρᾶγμα.

9[b] τεχνικῶς δὲ δοκεῖ φωρᾶσαι, ὅτι τὰς πεμπομένας
παρὰ τοῦ ἀνθρώπου οὐκ ἀπέλαβεν·[2] ἦν γὰρ αὐτοῖς
ἀρνηθῆναι καὶ φάσκειν ἐπιβουλεύεσθαι ὑπό τινος.
τὰς δ' ἀνταποστελλομένας λαβὼν ἀναντιλέκτως[3]
ἤλεγξεν.

10 Κομίζεται δὲ καὶ ὧδε. κύστιν ἰσομεγέθη
ληκύθῳ ὁπόσῃ ἂν βούλῃ[4] πρὸς τὸ πλῆθος
τῶν γραφησομένων φυσήσαντα καὶ ἀποδήσαντα[5]
σφόδρα ξηρᾶναι, ἔπειτα ἐπ' αὐτῆς γράψαι ὅ τι ἂν

11 βούλῃ[6] μέλανι κατακόλλῳ. ξηρανθέντων δὲ τῶν
γραμμάτων ἐξελεῖν[7] τὴν πνοὴν τῆς κύστιδος καὶ
συμπιέσαντα[8] εἰς τὴν[9] λήκυθον ἐνθεῖναι· τὸ δὲ
στόμα τῆς κύστιδος ὑπερεχέτω τοῦ στόματος[10]

12 τῆς ληκύθου. ἔπειτα φυσήσαντα τὴν κύστιν ἐν
τῇ ληκύθῳ ἐνοῦσαν, ἵνα διευρυνθῇ[11] ὡς μάλιστα,
καὶ[12] ἐλαίου ἐμπλήσαντα περιτεμεῖν τῆς κύστιδος τὸ ὑπερέχον τῆς ληκύθου καὶ προσαρμόσαι
τῷ στόματι ὡς ἀδηλότατα, καὶ βύσαντα τὴν
λήκυθον κομίζειν φανερῶς. διαφανές τε οὖν τὸ
ἔλαιον ἔσται ἐν τῇ ληκύθῳ καὶ οὐδὲν ἄλλο φανεῖται

13 ἐνόν. ὅταν δὲ ἔλθῃ παρ' ὃν δεῖ, ἐξεράσας τὸ
ἔλαιον ἀναγνώσεται φυσήσας τὴν κύστιν· καὶ
ἐκσπογγίσας καὶ κατὰ ταὐτὰ εἰς τὴν αὐτὴν γράψας

14 ἀποστελλέτω. ἤδη δέ τις[13] ἐν δέλτου[14] ξύλῳ

---

[1] Köchly and Rüstow : αὐτὸν M.
[2] Hertlein (οὐκ ἔλαβε Casaubon) : ὅτι καὶ ἔλαβεν M.
[3] Casaubon : ἂν ἀντιλεπτως M.
[4] Casaubon (βούλῃ Lange) : ὁπόσῃ ἀντιβούλει M : ὁπόσῃ
ἀντιβολεῖ Eberhard : ὁπόσῃ ἂν βούλῃ Lange.
[5] Köchly and Rüstow : φυσήσασ καὶ ἀποδήσασ M.
[6] Meier : βούλει M.

marks of the seals which they admitted to be their own, and, opening the letters, exposed the matter. And he seems to have detected this skilfully in that he did not accept from the man the letters that were sent. For then it would have been possible for the men to deny it and claim that someone was plotting against them. But by taking the letters that were sent in answer he proved the case incontestably.

Messages are sent also in this way. Take a bladder in size equal to a flask large enough for your purpose; inflate it, tie it tightly, and let it dry; then write on it whatever you wish, in ink mixed with glue. When the writing is dry, let the air out of the bladder, and press it into the flask, letting the mouth of the bladder protrude from the mouth of the flask. Then inflate the bladder inside the flask in order to expand it as much as possible, and filling it with oil, cut off the part of the bladder that comes over the top of the flask, fitting it in the mouth as inconspicuously as you can, and, corking the bottle, carry it openly. Hence the oil will be visible in the flask, but nothing else. When it comes to the appropriate person, he will pour out the oil, inflate the bladder, and read the writing. And washing it off with a sponge, let him write on it in the same manner and send it back. It has actually happened that someone has written on the wooden part

---

7 Köchly and Rüstow: ἔξελε M.
8 Köchly and Rüstow: συμπιέσαντασ M.
9 Added by Hercher.
10 Köchly and Rüstow: τοῦ πωματοσ M.
11 Gronov: διερβυθῆ M.
12 Added by Köchly and Rüstow.
13 Casaubon: τινεσ M.
14 Hercher: δέλτω M: τῷ τῆς δέλτου ξύλῳ J. Afr.

γράψας κηρὸν ἐπέτηξεν[1] καὶ ἄλλα εἰς τὸν κηρὸν
ἐνέγραψεν. εἶτα ὅταν ἔλθῃ παρ' ὃν ἔδει,[2] ἐκκνήσας[3] τὸν κηρὸν καὶ ἀναγνοὺς γράψας πάλιν
ὡσαύτως[4] ἐπέστειλεν. ἐνδέχεται[5] δὲ καὶ εἰς πυξίον
γράψαντα μέλανι ὡς βελτίστῳ ἐᾶν ξηρανθῆναι,
ἔπειτα λευκώσαντα ἀφανίζειν τὰ γράμματα. ὅταν
οὖν ἀφίκηται παρὰ τὸν πεμπόμενον, λαβόντα εἰς
ὕδωρ θεῖναι τὸ πυξίον· φανεῖται οὖν ἐν τῷ ὕδατι
15 ἀκριβῶς ἅπαντα τὰ γεγραμμένα. γράφοιτο δ'
ἂν καὶ εἰς πινάκιον ἡρωϊκὸν[6] ἅπερ ἂν βούλῃ.[7]
ἔπειτα καταλευκῶσαι καὶ ξηράναντα γράψαι ἱππέα
φωσφόρον ἢ ὅ τι ἂν βούλῃ,[7] ἔχοντα[8] ἱματισμὸν
λευκὸν καὶ τὸν ἵππον λευκόν· εἰ δὲ μή, καὶ ἄλλῳ
χρώματι, πλὴν μέλανος. ἔπειτα δοῦναί τινι ἀνα-
θεῖναι ἐγγὺς τῆς πόλεως εἰς ὃ ἂν[9] τύχῃ ἱερὸν ὡς
16 εὐξάμενος.[10] ὃν[11] δὲ δεῖ ἀναγνῶναι τὰ γεγραμμένα,
χρὴ ἐλθόντα εἰς τὸ ἱερὸν καὶ γνόντα τὸ πινάκιον συσ-
σήμῳ τινὶ προσυγκειμένῳ, ἀπενέγκαντα εἰς οἶκον
θεῖναι εἰς ἔλαιον· πάντα οὖν τὰ γεγραμμένα φανεῖται.

Πασῶν δὲ ἀδηλοτάτη πέμψις, πραγματωδεστάτη[12]
δὲ νῦν μοι ἡ[13] δι' ἀγραμμάτων[14] ἐμφανισθήσεται·
17 ἔστι δὲ τοιάδε. ἀστράγαλον εὐμεγέθη τρυπῆσαι
τρυπήματα[15] εἴκοσι καὶ τέτταρα, ἓξ εἰς ἑκάστην

---

[1] Valckenaer: ἐπέθηκεν M: ἐπέτηξαν J. Afr.
    [2] Meier: παρὸν δεῖ M.
[3] Köchly and Rüstow: ἐκκνίσασ M: ἐκκινήσας J. Afr.
[4] ὦῦς αως M.   [5] Kirchhoff: λέγεται M.
[6] ἀκήρωτον Hercher: ζωγραφικὸν Meier.
[7] Meier: βούλει M.
[8] Suggested by Diels.   [9] Meier: ἐὰν M.
[10] Casaubon and Stahl: εὐξόμενος M: εὐξάμενον Meier.
[11] Meineke: ὅσον M.   [12] πραγματοδεστάτη M.
[13] Added by Meineke. [14] Herm. Schöne: διὰ γραμμάτων M.
[15] J. Afr.: not in M.

of a tablet, poured wax over it, and written something else on the wax. Then when it came to the appointed person, he, scraping off the wax and reading the writing, again in the same way has sent back a message.[1] It would be possible, also, to write on a boxwood tablet with the best quality of ink, let it dry, and then by whitening the tablet to make the letters invisible. When, then, the tablet comes to the recipient, he should take it and put it into water; and so in the water there will clearly appear all that was written. You might also write on a tablet for a hero's chapel whatever you desire. Then it should be whitened and dried, and a light-bringing horseman painted on it, or anything else you please, with white apparel and his horse white; or if not white, any colour except black. Then it should be given to somebody, to be hung up near the city in whatever shrine he may chance upon, as though it were a votive offering. And he whose part it is to read the message must go to the shrine, and recognizing the tablet by some prearranged sign, must take it back home and put it into oil. And so everything written on it will become visible.

The most secret method of all for sending messages, but the most difficult, namely, that without writing, I shall now make clear. It is this.[2] In a sufficiently large astragal[3] bore twenty-four holes, six

---

[1] This was done by Demaratus, the exiled Spartan king at the time of the expedition of Xerxes, as told by Herodotus vii. 239, whose account Aeneas follows closely here. Compare also Polyaenus ii. 20; Justin ii. 10. 13 f.; A. Gellius xvii. 9. 16 f. for this stratagem.

[2] The detail with which Aeneas describes this device makes it certain that it was an invention of his own.

[3] Astragals, or knuckle-bones of sheep, were often used like dice and were among the familiar playthings of children.

πλευρὰν τοῦ ἀστραγάλου· ἔστω δὲ τὰ τρυπή-
18 ματα τοῦ ἀστραγάλου στοιχεῖα.[1] διαμνημόνευε[1]
δ'[2] ἀφ' ἧς ἂν πλευρᾶς ἄρξῃ[3] τὸ ἄλφα καὶ
τὰ ἐχόμενα ἅπερ ἐν ἑκάστῃ πλευρᾷ γέγραπται.
μετὰ δὲ ταῦτα, ὅταν τινὰ θέλῃς ἐν αὐτοῖς
τίθεσθαι λόγον, λίνον διείρειν, οἷον,[4] ἐὰν θέλῃς
Αἰνείαν[5] δηλοῦν ἐν τῇ διέρσει[6] τοῦ λίνου
ἀρξάμενος ἐκ τῆς πλευρᾶς τοῦ ἀστραγάλου ἐν ᾗ
τὸ ἄλφα ἐστίν, δίειρον,[7] καὶ[8] παρελθὼν τὰ ἐχόμενα
τούτου[9] παραγράμματα, ὅταν ἔλθῃς[10] εἰς πλευρὰν
οὗ τὸ ἰῶτά[11] ἐστιν, δίειρον πάλιν, παρεὶς δὲ τούτου
τὰ ἐχόμενα, ὅπου συμβαίνει τὸ νῦ[12] εἶναι, δίειρον[13]
καὶ πάλιν παρεὶς τὰ[14] ἐχόμενα τούτου, ὅπου τὸ[15]
εἶ ἐστιν,[16] δίειρον τὸ λίνον,[17] καὶ οὕτω τὰ ἐπίλοιπα
τοῦ λόγου ἀντιγράφων ἔνειρε εἰς τὰ τρυπήματα,
19 ὥσπερ ὃ ἄρτι ἐθέμεθα[18] ὄνομα. ἔσται οὖν περὶ
τὸν ἀστράγαλον ἀγαθὶς λίνου τετολοπευμένη,[19]
δεήσει δὲ τὸν[1] ἀναγιγνώσκοντα[20] ἀναγράφεσθαι
εἰς δέλτον τὰ δηλούμενα γράμματα ἐκ τῶν τρυπημάτων. ἀνάπαλιν δὲ γίγνεται ἡ ἔξερσις[21] τῇ

---

[1] J. Afr.: not in M.
[2] ὃ M: δὲ J. Afr.   [3] ἄρξηται J. Afr.
[4] Köchly and Rüstow: λίνω διαιρεῖν ἐὰν M.
[5] Haase (Αἰνείας: Αἰνείαν Hercher: Αἰνέαν also is possible
—R. Schöne): ελληδινη αλι M (with marks of corruption over
the first η and the second ι).
[6] Casaubon: διαιρέσει M.
[7] Added by Williams.   [8] Added by R. Schöne.
[9] Hercher: τούτων M: τοῦ ἰῶτα J. Afr.: τοῦ ἄλφα Köchly
and Rüstow.
[10] J. Afr. (ἔλθῃς): ἔλθη M.
[11] Orelli: οντο τω τα M: οὗ τὸ ἰῶτα γράμμα J. Afr.
[12] Williams (ν̄ Orelli): τον ειναι M (with mark of corruption
over ε).
[13] Köchly and Rüstow from J. Afr. διήρον.

on each side. Let the holes stand for letters, and note clearly on which side begins Alpha and the following letters that have been written on each particular side. Then, whenever you wish to communicate any word by them, draw a thread through them, as, for instance, if you wish to express Αἰνείαν by the drawing through of a thread, begin from the side of the astragal on which Alpha is found, pass the thread through, and omitting the characters placed next to Alpha, draw through again when you come to the side where Iota belongs ; and disregarding the characters following this, again pass the thread through where Nu happens to be. And again passing by the succeeding letters draw the thread through where Ei[1] is found. Now continuing in this way to write the rest of the communication, pass the thread into the holes in such a manner as that in which we just now wrote the name. Accordingly, there will be a ball of thread wound around the astragal, and it will be necessary for the one who is to read the information to write down upon a tablet the characters revealed by the holes. The unthreading takes place in the reverse order to that of

---

[1] The original name for ε, whereas the name Epsilon is due to a later misunderstanding of Byzantine usage.

---

[14] τὸν τὰ M.   [15] Added by Köchly and Rüstow.
[16] Haase : ἔνεστιν M.
[17] R. Schöne thinks that directions for spelling the rest of the name are missing here, but the author may have stopped at this point after making the method clear.
[18] Sauppe : ὥσπερ αρ τιαι μεθα M (with marks of corruption over the first ι and the second ε).
[19] Herm. Schöne : πεμπομένη M.
[20] Hercher : ἀναγινώσκοντα M.
[21] Boivin, Köchly and Rüstow : ἐξίεσις M.

ἐνέρσει.¹ διαφέρει δὲ οὐδὲν τὰ γράμματα ἀνάπαλιν γραφῆναι εἰς τὴν² δέλτον· οὐδὲν γὰρ ἧττον
γνωσθήσεται. καταμαθεῖν δὲ πλεῖον³ ἔργον ἐστὶν
20 τὰ γεγραμμένα ἢ τὸ ἔργον αὐτὸ γενέσθαι. εὐ-
τρεπέστερον⁴ δ' ἂν τοῦτο γίγνοιτο ξύλου ὡς
σπιθαμιαίου⁵ τρυπηθέντος ὅσα γε⁶ τὰ στοιχεῖα
τῶν γραμμάτων· ἔπειτα ὡσαύτως ἐνείρειν τὸ
λίνον εἰς τὰ τρυπήματα. ὅπου δ' ἂν εἰς τὸ αὐτὸ
τρύπημα συμβῇ δὶς ἐνείρεσθαι, ὥσπερ τὸ αὐτὸ
γράμμα δὶς ἐφεξῆς γράφεσθαι, προπεριελίξαντα
τὸ λίνον περὶ τὸ ξύλον ἐνείρειν. γίγνοιτο δ'
21 ἂν καὶ ὧδε. ἀντὶ τοῦ ἀστραγάλου καὶ ξύλου
ποιήσαντα⁷ κύκλον ξύλινον λεᾶναι, καὶ τρῆσαι
ἐφεξῆς κύκλῳ τὰ στοιχεῖα τῶν γραμμάτων τέτταρα
καὶ εἴκοσι· ὑποψίας δ' ἕνεκεν καὶ ἄλλα ἐν μέσῳ
τοῦ κύκλου τρυπῆσαι, ἔπειτα οὕτω εἰς τὰ στοιχεῖα
22 ἐφεξῆς ὄντα τὸ λίνον ἐνείρειν. ὅταν δὲ δὶς τὸ
αὐτὸ γράμμα συμβαίνῃ⁸ γράφειν, ἐκ τῶν ἐν μέσῳ
τρυπημάτων προενείραντα εἰς τὸ αὐτὸ γράμμα
ἐνεῖραι· γράμμα⁹ δὲ λέγω τὸ τρύπημα.
23 Ἤδη δέ τινες εἴς τι¹⁰ βιβλίον γράψαντες ὡς
λεπτότατον μακροὺς¹¹ στίχους καὶ λεπτὰ γράμματα,
ἵν' ὡς εὐογκοτάτη γένηται¹² ἡ ἐπιστολή, εἶτα ἐπὶ
τῷ ὤμῳ τοῦ χιτῶνος ὑποθέντες καὶ ἀποπτύξαντες
τοῦ χιτωνίσκου ἐπὶ τῷ ὤμῳ, ἀνύποπτος δὴ δοκεῖ

---

¹ Casaubon: ἐνέρξει M.   ² Added by Hercher.
³ Orelli: πλεῖστον M.   ⁴ Hercher: εὐπρεπέστερον M.
⁵ C: σπιθαμαίου M.   ⁶ Casaubon: ὅσατε M.
⁷ Hertlein: ποιήσασ M.   ⁸ Meier: συμβαίνει M.
⁹ Hercher: γράμματα M.
¹⁰ Köchly and Rüstow: τὸ M : εἰς βιβλίον J. Afr.
¹¹ μικροὺς one ms. of J. Afr. and Birt.
¹² J. Afr.: γίνηται M.

the threading. But it makes no difference that the letters are written upon the tablet in reverse order, for none the less will the message be read, although to understand what has been written is a greater task than to prepare it. But this would be accomplished more easily if a piece of wood about a span long were perforated just as many times as there are letters in the alphabet, and the thread were then in the same way drawn into the holes. Wherever two insertions into the same hole occur, the same character being written twice in succession, you should wind the thread around the wood before inserting it. Or it could even be done as follows. Instead of the astragal or the piece of wood, make a disc of wood, polish it, and bore successively on the disc the twenty-four characters of the alphabet ; but to avoid suspicion you should bore other holes also in the centre of the disc, and then in this way run the thread through the characters, which are in their regular order. But whenever the writing of the same letter occurs twice in succession, you must insert the thread in the holes bored in the centre of the disc before running it into the same letter ; and by *letter* I mean the *hole*.[1]

Again, some persons, after writing long lines with fine characters upon some very thin papyrus, so that the message may be as compact as possible, have then placed it on the shoulder of the tunic and spread a part of the over-tunic out on the shoulder. Naturally the transmitting of the letter is un-

[1] For a diagram and explanation see H. Diels, *Antike Technik²*, 1920, 74-75.

εἶναι ἡ κομιδὴ τῆς ἐπιστολῆς καὶ ἐνδεδυκότος
τινὸς τὸν χιτωνίσκον καὶ οὕτω φερομένου.

24 Μαρτύριον δὲ ὅτι τὰ εἰσπεμπόμενα μετὰ ἐπιβουλῆς χαλεπὸν φυλάξαι. οἱ γοῦν περὶ Ἴλιον[1] ἄνθρωποι καὶ ἐκ τοσούτου χρόνου καὶ οὕτω διατετα-
μένοι[2] οὔπω[3] δύνανται φυλάξαι μὴ εἰσελθεῖν αὐτοῖς
τὰς Λοκρίδας· καίτοι τοσοῦτον αὐτοῖς ἐστιν ἡ
σπουδὴ καὶ ἡ φυλακή. ἀλλ' ὀλίγοι, προσέχοντες
τῷ λαθεῖν, λανθάνουσιν ἀνὰ ἔτεα[4] πολλὰ εἰσάγοντες
25 σώματα. παρὰ δὲ τοῖς παλαιοτέροις καὶ τοιόνδε
ποτὲ ἐτεχνάσθη. Ποτίδαιαν γὰρ θέλων προδοῦναι
Τιμόξενος Ἀρταβάζῳ προσυνέθεντο ἀλλήλοις ὁ μὲν
26 τῆς πόλεώς τι χωρίον, ὁ δὲ τοῦ στρατοπέδου, εἰς
ὅπερ ἐτόξευον πᾶν ὅ τι[5] ἤθελον ἀλλήλοις ἐμφανίσαι.
ἐτεχνάζετο δὲ ὧδε[6]· τοῦ τοξεύματος περὶ τὰς
γλυφίδας[7] ἑλίξαντες τὸ βιβλίον καὶ πτερώσαντες
27 ἐτόξευον εἰς τὰ προσυγκείμενα χωρία. ἐγένετο δὲ
καταφανὴς ὁ Τιμόξενος προδιδοὺς τὴν Ποτίδαιαν·
τοξεύων γὰρ ὁ Ἀρτάβαζος εἰς τὸ προσυγκείμενον,
ἁμαρτὼν τοῦ χωρίου διὰ πνεῦμα καὶ φαύλην

---

[1] M has a space of four letters after this word.
[2] Hertlein: διατεταγμένοι M.   [3] Casaubon: ὄντω M.
[4] Orelli: ανετεα M (with sign of corruption over the first ε).
[5] Herm. Schöne: ὅ τι ἄντι M.
[6] Herm. Schöne: αξετο δὲ τοῦ M (with mark of corruption over the first ε).
[7] Casaubon: πύλασ γλυφὰσ M.

---

[1] This is the earliest of a long series of references in ancient
authors to a singular custom whereby the Locrians sent
annually for many centuries two maidens to the service of
Athena at Ilium as an atonement for the injury done to Cas-
sandra by Aias the Locrian. The inhabitants of the city
were expected to prevent their introduction, killing those
who were caught and burning their bodies. Only recently

suspected, if one puts on an over-tunic and wears it in this manner.

There is proof, however, of the fact that it is difficult to guard against anything sent in by artifice. At any rate the people at Ilium who have been so long and so well prepared, are not yet able to prevent the coming of the Locrian maidens[1] into their town, although they use such great care and watchfulness. But a few men, bent on deceiving, succeed in secretly bringing in many maidens, at yearly intervals.[2] And among the ancients the following scheme was once contrived. When Timoxenus wished to hand over Potidaea to Artabazus,[3] they prearranged, the one a certain spot in the city, the other one in the camp, to which they used to shoot whatever they wished to communicate with each other. They adopted the device of winding a sheet of writing around the notched end of the arrow, and, after feathering it, they shot it into the places previously determined. But Timoxenus was discovered in the attempt to betray Potidaea. For Artabazus, shooting toward the designated area, missed the spot because of the wind and because the arrow was

a remarkable inscription has been discovered in West Locris which makes special provisions for the selection of the maidens. The best discussion at present of the whole matter is by A. Wilhelm, " Die lokrische Mädcheninschrift," *Jahresh. d. österr. arch. Inst.*, 1911, xiv. : 163–256.

[2] Possibly πολλὰ should be construed with ἔτεα. The sense will then be : " have been secretly each year for many years bringing in maidens."

[3] The incident is taken direct from Herodotus viii. 128. This device was often employed in ancient times, the best known case, perhaps, being that in which Caesar contrived in this way to get word to the beleaguered Quintus Cicero. Caesar, *Bell. Gall.* v. 48.

AENEAS TACTICUS

πτέρωσιν, βάλλει ἀνδρὸς Ποτιδαιάτου τὸν ὦμον,
τὸν δὲ βληθέντα[1] περιέδραμεν ὄχλος, οἷα φιλεῖ
γίγνεσθαι ἐν τῷ πολέμῳ· αὐτίκα δὲ τὸ τόξευμα
λαβόντες ἔφερον ἐπὶ τοὺς στρατηγούς, καὶ οὕτως
28 καταφανὴς ἐγένετο ἡ πρᾶξις. Ἱστιαῖος δὲ βουλόμενος τῷ Ἀρισταγόρᾳ σημῆναι ἀποστῆναι,[2]
ἄλλως μὲν οὐδαμῶς εἶχεν ἀσφαλῶς[3] δηλῶσαι, ἅτε
φυλασσομένων τῶν ὁδῶν καὶ οὐκ εὔπορον ὂν[4]
γράμματα λαθεῖν φέροντα, τῶν δὲ[5] δούλων τὸν
πιστότατον ἀποξυρήσας ἔστιξεν καὶ ἐπέσχεν ἕως
29 ἀνέφυσαν[6] αἱ τρίχες. ὡς δὲ ἀνέφυσαν[7] τάχιστα,
ἔπεμπεν εἰς Μίλητον, ἐπιστείλας τῷ ἐπεστιγμένῳ[8]
ἄλλο μὲν οὐδέν, ἐπειδὰν δ' ἀφίκηται εἰς Μίλητον πρὸς
Ἀρισταγόραν, κελεύειν ξυρήσαντα κατιδεῖν εἰς τὴν
κεφαλήν. τὰ δὲ στίγματα ἐσήμαινεν ἃ ἔδει[9] ποιεῖν.
30 Γράφειν δὲ καὶ ὧδε. προσυνθέμενον τὰ φωνή-
εντα γράμματα ἐν κεντήμασι τίθεσθαι, ὁπόστον
δ'[10] ἂν τύχῃ ἕκαστον ὄν,[11] ἐν τοῖς γραφομένοις
31 τοσαύτας στιγμὰς εἶναι. οἷον τόδε·

Διονύσιος κόλος [12]
Δ∷∶∶N∷∶C∷∷∶C K∷∶Λ∶∶C
Ἡρακλείδας ἡκέτω
∶·P·ΚΛ··∷∶Δ·C∶·K··T∷∶· [13]

[1] Hercher (from Herodotus): προβληθέντα M.
[2] Added by Casaubon from Herodotus.
[3] ἀσφαλῷ M.   [4] Added by Valckenaer.
[5] Added by Köchly and Rüstow.
[6] Meier: ἂν ἔφυσαν M.
[7] These three words added by Hercher from Herodotus.
[8] Casaubon: ἐπιστιγένῳ M.
[9] Meineke: δεῖ M.   [10] Added by Hercher.
[11] Casaubon: ὂν M.
[12] Herm. Schöne: καλόσ M (cf. Introduction, p. 6): κακῶς
Diels and Fischer.

170

badly feathered, and hit a man of Potidaea on the shoulder, and a crowd gathered around the wounded man, as often happens in war. And immediately picking up the arrow, they brought it to the generals, and thus the plot was revealed. Again, Histiaeus, wishing to tell Aristagoras to revolt,[1] had no other safe means of communicating, since the roads were guarded and it was not easy for a letter-carrier to escape notice, but shaving the head of his most faithful slave, he tattooed it and detained him until the hair had grown again. And as soon as it had grown, he dispatched him to Miletus and gave the tattooed man no other orders except that when he had come to Miletus, into the presence of Aristagoras, he should request him to shave his head and examine it, whereupon the marks indicated what was to be done.

But it is also possible to write as follows. It should be arranged in advance to express the vowels by dots, and whatever the number of each vowel happens to be, so many dots are to be placed in the writing. As for example the following:[2]

" DIONYSIUS DOCKED "

D : . : : N : : : S : . : · : S D : : CK : D

" LET HERACLEIDES COME "

L : T H : R . CL : : . D : S C : : M :

---

[1] The story is from Herodotus v. 35.
[2] See Introduction, pp. 5-7.

---

[13] In M only the consonants are given: Casaubon added the dots for the vowels. In this scheme the vowels from α to ω would bear the numbers one to seven. In English the correspondences will necessarily vary somewhat because of the different number and order.

καὶ τόδε ἄλλο· ἀντὶ τῶν φωνηέντων γραμμάτων τίθεσθαι ὅ τι δή.[1]   καὶ τάδε· τὰ πεμπόμενα γράμματα εἴς τινα τόπον . . .[2] τῷ πεμπομένῳ δῆλον
γίγνεσθαι ἐλθόντος τοῦ ἀνθρώπου εἰς τὴν πόλιν καὶ
πωλοῦντός τι ἢ ὠνουμένου, ὅτι ἥκει αὐτῷ γράμματα
καὶ κεῖται ἐν τῷ προρρηθέντι[3] τόπῳ. καὶ οὕτως
οὔτε ὁ φέρων οἶδεν ὅτῳ ἠνέχθη οὔτε ὁ λαβὼν γνω-
στὸς ἔσται ὅτι ἔχει. πολλοὶ δὲ κατ᾽ Ἤπειρον
32 κυσὶν ἐχρήσαντο ὧδε. ἀπαγαγόντες δέσμιον[4]
περιέθηκαν περὶ τὸν αὐχένα ἱμάντα, ἐν ᾧ ἐπιστολὴ
ἐνέρραπτο.[5] εἶτα ἀφῆκαν νυκτὸς ἢ μεθ᾽ ἡμέραν
πρὸς ὃν ἐξ ἀνάγκης ἔμελλεν ἥξειν ὅθεν ἀπήχθη.
ἔστι δὲ τοῦτο καὶ[6] Θεσσαλόν.[7]

33 Χρὴ δὲ τὰς παραγιγνομένας εὐθὺς ἀνοίγειν
δέλτους. Ἀστυάνακτι δὴ τυράννῳ Λαμψάκου
πεμφθείσης ἐπιστολῆς ἐν ᾗ γεγραμμένα ἦν μη-
νύοντα τὴν ἐπιβουλὴν ἀφ᾽ ἧς ἀνῃρέθη, παρὰ τὸ μὴ
εὐθὺς ἀνοῖξαι καὶ ἀναγνῶναι τὰ γεγραμμένα ἀλλὰ
ἀμελήσαντος αὐτοῦ, πρὸς ἄλλοις δὲ γενομένου
πρότερον, διεφθάρη, τὴν ἐπιστολὴν ἔχων περὶ τοὺς
34 δακτύλους. διὰ τὴν αὐτὴν αἰτίαν καὶ ἐν Θήβαις
ἡ Καδμεία κατελήφθη, τῆς τε Λέσβου ἐν Μυτιλήνῃ
παραπλήσια τούτοις ἐπράχθη.

---

[1] Haase: τί δαὶ M.
[2] R. Schöne sets a lacuna here, suggesting the following:
τῷ πεμπομένῳ γνωστὸν ὑπ᾽ ἀνθρώπου κατατίθεσθαι γνωστοῦ καὶ
αὐτοῦ, τῷ δὲ πεμπομένῳ δῆλον κτλ. The translation follows
what seems most plausible in the suggestion, i.e., . . . ὑπ᾽
ἀνθρώπου γνωστοῦ τῷ πεμπομένῳ δῆλον. Other (briefer)
supplements require emendation as well.
[3] Casaubon: πορρηθέντι M.   [4] Casaubon: δεσμὸν M.
[5] Köchly and Rüstow: ἐγέγραπτο M.
[6] Added by Köchly and Rüstow.
[7] J. Afr. (Θετταλόν): Θεσσαλονικόν M.

And here is another way: Instead of the vowels, put in anything whatever. And again, the following. The letter should be sent to a certain place [. . . by a man known to the recipient] and it should be indicated to him that a message has come for him and is in the appointed spot, by the fact that the man comes to the city and buys or sells something. And by this method neither does the bearer know to whom the message has been brought nor will the recipient be known as having the letter. Many in Epirus used to employ dogs in the following manner. After leading the dog away in leash they placed around his neck a strap, inside of which was sewed a letter. Then at night or during the daytime, they dispatched the dog to the person to whom he was sure to go, that is, to the one from whom he had been taken away. And this is also a Thessalian custom.

But the letters must be opened as soon as received. In fact Astyanax, tyrant of Lampsacus, did not at once open and read a letter sent to him in which was related evidence of the plot by which he was destroyed, but neglecting it, and attending first to other matters, he was killed while still holding the letter in his fingers.[1] For the same reason also the Cadmea in Thebes was captured,[2] and in Mytilene in Lesbos something similar happened.

---

[1] Nothing further is known of this Astyanax. The same thing happened to Julius Caesar. At the very moment when he was struck down he held in his hands a paper given him by Artemidorus which contained a full statement of the conspiracy.

[2] This was referred to also in Ch. xxiv. 18. The particular incident in the mind of the author was, no doubt, the occasion when Archias, the oligarchic leader, was given a paper

35 Γλοῦς δὲ βασιλέως ναύαρχος παρὰ βασιλέα ἀνα-
βάς, ἐπεὶ οὐχ οἷόν τε ἦν ὑπομνήματα ἐν βιβλίῳ
ἔχοντα εἰσιέναι παρὰ βασιλέα (ἦν δὲ αὐτῷ περὶ
πολλῶν τε καὶ μεγάλων διαμνημονευτέον), ἐγρά-
ψατο εἰς τὰ διαστήματα τῆς χειρὸς τῶν δακτύλων
περὶ ὧν ῥητέον ἦν αὐτῷ.

Περὶ τὴν τῶν τοιούτων ἐπιμέλειαν τῷ πυλωρῷ
πονητέον,[1] ὡς ἂν μηδὲν[2] λανθάνῃ[3] εἰς τὴν πόλιν
εἰσφερόμενον μήτε ὅπλον μήτε γράμματα.

XXXII. [Ἀντιμηχανήματα]

Πρὸς δὲ τὰς τῶν ἐναντίων προσαγωγὰς μηχανήμασιν ἢ σώμασιν ἐναντιοῦσθαι ὧδε. πρῶτον μὲν
εἰς τὰ ὑπεραιρόμενα ἐκ πύργων ἢ ἱστῶν[4] ἢ τῶν
ὁμοτρόπων τούτοις ἱστία,[5] οἷς τὰ[5] προσαχθέντα
ὑπεραίρειν[6] χρή, τισὶν ἀδιατμήτοις περιβληθέντα
κατατετάσθαι ὑπὸ τενόντων.[7] ἄλλα τε[8] καὶ ὑπο-
θυμιᾶν καπνὸν πολὺν ἱέντα[5] καὶ[5] ὑφάπτειν ὡς μέ-

---

[1] Herm. Schöne: ποιητέον M.
[2] μηθὲν M.
[3] L. Dindorf: λανθάνηται M.
[4] Casaubon: ἱστίων M.
[5] Added by Köchly and Rüstow.
[6] Köchly and Rüstow: ὑπεραιρατο M.
[7] Köchly and Rüstow: ὑπονεόντων M.
[8] Köchly and Rüstow: δὲ M.

---

telling about the design on his life, while sitting at table the
evening of the night on which he was murdered. He thrust
the paper under a cushion with the remark " Serious business
to-morrow."

174

Glus,[1] the admiral of the great king, came up before the king, and since it was forbidden to come into the king's presence with a sheet of notes (and he had to report upon many important affairs), he wrote in the spaces between the fingers of his hands the things he had to say to the king.

The gate-keeper ought to be watchful about such matters as these, so that nothing brought into the city may escape him, whether it be weapon or message.

XXXII. [Counter-devices]

Against the approaches of the foe you must take the following measures with engines or with infantry.[2] In the first place, against objects raised higher than the wall from towers or masts or devices similar to these, there should be stretched on thongs and covered with some impenetrable substance sails which will have to be overshot by the missiles. And in particular one must set smoking materials that will send up a great smudge from beneath, and must kindle those which will rouse as great a blaze

[1] Glus (the correct form is Glos) is well known from the *Anabasis* as one of those who supported the younger Cyrus in the revolt against his brother. He was admiral of the great king's forces in the war against Evagoras of Cyprus, between 387-6 b.c. and 380-79, the year in which he was murdered.

[2] In this chapter there are many echoes of the devices employed by the Spartans in the long siege of Plataea, 428-7 b.c., which seems to have made an epoch in ancient siege operations. A full account of the events at Plataea is given by Thucydides ii. 75-8.

2 γιστον πῦρ πνέοντα· ἀνταείρεσθαι πύργους ξυλίνους
ἢ ἄλλα ὕψη ἐκ φορμῶν πληρουμένων ψάμμου ἢ ἐκ
λίθων ἢ ἐκ πλίνθων. ἴσχοιεν[1] δ᾿ ἂν τὰ βέλη καὶ[2]
καλάμων ταρσοὶ ὀρθίων καὶ πλαγίων συντιθεμένων.
3 ἡτοιμάσθαι[3] δὲ καὶ τοῖς εἰς τὰ χείλη μηχανήμασιν
εἰσπίπτουσιν[4] κριῷ καὶ τοῖς ὁμοτρόποις τούτῳ,[5]
ἐρύματα, σάκκους ἀχύρων πληροῦντα προκρεμαν-
νύειν[6] καὶ[7] ἀγγεῖα ἐρίων καὶ ἀσκοὺς βοείους
νεοδάρτους πεφυσημένους ἢ πεπληρωμένους[8] τινῶν
4 καὶ[9] ἄλλα τούτοις ὁμότροπα. καὶ ὅταν ᾖ πύλην ἢ
ἄλλο τι τοῦ τείχους διακόπτῃ, χρὴ βρόχῳ τὸ προΐ-
σχον[10] ἀναλαμβάνεσθαι, ἵνα μὴ δύνηται προσπίπτειν
5 τὸ μηχάνημα. καὶ παρασκευάζεσθαι δὲ ὅπως
λίθος ἁμαξοπληθὴς ἀφιέμενος ἐμπίπτῃ καὶ συντρίβῃ
τὸ[11] τρύπανον· τὸν δὲ λίθον ἀφίεσθαι ἀπὸ τῶν
6 προωστῶν, ἐχόμενον ὑπὸ καρκίνων. ὅπως δὲ μὴ
ἁμαρτάνῃ τοῦ τρυπάνου ὁ λίθος φερόμενος, κάθετον[12]
χρὴ προαφίεσθαι, καὶ ὅταν αὕτη πέσῃ ἐπὶ τὸ τρύπα-
7 νον, εὐθὺ τὸν λίθον ἐπαφίεσθαι. ἄριστον δὲ πρὸς
τὰ διακόπτοντα τὸ τεῖχος καὶ τόδε παρεσκευάσθαι.
ὅταν γνῷς ᾖ[13] προσάγεσθαι τοῦ τείχους, ταύτῃ χρὴ
ἔσωθεν ἀντιπαρασκευάζειν ἀντίκριον, διορύξαντα
τοῦ τείχους μέχρι τοῦ ἄλλου μέρους τῶν πλίνθων,[14]
ἵνα μὴ προΐδωσιν πρότερον οἱ πολέμιοι· ὅταν δὲ
ἐγγὺς ᾖ τὸ διακόπτον, οὕτως ἔσωθεν τῷ ἀντικρίῳ

---

[1] Hertlein : ἴσχοι M.
[2] Added by R. Schöne (Köchly and Rüstow).
[3] Hertlein : ἡτοίμασται M.
[4] Casaubon : εἰσπουσιν M.
[5] Hertlein : τούτων M.
[6] Casaubon : προσκρεμαννύειν M.
[7] Added by Köchly and Rüstow.
[8] Casaubon : πεπληρωμένων M.

as possible, and build in opposition wooden towers, or other high structures with baskets filled with sand, or built of stones or bricks. And even basket-work made of reeds, upright and transverse, woven together, may stop the missiles. Against contrivances for attacking the battlements, such as a ram or other like instrument, you must also make ready protective devices to hang in front of them, sacks full of chaff, and bags of wool, fresh hides inflated or filled with something, and other things similar to these. And when the ram is battering a gate or some other part of the wall, you must catch up with a noose the projecting part of the engine, so that it cannot strike again. And you must make ready a stone large enough to fill a wagon so that it may be let fall upon the drill and crush it. The stone, held in place with grappling hooks, must be dropped from the projecting beams, and in order that in its descent it may not miss the drill, a plumb-line should be lowered in advance, and when it hangs over the drill, then the stone should at once be dropped after it. It is best to adopt this measure also against the engines that are battering the wall: When you see what part of the wall is being attacked, you should prepare a counter-ram at that point, inside the wall, and excavate the wall just as far as the outer layer of bricks, so that the enemy may not be aware in advance. And when the ram is close at hand you must strike from within with the counter-ram, which must

---

[9] Added by Hercher: ἢ Köchly and Rüstow.
[10] Casaubon: προσΐσχον M.   [11] Casaubon: τὸν M.
[12] Hercher: καθέτην M.   [13] Köchly and Rüstow: ἢ M.
[14] Casaubon: τὸν πλίνθον M.

be much more powerful. Furthermore, against the large engines on which many troops are moved up, and from which missiles are shot, and especially catapults and slings, and incendiary arrows against the thatched roofs—against all these, I say, those in the city must, in the first place, secretly dig beneath where the engine is to be applied, so that the wheels of the engines may sink and fall into the excavations. Then, on the inside, you must build a defence of baskets of sand and of stones from what you have near by, which will overtop the engine and render the missiles of the enemy useless. At the same time you must spread out from the inside of the wall thick curtains or sails as a protection from the oncoming shafts, which will stop the missiles that fall over the wall, so that they will be easy to gather up and none will fall to the ground. The same must be done at any other part of the wall where the missiles might come over and injure or wound the helpers and passers-by. And at whatever part of the wall by bringing up a pent-house a portion of the wall can be dug through or broken down, there counter-preparation must be made. To forestall the piercing of the wall a large fire should be built, and to provide against a breach of the wall a trench must be dug inside, so that the enemy may not enter. At the same time you should build a counter-rampart where the breach is being made, before the wall collapses, if you cannot otherwise stop the enemy.

XXXIII. ['Εμπρησις]

Χρὴ δὲ ταῖς προσενεχθείσαις χελώναις ἐπιχεῖν
πίσσαν καὶ στυππεῖον[1] καὶ θεῖον ἐπιβάλλειν,
ἔπειτα φλογωθέντα[2] φάκελλον καὶ ἐξάψαντα ἐπ-
αφιέναι σχοίνῳ ἐπὶ τὴν χελώνην. τὰ δὲ τοιαῦτα
προτεινόμενα[3] ἀπὸ τοῦ τείχους ἐπιβάλλεται τοῖς
προσαγομένοις μηχανήμασι. πιμπράναι χρὴ ταῦτα
2 ὧδε. παρεσκευάσθω ξύλα οἷον ὕπερα, μεγέθει[4]
δὲ πολλῷ μείζω· καὶ εἰς μὲν τὰ ἄκρα τοῦ ξύλου
κροῦσαι σιδήρια ὀξέα μικρότερα[5] καὶ μείζω,
περὶ δὲ τὰ ἄλλα μέρη τοῦ ξύλου καὶ ἄνω καὶ
κάτω χωρὶς πυρὸς σκευασίας ἰσχυράς· τὸ δὲ
εἶδος γενέσθω οἷον κεραυνὸς τῶν γραφομένων.[6]
τοῦτο δὲ ἀφίεσθαι χρὴ ἐς τὸ προσαγόμενον μηχάνημα ἐσκευασμένον οὕτως ὥστε ἐμπήγνυσθαι
εἰς τὸ μηχάνημα, καὶ ἐπιμένειν τὸ πῦρ ἐμπα-
3 γέντος αὐτοῦ. ἔπειτ' ἄν τινες ὦσι τῆς πόλεως
ξύλινοι μόσυνες ἢ τοῦ τείχεός τι, χρὴ τούτοις
ὑπάρχειν πρὸς τὸ μὴ ἐμπίμπρασθαι[7] ὑπὸ τῶν
πολεμίων πίλους[8] καὶ βύρσας πρὸς τὴν ἔπαλξιν.[9]
4 ἐὰν δὲ ἐμπρησθῶσιν πύλαι, προσφέρεσθαι ξύλα,
καὶ ἐμβάλλοντα ὡς μέγιστον τὸ πῦρ ποιεῖν,
μέχρι οὗ ἂν[10] ταφρεύσῃς[11] τὰ ἔσωθεν, καὶ ἀντι-
δείμῃς[12] ἐκ τῶν σοι συνυπαρχόντων[13] τάχιστα·
εἰ δὲ μή, ἐκ τῶν ἐγγύτατα οἰκιῶν καθαιροῦντα.

---

[1] Casaubon: στίππυον M.
[2] φλογώσαντα J. Afr., Hercher.
[3] Boivin (after Casaubon): προτεινόμενος M.
[4] Gronov and Köchly and Rüstow: ὑπερμεγέθη M.
[5] Suggested by R. Schöne.   [6] Hertlein: τὸ γραφόμενον M.
[7] Köchly and Rüstow: ἐμπίπρασθαι M.   [8] Koraes: πλείους M.
[9] Köchly and Rüstow: τάξιν.   [10] Added by Meineke.
[11] Boivin, Hertlein: ταφρεύσῃ M.

XXXIII. [*Setting on Fire*]

You must pour pitch and cast tow and sulphur on the pent-houses that have been brought up, and then a fagot fastened to a cord must be let down in flames upon the pent-house. And such things as these, held out from the walls, are hurled at the engines as they are being moved up, by which the latter are to be thus set on fire. Let sticks be prepared shaped like pestles[1] but much larger, and into the ends of each stick drive sharp irons, larger and smaller, and around the other parts of the stick, above and below, separately, place powerful combustibles. In appearance it[2] should be like bolts of lightning as drawn by artists. Let this be dropped upon the engine as it is being pushed up, fashioned so as to stick into it, and so that the fire will last after the stick has been made fast. Then, if there are any wooden towers, or if a part of the wall is of wood, covers of felt or raw hide must be provided to protect the parapet so that they cannot be ignited by the enemy. If the gate is set on fire you must bring up wood and throw it on to make as large a fire as possible, until a trench can be dug inside and a counter-defence be quickly built from the materials you have at hand, and if you have none, then by tearing down the nearest houses.

[1] The pestle meant by the word ὕπερον here is the large instrument (three cubits long according to the advice of Hesiod, *Works and Days*, 423) used to stir the meal or dough in the large kneading-trough.
[2] That is, the end of the pestle, bristling with iron points.

---

[12] R. Schöne: ἄν τι δέη M (*cf.* xxiii. 5 and xxxii. 12).
[13] ὑπαρχόντων J. Afr.

AENEAS TACTICUS

XXXIV. [Πυρὸς σβεστήρια πρὸς τὰ ἐμπιμπράμενα]

Ἐὰν δέ τι οἱ πολέμιοι πειρῶνται ἐμπιμπράναι ἰσχυρᾷ σκευασίᾳ πυρός, σβεννύειν[1] χρὴ αὐτὸ ὄξει· οὐ γὰρ ἔτι ῥᾳδίως[2] ἐξάπτεται. μᾶλλον δὲ ἰξῷ[3] προαλείφειν· τούτου γὰρ πῦρ οὐχ ἅπτε-
2 ται. τοὺς δὲ κατασβεννύντας ἀπὸ τῶν ὑψηλο- τέρων ἔχειν περὶ τὸ πρόσωπον ἔρυμα, ἵνα ἧσσον ὀχλῶνται προσαϊσσούσης αὐτοῖς τῆς φλογός.

XXXV. [Πυρὸς σκευασία]

Αὐτὸν δὲ πῦρ σκευάζειν ἰσχυρὸν ὧδε, ὅπερ οὐ πάνυ τι[4] κατασβέννυται. πίσσαν, θεῖον, στυπ- πεῖον,[5] μάνναν λιβανωτοῦ, δᾳδὸς πρίσματα ἐν ἀγγείοις[6] ἐξάπτοντα προσφέρειν, ἐὰν βούλῃ[7] τῶν πολεμίων τι ἐμπρησθῆναι.

XXXVI. [Κλιμάκων προσθέσει κωλύματα]

Ταῖς δὲ τῶν κλιμάκων προσθέσεσιν ἀντιοῦσθαι ὧδε.[8] ἐὰν μὲν ὑπερέχῃ τοῦ τείχους ἡ κλῖμαξ προστεθεῖσα, χρή, ὅταν ἐπ᾽ ἄκρων ᾖ ὅ[9] ἀναβαί-

---

[1] R. Schöne and Lange using some older conjectures: τινες πολέμιοι   παι (with mark of corruption over ι) . . . ται ἐμπιμπράμεναι ἰσχυραὶ σκευασίαι πρὸς τὸ πῦρ σβεννύειν M.
[2] C: ῥάιωσ M.
[3] Added by Meineke: ὄξος J. Afr. and Polyaenus vi. 3.
[4] Meineke: πάντη〉 πάνυτη M.
[5] στυπεῖον M.   [6] Orelli: ἐναντίως M.
[7] Hertlein: βούλει M.
[8] Added by Hercher.
[9] Added by Köchly and Rüstow.

182

XXXIV. [Fire-extinguishers]

If the enemy tries to set anything on fire with a powerful incendiary equipment you must put out the fire with vinegar, for then it cannot easily be ignited again, or rather it should be smeared beforehand with birdlime,[1] for this does not catch fire. Those who put out the fire from places above it must have a protection for the face, so that they will be less annoyed when the flame darts toward them.

XXXV. [Incendiary Equipment]

And fire itself which is to be powerful and quite inextinguishable is to be prepared as follows. Pitch, sulphur, tow, granulated frankincense, and pine sawdust in sacks you should ignite and bring up if you wish to set any of the enemy's works on fire.

XXXVI. [How to Prevent the Placing of Ladders]

The placing of ladders must be prevented thus. If the ladder when in place overtops the wall, you must, when the person who mounts it is at the top,

---

[1] This word is omitted in the original, but despite Julius Africanus and Polyaenus vi. 3, who write ὄξος, birdlime is certainly meant, partly because vinegar has already been mentioned, and partly because ' smear ' (προαλείφειν) is appropriately used only of a substance like birdlime, certainly not of a liquid like vinegar. Philo Mechanicus v. 90. 17 (Schöne) mentions birdlime as one of the important objects with which to be supplied in case of a siege, and (99. 26 ff.) recommends that wood which is in danger of being set on fire be smeared with birdlime or a mixture of blood and ashes. Thus Theophrastus also, De igne 61, notes that things smeared with birdlime do not take fire ; cf. Pliny, N.H. xxxiii. 94.

AENEAS TACTICUS

νων, τότε ἀπῶσαι τὸν ἄνδρα ἢ τὴν κλίμακα ξύλῳ
δικρῷ, ἐὰν μὴ ἄλλως κωλύειν δύνῃ διὰ τὸ ὑποτο-
2 ξεύεσθαι· ἐὰν δὲ ἀρτία ἦ[1] τῷ τείχει[2] ἡ κλίμαξ,
τὴν μὲν κλίμακα οὐχ οἷόν τε ἀπωθεῖν, τὰ δὲ
ὑπερβαίνοντα χρὴ ἀπῶσαι. ἐὰν δὲ ταῦτα μὲν
ἀδύνατα[3] δοκῇ εἶναι, πεποιῆσθαι χρὴ οἷον θύραν
ἐκ σανίδων, ἔπειτ' ἐπὰν προσφέρηται ἡ κλίμαξ,
προϋποτιθέναι[4] τῇ κλίμακι τῇ προσφερομένῃ· ὅταν
δὲ προσίη ἡ κλίμαξ πρὸς τὴν θύραν, ἐξ ἀνάγκης
ὑπαχθείσης τῆς θύρας ἡ κλίμαξ πίπτει, σπονδύλου
προϋποτιθεμένου, οὐδὲ προσσταθῆναι[5] δυνήσεται.

XXXVII. [Ὑπορυσσόντων γνῶσις καὶ κώλυσις]

Τοὺς δὲ ὑπορύσσοντας ὧδε κωλύειν. ἐὰν δο-
κῇς[6] ὑπορύσσεσθαι, ὡς βαθυτάτην ἐκτὸς χρὴ
τὴν τάφρον ὀρύσσεσθαι, ὅπως εἰς τὴν τάφρον τὸ
ὑπόρυγμα ἀφίκηται καὶ οἱ ὑπορύσσοντες ὀφθῶσιν.
2 ἐὰν δέ σοι ὑπάρχῃ, καὶ τειχίον τειχίσαι εἰς αὐτὴν
ὡς ἰσχυροτάτων[7] καὶ μεγίστων λίθων. ἐὰν
3 δὲ μὴ ὑπάρχῃ τειχίσαι λίθοις,[8] ξύλων φορυτὸν
κομίσαντα . . .[9] ἂν δὲ τὰ ὑπορύγματα τῆς τά-
φρου πῃ[10] προσπέσῃ, ταύτῃ ἐπιβάλλοντα[11] ξύλα
καὶ τὸν φορυτὸν ἐμπρῆσαι καὶ τὰ ἄλλα κατα-
σκεπάσαι, ὅπως ὁ καπνὸς εἰς τὸ διόρυγμα πορεύσηται καὶ κακῶς ποιήσῃ[12] τοὺς ἐν τῷ ὀρύγματι

---

[1] Meineke: ἄρ τι ἀνῃ M.
[2] Orelli: τω τε σχει M (with mark of corruption over σ).
[3] Added by Casaubon.   [4] Hertlein: ὑποπροτιθέναι M.
[5] R. Schöne: προσταθῆναι M.
[6] δοκῇ J. Afr., C, Casaubon, Hercher
[7] J. Afr.: ἰσχυροτάτην M.   [8] J. Afr.: λίθους M.
[9] R. Schöne recognizes a lacuna here.

184

thrust him or the ladder away with a forked pole, if you cannot keep him away otherwise because of arrows shot from below. And if the ladder is even with the wall it cannot be pushed away, but those who climb over the wall should be thrust off. And if even this seems impossible, there must be made a sort of door-frame of planks and when the ladder is being raised, the frame should be placed in advance underneath it. When, then, the ladder approaches the frame, at the raising of the frame from beneath, if a roller has previously been attached to the edge of it, the ladder necessarily falls, and it will not be possible to set it up.

XXXVII. [*Detection and Prevention of Mining Operations*]

Those who are constructing mines are to be prevented in the following manner. If you think a mine is being made you should dig the moat outside the wall as deep as possible so that the mine may open into the moat and those who are digging it may be exposed to view. And if you have a chance, a wall should also be built in the moat, of the very hardest and largest stones available. But if you have no chance to build a stone wall you should bring up logs and rubbish . . ., and if the mines at any point open into the moat, there you should dump the wood and set fire to the rubbish and cover the rest over in order that the smoke may penetrate the opening and injure those in the mine. It is

---

[10] Added by Meineke.
[11] Köchly and Rüstow: ἐπιβάλλοντες M, ἐμβάλλοντας J. Afr.
[12] R. Schöne: ποιῆι·ἡ M.

ὄντας· ἐνδέχεται δὲ καὶ πολλοὺς ἀπολέσθαι
4 αὐτῶν ὑπὸ τοῦ καπνοῦ. ἤδη δέ τινες καὶ σφῆκας[1] καὶ μελίσσας εἰς τὸ διόρυγμα ἀφέντες
5 ἐλυμήναντο τοὺς ἐν τῷ ὀρύγματι ὄντας. χρὴ δὲ
ἁπλῶς εἰπεῖν[2] καθ' ὃν τινα τόπον[3] ὀρύσσουσιν
ἀνθυπορύσσειν καὶ ἀντιοῦσθαι καὶ ἐμπιμπράναι
6 . . .[4] τὸ ἐν τῷ ὀρύγματι μαχόμενον. παλαιὸν
δέ τι λέγεται . . .[5] Ἄμασιν Βαρκαίους πολιορκοῦντα,[6] ἐπεὶ ἐπεχείρει ὀρύσσειν. οἱ δὲ Βαρκαῖοι
αἰσθόμενοι τὸ[7] ἐπιχείρημα τοῦ Ἀμάσιδος, ἠπο-
ροῦντο μὴ λάθῃ ἢ φθάσῃ, ἔπειτα ἀνὴρ χαλκεὺς
ἀνεῦρεν ἐνθυμήσας· ἀσπίδος χάλκωμα περιφέρων[8]
ἐντὸς[9] τοῦ τείχεος ἐπάνω προσίσχεν[10] πρὸς τὸ
7 δάπεδον.[11] τῇ μὲν δὴ ἄλλῃ κωφὰ ἦν πρὸς ἃ
προσίσχοι τὸ χάλκωμα· ᾗ δὲ ὑπωρύσσετο,[12]
ἀντήχει. ἀντορύσσοντες οὖν οἱ Βαρκαῖοι ταύτῃ,
ἀπέκτειναν πολλοὺς τῶν ὑπορυσσόντων. ὅθεν καὶ
νῦν χρῶνται τούτῳ τῷ ἐνθυμήματι[13] γνωρίζοντες
ᾗ ὑπορύσσεται.

8 Καὶ οἷς μὲν προσήκει[14] τὰ[15] ἐκ τῶν ἐναντίων
τεχνάσματα καταντῶντα[16] ἀμύνειν[17] δεδήλωται·
τοῖς δὲ ὑπορύσσειν μέλλουσιν ὧδ' ἂν γένοιτο
9 ἰσχυρότατον φράγμα. χρὴ δύο ἁμαξῶν τοὺς ῥυμοὺς εἰς τὸ αὐτὸ δῆσαι, συμπετάσαντα κατὰ τὸ

[1] Casaubon: σφίκασ M.
[2] Herm. Schöne: αγνωσσειν M.
[3] J. Afr.: τρόπον M.
[4] For the lacuna which he recognizes here R. Schöne
suggests φορυτὸν καὶ οὕτω διαφθείρειν τὸ κτλ.
[5] The lacuna is indicated by Rouse.
[6] Casaubon: πολιορκοῦντασ M.   [7] Added by C.
[8] Köchly and Rüstow (from Herodotus): ἐπιφέρων M.
[9] Wesseling: ὄντοσ M.   [10] Casaubon: προσίσχειν M.
[11] Wesseling (from Herodotus): τάδε M.

even possible that many of these may be killed by
the smoke. And in some instances, by releasing
wasps and bees into the opening, men have worked
mischief with those in the mine. One must, in a
word, at whatever point the enemy are digging,
construct a countermine beneath and against them,
and by setting fire to [rubbish in the countermine
thus destroy the] fighting force in the mine itself.
Now an old incident is told . . . of Amasis in his siege
of Barca, when he was trying to dig a mine.[1] The
people of Barca, who were aware of the attempt of
Amasis, were concerned lest he might elude or anticipate them, until a coppersmith thought out a device.
Carrying a bronze shield around inside the wall he
held it against the ground above various points.
And of course at all other points the parts to which he
applied the bronze were without sound, but where
the digging was in progress beneath the shield
became resonant. So the people of Barca dug a
countermine at this point and killed many of the
enemy's miners, and as a result even now men use
this means of ascertaining where mines are being
dug.
I have already explained by what means one
should oppose and ward off the devices of the enemy.
For those, on the other hand, who are to construct
mines, a very effective form of protection would be
this. One should fasten together the poles of two
wagons, having first turned them back each in the

---

[1] The incident is taken from Herodotus iv. 200.

<hr>

[12] Casaubon: ὑπορυσσετο M.
[13] Hertlein: αὐτῷ ἐν τῇ νυκτὶ M.
[14] Hertlein: προσῆκεν M.   [15] Casaubon: καὶ M.
[16] R. Schöne: καὶ αντιωμεθα M.   [17] C: ἀμύνη M.

ἕτερον μέρος τῆς ἁμάξης, ὅπως μετεωρισθῶσιν
οἱ ῥυμοὶ εἰς τὸ αὐτὸ νεύοντες· ἔπειτα οὕτως[1]
ἐπισυνδεῖν ἄλλα ξύλα καὶ ῥίπους καὶ ἄλλα φράγματα ἐπάνω, ταῦτα[2] δὲ πηλῷ καταλεῖψαι.
ἔσται οὖν τοῦτο καὶ προσαγαγεῖν ὅπου βούλει
τοὺς τροχοὺς καὶ ἀπαγαγεῖν, ὑπὸ δὲ τούτῳ τῷ
φράγματι τοὺς ὑπορύσσοντας εἶναι.

XXXVIII. [Ἐπικουρητικά]

Ἐν δὲ ταῖς προσβολαῖς τῶν πολεμίων πρὸς
τὸ τεῖχος μηχανήμασιν ἢ καὶ σώμασι χρὴ δια-
τετάχθαι τοὺς ἐν τῇ πόλει μαχομένους τρία μέρη,
ὅπως οἱ μὲν μάχωνται, οἱ δὲ ἀναπαύωνται, οἱ
δὲ παρασκευάζωνται, καὶ νεοκμῆτες[3] ἀεὶ ἐπὶ
2 τοῦ τείχους ὦσιν.[4] δεῖ δέ τινας καὶ ἄλλους
ἐπιλελεγμένους πλήθει πλείονι μετὰ τοῦ στρατηγοῦ ξυμπεριιέναι κύκλῳ τὸ τεῖχος, ἐπικου-
ροῦντας ἀεί τινι πονουμένῳ μέρει· τὸ γὰρ ἐπιὸν
μᾶλλον οἱ πολέμιοι φοβοῦνται τοῦ ὑπάρχοντος
καὶ παρόντος ἤδη. τάς τε κύνας δεσμεῖν τὸν
3 καιρὸν τοῦτον· μετὰ γὰρ ὅπλων καὶ θορύβου
τῶν ἀνθρώπων[5] τρεχόντων κατὰ τὴν πόλιν δι᾽

[1] J. Afr.: ὅπωσ M.
[2] Köchly and Rüstow: σπανιώτατα M: ἐπάνω, τὰ J. Afr.
[3] Casaubon: νεοχμῆτες M.   [4] Casaubon: σώμασιν M.
[5] Haase: θορυβούντων καὶ ἀνθρώπων M.

[1] Apparently the poles, which seem to have been hinged
at the point of attachment, are thought of as being turned
(or 'spread back' συμπετάννυμι) in a direction which eventually would bring them back upon the body of the wagon

188

direction of the other part of its wagon, in such a way that the poles may be raised aloft, inclining toward the same point.[1] Then when this has been done, one should fasten on in addition other timbers and hurdles and other sorts of covering above and smear these over with clay. This device, then, can be advanced and withdrawn on its wheels wherever you desire, and those who are excavating can keep under this protection.

XXXVIII. [*Use of Reserves*]

During the attacks of the enemy upon the wall with engines of war, or even with infantry, the defenders within the town should be divided into three groups, so that one group may be fighting, another resting, and the third preparing for action, and that there may always be on the wall soldiers who are fresh. And certain other picked troops, in considerable number, must go around the wall with the general, constantly relieving any section that is hard pressed. For the enemy fear the reserves more than the force already on duty before them. And the dogs should be tied up at this time, for when men are hurrying through the town, with noise of arms and confusion, if the dogs in addition, because

(κατὰ τὸ ἕτερον μέρος), but they are actually lifted only to an angle, say, of 45° to 60°, and their tips are then firmly fastened together. From the point of convergence timbers are extended to the sides and covers of the wagon-bodies and then a roof in the shape of an oblong pyramid is constructed. The passage is very obscure, however, and a corruption may lurk in the words συμπετάσαντα κατά.

ἀήθειαν[1] ὁρμῶσαι[2] αἱ κύνες ὀχλοῖεν ἂν προσκείμεναι.

4 Τοῖς τε ἐπὶ τῷ τείχει μαχομένοις παραινεῖν οἷα ἑκάστῳ δεῖ, τοὺς μὲν ἐπαινοῦντα,[3] τῶν δὲ δεόμενον·[4] ὀργῇ δὲ μηδένα[5] μετιέναι[6] μηδὲ[7] τῶν
5 τυχόντων ἀνθρώπων· ἀθυμότεροι γὰρ εἶεν ἄν. εἰ δέ τινας δεῖ μετιέναι ἀμελοῦντας καὶ ἀκοσμοῦντας, τοὺς τὰ πλεῖστα κεκτημένους καὶ ἐν τῇ πόλει δυνάμεως[8] μάλιστα μετέχοντας· εἴη γὰρ ἄν τι τοιοῦτο καὶ τοῖς ἄλλοις παράδειγμα. ἐν οἷς καιροῖς ἕκαστα τούτων δεῖ παρεῖναι,[9] ἐν τοῖς Ἀκούσμασι
6 γέγραπται. χερμάδια δὲ μὴ ἐπιτρέπειν ἀκαίρως ἀφιέναι, παρεσκευάσθαι δὲ[10] ὅπως καὶ τὰ ἀφεθέντα
7 ἐν τῇ ἡμέρᾳ ἐν νυκτὶ ἀναλέγηται ὧδε. κατακρεμαννύειν χρὴ ἐν κοφίνοις ἄνδρας κατὰ τοῦ τείχεος οἵτινες ἀναλέξουσιν· τοὺς[11] δὲ ἄνδρας χρὴ τοὺς ἀναλέξαντας[12] τὰ χερμάδια ἀναβαίνειν εἰς τὸ τεῖχος, κατακρεμασθέντων δικτύων συείων ἢ ἐλαφείων[13] ἢ ταῖς ἐκ τῶν σχοινίων κλίμαξι πεποιη-
8 μέναις. ταύτας δ' ἴσας[14] εἶναι τὸν ἀριθμὸν τοῖς ἀναλέγουσιν ἀνθρώποις, ὅπως, ἐάν τινες πονῶσιν, ταχὺ ἀναβαίνωσιν· πύλας γὰρ μὴ ἀνοίγεσθαι νυκτός, ἀλλὰ ταῖς τοιαύταις κλίμαξι χρῆσθαι καὶ ἂν τινα βούλησθε.

[1] Casaubon: ἀλήθειαν M.   [2] Lange: ὁρῶσαι M.
[3] Meineke: ἐπαινοῦντασ M.
[4] Casaubon: τῶν δεδεμένων M.
[5] μηθένα M.   [6] Added by Casaubon.
[7] Added by R. Schöne.   [8] Orelli: δυναμένους M.
[9] From παρίημι; for the sense compare 26. 8 (Pease): παραινεῖν Köchly and Rüstow: ποιεῖν Hercher: περαίνειν Oldfather.

of the unusual doings, should begin to run amuck, they would make trouble.

And to those who are fighting on the wall the general should give such advice as is necessary for each, to some commendation and to others an appeal, but he should not in anger reprimand anyone, even of the common soldiers, for that would dishearten them the more. If, however, it is necessary to reprimand anyone for neglect and lack of discipline, it should be those who are most wealthy and influential in the city, for such a case would be an example to the others also. The occasions on which it is expedient to overlook each of these matters I have discussed in the work on *Admonitions*. And one should not permit the throwing of small stones at unsuitable times, but should provide that even those thrown during the day may be gathered again during the night, in the following manner. Men should be let down from the wall in baskets to pick the stones up again, and when they have gathered them they should regain the wall by means of boar- or stag-nets which have been let down, or else by rope ladders, which should be equal in number to the men who are gathering the stones, so that if any are hard pressed they may quickly climb up again. For the gates must not be opened during the night, but ladders of this sort should be used, and other devices you may choose.

---

[10] Casaubon: ὁ δὲ M.   [11] Hercher: ὄντωσ M.
[12] Hertlein: ἀναλέξοντασ M
[13] Orelli: δακτυλίων ιστων πελαφιων M (with marks of corruption over the second ι and the ε).
[14] Kirchhoff: δισσὰσ M.

XXXIX. [Δολεύματα]

Χρὴ δὲ πολιορκουμένους καὶ τὰ τοιαῦτα τεχνά-
ζειν. ἐν ταῖς πύλαις καὶ εἰς τὸ ἔσω μᾶλλον
μέρος ὀρύξαντα τάφρον ἔνθεν καὶ ἔνθεν πάροδον
λιπόντα, ἔπειτα ἐπεξελθόντας τινὰς ἀκροβολίζεσθαι
καὶ προάγειν[1] τῶν πολεμίων ὥστε συνεισδραμεῖν
2 εἰς τὴν πόλιν. τοὺς μὲν οὖν ἐκ τῆς πόλεως κατα-
φεύγοντας εἰς τὴν πόλιν χρὴ ἔνθεν καὶ ἔνθεν παρὰ
τὰς λελειμμένας παρόδους εἰστρέχειν· τοὺς δὲ
τῶν πολεμίων συνειστρέχοντας εἰκός[2] ἐστι, μὴ
προειδότας τὴν τάφρον, ἅμα τε καὶ κεκρυμμένης
οὔσης, εἰσπίπτειν καὶ φθείρεσθαι ὑπὸ τῶν[3] ἔσω
τῆς πόλεως ἐν τῷ καιρῷ τούτῳ.[4] τούτων δ' εἶναι
συντεταγμένους τινὰς ἐν ταῖς διόδοις καὶ πρὸς[5]
3 τοῖς ὀρύγμασι τῶν[6] πυλῶν χώραις. ἐὰν δὲ
πλείονες τῶν πολεμίων ἐπεισφέρωνται καὶ βούλῃ[7]
αὐτοὺς κατέχειν,[8] χρὴ ἡτοιμάσθαι ἄνωθεν[9] ἀπὸ
τοῦ μεσοπύλου πύλην ξύλων[10] ὡς παχυτάτων καὶ
4 σεσιδηρῶσθαι αὐτήν. ὅταν οὖν βούλῃ[7] ἀπολα-
βεῖν[11] τοὺς εἰστρέχοντας πολεμίους, ταύτην ἀφιέναι
ὀρθήν· καὶ αὐτή τέ τινας ἡ πύλη φερομένη διαφθερεῖ[12] καὶ τοὺς πολεμίους σχήσει μὴ εἰσιέναι,
ἅμα δὲ καὶ τῶν ἐπὶ τῷ τείχει βαλλόντων τοὺς
5 πρὸς ταῖς πύλαις πολεμίους. χρὴ δὲ τοῖς φίλοις
ἀεὶ προειρῆσθαι, ἐάν ποτε αὐτοῖς[13] πολέμιοι

---

[1] J. Afr.: προσάγειν M.   [2] Casaubon: εἴη ὅσ M.
[3] Added by R. Schöne: φθείρεσθαι ἔσω M.
[4] Added by Hercher.   [5] Casaubon: πρω M.
[6] Added by Köchly and Rüstow.
[7] Meier: βούλει M.   [8] J. Afr.: ἔχειν M.
[9] Casaubon: ανθεν M (with sign of corruption over α).
[10] Orelli (after Casaubon): πύλη πυλῶν M.

XXXIX. [*Stratagems*]

Those undergoing siege should also contrive such measures as these. At the gates and somewhat inside them they should dig a trench and leave a passage on this side and on that. Then some of them should go out and engage in skirmishing and lure the enemy to make a dash into the town with them. Of course the men from the town, as they retire into it, are to run along the passages that have been left on either side, but it is likely that those of the enemy who run in with them, being unaware of the trench, especially since it is concealed, will fall into it and be killed at that instant by those within the city. And of these some should be stationed in the passages and in places at the trenches near the gate. And if a larger number of the enemy come in after these and you wish to catch them, you should have ready above the centre of the gate a portcullis of the stoutest possible timbers overlaid with iron.[1] When, then, you wish to cut off the enemy as they rush in, you should let this drop down, and the portcullis itself will not only as it falls destroy some of them, but will also keep the foe from entering, while at the same time the forces on the wall are shooting the enemy at the gate. And you should always give instructions in advance to your own party, in case the enemy rush

---

[1] Vegetius iv. 4 speaks of this device as one *quod invenit antiquitas*. It was employed successfully by the men of Salapia in 208 B.C. against Hannibal (Livy xxvii. 28. 10-12), and by the Lycians of Xanthus against M. Junius Brutus in 42 B.C. (Appian, *Bell. Civ.* iv. 78).

---

[11] Hertlein: ὑπολαβεῖν M.
[12] Orelli: πολυφερομενη διαφέρει M.
[13] Hertlein: ἀυθισ M.

συνεισπίπτωσιν, ὅπῃ τῆς πόλεως συναθροισθήσονται, ὅπως τῷ τόπῳ οἱ φίλοι διαγιγνώσκωνται·
οὐ γὰρ ῥᾴδιον μιγάδας τε ὄντας μεθ' ὅπλων καὶ
μετὰ θορύβων συνεισπίπτοντας διαγιγνώσκεσθαι.
6 ἤδη δὲ τοῖς θρασυνομένοις τε λίαν[1] καὶ προσ-
πελάζουσι τῷ τείχει ἐγγυτέρω τοῦ προσήκοντος
νυκτὸς ἢ μεθ' ἡμέραν, βρόχους ἡμέρας μὲν κρυφαίως
κατεσκεύασαν νυκτὸς δὲ ἀκρύπτους, οἷς προ-
καλούμενοι[2] ἀκροβολισμοῖς τὸν εἰσπεσόντα ἀνα-
7 σπάσουσιν. ἔστω δὲ ὁ μὲν βρόχος ὅπλου ὡς
ἰσχυροτάτου, τὸ δὲ ἕλκον ἐπὶ δύο πήχεις ἄλυσις,[3]
τοῦ μὴ διατμηθῆναι· τὸ δ' ἄλλο, ὅθεν ἕλκουσι,
σχοίνου. ὅλος[4] δὲ ἔσω κατακρέμαται καὶ ἀνα-
σπᾶται ὅπλοις ἢ κηλωνείοις.[5] οἱ δὲ πολέμιοι
ἐὰν διατέμνειν ἐπιχειρῶσι, πρὸς ταῦτα πάλιν οἱ
ἔσωθεν κηλωνείοις χρῶνται καθιέντες, ἵνα μὴ δια-
τέμνηται· αἱ γὰρ ἀλύσεις πρὸς τὰ τοιαῦτα πραγ-
ματῶδες καὶ δυσμεταχείριστον, ἅμα δὲ καὶ
ἀλυσιτελές.[6]

XL. [Φυλακὴ πόλεως]

Ἂν ᾖ ἡ πόλις μεγάλη καὶ μὴ ἱκανοὶ ὦσιν οἱ ἐν
τῇ πόλει ἄνθρωποι περίστασθαι ἐν κύκλῳ τὴν
πόλιν, τοῖς δὲ ὑπάρχουσι θέλῃς αὐτὴν διαφυλάξαι,
χρὴ τῆς πόλεως ὅσα ἂν ᾖ εὐπρόσοδα οἰκοδομεῖν
ὕψη[7] ἐκ τῶν ὑπαρχόντων, ἵνα, ἄν τινες τῶν
πολεμίων ἢ λαθραίως ἢ βίᾳ ἀναβῶσιν, ἐν ἀπειρίᾳ[8]

---

[1] Hercher: τέλεον M.
[2] Köchly and Rüstow: προσκαλούμενοι M.
[3] Casaubon: ἀλυσεισ M, ἄλυσις C.
[4] Köchly and Rüstow: ὅλως M.
[5] Casaubon: αλωνίοισ M.   [6] Casaubon: λυσιτελέσ M.
[7] Meineke (or ὕψι): ὕψει M: ὑψηλὰ J. Afr.

194

in with them, in what place in the city they are to
make their rendezvous, in order that your friends
may be distinguished by their position. For it is
not easy to distinguish between men in a promiscuous
armed throng, rushing confusedly in together. And
on some occasions, against enemies who were
over-confident and were approaching the wall more
closely than was prudent, either by night or by day,
the defenders have made ready nets, secretly by day,
but by night without attempt at concealment, and
luring the enemy forward by skirmishes have hauled
up those who became entangled. The net should
be of the very strongest rope, and the line that lifts
it should be of chain for a distance of two cubits,
to prevent its being severed, but the rest, from the
point where they are pulling it, may be of rope.
The whole device is let down and hauled up from
within the wall by ropes or by swing-beams. If,
however, the enemy try to cut their way out, then to
meet this the besieged should again use swing-beams,
letting them down so that the net may not be cut;
for to use chains to prevent such an occurrence is
troublesome and inconvenient, as well as too costly.

XL. [*Guarding a City*]

If the city is a large one and the men in the city
are not numerous enough to man its walls all the
way around, and yet you wish to keep it closely
guarded with the men you have, you should, from
the materials at hand, build up high all the easily
assailable parts of the city wall, so that if any of the
enemy shall scale them, either by stealth or by

---

[8] ἀπορίᾳ Casaubon, Hercher, Capps.

γενόμενοι μὴ δύνωνται καταπηδᾶν ἀφ' ὑψηλῶν, ἅμα παντάπασι[1] μὴ ἔχοντες ὅπη καταβαίνωσιν. παρὰ δὲ τὰ ᾠκοδομημένα ἔνθεν καὶ ἔνθεν φυλασσόντων ἐκ τῶν[2] ὑπαρχόντων ἀνθρώπων, ἵνα τοὺς καταπηδῶντας ἀπὸ τῶν ὑψηλῶν διαφθείρωσιν.

2 Διονύσιος δὲ πόλιν ὑποχείριον ποιησάμενος, ἀνδρῶν τῶν μὲν[3] ἐν τῇ πόλει τεθνηκότων, τῶν δὲ πεφευγότων, ἠθέλησε κατασχεῖν· ἦν δὲ μείζων ἢ 3 ὥστε ὑπ' ὀλίγων φυλάσσεσθαι. ἐπιμελητὰς μὲν οὖν τινὰς μετ' ὀλίγων οὓς ἐνεδέχετο ἐπέστησε,[4] τῶν δὲ ἐν τῇ πόλει τὰ μέγιστα δυναμένων τοῖς οἰκέταις[5] συνῴκισεν τῶν δεσποτῶν τὰς θυγατέρας καὶ γυναῖκας καὶ ἀδελφάς· οὕτω γὰρ οὖν[6] ᾤετο μάλιστα πολεμιωτάτους ἔσεσθαι τοῖς δεσπόταις 4 καὶ αὐτῷ[7] πιστοτέρους. Σινωπεῖς δὲ πρὸς Δαταμᾶν πολεμοῦντες ἐπεὶ ἐν κινδύνῳ ἦσαν καὶ σπάνει ἀνδρῶν, τῶν γυναικῶν τὰ ἐπιεικέστατα σώματα μορφώσαντες καὶ ὁπλίσαντες ὡς ἐς ἄνδρας μάλιστα, ἀντὶ ὅπλων καὶ περικεφαλαίων τούς τε κάδους καὶ τὰ ὁμότροπα τούτοις δόντες χαλκώματα, περιῆγον τοῦ τείχους ᾗ μάλιστα οἱ πολέμιοι ὄψεσθαι 5 ἔμελλον. βάλλειν δὲ[4] οὐκ εἴων αὐτάς· πόρρωθεν γὰρ κατάδηλος βάλλουσα γυνή. ποιοῦντες δὲ ταῦτα τοὺς αὐτομόλους ἐφύλασσον μὴ διαγγελθῇ.

6 Ἐὰν δὲ θέλῃς ἐπὶ τῷ τείχει περιόδους πλείους

---

[1] Oldfather (or ἄλλῃ): ἀλλὰ πασιναπασι M (with mark of corruption over the third and the fourth a): πάλιν ἀπίωσι Orelli: ἀλλ' ἀπορῶσι τοῖς πᾶσι Casaubon.
[2] ἐκ τῶν added by Casaubon: οἱ ὑπάρχοντες ἄνθρωποι J. Afr.
[3] Added by Lincke (Philol., 1914, 157).
[4] Added by Casaubon.
[5] Köchly and Rüstow: δυναμένους οἰκέτας M.
[6] Meineke: ἂν M.   [7] Sauppe: αὐτῶ M.

force, from their unfamiliarity they may not be able to leap down from great heights, being at the same time completely at a loss for any place to descend. And at either side of the parts that have been built up some of the available men should keep watch to destroy those who may leap from the high points.

When Dionysius [1] had subjugated a certain city and some of its defenders had been killed and the others had fled, he wished to retain the place, but it was too large to be guarded by a small force. Accordingly he left some in charge with a few available men, and to the slaves of the most influential men in the city he married the daughters, wives, and sisters of their masters; for in this relation he thought that the slaves would be most hostile to their masters and more faithful to him. Again, the people of Sinope in their war against Datamas, [2] when they were in danger and in need of men, disguised the most able-bodied of their women and armed them as much like men as they could, giving them in place of shields and helmets their jars and similar bronze utensils, and marched them around the wall where the enemy were most likely to see them. But they did not allow them to throw missiles, for even a long way off a woman betrays her sex when she tries to throw. While they were doing this they took care that deserters should not disclose the stratagem.

If you wish the patrolmen upon the wall to appear

[1] Clearly Dionysius I. of Syracuse, but the precise occasion is unknown.

[2] His active career extended from *circa* 384 to 362 B.C. Köchly in a note sets this event in 379-8, but the reasoning is not very cogent.

more numerous than they are,[1] you should make them go their rounds two abreast, one rank with their spears upon the left shoulder, the other with their spears upon the right, and thus they will appear to be four abreast. And if they go about three abreast, the first man should have his spear upon his right shoulder, the next upon his left, and the others similarly, and in this way each man will look like two.

Now about wheatless rations and things of which there is a scarcity during a siege, and about how waters are to be rendered drinkable, I have explained in the book on *Military Preparations.* And inasmuch as these points have been described I shall pass on to naval manœuvres.

Of a naval armament there are two forms of equipment. . . .

[1] See the critical note for a discussion of this passage.

---

his left shoulder, and the other on his right, and thus they will appear to be four abreast. And if they go about three abreast, the first man should have one spear on his right shoulder, and the other on his left, and the others similarly, and in this way each separate man will look like two."

[4] The subscription in M runs Αἰνείου πολιορκητικά· ἢ Αἰλιανοῦ καθὼς ἡ ἀρχή· followed by an erasure of 13 letters. See the Introduction, p. 2.

TESTIMONIA ET FRAGMENTA

I.

Aelian, *Tact.* i. 2 καὶ περὶ τῆς καθ᾽ Ὅμηρον τακτικῆς ἐνετύχομεν συγγραφεῦσι Στρατοκλεῖ καὶ Ἑρμείᾳ καὶ Φρόντωνι τῷ καθ᾽ ἡμᾶς ἀνδρὶ ὑπατικῷ. ἐξειργάσαντο δὲ τὴν θεωρίαν Αἰνείας τε διὰ πλειόνων ὁ καὶ στρατηγικὰ βιβλία ἱκανὰ συνταξάμενος, ὧν ἐπιτομὴν ὁ Θετταλὸς Κινέας ἐποίησε, Πύρρος τε ὁ Ἠπειρώτης τακτικὰ συνέταξε καὶ Ἀλέξανδρος ὁ τούτου υἱὸς καὶ Κλέαρχος.

II.

Aelian, *Tact.* iii. 4 ὅρον δὲ αὐτῆς (*sc.* τῆς τακτικῆς) ἔθεντο Αἰνείας μὲν ἐπιστήμην εἶναι πολεμικῶν κινήσεων, Πολύβιος δέ, ἐάν τις πλῆθος ἄτακτον παραλαβὼν τοῦτο συγκρίνῃ καὶ καταλοχίσας συλλοχίσῃ παιδεύσῃ τε χρησίμως τὰ πρὸς τὸν πόλεμον.

III.

Polybius x. 44 Αἰνείας δὲ βουληθεὶς διορθώσασθαι τὴν τοιαύτην ἀπορίαν, ὁ τὰ περὶ τῶν στρατηγικῶν ὑπομνήματα συντεταγμένος, βραχὺ μέν τι προεβίβασε, τοῦ γε μὴν δέοντος ἀκμὴν πάμπολυ τὸ[1] κατὰ τὴν ἐπίνοιαν ἀπελείφθη. γνοίη δ᾽ ἄν τις ἐκ τούτων. φησὶ γὰρ δεῖν τοὺς μέλλοντας

200

ATTESTATIONS AND FRAGMENTS

I.

And upon the subject of tactics in Homer we have read Stratocles and Hermeas and Fronto the exconsul of our own time. Now the theory has been elaborated both by Aeneas in detail (and he also composed a considerable number of military manuals, of which Cineas the Thessalian made an epitome), and by Pyrrhus of Epirus, who composed a treatise on tactics, and by Alexander his son, and by Clearchus.

II.

Aeneas defined it (*sc.* tactics) as the science of military movements, but the definition of Polybius was, that tactics was when a man took an unorganized crowd, arranged it, divided it into companies, grouped them together, and gave them a practical military training.

III.

Aeneas, therefore, the writer of the treatise on tactics, wished to correct this defect, and did in fact make some improvement; but his invention still fell very far short of what was wanted, as the following passage from his treatise will show. " Let

---

[1] Reiske: τοῦ MSS.

ἀλλήλοις διὰ τῶν πυρσῶν δηλοῦν τὸ κατεπεῖγον
ἀγγεῖα κατασκευάσαι κεραμεᾶ[1] κατά τε τὸ πλάτος
καὶ κατὰ τὸ βάθος ἰσομεγέθη πρὸς ἀκρίβειαν·
εἶναι δὲ μάλιστα τὸ μὲν βάθος τριῶν πηχῶν, τὸ
δὲ πλάτος πήχεος. εἶτα παρασκευάσαι φελλοὺς
βραχὺ κατὰ πλάτος ἐνδεεῖς τῶν στομάτων, ἐν δὲ
τούτοις μέσοις ἐμπεπηγέναι βακτηρίας διῃρημένας[2]
ἴσα μέρη τριδάκτυλα, καθ' ἕκαστον δὲ μέρος
εἶναι περιγραφὴν εὔσημον. ἐν ἑκάστῳ δὲ μέρει
γεγράφθαι τὰ προφανέστατα καὶ καθολικώτατα
τῶν ἐν τοῖς πολεμικοῖς συμβαινόντων, οἷον εὐθέως
ἐν τῷ πρώτῳ διότι πάρεισιν ἱππεῖς εἰς τὴν χώραν,
ἐν δὲ τῷ δευτέρῳ διότι πεζοὶ βαρεῖς, ἐν δὲ τῷ
τρίτῳ ψιλοί, τούτων δ' ἑξῆς πεζοὶ μεθ' ἱππέων,
εἶτα πλοῖα, μετὰ δὲ ταῦτα σῖτος, καὶ[3] κατὰ τὸ
συνεχὲς οὕτω, μέχρις[4] ἂν ἐν πάσαις γραφῇ ταῖς
χώραις τὰ μάλιστ' ἂν ἐκ τῶν εὐλόγων προνοίας
τυγχάνοντα καὶ συμβαίνοντα κατὰ τοὺς ἐνεστῶτας
καιροὺς ἐκ τῶν πολεμικῶν. τούτων δὲ γενομένων
ἀμφότερα κελεύει τρῆσαι[5] τὰ ἀγγεῖα πρὸς ἀκρί-
βειαν, ὥστε τοὺς αὐλίσκους ἴσους εἶναι καὶ κατ'
ἴσον ἀπορρεῖν· εἶτα πληρώσαντας ὕδατος ἐπιθεῖναι
τοὺς φελλοὺς ἔχοντας τὰς[6] βακτηρίας, κἄπειτα
τοὺς αὐλίσκους ἀφεῖναι ῥεῖν ἅμα. τούτου δὲ
συμβαίνοντος δῆλον ὡς ἀνάγκη, πάντων ἴσων καὶ
ὁμοίων ὄντων, καθ' ὅσον ἂν ἀπορρέῃ τὸ ὑγρόν,
κατὰ τοσοῦτον τοὺς φελλοὺς καταβαίνειν καὶ τὰς
βακτηρίας κρύπτεσθαι κατὰ τῶν ἀγγείων. ὅταν
δὲ τὰ προειρημένα γένηται κατὰ τὸν χειρισμὸν
ἰσοταχῆ καὶ σύμφωνα, τότε κομίσαντας ἐπὶ τοὺς

---

[1] Dindorf: κεραμμαῖα or κεραμαῖα MSS.
[2] These two words added by Casaubon.

those who wish," he says, " to communicate any matter of pressing importance to each other by fire-signals prepare two earthenware vessels of exactly equal size both as to diameter and depth. Let the depth be three cubits, the diameter one. Then prepare corks of a little shorter diameter than that of the mouths of the vessels : and in the middle of these corks fix rods divided into equal portions of three fingers' breadth, and let each of these portions be marked with a clearly distinguishable line ; and in each let there be written one of the most obvious and universal of those events which occur in war ; for instance in the first ' cavalry have entered the country,' in the second ' hoplites,' in the third ' light-armed,' in the next ' infantry and cavalry,' in another ' ships,' in another ' corn,' and so on, until all the portions have had written on them the measures on the part of the enemy which may reasonably be foreseen and are most likely to occur in the present emergency. Then carefully pierce both the vessels in such a way that the taps shall be exactly equal and carry off the same amount of water. Fill the vessels with water and lay the corks with their rods upon its surface and set both taps running together. This being done, it is evident that, if there is perfect equality in every respect between them, both corks will sink exactly in proportion as the water runs away, and both rods will disappear to the same extent into the vessels. When they have been tested and the rate of the discharge of the water has been found to be exactly equal in both, then the vessels should be taken

---

[3] Added by Casaubon.   [4] Casaubon : μέχρι MSS.
[5] Scaliger : τηρῆσαι MSS.   [6] Added by Reiske.

τόπους ἐν οἷς ἑκάτεροι μέλλουσιν συντηρεῖν τὰς
πυρσείας, ἑκάτερον θεῖναι τῶν ἀγγείων. εἶτ᾽
ἐπὰν ἐμπέσῃ τι τῶν ἐν τῇ βακτηρίᾳ γεγραμμένων,
πυρσὸν ἆραι κελεύει, καὶ μένειν ἕως ἂν ἀνταίρωσιν
οἱ συντεταγμένοι· γενομένων δὲ φανερῶν ἀμφοτέρων ἅμα τῶν πυρσῶν καθελεῖν, εἶτ᾽ εὐθέως
ἀφεῖναι τοὺς αὐλίσκους ῥεῖν. ὅταν δὲ κατα-
βαίνοντος τοῦ φελλοῦ καὶ τῆς βακτηρίας ἔλθῃ
τῶν γεγραμμένων ὃ βούλει δηλοῦν κατὰ τὸ χεῖλος
τοῦ τεύχους, ἆραι κελεύει τὸν πυρσόν· τοὺς δ᾽
ἑτέρους ἐπιλαβεῖν εὐθέως τὸν αὐλίσκον, καὶ σκοπεῖν τί κατὰ τὸ χεῖλός ἐστι τῶν ἐν τῇ βακτηρίᾳ
γεγραμμένων· ἔσται δὲ τοῦτο τὸ δηλούμενον,
πάντων ἰσοταχῶς παρ᾽ ἀμφοτέροις κινουμένων.

Suidas Αἰνείας· οὗτος ἔγραψε περὶ πυρσῶν,
ὥς φησι Πολύβιος, καὶ περὶ στρατηγημάτων
ὑπόμνημα.

IV.

Jul. Africanus, Κεστοί c. 37 p. 302[a] Thev. (according to mss. EP[1]) φασὶ δέ τινες τῶν ἀρχαίων ὅτι
καὶ ⟨ὁ⟩ τοῦ ἐχέως ἰὸς καὶ ἀσπίδος σαλαμάνδρης
τε εἰς τοῦτο (sc. χρῖσμα βελῶν) ἀπαράβατος.

V.

Johannes Lydus, Περὶ ἀρχῶν τῆς Ῥωμαίων
πολιτείας i. 47, in defining ἀδωράτορες and βετε-
ρανοί, cites a series of Roman authorities and then:
Ἑλλήνων δὲ Αἰλιανὸς καὶ Ἀρριανός, Αἰνείας,

---

[1] Shuckburgh's translation, slightly revised.
[2] This notice is clearly taken direct from Polybius.
[3] The same substances are mentioned in Philo Mechanicus

respectively to the two places from which the two parties intend to watch for fire-signals. As soon as any one of these eventualities which are inscribed upon the rods takes place, Aeneas bids raise a lighted torch, and wait until the signal is answered by a torch from the others ; then, when both torches have been simultaneously visible, lower them, and then immediately set the taps running. When the cork and rod on the signalling side has sunk low enough to bring the ring containing the words which give the desired information on a level with the rim of the vessel, a torch is to be raised again. Those on the receiving side are then at once to stop the tap, and to see which of the messages written on the rod is on a level with the rim of their vessel. This will be the same as that on the signalling side, assuming everything to be done at the same speed on both sides." [1]

Aeneas wrote on signal-fires, as Polybius said, and a treatise on stratagems. [2]

IV.

Some of the ancients say that the poison of the viper, asp, and salamander does not lose its virtue for this purpose (*i.e.* the smearing of missiles). [3]

V.

And of the Greeks, Aelian and Arrian, Aeneas,

v. 90. 17 ff. as necessary supplies in a beleaguered city. Such topics as this must have been treated by Aeneas in his Παρασκευαστικὴ βίβλος, *On Military Preparations.* See 8. 2-5 ; 40. 8, and the Introduction, p. 8.

Ὀνήσανδρος, Πάτρων, Ἀπολλόδωρος ἐν τοῖς
πολιορκητικοῖς, κτλ.[1]

JULII AFRICANI Κεστῶν CAPITA EX AENEA EXCERPTA[2]

XXXVIII. Πῶς πῦρ δυνάμεθα σβέσαι (= Ch. 34)

Ἐὰν ἡμῶν οἱ πολέμιοι πυρὶ κατασκευαστῷ
τεῖχος ἤ τι ἕτερον ἐμπρήσουσι, πῶς σβέσαι
δυνάμεθα; σβέσομεν αὐτὸ συντόμως καταχέοντες
ὄξος. τοὺς δὲ σβεννῦντας ἀπὸ τῶν ὑψηλοτέρων
δεῖ περὶ τὸ πρόσωπον ἔχειν ἔρυμά τι[3] ἵνα ἧσσον
ὀχλοῦνται προσαϊσσούσης αὐτοῖς τῆς φλογός. εἰ
δὲ σὺ προγνῷς τὰ μέλλοντα καίεσθαι, χρῖσον
ἔξωθεν ὄξος, καὶ τούτοις οὐ πρόεισι πῦρ.

XLV. Πῶς ἡμεῖς ἐμπρήσωμεν; (= Ch. 33. 1)

Ἐμπρήσωμεν ἡμεῖς καθ᾽ ἡμῶν ἐρχόμενον μάγ-
γανον ἢ ναῦν[4] ἢ πύργον πολέμιον οὕτως· ἐπιχεῖν[5]
δεῖ πίσσαν καὶ θεῖον ἐπιβάλλειν, ἔπειτα φλογώσαντα φάκελλον ἐπαφεῖναι[6] σχοινίῳ ἐφ᾽ ὅπερ
θέλομεν. τὰ δὲ τοιαῦτα προτεινόμενα[7] ἀφ᾽ ὧν
ἱστάμεθα τόπων ἐπιβάλλεται τοῖς ἐπιφερομένοις.

XLVI. Πρὸς καιομένας πύλας (= Ch. 33. 4)

Ἐὰν ἐμπρησθῶσιν αἱ πύλαι, δεῖ προσφέρεσθαι
ξύλον καὶ ἐμβάλλοντα[8] ὡς μέγιστον τὸ πῦρ ποιεῖν,

---

[1] This testimony is not given by R. Schöne. The citation of Aeneas involves an obvious anachronism.

[2] For these excerpts we give R. Schöne's constitution of the text, noting only those points at which some change seems necessary.   [3] Meursius: ἐρύματι MSS.

[4] Boivin: ἵνα οὖν MSS.   [5] Boivin: ἐπισχεῖν MSS.

FRAGMENTS

Onesander, Patro, and Apollodorus, in their works on the besieging of cities.

EXCERPTS FROM AENEAS IN THE Κεστοί OF JULIUS AFRICANUS

XXXVIII. *How we can put out Fire*

If our enemies shall set on fire a palisade or anything else with an incendiary preparation, how can we put out the fire? By pouring vinegar over it we shall at once put it out. Those who put out the fire from places above it must have some protection for the face, that they may be less annoyed when the flame darts toward them. And if you know in advance the parts that are likely to be set on fire, rub vinegar[1] on the outside, and the flame will not advance on them.

XLV. *How shall we ourselves set Things on Fire?*

Let us set on fire an engine coming against us or a ship or a hostile tower in this manner. One must pour pitch and cast sulphur, then set on fire a fagot and let it down by a rope upon the particular object we wish. And such things as these, held out from the places in which we are standing, are hurled at the approaching engines.

XLVI. *Against the Burning of a Gate*

If the gate is set on fire you must bring up wood and throw it on to make as large a fire as possible,

---

[1] See note on Aeneas, ch. 34. 1.

6 Cod. Monac. 195 m².   7 Boivin: προτεινομένων MSS.
    8 Aeneas: ἐμβάλλονται or ἐμβάλλονταs MSS.

207

μέχρις οὗ ταφρεύσει τὰ ἔσωθεν, καὶ ἐάν τι δέῃ[1]
ἐκ τῶν σοι ὑπαρχόντων οἴκοι καθαίρειν.[2]

XLVIII. Περὶ κλεψύδρας (=Ch. 22. 24 f.)

Κλεψύδρα πάνυ χρήσιμον[3] κτῆμα πρὸς τοὺς
νύκτωρ φυλάσσοντας, μακροτέρων ἢ βραχυτέρων
νυκτῶν γινομένων· αὕτη δὲ συμβάλλεται οὕτως.
χρὴ κεκηρῶσθαι αὐτῆς τὰ ἔσωθεν καὶ μακροτέρων
γινομένων τῶν νυκτῶν ἀφαιρεῖσθαι τοῦ κηροῦ,
ἵνα πλέον ὕδωρ χωρῇ, βραχυτέρων δὲ προσπλάσσεσθαι, ἵνα ἔλασσον δέχηται. τὴν δὲ ταύτης
ὀπὴν ἀκριβῶς δεῖ ποιεῖσθαι,[4] δι᾽ ἧς τὸ τῆς προ-
θεσμίας ὕδωρ ἐκρεῖ.

XLIX. Πυλωρικόν (=Ch. 28. 1-4; 29. 12)

Ἐν φόβῳ μενούσης[5] πόλεως τάδε δεῖ προνοεῖσθαι. πύλας τὰς μὲν ἄλλας κεκλεῖσθαι, μίαν
δὲ ἀνεῷχθαι, δι᾽ ἧς ἂν δυσπροσοδώτατον ᾖ[6] τῆς
πόλεως καὶ ἐπὶ πλεῖστον ἀπ᾽ αὐτῶν μέλλουσιν
ὁρᾶσθαι οἱ προϊόντες. καὶ ἐν αὐτῇ τῇ πύλῃ δεῖ
ἐκτομάδα,[7] ἵνα σώματα μὲν ἀνθρώπων δι᾽ αὐτῆς
εἰσίῃ[8] ἐν καθ᾽ ἕν· οὕτως γὰρ ἂν ἥκιστά τις
λανθάνῃ[9] καὶ δι᾽ αὐτῆς εἰσιὼν αὐτόμολος[10] ἢ
κατάσκοπος, ἐάνπερ ὁ πυλωρὸς ᾖ νοηρός. πᾶν
δὲ ἀνοίγεσθαι[11] ὑποζυγίων ἕνεκεν καὶ ἁμαξῶν καὶ
ἄλλων ἀγωγίμων ἀποτρέπω. εἰ δέ τι τούτων

---

[1] Aeneas: δὲ ἐνί MSS.   [2] Paris. 2441.
[3] After this word the MSS. have τὸ.
[4] Boivin: πνεῖσθαι MSS.   [5] μὲν οὔσης Boivin.
[6] δυσπροσοδώτατον ᾖ later MSS.: others δυσπροσοδότατον ἡ.
[7] Boivin adds εἶναι.   [8] Aeneas: εἰσίν MSS.

even if it be necessary to tear down some one of the buildings that stand in your town, until you can dig your trench inside.

XLVIII. *On the Water-Clock*

A water-clock is a very useful thing for those who are keeping guard at night, according as the nights become longer or shorter, and it is constructed as follows. One should smear the interior of the clock with wax, and then remove some of the wax when the nights grow longer, so that the clock may contain more water. When, on the other hand, the nights grow shorter, more wax should be added in order that the clock's capacity may be less. And its orifice, through which the water for a particular period flows out, must be made with exactness.

XLIX. *On Gates*

When a city is in constant fear precautions must be taken as follows. Close the other gates but leave one open, where access to the city is most difficult, and where those who advance are going to be in plain sight for the longest distance. And in this gate there should be a wicket-gate, so that men may pass through it singly. For in this way anyone, whether deserter or spy, is least able to escape notice if he should enter, if the gate-keeper is sharp-witted. Yet I advise against opening the whole gate for beasts of burden, wagons, and other things that are brought in. But if it shall be necessary to bring

---

⁹ Boivin : λανθάνει MSS.   ¹⁰ Boivin : αὐτόμολις MSS.
¹¹ Aeneas : ἀνύεσθαι MSS.

ἀναγκαίως δεήσει δι' ἁμαξῶν εἰσκομίζεσθαι, σίτου
ἢ οἴνου ἢ ἐλαίου ἢ τῶν τοιούτων τι, σωμάτων
πλήθει ταῦτα εἰσκομίζεσθαι δεῖ προεξιόντος στρατεύματος. τὸ δὲ ὅλον πρᾶγμα πύλας πρωῒ μὴ
ἀνοίγεσθαι, ὀψίτερόν τε μηθένα ἔξω ἀφίεσθαι,
πρὶν ἂν ἐξερευνήσῃ τὰ περὶ τὴν πόλιν. ἔτι τε
μήτε πλοῖα κατ' αὐτὰς ὁρμίζεσθαι, ἀλλὰ ἀποτέρω[1]
(29. 12) χρὴ γὰρ καὶ τοὺς ἑλλιμενιστὰς[2] προσ-
ορμιζομένων πλοίων νυκτὸς ἢ ἡμέρας περὶ τούτων
μὴ[3] ἀδιασκέπτως ἔχειν, ἀλλ' ἐμβαίνοντας[4] ἰδεῖν
αὐτοὺς τὰ ἀγώγιμα, ἐνθυμουμένους ὅτι τούτων
καταμελήσαντες τὰ μεγάλα ἐσφάλησαν.

L. Ὅπλων λάθρᾳ εἰσκομιδή (=Ch. 29. 1-12)

Περὶ τῆς τῶν ὅπλων λάθρᾳ εἰσκομιδῆς ἥτις
ἐστὶν αὕτη ἐκτέθειται[5] τοῖς μὲν παλαιοῖς πολλάκις πεπραγμένη, ἡμῖν δὲ παράδειγμα γινομένη
πρὸς τὸ πράττειν ᾗ[6] θέλομεν, καὶ μὴ πάσχειν ὡς
εἰδότες. εἰ[7] μὲν οὖν ἐστιν ἑορτὴ πάνδημος τοῖς
ἀφ' ἡμῶν ἐκεῖσε προενδημοῦσι ξένοις καὶ προδόταις ὡς εἰς τὸ μέλλον ἡμῖν συμπράττουσιν,
εἰσκομίζεσθαι δεῖ θώρακας λινέους καὶ στολίδας
καὶ περικεφαλαίας ὅπλα κνημῖδας μαχαίρας τόξα[8]
τοξεύματα ἐν κιβωτίοις ὡς φορταγωγοῖς κατεσκευασμένα, ὡς ἱματίων[9] ἐνόντων καὶ ἄλλων
ἀγωγίμων. ἅπερ οἱ ἑλλιμενισταὶ[10] ἀνοίξαντες

---

[1] Aeneas: ἀποτέρων MSS.
[2] Meursius and Cod. Paris. 2437.   [3] Cod. Paris. 2437.
[4] Boivin: ἐμβαίνοντα MSS.   [5] Boivin: ἐκτέθηται MSS.
[6] Boivin: ἢ MSS.   [7] Later MSS.: ἡ older MSS.
[8] Aeneas: τοξότοξεύματα MSS.
[9] Aeneas: ἱμάτιον MSS.   [10] Aeneas: ἐνλιμενισταὶ MSS.

in any of these things in wagons—some grain, or wine, or oil, or such supplies—you should send the army out beforehand, and bring the goods in with a gang of men. In general, the gates must not be opened early in the day, and even later no one should be let out until the region around the city has been reconnoitred. Again, boats are not to be moored at the gates but at a distance. For the revenue officers also must be watchful of vessels which anchor near by, night or day, and they must go on board and personally see the wares, having in mind that men who have neglected these precautions have suffered serious disasters.

L. *Importation of Arms by Stealth*

Concerning the stealthy importation of arms, as to just what it is, this has often been set forth by the old writers, and has become to us a model for accomplishing what we desire, and, through this knowledge, for avoiding mishap. So, if there is a public holiday, there must be brought in for the aliens [1] on our side who have previously established themselves there, and traitors co-operating with us in what is to take place, linen corslets and cloaks and helmets, shields, greaves, short swords, bows, arrows, stowed away in chests like those of merchants, just as if clothing and other merchandise were in them. The revenue officers opening these

---

[1] These may have been mercenaries hired by ' us,' *i.e.*, by the exiled faction which is seeking to regain possession of the city. The original in Aeneas is written from the point of view of the defenders of the town.

AENEAS TACTICUS

καὶ ἰδόντες, ὡς ἱμάτια μόνον τιμήσονται. εἶτ᾽ αὐτὰ[1] εἰσάγεσθαι καὶ τιθέναι πρὸ τῆς ἀγορᾶς· ἐν δὲ ταρσοῖς καὶ ῥίποις[2] καὶ ἱστίοις[3] ἡμιυφαντιαίοις δοράτια καὶ ἀκόντια ἐνειλημένα, ἐν δὲ ἄγγεσιν[4] ἀχύρων πέλται καὶ μικρὰ ἀσπιδίσκια κεκρυμμένα, καὶ τὰ τούτων εὐογκότερα ἐν σαργάναις[5] ἀσταφίδων καὶ σύκων πλήρεσι, ἐγχειρίδια δὲ ἐν ἀμφιφορεῦσι[6] πυρῶν καὶ ἰσχάδων καὶ ἐλαιῶν, τὸν δὲ τῆς ἐπιβουλῆς ἡγεμόνα φρυγάνων ἐν ἐμφορήματι. καὶ εἰ μὲν μὴ γνωσθεῖεν[7] ὑπὸ τῶν ἐν τῇ πόλει, νυκτὸς γινομένης ἀθροίζεσθαι τοὺς ἐπιθησομένους δεῖ[8] καιρῷ ἐν ᾧ οἰκοῦνται οἱ πολῖται. καὶ πρῶτον μὲν λυθήτω[9] τὸ φόρημα διὰ τὸν ἡγεμόνα, ἔπειτα τοὺς ἄλλους τὰ ἄλλα λύσαντας δεῖ λαμβάνειν, καὶ τοὺς ἀμφιφορέας συντρίβειν διὰ τὸ συντόμως ἐπαίρειν· ἀπὸ σημείου τε[10] ἕκαστον προσηκόντως ὁπλίζεσθαι. καὶ τούτων τινὰς ἔχεσθαι πύργων τε καὶ τῶν τοῦ τείχους πυλῶν· καὶ πύργων μὲν διὰ τὸ διὰ σκάλης ἑτέρους ἀναδέχεσθαι, πυλῶν δὲ διὰ τὸ εἰσδέχεσθαι· καὶ τοὺς ἄλλους εἴς τε τὰ ἀρχεῖα[11] καὶ τὰς πολεμίας[12] οἰκίας[13] εἰστρέχειν.[14] εἰ δὲ πρὸ τῆς ἑσπέρας γνωσθεῖεν, τοῦ ἔργου δεῖ παραυτίκα[15] τούτους[16] ἔχεσθαι καθὼς προεδηλώθη· οὐ γὰρ ἄλλως εὖ βουλεύσῃ.

[1] R. Schöne: εἰ ταῦτα MSS.   [2] Aeneas: ῥιπτοῖς MSS.
[3] Köchly and Rüstow in Aeneas: ἱστοῖς MSS.
[4] Aeneas: ἄγεσιν MSS.   [5] Aeneas: σπαργάναις MSS.
[6] ἀμβιβορεῦσι, ἀμφιβορεῦσι MSS.

212

and inspecting them, will appraise them as mere clothing. Then these must be brought in, and set at the edge of the market-place; and also in crates and wicker-frames and wrapped in half-woven sailcloth spears and javelins and, in baskets of chaff, bucklers and small shields concealed, and the things that are smaller than these in baskets full of raisins and figs, as well as daggers in jars of wheat and dried figs and olives, and the leader of the plot in a load of fagots. And if they should not be discovered by the men in the city, then, when night has fallen, those who are to make the attack should be assembled at a time when the citizens are intoxicated. And first of all the load is to be loosened, so as to get the leader, then the others must unpack and take the rest of the things, and smash the jars so as to get the contents quickly, and at a signal each is to arm himself appropriately. And some of these men are to seize the towers and the gates of the wall—the towers so as to take up others by a ladder, and the gates so as to let them in —while the rest should run to the city hall and the houses of their opponents. But if they should be discovered before evening, they must begin at once as already set forth; for any other course would be ill-advised.

---

[7] Editors: ἡ μὲν μὴ ἐγνώσθη MSS. (The text before Boivin had εἰ.)   [8] Boivin: δὴ MSS.
[9] R. Schöne: λυθῇ MSS.   [10] Boivin: σημειοῦται MSS.
[11] Boivin: ἀρχαῖα MSS.   [12] Editors: πολέμου MSS.
[13] Boivin: οἰκείας MSS.   [14] Cod. Paris. 2441.
[15] Boivin: παρ' αὐτὰ MSS.   [16] Editors: τούτου MSS.

AENEAS TACTICUS

LI. Περὶ κρυφίας ἐπιστολῶν εἰσπομπῆς
(=Ch. 31. 4 f.)

Τοῖς κεχρημένοις προδόταις ἀναγκαῖον εἰδέναι
πῶς ἐπιστολὰς δεῖ αὐτοὺς εἰσπέμπειν. ἀπόστελλε
γοῦν οὕτως. πεμπέσθω ἀνὴρ ἐν τῷ φανερῷ
φέρων[1] ἐπιστολήν τινα περὶ ἄλλων πραγμάτων.
τοῦ δὲ πορεύεσθαι μέλλοντος κρυφαίως αὐτοῦ εἰς
τὸ τῶν ὑποδημάτων πέλμα ἐντεθήτω εἰς τὸ
μεταξὺ βιβλίον καὶ καταραπτέσθω· πρὸς δὲ τοὺς
πηλοὺς καὶ τὰ ὕδατα εἰς κασσίτερον ἐληλασμένον[2]
γραφέσθω πρὸς τὸ μὴ ἀφανίζεσθαι ὑπὸ τῶν
ὑδάτων τὰ γράμματα. ἀφικομένου δὲ πρὸς ὃν
δεῖ[3] καὶ ἀναπαυομένου νυκτὸς ἀναλυέτω τὰς
ῥαφὰς τῶν ὑποδημάτων καὶ ἐξελὼν ἀναγνούς τε
καὶ[4] ἄλλα γράψας λάθρᾳ ἀποστελλέτω τὸν ἄνδρα,
ἀνταποστείλας καὶ δούς τι[5] φέρειν φανερῶς· οὕτως
γὰρ οὔτε ἄλλος οὔτε ὁ φέρων εἰδήσει.

LII. Ἕτερον ἄλλο πανουργότερον (=Ch. 31. 16-19)

Ἀστράγαλον εὐμεγέθη δεῖ σε τρυπῆσαι τρυπήματα κδ, ἐξ[6] εἰς ἑκάστην πλευρὰν τοῦ ἀστραγάλου·
ἔστω δὲ τὰ τρυπήματα στοιχεῖα. διαμνημόνευε
δὲ ἀφ᾽ ἧς ἂν πλευρᾶς ἄρξηται τὸ ἄλφα καὶ τὰ
ἐχόμενα ἅπερ ἐν ἑκάστῃ πλευρᾷ γέγραπται. μετὰ
δὲ ταῦτα ὅταν τινὰ θέλῃς ἐν αὐτῷ τίθεσθαι, λίνῳ
δῆσαι. διαιροῦντα[7] δὲ δηλοῦν ἐν τῇ τοῦ λίνου
διέρσει,[8] ἀρξάμενος ἐκ τῆς πλευρᾶς τοῦ ἀστραγάλου, ἐν ᾗ τὸ ἄλφα ἐστί, παρελθὼν τὰ ἐχόμενα

---

[1] Boivin : φανερῶν mss.
[2] Meineke on Aeneas: ἠλασμένον mss.
[3] Later mss.: δὴ earlier mss.   [4] Boivin : τὰ mss.

214

FRAGMENTS

LI. *On the secret Sending of Messages*

Those who employ traitors must know how they should send in messages. Dispatch them, then, like this. Let a man be sent openly bearing some message about other matters. Let the letter be inserted without the knowledge of the bearer in the sole of his sandals and be sewed in, and, to guard against mud and water, have it written on beaten tin so that the writing will not be effaced by the water. And when he reaches the one intended and goes to rest for the night, this person should pull out the stitches of the sandals, take out and read the letter, and, writing another secretly, let him send the man back, having dispatched some reply and having given him something to carry openly. For in this way no one else, not even the messenger, will know the message.

LII. *Yet another shrewder Device*

In a sufficiently large astragal you must bore twenty-four holes, six on each side. Let the holes stand for letters, and note clearly on which side begins Alpha and which of the following letters have been written on each particular side. Then whenever you wish to make some communication by means of it, tie a thread to it. And you are to make clear your differentiation between the letters by the drawing through of the thread, beginning from the side of the astragal on which Alpha is found, omitting the characters placed next to Alpha

---

[5] Boivin: τε MSS. [6] Aeneas: ἐξ ὧν MSS.
[7] Editors: διαιροῦνται MSS.
[8] Casaubon on Aeneas: διαιρέσει MSS.

215

τούτου[1] γράμματα, ὅταν ἔλθῃς εἰς πλευρὰν οὗ τὸ
ἰῶτα γράμμα ἐστί, δίειρον[2] καὶ πάλιν παρεὶς τὰ
ἐχόμενα, ὅπου τὸ νῦ[3] εἶναι συμβαίνει δίειρον,[2]
καὶ οὕτως τὰ τοῦ λόγου ἀντιγραφεῖεν ἂν εἰς τὰ[4]
τρυπήματα. δεήσεται δὲ τὸν ἀναγινώσκοντα ἀναγράφεσθαι εἰς δέλτον τὰ[5] δηλούμενα γράμματα ἐκ
τῶν τρυπημάτων, ἀνάπαλιν γινομένης τῆς ἐξέρ-
σεως[6] τῇ ἐνέρσει.[7]

LIII. Ἕτερα περὶ τούτου παρὰ τῶν παλαιῶν
πραχθέντα (=Ch. 31. 31 f.; 31. 23; 31. 14;
31. 33; 31. 24)

Ἐπέμφθη γράμματά ποτε πολλάκις κατ᾽ Ἤπειρον[8] οὕτως χρησαμένων αὐτῶν. κυνὶ δεσμὸν[9]
τεθεικότες περὶ τὸν αὐχένα ἐνέβαλον τοῦ ἱμάντος
ἔσωθεν ἐπιστολήν, εἶτα[10] νυκτὸς τοῦτον ἀφῆκαν
ἢ μεθ᾽ ἡμέραν πρὸς ὃν ἐξ ἀνάγκης ἤμελλεν ἤξειν,
ὅθεν ἀπηνέχθη. ἔστι δὲ τοῦτο Θετταλόν.

(31. 23) Ἄλλοι τινὲς εἰς βιβλίον γράψαντες ὡς
λεπτότατον μακροὺς στίχους καὶ λεπτὰ γράμματα,
ἵνα εὐογκότατα γένηται, εἶτα[11] ἐπὶ τοῦ ὤμου τοῦ
χιτωνίσκου ὑποθέντες καὶ ἀποπτύξαντες, ἀν-
ύποπτον ἐποίουν τὴν κομιδὴν τῆς ἐπιστολῆς.

(31. 14) Ἄλλοι πάλιν ἐν τῷ τῆς δέλτου ξύλῳ
γράψαντες κηρὸν ἐπέτηξαν καὶ ἄλλα εἰς τὸν κηρὸν
ἔγραψαν. εἶτα ὅταν ἔλθῃ[12] παρ᾽ ὃν δεῖ[13] τὸν κηρὸν

---

[1] Hercher on Aeneas: τοῦ ἰῶτα MSS.
[2] Aeneas: διήρον MSS.
[3] Orelli and Williams on Aeneas: ὅπου εἶναι MSS.
[4] Boivin: ἀντιγράφειεν ἄριστα MSS. (ἀντιγράφει ἐν P[1]).
[5] Aeneas: δέλτα τὸν MSS. [6] Boivin · ἐξισώσεως MSS.
[7] Casaubon on Aeneas: ἐνάρξει MSS.

when you come to the side where the letter Iota is marked, pass the thread through, and again, disregarding the characters following this, pass the thread through where Nu happens to be, and thus the elements of the word would be indicated in the holes. And it will be necessary for the one who is to read the information to write down upon a tablet the characters revealed by the holes, the unthreading taking place in the reverse order to that of the threading.

LIII. *Other Devices for this from the Ancients*

Letters were often sent in Epirus by the employment of the following method. After getting a collar around a dog's neck, they placed inside the strap a letter; then at night or during the daytime they dispatched the dog to the person to whom he was sure to go, that is, to the one from whom he had been brought. And this is a Thessalian custom.

Certain others, by writing long lines with fine characters upon some very thin papyrus, so that they may be as compact as possible, then by placing it on the shoulder under the over-tunic and spreading that out, have caused the letter to be transmitted without suspicion. Others, again, after writing on the wooden part of the tablet, have poured wax over it and written something else on the wax. Then when it came to the appointed person, he, scraping

---

[8] Aeneas: κατήπειρον MSS.

[9] Boivin: δεσμῶν or δεσμῶν MSS.

[10] Added by Boivin.   [11] Aeneas: εἰς τὸν MSS.

[12] Aeneas: ὅτε ἦλθες MSS.   [13] Aeneas: δὴ MSS.

ἐκκνήσας[1] καὶ ἀναγνοὺς ὁμοιοτρόπως ἀνταπέστειλεν. (31. 33) ἐγὼ δὲ τὰς παραγινομένας δέλτους[2] εὐθὺς ἀνοίγειν παραινῶ, (31. 24) διότι τὰ εἰσπεμπόμενα μετὰ ἐπιβουλῆς πάνυ χαλεπὸν φυλάξαι.

LIV. Ὑπορυσσόντων γνῶσις καὶ κώλυσις
(= Ch. 37. 1-4)

Δεῖ τοὺς ὑπορύσσοντας ὧδε κωλύειν. ἐὰν δοκῇ ὑπορύσσεσθαι, ὡς βαθυτάτην[3] χρὴ τὴν ἐκτὸς τάφρον ὀρύσσεσθαι, ὅπως εἰς τὴν τάφρον τὸ ὑπόρυγμα ἀφίκηται καὶ οἱ[4] ὑπορύσσοντες ὀφθῶσιν. ἐὰν δέ σοι ὑπάρχῃ καὶ τειχίον τειχίσαι εἰς αὐτὴν ὡς ἰσχυροτάτων καὶ μεγίστων λίθων.[5] ἐὰν δὲ μὴ ὑπάρχῃ τειχίσαι λίθοις, ξύλων φορυτὸν[6] κόμιζε. ἐὰν δὲ τὰ ὑπορύγματα τῇ τάφρῳ προσπέσῃ, ἐμβάλλων τὸν[7] φορυτὸν ἔμπρησον καὶ τὰ ἄλλα κατασκέπασον, ὅπως ὁ καπνὸς εἰς τὸ διόρυγμα πορεύσηται καὶ κακῶς ποιῇ[8] τοὺς ἐν τῷ ὀρύγματι ὄντας· συμβαίνει γὰρ πολλοὺς ὑπὸ καπνοῦ ἀπολέσθαι. λυμανεῖ δὲ τοὺς ὑπορύσσοντας[9] σφῆκας καὶ μελίσσας ἀφεὶς εἰς τὸ διόρυγμα. χρὴ δὲ καθ' ὃν ἂν ὀρύσσουσι τόπον ἀντορύσσειν καὶ ὑπαντᾶν.

LV. Περὶ τοῦ τοὺς ὑπορύσσοντας μὴ βλάπτεσθαι
(= Ch. 37. 8 f.)

Τοῖς ὑπορύσσειν μέλλουσιν οὕτως ἂν γένοιτο περίφραγμα ἰσχυρώτατον. χρὴ δύο ἁμαξῶν τοὺς

---

[1] Aeneas: ἐκκινήσας mss.
[2] Added by the editors from Aeneas.
[3] Aeneas: βαθὺ mss.   [4] Added from Aeneas.
[5] Aeneas: μεγιστοτάτων mss.   [6] Aeneas: ξυλοφευκτὸν mss.

off the wax and reading the writing, sent back a reply in a similar manner. And I advise that letters be opened as soon as received, because it is very difficult to guard against anything sent in by artifice.

LIV. *Detection and Prevention of Mines*

Those who are constructing mines must be prevented in the following manner. If it appears that a mine is being made you should dig the moat outside the wall as deep as possible, so that the mine may open into the moat and those who are digging it may be exposed to view. And if you have a chance, a wall should also be built in the moat, of the very hardest and largest stones available. But if you have no chance to build a stone wall, bring up logs and rubbish. And if the mines open into the moat, dump the rubbish, set fire to it, and cover the rest over in order that the smoke may penetrate the opening and injure those in the mine, for it happens that many are killed by smoke. And by releasing wasps and bees into the opening one will work mischief with those in the mine. One must, at whatever point the enemy are digging, construct a countermine and oppose them.

LV. *To protect from Injury those who are digging Mines*

For those who are to construct mines a very effective form of protection would be this. One

---

[7] Boivin: ἐμβάλλοντας MSS.   [8] Aeneas: ποιεῖ MSS.
[9] R. Schöne (κατορύσσοντας or ἀντορύσσοντας Boivin): τορύσσον τὰς MSS.

ῥυμοὺς εἰς ταὐτὸ συνδῆσαι, συμπετάσαντα κατὰ
τὸ ἕτερον μέρος τῆς ἁμάξης, ὅπως μετεωρισθῶσιν
οἱ ῥυμοὶ εἰς ταὐτὸ νεύοντες. ἔπειτα οὕτως
ἐπισυνδεῖν ἄλλα ξύλα τοῖς[1] ῥυμοῖς καὶ ἄλλα περι-
φράγματα ἐπάνω, τὰ δὲ πηλῷ καλύψαι. εἴη ἂν
οὖν τοῦτο[2] προσάγειν ὅπου βούλει τοὺς τροχοὺς
καὶ ἀπάγειν,[3] ὑπὸ δὲ τούτῳ τῷ φράγματι τοὺς
ὑπορύσσοντας εἶναι.

LVI. Δολίευμα (=Ch. 39. 1 f.)

Τοὺς πολιορκουμένους οὕτως δεῖ δολιεύεσθαι·
ἐν ταῖς πύλαις εἰς τὸ ἔσω μᾶλλον μέρος ὀρύξαντας
τάφρον ἔνθεν καὶ ἔνθεν πάροδον λιπεῖν καὶ προάγειν τῶν πολεμίων, ὥστε τινας συνδραμεῖν εἰς
τὴν πόλιν. χρὴ γοῦν ἔνθεν καὶ ἔνθεν παρὰ τὰς
λελειμμένας[4] παρόδους εἰστρέχειν. τοὺς δὲ τῶν
πολεμίων συντρέχοντας εἰκός ἐστιν ἐμπεσεῖν μὴ[5]
προειδότας τὴν τάφρον κεκρυμμένης αὐτῆς οὔσης.

LVIa. Ἄλλο δι' οὗπερ ὅσους ἂν θέλωμεν τῶν
πολεμίων κατάσχωμεν (=Ch. 39. 2-4)

Τῶν εἰσερχομένων πολεμίων ὅσους κατέχειν
βουληθῶμεν ἄν, οὕτως[6] ποιήσωμεν. ἐάσωμεν
εἰσιέναι ὅσους ἂν ἡμῖν ᾖ[7] εὐχερὲς κτεῖναι· προ-
ετοιμάσθω δὲ ἄνωθεν ἀπὸ τοῦ μεσοπύλου ἔσω[8]
τῶν πυλῶν πύλη[9] ὡς παχυτάτη· καὶ σεσιδη-

---

[1] Editors : ἴ mss.
[2] Editors : εἴη οὖν τούτους mss. (τοῦτο Boivin).
[3] Boivin : ἐπάγειν mss.   [4] Aeneas : λελημένας mss.
[5] Added from the text of Aeneas.
[6] Editors : οὕτως ἂν mss.   [7] Editors : ἐστὶν mss.

should fasten together the poles of two wagons, having first turned them back each in the direction of the other part of its wagon in such a way that the poles may be raised aloft, inclining toward the same point. Then, when this has been done, one should fasten on to the poles in addition other timbers and sorts of covering above, and cover them over with clay. This device, then, could be advanced and withdrawn on its wheels wherever you desire, and those who are excavating could keep under this protection.

LVI. *A Stratagem*

Those undergoing siege ought to contrive thus. At the gateway and somewhat within it they should dig a trench and leave a passage on this side and on that, and should lure some of the enemy to make a dash into the town with them. Of course they must themselves run in along the passages that have been left on either side. But it is likely that those of the enemy who run in with them, being unaware of the trench, since it is concealed, will fall in.

LVIa. *Another Method by which we may catch as many of the Enemy as we please*

However many of the enemy we may wish to catch as they come in—let us do it in this way. Let us allow to enter as many as it is convenient for us to kill. You should have ready inside, above the centre of the gate, as stout a portcullis as possible,

---

[8] Editors : ἕως MSS.
[9] Added by the editors from Aeneas.

AENEAS TACTICUS

ρῶσθαι αὐτὴν ἢ[1] ὅταν οὐ βούλῃ ὑπολαβεῖν τοὺς
εἰστρέχοντας πολεμίους σχῇ. ταύτην ἄφες ὀρθὴν
καὶ αὕτη τέ τινας ἢ πολλοὺς φερομένους διαφθερεῖ[2]
καὶ τοὺς πολεμίους σχήσει[3] μὴ εἰσιέναι· ἅμα δὲ
καὶ οἱ ἐπὶ τῷ τείχει βαλλέτωσαν πρὸς[4] ταῖς
πύλαις πολεμίους.

LVII. Πῶς δι᾿ ὀλίγων ἀνθρώπων μεγάλης πόλεως
φυλακὴ γενήσεται (= Ch. 40. 1 ; 40. 4 f.)

Ἐὰν ἡ πόλις μεγάλη ᾖ, καὶ μὴ ἱκανοὶ ὦσιν οἱ
ἐν τῇ πόλει ἄνθρωποι περιίστασθαι καὶ κυκλοῦν
τὴν πόλιν, τοῖς δὲ ὑπάρχουσι θέλῃς αὐτὴν διαφυλάξαι, δεῖ τῆς πόλεως ὅσα ἂν ᾖ εὐπρόσοδα οἰκοδομεῖν ὑψηλὰ ἐκ τῶν ὑπαρχόντων, ὡς ἐάν τινες
τῶν πολεμίων βίᾳ ἢ λάθρα ἀναβῶσιν ἐν ἀπειρίᾳ
γινόμενοι μὴ δύνωνται καταπηδᾶν. παρὰ δὲ τὰ
ᾠκοδομημένα[5] ἔνθεν καὶ ἔνθεν φυλασσόντων οἱ
ὑπάρχοντες ἄνθρωποι, ἵνα τοὺς καταπηδῶντας ἀπὸ
τῶν ὑψηλῶν διαφθείρωσιν. (40. 4 f.) ἀλλὰ μὴν
καὶ γυναίων ἐνόντων καὶ γερόντων καὶ παιδαρίων,
τούτων ἐπιεικέστατα σώματα διαμορφοῦν καὶ
ὁπλίζειν ὡς εἰς ἄνδρας μάλιστα. ἀντὶ δὲ ὅπλων
διδόναι τούς τε κάδους[6] καὶ τὰ τούτοις ὁμότροπα
δόντας[7] χαλκώματα περιάγειν τοῦ τείχους, βάλλειν
δὲ ἢ καὶ ἀκοντίζειν μηδαμῶς ἐᾶν· κατάδηλον γὰρ
γύναιον πόρρωθεν βάλλον.[8]

[1] Editors : ὡς καὶ . . . ἢ MSS. (ἢ Boivin).
[2] Capps from Orelli on Aeneas : διαφθείρει MSS.
[3] Added from Aeneas.   [4] Aeneas : πρὸ MSS.
[5] Aeneas : οἰκοδομημένα MSS.

and this should be overlaid with iron, so that when you do not wish to admit the enemy as they run in, it may keep them from entering. Drop this, and the portcullis itself not only will destroy some few or many of them as they sweep in, but also will keep the foe from entering; at the same time let the forces on the wall keep shooting at the enemy by the gate.

LVII. *How a large City can be guarded by a few Men*

If the city is a large one and the men in it are not numerous enough to man its walls all the way around, and yet you wish to keep it closely guarded with the men you have, you must from the materials at hand build up high all the easily assailable parts of the city wall, so that, if any of the enemy shall scale it, either by force or by stealth, from their unfamiliarity they may not be able to leap down. And on either side of the parts that have been built up the available men should keep watch to destroy those who may leap from the high points. Moreover, you should disguise the most able-bodied of the women, old men, and boys that are in the town, and arm them as much like men as you can. And in place of arms give them their jars and similar bronze utensils, and march them around the wall, but do not by any means allow them to throw missiles or yet to hurl a javelin, for even a long way off a female betrays her sex when she tries to throw.

---

[6] Aeneas: κλάδους MSS.   [7] Aeneas: δόντες MSS.
[8] Editors from Aeneas: μᾶλλον MSS.

LVIII. Περὶ τοῦ στρατιώτας ὀλίγους ὄντας
πολλοὺς φαίνεσθαι (= Ch. 40. 6 f.)

Ἐὰν ἐπὶ τῷ τείχει ἢ χάρακι βούλῃ τοὺς περιόδους πλείω τῶν ὄντων φαίνεσθαι, χρὴ περιιέναι
ἐπὶ δύο, ἔχοντας τὰ δόρατα τὸν πρῶτον στίχον ἐπὶ
τῷ ἀριστερῷ ὤμῳ, τὸν δὲ ἕτερον ἐπὶ τῷ δεξιῷ·
καὶ οὕτως φανοῦνται εἰς τέσσαρας. ἐὰν δὲ ἐπὶ[1]
τρία περιῶσι,[2] τὸν μὲν πρῶτον ἄνδρα ἐπὶ τῷ
δεξιῷ ὤμῳ ἔχειν τὸ δόρυ, τὸν δὲ ἕτερον ἐπὶ τῷ
ἀριστερῷ, καὶ οὕτω φανοῦνται εἰς[3] δύο.

[1] Added by Boivin. [2] Later MSS. : περιῶσι earlier MSS.
[3] Aeneas : εἰς MSS.

LVIII. *How Soldiers who are few may appear to be many*

If you wish the patrolmen upon the wall or rampart to appear more numerous than they are, you should make them go their rounds two abreast, the first rank with their spears upon the left shoulder, the other with their spears upon the right, and thus they will appear to be four abreast. And if they go about three abreast, the first man should have his spear upon his right shoulder, the next upon his left, and in this way each man will look like two.

ASCLEPIODOTUS

INTRODUCTION

In a manuscript of the tenth or eleventh century, now at Florence, is found the *Outline of Tactics by Asclepiodotus the Philosopher*. The early date of this manuscript, which is the archetype of all the others which contain this work, can leave little doubt that the name is genuine. When we come, however, to inquire further about the author, we find no certain landmarks. Among the men of that name in antiquity he can be identified, with any degree of probability, only with the Asclepiodotus who is mentioned in five places by Seneca in his *Naturales Quaestiones* as a source for his illustrations, in two of which he is further described as a pupil (*auditor*) of Poseidonius. That he stood in such a relation to the great Stoic is all the more probable since Aelian in the beginning of his work on tactics says that Poseidonius also wrote on the same subject, giving the title of his work as Τέχνη τακτική.[1] We know from

---

[1] This work by Poseidonius must have been in the mind of Philodemus, his younger contemporary, when he raised the question in his Περὶ τοῦ καθ᾽ Ὅμηρον ἀγαθοῦ βασιλέως, p. 33 ed. Olivieri (1909), εἰ δὲ τῷ φιλοσόφῳ πρέπει τὰ περὶ στρατεύματος εὐπρεπῶς καὶ δι᾽ εὐκοσμίας γράφειν. Unfortunately the lines immediately following are so injured that we cannot tell what his answer was. But he proceeds to present the views of Homer on the same subject at some length, and can hardly, therefore, in principle have denied the propriety of a philosopher handling the question.

INTRODUCTION

Seneca that on other subjects, such as earthquakes and volcanic eruptions, Asclepiodotus wrote along the same lines as his master, and he may very well have followed him into the field of military science.

After Aeneas Tacticus, who belongs to the earlier group of military writers, Asclepiodotus, the earliest among the later tacticians, is the first whose work has come down to us. While the former was in all probability a general, or at least a man intimately acquainted with military affairs, in the case of the latter we find that the discussion of tactics has become the subject matter for lectures by philosophers and theorists. Nor is this without good reason. Aeneas wrote in the middle of the fourth century B.C., when the quarrels and battles of Greek states were still the most important political events of the Mediterranean world, and the Greek phalanx was of all battle arrays the most formidable ; Asclepiodotus wrote when no Greek state possessed a military establishment of any power and the cumbersome phalanx had long since bowed before the mobile maniples of Italy. A spirited treatment, therefore, of the old Greek phalanx could hardly be expected. No treatment of the subject, indeed, would have been written at all had not the philosophers in laying claim to all branches of learning included tactics as well.[1] The tramp of the phalanx, that had once

---

The sad experience of the Peripatetic Phormio, who undertook to instruct even Hannibal at the court of Antiochus *de imperatoris officio et de omni re militari*, is reported at length by Cicero, *De oratore*, ii. 75 f.

[1] This seems to have been true, in particular, of Poseidonius, who found the basis of all practical affairs, even of carpentry and bread-making, in philosophy. *Cf.* Seneca, *Epist.* lxxxviii. 21 ff. ; xc. 7 ff.

reverberated among the hills around Thermopylae and Marathon, now echoed feebly in the halls of theorists and rhetoricians.

A corresponding flagging of interest would be expected in the form of the discussion also, and in consequence the style of Asclepiodotus does not cause surprise. There is not a single illustration drawn either from history or from experience ; little effort is made to vary the almost inevitable monotony of a treatise on such a subject ; the sentences are short and stiff, the language unimaginative ; not even an extra sentence is spent upon an introduction. The whole is a dry, but most orderly, exposition of the different branches of the army, their equipment, their number, their manœuvres, etc. So sketchy, indeed, is this little work of twelve chapters, that those who hold that Asclepiodotus merely edited the work of his master, think it the outline of the latter's lectures which he amplified before his class ; and the nature of the treatise to some extent bears out their contention : no historical material to confuse the pupil, everything very clear, the most important facts stressed, diagram and figures employed. It would thus be very similar to the material dictated by the medieval professor to his students, and then lectured upon. In a sense it is a study only of antiquarian interest, as was freely confessed by Aelian in the introduction to his work, a funeral oration upon the past glory of the Grecian Phalanx, although, without the personal interest of the orator, it becomes rather the coroner's stilted verdict on a tragic death.

It would be a mistake, however, to think too lightly of the value of even these late theoretical works upon phalanx tactics. They must consist in large part of quotations from early military handbooks, and these quotations are of the utmost historical value, even though they may be sometimes misunderstood, improperly elaborated, and occasionally treated in too theoretical a fashion. The materials for a reconstruction of Macedonian tactics are after all in a large measure preserved here, and it is the proper task of criticism to understand and interpret them. This attitude which Lammert takes (see Bibliography), in contrast with the occasionally almost supercilious comments of Köchly and Rüstow, is, without a doubt, the proper one to assume towards the later tacticians.

In a papyrus of Herculaneum containing an index of Stoic philosophers there appears a certain Asclepiodotus of Nicaea, son of Asclepiodotus and pupil of Panaetius. Comparetti in his reconstruction of the lines following reads ' who was also a pupil of Poseidonius.' [1] The reading was attractive and was accepted by Gomperz, Diels, and Susemihl, notwithstanding considerable chronological difficulties. For Panaetius died in 110-109 B.C., and the dates of birth and death for Poseidonius are given as 135 (or 130)–51 (or 46) B.C., the earlier date allowing him to be about twenty-five years of age when his teacher died. If Asclepiodotus was the pupil of both Panaetius and Poseidonius, he would have had to be nearly as old as his second teacher, and survive him, writing his edition of his master's *Tactics* after the latter's death at the advanced age of eighty-four. That Asclepiodotus attained such an age is possible, but the attempted identification of the

[1] *Rivista di filologia*, 1875, iii. 543.

pupil of Panaetius with the pupil of Poseidonius will probably have to be given up since Crönert has shown that Comparetti's reconstruction of the text is impossible.[1] The lines, properly restored, merely inform us that the pupil of Panaetius ' also visited Rome,' and so Zeller's insistence upon an older philosopher Asclepiodotus, a pupil of Panaetius, and a younger, a pupil of Poseidonius, is probably justified. It is unlikely that Asclepiodotus was older than his teacher, nor could he have been much younger than twenty-five in 51 (or 46) B.C. when Poseidonius died, since a younger man would scarcely have won the distinction of being one of the three pupils of Poseidonius and have been able to continue his master's work. The date of his birth, therefore, must fall somewhere in the period 135 (or 130)–76 (or 71) B.C.[2]

---

[1] Sitzb. d. k. preuss. Ak. d. Wiss., 1904, 480.

[2] It is not, indeed, impossible for Asclepiodotus to have been a pupil of Panaetius and Posidonius and to have survived the latter, for this was the relation of Philippus of Opus to Socrates and Plato, and Plato lived to be at least eighty years of age. Philippus was Σωκράτους καὶ αὐτοῦ Πλάτωνος ἀκουστής (Suidas), and survived Plato, editing his Laws and adding thereto his own Epinomis (Philologus, 1908, lxvii. pp. 452 ff.). The determining reasons, however, for rejecting the identity of those Asclepiodoti are that Asclepiodotus the pupil of Panaetius being listed immediately after one who died during his master's lifetime, is presumably to be reckoned among the older pupils and not the very youngest (so Crönert); and that in the very brief remarks characterizing the several pupils, surely if this Asclepiodotus had been the pupil also of Poseidonius and edited certain works of his, that circumstance would much more naturally have been selected for purposes of characterization than the trivial fact that he also visited Rome.

INTRODUCTION

Our knowledge, then, of Asclepiodotus, the author of the present work, is limited to the five times Seneca mentions him, and to any inferences we may draw from his *Tactics*. From the latter we may well conclude that he was not a military man, nor even greatly interested in military matters, for a real enthusiasm for one's subject cannot be consistently repressed into such a cold and methodical style ; rather he was a chair-strategist, as Köchly and Rüstow denominate him, although not all their strictures are just. He was rightly termed ' the philosopher,' for certain sections of his work can scarcely be brought down from the heaven of pure theory. So, for instance, his repetition of the advice of ' most tacticians ' that the phalanx consist of 16,384 men, since this number is evenly divisible by two down to unity ; his strong dependence upon mathematical forms and proportions, so that one feels that he is dealing more with numbers than with men, his pedantic divisions of the chariots and elephants,[1] or his elaborations upon the array of an army in march, some of which are obviously impracticable and of use only on the drill-ground.[2]

From the citations in Seneca it appears that he continued the meteorological studies of his teacher. Of the five references, three have to do with phenomena attendant on earthquakes and volcanic eruptions,[3] one with the nature of winds,[4] and the last with the character of subterranean water.[5] All these subjects fall quite properly under the

---

[1] Ch. viii. 10.　　　　　　[2] Ch. xi. 1.
[3] Seneca, *Quaest. nat.* ii. 26. 6 ; 30. 1 ; vi. 22. 2.
[4] *Ibid.* vi. 17. 3.　　　　[5] *Ibid.* v. 15. 1.

title of his work as given by Seneca, *Causes of natural Phenomena*.[1]

The work of Asclepiodotus was drawn upon by the tactician Aelian, who wrote in the time of the Emperor Trajan, to whom he dedicated his discussion of tactics. In connexion with this use by Aelian arises a most interesting question. In his opening chapter, Aelian mentions by name several writers, who had published works in more recent times on tactics, such as Aeneas, Cineas, Pyrrhus of Epirus and his son Alexander, Clearchus, Poseidonius, and others, and acknowledges his indebtedness to many whom he does not name. But he makes no mention of Asclepiodotus who was certainly his main source. K. K. Müller gives two possible explanations for his failure to acknowledge such a debt of obligation.[2] Aelian may include Asclepiodotus under the other writers whom he has read, and intentionally fails, perhaps, to mention his name in order that attention may not be called to the extent of his obligation. Or Asclepiodotus bore a very unusual relation to the work which we have now under his name, a relation well known in antiquity, but obscured in the course of centuries. Because Seneca speaks of Asclepiodotus as if he were the medium through which the teachings of Poseidonius had come to him, and because of parallel instances, Müller feels that Asclepiodotus merely transmitted the work of Poseidonius on tactics, for the knowledge of which Aelian is our only source. Then, as time

---

[1] *Ibid.* vi. 17. 3 . . . id apud Asclepiodotum invenies, auditorem Posidonii, in his ipsis Quaestionum naturalium Causis.

[2] Pauly-Wissowa, *Realencyklop.* ii. 1638.

passed, the relations of the master and of his pupil to this work became increasingly obscure and some attributed it to Poseidonius, others to Asclepiodotus. The manuscript preserved to us would thus have come from the latter group, or else part of the original subscription has been lost.

The question how closely Asclepiodotus followed the lost work of Poseidonius must remain unanswered. The *Tactics* have the appearance as much of an abridgement of a larger work as of an outline for lectures—an abridgement in which the author resolved to strike out everything but the cold facts and succeeded only too well. Neither in this subject nor in his work on meteorology are the titles of the books of Asclepiodotus the same as those of his master's, and, as he is quoted in Seneca, there is something to be said for the view that he may have departed at times perhaps widely from the tradition of his teacher.[1]

The value of the work depends, of course, upon the use and the nature of its sources. The fact that Poseidonius continued in his history the writings of Polybius, makes it highly probable that the latter's work on tactics was drawn upon, and other writers on tactics, mentioned by Aelian, may well have been put under contribution. But the fact that all these earlier treatises have disappeared, coupled with the cursory nature of the work itself, precludes any answer to this most important question. It must be borne in mind, however, that probably Asclepiodotus, and certainly his master Poseidonius, were not intimately acquainted with the arts of war, and that at all times, and perhaps especially in the Hellenistic

[1] *Cf.* E. Oder, *Philologus, Supplb.* vii., 1899, 302 f.

period, works of this nature contained much material which was confined to drill-grounds and never intended for actual employment upon the battle-field.[1]

BIBLIOGRAPHY

A. Bauer: Die griechischen Kriegsaltertümer, in Müller's *Handbuch der klassischen Altertumswissenschaft*, iv. 1 (2nd ed.), 279 f., 287, 422, 425, 450.

W. Capelle: Der Physiker Arrian und Poseidonios, *Hermes*, 1905, xl. 633 f.

W. Capelle: Zur Geschichte der meteorologischen Litteratur, *Hermes*, 1913, xlviii. 344 f.

W. Christ: Griechische Literaturgeschichte, in Müller's *Handbuch der klassischen Altertumswissenschaft*, vii. 2 (6th ed. by Schmid and Stählin), 354, 7.

D. Comparetti: Papiro ercolanese inedito, *Rivista di filologia*, 1875, iii. 543.

W. Crönert: Eine attische Stoikerinschrift, *Sitzb. der k. preuss. Akademie der Wissenschaften*, 1904, 480.

H. Delbrück: Geschichte der Kriegskunst im Rahmen der politischen Geschichte, Berlin, 1901, ii. 1, 200.

H. Delbrück: Die Perserkriege und die Burgunderkriege, Berlin, 1887, 305 ff.

H. Delbrück: Die Manipularlegion und die Schlacht bei Cannae, *Hermes*, 1886, xxi. 64-90, esp. 83 ff.

H. Diels: Doxographi Graeci, Berlin, 1879, 19 and 225.

R. Förster: Studien zu den griechischen Taktikern, *Hermes*, 1877, xii. 431 f.

F. Haase: Ueber die griechischen und lateinischen

[1] The vexed question of the precise relations of Aelian and Arrian to one another and to Asclepiodotus belongs properly in a discussion of the later authors. Both drew largely from Asclepiodotus.

238

INTRODUCTION

Kriegsschriftsteller, *Neue Jahrbücher für Philologie*, 1835, xiv. 115 ff.

F. Haase: De militarium Scriptorum Graecorum et Latinorum omnium Editione instituenda, Berolini, 1847, 8, 27 ff., 32 ff.

Max Jähns: Handbuch einer Geschichte des Kriegswesens, etc., Technischer Teil, Leipzig, 1880, 117 ff.

Max Jähns: Geschichte der Kriegswissenschaften vornehmlich in Deutschland, München und Leipzig, 1889, i. 5 f. ; 67 f. ; 130 ff.

H. Köchly : De Libris tacticis, qui Arriani et Aeliani feruntur, Supplementum, Turici, 1852, 33 ff.

H. Köchly : De Scriptorum militarium Graecorum Codice Bernensi, Diss. Turici, 1854, especially 27.

H. Köchly und W. Rüstow : Griechische Kriegsschriftsteller, Leipzig, 1855 ; i. Introduction, Asclepiodotus, Greek text and translation ; ii. Introduction and critical notes.

E. Lammert : Polybios und die römische Taktik, Program des königlichen Gymnasiums zur Leipzig, 1889, 11 ff., especially 13.

Angelo Mai : Spicilegium Romanum, tomus iv., Romae, 1840. Pages 577-81 contain a reproduction of the first two chapters of the Laurentian MS. as copied by Leo Allatius.

K. K. Müller : Article " Asklepiodotos," Pauly-Wissowa *Realencyclop.* ii. col. 1637-1641.

K. K. Müller : Festschrift für L. Urlichs, Würzburg, 1880, 106 f.

K. K. Müller : Festgabe zur dritten Säcularfeier der Julius-Maximilians - Universität zu Würzburg, Würzburg, 1887, 30 f.

E. Oder : Quellensucher im Altertum, *Philologus, Supplementband*, 1899, vii. 290 ff.

F. Osann : Der Taktiker Asklepiodot, *Zeitschrift für die Altertumswissenschaft*, 1853, xi. 311 ff.

W. Rüstow und H. Köchly : Geschichte des griechischen Kriegswesens von der ältesten Zeit bis auf Pyrrhos, Aarau, 1852.

ASCLEPIODOTUS

R. Schneider : Legion und Phalanx, Berlin, 1893, 70 ff.

S. Sudhaus : Aetna, Leipzig, 1898, 61 f.

Franz Susemihl : Geschichte der griechischen Litteratur in der Alexandrinerzeit, Leipzig, 1892, ii. 144, 244 f.

E. Zeller : Die Philosophie der Griechen in ihrer geschichtlichen Entwicklung, 3rd ed., 1880, iii. 1, 569, 585 ; 4th ed., 1909, iii. 590.

For some other references of minor importance see the detailed list in K. K. Müller's learned and thorough article ' Asklepiodotos,' given above.

EDITION AND MANUSCRIPTS

The only edition of Asclepiodotus is that by H. Köchly and W. Rüstow, Leipzig, 1855 (see Bibliography). It was based upon collations of three Paris MSS., but Köchly had no knowledge of the Florentine MS., from which they are descended, Laurentianus LV 4, a parchment codex of the tenth or eleventh century. The present text represents, therefore, a new recension made from a collation of the text of the Florentine MS. and copies of its diagrams, prepared for this purpose by the accomplished scholar Professor Dr. Enrico Rostagno of the Bibliotheca Mediceo-Laurenziana at Florence, to whom we take this occasion to express publicly our great indebtedness. For a brief discussion of the archetype and its descendants, together with some remarks upon the text of Asclepiodotus, those who seek further information may be referred to an article by W. A. Oldfather in *The Amer. Journ. of Philol.*, 1920, xli. 127 ff.

Suffice it to say here that the variant readings in

INTRODUCTION

the descendants have independent value only as emendations, those in the MS. copied by Salmasius being, of course, the most important in this respect. Mere errors and omissions are, therefore, not recorded. Our knowledge of the first three (A, B, C) of these MSS. we owe to the *apparatus criticus* in Köchly and Rüstow, of the fourth (V) to Mai's reprint which, although employed by Köchly and Rüstow, was newly collated for this edition, and of the last three to specimen photographs of a few folios from the beginning of each (covering the whole of Chapters i, iv-vi, and parts of ii, iii, and vii), these being sufficient to determine the fact that they are practically worthless.

SYMBOLS

F = Cod. Laurentianus LV, 4. s. X-XI.

A = Cod. Parisinus 2522. s. XV.

B = Cod. Parisinus 2435. s. XVI.

C = Cod. Parisinus 2528. s. XVII. This MS. was copied by Salmasius.

D = Cod. Parisinus 2447. s. XVI.

E = Cod. Parisinus Suppl. Gr. s. XVII. This MS. was copied by P. D. Huet at Stockholm in 1642.

V = Copy of the Laurentian MS. by Leo Allatius, in the Bibliotheca Vallicellana at Rome. Chapters i and ii were printed from this MS. by Angelo Mai, *Spicilegium Romanum.* vol. iv (see Bibliography).

ASCLEPIODOTUS

The text of Asclepiodotus may be not infrequently controlled by the works on tactics which are current under the names of Arrian and Aelian. Whether they derive in part directly from Asclepiodotus, or merely employ in large measure the same sources, has not been decided as yet, but in any event they frequently discuss the same topics in very much the same fashion, and they throw light accordingly upon a number of corrupt or lacunose passages.

In the *Lexicon militare* [1] also we possess an important *subsidium* for determining the text. This work of uncertain date, but anterior to the Byzantine period, was drawn in very large part direct from Asclepiodotus, Arrian, and Aelian, numerous passages from whom it repeats *verbatim*, and others with only slight variations. Its quotations from Asclepiodotus, therefore, in so far as they have not themselves become garbled,[2] give the text as it stood several centuries before the time of F. In a score of cases emendations of F supported by the *Lex. mil.* (so designated in the notes) have been introduced into the present edition, while in two other instances the reading in the *Lex. mil.*, as being more easy and natural, may possibly be correct.

In the notes to the translation we have given references to the treatment of the same general topic in Aelian's *Tactics*. Since, in the edition of

---

[1] Best edited by Köchly and Rüstow, *Griech. Kriegsschriftsteller*, ii. 2. Leipzig, 1855, 217 ff. It appears ordinarily as an appendix to the lexicon of Suidas. For a discussion of the sources and the text-critical value of the work see a note by W. A. Oldfather and J. B. Titchener in *Class. Philol.*, 1921, xvi, 74-76.

[2] Thus it gives ἔκτατοι like F, alongside of ἔκτακτοι in § 14 (=Ascl. ii. 9).

Köchly and Rüstow, Arrian's *Tactics* have the same chapter and paragraph enumeration as Aelian's, we have not thought it necessary to add Arrian's name.

THE DIAGRAMS

A notable feature of the great Florentine MS. is its series of diagrams which go back to Asclepiodotus himself, as is clear from the way in which mention is made of them in the body of the text. These have been reproduced in this edition from tracings prepared by Dr. E. Rostagno. In a few instances where the inscriptions in F have faded since the copies A and B were made, the inscriptions in these latter MSS. have been given in the notes. As might be expected in a thousand years or more of copying, a number of demonstrable errors have crept into the diagrams, so that in nearly every instance it has been found necessary to supplement the originals in the text with the reconstructed figures of Köchly and Rüstow in the notes. Even though frequently in one respect or another these diagrams in the MS. are erroneous, it seems desirable to retain them as an indication of the approximate appearance of the work as it left the hand of the author, of the degree to which they have been modified in copying, and of the evidence upon which the revised figures were constructed.

ΑΣΚΛΗΠΙΟΔΟΤΟΥ

ΦΙΛΟΣΟΦΟΥ

ΤΑΚΤΙΚΑ ΚΕΦΑΛΑΙΑ

[1] ζ΄ F.   [2] ΚΟΙΝΗ F.

CHAPTER HEADINGS OF THE TACTICS

OF ASCLEPIODOTUS THE PHILOSOPHER

ΤΕΧΝΗ ΤΑΚΤΙΚΗ

I. Περὶ τῆς φαλάγγων διαφορᾶς

Τῆς τελείας παρασκευῆς πρὸς πόλεμον διττῆς οὔσης, χερσαίας τε καὶ ναυτικῆς, περὶ τῆς χερσαίας τὰ νῦν λεκτέον. ταύτης τοίνυν τὸ μέν ἐστι μάχιμον, τὸ δ' εἰς τὴν τούτου χρείαν ὑπηρετοῦν, οἷον ἰατρῶν καὶ σκευοφόρων καὶ τῶν ὁμοίων.

Τοῦ δὲ μαχίμου τὸ μέν ἐστι πεζόν, τὸ δ' ὀχηματικόν· τὸ μὲν γὰρ ποσὶ χρῆται πρὸς τὴν μάχην, τὸ δ' ἐπί τινος ὀχεῖται.

2 Τοῦ δὲ δὴ πεζοῦ τὸ μέν ἐστιν ὁπλιτῶν σύστημα, τὸ δὲ πελταστῶν, τὸ δὲ τῶν καλουμένων ψιλῶν. τὸ μὲν οὖν τῶν ὁπλιτῶν ἅτε ἐγγύθεν μαχόμενον βαρυτάτῃ κέχρηται σκευῇ—ἀσπίσι τε γὰρ μεγίσταις καὶ θώραξι καὶ ταῖς κνημῖσι σκέπεται—καὶ δόρασι μακροῖς κατὰ τὸν ῥηθησόμενον Μακεδόνιον τρόπον· τὸ δὲ τῶν ψιλῶν τούτοις ἀπ' ἐναντίας κουφοτάτῃ κέχρηται τῇ σκευῇ διὰ τὸ πόρρωθεν βάλλειν, οὔτε προκνημῖσιν οὔτε θώραξι κεκοσμημένον,[1] ἀκοντίοις δὲ καὶ σφενδόναις καὶ ὅλως τοῖς

---

[1] κοσμούμενον V (Leo Allatius).

---

[1] For this use of φάλαγξ as applying to any kind of military fighting force (not recorded in the lexica) see below, ch. i. 4.

246

TACTICS

I. *The different Branches of the Army* [1]

WHEREAS the complete equipment for warfare is of two kinds, namely land and naval forces, we are now to speak of the land force. This, then, consists on the one hand of the fighting men, and on the other of those who serve their needs, as, for example, surgeons, baggage-carriers, and the like.

Of the fighting men, some are infantry, the others mounted ; for some fight on foot, the others on their mounts.

The infantry is divided into the corps of hoplites, the corps of targeteers, and the corps of so-called light infantry (*psiloi*). Now the corps of hoplites, since it fights at close quarters, uses very heavy equipment—for the men are protected by shields of the largest size, cuirasses, and greaves—and long spears of the type which will here be called ' Macedonian.' The corps of the light infantry on the contrary uses the lightest equipment because it shoots from a distance, and is provided with neither greaves nor cuirasses, but with javelins and slings, and in general

Asclep. i. 1=Ael. ii. 1-3 (=Arrian ii. 1-3 in Köchly and Rüstow's parallel column edition, so that references to Aelian below are understood to include Arrian as well).

Asclep. i. 2=Ael. ii. 7-9.

ἐξ ἀποστήματος λεγομένοις τοξεύμασιν.[1] τούτων
δ' ἐν μέσῳ πώς ἐστι τὸ πελταστικὸν σύστημα·
ἥ τε γὰρ πέλτη μικρά τίς ἐστιν ἀσπιδίσκη καὶ
κούφη, τά τε δόρατα πολὺ τῶν ὁπλιτῶν μεγέθει
λειπόμενα.

3 Κατὰ τὰ αὐτὰ δὴ καὶ τῆς ὀχηματικῆς δυνάμεως
τρεῖς 'εἰσι διαφοραί· ἡ μὲν γάρ ἐστιν ἱππική, ἡ
δὲ δι' ἁρμάτων ἐπιτελεῖται, ἡ τρίτη δὲ δι' ἐλε-
φάντων· ἀλλ' ἁρμάτων τε πέρι καὶ ἐλεφάντων
ὡς οὐκ εὐφυῶν εἰς μάχην ὁ λόγος εἰς ὕστερον
ἀναβεβλήσθω· τὴν δὲ[2] ἱππικὴν ὡς πολλὴν καὶ
παρὰ πολλοῖς καιροῖς χρησιμωτέραν[3] ταῖς μάχαις
νῦν διελοῦμεν· ἔστι γὰρ αὐτῆς εἴδη τρία, τὸ μὲν
τὸ[4] ἐγγύθεν μαχόμενον, τὸ δὲ πόρρωθεν, τὸ δὲ
μέσον. καὶ τὸ μὲν ἐγγύθεν ὁμοίως βαρυτάτῃ
κέχρηται σκευῇ, τούς τε[5] ἵππους καὶ τοὺς ἄνδρας
πανταχόθεν θώραξι περισκέπον,[6] μακροῖς μέντοι[7]
χρώμενον καὶ αὐτὸ τοῖς δόρασιν, δι'[8] ὃ καὶ δορα-
τοφόρον τοῦτο καὶ ξυστοφόρον προσαγορεύεται,
ἢ καὶ[9] θυρεοφόρον, ὅτ' ἂν καὶ ἀσπίδας ἔνιοι φορῶσι
παραμήκεις διὰ τὸ συνεπισκέπεσθαι[10] καὶ τὸν
ἵππον. τὸ δὲ πόρρωθεν μαχόμενον τοξοτῶν τε
καὶ Σκυθῶν λέγεται· μέσον δὲ τὸ τῶν καλουμένων ἀκροβολιστῶν, οἳ δὴ τοῖς ἄκροις ἐπικοινω-

---

[1] σφενδόναις καὶ τοξεύμασι καὶ ὅλως ὅπλοις τοῖς ἐξ ἀποστήματος
λεγομένοις K. and R.   [2] γὰρ C (Salmasius).

[3] K. and R.: πολλοῖς καὶ χρησίμως ἐρᾶν F.

[4] K. and R.: μέν τι F: μέντοι ABCV.

[5] μὲν K. and R.: δὲ ABC.

[6] περισκέπων corrected to -έπον F (first hand probably).

[7] μὲν F: δὲ K. and R.   [8] Supplied by Oldfather.

[9] F has καὶ τοῦτο καὶ in the line above and ἢ θυραιοφόρον
here. K. and R. saw that the καὶ belongs after ἤ.

[10] συνεπισκέπτεσθαι F: corrected in V (Leo Allatius).

with those missiles which we call 'long-distance
missiles.' The corps of the targeteers stands in a sense
between these two, for the targe (*pelte*) is a kind of
small, light shield, and their spears are much shorter
than those of the hoplites.

In the same way there are three branches of the
mounted force: the first is cavalry, the second is
furnished with chariots, and the third with elephants;
but let the consideration of chariots and elephants,
since they are not naturally well adapted for fighting
purposes, be deferred to a later time, and we shall
now discuss the cavalry, since it is much employed and
upon many occasions more useful in battles. There
are, then, three branches of the cavalry service: the
first which fights at close quarters, the second which
fights at a distance, and the third which is intermediate. Now the cavalry which fights at close
quarters uses, similarly,[1] a very heavy equipment,
fully protecting both horses and men with defensive
armour, and employing, like the hoplites, long spears,
for which reason this arm of the service is also called
the spear-bearing and the lance-bearing cavalry,
or even the shield-bearing cavalry, when it, sometimes, carries unusually long[2] shields for the purpose
of protecting the mount as well as the rider. The
branch which fights at long range is called both
the archer-cavalry and the Scythian cavalry; and
the intermediate variety, the skirmishers. These
latter are posted on the flanks and do their fighting,

---

[1] That is, like the heavy-armed infantry.

[2] For ἀσπίς used of long shields, as here, compare
Xenophon, *Anab.* i. 8. 9, who says that the Egyptian
γερροφόροι were equipped with ποδήρεσι ξυλίναις ἀσπίσιν (*cf.*
ibid. ii. 1. 6).

Asclep. i. 3=Ael. ii. 11-13.

νοῦντες οἱ μὲν τόξοις, οἱ δὲ ἀκοντίοις μάχονται,
καὶ τῇ ἄλλῃ[1] χρώμενοι σκευῇ οἱ μὲν οὕτως, οἱ
δὲ ἐκείνως· ὧν μὲν ἔνιοι[2] μετὰ τὴν ἀκόντισιν
ἐγγύθεν μάχονται, οὓς ἰδίως ἐλαφροὺς ὀνομάζουσιν·
ὅτ᾽ ἂν δὲ πόρρωθεν ἀκοντίζωσι μόνον, Ταραντίνους.

4   Εἰσὶν οὖν αἱ πᾶσαι τῶν τάξεων διαφοραὶ αἵδε,[3]
ὧν ἑκάστη φάλαγξ προσαγορεύεται περιέχουσα
συστήματα κατὰ ἀριθμὸν ἐπιτήδειον καὶ ἡγεμόνας
αὐτῶν πρὸς τὸ ῥᾳδίως ποιεῖν τὰ παρακελευόμενα
πρὸς τὴν ἐφήμερον γυμνασίαν τε καὶ ἄσκησιν τῆς
πορείας καὶ στρατοπεδεύσεως καὶ παρατάξεως καὶ
πρὸς τοὺς ἐπ᾽ ἀληθείας ἀγῶνας.

II. Περὶ μερῶν τῆς φάλαγγος τῶν ὁπλιτῶν τῆς
τε ὀνομασίας αὐτῶν καὶ τοῦ ἀριθμοῦ

Ἀναγκαῖον δὲ πρῶτον τὴν φάλαγγα καταλοχίσαι·
τοῦτο δέ ἐστι καταμερίσαι εἰς λόχους. ὁ δὲ λόχος
ἐστὶν ἀριθμὸς ἀνδρῶν εἰς σύμμετρα διαιρῶν τὴν
φάλαγγα· σύμμετρα δέ ἐστι τὰ τιθέμενα μέρη, ἃ[4]
μηδὲν τὴν φάλαγγα πρὸς τὴν μάχην λυμαίνεται·[5]
δι᾽ ὃ τὸν ἀριθμὸν τοῦ λόχου οἱ μὲν ὀκτώ, οἱ δὲ

[1] ἄλλῃ (and similarly τῇ and σκευῇ) F: αὐτῇ V (Leo Allatius) K. and R.   [2] ἔνιοι μὲν K. and R.

[3] Added by K. and R.: ὃ D.

[4] C (Salmasius): ἐστι θέμενα τὰ τιθέμενα τὰ μέρη μηδὲν F: ἐστι θέμενα τὰ μέρη ἃ μηδὲν V (Leo Allatius).

[5] λυμαίνηται F.

---

[1] There seems to be no trace in actual practice of this threefold division in the cavalry. The author seems especially fond of such groupings by three, even to the point, one is inclined to suspect, of inventing some. Compare x. 15 and xi. This seems to be a trace of earlier rhetorical training.

[2] i.e., mutually interchangeable.

[3] If the text be sound, and it will be noted that it depends

some with bows and some with javelins, the former using the general equipment of the light cavalry, the others that of the heavy cavalry. Of this intermediate variety some, who in a narrower sense are called the light cavalry, after hurling their javelins fight at close quarters, but when they merely hurl their javelins from a distance, they are called Tarentine cavalry.[1]

These, then, are all the different military forces, each one of which is called a phalanx and includes divisions of a suitable size and officers sufficient in number to put orders into effect easily, both in daily exercises and in service upon the march, in camp, in battle formation, and in actual fighting.

II. *The Subdivisions of the Phalanx of Hoplites, their Names and their Strength*

It is necessary, first of all, to divide the phalanx, that is, to break it up into files. Now a file is a number of men dividing the phalanx into symmetrical[2] units, and by 'symmetrical' I mean those which do not interfere with the fighting efficiency of the phalanx.[3] Accordingly some have formed the file of eight men, others of

in part upon an emendation by Salmasius, the definition of a file is somewhat unsatisfactory. The file, the smallest unit of the phalanx, corresponds in formation to the file in modern armies, except that it was normally of eight to sixteen men, but in actual use to the squad, being the basic tactical unit. The second part of the sentence seems to suggest that any scheme of formation for purposes of marching or manœuvring is to be subordinated to the fighting efficiency of the phalanx as a unit.

Asclep. i. 4＝Ael. iii. **3**.　　　Asclep. ii. 1＝Ael. iv. 1-3.

δέκα, οἱ δὲ δυοκαίδεκα ἀνδρῶν πεποιήκασιν, ἕτεροι
δὲ ἐξκαίδεκα πρὸς τὸ συμμέτρως ἔχειν τὴν
φάλαγγα[1] εἴς τε τὸ διπλασιάσαι πρὸς[2] τὰς ῥηθη-
σομένας χρείας ἐπὶ δύο καὶ τριάκοντα ἄνδρα
καὶ εἰς τὸ συναιρεῖσθαι εἰς ἥμισυ ἐπ᾽ ἄνδρα,
ὀκτώ· οὐδὲν γὰρ ἔμποδον[3] ἔσται τοῖς ὄπισθεν
μαχομένοις ψιλοῖς ἀκοντίζουσιν ἢ σφενδονῶσιν ἢ
καὶ τοξεύουσιν· ὑπερβήσονται γὰρ τὸ τῆς φάλαγγος
βάθος.

2   Ἐκαλεῖτο δὲ ὁ λόχος πάλαι καὶ στίχος καὶ
συνωμοτία[4] καὶ δεκανία,[5] καὶ ὁ μὲν ἄριστος καὶ
ἡγεμὼν τοῦ στίχου λοχαγός, ὁ δὲ ἔσχατος οὐραγός·
ὕστερον δὲ μεταταχθεὶς ὁ στίχος διαφόρους ἔσχεν
τῶν μερῶν ἐπωνυμίας· τό τε γὰρ ἥμισυ ἡμιλόχιον
ὠνόμασται[6] καὶ διμοιρία, τὸ μὲν ὡς πρὸς τὸ τῶν
δεκαὲξ ἀνδρῶν πλῆθος, τὸ δὲ ὡς πρὸς τὸ τῶν
δώδεκα, καὶ ὁ ἡγεμὼν ἡμιλοχίτης καὶ διμοιρίτης,
καὶ τὸ τέταρτον ἐνωμοτία καὶ ἐνωμοτάρχης ὁ
ἡγούμενος.

3   ⟨Ὁ δὲ ἡγούμενος ὠνόμασται καὶ πρωτοστάτης⟩,[7]
ἐπιστάτης δὲ ὁ ἑπόμενος, ὥστε καθ᾽ ὅλον[8] τὸν
στίχον εἶναι πρῶτον[9] πρωτοστάτην,[10] εἶτα ἐπιστά-

---

[1] K. and R. (after C?): τῆς φάλαγγοσ F.
[2] διπλασιάσαι K. and R.: πρὸς C (Salmasius): διπλάσια τὰς
F: διπλασίονα (?) πρὸς C (Salmasius).
[3] γὰρ εμποδον F: δὲ ἔμποδον K. and R.
[4] AC (Salmasius): συνωμετια FB (ὁ in marg.): συνωμοτιὰ
V (Leo Allatius): ἐνωμοτία K. and R.
[5] δεκανια F.
[6] ὠνόμαστο K. and R.
[7] Supplied by K. and R. to fill the evident lacuna.
[8] K. and R. (note): καθόλου F.
[9] Added by K. and R. (note).
[10] πρωτοστατῶν K. and R. (text).

ten, others of twelve, and yet others of sixteen
men, so that the phalanx will be symmetrical both
for doubling the depth of its units, in circumstances
to be described later, so that it may consist of thirty-
two men, and also for reducing it by one-half, *i.e.*, to
eight men ; for thus it will not interfere with the
light infantry who fight in the rear, since, as they
use javelins, slings, or also bows, they will be able
to shoot their missiles over a phalanx of this
depth.[1]

Now the file was formerly called a row, a
synomoty, and a decury, and the best man and the
leader of the row was called the file-leader (*lochagos*),
while the last man was called the file-closer (*ouragos*).
But when later on the row was reorganized its parts
received different names ; for the half is now called
the half-file (*hemilochion*), or the double quarter
(*dimoiria*), the former term being used for a file of
sixteen men, the latter for one of twelve, and the
leader is now called the half-file-leader (*hemi-
lochites*) and the double-quarter-leader (*dimoirites*),
and the quarter is called an enomoty and its leader
an enomotarch.

[The leading man has been given the name of
the front-rank-man (*protostates*)], while the one who
follows him is called the rear-rank-man (*epistates*),
so that in the whole file there comes first a front-
rank-man, then a rear-rank-man, then successively

---

[1] In the classical period down to the innovations of
Epaminondas the battle-line of the Greeks was usually
eight men deep, the Lacedaemonians only extending this
at times to twelve men. Our author's ideal for the depth
of the perfect phalanx is sixteen men.

Asclep. ii. 2 = Ael. v. 1-2.   Asclep. ii. 3 = Ael. v. 4.

τὴν,[1] εἶθ' ἑξῆς πρωτοστάτην, εἶτα ἐπιστάτην, καὶ
τοῦτο παρ' ἕνα μέχρις οὐραγοῦ, καθ' ἃ ὑπογέγραπται·

πρωτοστάτης	λοχαγός	παραστάται
ἐπιστάτης		παραστάται
πρωτοστάτης		παραστάται
ἐπιστάτης		παραστάται
πρωτοστάτης[2]		παραστάται
ἐπιστάτης	οὐραγός	παραστάται

4 Ὅτ' ἂν δὲ λόχῳ λόχος παρατεθῇ, ὥστε λοχαγὸν
λοχαγῷ καὶ οὐραγὸν οὐραγῷ καὶ τοὺς μεταξὺ
τοῖς ὁμοζύγοις παρίστασθαι, συλλοχισμὸς ἔσται
τὸ τοιοῦτον, οἱ δὲ ὁμόζυγοι[3] τῶν λόχων πρωτοστάται ἢ ἐπιστάται διὰ τὸ παραλλήλους[4] ἵστασθαι
παραστάται κεκλήσονται.

5 Ὁ δὲ ἐκ πάντων συλλοχισμὸς φάλαγξ, ἧς[5] τὸ
τῶν λοχαγῶν[6] τάγμα μέτωπον καὶ μῆκος καὶ
πρόσωπον καὶ στόμα καὶ παράταξις καὶ πρωτολοχία
καλεῖται καὶ πρῶτον ζυγόν· ὁ δὲ κατόπιν κείμενος
μετὰ[7] τοῦτον στίχος τῶν ἐπιστατῶν κατὰ μῆκος
τῆς φάλαγγος δεύτερον ζυγόν, καὶ ὁ τούτῳ παράλ-
ληλος ὑπ' αὐτὸν τρίτον, καὶ τέταρτόν ἐστι[8] τὸ ὑπὸ
τοῦτον[9] ζυγὸν καὶ πέμπτον ὡς αὕτως[10] καὶ ἕκτον
καὶ ἑξῆς μέχρις οὐραγοῦ· κοινῶς δὲ πᾶν τὸ μετὰ
τὸ μέτωπον τῆς φάλαγγος βάθος ἐπονομάζεται
καὶ ὁ ἀπὸ λοχαγοῦ ἐπ' οὐραγὸν στίχος κατὰ
βάθος.

[1] ἐπιστατῶν K. and R. (text).   [2] πρωτοστατης F.
[3] *Lex. mil.* 8, quoting this passage. K. and R. : δεσμοζευγοι F.
[4] παρ' ἀλλήλοις *Lex. mil.* K. and R.
[5] καὶ K. and R.   [6] K. and R. : λόχων F.
[7] K. and R. (F ?): παρὰ ABCV.
[8] εἴ τι B : εἰσι A : εἴη V.
[9] τοῦ τὸν F.   [10] αὕτωσ F.

a front-rank-man and a rear-rank-man, and so on, one after the other, until one reaches the file-closer, according to the following diagram :

Front-rank-man (= file-leader)	comrades-in-rank
Rear-rank-man	comrades-in-rank
Front-rank-man	comrades-in-rank
Rear-rank-man	comrades-in-rank
Front-rank-man	comrades-in-rank
Rear-rank-man (= file-closer)	comrades-in-rank

Now when one file is placed beside another, so that file-leader stands beside file-leader, file-closer beside file-closer, and the men in between beside their comrades-in-rank, such an arrangement will be a formation by file (*syllochismos*), and the men of the files forming the same rank, front-rank-men, and rear-rank-men, will be called comrades-in-rank because they stand side by side.

The assembly (*syllochismos*) of all the files constitutes a phalanx, in which the rank of the file-leaders is called the front (*metopon*), the length (*mekos*), the face (*prosopon*), the mouth (*stoma*), the marshalling (*parataxis*), the head of the files (*protolochia*), and the first line (*proton zygon*); and the rank behind this consisting of rear-rank-men running the length of the phalanx, is the second line, and the rank parallel and behind this the third line, and the line behind this is the fourth, and similarly the fifth and the sixth and so on down to the file-closer ; but taken all together everything behind the front of the phalanx is called its depth, and the file, from file-leader to file-closer, is the file in depth.

Asclep. ii. 4 = Ael. vi.   Asclep. ii. 5 = Ael. vii. 1-3.

6 Καὶ οἱ μὲν τούτῳ ἐπ' εὐθείας κείμενοι[2] στοιχεῖν
λέγονται, οἱ δὲ τῷ[3] κατὰ μῆκος στίχῳ ζυγεῖν·
διαιρεθείσης δὲ τῆς φάλαγγος δίχα κατὰ τὸ μῆκος
τὸ μὲν ἥμισυ κέρας προσαγορεύεται δεξιόν τε καὶ
λαιόν, αὕτη δὲ ἡ διχοτομία ὀμφαλός τε καὶ ἀραρός.

7 Ὁπόσον δὲ δεῖ τὸ πλῆθος εἶναι τῆς φάλαγγος
οὐκ εὔλογον διορίζειν· πρὸς γὰρ ἣν ἕκαστος ἔχει
παρασκευὴν τοῦ πλήθους καὶ τὸν ἀριθμὸν διοριστέον,
πλὴν ἐπιτήδειον ἑκάστοτε εἶναι δεῖ πρὸς τοὺς
μετασχηματισμοὺς τῶν ταγμάτων, λέγω δὲ τὰς
συναιρέσεις ἤτ'[4] αὐξήσεις· δι' ὃ τοὺς ἀρτιάκις
ἀρτίους μᾶλλον ἐκλεκτέον ὡς μέχρι μονάδος
διαιρεῖσθαι δυναμένους· καὶ τούς γε πλείονας
τῶν τακτικῶν εὑρήσεις πεποιηκότας τὴν φάλαγγα
τῶν ὁπλιτῶν μυρίων ἑξακισχιλίων τριακοσίων
ὀγδοήκοντα τεσσάρων, ὡς δίχα διαιρουμένην
μέχρι μονάδος, ταύτης δὲ ἡμίσειαν τὴν τῶν ψιλῶν.
ὑποκείσθω δ'[5] οὖν καὶ ἡμῖν τοσούτων ἀνδρῶν
εἶναι τὴν φάλαγγα, τὸν δὲ λόχον ἑκκαίδεκα.

---

[1] The diagram in K. and R. contains 13 in a row.
[2] K. and R. suggest that κείμενοι or ὄντες is to be supplied.
I have introduced the former from κεῖσθαι in *Lex. mil.* § 22.
[3] K. and R. : τὸ F.
[4] K. and R. suggest ἤ.   [5] Om. K. and R.

---

[1] That is, numbers, which when divided by 2 remain
even, as 4, 8, 16, etc.

```
o   o   o   o   o   o   o   o   o   o   o   o rank
o   o   o   o   o   o   o   o   o   o   o   o rank
o   o   o   o   o   o   o   o   o   o   o   o rank
o   o   o   o   o   o   o   o   o   o   o   o last rank
```

And those who stand behind one another in this formation are said to form a file (*stoichein*), but those who stand side by side are said to form a rank (*zygein*). When the phalanx is bisected by a line running from front to rear, one half is called the right wing and the other the left wing, while the point of division is called the navel and the joint.

How great the strength of the phalanx ought to be is not easy to determine, for the strength must be determined in proportion to the number which each commander is able to equip; only the strength must in every instance be suitable to the changes in form of the detachments, I mean the decrease and increase of their depth. Accordingly you should rather select numbers which are evenly divisible by two down to unity,[1] and you will find that most tacticians have made the phalanx to consist of 16,384 hoplites, because this number is divisible by two down to unity, and half that number (*i.e.,* 8192) for the phalanx of the light infantry.[2] So let us also assume that the phalanx will consist of this number of men, and the file of sixteen men.

[1] The number 16,384 represents, of course, only an ideal for tactical convenience and exactness in manœuvres. As an ideal or standard theoretical number it does no harm, since no one would dream of allowing it to interfere with practical considerations.

Asclep. ii. 6 = Ael. xxvi. 1-2 ; vii. 3.   Asclep. ii. 7 = Ael. viii.

8 Ἔσονται δὴ οἱ μὲν δύο λόχοι διλοχία καὶ ὁ ἐπ᾽ αὐτοῖς ἄρχων διλοχίτης, οἱ δὲ τούτων διπλάσιοι τετραρχία καὶ ὁ ἐπ᾽ αὐτοῖς τετράρχης, οἱ δὲ ἔτι[1] τούτων διπλάσιοι τάξις καὶ ὁ ἡγεμὼν ταξίαρχος μὲν πάλαι, νῦν δὲ καὶ ἑκατοντάρχης, οἱ δὲ τῆς τάξεως διπλάσιοι σύνταγμα καὶ ὁ ἐπὶ τούτοις συνταγματάρχης.

9 Τοὺς δὲ ἐκτάκτους[2] τὸ μὲν παλαιὸν ἡ τάξις εἶχεν, ὡς καὶ τοὔνομα σημαίνει, δι᾽ ὅτι τῆς τάξεως ἐξάριθμοι[3] ὑπῆρχον, στρατοκήρυκα, σημειοφόρον,[4] σαλπιγκτήν, ὑπηρέτην, οὐραγόν· τὸν μέν, ὅπως τῇ φωνῇ σημαίνοι τὸ προστατττόμενον, τὸν δὲ σημείῳ, εἰ[5] μὴ φωνῆς κατακούειν ἐνδέχοιτο διὰ θόρυβον, τὸν δὲ τῇ σάλπιγγι, ὁπότε μηδὲ σημεῖον[6] βλέποιεν διὰ κονιορτόν, καὶ τὸν ὑπηρέτην, ὥστε τι παρακομίσαι τῶν εἰς τὴν χρείαν, τόν γε[7] μὴν ἔκτακτον οὐραγὸν πρὸς τὸ ἐπανάγειν τὸν ἀπολειπόμενον ἐν[8] τῇ τάξει. ὀκτὼ γὰρ ἀνδρῶν ὄντος τοῦ λόχου ὀκταλοχία τὸ τετράγωνον ἐποίει σχῆμα, ὅπερ διὰ τὴν πανταχόθεν ἰσότητα μόνον τῶν μερῶν τῆς φάλαγγος ὁμοίως κατακούειν τῶν προστατττομένων δυνάμενον εὐλόγως τάξις ἐπωνό-

---

[1] K. and R. : ἐπὶ F.

[2] C (Salmasius), *Lex. mil.* § 14, K. and R. : ἐκτάτους F.

[3] K. and R. : ἐξ ἀριθμοὶ F : ἐξ ἀρίθμῳ [sic] C (Salmasius) : ἐνάριθμοι V (Leo Allatius).

[4] σαλπιγκτην. ἡμιάφορον F : σημειοφόρον K. and R. I have changed the order of these words to correspond with the sequence in which they are defined below; it is also the order in the *Lex. mil.* § 14.

[5] C (Salmasius), *Lex. mil.* § 14, K. and R. : δ᾽ οηωι ει F.

[6] C (Salmasius), *Lex. mil.* § 14, K. and R.: ὁποτε δ᾽ εμη δ εσημε. ὸν F.   [7] *Lex. mil.* § 14, K. and R.: τόγε F.

[8] ἐπὶ K. and R. : ἐπὶ τὴν τάξιν *Lex. mil.* § 14.

Now two files will form a double-file (*dilochia*) and the officer in command will be a double-file-leader (*dilochites*), and twice this number will be a platoon (*tetrarchia*), and the officer in command a platoon-commander (*tetrarches*), and twice this latter number will be a company (*taxis*), and the officer in command a company-commander (*taxiarchos*), as he used to be called, but nowadays also a captain-of-a-hundred (*hekatontarches*), and twice the number of a company will be a battalion (*syntagma*), and the officer in command a battalion-commander (*syntagmatarches*).[1]

The supernumeraries were formerly attached to the company, as their name (*ektaktoi*)[2] indicates, because they were not included in the number of the company : an army-herald, a signalman, a bugler, an aide, and a file-closer. The first was to pass on the command by a spoken order, the second by a signal, in case the order could not be heard because of the uproar, the third by the bugle, whenever the signal could not be seen for the dust ; the aide was there to fetch whatever was needed, while the supernumerary file-closer was to bring up the straggler to his position in the company. For when the file consisted of eight men, eight files constituted the square, which, alone of all the detachments, by reason of the equal length of the sides of the formation could hear equally well the commands from every quarter and so was properly

---

[1] The file has thus 16, the double-file 32, the half-company 64, the company 128, and the battalion 256.

[2] That is, ' a body of men outside the company ' (*taxis*).

Asclep. ii. 8=Ael. ix. 1-4a.   Asclep. ii. 9=Ael. ix. 4b.

μαστο· διπλασιασθέντος δ' ὕστερον τοῦ λόχου ἡ
συνταξιαρχία[1] τὸ τετράγωνον ἀπετέλεσεν, δι' ἃ[2]
εἰς ταύτην μετῆλθον οἱ ἔκτακτοι.[3]

10 Τὸ διπλάσιον δὲ τοῦ συντάγματος πεντακοσιαρ-
χίαν καὶ τὸν ἐπὶ τούτῳ πεντακοσιάρχην ὠνόμασαν,
τὸ δὲ τούτου διπλάσιον χιλιαρχίαν καὶ τὸν ἡγεμόνα
χιλιάρχην, τὰς δὲ δύο χιλιαρχίας πάλαι μὲν κέρας
καὶ τέλος καὶ τελάρχην τὸν ἡγούμενον, ὕστερον
δὲ μεραρχίαν καὶ μεράρχην· δι' ὃ καὶ τὸ τούτου
διπλάσιον φαλαγγαρχία καὶ νῦν ἔτι καλεῖται, πλὴν
καὶ ἀποτομὴ κέρατος, καὶ ὁ ἡγεμὼν πάλαι μὲν
στρατηγός, νῦν δὲ φαλαγγάρχης· τὸ δὲ τῆς
φαλαγγαρχίας[4] ἤτοι ἀποτομῆς διπλοῦν διφαλαγγία
καὶ κέρας καὶ ὁ ἐπ' αὐτῇ κεράρχης, αὐτὸ δὲ τὸ ἐκ
τῶν δυεῖν κεράτων ἡ φάλαγξ, ἐφ' ᾗ ὁ στρατηγός,
κέρατα ἔχουσα δύο, φαλαγγαρχίας ἤτοι ἀποτομὰς
δ, μεραρχίας[5] η̄, χιλιαρχίας ῑϛ̄,[6] πεντακοσιαρχίας
λβ̄, συνταξιαρχίας ξδ̄, ταξιαρχίας ρκη̄, τετραρχίας
σνϛ̄,[7] διλοχίας φιβ̄,[8] λόχους ᾱκδ̄.

1 K. and R. : συνταξία F (cf. § 10).
2 δι' ὃ K. and R.
3 C (Salmasius), K. and R. : ἔκτατοι F.
4 Lex. mil. § 18, K. and R. : φάλαγγος F.
5 K. and R. (after B and C ?) : δηεραρχίας F.
6 BC (Salmasius), K. and R. : κ̄ F.
7 ϛβϛ̄ (sic) K. and R.
8 ABC (Salmasius) V (Leo Allatius), K. and R. : φιε F
(but φιβ below).

1 Or 'command,' to preserve in the translation the
suggested etymological connexion between τῶν προσταττο-
μένων and τάξις.

called a company;[1] when, however, the file was later doubled, the battalion (*syntaxiarchia*) constituted the square, and, as a consequence, included the supernumeraries.[2]

Two battalions are called a regiment (*pentakosiarchia*), and its commander a colonel (*pentakosiarches*), and two regiments a brigade (*chiliarchia*), and its commander a brigadier-general (*chiliarches*), and two brigades were formerly called a wing and a complement (*telos*), and its leader a complement-commander (*telarches*), but later it was called a division (*merarchia*), and its leader a division-commander (*merarches*) ; two divisions, consequently, are even yet called a corps (*phalangarchia*), as well as a half-wing (*apotome keratos*), and its commander, formerly a general, is now a corps-commander (*phalangarches*) ; when the corps or half-wing is doubled it is a double-corps (*diphalangia*) and wing (*keras*), and its commander a wing-commander (*kerarches*) ; and, finally, the union of the two wings is called the army (*phalanx*), under the command of the general, comprising 2 wings, 4 corps or half-wings, 8 divisions, 16 brigades, 32 regiments, 64 battalions, 128 companies, 256 platoons, 512 double-files, and 1024 files.

[2] The battalion is the real unit of the phalanx, a perfect square of 16 ranks and 16 files. As a square it became the tactical unit for all the quarter-turns, etc., of the phalanx, pivoting on the men at the four corners, and so is the smallest unit to have its own officers outside the ranks. It was known under several names, in Asclepiodotus as *syntagma* and *syntaxiarchia* (ii. 9), in the Anonymus Byzantinus as *tagma*.

Asclep. ii. 10=Ael. ix. 5-10.

$\bar{\beta}^1$ κέρας $\bar{\xi}\bar{\delta}$ συνταξιαρχία

$\bar{\delta}$ ἀποτομή $\bar{\rho}\bar{\kappa}\bar{\eta}$ τάξις

$\bar{\eta}$ μεραρχία $\overline{σν\varsigma}$ τετραχία

$\overline{ι\varsigma}$ χιλιαρχία $\overline{φ ι β}$ διλοχία

$\bar{\lambda}\bar{\beta}$ πεντακοσιαρχία $\overline{α κ δ}$ λόχος

III. Περὶ διατάξεως τῶν ἀνδρῶν καθ' ὅλην τε
τὴν φάλαγγα ἢ² κατὰ τὰ³ μέρη

Διατέτακται δὲ ἥ τε ὅλη φάλαγξ καὶ τὰ μέρη
κατὰ τετράδα, ὥστε τῶν τεσσάρων ἀποτομῶν τὴν
μὲν ἀρίστην κατ' ἀρετὴν τοῦ δεξιοῦ κέρατος τετάχθαι
δεξιάν, τὴν δὲ δευτέραν ἀριστερὰν τοῦ λαιοῦ καὶ
δεξιὰν τὴν τρίτην, τὴν δὲ τετάρτην τοῦ δεξιοῦ
λαιάν. οὕτω γὰρ⁴ διατεταγμένων ἴσον⁵ εἶναι
συμβήσεται κατὰ δύναμιν τὸ δεξιὸν κέρας τῷ
λαιῷ· τὸ γὰρ ὑπὸ πρώτου⁶ καὶ τετάρτου, φασὶ
γεωμέτριοι,⁷ ἴσον ἔσται τῷ ὑπὸ δευτέρου καὶ
τρίτου, ἐὰν τὰ⁸ τέσσαρα ἀνὰ λόγον⁹ ᾖ.

2   Τὸν αὐτὸν δὲ τρόπον καὶ ἑκάστην ἀποτομὴν ἤτοι
φαλαγγαρχίαν διακοσμήσομεν· ἐπεὶ¹⁰ γὰρ ἥμισυ
μὲν αὐτῆς ἐστιν ἡ μεραρχία, τέταρτον δὲ ἡ χιλι-
αρχία· τὴν μὲν ἀρίστην χιλιαρχίαν τῆς δεξιᾶς

---

¹ $\overline{\varsigma}$ F.   ² καὶ K. and R.

³ Om. AC (Salmasius), K. and R.

⁴ δὲ C (Salmasius).

⁵ K. and R. : ἴσην F.

⁶ ABC (Salmasius), K. and R. : πρώτον F.

⁷ γεώμετροι K. and R. If it is necessary to emend I
should prefer γεωμετρικοί or γεωμέτραι.

⁸ Added by Oldfather.

⁹ ἀνάλογα C (Salmasius), K. and R.

¹⁰ καὶ K. and R. in the text, but it would seem from the
note that ἐπεὶ was intended : ἐπὶ C (Salmasius).

2	wings	64	battalions [1]
4	half-wings	128	companies (*taxis*) [2]
8	divisions	256	platoons
16	brigades	512	double-files
32	regiments	1024	files.

III. *The Disposition of the Men both in the entire Army and in its Subdivisions*

The entire army as well as its units is disposed on the basis of a fourfold division, so that of the four half-wings the bravest holds the right of the right wing, the second and third in point of valour the left and right, respectively, of the left wing, and the fourth the left of the right wing. For with the units ordered in this manner the right wing will have the same strength as the left, since, as the geometricians say, the product of the first and the fourth will equal that of the second and third, if the four be proportionate.[3]

In the same way we shall arrange each half-wing or corps ; since, indeed, a half of it is the division and a fourth the brigade ; we shall station the bravest brigade on the right of the right-hand corps, the

---

[1] Called a *syntagma* in ii. 8.

[2] Just above this unit has been called a *taxiarchia*.

[3] There is some point to this arrangement, if one thinks of an arithmetical series, where, *e.g.*, in the series 5, 7, 9, 11, $5+11=7+9$; but the words clearly refer to a geometrical series 2, 4, 8, 16, or a proportion 2 : 4 :: 8 : 16, where $2 \times 16 = 4 \times 8$, although it is difficult to see how one multiplies strength by merely adding together units.

With Asclep. iii. 1-3 *cf.* Ael. x.

μεραρχίας τάξομεν δεξιάν, τὴν δὲ δευτέραν κατ᾽
ἀρετὴν τῆς λαιᾶς ἀριστεράν, δεξιὰν δὲ τὴν[1] τρίτην,
τὴν δὲ ὑπολειπομένην λαιὰν[2] τῆς δεξιᾶς. οὕτω γὰρ
ἰσοσθενήσουσι καὶ αἱ μεραρχίαι.

3 Καὶ τὰς χιλιαρχίας δὲ ὡς αὔτως διαθήσομεν.
καὶ γὰρ τούτων ἥμισυ μέν ἐστιν ἡ πεντακοσιαρχία, τέταρτον δὲ ἡ συνταξιαρχία· οὐκοῦν τὴν
μὲν πρώτην καὶ τετάρτην συνταξιαρχίαν τῇ
δεξιᾷ πεντακοσιαρχίᾳ νεμοῦμεν τὴν πρώτην ἐν
τοῖς δεξιοῖς αὐτῆς μέρισι τιθέντες, δευτέραν δὲ
καὶ τρίτην συνταξιαρχίαν τῇ λαιᾷ πεντακοσιαρχίᾳ προσνεμοῦμεν κατὰ τὸ ἴσον μέρος αὐτῆς
τιθέντες.

4 Τὴν δὲ πάλιν[3] συνταξιαρχίαν ἑκάστην ἥμισυ
μὲν ἔχουσαν τὴν ταξιαρχίαν, τέταρτον δὲ τὴν
τετραρχίαν κατὰ τὸν αὐτὸν λόγον διαθήσομεν,
ὥστε τὰς ἐν αὐτῇ ταξιαρχίας ἰσοσθενεῖν. τὸ δ᾽
ὅμοιον γέγονε καὶ[4] ἐπὶ τῆς τετραρχίας·[5] καὶ
γὰρ ταύτης ἥμισυ μὲν ἡ διλοχία,[6] τέταρτον δὲ ὁ
λόχος.

5 Τὸν μέντοι γε λόχον οὐ κατὰ ταὐτὰ[7] διατάξομεν,
ἀλλὰ τοὺς μὲν πρόσω τῶν ἀνδρῶν κατὰ τὴν ῥώμην,
τοὺς δ᾽ ὀπίσω κατὰ τὴν φρόνησιν διαφέροντας,
αὐτῶν δὲ τῶν πρόσω τοὺς λοχαγοὺς μεγέθει τε
καὶ ῥώμῃ καὶ ἐμπειρίᾳ προὔχοντας[8] τῶν ἄλλων·
τοῦτο γὰρ τὸ ζυγὸν συνέχει τὴν φάλαγγα καὶ

---

[1] C (Salmasius), K. and R. : δεξιάν· τὴν δὲ F.
[2] K. and R. : λιαν F.
[3] K. and R. : δευτέραν πάλιν F.
[4] K. and R. : τῶ καὶ F.
[5] τεταρχίας F.
[6] διχολοχία F.
[7] K. and R. : αὐτὰ F.
[8] προύχοντ(ας) F.

second and third in point of valour on the left and right of the left-hand corps, and the remaining brigade on the left of the right-hand corps ; for thus the several corps will have a uniform strength.

The brigades also we shall order in the same manner, since a half of these is the regiment, and a fourth the battalion. We shall, then, assign the first and fourth battalion to the right-hand regiment, setting the first among its right-hand units, and we shall, further, assign the second and third battalion to the left-hand regiment, disposing them in the regiment on exactly the same principle.

Each battalion also, since it has as its half the company and as its quarter the platoon, will be ordered in like manner, that its companies may have an equal strength. The same arrangement applies also to the platoon. For its half is the double-file, and its quarter the file.[1]

We shall not, however, arrange the file as above, but we shall place the strongest in the front rank and behind them the most intelligent, and of the former the file-leaders shall be those who excel in size, strength, and skill ; because this line of file-leaders binds the phalanx together and is like the

---

[1] Aelian, in the parallel account, follows our author, but arranges the divisions of the army on the basis of the strength of the commanders and not of the men. This is worse than the arrangement proposed by Asclepiodotus, for in practical operations we know of such a distribution of strength only in the largest divisions of the army. It remained for the philosophers to seize upon an arrangement applicable only to large masses and apply it down to the very lowest unit, the file, and, as in Aelian, even down to the individual officers !

With Asclep. iii. 4 *cf.* Ael. x.   Asclep. iii. 5 = Ael. xiii. 1-2.

οἷον τῆς μαχαίρας ἐστὶ τὸ στόμα, ὅθεν καὶ ἀμφιστόμους καλοῦσι τὰς ἀμφοτέρωθεν[1] λοχαγοῖς συν-
εχομένας τάξεις.

6 Δεῖ δὲ καὶ τὸ δεύτερον ζυγὸν μὴ πάνυ χεῖρον
εἶναι, ἵνα πεσόντος τοῦ λοχαγοῦ ὁ παρεδρεύων
προελθὼν εἰς τὸ πρόσω συνέχῃ τὴν φάλαγγα.   οἱ
δὲ οὐραγοὶ οἵ τ' ἐν τοῖς λόχοις καὶ οἱ ἔκτακτοι[2]
συνέσει τῶν ἄλλων διαφερέτωσαν, οἱ μέν, ἵνα τοὺς
ἰδίους κατευθύνωσι λόχους, οἱ δ' ὅπως στοιχῶσί
τε τὰ συντάγματα καὶ ζυγῶσιν ἀλλήλοις τούς τε
λειποτακτοῦντας[3] διὰ δειλίαν εἰς τάξιν ἐπαν-
άγοιεν καὶ ἐν τοῖς συνασπισμοῖς συνεδρεύειν[4]
ἀναγκάζοιεν.

IV. Περὶ διαστημάτων

Τοῦτον δὴ τὸν τρόπον ἐξομοιωθέντων τῷ ὅλῳ
τῶν μορίων ἑξῆς ἂν εἴη ῥητέον περὶ διαστημάτων[5]
κατά τε μῆκος καὶ βάθος· τριττὰ γὰρ ἐξηύρηται[6]
πρὸς τὰς τῶν πολεμίων[7] χρείας, τό τε ἀραιότατον,
καθ' ὃ ἀλλήλων ἀπέχουσι κατά τε μῆκος καὶ
βάθος ἕκαστοι πήχεις τέσσαρας, καὶ τὸ πυκνότατον,
καθ' ὃ συνησπικὼς ἕκαστος ἀπὸ τῶν ἄλλων
πανταχόθεν διέστηκεν πηχυαῖον διάστημα, τό τε

---

[1] K. and R. : ἀμφοτέροθεν F.
[2] C (Salmasius) D, K. and R. : ἔκτατοι F.
[3] λιποτακτοῦντας C (Salmasius).
[4] συνερείδειν K. and R. perhaps rightly ; cf. Polyb. xii.
21. 3.
[5] A (2nd hand), K. and R. : περιδιαστηκασι F.
[6] ἐξεύρηται C (Salmasius) E.
[7] πολεμικῶν K. and R.

cutting edge of the sword, for which reason the companies, when covered on both flanks by file-leaders, are called double-edged (*amphistomoi*).

The second line must also be not much inferior to the first, so that when a file-leader falls his comrade behind may move forward and hold the line together; and the file-closers, both those in the files and those attached to larger units, should be men who surpass the rest in presence of mind, the former to hold their own files straight, the latter to keep the battalions in file and rank with one another besides bringing back to position any who may leave their places through fear, and forcing them to close up in case they lock shields.[1]

IV. *Intervals*

Now that the parts of the army have been brought into due relation with the entire force, we may well speak of the intervals in both length and depth. The needs of warfare have brought forth three systems of intervals: the most open order, in which the men are spaced both in length and depth four cubits apart,[2] the most compact, in which with locked shields each man is a cubit distant on all sides from his comrades, and the intermediate, also

[1] The importance of the ranks of file-leaders and file-closers can scarcely be exaggerated; the former were the first to meet the enemy and in between them and the file-closers were included the less brave.

[2] The cubit may be taken as approximately eighteen inches.

Asclep. iii. 6 = Ael. xiii. 3, 5 ; xi. **3.**
Asclep. iv. 1 = Ael. xi. 1-4.

ASCLEPIODOTUS

μέσον, ὃ καὶ πύκνωσιν ἐπονομάζουσιν, ᾧ διεστήκασι
πανταχόθεν δύο πήχεις ἀπ' ἀλλήλων.

2 Γίνεται δὲ μεταβολὴ κατὰ τὰς χρείας ἔκ τινος
τούτων εἴς τι τῶν λοιπῶν, καὶ ἤτοι κατὰ μῆκος
μόνον, ὃ καὶ ζυγεῖν ἔφαμεν λέγεσθαι, ἢ κατὰ
βάθος, τὸ καὶ στοιχεῖν,[1] ἢ κατ' ἄμφω, ὅπερ ὀνομάζεται κατὰ παραστάτην καὶ ἐπιστάτην.[2]

3 Δοκεῖ δὲ τὸ τετράπηχυ κατὰ φύσιν εἶναι, ὅθεν
οὐδὲ κεῖται ἐπ' αὐτῷ ὄνομα· ἀναγκαῖον δὲ τὸ
δίπηχυ[3] καὶ ἔτι[4] μᾶλλον τὸ πηχυαῖον. τούτων
δὲ τὸ μὲν δίπηχυ κατὰ πύκνωσιν, ἔφην, ἐπωνό-
μασται, τὸ δὲ πηχυαῖον κατὰ[5] συνασπισμόν.
γίνεται δὲ ἡ μὲν πύκνωσις, ὅτ' ἂν ἡμεῖς τοῖς πολεμίοις τὴν φάλαγγα ἐπάγωμεν,[6] ὁ δὲ συνασπισμός, ὅτ' ἂν οἱ πολέμιοι ἡμῖν ἐπάγωνται.

4 Ἐπεὶ οὖν χίλιοι εἴκοσι τέσσαρές εἰσιν οἱ κατὰ
μέτωπον τῆς φάλαγγος ἀφωρισμένοι λοχαγοί,
δῆλον ὅτι τεταγμένοι μὲν ἐφέξουσι πήχεις ἓξ
καὶ ἐνενήκοντα καὶ τετρακισχιλίους, ὅπερ ἐστὶ
στάδια δέκα καὶ πήχεις ἐνενήκοντα ἕξ, πεπυ-
κνωκότες δὲ σταδίους πέντε καὶ πήχεις μῆ,[7]
συνησπικότες δὲ σταδίους δύο καὶ ἥμισυ καὶ

---

[1] Oldfather: τὲ καὶ στοῖχον F. ὅπερ καὶ στοιχεῖν was suggested by K. and R.; possibly ὃ καὶ should be read.
[2] C (Salmasius), K. and R.: καὶ παραστάτην ἐπιστάτην F.
Perhaps one should read καὶ παραστατεῖν καὶ ἐπιστατεῖν.
[3] B (margin) C (Salmasius) E, K. and R.: ὁ πηχυ F.
[4] K. and R.: ἔστι F.
[5] B (margin) DE, K. and R: κα F.
[6] B (margin) E, K. and R.: ἔπωμεν F.
[7] B (margin) C (Salmasius) DE, K. and R.: πήχει· μὴ F.

---

[1] It must be borne in mind that one soldier is included
in the interval, i.e., the distance is from right shoulder to
268

called a 'compact formation,' in which they are distant two cubits from one another on all sides.[1]

As occasion demands a change is made from one of these intervals to one of the others, and this, either in length only, which, as we have noted before, is called forming by rank,[2] or in depth, *i.e.*, forming by file, or in both rank and file, which last is called ' by comrade-in-rank ' and ' by rear-rank-man.'

The interval of four cubits seems to be the natural one and has, therefore, no special name ; the one of two cubits and especially that of one cubit are forced formations. I have stated[3] that of these two spacings the one of two cubits is called ' compact spacing ' and the one of a single cubit ' with locked shields.' The former is used when we are marching the phalanx upon the enemy, the latter when the enemy is marching upon us.

Now since the file-leaders, forming the front of the phalanx, number 1024, it is clear that, drawn up in the most open formation,[4] they will cover 4096 cubits, which is 10 stades and 96 cubits ; in the compact formation, 5 stades and 48 cubits ; and with locked shields 2½ stades and 24 cubits.[5]

---

[1] right shoulder or from breast to breast. The interval of one cubit seems hardly enough, but it was used only in receiving a charge (*cf.* § 3 below) and is the interval of the Swiss pikemen of the fifteenth and sixteenth centuries (*cf.* R. Schneider, *Legion und Phalanx*, 70).

[2] The reference is to ii. 6.

[3] *Cf.* § 1, above.

[4] Τάττω ('draw up') is used here without qualifying phrase, since the formation has no special name (*cf.* § 3 above).

[5] That is, the phalanx of 16,384, drawn up 16 deep, would occupy 2048 yards, 1024 yards, and 512 yards respectively.

Asclep. iv. 2 = Ael. xi. 1-4.   Asclep. iv. 3 = Ael. xi. 5.
  Asclep. iv. 4 = Ael. xi. 6.

πήχεις εἴκοσι τέσσαρας, πρὸς ὃ σε[1] δεήσει καὶ τῶν χωρίων τὰς ἐκλογὰς ποιεῖσθαι.

V. Περὶ ὅπλων ἰδέας[2] τε καὶ συμμετρίας

Τῶν δὲ φάλαγγος ἀσπίδων ἀρίστη ἡ Μακεδονικὴ χαλκῆ ὀκτωπάλαιστος, οὐ λίαν κοίλη· δόρυ δὲ αὖ οὐκ ἔλαττον δεκαπήχεος, ὥστε τὸ προπῖπτον αὐτοῦ εἶναι οὐκ ἔλαττον ἢ ὀκτάπηχυ, οὐ μὴν οὐδὲ μεῖζον ἐτέλεσαν δύο[3] καὶ δέκα πηχέων,[4] ὥστε τὴν πρόπτωσιν εἶναι δεκάπηχυν, ᾧ δὴ καὶ[5] ἡ Μακεδονικὴ φάλαγξ χρωμένη ἐν καταπύκνῳ στάσει ἀνύποιστος εἶναι ἐδόκει[6] τοῖς πολεμίοις. εὔδηλον γάρ, ὅτι τῶν μέχρι τοῦ πέμπτου[7] ζυγοῦ τὰ δόρατα προπίπτει τοῦ μετώπου· οἱ μὲν γὰρ ἐν τῷ δευτέρῳ ζυγῷ πήχεσι δυσὶν ὑποβεβηκότες ὀκτὼ πηχέων[8] τὴν τοῦ μετώπου ποιοῦνται πρόπτωσιν, ἐξ δὲ οἱ ἐν τῷ τρίτῳ ζυγῷ, οἱ δ' ἐν τῷ τετάρτῳ τεσσάρων, δύο δὲ οἱ ἐν τῷ πέμπτῳ, προβεβλημέναι[9] δὲ τοῦ πρώτου ζυγοῦ πέντε σά-
2 ρισσαι.   καὶ Μακεδόνες μὲν[10] οὕτω τῷ στοίχῳ,[11] φασί, τῶν δοράτων οὐ μόνον τῇ ὄψει τοὺς πολεμίους ἐκπλήττουσιν, ἀλλὰ καὶ τῶν λοχαγῶν ἕκαστον

[1] K. and R. (note): οὖσ F.   [2] D: εἰδέας F.
[3] K. and R.: μει ζολατεσ σαν καὶ F: μείζονα θέσαν καὶ C (Salmasius).
[4] πηχέων F. In a strict Atticist one should, of course, accent πήχεων, but F (below, note 8) testifies apparently to πηχέων (πηχαίων), and perhaps K. and R. are right in accenting the word thus.   [5] Om. C (Salmasius).
[6] Added by C (Salmasius) in the margin.
[7] K. and R.: μέχρι πέμπτον F (πέμπτου DE).
[8] πηχαίων F.   [9] K. and R.: προβεβλημένοι F.
[10] K. and R.: πεντε τεσσαρεσ· καὶ βαβυλώνιοι γὰρ οὕτω F:

It will be necessary, therefore, for you to select your terrain with all this in mind.

V. *The Character and appropriate Size of Arms*

The best shield for use in the phalanx is the Macedonian, of bronze, eight palms [1] in diameter, and not too concave; and their spear, moreover, is not shorter than ten cubits, so that the part which projects in front of the rank is to be no less than eight cubits—in no case, however, is it longer than twelve cubits, so as to project ten cubits. Now when the Macedonian phalanx used such a spear in a compact formation it appeared to the enemy irresistible. For it is obvious that the spears of the first five ranks project beyond the front, since the soldiers in the second rank, being two cubits back, extend their spears eight cubits beyond the front, those in the third rank six cubits, those in the fourth rank four cubits, those in the fifth rank two cubits, and so five spears extend beyond the first rank. And the Macedonians, men say, with this line of spears do not merely terrify the enemy by their appearance, but also embolden every file-leader,

---

[1] The ' palm ' may be considered as approximately three inches.

Asclep. v. 1-2 = Ael. xii.; xiv.

πέντε τέσσαρες. καὶ βαβυλώνιοι γὰρ προβεβλημμένα δὲ τοῦ πρώτου ζυγοῦ πέντε σαρίσσα καὶ μακεδόνες μὲν C (Salmasius): K. and R. suggest also the possibility of a lacuna. The ' Babylonians' here are probably due to a bold attempt to emend a dittography of προβεβλημέναι (or ·μένοι as it appears in F).

[11] B (margin) E, K. and R. : τὸν στοῖχον F.

ASCLEPIODOTUS

παραθαρσύνουσι πέντε δυνάμεσι πεφρουρημένον.[1]
οἱ δὲ μετὰ τὸ[2] πέμπτον ζυγόν, εἰ[3] καὶ μὴ τὰς
σαρίσσας[4] προάγουσι τοῦ μετώπου, ἀλλὰ τοῖς
γε σώμασιν ἐπιβρίθοντες ἀνελπιστίαν τοῖς πρωτο-
στάταις φυγῆς παρέχονται. ἔνιοι δὲ τὰς τοῦ
μετώπου προπιπτούσας ἀκμὰς ἐξισοῦσθαι βουλόμενοι τὰ δόρατα τῶν ὀπίσω ζυγῶν αὔξουσιν.

VI. Περὶ ψιλῶν τε καὶ πελταστῶν

Οἱ δὲ ψιλοί τε καὶ πελτασταὶ πρὸς τὰς ἁρμοζούσας
χρείας ὑπὸ τοῦ στρατηγοῦ ταγήσονται τοτὲ μὲν
πρὸ[5] τῆς φάλαγγος, τοτὲ δὲ ὑπὸ τῇ φάλαγγι,
ἄλλοτε δὲ κατὰ δεξιά τε καὶ ἀριστερά· ὀνομάζεται
δὲ τὸ μὲν πρόταξις, τὸ δ' ὑπόταξις, τὸ δὲ προσέν-
ταξις· ἔστι δ' ὅτε καὶ ἐμπλεκόμενοι τῇ φάλαγγι
παρ' ἄνδρα τάττονται· λέγεται[6] δὲ καὶ τοῦτο
παρένταξις, δι' ὅτι ἀνομοίων ἐστὶ παρένθεσις,
οἷον ψιλῶν παρ' ὁπλίτας· τὴν γοῦν τῶν ὁμοίων
παρένθεσιν, οἷον ὁπλιτῶν παρ' ὁπλίτας ἢ ψιλῶν
παρὰ ψιλούς—ῥηθήσεται[7] γὰρ καὶ ἡ τούτων

---

[1] K. and R. suggest πεφραγμένον which appears in the
parallel passage, Aelian, *Tactica*, xiv. 5.
[2] τὸν F.
[3] B (margin) C (Salmasius) D, K. and R. : εἶναι F.
[4] D, K. and R. : τασ σαρισ F (at end of line) : ταῖς σαρίσσαις
B (margin) C (Salmasius) E.
[5] πρὸσ F.
[6] DE, *Lex. mil.* § 28, K. and R. : λέγονται F.
[7] K. and R. suggest εὑρεθήσεται.

---

[1] This includes the file-leader himself.

protected as he is by the strength of five[1]; while
the men in the lines behind the fifth, though they
cannot extend their spears beyond the front of the
phalanx, nevertheless bear forward with their
bodies at all events and deprive their comrades in
the front ranks of any hope of flight. But some,
who wish to bring all the projecting spear-points to
the same distance in front of the line, increase the
length of the spears of the rear ranks.[2]

VI. *Light Infantry and Targeteers*

The light infantry and targeteers will be stationed
by the general as the situation demands, sometimes
before the line of battle, sometimes behind it, and
on other occasions now on the right flank and again
on the left; the first is called van-position (*protaxis*),
the second rear-position (*hypotaxis*), and the third
flank-position (*prosentaxis*).[3] Sometimes they are
incorporated in the phalanx and stationed one
beside each man; and this is called insert-position
(*parentaxis*), because there is an insertion of
different branches of the service, *e.g.*, light infantry
with hoplites; but the incorporation of like arms,
such as hoplites beside hoplites or light infantry
beside light infantry—the reason for this will be

[2] *Cf.* Aelian xiv. 7 and the Scholiast on the *Iliad*, N 130;
but it is very doubtful if this was ever actually done.
[3] The reasons for such positions are clear. The rear-
position was the first in order of development, when the
lighter troops served merely as reserves. Later they
became an offensive weapon for the army.

Asclep. vi. 1 = Ael. vii. 4-5; xv. 1; xxxi.

273

χρεία—, παρένταξιν[1] μὲν οὐκέτι, παρεμβολὴν δὲ
ἐπονομάζουσι.

2 Λόχους μὲν δὴ καὶ οὗτοι τέσσαρας καὶ εἴκοσι
καὶ χιλίους ἕξουσιν, εἰ μέλλουσι συμπαρεκτεί-
νεσθαι τῇ φάλαγγι τῶν ὁπλιτῶν ὑποταττόμενοι,
οὐ μὴν[2] ἀπὸ ἑξκαίδεκα ἀνδρῶν—ἥμισυ γὰρ αὐτῶν
ἐστι τὸ πλῆθος—, ἀλλ᾽ ἐξ ὀκτὼ δηλονότι.

3 Ἔσται δὲ κἀπὶ τούτων τὸ μὲν ἐκ δ[3] λόχων
σύστασις ἔτι δὲ ἐκ δυεῖν συστάσεων[4] πεντηκονταρχία, τὸ δὲ τούτου διπλάσιον ἑκατονταρχία, ἐφ᾽
ἧς ἔσονται οἱ ἔκτακτοι,[5] πέντε τὸν ἀριθμόν,
στρατοκῆρύξ τε καὶ σημειοφόρος καὶ σαλπιγκτής,
ὑπηρέτης τε καὶ οὐραγός· τὸ δὲ τῆς ἑκατονταρχίας
διπλάσιον ⟨ψιλαγία, τὸ δὲ τούτου διπλάσιον
ξεναγία, ἧς τὸ διπλάσιον[6]⟩ σύστρεμμα, τούτου
δὲ τὸ διπλοῦν ἐπιξεναγία, ἧς πάλιν τὸ διπλάσιον
στῖφος, οὗ δὴ συντεθέντος ἡ τῶν ψιλῶν γίνεται
φάλαγξ, ἣν καὶ ἐπίταγμα καλοῦσιν ἔνιοι. ταύτης
δὲ ἔκτακτοι[5] ἄνδρες ὀκτώ, ἐπιξεναγοὶ[7] μὲν τέσσαρες,
συστρεμματάρχαι[8] δὲ οἱ λοιποί.

[1] B (margin) C (Salmasius) E, K. and R.: παρ᾽ ὧν τάξιν F.
[2] C (Salmasius), K. and R.: ὑμῖν F.
[3] *Lex. mil.* § 30, K. and R.: δύο F.
[4] D, K. and R.: συστάσεσι F.
[5] C (Salmasius), K. and R.: ἔκτατοι F.
[6] These bracketed words are supplied by K. and R. from
the corresponding passage in Aelian, *Tactica*, xvi. 3. See
also *Lex. mil.* § 30. In substance they are without doubt
correct and necessary.
[7] K. and R. (*cf.* Aelian, *Tactica*, xvi. 4; *Lex. mil.* § 30):
ξεναγοὶ F.
[8] οἱ συστρ. K. and R. The omission of the article is
attested also by the verbatim quotation in *Lex. mil.* § 30.

discussed later [1]—is not called insert-position, but rather interjection (*parembole*).[2]

Now these light infantry will also have 1024 files, if they are to stand behind the phalanx of the hoplites and extend the same distance, without, however, a depth of sixteen men—for they are only one-half as strong—but obviously of eight men.

With these, also, four files will form a squad (*systasis*), two squads a platoon (*pentekontarchia*), and double the platoon a company (*hekatontarchia*), to which will be attached the supernumeraries, five in number, an army-herald, a signal-man, a bugler, an aide-de-camp, and a file-closer. Two companies will form a battalion (*psilagia*), two of these a regiment (*xenagia*), the double of which will be a brigade (*systremma*), two brigades a division (*epixenagia*), the double of which will form a corps (*stiphos*), and where this is doubled we have the phalanx of light infantry, which some call also a supporting force (*epitagma*). To this are attached eight men as supernumeraries, four of whom are generals and the others brigadier-generals (*systremmatarchai*) [3]

---

[1] *Cf.* x. 17 below.

[2] In the definition of some of these terms Asclepiodotus differs from Aelian.

[3] The importance of the light infantry is not adequately appreciated by Asclepiodotus. With each increase in the depth of the phalanx and, consequently, in its immobility, the light infantry became more necessary, until the Macedonian phalanx was helpless without it.

Asclep. vi. 2 = Ael. xv. 2.   Asclep. vi. 3 = Ael. xvi.

VII. Περὶ τῶν ἱππέων

Οἱ δέ γε ἱππεῖς, ὥσπερ καὶ οἱ ψιλοί, πρὸς τὰς
παρακολουθούσας χρείας τὴν τάξιν λαμβάνουσιν,
καὶ μάλιστα αὐτῶν οἱ ἀκροβολισταί· οὗτοι γὰρ
οἱ ἐπιτηδειότατοι πρὸς τὸ κατάρξαι τραυμάτων
καὶ ἐκκαλέσασθαι πρὸς μάχην καὶ τὰς τάξεις
διαλῦσαι καὶ ἵππον ἀνακρούσασθαι καὶ τόπους
ἀμείνους προκαταλαβεῖν καὶ τοὺς προκατειλημ-
μένους ἀναλαβεῖν[1] καὶ τοὺς ὑπόπτους ἐρευνῆσαι
καὶ ἐνέδρας παρασκευάσαι καὶ τὸ ὅλον προαγωνί-
σασθαί τε καὶ συναγωνίσασθαι· πολλὰ γὰρ δι'
ὀξύτητα καὶ μεγάλα κατεργάζονται περὶ τὰς
μάχας.

2   Τὰς δὲ τάξεις αὐτῶν κατὰ σχῆμα οἱ μὲν τετράγωνον πεποίηνται, οἱ δὲ ἑτερόμηκες, ἄλλοι
δὲ ῥομβοειδές, καὶ ἕτεροι σφηνοειδὲς ἤτοι ἐμβολοειδές. κοινῶς δὲ ἅπαντες εἴλην[2] καλοῦσι τὸ
σύστημα τοῦ σχήματος. τῇ μὲν οὖν ῥομβοειδεῖ
τῶν εἰλῶν δοκοῦσι Θετταλοὶ κεχρῆσθαι πρῶτοι
ἐν ἱππικῇ πολὺ δυνηθέντες, πρός τε τὰς ἀποστροφὰς[3]
καὶ τὰς ἐπιστροφὰς τῶν ἵππων, ὅπως μὴ συν-
ταράττοιντο πρὸς πάσας τὰς πλευρὰς στρέφεσθαι
δυνάμενοι· τοὺς γὰρ ἀρίστους τῶν ἱππέων κατὰ
τὰς πλευρὰς ἔταττον,[4] πάλιν τοὺς ἐξέχοντας
ἀρετῇ κατὰ τὰς γωνίας· ἐκάλουν δὲ τὸν μὲν κατὰ
τὴν πρόσω γωνίαν ἰλάρχην, τὸν δὲ κατὰ τὴν ὀπίσω
οὐραγόν, τοὺς δὲ κατὰ τὴν δεξιὰν καὶ λαιὰν πλαγιοφύλακες.

---

[1] ἀναστεῖλαι K. and R.   [2] εἴλη F.
[3] Oldfather: ἀπορίασ F: ἀναστροφὰς K. and R.
[4] D, K. and R.: ἐλάττων F.

VII. *The Cavalry*

Now the cavalry, like the light infantry, take their positions according to the demands of battle, and especially is this true of the skirmishers ; for these are the most useful to draw first blood, to provoke the enemy to battle, to break their ranks, to repulse the horse, be the first to occupy points of advantage, carry such positions as the enemy have already occupied, reconnoitre terrain that looks suspicious, lay ambuscades, and in general to open and support the struggle ; for by their swift manœuvring they render many valuable services in battle.[1]

Now some order the horsemen in a square, others in an oblong rectangle, others in a rhomboid, and still others in a wedge-like or pointed formation. But all agree in calling the formation of the body a squadron. It appears that the Thessalians [2] were the first to use the rhomboid formation for their squadrons in cavalry fighting, and this with great success both in retreat and in attack, that they might not be thrown into disorder, since they were able to wheel in any direction ; for they placed their crack troopers on the sides and the very best of these at the angles ; and they called the man at the fore angle a squadron-commander (*ilarches*), the one at the rear angle a squadron-closer (*uragos*), and those on the right and left angles flank-guards (*plagiophylakes*).

---

[1] According to Aelian xvii these and other similar services are performed by the light infantry.
[2] Aelian adds that this was under Jason, but thinks that the formation was actually much older, and later attributed to him.

Asclep. vii. 1 = Ael. vii. 4-5. Asclep. vii. 2 = Ael. xviii. 1-3.

ASCLEPIODOTUS

3 Τὰς δ' ἐμβολοειδεῖς Σκύθας ἐξευρεῖν καὶ Θρᾶκας λέγεται, ὕστερον δὲ χρήσασθαι καὶ Μακεδόνας ταύταις, ὡς εὐχρηστοτέραις[1] τῶν τετραγώνων· τὸ γὰρ μέτωπον τῶν ἐμβόλων βραχὺ[2] γινόμενον ὥσπερ κἀπὶ τῶν ῥομβοειδῶν, ὧνπερ ἥμισύ ἐστι τὸ ἐμβολοειδές, ῥάστην ἐποίει τὴν διίππευσιν, μετὰ τοῦ καὶ τοὺς ἡγεμόνας προβεβλῆσθαι τῶν ἄλλων· καὶ τὰς ἀναστροφὰς εὐμαρεστέρας τῶν τετραγώνων ἐπὶ τούτοις γίνεσθαι, πρὸς ἕνα τὸν ἰλάρχην ἀποβλεπόντων ἁπάντων, ὡς καὶ ἐπὶ τῆς τῶν γεράνων πτήσεως γίνεται.

4 Ταῖς δὲ τετραγώνοις Πέρσαι τε καὶ Σικελοὶ καὶ Ἕλληνες ἐχρῶντο διὰ τὸ ἐν τούτοις δύνασθαι ζυγεῖν τε ἅμα καὶ στοιχεῖν τὰς εἴλας. πλὴν Ἕλληνες ἑτερομήκει τῷ πλήθει τὴν εἴλην ἐναλλάττοντες τῇ ὄψει τὸ σχῆμα τετράγωνον ἀπεδίδοσαν. δέκα γὰρ ἐξ κατὰ μῆκος, ὀκτὼ δὲ κατὰ βάθος[3] ἄνδρας ἔταττον, ἀλλ' ἐν διπλασίοις διαστήμασι διὰ τὰ τῶν ἵππων μεγέθη. ἔνιοι δὲ τριπλάσιον τὸ μῆκος τοῦ βάθους κατ' ἀριθμὸν ποιήσαντες τριπλάσιον διάστημα κατὰ βάθος ἀπέδοσαν, ὥστ' εἶναι πάλιν τὸ σχῆμα τετράγωνον, ὀρθότερον οὗτοι διανοηθέντες, οἶμαι· οὐδὲ[4] γὰρ τὸ ἱππικὸν βάθος τῷ πεζῷ τὴν αὐτὴν ὠφέλιαν παρέχει[5] προσερειδόν τε[6] καὶ συνέχον τὴν εἴλην,

[1] χρηστοτέραις C (Salmasius).

[2] σφόδρα ὀξὺ K. and R.; but βραχύ is supported by the parallel passage in Aelian, *Tactica*, xviii. 4, although the recension ascribed to Arrian xviii. 4 reads τὸ μέτωπον ἐς ὀξὺ ἀπολῆγον.

[3] K. and R.: πλάθοσ F.   [4] K. and R.: οὐχ ὅτι F.

[5] K. and R.: οὐ παρέχει F.   [6] προσερειδόν τὲ F.

---

[1] According to Aelian, under Philip.

It is said that the Scythians and Thracians invented the wedge formation, and that later the Macedonians used it,[1] since they considered it more practical than the square formation ; for the front of the wedge formation is narrow, as in the rhomboid, and only one-half as wide, and this made it easiest for them to break through, as well as brought the leaders in front of the rest, while wheeling was thus easier than in the square formation, since all have their eyes fixed on the single squadron-commander, as is the case also in the flight of cranes.[2]

The Persians, Sicilians, and Greeks regularly used the square formation since it can hold the squadrons in both rank and file ; but the Greeks modified the squadron formation by making it an oblong in mass, while giving it to the eye the appearance of a square. For they drew up the riders with a front of sixteen and a depth of eight, but they doubled the interval between the riders[3] because of the length of the horses. And some made the number of men in length three times that of the depth and then tripled the interval in depth, so that it again appeared to be a square, and these, in my opinion, had the better plan ; since the depth of the cavalry unit, provided it is enough to hold the squadron firm and in line, does not have the same importance as in the infantry, rather it may work

[2] Compare the numerous passages on the flight of cranes collected by J. B. Mayor and J. E. B. Mayor in the former's edition of Cicero, *De Natura Deorum*, on ii. 125. See also Greg. Naz. *Orat.* 28. 25 (*Patr. Gr.* 36. 61 A), where the invention is ascribed to Palamedes, and the Schol. of Elias Cretensis (*Patr. Gr.* 36. 788 B).

[3] That is, in the files, as compared with the interval between them in the ranks.

Asclep. vii. 3 = Ael. xviii. 4.   Asclep. vii. 4 = Ael. xviii. 5-9.

ἀλλὰ γὰρ[1] καὶ βλάβην ἐμποιεῖν οἶδε πλείω τῶν
πολεμίων· ἐπιβάλλοντες γὰρ ἀλλήλοις ἐκταράτ-
τουσι τοὺς ἵππους, ὅθεν τετραγώνου μὲν ὄντος
τοῦ[2] ἀριθμοῦ δεήσει τὸ σχῆμα ποιεῖν ἑτερόμηκες,
ἑτερομήκους δὲ ὄντος, ἐὰν δέῃ ποιεῖν τετράγωνον,
τριῶν ἢ τεττάρων ἱπποτῶν[3] εἶναι δεήσει τὸ βάθος
καὶ πρὸς τοῦτό γε τὸ μῆκος ἐξισοῦσθαι.

5 Πλὴν ἔδοξε τὸ ῥομβοειδὲς ἀναγκαιότερον[4] εἶναι
πρὸς τὰς μεταγωγὰς διὰ τὴν πρὸς ἡγεμόνα νεῦσιν,
καὶ δι᾽ ὅτι ὁμοίως τῷ τετραγώνῳ καὶ ζυγεῖν
δύναται καὶ στοιχεῖν, ὅθεν οἱ μὲν οὕτως αὐτὸ
συνέταξαν, ὥστε φροντίσαι τοῦ συναμφοτέρου,
ὅπως ἂν καὶ ζυγῇ καὶ στοιχῇ, οἱ δὲ οὔτε τοῦ
ζυγεῖν οὔτε τοῦ στοιχεῖν ἐφρόντισαν, ἔνιοι δὲ τοῦ
ζυγεῖν, οὐ μέντοι τοῦ στοιχεῖν, ἔνιοι δὲ ἀνάπαλιν.

6 Τοῖς μέντοι ζυγεῖν ἅμα καὶ στοιχεῖν αὐτὸ
προελομένοις τέτακται τὸ μέγιστον[5] ζυγὸν κατὰ
μέσον ἐκ περιττοῦ ἀριθμοῦ οἷον[6] δέκα καὶ ἑνάς,
οἷόν ἐστι τὸ ἐκ τῶν ᾱ ᾱ ἐν τῇ ὑποκειμένῃ δια-
γραφῇ   εἶτ᾽ ἐφ᾽ ἑκάτερα τοῦδε δύο ζυγὰ δυάδι
αὐτοῦ λειπόμενα,[7] πρόσω μὲν ὡς τὸ ἐκ τῶν β̄β̄
συγκείμενον, ὀπίσω δὲ ὡς τὸ ἐκ τῶν γ̄γ̄, ὥσθ᾽
ἕκαστον τῶν β̄ καὶ γ̄ στοιχεῖν ἑκάστῳ τῶν ᾱ πλὴν
τῶν ἄκρων ᾱ καὶ ᾱ· ἔπειτα ἑξῆς μετὰ μὲν τὸ β̄
ζυγὸν τὸ ἐκ τῶν δ̄δ̄ δυάδι αὐτοῦ λειπόμενον, μετὰ
δὲ τὸ γ̄ τὸ[8] ἐκ τῶν ε̄ε̄ καὶ τοῦτο δυάδι τοῦ γ̄
λειπόμενον, ὥστε ἕκαστόν τε τῶν δ̄δ̄ ἑκάστῳ τῶν

---

[1] Om. by K. and R.   [2] Om. C (Salmasius).
[3] ἵππων K. and R.   [4] K. and R. suggest ἐπιτηδειότερον.
[5] K. and R.: μέσον F.   [6] K. and R.: τῶν F.
[7] K. and R.: λιπόμενα F.   [8] Added by K. and R.

---

[1] The idea behind these words is more clearly expressed

more havoc than the enemy themselves, for when the riders run afoul of one another they frighten the horses. Hence, if the number of the cavalry is a square number, they will have to be drawn up in an oblong rectangle, but if the number of men is not a square number and a square must be formed, the depth will have to be fixed at three or four horsemen and the front arranged accordingly.[1]

And yet the rhomboid formation has seemed more necessary for manœuvring because it bears toward a leader and because, like the square, it is capable of both rank and file arrangement, for which reasons some have ordered it with this in mind, namely that attention be paid to both rank and file, others have paid attention to neither rank nor file, some to rank only and not to file, and still others the opposite.

Now by those who prefer to order the squadron by both rank and file the longest line is stationed in the middle, consisting of an odd number such as eleven, designated by the line $a\,a$ in the following diagram; then before and behind this line are two others, each two men less in number, the front $\beta\,\beta$, the rear $\gamma\,\gamma$, ordered so that each man in β and γ is in file with each in a except the two end men in a; then again after the line β there comes the line $\delta\,\delta$, also two less in number, and after the line γ there comes the line $\epsilon\,\epsilon$, and this also is two less than the line γ, so that each man in the line $\delta\,\delta$ is in file with

in Aelian xviii. 9 : " When the number of riders in rank equals the number in file, the number is a square number, but the formation is an oblong rectangle, the depth of which is greater than its length ; but when the formation of the squadron is a square the number of the horsemen in rank is different from that in file."

Asclep. vii. 5=Ael. xix. 1. 3.   Asclep. vii. 6=Ael. xix. 4.

each man in the line $\beta\,\beta$ except the end men, and
each man in the line $\epsilon\,\epsilon$ is in file with each man in
the line $\gamma\,\gamma$ except the last men; then the lines β
and γ will be formed of nine men, and the lines δ
and ϵ of seven men, and in the same manner will be
ordered the lines after these, *i.e.*, the lines $\zeta\,\zeta$ and $\eta\,\eta$
will have five men, and the lines θ and κ three men;
and of the remaining lines of one man each let the
front one λ be a squadron-commander (*ilarches*) and
the rear one μ be a squadron-closer (*uragos*); and
the flank-guards will be the men on the ends of line
α, so that the strength of the entire squadron will
be sixty-one men. The triangle from the middle
line to the squadron-commander is called a ram and
wedge-shaped. The figure follows:

```
              λ
            θ θ θ
          z z z z
        Δ Δ Δ Δ Δ Δ
      B B B B B B B B
    Δ Δ Δ Δ Δ Δ Δ Δ Δ Δ
      Γ Γ Γ Γ Γ Γ Γ Γ Γ
        ϵ ϵ ϵ ϵ ϵ ϵ ϵ
          H H H H H
            K K K
              M
```

Those who prefer to order the squadron by rank
and not by file, make the longest and centre rank
odd in number as above, as $\alpha\,\beta\,\gamma\,\delta\,\epsilon\,\zeta\,\eta$,[1] and then
place, before and behind, ranks one man less in
number, as the ranks $\theta\,\iota\,\kappa\,\lambda\,\mu\,\nu$, so that θ is not in

------

[1] From here on the diagram after § 9 is in mind.

ζυγόν, ὥστε τὸ θ̄ μήτε τῷ ᾱ μήτε τῷ β̄ στοιχεῖν,
ἀλλ᾽ ἐν τῷ μεταξὺ αὐτῶν κεῖσθαι εἰς τοὔμπροσθεν,
ὡς αὕτως δὲ καὶ τῶν β̄γ̄ τὸ ῑ καὶ τῶν γ̄δ̄ τὸ κ̄ καὶ
τὸ λ̄ τῶν δ̄ε̄, τὸ δὲ μ̄ τῶν ε̄ζ̄ καὶ τῶν ξ̄η̄ τὸ ν̄.
οὕτω γὰρ κειμένων οὐδὲ εἷς τῶν ἐν τῷ θ̄ῑκ̄λ̄μ̄ν̄[1]
ζυγῷ οὐδενὶ τῶν ἐν τῷ ᾱβ̄γ̄δ̄ε̄ζ̄η̄ στοιχήσει.
ὁμοίως δὲ καὶ τὸ ξ̄ο̄π̄ρ̄σ̄ ζυγὸν ἔμπροσθεν τοῦ
θ̄ῑκ̄λ̄μ̄ν̄ τάσσουσιν, ὥστε τὸ ξ̄ μήτε τῷ θ̄ μήτε
τῷ ῑ[2] ἐπ᾽ εὐθείας εἶναι, ἀλλ᾽ ἐν τῷ[3] μεταξὺ τόπῳ
καὶ κατὰ τὸ β̄ τοῦ πρώτου ζυγοῦ, καὶ τὸ ο̄ μεταξὺ
τοῦ ῑκ̄[4] ὡς κατὰ τὸ γ̄, καὶ τὸ π̄ μεταξὺ τῶν κ̄λ̄ ὡς
κατὰ τὸ δ̄, τὸ δὲ ρ̄ μεταξὺ τῶν λ̄μ̄ ὡς κατὰ τὸ ε̄,[5]
καὶ τὸ σ̄[6] μεταξὺ τῶν μ̄ν̄ κατὰ τὸ ζ̄.[7]   οὕτω γὰρ
τὸ ξ̄ο̄π̄ρ̄σ̄ ζυγὸν οὐδενὶ τῶν ἐν τῷ παρεδρεύοντι
ζυγῷ στοιχήσει, οἷον τῷ θ̄ῑκ̄λ̄μ̄ν̄, ἀλλὰ τῷ παρ᾽
ἕν,[8] οἷον τῷ ᾱβ̄γ̄δ̄ε̄ζ̄η̄.   ἔσται τοίνυν καὶ τὸ ἑξῆς
ζυγὸν οἷον τὸ τ̄ῡφ̄χ̄ τῷ μὲν πρὸ αὐτοῦ μὴ στοιχοῦν
τῷ ξ̄ο̄π̄ρ̄σ̄,[9] τῷ δὲ παρ᾽ ἕν, οἷον τῷ θ̄ῑκ̄λ̄μ̄ν̄, καὶ τὸ
ψ̄ω̄ϛ̄[10] τῷ[11] μὲν τ̄ῡφ̄χ̄ οὐ στοιχήσει,[12] τῷ δὲ παρὰ
τοῦτο ξ̄ο̄π̄ρ̄σ̄, τὸ δὲ ⳨⳨ οὐ στοιχήσει τῷ ψ̄ω̄ϛ̄,
τῷ δὲ παρὰ τοῦτο τ̄ῡφ̄χ̄.[13]   ὁ δὲ ᾱ ἰλάρχης μεταξὺ
μὲν ἔσται τῶν ⳨⳨,[14] ἐπ᾽ εὐθείας δέ τινι τῶν ἐν
τῷ ψ̄ω̄ϛ̄.[15]   καὶ τούτῳ δὲ τῷ ἐμβόλῳ καὶ τὸν
ὄπισθεν ἴσον τάξαντες συμπληροῦσι τὴν εἴλην, ἧς
ὁ μὲν ᾱ ἔσται ἰλάρχης, οὐραγὸς δὲ ᾱ[16] ὁ ἔσχατος
τῶν δυεῖν ἐμβόλων, οἱ δὲ ᾱη̄[17] πλαγιοφύλακες.
καὶ φανερόν, ὅτι τῆς τοιαύτης εἴλης εἰ καὶ μὴ

---

[1] ῑκ̄λ̄μ̄ν̄ F.   [2] K. and R. : κ̄ F.
[3] K. and R. : ἀλλὰ τῷ F.   [4] K. and R.: ῑ καὶ κ̄ F.
[5] K. and R. : ῑ F.   [6] K. and R. : Γ̄ F.
[7] K. and R. : ξ̄ F.   [8] K. and R. : ἕνα F.
[9] K. and R. added σ̄.

file with either α or β but stands before and between them, and in the same manner ι between β γ, κ between γ δ, λ between δ ε, μ between ε ζ, and ν between ζ η. When the ranks are so ordered not a man in the rank θ ι κ λ μ ν will be in file with a man in the rank α β γ δ ε ζ η. After the same fashion they place the rank ξ ο π ρ σ before the rank θ ι κ λ μ ν, so that ξ is not directly before either θ or ι, but is in their interval and in line with β of the first rank, ο is between ι κ and in line with γ, π is between κ λ and in line with δ, ρ between λ μ and in line with ε, and σ between μ ν and in line with ζ. For by this arrangement the rank ξ ο π ρ σ will not be in file with the nearest rank θ ι κ λ μ ν, but with the second rank α β γ δ ε ζ η. So also the next rank τ υ φ χ will not be in file with the one immediately preceding it ξ ο π ρ σ, but with the second rank θ ι κ λ μ ν, the rank ψ ω ς will not be in file with τ υ φ χ, but with the one beyond it ξ ο π ρ σ, and the rank ↑↑ will not be in file with the rank ψ ω ς, but with the one beyond it τ υ φ χ; and the squadron-commander α will be between ↑↑, and directly before someone in the rank ψ ω ς. Now since they place a wedge behind, exactly like the one in front, they complete the squadron, which will have α as a squadron-commander, α the last man in the two wedges as a squadron-closer, and αη as flank-guards. And it is apparent that in such a squadron, though the

---

[10] K. and R. added ς.   [11] K. and R. : καὶ τῷ F.
[12] C (Salmasius), K. and R. : συστοιχήσει F.
[13] K. and R. : a series of certain emendations for the corrupt παρὰ τοῦτο καὶ το ρ̄ς̄ τῷ παρὰ τὸ ψω̄ς F.
[14] K. and R. : τῷ ↑ς F.   [15] K. and R. : τῷ ψ̄ω̄ F.
[16] Supplied by K. and R.   [17] B (?), K. and R. : λ̄ η̄ F.

τὰ συνεχῆ ζυγὰ στοιχεῖ, ἀλλὰ τὰ ἓν παρ' ἓν
κείμενα.

8 Ἐπεὶ[1] δὲ συνέβη ζυγεῖν μέν, οὐ στοιχεῖν δέ,
τοῦτο ἡμῶν φροντιζόντων, στοιχεῖν λέγεται εἴ
γε μόνως ἐν τῇ τάξει φροντίζομεν πρώτου τοῦ[1]
κατὰ τὸν ἰλάρχην τε καὶ οὐραγὸν στίχου, οἷον
τοῦ ᾱ ω̄ π̄ δ̄ π̄ ω̄ ᾱ καὶ τῶν ἐφ' ἑκάτερα,[2] οἷον ↑ ῡ κ̄ κ̄ ῡ ↑[3]
καὶ ↑ φ̄ λ̄ φ̄ ↑,[4] ἔπειτα τῶν μετὰ τούσδε, οἷον τοῦ
τε ψ̄ ο̄ γ̄ ο̄ ψ̄[5] καὶ τοῦ ς̄ ρ̄ ε̄ ρ̄ ς̄,[6] εἶτα τῶν ἐφεξῆς, τοῦτ'
ἔστι τοῦ τε τ̄ ῑ ῑ τ̄[7] καὶ τοῦ χ̄ μ̄ μ̄ χ̄,[8] καὶ τῶν μετὰ
τούτους ξ̄ β̄ β̄ ξ̄[9] καὶ σ̄ ζ̄ σ̄, καὶ ἔτι τῶν παρὰ τούτους
τοῦ[10] τε θ̄ θ̄ καὶ τοῦ ν̄ ν̄ καὶ τελευταίων τῶν κατὰ
τοὺς πλαγιοφύλακες, καὶ[11] οὐδὲν μὲν διοίσει κατὰ
τὴν θέσιν τοῦ ζυγοῦντος[12] μέν, μὴ στοιχοῦντος δέ,
τῇ δ' ἡμετέρᾳ λήψει τῆς τάξεως καὶ τῇ φροντίδι
στοιχήσει μέν, δι' ὅτι οἱ τεταγμένοι κατὰ στοῖχον
ἀλλήλους συνέχουσιν, οὐ ζυγήσει δέ, ὅτι ὁ πρῶτος
τοῦ πρώτου στοίχου, οἷον ὁ ᾱ, τῷ τοῦ δευτέρου
πρώτῳ, οἷον τῷ ↑[13], οὐκ ἐπ' εὐθείας ἐστὶν κατὰ
τὸ ζυγεῖν.[14]

9 Ἀλλὰ[15] καὶ ὅσοι μήτε ζυγεῖν μήτε στοιχεῖν
μᾶλλον τὴν εἴλην προὐθυμήθησαν, ἄλλον τρόπον
εἰς ταύτην ἐπήνεσαν τὴν θέσιν.[15] τάσσουσι γὰρ

---

[1] The tentative restoration of this extremely corrupt
passage follows the lines marked out by K. and R., with
some simplifications. ἐπειδὴ συνέβημεν οὐ τοῦτο δὲ ἡμῶν
φροντιζόντων ζυγεῖν λέγεται μόνως ἔν γε (εἰ δὲ C) ἐν τῇ τάξει
φροντίζομεν τοῦ F: ἐπεὶ δὲ συνέβη ζυγεῖν μέν, οὐ στοιχεῖν δὲ τοῦτο
ἡμῶν φροντιζόντων, οὐ ζυγεῖν λέγεται μέν, στοιχεῖν δέ, εἴ γε μόνον
ἐν τῇ τάξει φροντίζομεν πρώτου τοῦ K. and R.
[2] ἑκατέρα F: ἑκατέρᾳ AC (Salmasius).
[3] K. and R.: ζ γ̄ κ̄ γ̄ς F.   [4] K. and R.: ↑ φ̄ λ̄ φ̄ ↑ F.
[5] K. and R.: ψ̄ ο̄ ϝ̄ ψ̄ F.   [6] K. and R.: ς̄ ρ̄ ε̄ ς̄ F.

successive ranks are not in file, the alternate ones are.

Though, when considered in the foregoing manner, the squadron happens to be ordered by ranks and not by files, it is still said to be in file formation, if only we regard the formation of the first file from squadron-commander to squadron-closer, namely the file α ω π δ π ω α, and those on each side of it, namely ↑υκκυ↑ and ↑φλλφ↑, then the following files ψογοψ and ϛρεριϛ, further the next in order τιιτ and χμμχ, then the next ξβξ and σζσ, the successive ones θθ and νν, and finally the flank-guards. Now such a formation will in no way differ from that called the ordering by rank and not by file, and yet in our apprehension and conception of the ordering it will be by file, because the men are contiguous in file, but it will not be by rank, since the first man in the first file, namely α, is not directly before the first man in the second file, namely ↑, by rank.

But those who wish to draw up the squadron neither by rank nor by file, prefer another arrangement for this formation; for they first station as a

Asclep. vii. 8 = Ael. xix. 11.   Asclep. vii. 9 = Ael. xix. 6-10.

---

[7] τοῦ τε ͞τ͞ι͞ι͞τ added by K. and R. after C (Salmasius), which has δέ (for τε).

[8] C (Salmasius), K. and R.: ἔστιν καὶ τοῦ ͞χ͞μ͞μ͞χ F.

[9] ͞ξ͞β͞ζ F, K. and R. (misprint).

[10] K. and R.: τῶν F.   [11] Added by K. and R.

[12] ζυγῶντος F.   [13] K. and R.: ͞ζ F.

[14] The last three words are added by K. and R. (from C?).

[15] K. and R., following in the main C (Salmasius), which, however, has μηδὲ στοιχεῖν . . . προθυμηθησαν . . . ἐπήνεσαν θέσιν: F has ὅσοι μή τε στοιχεῖν μὴ δὲ ζυγεῖν κατὰ τὸ τὸ ζυγὸν ἄλλον τρόπον μᾶλλον τὴν εἴλην προθυμηθεῖσαν εἰς ταύτην ἐπαινησον τὴν θέσιν.

πρῶτον τῆς εἴλης[1] πρόσωπον καὶ οἷον ζυγὸν τὰς
εἰς τοὔμπροσθεν δύο πλευρὰς τοῦ ῥομβοειδοῦς,
οἷον ā θ̄ ξ̄ τ̄ ψ̄ ↑ ā ↑ ⌐ χ̄ σ̄ ν̄ η̄,[2] λαβδοειδὲς[3] σχῆμα, εἶθ'
ἑξῆς ὑπὸ τοῦτο δυάδι αὐτοῦ λειπόμενον τὸ θ̄ β̄ ῑ ō ῡ ω̄
φ̄ ρ̄ μ̄ ζ̄ ν̄, εἶτα ξ̄ ῑ γ̄ κ̄ π̄ λ̄ ε̄ μ̄ σ̄[4] δυάδι καὶ τοῦτο τοῦ
πρὸ αὐτοῦ λειπόμενον,[5] ζυγαρχοῦντος τοῦ ἐν τῇ
κατὰ τὸ μέσον γωνίᾳ, οἷον τῶν ā ω̄ π̄, ἑξῆς δὲ
τούτῳ τὸ τ̄ ō κ̄ δ̄ λ̄ ρ̄ χ̄[6], οὗ ζυγάρχης ὁ δ̄,[7] καὶ ὑπὸ
τοῦτο τὸ[8] ψ̄ ῡ π̄ φ̄ ς̄, ὑφ' ὃ τὸ ↑ ω̄ ↑,[9] καὶ ἔσχατος
οὐραγὸς ὁ ā. φανερὸν οὖν ὅτι θέσει μὲν οὐδὲν
διοίσει τῶν προτέρων, λήψει δὲ μόνον, ὡς ἐκ τῆς
ὑπογραφῆς δῆλον ἔσται.

10 Τάττουσι δὲ τὰς εἴλας, ὥσπερ καὶ τὰ ψιλά,
τοτὲ μὲν πρὸ τῆς φάλαγγος,[10] τοτὲ δὲ ὑπὸ τῇ φά-

---

[1] εἴλησ F.   [2] K. and R.: ā θ̄ ξ̄ τ̄ ψ̄ς α ↑ ς χ̄ c ν̄ η̄ F.
[3] B (margin) C (Salmasius): λαβοειδὲσ F.
[4] K. and R.: θ̄ ʋ̄ ῑ ō ν̄ ω̄ φ̄ ρ̄ μ̄ ζ̄ ν̄ π̄ λ̄ ι μ ο F.
[5] K. and R.: λιπόμενον F.
[6] K. and R. (who read, however, σ̄ τ instead of τ̄ ō):
ζυγαρχοῦντοσ κἀν τῷ δεκατηγωνίαν οἷον τὸ π̄ ἑξῆς δὲ τούτῳ τὸ
κ̄ δ̄ λ̄ ρ̄ χ̄ F (τὸ ō τ̄ κ̄ δ̄ λ̄ ρ̄ χ̄ C).   [7] ō ā F.

288

face and a kind of rank of the squadron the opposite sides of the rhomboid α θ ξ τ ψ ↑ ↑ α ↑ ϛ χ σ ν η, like the letter Λ, then, in order, the line two men less in number θ β ι ο υ ω φ ρ μ ζ ν, then the line ξ ι γ κ π λ ε μ σ also two men less than the one before it, with the man at the centre corner leading each line, *i.e.*, the men α ω π; then the line τ ο κ δ λ ρ χ whose leader is δ, then the line ψ υ π φ ϛ, behind it ↑ ω ↑, and last a squadron-closer α. It is clear, then, that such an arrangement will not differ from the former ones save in conception only, as will be evident from the diagram.[1]

The cavalry force is stationed, like the light infantry, sometimes before the phalanx, sometimes

[1] After one has observed the great care with which our author dwells upon these different formations, man by man, rank by rank, file by file, he is rather surprised to find that they differ only in the way one looks at them—that, in fact, paragraphs 7-9 are to be taken in a Pickwickian sense.

Asclep. vii. 10=Ael. xx. 1.

[8] Supplied by K. and R.   [9] K. and R. : ϛ ῶ↑F.
[10] After φάλαγγος F has the dittography τότε δὲ ὑπὸ τῆς φάλαγγοσ · τότε δὲ ὑπὸ τῇ φάλαγγι.

289

λαγγι, ἄλλοτε δ' ἐκ πλαγίων, ὅθεν καὶ τούτων τὸ
πλῆθος φάλαγγα μὲν οὐ καλοῦσιν, ἐπίταγμα δέ,
ὥσπερ καὶ τὸ τῶν ψιλῶν, δι' ὅτι ἐπὶ τῇ φάλαγγι
τάττονται[1] πρὸς τὰς παρακαλούσας αὐτὴν χρείας.

1 Τὰς μὲν οὖν δύο εἴλας ἐπιλαρχίαν ὠνόμασαν,
τὰς δὲ δύο ἐπιλαρχίας Ταραντιναρχίαν,[2] τὰς δὲ
δύο Ταραντιναρχίας[2] ἱππαρχίαν, τὰς δὲ δύο ἱππαρ-
χίας ἐφιππαρχίαν, τὸ δὲ διπλοῦν τῆς ἐφιππαρχίας
τέλος ἀνάλογον τῷ κέρατι τῆς φάλαγγος. ἀπὸ
γοῦν τῶν δύο τελῶν τὸ ὅλον ἐπίταγμα γίνεται
ἀνάλογον τῇ φάλαγγι.

VIII. Περὶ ἁρμάτων

Τῶν δὲ ἁρμάτων καὶ ἐλεφάντων εἰ καὶ τὴν
χρῆσιν σπανίζουσαν εὑρίσκομεν, ἀλλ' ὅμως πρὸς
τὸ τέλειον τῆς γραφῆς τὰς ὀνομασίας ἐκθησόμεθα.
καλουσι τοίνυν τὰ μὲν δύο ἅρματα ζυγαρχίαν, τὰς
δὲ δύο ζυγαρχίας συζυγίαν, δύο δὲ συζυγίας
ἐπισυζυγίαν, δύο δὲ ἐπισυζυγίας ἁρματαρχίαν,
καὶ τὸ ἐκ τῶν[3] ἁρματαρχιῶν κέρας, οὗ τὸ διπλάσιον φάλαγγα. πλείοσι δὲ φάλαγξι ἁρμάτων
χρώμενον[4] ἔξεστι ταῖς αὐταῖς ὀνομασίαις συγκε-
χρῆσθαι.[5] ἔστι δὲ τῶν ἁρμάτων τὰ μὲν ψιλά,
τὰ δὲ δρεπανηφόρα κατὰ τοὺς ἄξονας.

IX. Περὶ ἐλεφάντων

Ἐπὶ δὲ τῶν ἐλεφάντων ὁ μὲν ἑνὸς ἐλέφαντος
ἄρχων ζώαρχος ὀνομάζεται, ὁ δὲ δυεῖν θήραρχος

---

[1] K. and R. : τάττειν F.
[2] K. and R. (from Arrian and Ael. *Tact.* xx. 2; *Lex. mil.* § 32):
ταραντιαρχίαν and -τιαρχίας F.　　　　[3] δυοῖν K. and R.

behind it, and at other times on the flanks, for which reason this arm of the service is called a supporting force (*epitagma*), as in the case of the light infantry, and not a phalanx, because it is attached to the phalanx according as need for it arises.

Now two squadrons are called a battalion (*epilarchia*), two battalions a Tarentine regiment (*Tarantinarchia*), two Tarentine regiments a brigade (*hipparchia*), two brigades a division (*ephipparchia*), and the double of the division a complement (*telos*), corresponding to the wing of the phalanx. The two complements form the entire supporting force (*epitagma*), corresponding to the phalanx.[1]

VIII. *Chariots*

Although we rarely find any use for chariots and elephants, we shall, nevertheless, set forth their nomenclature to complete this discussion. Two chariots are called a pair (*zygarchia*), two pairs a double-pair (*syzygia*), two double-pairs a chariot-unit (*episyzygia*), two chariot-units a chariot-line (*harmatarchia*), two chariot-lines a wing (*keras*), and the double of this a phalanx. If several phalanxes of chariots are to be used, the same nomenclature may be employed. Some of the chariots have no offensive weapons, while others carry scythes on the axles.

IX. *Elephants*

In the branch of the elephants the leader of a single elephant is called an animal-commander

[1] That is, the phalanx of light infantry (*cf.* vi. 3).
Asclep. vii. 11 = Ael. xx. 2.   Asclep. viii = Ael. xxii.
Asclep. ix = Ael. xxiii.

---

[4] χρωμένῳ K. and R.   [5] συνκεχρῆσθαι F.

καὶ τὸ σύστημα θηραρχία, ὁ δὲ τεσσάρων ἐπιθήραρχος καὶ ἐπιθηραρχία τὸ σύστημα, ὁ δὲ τῶν
ὀκτὼ ἰλάρχης, τῶν δὲ ἑξκαίδεκα ἐλεφαντάρχης,
κεράρχης δὲ ὁ τῶν δύο καὶ τριάκοντα, ὁ δὲ τῶν
διπλασιόνων φαλαγγάρχης, καὶ ὁμωνύμως τὸ
σύστημα καθ᾽ ἑκάστην ἀρχὴν κεκλήσεται.

X. Περὶ τῶν κατὰ τὴν κίνησιν ὀνομασιῶν

Τὰ μὲν οὖν εἴδη τῆς τελείας δυνάμεως καὶ τὰ
ὀνόματα τῶν ἐν αὐτῇ ταγμάτων εἴρηται· ἑξῆς
δὲ περὶ τῶν ὀνομάτων ἀκόλουθον λέγειν, οἷς
χρώμενοι μεταρρυθμίζουσιν[1] οἱ στρατηγοὶ τὰς
φάλαγγας· φασὶ γὰρ τὸ μέν τι κλίσιν[2] ἐπὶ δόρυ
ἢ ἐπ᾽ ἀσπίδα, τὸ δὲ μεταβολὴν καὶ ἐπιστροφήν,
ἄλλο καὶ ἀναστροφήν, ἕτερον καὶ περισπασμὸν[3]
καὶ ἐκπερισπασμόν, ἀποκατάστασίν τε καὶ ἐπι-
καταστάσιν, στοιχεῖν τε καὶ ζυγεῖν[4] καὶ εἰς ὀρθὸν
ἀποδοῦναι καὶ ἐξελίσσειν[5] καὶ διπλασιάζειν· φασὶ
δέ τι καὶ ἐπαγωγὴν καὶ παραγωγὴν δεξιὰν ἢ
λαιὰν καὶ[6] πλαγίαν φάλαγγα καὶ ὀρθίαν καὶ λοξήν,
καὶ παρεμβολὴν καὶ παρένθεσιν, πρόταξίν[7] τε καὶ

[1] K. and R. write with one ρ and so apparently F.
[2] K. and R.: κλῆσιν F.
[3] Added by K. and R. from Arrian and Aelian, *Tactica*,
xxiv. 2 (*cf.* § 7 below): ἕτερον καὶ ἐκπερισπασμὸν F.
[4] These four words are omitted by K. and R. but
supported by the parallel passage in Arrian and Aelian,
Tactica, xxiv. 2; *cf.* ch. x. § 11 below, last note.
[5] K. and R.: ἐξελεῖν F.
[6] K. and R.: καὶ κατὰ F (but *cf.* Arrian and Aelian, *l.c.*,
§ 3, and § 21 below).
[7] K. and R.: ταξιν F.

(*zoarchos*), the commander of two a beast-commander (*therarchos*) and his command a beast-unit (*therarchia*), the commander of four a top-beast-commander (*epitherarchos*) and his command a top-beast-unit (*epitherarchia*), the commander of eight a troop-commander (*ilarches*), of sixteen an elephant-commander (*elephantarches*), of thirty-two a wing-commander (*kerarches*), and of double this number a phalanx-commander (*phalangarches*); corresponding names will be given to each unit.[1]

X. *The Terms used for military Evolutions*

The different branches of the entire army and the names of its lesser divisions have now been given; it remains to consider in turn the terms used by the commanders in manœuvring the divisions of the phalanx. For they use first 'right-' or 'left-face' (*klisis*), then 'about-face' (*metabole*) and 'quarter-turn' (*epistrophe*), also 'back-turn' (*anastrophe*), further 'half-turn' (*perispasmos*) and 'three-quarter-turn' (*ekperispasmos*) and 'return-to-original-position' (*apokatastasis*) and 'advance-to-original-position' (*epikatastasis*), 'order files' (*stoichein*) and 'order ranks' (*zygein*), also 'lines front' (*eis orthon apodunai*) and 'counter-march' (*exeligmos*) and 'doubling' (*diplasiasmos*); they use also 'march-in-column' (*epagoge*) and 'march-in-line' (*paragoge*), and these either 'to the right' or 'to the left,' 'extended front,' 'column formation,' and 'oblique front' (*plagia, orthia, loxe phalanx*), 'interjection' (*parembole*) and 'insertion' (*parenthesis*), and

---

[1] It is very doubtful if such terms as these were known outside the class-rooms of the philosophic strategists.

Asclep. x. 1 = Ael. xxiv.

ὑπόταξιν[1] καὶ ἐπίταξιν, ὧν ἕκαστον ὅ τι σημαίνει,
δηλῶσαι διὰ βραχέων πειρασόμεθα.

2 Κλίσις μὲν οὖν ἐστιν ἡ κατ' ἄνδρα κίνησις, ἐπὶ
δόρυ μὲν ἡ ἐπὶ δεξιά, ἐπ' ἀσπίδα δὲ ἡ ἐπ' ἀριστερά, ἐπὶ δὲ τῶν ἱπποτῶν[2] ἐφ' ἡνίαν· γίνεται δὲ
κατὰ τὰς ἐκ πλαγίων ἐφόδους τῶν πολεμίων
ἀντιπορίας χάριν ἢ ὑπερκεράσεως[3] ὅπερ ἐστὶν
ὑπερβαλέσθαι τὸ κέρας τῶν πολεμίων.

3 Ἡ δὲ δὶς ἐπὶ τὸ αὐτὸ γινομένη[4] κλίσις κατὰ
νώτου τὰς τῶν ὁπλιτῶν ὄψεις μετατιθεῖσα καλεῖται
μεταβολή, ἧς δύο διαφοραί, ἡ μὲν ἀπὸ τῶν πολεμίων, ἣν καὶ ἐπ' οὐρὰν ἐπονομάζουσιν, ἡ δ'
ἐπὶ τοὺς πολεμίους ἀπ' οὐρᾶς[5] καλουμένη.

4 Ἐπιστροφὴ δέ ἐστιν, ὅτ' ἂν πυκνώσαντες ὅλον
τὸ σύνταγμα κατὰ λόχον τε καὶ ζυγὸν ὡς ἑνὸς
ἀνδρὸς σῶμα κλίνωμεν, ὡς ἂν περὶ κέντρον περὶ
τὸν πρῶτον λοχαγόν,[6] εἰ μὲν ἐπὶ δόρυ, τὸν δεξιόν,
εἰ δὲ ἐπ' ἀσπίδα, τὸν ἀριστερὸν ὅλου[7] τοῦ συντάγματος περιενεχθέντος καὶ μεταλαβόντος[8] τὸν
ἔμπροσθεν τόπον καὶ ἐπιφάνειαν, ἐπὶ δόρυ μὲν
τὴν ἐκ δεξιῶν, ἐπ' ἀσπίδα δὲ τὴν ἐπὶ λαιάν.

5 Οἷον ἔστω σύνταγμα τὸ ᾱβ̄γ̄δ̄,[9] λοχαγῶν[10] δ' ἐν
αὐτῷ ζυγὸν τὸ ᾱβ̄· δῆλον δέ, ὅτι δεξιὸς μὲν
ἔσται λοχαγὸς ὁ[11] κατὰ τὸ β̄, λαιὸς δὲ ὁ κατὰ τὸ ᾱ,

---

[1] ὑπίταξιν F.   [2] K. and R. suggest ἱππέων.
[3] A and B in margin, K. and R.: ἡ ὑπερασσω F.
[4] γιγνομένη K. and R.: γινομένη is attested also in Lex. mil.
§ 34.   [5] ἀπουραο F.
[6] K. and R. (λοχαγὸν C, the second περὶ suggested by K.
and R.): περικεντρον πρώτον λόγον F.   [7] ὅλον F.
[8] K. and R.: μεταβάλλοντοσ F.   [9] ᾱβ̄γ̄ F.
[10] K. and R.: λοχαγὸν F.   [11] Supplied by K. and R.

---

[1] The great confusion of these terms during this period

' van-position' (*protaxis*), ' rear-position' (*hypotaxis*), and 'supporting-position' (*epitaxis*). The signification of each of these terms we shall endeavour to explain as briefly as possible.[1]

Right- or left-facing, then, is the movement of the individual men, ' by spear ' to the right, and 'by shield' —called in the cavalry 'by rein'—to the left; this takes place when the enemy falls upon the flanks and we wish either to counter-attack, or else to envelop his wing, *i.e.*, overlap the wing of the enemy.

The double turning, which is performed in the same way, whereby the soldiers face about to the rear, is called an about-face (*metabole*), of which there are two kinds, the one from the enemy, called ' to the rear' (*ep' uran*), and the other toward the enemy, called 'from the rear' (*ap' uras*).

It is a quarter-turn, when we close up the entire battalion by file and rank in the compact formation[2] and move it like the body of one man in such a manner that the entire force swings on the first file-leader as on a pivot, if to the right on the right file-leader, and if to the left on the left file-leader, and at the same time takes a position in advance and faces 'by spear' if pivoting right and ' by shield' if pivoting left.

Let the battalion, for example,[3] be α β γ δ, and α β its rank of file-leaders; it is clear, then, that the right file-leader will be the one at β and the left the

was probably due to the fact that such discussions had lost all contact with the drill-ground.

[2] That is, two cubits apart.

[3] The diagrams to explain this and the following evolutions will be found on p. 301.

Asclep. x. 2 = Ael. xxv. 1.   Asclep. x. 3 = Ael. xxv. 2-4.
Asclep. x. 4 = Ael. xxv. 5.

ASCLEPIODOTUS

καὶ ἐπὶ δόρυ μὲν τὰ κατὰ τὸ $\bar{\beta}$ μέρη, ἐπ' ἀσπίδα
δὲ τὰ κατὰ τὸ $\bar{a}$· μένοντος τοίνυν τοῦ $\bar{\beta}$, εἰ ἐπι-
στρέφομεν ὅλον τὸ $\bar{a}\bar{\beta}\bar{\gamma}\bar{\delta}$ σύνταγμα ἐπὶ δόρυ, τὸ
κατὰ τὴν $\bar{a}\bar{\beta}$ ζυγὸν μεταστήσεται ἐπὶ τὴν πρὸς
ὀρθὰς αὐτῷ θέσιν τὴν $\bar{\beta}\bar{\epsilon}$ καὶ ὅλον τὸ $\bar{\beta}\bar{a}\bar{\delta}\bar{\gamma}^1$ ἔσται
ὡς τὸ $\bar{\beta}\bar{\epsilon}\bar{\zeta}\bar{\eta}$ ἐπεστραμμένον ἐπὶ δόρυ καὶ κατ-
ειληφὸς[2] τόπον μὲν τὸν ἔμπροσθεν, ἐπιφάνειαν δὲ
τὴν δεξιάν.

6 Ἀναστροφὴ δέ ἐστιν ἀποκατάστασις τῆς ἐπιστροφῆς εἰς ὃν[3] προκατεῖχε τὸ σύνταγμα τόπον,
οἷον τὸν κατὰ τὸ $\bar{a}\bar{\beta}\bar{\gamma}\bar{\delta}$.[4]

7 Περισπασμὸς δέ ἐστιν ἡ[5] ἐκ δυεῖν ἐπιστροφῶν
τοῦ συντάγματος κίνησις κατὰ τὸ αὐτὸ μέρος ὡς
τὸ $\bar{\beta}\bar{\theta}\bar{\kappa}\bar{\lambda}$· τῆς μὲν γὰρ πρώτης ἐπιστροφῆς τῆς
κατὰ τὸ $\bar{\beta}\bar{\epsilon}\bar{\zeta}\bar{\eta}$ ἐπέχει τόπον μὲν τὸν ἔμπροσθεν,
ἐπιφάνειαν δὲ τὴν δεξιάν, τῆς δ' ἐξ ἀρχῆς θέσεως
τῆς $\bar{a}\bar{\beta}\bar{\gamma}\bar{\delta}$ εἰς[6] τοὐπίσω βλέπει.

8 Ἐκπερισπασμὸς δέ ἐστιν, ὅτ' ἂν ἐκ τριῶν ἐπιστροφῶν[7] ἐπὶ τὰ αὐτὰ συνεχῶν κινῆται[8] τὰ συντάγματα εἰς τὸν ὄπιθεν τόπον καὶ τὴν εἰς λαιὸν
ἐπιφάνειαν, καθάπερ ἔχει τὸ $\bar{\beta}\bar{\mu}\bar{\nu}\bar{\xi}$, τοῦ μὲν $\bar{\beta}\bar{\theta}\bar{\kappa}\bar{\lambda}$ εἰς
τοὔμπροσθεν κατὰ τὴν δεξιὰν κείμενον ἐπιφάνειαν,
τοῦ δὲ κατὰ τὴν ἐξ ἀρχῆς θέσιν $\bar{\beta}\bar{a}\bar{\delta}\bar{\gamma}$ εἰς τοὐπισθέν
τε μεταπεσὸν καὶ τὴν ἀριστερὰν βλέπον ἐπιφάνειαν.

9 Καὶ φανερόν, ὅτι τὸν ἐκπερισπασμὸν οὐ κατὰ

---

[1] $\bar{\beta}\bar{\epsilon}\bar{a}\bar{\gamma}$ F.   [2] K. and R.: κατειληφῶσ F.

[3] K. and R.: ἢν F.

[4] $\bar{\beta}o\bar{a}\bar{\beta}\bar{\gamma}\bar{\delta}$ F: K. and R. delete $\bar{\beta}o$. It is, however, a mistake for τό, which I have introduced into the text.

[5] *Lex. mil.* § 37, K. and R.: om. F.

[6] Omitted by K. and R.

[7] B (margin) C (Salmasius), *Lex. mil.* § 37, K. and R.:
τεριστρέφων F.

one at α, and the divisions of the force at β will be on the right, and the divisions at α will be on the left; if, then, we make the entire battalion α β γ δ quarter-turn to the right, while β holds his position, the line α β will occupy the position β ε at a right angle with α β, and the entire unit will be swung to the right into the position β ε ζ η, occupying a position in advance and facing to the right.

A back-turn is the reversal of the forward-turn to the position the battalion originally held, as to α β γ δ.

A half-turn is the movement of the battalion by two quarter-turns in the same direction, as β θ κ λ; it proceeds from the first forward-turn position β ε ζ η, takes a position in advance, and faces to the right, and, if considered from its original position α β γ δ, it faces to the rear.[1]

It is a three-quarter-turn when the battalions move by three quarter-turns in the same direction to the position behind and facing left from the original station, as β μ ν ξ, a position which, considered from β θ κ λ, lies before and faces the right, and considered from the original station β α δ γ, lies behind and faces the left.[2]

It is obviously impracticable to revert by a back-

---

[1] Such an evolution could scarcely ever have been used in actual warfare.

[2] This evolution must have been confined to the drill-ground, where for purposes of discipline and exercise formations are still taught which find no place in actual battle.

Asclep. x. 6 = Ael. xxv. 7.   Asclep. x. 7 = Ael. xxv. 8.
Asclep. x. 8 = Ael. xxv. 9.

---

[8] B (mar in) C (Salmasius), K. and R.: συνέχων γίνηται F.

ASCLEPIODOTUS

ἀναστροφὴν ἀποκαθιστάνειν[1] προσήκει — δεησό-
μεθα γὰρ τριῶν ἀναστροφῶν, ἵνα ἀποκαταστῇ,
τῆς τε ἐπὶ τὸ β̄θ̄κ̄λ̄ καὶ τῆς ἐπὶ τὸ β̄ε̄ζ̄η̄ καὶ ἔτι
τῆς ἐπὶ τὸ β̄ᾱδ̄γ̄,[2]—ἀλλὰ κατ' ἐπιστροφὴν μίαν
τὴν ἐπὶ τὸ δόρυ, δι' ὅτι τὸ β̄ᾱδ̄γ̄[2] τοῦ β̄μ̄ν̄ξ̄ τόπον
μὲν ἔχει τὸν ἔμπροσθεν,[3] ἐπιφάνειαν δὲ τὴν ἐκ
δεξιῶν. καλεῖται δὲ ἡ κατ' ἐπιστροφὴν εἰς τὸ
ἐξ ἀρχῆς ἀποκατάστασις[4] ἐπικατάστασις.

10 Ἡ μὲν οὖν πρώτη ἐπιστροφὴ καὶ ἡ τρίτη καλουμένη ἐκπερισπασμὸς μοναχῶς ἀποκαθίστανται,[5]
ἡ μὲν κατὰ ἀναστροφὴν μόνως ἡ β̄ε̄ζ̄η̄, ἡ δὲ κατ'
ἐπιστροφὴν μόνως ἡ β̄μ̄ν̄ξ̄· ἡ δὲ δὴ μέση τούτων
ἡ β̄θ̄κ̄λ̄, ἣν καὶ περισπασμὸν καλοῦμεν, διχῶς
ἀποκαθίσταται,[6] δι' ὅτι ἡ κατὰ ἀναστροφὴν
κίνησις αὐτῆς ἴση ἐστὶ τῇ κατ' ἐπιστροφήν· δύο
γὰρ ἀναστροφαῖς ἀποκαταστήσεται τῇ τε εἰς τὸ
β̄ε̄ζ̄η̄ καὶ τῇ εἰς τὸ β̄ᾱδ̄γ̄,[7] καὶ δύο ἐπιστροφαῖς
ἐπικαταστήσεται, τῇ τε εἰς τὸ β̄μ̄ν̄ξ̄ καὶ τῇ εἰς τὸ
β̄ᾱδ̄γ̄.[8]

11 Εἰ δ' ἐπ' ἀσπίδα ποιοίμεθα[9] τὴν ἐπιστροφήν,
τόπον ἐφέξει τὸ σύνταγμα καὶ οὕτω τὸν ἔμπροσθεν,
ἐπιφάνειαν δὲ ἐναντίαν τὴν κατ' ἀριστεράν·[10]
μεταταχθὲν γὰρ τὸ ᾱβ̄γ̄δ̄ περὶ μένοντα τὸν ᾱ
λοχαγὸν θέσιν ἕξει τὴν[11] ᾱο̄π̄ρ̄ κατὰ πρώτην ἐπιστροφήν, κατὰ δὲ περισπασμὸν τὴν ᾱσ̄τ̄ῡ,[12] ἐκπερι-

---

[1] ἀποκαθιστάναι K. and R.   [2] K. and R. : β̄ᾱγ̄δ̄ F.
[3] K. and R. : τὸν εμεν (space of three letters) F.
[4] K. and R. : κατάστασισ F.
[5] K. and R. : μοναχῶ καθίστανται F.
[6] K. and R. : καθίσταται F.
[7] β̄ᾱ (erasure of one letter) δ̄γ̄ F.
[8] The words from καὶ δύο to the end stand thus in F
(except τῇ twice), but have fallen out in ABC.

298

turn from the three-quarter-turn to the original position, for we shall require three back-turns to do this, one to the position $\beta\,\theta\,\kappa\,\lambda$, one to $\beta\,\epsilon\,\zeta\,\eta$, and one to $\beta\,a\,\delta\,\gamma$; but it is practicable by a quarter-turn to the right, because $\beta\,a\,\delta\,\gamma$ occupies a position before $\beta\,\mu\,\nu\,\xi$ and faces to its right. The return by a quarter-turn to the original position is called advance-to-original-position (*epikatastasis*).

Now the first position, the quarter-turn, and the third, called the three-quarter-turn, can be restored to the original position by a single evolution, the first $\beta\,\epsilon\,\zeta\,\eta$, by a single back-turn, the second $\beta\,\mu\,\nu\,\xi$ by a single quarter-turn; but the position between these two, $\beta\,\theta\,\kappa\,\lambda$, which we also call a half-turn, can resume its original station equally well by two evolutions, because its movement by a back-turn equals that by a quarter-turn; since it requires two back-turns to revert to the original position, first to $\beta\,\epsilon\,\zeta\,\eta$ and then to $\beta\,a\,\delta\,\gamma$, and also two quarter-turns to advance to the original position, first to $\beta\,\mu\,\nu\,\xi$ and then to $\beta\,a\,\delta\,\gamma$.

If we should make the quarter-turn to the left, then the battalion will in the same way occupy the position in advance, with its face, however, to the left; since $a\,\beta\,\gamma\,\delta$, by pivoting upon the stationary file-leader a, will by the first quarter-turn take the position $a\,o\,\pi\,\rho$, by the half-turn the position $a\,\sigma\,\tau\,\upsilon$,

With Asclep. x. 11 *cf.* Ael. xxxiv. 1.

⁹ ποιούμεθα K. and R.   ¹⁰ K. and R. : ἀριστερόν F.
   ¹¹ K. and R.: ὡσ τὴν F : ὡς C (Salmasius).
   ¹² K. and R.: περισπασμόν τινα C̅T̅Γ̅ F.

σπασθεῖσα δὲ τὴν ᾱϕ̄χ̄ψ̄ καὶ ἐπικατασταθεῖσα τὴν[1] ᾱβ̄γ̄δ. ἡ δὲ τῶν ἀποκαταστάσεων[2] διαϕορὰ ὁμοία ταῖς ἐπὶ δόρυ σοι νοείσθω.

Ταῦτα δὲ γίνεται ὁπότ' ἂν οἱ πολέμιοι παραϕαίνωνται κατὰ πλευρὰν τῆς ϕάλαγγος.[3]

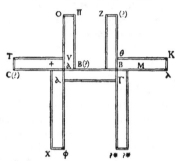

(†) litterae evanidae.   (?)* litterae bibliopegi incuria abscisae (Rostagno).

(In place of this figure which contains some errors and is not easy to understand, K. and R. have substituted two which will be found on the opposite page. On these figures in general see the Introduction.)

12 Εἰς ὀρθὸν δέ ἐστιν ἀποδοῦναι τὸ ἐπὶ τὴν ἐξ ἀρχῆς θέσιν ἀποκαταστῆσαι ἄνδρα ἕκαστον ὥστε, εἰ ἐπὶ δόρυ κλίνειν ἐκ τῶν πολεμίων κελεύοιντο εἶτα αὖθις ἐπ'[4] ὀρθὸν ἀποδοῦναι, δεήσει ἐπὶ τοὺς πολεμίους πάλιν τρέπεσθαι.

13 Ἐξελιγμὸς[5] δὲ γίνεται τριχῶς, Μακεδονικός τε

---

[1] K. and R.: ἐπικαταστάσα τη F.
[2] K. and R.: καταστάσεων F.
[3] A lacuna is assumed here by K. and R. since an explanation of στοιχεῖν τε καὶ ζυγεῖν in § 1 above is not given at this point, although an extremely verbose one appears in Arrian and Aelian, *Tactica*, xxvi. 1, in this same relative position.

by the three-quarter-turn the position α φ χ ψ, and by the advance-to-original-position, the position α β γ δ. The different ways of returning to the original position you may consider similar to those used in evolutions to the right.

These evolutions are used whenever the enemy appears on a flank of the army.

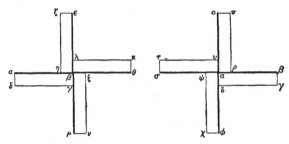

It is called lines-front when man by man the force reverts[1] to its original position, so that in case the command has been given to turn to the right from the enemy and then to form lines-front, the men will have to turn back so as to face the enemy.

There are three types of the counter-march, the

[1] That is, from a turn to the right or to the left.

Asclep. x. 12 = Ael. xxvi. 3.
Asclep. x. 13 = Ael xxvii. 1-2 ; xxviii. 1.

These terms were defined, however, in ch. ii. 6, above, and, as nothing new is to be added, Asclepiodotus may have been satisfied with that.

[4] K. and R. suggest εἰς or ἐς ὀρθὸν which is more natural, is supported by Aelian and Arrian, *Tactica*, xxvi. 3, and *Lex. mil.* § 38, and is perhaps correct.

[5]]ξελιγμὸς (at beginning of a line) F.

καὶ Λακωνικὸς καὶ ἔτι Κρητικὸς ἤτοι Περσικός· τοῦτο δὲ γίνεται διχῶς, ἢ κατὰ στοῖχον ἢ κατὰ ζυγόν.[1]

Μακεδονικὸς μὲν οὖν ἐστιν ἐξελιγμός, ὅτ' ἂν τοῦ λοχαγοῦντος ζυγοῦ τὸν οἰκεῖον τόπον ἐπέχοντος τὰ ὀπίσω ζυγὰ τὸν ἔμπροσθεν καταλάβῃ τόπον[2] μεθισταμένων μέχρις οὐραγοῦ, εἶτα κατ' ἄνδρα μεταβαλλόντων· οἷον εἰ τοῦ ᾱβ̄γ̄δ̄ε̄[3] ζυγοῦ λοχαγοῦντος καὶ μένοντος ἐπὶ ταὐτοῦ τὰ εἰς τοὐπίσω τὸ[4] ζ̄η̄θ̄ῑκ̄ καὶ τὸ λ̄μ̄ν̄ξ̄ο̄ εἰς τὸ πρόσω καθίσταται, ἤτοι κατὰ ζυγόν, ὥστε τὸ ζ̄η̄θ̄ῑκ̄ μεταστῆναι πρότερον καὶ γενέσθαι κατὰ[5] τὸ π̄ρ̄σ̄τ̄ῡ, ἔπειτα τὸ λ̄μ̄ν̄ξ̄ο̄ κατὰ τὸ φ̄χ̄ψ̄ω̄ς̄, ἢ κατὰ στοῖχον, ὥστε τὰ μὲν κ̄ο̄ γενέσθαι κατὰ τὰ ῡς̄, τὰ δὲ ῑξ̄ κατὰ τὰ τ̄ω̄[6] καὶ τὰ ἑξῆς, οἷον τὰ θ̄ν̄ κατὰ τὰ σ̄ψ̄ καὶ τὰ[8] η̄μ̄ κατὰ τὰ ῥ̄χ̄ καὶ τὰ[9] ζ̄λ̄[10] κατὰ τὰ π̄φ̄· εἶτα καὶ κατ' ἄνδρα μεταβάλωσιν ἀπὸ οὐραγοῦ, τόδε[11] ἐστὶν ἀπεστράφθαι μὲν τὰ π̄ρ̄σ̄τ̄ῡ καὶ τὰ φ̄χ̄ψ̄ω̄ [12] μέρη, βλέπειν δὲ κατὰ τὰ ᾱβ̄γ̄δ̄ε̄ διὰ τὸ ὄπιθεν ὀφθῆναι τοὺς πολεμίους. φανερὸν δὲ ὅτι κατὰ τοῦτον τὸν ἐξελιγμὸν ἡ φάλαγξ δόξειεν ἂν ὑποχωρεῖν τοῦ οἰκείου τόπου καὶ φυγῇ παραπλήσιον ποιεῖν, ὃ δὴ θαρραλεωτέρους μὲν ποιεῖ τοὺς πολεμίους, ἀσθενεστέρους δὲ τοὺς ἐξελίσσοντας.

14 Ὁ δὲ Λακωνικὸς ἐξελιγμὸς τὸν ἐναντίον τούτῳ

---

[1] This whole sentence beginning with τοῦτο δὲ does not appear here in F, where, as K. and R. saw, it belongs, but between the words τόπον and μεθισταμένων in the middle of the next sentence. [2] See preceding note.
[3] K. and R. : ᾱβ̄ γ̄δ̄ F. [4] K. and R. : τουπίσω τε F.
[5] K. and R.: μετὰ F. [6] K. and R.: ζ̄ω̄ F.
[7] C (Salmasius), K. and R.: κατὰ F.
[8] K. and R. : κατὰ F.

Macedonian, the Laconian, and also the Cretan or Persian; and each of these, again, is performed in two ways, either by file or by rank.[1]

It is a Macedonian counter-march when the rank of file-leaders holds its original position, and the rear ranks down to the file-closers march through to a forward position and then each man about-faces; thus $\alpha\,\beta\,\gamma\,\delta\,\epsilon$ is the rank of file-leaders and remains in the same place, and the back ranks $\zeta\,\eta\,\theta\,\iota\,\kappa$ and $\lambda\,\mu\,\nu\,\xi\,o$ move forward, either by rank so that $\zeta\,\eta\,\theta\,\iota\,\kappa$ marches through first and becomes $\pi\,\rho\,\sigma\,\tau\,\upsilon$ and $\lambda\,\mu\,\nu\,\xi\,o$ becomes $\phi\,\chi\,\psi\,\omega\,\varsigma$, or by file so that $\kappa\,o$ takes the place of $\upsilon\,\varsigma$, $\iota\,\xi$ of $\tau\,\omega$, and so on, as $\theta\,\nu$ of $\sigma\,\psi$, $\eta\,\mu$ of $\rho\,\chi$, and $\zeta\,\lambda$ of $\pi\,\phi$; and then each man from the file-closer on about-faces, i.e., $\pi\,\rho\,\sigma\,\tau\,\upsilon$ and $\phi\,\chi\,\psi\,\omega\,\varsigma$ turn about and face with $\alpha\,\beta\,\gamma\,\delta\,\epsilon$ as their front line, because the enemy was seen in the rear.[2] It is clear that in this kind of counter-march the phalanx would seem to yield ground and to be almost in flight, which emboldens the enemy and disheartens those who are counter-marching.

The Laconian counter-march takes up a position

[1] The importance of the counter-march by files is evident, when one bears in mind that in the front lines of the ancient phalanx were stationed the best soldiers (cf. iii. 5-6).

[2] The following diagram will explain this manœuvre:

$$\phi\ \chi\ \psi\ \omega\ \varsigma$$
$$\pi\ \rho\ \sigma\ \tau\ \nu$$
$$\alpha\ \beta\ \gamma\ \delta\ \epsilon$$
$$\zeta\ \eta\ \theta\ \iota\ \kappa$$
$$\lambda\ \mu\ \nu\ \xi\ o$$

Asclep. x. 14 = Ael. xxvii. 3 ; xxviii. 2 ; cf. xxxiv. 4.

[9] Supplied by C (Salmasius), K. and R.
[10] K. and R. : $\overline{\lambda z}$ F.   [11] $\tau\acute{a}\delta\epsilon$ K. and R. : $\tau\grave{o}$ $\delta\grave{\epsilon}$ F.
[12] The additions were made by K. and R. : $\mu\grave{\epsilon}\nu$ $\tau\grave{a}$ $\overline{\phi\chi\psi}$ F.

μεταλαμβάνει τόπον· μεταβάλλει γὰρ ἕκαστος
ἐπ᾽ οὐράν, μένοντος τοῦ οὐραγοῦντος ζυγοῦ οἷον
τοῦ λ͞μ͞ν͞ξ͞ο̄· τὰ γὰρ λοιπά, τό τε ζ͞η͞θ͞ι͞κ̄ καὶ τὸ
ᾱ͞β͞γ͞δ͞ε̄ μεθίσταται ἐφ᾽ ἑκάτερα . . .[1] τοῦ οὐραγοῦντος, διχῶς δῆλον ὅτι, ἤτοι κατὰ στοῖχον
ἢ κατὰ ζυγόν, καὶ θέσιν ἔχει τὸ μὲν ζ͞η͞θ͞ι͞κ̄[2] τὴν
τοῦ ΖΗΘΙΚ,[2] τὸ δὲ ᾱ͞β͞γ͞δ͞ε̄[3] τὴν τοῦ ΑΒΓΔΕ.[3]
τοῦτο δὴ ποιῶν ὁ Λακωνικὸς ἐξελιγμὸς τὴν ἐναντίαν
κατὰ τὸν Μακεδονικὸν τοῖς πολεμίοις παρέχεται
δόξαν· ἐφορμᾶν γὰρ καὶ ἐπιέναι δόξειεν ἂν ὄπιθεν
παραφανεῖσιν, ὥστε καταπλῆξαι αὐτούς[4] καὶ δειλίαν ἐκ τοῦδε γενέσθαι.

15   Ὁ Κρητικὸς δὲ καὶ Περσικὸς καλούμενος μέσος
ἐστὶν ἀμφοῖν· οὐ γὰρ τὸν ὄπιθεν τῆς φάλαγγος
μεταλαμβάνει τόπον, ὡς ὁ Μακεδονικός, οὔτε
τὸν ἔμπροσθεν, ὡς ὁ Λακωνικός, ἀλλ᾽ ἐπὶ τοῦ

Φ Χ † Ω ϟ
Π Ρ Σ Τ Υ
Α Β Γ Δ Ε
Ζ Η Θ Ι Κ
Λ Μ Ν Ξ Ο

Ζ Η Θ Ι Κ

Δ ? Γ Δ ?

† litterae evanidae (Rostagno).

αὐτοῦ χωρίου ὁ μὲν λοχαγὸς τοῦ οὐραγοῦ τὸν
τόπον[5] μεταλαμβάνει καὶ οἱ κατὰ τὸ ἑξῆς ἐπι-

the opposite of that shown above; for each soldier about-faces to the rear, while the rank of file-closers λ μ ν ξ o holds its position; and the other ranks ζ η θ ι κ and α β γ δ ε march through on either side [to a position behind the] file-closer—and this, clearly, in two ways, either by file or by rank—and ζ η θ ι κ take the position Z H Θ I K, and α β γ δ ε the position A B Γ Δ E.[1] By this form of manœuvre the Laconian counter-march arouses a feeling in the enemy just opposite to that aroused by the Macedonian; for they would seem to those who have appeared in the rear to be making for and charging upon them, so that they dismay the enemy and arouse fear among them.

The so-called Cretan and Persian counter-march is an intermediate between these two; for it does not occupy the position behind the phalanx, as the Macedonian, nor the one before the phalanx, as the Laconian, but occupies the same ground, while the file-leader takes the place of the file-closer, and in like manner the rear-rank-men those of the front-

---

[1] To explain the manœuvre:

$$
\begin{array}{ccccc}
α & β & γ & δ & ε \\
ζ & η & θ & ι & κ \\
λ & μ & ν & ξ & o \\
Z & H & Θ & I & K \\
A & B & Γ & Δ & E \\
\end{array}
$$

Asclep. x. 15=Ael. xxvii. 4; xxviii. 3; *cf.* xxxiv. 5.

---

[1] For the lacuna which K. and R. recognized at this point they suggest παριόντα εἰς τὸν ὄπιθεν τόπον.
[2] K. and R.: z͞Hθι͞κ F.   [3] K. and R.: α͞βΓ͞δε F.
[4] K. and R.: αὐτοῖσ F.   [5] K. and R.: τομὲν F.

στάται καὶ πρωτοστάται[1] καὶ . . .[2] παραπορευόμενοι κἀνταῦθα διχῶς ἢ[3] κατὰ λόχον ἢ κατὰ
ζυγόν, ἄχρις ἂν ὁ οὐραγὸς τὸν τοῦ λοχαγοῦ τόπον
ἀντιμεταλάβῃ, οἷον λοχαγοῦντος τοῦ ᾱβ̄γ̄δ̄ε̄[4] καὶ
ἑξῆς ἐπιστατοῦντος[5] τοῦ ζ̄η̄θ̄ῑκ̄ καὶ ἐφ᾽ ἑξῆς τοῦ
λ̄μ̄ν̄ξ̄ο̄, καὶ μετὰ τοῦτο τοῦ π̄ρ̄σ̄τ̄ῡ—ἔστω δὲ τοῦτο
οὐραγοῦν—ὅτ᾽ ἂν τὸ μὲν ᾱβ̄γ̄δε̄ τὸν τοῦ π̄ρ̄σ̄τ̄ῡ
τόπον μεταλαμβάνῃ, τὸ δὲ ζ̄η̄θ̄ῑκ̄ τὸν τοῦ λ̄μ̄ν̄ξ̄ο̄,
τὸ δὲ λ̄μ̄ν̄ξ̄ο̄ τὸν τοῦ ζ̄η̄θ̄ῑκ̄, τὸ δὲ π̄ρ̄σ̄τ̄ῡ τὸν τοῦ
ᾱβ̄γ̄δ̄ε̄. οὕτω γὰρ ὁ ἐξελιγμὸς οὐκ ἀποστήσει
τοῦ αὐτοῦ χωρίου τὴν φάλαγγα, ὅπερ ἡμῖν ἔσται
χρήσιμον, ὁπότ᾽ ἂν ὦσιν οἱ ἑκατέρωθεν τόποι
φαυλότεροι.

16 Γίνονται δὲ κατὰ ζυγὸν ἐξελιγμοί, ὅτ᾽ ἂν τὰ
κέρατα μεθίστηται τῶν ἀποτομῶν· διὰ ταῦτα[6]
γὰρ ἰσχυρὰ ποιεῖται[7] τὰ μέσα τῆς φάλαγγος.
ἐνίοτε δὲ κατὰ ἀποτομὰς οὐκ ἐγχωρεῖ τοὺς
ἐξελιγμοὺς ποιήσασθαι, ὅτ᾽ ἂν ἐγγὺς ὦσιν οἱ
πολέμιοι, ἀλλὰ κατὰ σύνταγμα, ὥστε τὸ τοῦ
συντάγματος δεξιὸν ἀντιμεταλαμβάνειν τὰ λαιὰ
καὶ ἀνάπαλιν.[8]

---

[1] K. and R. : προστάται F.
[2] For the lacuna which K. and R. recognize at this point
they suggest πρωτοστάται ὡς αὕτως τὸν τόπον ἐφεξῆς μεταλαμ-
βάνουσι παραπορευόμενοι, but, since the actual words are
uncertain, they leave καὶ in the text.
[3] Supplied by K. and R.   [4] K. and R. : ᾱβ̄γ̄δ F.
[5] C (Salmasius), K. and R. : ἐξησατος F.
[6] K. and R. : διὰ τῶν ἀποτόμων ταύταις F.
[7] ἰσχυροποιεῖται C (Salmasius), K. and R.
[8] K. and R : τὸν τοῦ δεξιοῦ συντάγματος ἀντιμεταλαμβάνειν
τὰ λαιὰ καὶ ἀνὰ πᾶσιν F. C (Salmasius) wrote in the margin
καὶ τὸν λαιὸν τὰ δεξιά, which would require τὸν δεξιὸν τοῦ
συντάγματος above.

rank-men . . . marching past each other, and this
in two ways, either by file or by rank, until the file-
closer has in turn taken the place of the file-leader.
That is, consider the line of file-leaders $a \beta \gamma \delta \epsilon$, of
rear-rank-men $\zeta \eta \theta \iota \kappa$, then $\lambda \mu \nu \xi o$, and after it as
the rank of file-closers $\pi \rho \sigma \tau \nu$; then $a \beta \gamma \delta \epsilon$ takes
the position of $\pi \rho \sigma \tau \nu$, $\zeta \eta \theta \iota \kappa$ of $\lambda \mu \nu \xi o$, $\lambda \mu \nu \xi o$
that of $\zeta \eta \theta \iota \kappa$, and $\pi \rho \sigma \tau \nu$ that of $a \beta \gamma \delta \epsilon$.[1] By
this counter-march the phalanx will not change its
ground, and this we shall find advantageous, whenever
the terrain before and behind is less favourable.

Counter - marches are made by rank, when the
half-wings exchange positions each within its own
wing,[2] for this strengthens the centre of the phalanx.
Sometimes it is not advisable to make the counter-
marches by half-wings, when the enemy is near by,
but rather by battalions, so that the right wing of
the battalion occupies the left and *vice versa.*

[1] *Cf.* the diagram :

[2] Since the strongest half-wing occupies the right flank,
the second strongest the left, and the others the centre, by
this evolution the two stronger half-wings will exchange
places with the two weaker, and so the centre will be
strengthened and the wings weakened.

Asclep. x. 16 = Ael. xxvii. 5 ; xxviii. 4.

```
Α  Β  Γ  Δ  Ε
Ζ  Η  Θ  Ι  Κ
Λ  Μ  Ν  Ξ  Ο
Π  Ρ  Σ  Τ  Υ
```

17 Διπλασιάσαι δὲ λέγεται διχῶς· ἢ γὰρ τόπον,
ἐν ᾧ ἡ φάλαγξ, μένοντος τοῦ πλήθους τῶν ἀνδρῶν,
ἢ τὸν ἀριθμὸν αὐτῶν· γίνεται δὲ ἑκάτερον διχῶς
κατὰ λόχον ἢ κατὰ ζυγόν, ταὐτὸν δὲ εἰπεῖν κατὰ
βάθος ἢ κατὰ μῆκος. κατὰ μῆκος μὲν οὖν
γίνεται διπλασιασμὸς ἀνδρῶν, ὅτ᾽ ἂν μεταξὺ
τῶν προϋπαρχόντων λόχων παρεμβάλωμεν ἢ παρεμπλέκωμεν ἄλλους αὐτοῖς[1] ἰσαρίθμους τὸ μῆκος
τῆς φάλαγγος φυλάττοντες, ὥστε πύκνωσιν γενέσθαι μόνην ἐκ τῆς τῶν ἀνδρῶν διπλασιάσεως·
κατὰ βάθος δέ, ὅτ᾽ ἂν μεταξὺ τῶν προϋπαρχόντων
ζυγῶν ἄλλα αὐτοῖς ἰσάριθμα παρεμβάλωμεν[2] ὥστε
κατὰ βάθος εἶναι πύκνωσιν μόνην· τί δὲ διενήνοχε
παρεμβολὴ παρεμπλοκῆς, εἴρηται πρότερον.

18 Τόπου δὲ γίνεται διπλασιασμὸς κατὰ μῆκος μέν,
ὅτ᾽ ἂν τὴν προειρημένην κατὰ μῆκος πύκνωσιν
μανότητι μετατάττωμεν, ἢ[3] οἱ παρεντεθέντες[4]
ἐξελίξωσι κατὰ μῆκος πρὸς[5] τὸ μὴ[5] ὑπερκερασθῆναι
ὑπὸ τῶν πολεμίων ἢ[5] ὅτ᾽ ἂν ὑπερκερᾶσαι βουλώμεθα
τοὺς πολεμίους· τὸ δ᾽ ὑπερκερᾶσαι ἐστιν τὸ τῷ[6]

---

[1] ἄλλους αὐτοῖς Lex. mil. § 40 (cf. below ἄλλα αὐτοῖς), K.
and R. (in note, ἄλλους alone in text): ἀλλήλους F.

[2] K. and R. after C (Salmasius), which, however, omits
αὐτοῖς: προϋπαρχόντων ἀλλὰ αὐτοῖς ἰσάριθμα ὥστε F.: Lex. mil.
§ 40 reads παρεμβάλωμεν ἢ παρεμπλέκωμεν ἄλλα αὐτοῖς κτλ.

The term doubling is used in two ways : either of the place occupied by the phalanx, while the number of the men remains the same, or of the number of the men ; and each of these may be by file or by rank, also called by depth or by length. Doubling of men, then, takes place by length when we interject or insert between the original files other files of equal strength, maintaining all the while the length of the phalanx, so that a compact order arises only from the doubling of the men ; doubling takes place by depth when we interject between the original ranks others of equal strength, so that a compact order arises only by depth. The difference between insertion and interjection has been explained before.[1]

Doubling of place occurs by length when we change the above mentioned compact formation by length into a loose formation, or when the interjected men counter-march by rank, either to prevent being outflanked by the enemy or when we wish to outflank the enemy ; by outflanking is understood

[1] *Cf.* vi. 1, where, however, a slightly different word is used for ' insertion.'

Asclep. x. 17=Ael. xxix. 1 ; 2 ; 8.
Asclep. x. 18=xxix. 7 ; 9 ; xxxviii. 1-2.

---

[3] μανοτητι μετατατταμένη οι F.

[4] παρεντιθεντεσ F : παρεντεθέντες *Lex. mil.* § 40.

[5] Thus have K. and R. reconstructed the confused passage which runs in F : κατὰ μῆκοσ. τοῦτο δὲ γίνεται ὅτ' ἂν ὑπερκεράσαι βουλώμεθα τοὺς πολεμίουσ. τὸ δ' ὑπερκεράσαι ἐστὶν τὸ τῷ κέρατι ὑπερβαλέσθαι τὸ ἐκείνων κέρας τοῦ ἑτέρου· ἐνίοτε καὶ ἐλλίποντοσ διολιγότητα ἀνδρῶν . . . 19 . . . ἐξελίξωσι κατὰ βάθοσ πρὸς τὸ ὑπερκερασθῆναι ὑπὸ τῶν πολεμίων.

ASCLEPIODOTUS

κέρατι τῷ ἑτέρῳ[1] ὑπερβαλέσθαι τὸ ἐκείνων κέρας[1]—
τοῦτο[1] δὲ γίνεται[1] ἐνίοτε καὶ τοῦ ἑτέρου[1] ἐλλεί-
ποντος[1] δι' ὀλιγότητα[1] ἀνδρῶν, ὡς, ὅτ' ἄν γε καθ'
ἑκάτερον κέρας ὑπερβάλλωσιν, ὑπερφαλαγγεῖν[2]
λέγεται.

19 Κατὰ βάθος δὲ γίνεται τόπου διπλασιασμός,
ὅτ' ἂν τὴν προειρημένην κατὰ βάθος πύκνωσιν
μανότητι μετατάττομεν ἢ[3] οἱ παρεντεθέντες[4] ἐξελίξωσι κατὰ βάθος.[1]

20 Ἀποκαταστῆσαι δὲ ὅτ' ἂν βουλώμεθα ἐπὶ τὰ[5]
ἐξ ἀρχῆς, παραγγελοῦμεν ἐξελίσσειν τοὺς μετα-
τεταγμένους εἰς οὓς προεῖχον τόπους. ἔνιοι δὲ
τοὺς τοιούτους διπλασιασμοὺς ἀποδοκιμάζουσιν
καὶ μάλιστα ἐγγὺς ὄντων τῶν πολεμίων, ἐφ'
ἑκάτερα δὲ τῶν κεράτων τοὺς ψιλοὺς καὶ τοὺς
ἱππέας ἐπεκτείνοντες τὴν[6] ὄψιν τοῦ[7] διπλασιασμοῦ
χωρὶς ταραχῆς τῆς φάλαγγος ἀποδιδόασιν.

21 Γίνεται δὲ ἐκ τῶν τοιούτων σχηματισμῶν
φάλαγξ τοτὲ μὲν τετράγωνος, τοτὲ δὲ παραμήκης
καὶ ἤτοι πλαγία, ὅτ' ἂν τὸ μῆκος τοῦ βάθους
πολλαπλάσιον ᾖ,[8] ἢ[9] ὀρθία ὅτ' ἂν ἀνάπαλιν τὸ
βάθος τοῦ μήκους· τούτων δ' ἀνὰ μέσον ἡ λοξή,[10]
ἢ[11] θάτερον κέρας πλησίον ἔχουσα τῶν πολεμίων
καὶ ἐν αὐτῷ τὸν ἀγῶνα ποιουμένη, θάτερον[11] δ' ἐν

---

[1] See note 5 on p. 309.
[2] C (Salmasius)? K. and R.: ὑπερφαλαγγιν F.
[3] μανοτητι μεταταττομενη οἱ F.   [4] παρεντιθέντες F.
[5] C (Salmasius), K. and R.: ἔπειτα F.
[6] C (Salmasius), K. and R.: ἢ ἐκτείνοντες F.
[7] K. and R. (B? C?): ἢ τοῦ F.
[8] Added by K. and R.
[9] Added by C (Salmasius)? K. and R.   [10] λοχη F.
[11] K. and R.: καὶ F.

310

the throwing of one wing about the wing of the enemy—and this is done sometimes even when a wing is numerically inferior to that of the enemy—as when both wings are used in a flanking movement, it is called a double outflanking.

Doubling of place is performed by depth when we change the above mentioned compact formation by depth into a loose formation, or when the interjected men counter-march by file.

Whenever we wish to return this compact formation to its original position, we shall command the men who have changed their position to countermarch to their original stations. Some condemn such doublings, especially when the enemy is near, and, by extending the light infantry and cavalry on both wings, give the appearance of the doubling without disturbing the phalanx.

By such evolutions a phalanx assumes the form sometimes of a square, sometimes of an oblong rectangle, or, again, of an extended front when the length is many times as great as the depth, or of an extended depth when the depth is many times as great as the length; an oblique front lies midway between the last two. In this formation one wing is drawn up close to the enemy and fights the contest, while the other is partly withdrawn and refused;

Asclep. x. 19=Ael. xxix. 9.
Asclep. x. 20=Ael. xxix. 3; 5; 6; 10.
Asclep. x. 21=Ael. xxx.

ἀποστάσει δι' ὑποστολῆς[1] ἔχουσα, δεξιὰ μὲν ἥ[2] τὸ δεξιὸν[3] προβεβλημένη, λαιὰ δὲ ἡ τὸ λαιόν.[4]

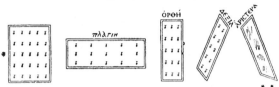

* hic litterarum vestigia sunt tam evanida, ut quid legeretur scriptum deprehendi non possit.

** quid pictum esset in tabula ἀριστερά inscripta non patet (Rostagno).

22   Πολλὰ δὲ καὶ ἄλλα σχήματα οὐ μόνον ἐν ταῖς μάχαις, ἀλλὰ κἂν ταῖς πορείαις ἴσχει πρὸς τὰς ἐξαίφνης τῶν πολεμίων ἐφόδους· καταδιαιρεῖται γὰρ εἰς τὰ μέρη τοτὲ μὲν τὰ μείζω, τοτὲ δὲ τὰ ἐλάττω, οἷον κέρατα καὶ ἀποτομάς, ὥστ' ἐν τῇ συζεύξει τὰς μοίρας τοτὲ μὲν ἀντιστόμους γενέσθαι, τοτὲ δὲ ἀμφιστόμους, ἄλλοτε δὲ ὁμοιοστόμους ἢ ἑτεροστόμους.

Ἡ γὰρ ἐξ ἑνὸς μέρους ὑφορῶνται τοὺς πολεμίους ἢ ἐκ δυεῖν[5] ἢ τριῶν ἢ πανταχόθεν, περὶ ὧν ἑξῆς εἴρηται.

XI. Περὶ πορειῶν

Παραγωγὴ καλεῖται ἡ τῆς φάλαγγος ἤτοι καθ' ὅλην ἢ κατὰ μέρη καί, εἰ καθ' ὅλην, ἢ[6] πλαγία λέγεται, ὅτ' ἂν κατὰ τὴν πλαγίαν θέσιν βαδίζῃ, ἢ ὀρθία, ὅτ' ἂν κατὰ τὴν ὀρθίαν· καὶ εἰ πλαγία πορεύοιτο, ἤτοι κατ' ὀρθόν,[7] ὅτ' ἂν κατὰ τοὺς

[1] K. and R.: διϋποστολὴν F.
[2] K. and R. (in mss. ?): ἢ F.   [3] K. and R.: τὰ δεξιὰ F.
[4] A lacuna is perhaps to be assumed here since an explanation of παρεμβολή, παρένθεσις, πρόταξις, ὑπόταξις, and

it is called the right oblique when the right wing is advanced, and the left oblique when the left wing is advanced.[1]

Many other formations are in use, not merely in battle, but also on the march to guard against the sudden attacks of the enemy ; for the entire army is broken up into its parts, sometimes large and sometimes small, such as wings and half-wings, so that when the parts are combined the army may face the enemy with inner fronts or with outer fronts, and at other times with corresponding or again with different fronts.

For the enemy is descried either on one side, or on two, or three, or on all sides. Each of these situations has been discussed in order.

XI. *Formations in Marching*

A march in line (*paragoge*) is the march of the phalanx, either as a whole or by its parts ; as a whole, it is called either a march by front when it advances with extended front, or a march by file when it advances in file. And if it march with an extended front it is either forward by the rank of file-

---

[1] The figures to explain these formations will be found below : square (Fig. 21), extended front (Figs. 1 and 2), extended depth (Figs. 3 and 4), right oblique (Fig. 6), and left oblique (Fig. 5).

With Asclep. x. 22 *cf.* Ael. xxiv. 1.
With Asclep. xi. 1-2 *cf.* Ael. xxxvi.

ἐπίταξις in § 1 above is not given ; but the first four terms are defined in vi. 1, and ἐπίταξις is clear from the definition of ἐπίταγμα in vii. 10, so that Asclepiodotus himself may have omitted the definitions here.

[5] C (Salmasius), K. and R. : ηεκαχεινη F.
[6] K. and R. (ABC?) : ἡ F.   [7] K. and R. : κατορθόν F.

ASCLEPIODOTUS

λοχαγούς, ἢ ἐπ᾽ οὐράν, ὅτ᾽ ἂν κατὰ τοὺς οὐραγούς·
ὀρθία δὲ εἰ φέροιτο καὶ τὸ λοχαγοῦν ζυγόν, ὃ δὴ
καὶ στόμα λέγεται, δεξιὸν ἔχει[1], δεξιὰ καλεῖται,
εἰ δὲ λαιόν, ἀριστερά· λοξὴ δὲ ὡς αὕτως λαιά τε
καὶ δεξιὰ ἡ τὸ προῦχον[2] ἔχουσα κέρας ὁμώνυμον,
κυρτὴ δὲ καὶ κοίλη καὶ ἐπικάμπιος εἰς τοὐπίσω
ἢ[3] καὶ πρόσω ἢ τὸ στόμα κοῖλον ἢ κυρτὸν ἢ εἰς
τοὐπίσω ἢ καὶ πρόσω ἐπικεκαμμένον[3] ἔχουσα, ὡς
ἔχει τὰ ὑπογεγραμμένα.

Omnia sunt tam evanida, ut aciem oculorum penitus effugiant (Rostagno).[4]

[1] ἔχοι K. and R.   [2] K. and R. : προῦχον F.
[3] K. and R. from the inscriptions on the accompanying
diagrams.   F has only τοὐπίσω δὲ καὶ πρόσω τὸ στόμα κοῖλον ἢ
κυρτὸν ἢ ἐπικεκαμμένον.
[4] In ABC the following inscriptions, which must have
stood at one time in F, as there are still faint traces,
especially above Fig. 7 where κ of κυρτή is still legible, are
attached to the illustrations: πλαγεία κατευθεῖαν (l. πλαγία
κατ᾽ ὀρθόν), πλαγεία (l. πλαγία) ἐπ᾽ οὐράν, ὀρθία δεξιά, ὀρθία
ἀριστερά, ἀριστερά (l. λοξὴ ἀριστερά), δεξιά (l. λοξὴ δεξιά), κυρτή,
κοίλη, ἐπικάμπιος ὀπίσω, ἐπικάμπιος πρόσω.   These figures have
been reconstructed by K. and R. and in that form are reproduced on the opposite page.

314

leaders (Fig. 1), or backward by the rank of file-closers (Fig. 2); but if it move in column, if the line of file-leaders, which is also called the mouth, is on the right, it is called by the right (Fig. 3), and if on the left, it is called by the left (Fig. 4); also a left (Fig. 5) and right (Fig. 6) oblique march-in-line when the corresponding wing is advanced; a convex (Fig. 7), concave [1] (Fig. 8), and a half-square march backwards (Fig. 9) and the same forward (Fig. 10), when the front is bent concave, convex, or as a half-square forward or backward, as in the following diagrams.[2]

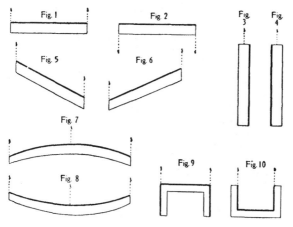

[1] Most unusual formations, certainly, for marching.
[2] The treatment of this and the following paragraphs in Aelian is very different.

ASCLEPIODOTUS

2 Τὸ δ' ὄρθιον[1] τοῦτο καὶ πλάγιον οὐ μόνον ἐπὶ
τῆς ὅλης φάλαγγος ἐκδέχεσθαι δεῖ,[2] ἀλλὰ γὰρ[3]
καὶ ἐπὶ τῶν μερῶν· εἰ γὰρ[4] κατὰ κέρατα βαδίζοι
ἡ φάλαγξ, ἢ κατ' ὄρθια[5] ἢ πλάγια, καί, εἴτε κατ'
ὄρθια εἴτε[6] πλάγια, ἢ κατ' ἐπαγωγὴν ἤτοι σύζευξιν·
ἔστι δὲ κατ' ἐπαγωγὴν μέν, ὅτ' ἂν τὸ δεύτερον
ἔπηται τῷ προτέρῳ, κατὰ σύζευξιν δέ, ὅτ' ἂν
μηδ' ἕτερον θατέρου προηγῆται.

3 Τοῦ δ' ὀρθίου[7] κατὰ σύζευξιν εἴδη τέσσαρα· ἢ
γὰρ δεξιά ἐστιν ἄμφω τὰ στόματα[8] ἢ λαιὰ καὶ
καλεῖται ἡ φάλαγξ[9] ὁμοιόστομος, ἡ μὲν δεξιά, ἡ
δὲ λαιά, ἢ[10] ἐναντίως ἔχει τὰ στόματα, καὶ εἰ μὲν
κατὰ ταῦτα συνάπτοιεν ἀλλήλοις[11], ἀντίστομος
ἐπονομάζεται, εἰ δὲ κατὰ τοὺς οὐραγούς, ἀμφίστομος.

4 Τῶν δὲ κατ' ἐπαγωγὴν πορευομένων[12] ποιεῖν
ἔστιν ὄρθια ἑτεροστόμως[13] μόνον, ὥστε[14] τὸ μὲν
ἔχει δεξιόν, τὸ δὲ λαιὸν στόμα· οὐ γὰρ οἷόν τε[15]
ἐπὶ τὰ αὐτὰ ἔχειν ἄμφω, οὐδὲν γὰρ διοίσει τῆς
ὅλης τὰ κέρατα, δι'[16] ὃ καὶ τὰ πλάγια οὕτως μόνον
συζευχθήσονται· κατ' ἐπαγωγὴν[16] γὰρ τὰ[17] πλάγια

---

[1] K. and R.: Τοῦ' ὀρθὸν F.
[2] ἐπιδέχεσθαι χρή K. and R. after C (Salmasius), which,
however, has χρῆ.
[3] K. and R. delete γάρ.   [4] εἰ γε F.
[5] K. and R.: βαδίζοι ἢ γὰρ κατορθὰ F.
[6] K. and R.: καὶ εἰ πλάγια F.
[7] K. and R.: τοῦ δὲ κατὰ F.
[8] τὰ στόματα added by K. and R.
[9] Added by K. and R. (after AB).   [10] K. and R.: εἰ F.
[11] C (Salmasius) in margin, K. and R.: ειλη F.
[12] K. and R.: δετεπαγωγὴν ορευομένων F. As K. and R.
suggest, τὰ στόματα is to be understood, if not actually
supplied.
[13] K. and R.: ἑτερόστομοσ F.   [14] K. and R.: δι' ὅτι F.

316

The march by flank [1] and the march by front need apply not merely to the entire phalanx, but also to its parts ; for if the phalanx should march by wings, it may be either by column or by front, and each of these again either in sequence (*epagoge*) or in parallel formation (*syzeuxis*) ; it is a march in sequence when the second wing follows the first, and in parallel formation when neither precedes the other.[2]

There are four kinds of march in column in parallel formation : for the fronts may be either right or left, which is called the order with corresponding front, right (Fig. 11), or left (Fig. 12) ; or the fronts may be opposite, and if the men should march with fronts side by side it is called a march with inner fronts (Fig. 13), but if with file-closers side by side a march with outer fronts (Fig. 14).

When the army advances in sequence formation and in column, it can do so only with different fronts, so that one wing has its front right and the other its front left (Fig. 15), it being impossible for the fronts to be on the same side, for the march by wings would then differ in no respect from that of the phalanx in a body,[3] since in this way the fronts will follow one behind the other ; but when the army advances in

[1] That is, in file, or in column.
[2] That is, when the wings are side by side.
[3] As in Figs. 3 and 4.

Asclep. xi. 3 = Ael. xxxvii. 2 ; 3 ; 5.
Asclep. xi. 4 = Ael. xxxvii. 4.

---

[15] K. and R. : οιονται F.
[16] These words, δι' δ . . . ἐπαγωγὴν, are supplied by K. and R.   [17] τὰ γάρ F.

ἢ ὁμοιοστόμως συντεθήσονται[1] ἢ ἀμφιστόμως·
τοῖς γὰρ οὐραγοῖς τοῦ ἡγουμένου τοτὲ μὲν οἱ
λοχαγοί, τοτὲ δὲ οἱ οὐραγοὶ τοῦ ἑπομένου μετα-
ταγήσονται.[2]

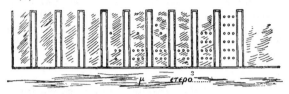

5 Καὶ τὰ λοξὰ δὲ συντιθέμενα διττὰς ἔχουσι
διαφοράς· ἢ γὰρ λαιὸν ἐν λαιῷ τάττεται μέρει[4]
καὶ δεξιὸν ἐνδεξιῷ καὶ καλεῖται ἡ ὅλη κοιλέμβολος, ἢ ἀνάπαλιν καὶ λέγεται ἔμβολος, ὡς τὰ
ὑποτεταγμένα σχήματα.

(These figures as reconstructed by K. and R. are given on the opposite page.)

6 Ἔστι δ' ὅτε καὶ τετραμερίᾳ πορεύονται κατὰ
ἀποτομὰς παντοχόθεν φυλαττόμενοι τοὺς πολεμίους καὶ γίνεται τετράπλευρον[5] περίστομον τοτὲ

---

[1] K. and R.: συζευχθήσονται F, which, though impossible
here, supplied the clue to the supplement of K. and R.
above.   [2] K. and R.: παραταγήσονται F.
[3] In ABC apparently the following inscriptions, which
must have been in F, where a few letters of ἑτερόστομος are
still visible, are attached to the illustrations: δεξιὰ ὁμοιόστομος, ἀριστερὰ ὁμοιόστομος, ἀμφίστομος, ἀντίστομος, ἑτερόστομος.

sequence formation and with extended front it will
have either corresponding fronts or outer fronts, *i.e.*,
behind the file-closers of the leading wing will follow
either the file-leaders (Fig. 16) or the file-closers
(Fig. 17) of the second wing.

The wings also, when in oblique formation, have
two different positions : either the left wing is advanced on the left side and the right wing on the
right, in which array the entire phalanx is called
a hollow-wedge (*koilembolos*, Fig. 18), or just the
opposite formation is assumed, when it is called a
wedge (*embolos*, Fig. 19) ; see the following diagrams.

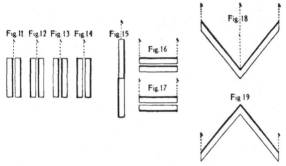

Fig. 11 Fig. 12 Fig. 13 Fig. 14   Fig. 15   Fig. 16   Fig. 17   Fig. 18   Fig 19

Sometimes the army marches in four parts by
divisions, on its guard upon every side against the
enemy, and we have a four-sided figure fronting on

Asclep. xi. 5 = Ael. xxxvii. 6-7.
Asclep. xi. 6 = Ael. xxxvii. 8-9.

The figures as reconstructed by K. and R. are given on this
page.
[4] C (Salmasius), K. and R. : μει ει F.
[5] K. and R. : τετράπλευραν F.

ASCLEPIODOTUS

μὲν ἑτερόμηκες, τοτὲ δὲ τετράγωνον, πανταχόθεν ἔχον στόματα ὡς τὸ ὑπογεγραμμένον.

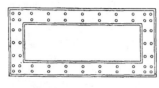 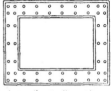

(These figures as reconstructed by K. and R. are given on the opposite page.)

7 "Οτ' ἂν δὲ κατὰ πλείω μέρη πορεύωνται, ἢ
ἐσπαρμένα συντάγματα πορεύσεται ἢ πεπλεγ-
μένα· πεπλεγμένα δέ[1] ἐστιν ὅτ' ἂν λοξὰ πο-
ρεύηται[2] νοειδῆ[3] τὴν ὅλην ποιοῦντα φάλαγγα·
ἐσπαρμένα δὲ ὁπότ' ἂν κατὰ παραλληλόγραμμα[4]
μόναις ταῖς γωνίαις[5] συνάπτοντα ἀλλήλοις, ταῖς
δὲ πλευραῖς ἐπὶ τὸ πρόσω βλέποντα. καὶ ὁ
τούτων δὲ τύπος ἐκ τῆς ὑπογραφῆς ἔσται φανερός·[6]
γένοιτο δ' ἂν κατὰ τὸ εἰκὸς καὶ ἕτερα σχήματα
πρὸς τὰς ἀνακυπτούσας ἁρμόζοντα χρείας.

8 Ἀναγκαιοτάτη δ' οὖσα[7] καὶ ἡ τῶν σκευοφόρων
ἀγωγὴ ἡγεμόνος δεομένη κατὰ τρόπους γίνεται

[1] καὶ πεπλεγμένα μέν K. and R. who report ABC as having
only ἢ πεπλεγμένα δέ. If so F confirms the essential correct-
ness of their reading.   [2] K. and R.: πορεύεται F.
[3] K. and R.: νοειδῆ F. The smooth breathing is etymo-
logically correct and I see no reason to follow the lexicons
and introduce the rough.
[4] παραλληλόγραμμον K. and R. after C (Salmasius).
[5] K. and R.: γονίαις F.
[6] φανερόν K. and R. (apparently from A and B, for the
phrase is omitted by C).
[7] οὖσα F (the δ' added by the first hand).

each side, an oblong rectangle (Fig. 20) or a square (Fig. 21) which fronts on all sides, as the following diagram shows.[1]

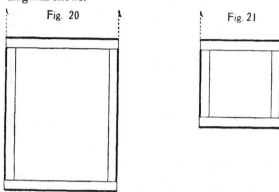

When the army marches in several divisions, the battalions will be either in loose or close formation : it is the close formation when the march is by battalions *en échelon*, the entire phalanx assuming the form of a V (Fig. 22) ; the loose formation, when the battalions form parallelograms with only the corners touching one another, but with the fronts facing forward (Fig. 23). The form of these dispositions will be clear from the following figure. There might, of course, be other orders of march, meeting the situations that arise.

The baggage-train, which is very essential and requires its own commander, is convoyed in five

---

[1] The *locus classicus* for this order of march is the *Anabasis* of Xenophon iii. 4. 19-23.

Asclep. xi. 7 = Ael. xlviii. 2-3.   Asclep. xi. 8 = Ael. xxxix.

ASCLEPIODOTUS

πέντε· ἢ γὰρ προάγειν δεῖ τῆς φάλαγγος, ὅτ᾿ ἂν
ἐκ πολεμίων ἀπίῃ,[1] ἢ ἐπακολουθεῖν, ὅτ᾿ ἂν εἰς
πολεμίους ἐμβάλλῃ, ἢ παρὰ τὴν φάλαγγα κατὰ

(This figure as reconstructed by K. and R. is given on the opposite page.)

λαιὰ ἢ δεξιὰ εἶναι, ὁπότ᾿ ἂν φοβῆται[2] τἀναντία
μέρη, ἢ τό γε λειπόμενον ἀγόμενα ἐντὸς κοίλῃ τῇ[3]
φάλαγγι περιέχεσθαι πανταχόθεν ὄντος τοῦ δέους.

XII. Περὶ τῶν κατὰ τὰς κινήσεις προσταγμάτων

Τοσούτων δὲ ὄντων καὶ τοιούτων σχηματισμῶν
ἑπόμενον ἂν εἴη τοῖς περὶ αὐτῶν ἐπιέναι προστάγ-
μασι, καθ᾿ ἃ[4] σχηματίζειν τε αὐτὰ καὶ κινεῖν
δυνησόμεθα καὶ ἀποκαθιστάνειν[5] εἰς τὴν προϋπάρ-
χουσαν τάξιν. τοῦτο γὰρ ἦν ἔτι λειπόμενον.

2 Ὅτ᾿ ἂν μὲν οὖν ἐπὶ δόρυ τὰ συντάγματα ἐπιστρέφειν βουλώμεθα, παραγγελοῦμεν τὸν ἐπὶ τοῦ
δεξιοῦ λόχον[6] ἡσυχίαν ἄγειν, ἕκαστον δὲ τῶν ἐν
τοῖς ἄλλοις λόχοις ἐπὶ δόρυ κλίνειν, προσάγειν[7] τε
ἐπὶ τὸ δεξιόν, εἶτα εἰς ὀρθὸν ἀποδοῦναι, ἔπειτα

[1] K. and R.: ἀπείη F.   [2] K. and R.: φοβεῖται F.
[3] K. and R.: ἀγόμενον. ἡ κοίλη τῇ F.
[4] K. and R.: καθά F.   [5] ἀποκαθιστάναι K. and R.
[6] K. and R.: λοξὸν F: λοχαγὸν C (Salmasius).
[7] F (K. and R. had emended to this the form προάγειν in ABC).

[1] The importance of the heavy baggage-train to the

322

ways : it must precede the phalanx when the march is away from the enemy's country, or follow it, when the march is into the enemy's country, or parallel

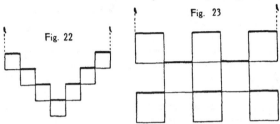

Fig. 22

Fig. 23

the phalanx on the right or left side, whenever danger is suspected from the opposite side, or, finally, it may be convoyed within the hollow square of the phalanx, when danger threatens on all sides.[1]

XII. *The Commands used in military Evolutions*

Such being the number and character of the evolutions, there would naturally follow a discussion of the commands used in these movements, by which we can order and move the troops, and return them to their original station ; for this is the one thing we have left to do.

When, therefore, we wish the battalions to quarter turn to the right, we shall command the right file to hold its position and each man in the rest of the files to right face, to advance to the right, and then to face to the front ; then we shall command

ancient army is hardly appreciated by our author, who dismisses it in these few words.

Asclep. xii. 1-2 = Ael. xxxii. **2.**

ASCLEPIODOTUS

προσάγειν[1] τὰ ὀπίσω ζυγά, καὶ ταύτης γενομένης
τῆς πυκνώσεως ἐπιστρέφειν ἐπὶ δόρυ, καὶ ἔσται
τὸ σύνταγμα ἐπεστραμμένον.

3 Ἐὰν δὲ ἐπὶ τὴν ἐξ ἀρχῆς[2] θέσιν ἀποκαταστῆσαι
βουλώμεθα, ἐπ' ἀσπίδα μεταβάλλεσθαι παραγγελοῦμεν — ἡ δὲ μεταβολὴ τί σημαίνει πρότερον
εἴρηται —, εἶτ' ἀναστρέφειν ὅλον τὸ σύνταγμα,
ἔπειτα ἐξ ἀρχῆς[2] τῶν λοχαγῶν ἠρεμούντων οἱ
λοιποὶ κατὰ ζυγὰ προαγέτωσαν, ἔπειτα μεταβαλλέσθωσαν, ἐφ' ἃ ἐξ ἀρχῆς[2] ἔνευον· ἔπειτα ὁ
δεξιὸς ἠρεμείτω λόχος,[3] οἱ δὲ λοιποὶ ἐπ' ἀσπίδα
κλινέτωσαν καὶ προάγοντες ἀποκαθιστάθωσαν.
οὕτω γὰρ τὴν τάξιν, ἣν πρότερον εἶχεν, ἕκαστος
ἀπολήψεται.

4 Εἰ δ' ἐπ' ἀσπίδα βουλοίμεθα[4] ἐπιστρέφειν,
παραγγελοῦμεν ἑκάστου συντάγματος τὸν λαιὸν
λόχον[5] ἠρεμεῖν, τῶν δὲ ἄλλων ἕκαστον ἐπ' ἀσπίδα
κλῖναι καὶ προσάγειν[1] εἰς τὰ λαιά, εἶτα εἰς ὀρθὸν
ἀποδοῦναι, ἔπειτα προσάγειν[1] τὰ ὀπίσω ζυγά,
καὶ γενομένης τῆς πυκνώσεως ἐπ' ἀσπίδα ἐπιστρέφειν περὶ τὸν λαιὸν λοχαγόν, καὶ γέγονε τὸ
παραγγελθέν.

5 Ἀποκαταστῆσαι δὲ βουλόμενοι ἕκαστον μετα-
βαλοῦμεν, εἶτα σύνταγμα ἀναστρεψάτω, εἶτα οἱ

---

[1] F (K. and R. had emended to this the form προάγειν in
ABC).
[2] The repetition of the phrase before τῶν λοχαγῶν seems
to have no precise meaning and is probably due, as K. and
R. suggested, to the appearance of the same phrase at two
other places in the paragraph, especially the one just below.
[3] λοχαγὸς (suprascr.) C (Salmasius).
[4] βουλόμεθα K. and R.
[5] λοχαγὸς above λόχος C (Salmasius).

the rear ranks to advance, and, when in this way we have the compact formation, to quarter turn to the right,[1] and the battalion will be swung to the right.

If we wish the battalion to resume the original position, we shall give the command to left about face—the meaning of 'about face' has been explained above [2]—and then for the entire battalion to resume its original position;[3] after that, while the rank of file-leaders holds its position, let the other soldiers advance by rank and about face in the direction originally faced; next let the right file hold its position and the rest of the soldiers left face, and advancing wheel to original position. In this manner each man will resume his former place.

If we wish to quarter turn to the left, we shall command the left file of each battalion to hold its position, and the other files to left face, to advance to the left, and then to face to the front; after that we shall command the rear ranks to advance and, when in this way we have the compact formation, to quarter turn to the left on the left file-leader, and the command is carried out.

If we wish the battalions to return to their original position, we shall make each man about face, and each battalion resume its original place; let the

---

[1] The verb used here, as defined in x. 4, means to 'pivot on the right file-leader,' and so the evolution is clear. *Cf.* the opposite evolution in § 4 below.

[2] That is, in x. 3.

[3] That is, the battalion shall pivot on the right file-closer, who now, because of the about-face, is the left file-leader.

Asclep. xii. 3 = Ael. xxxii. 3.   Asclep. xii. 4 = Ael. xxxii. 4.
Asclep. xii. 5 = Ael. xxxii. 5.

λοχαγοὶ ἠρεμείτωσαν, οἱ δὲ λοιποὶ κατὰ ζυγὰ
προαγέτωσαν, ἔπειτα μεταβαλλέσθωσαν[1] ἐφ' ἃ ἐξ
ἀρχῆς ἔνευον, ἔπειτα[1] ὁ λαιὸς λόχος ἠρεμείτω, οἱ
δὲ λοιποὶ ἐπὶ δόρυ κλίναντες προαγέτωσαν,[2] ἕως
ἂν ἀποκαταστῇ τὰ διαστήματα, εἶτα εἰς ὀρθὸν[3]
ἀποδότωσαν, καὶ πάντες ἕξουσι τὴν τάξιν ἣν
πρότερον εἶχον.

6 Ἐὰν δὲ ἐπὶ δόρυ περισπᾶν βουλώμεθα, δύο
ἐπιστροφὰς ἐπὶ τὸ αὐτὸ[4] ποιῆσαι παραγγελοῦμεν·
ἀποκαταστῆσαι[5] δὲ βουλόμενοι παραγγελοῦμεν ἔτι
ἐπὶ δόρυ περισπᾶν—ἐκ τεσσάρων γὰρ ἐπιστροφῶν
εἰς τὸ αὐτὸ πάλιν ἀποκαθίσταται—, τούτων δὲ
γενομένων[6] ἔτι παραγγελοῦμεν τοὺς λοχαγοὺς
ἠρεμεῖν, τοὺς δὲ λοιποὺς μεταβάλλεσθαι[7] καὶ[7]
ἀπιέναι τὰ ὀπίσω ζυγά, εἶτα πάλιν[7] μεταβάλλεσθαι, τὸν δεξιὸν δὲ λόχον ἠρεμεῖν καὶ τοὺς λοιποὺς
ἐπ' ἀσπίδα κλίναντες προάγειν καὶ ἀποκαθιστάνειν[8]
εἰς τὸ ἐξ ἀρχῆς διάστημα, εἶτα[7] εἰς ὀρθὸν ἀποδοῦναι, καὶ οὕτως ἔσται εἰς τὸ ἐξ ἀρχῆς καθ-
εστῶτα.

7 Εἰ δὲ ἐπ' ἀσπίδα βουλόμεθα περισπᾶν, τοῖς ἐναντίοις παραγγελοῦμεν ἐπ' ἀσπίδα δὶς ἐπιστρέφειν,[9]

[1] The words from μεταβαλλέσθωσαν to ἔπειτα are supplied
by K. and R. from the parallel passage in Aelian, *Tactica*,
xxxii. 5.   [2] K. and R.: προσαγέτωσαν F.
[3] K. and R.: ὀρθὴν F.
[4] τοαυτὸ δόρυ F: τὸ αὐτὸ τουτέστιν ἐπὶ δόρυ K. and R.   But
δόρυ derives probably from a gloss on τὸ αὐτό and does not
appear in the parallel passage in Aelian, *Tactica*, xxxii. 6.
[5] K. and R.: παρακαταστῆσαι F.
[6] The contraction for ομενων is by a much later hand in
an erasure of about three letters (Rostagno).
[7] Supplied by K. and R. from the parallel passage in
Aelian, *Tactica*, xxxii. 7.
326

file-leaders hold their position and the rest advance by rank and about face in the direction originally faced, then let the left file hold its position and the rest right face, advance until the intervals between them are resumed, and then face to the front ; and all will have the original line.

If we wish them to half turn to the right, we shall command them to make two quarter-turns in that direction ; and when we wish them to resume the original position, we shall command them to half turn to the right—for the original position is again taken by four quarter-turns in the same direction—; when this has been done we shall command the file-leaders to hold their position, the rest to about face, and the rear ranks to advance and then about face ; and we shall now command the right file to hold its position, and the rest to left face, advance, resume the original interval from one another, and then face to the front ; and in this way the battalion will return to the original position.[1]

If we wish to half turn to the left, we shall give the command in just the opposite way, to quarter

---

[1] These marchings are necessary to change from the compact formation, in which all wheeling by battalions is done, to the normal formation with interval of three cubits.

Asclep. xii. 6 = Ael. xxxii. 6-7.
Asclep. xii.7 = Ael. xxxii. 8-9.

---

[8] ἀποκαθιστάναι K. and R.

[9] For what has obviously fallen out (the εἰ below after δόρυ in F is probably a remnant of it, as K. and R. saw), K. and R. suggest εἶτα ἀποκαταστῆσαι βουλόμενοι πάλιν ἐπ' ἀσπίδα δὶς ἐπιστρέφειν ; compare Aelian, Tactica, xxxii. 8.

. . . ἀλλὰ μὴ ἐπὶ δόρυ, καὶ[1] ταῖς ὁμοίαις ἀγωγαῖς χρήσασθαι. ὁμοίως δὲ καὶ ἐκπερισπάσαι βουλόμενοι τρὶς ἐπιστρέψομεν τὰ συντάγματα.

8 Ἐὰν δὲ κατὰ κέρας τὴν φάλαγγα πυκνῶσαι δέῃ, παραγγελοῦμεν ἐπὶ τοῦ δεξιοῦ τὸν δεξιὸν λόχον ἠρεμεῖν, τοὺς δὲ λοιποὺς ἐπὶ δόρυ κλίναντας προσάγειν ἐπὶ τὸ δεξιόν, ἔπειτα εἰς ὀρθὸν ἀποδιδόναι, καὶ προσάγειν τὰ ὀπίσω ζυγά. ἀποκαταστῆσαι δὲ προαιρούμενοι παραγγελοῦμεν τὸ μὲν λοχαγοῦν ζυγὸν ἠρεμεῖν, τὰ δ' ὀπίσω ζυγὰ μεταβαλλόμενα ἀνιέναι,[2] εἶτα πάλιν μεταβάλλεσθαι, ἔπειτα τοῦ δεξιοῦ λόχου ἠρεμοῦντος οἱ λοιποὶ ἐπ' ἀσπίδα κλίναντες προαγέτωσαν, ἕως ἂν τὰ ἐξ ἀρχῆς διαστήματα συντηρήσαντες εἰς ὀρθὸν ἀποδῶσιν.[3]

9 Εἰ δὲ τὸ λαιὸν κέρας πυκνῶσαι δέῃ, τἀναντία παραγγελοῦμεν, εἰ δὲ τὸ[4] μέσον τῆς φάλαγγος, τὴν δεξιὰν ἀποτομὴν ἐπ' ἀσπίδα κλίναντες, τὴν δὲ λαιὰν ἐπὶ δόρυ, εἶτα προσάγειν[5] κελεύοντες ἐπὶ τὸν ὀμφαλὸν τῆς φάλαγγος, ἔπειτα εἰς ὀρθὸν ἀποδοῦναι καὶ[6] προσάγειν τὰ ὀπίσω ζυγά, ἕξομεν ὃ προαιρούμεθα. ἀποκαταστῆσαι δὲ βουλόμενοι μεταβάλλεσθαι παραγγελοῦμεν καὶ προάγειν κατὰ ζυγὰ χωρὶς τοῦ πρώτου, ἔπειτα πάλιν μεταβάλλεσθαι, καὶ τὴν μὲν δεξιὰν διφαλαγγίαν ἐπὶ δόρυ,

[1] C (Salmasius), K. and R.: εἰ F.
[2] K. and R. (ABἴ): ἀνίεσθαι F (C).
[3] K. and R.: ἀποδώσειν F.
[4] K. and R.: τὸν F.
[5] K. and R. (Aelian, *Tactica*, xxxiii. 4): προάγειν F.
[6] Supplied by K. and R.

[1] As in § 6 above.
[2] That is, the centre, the point of division between the two wings.

turn twice to the left, [and then, wishing to return to the original position, we shall command them to quarter turn twice to the left,] not to the right, and to perform the similar [1] evolutions. In the same way, when we wish to make the three-quarter-turn, we shall make the battalions perform three quarter-turns.

If the phalanx must assume the compact formation by wings, we shall give the command, if on the right wing, for the right file to hold its position and for the other files to right face, close up to the right, and then face to the front, and for the rear ranks to advance. Then, if we wish to resume the original position, we shall command the rank of file-leaders to hold its position, the rear ranks to about face and advance, and then again to about face; after that, while the right file holds its position, let the other files left face and advance, until they have resumed their original intervals, when they face to the front.

If the left wing must assume the compact formation, we shall give the opposite commands. If the centre must assume the compact formation, we shall command the right wing to left face and the left wing to right face, then to advance to the navel [2] of the phalanx, to face to the front, and to advance the rear ranks, and we shall have the desired formation. If we wish the wings to resume their former position, we shall command them to about face and all the ranks save the first to advance and then about face; and we shall order the right wing to

Asclep. xii. 8 = Ael. xxxiii. 1-2.
Asclep. xii. 9 = Ael. xxxiii. 4-6.

τὴν δὲ λαιὰν ἐπ᾽ ἀσπίδα κλῖναι, εἶτα κατὰ λόχους
ἀκολουθεῖν τοῖς ἡγουμένοις, ἄχρις ἂν τὰ ἐξ ἀρχῆς
λάβωσι διαστήματα, εἶτα εἰς ὀρθὸν ἀποδοῦναι.

Δεῖ δὲ ἄνω τὰ[1] δόρατα εἶναι ἐν ταῖς πυκνώσεσι
πρὸς τὸ μὴ ἐμποδὼν[2] ταῖς κλίσεσι γίνεσθαι.

10 Ταῖς δ᾽ αὐταῖς ἀγωγαῖς χρησίμαις οὔσαις πρὸς
τὰς τῶν πολεμίων αἰφνιδίους ἐπιφανείας[3] καὶ[4]
τοὺς ψιλοὺς ἀσκήσομεν.

. . .[5] τὰ μὲν φωνῇ, τὰ δὲ διὰ σημείων ὁρατῶν,
ἔνια δὲ καὶ διὰ τῆς σάλπιγγος. σαφέστατα μὲν
γάρ ἐστι τὰ[6] διὰ φωνῆς δηλούμενα—οὐ μὴν πάντοτε
δυνατὸν διὰ κτύπου τῶν ὅπλων ἢ διὰ πνευμάτων
σφοδρῶν ἐμβολάς, ἀθορυβώτερα δὲ τὰ διὰ τῶν
σημείων· ἀλλ᾽ ἐνίοτε καὶ τούτοις ἐπιπροσθοίη[7]
ἢ[8] ἡλίου ἀνταύγεια ἢ παχύτης ἀέρος καὶ κονιορτοῦ
ἢ καὶ ὄμβρου πλῆθος, δι᾽ ὃ οὐ ῥᾴδιον πρὸς πάσας
τὰς ἀνακυπτούσας[9] χρείας εὐπορῆσαι σημείων,
οἷς προσήθισται[10] ἡ φάλαγξ, ἀλλ᾽ ἐνίοτε[11] πρὸς
τοὺς καιροὺς ἀνάγκη καινὰ προσευρίσκειν, πλὴν
ἀδύνατον ἅπαντα συμπεσεῖν, ὥστ᾽ ἄδηλον εἶναι
καὶ σάλπιγγι καὶ φωνῇ καὶ σημείῳ τὸ παράγγελμα.

11 Τὰ μέντοι διὰ φωνῆς σύντομά[12] τε εἶναι δεῖ καὶ
ἀναμφίβολα. τοῦτο ἂν[13] γένοιτο, εἰ τὰ ἰδικὰ[14]
τῶν γενῶν τε καὶ κοινῶν προτάττοιμεν· ἀμφί-

---

[1] τα F.   [2] ἐμποδον F.
[3] αἰφνιδίους ἐπιφανείας τῶν πολεμίων C (Salmasius), K. and R.
[4] Added by K. and R.
[5] For the obvious lacuna K. and R. suggest from the
parallel passage in Aelian and Arrian, op. cit., xxxv. 1 Τὰ
δὲ παραγγέλματα ὀξέως δέχεσθαι τὴν στρατιὰν ἀσκήσομεν, τὰ μὲν
κτλ.   [6] Supplied by K. and R.
[7] K. and R. : ἐπιπροσθείη F.
[8] Supplied by K. and R. (without any note : in ABC?).
[9] ἀντικυπτούσας K. and R. (probably a mere misprint).

right face and the left wing to left face, to follow by files the leading files until they have the original intervals, and then to face to the front.

In the compact formations the spears must be elevated, so as not to interfere in the turnings.

We shall train the light infantry also in the same evolutions, which are so advantageous in case the enemy appears suddenly.

[We shall, furthermore, train the army to distinguish sharply the commands] given sometimes by the voice, sometimes by visible signals, and sometimes by the bugle. The most distinct commands are those given by the voice, but they may not carry at all times because of the clash of arms or heavy gusts of wind ; less affected by uproar are the commands given by signals ; but even these may be interfered with now and then by the sun's glare, thick fog and dust, or heavy rain. One cannot, therefore, find signals, to which the phalanx has been accustomed, suitable for every circumstance that arises, but now and then new signals must be found to meet the situation ; but it is hardly likely that all the difficulties appear at the same time, so that a command will be indistinguishable both by bugle, voice, and signal.

Now the commands by voice must be short and unambiguous. This would be attained if the particular command should precede the general,

Asclep. xii. 10 = Ael. xxxv. Asclep. xii. 11 = Ael. xl-xlii.

---

[10] προσείθισται K. and R. [11] ἀλλ ἐνίοται F.
[12] K. and R.: σύντονά F which might be defended ('sharp,' 'crisp') were it not that Arrian and Aelian, *op. cit.*, xl. 1, have σύντομα in the parallel passage.
[13] δ' ἂν K. and R. (AB?): om. δ' F (C). [14] εἰταϊδικὰ F.
331

βολα[1] γὰρ τὰ κοινά· οἷον οὐκ ἂν φήσαιμεν " κλῖναι
ἐπὶ δόρυ,"[2] ἀλλ' " ἐπὶ δόρυ κλῖναι," ἵνα μὴ διὰ
τὴν προθυμίαν οἱ μὲν ἐπ' ἄλλο, οἱ δὲ ἐπ' ἄλλο τῆς
κλίσεως προειρημένης νεύσωσιν,[3] ἀλλ' ὁμοῦ τὸ
αὐτὸ ποιήσωσιν· ὡς δὲ οὐδὲ " μεταβάλλου [4] ἐπὶ
δόρυ," ἀλλ' " ἐπὶ δόρυ μεταβάλλου[5] " φήσαιμεν,
οὐδ' " ἐξέλισσε[6] τὸν[7] Λάκωνα," ἀλλ' ἀνάπαλιν
" τὸν Λάκωνα ἐξέλισσε " καί . . .[8]

. . . παράστηθι ἐπὶ τὰ ὅπλα. ὁ σκευοφόρος
ἀποχωρείτω τῆς φάλαγγος. ἡσυχία δὲ ἔστω
καὶ προσέχετε τῷ παραγγέλματι. ὑπόλαβε[9] τὴν
σκευήν· ἀνάλαβε. διάστηθι. ἀνάλαβε τὸ δόρυ.
στοίχει, ζύγει,[10] παρόρα ἐπὶ τὸν ἡγούμενον. ὁ
οὐραγὸς ἀπευθυνέτω τὸν ἴδιον λόχον. συντήρει
τὰ ἐξ ἀρχῆς διαστήματα. ἐπὶ δόρυ κλῖνον,[11]
πρόαγε, ἔχου οὕτως. τὸ βάθος διπλασίαζε, ἀποκαταστήσον. τὸ βάθος ἡμισίαζε, ἀποκαταστήσον. τὸ μῆκος διπλασίαζε, ἀποκαταστήσον. τὸν
Λάκωνα[12] ἐξέλισσε, ἀποκαταστήσον. ἐπίστρεφε,
ἀποκαταστήσον. ἐπὶ δόρυ περίσπα,[13] ἀποκατά-
στησον ἢ ἐπικαταστήσον, κατὰ τὰ αὐτὰ καὶ ἐπ'[14]
ἀσπίδα.

Αὗται διὰ βραχέων αἱ τοῦ τακτικοῦ καθηγήσεις,
τοῖς μὲν χρωμένοις σωτηρίαν πορίζουσαι, τοῖς δ'
ἐναντίοις κινδύνους ἐπάγουσαι.

[1] ἀμφ·όλα F.
[2] ἐπιδου followed by space of four letters F (ἐπὶ δόρυ A
2nd hand in margin).
[3] νεύσωσιν K. and R. (perhaps a misprint, as there is no
note).   [4] K. and R.: ὥστε οὐδὲν μεταβάλλοι F.
[5] K. and R.: μεταβάλλειν F.
[6] K. and R.: ἐξελίσσαι F.   [7] K. and R.: τὴν F.
[8] What has been lost here, probably two or three sen-

since the general are ambiguous. For example, we would not say, " Face right ! " but " Right face ! ", so that in their eagerness some may not make the turn to the right and others to the left when the order to turn has been given first, but that all may do the same thing together ; nor do we say, " Face about right ! " but " Right about face ! " nor " Counter march Laconian ! " but " Laconian counter march ! " and . . . .

. . . Stand by to take arms ! Baggage-men fall out ! Silence in the ranks ! and Attention ! Take up arms ! Shoulder arms [1] ! Take distance ! Shoulder spear ! Dress files ! Dress ranks ! Dress files by the file-leader ! File-closer, dress file ! Keep your original distance ! Right face ! Forward march ! Halt ! Depth double ! As you were ! Depth half ! As you were ! Length double ! As you were ! Laconian counter march ! As you were ! Quarter turn ! As you were ! Right half turn ! As you were ! or Forward to position ! either Right ! [2] or Left !

These are in brief the principles of the tactician ; they mean safety to those who follow them and danger to those who disobey.

---

[1] ' Arms ' (σκευή) here probably mean merely the defensive equipment, shield and helmet.
[2] Literally, ' in the same direction,' *i.e.*, to the right.

---

tences containing further illustrations, the reason for this order in giving commands, and the sentence introductory to the following list of commands, can be recovered from the parallel passage in Arrian and Aelian, *op. cit.*, xl. 4-xlii. 1.
[9] K. and R.: ὑπέλαβε F.   [10] στοιχει ζυγει F.
[11] K. and R. (AB ?): κεινον F.   [12] λάκων F.
[13] περισπα F.   [14] K. and R. (AB ?): ἐπι F.

A LIST OF SOME OF THE MORE IMPORTANT
TECHNICAL TERMS IN ASCLEPIODOTUS [1]

ἀκροβολιστής, skirmisher; of horsemen, i. 3; vii. 7.

ἄκρον, wing of a line of battle, i. 3.

ἀμφίστομος -ον; πορεία ἀμφίστομος, when the main divisions of an army march in parallel or in column formation with the line of front-rank men on the outside, iii. 5; x. 22; xi. 3 and 4.

ἀναστρέφω, to wheel to the original position, after a military evolution, = ἀποκαθίστημι, ἀποκαθιστάνω, xii. 3.

ἀναστροφή, wheeling back to the original position, x. 1 and 6; wheeling in general, vii. 3 (also vii. 2 K. and R.).

ἀντιπορία, counter attack, or frontal attack, x. 2.

ἀντίστομος -ον; πορεία ἀντίστομος, when the main divisions of an army march in parallel formation with the line of front-rank men on the inside, xi. 3.

ἀποκαθίστημι, to return to the original position, xii. 11, etc.

ἀποκατάστασις, return to original position after wheeling or other evolutions, x. 1; 9 and 11. Cf. ἐπικατάστασις.

ἀπόστασις; ἐν ἀποστάσει, at a distance, at some interval, x. 21.

[ἀποστροφή, wheeling away (from the enemy), retreat, vii. 2 (Oldfather).]

ἀποτομή; ἀποτομή κέρατος, half-wing, or corps, theoretically 4096 men, ii. 10; iii. 1 and 2.

ἀραιός -ά -όν, open, wide, opposed to πυκνός, of the space between soldiers in array, iv. 1.

ἀραρός (neu. perf. ptcp. of ἀραρίσκω used as a substantive), joining - point, point of division between

[1] No attempt has been made to include every technical term, or all instances of each term cited, but only the most noteworthy or unusual.

LIST OF TECHNICAL TERMS

the two wings of an army, ii. 6.

ἁρματαρχία, unit of sixteen war-chariots, viii. 1.

ἀσπιδίσκη, small shield, i. 2.

ἀσπίς, shield; ἐπ' ἀσπίδα, to the left, x. 1, etc.

δεκανία, decury, older designation for a file (λόχος), ii. 2.

διάστημα, interval between soldiers in rank and in file, iv. 1.

δίππευσις, breaking through with cavalry, vii. 3.

δίστημι, to take distance, for the different spacings in the ranks, xii. 11; cf. διάστημα.

διλοχία, two files, ii. 8 and 10; iii. 4.

διλοχίτης, commander of two files, ii. 8.

διμοιρία, half-file, where the file had twelve men, ii. 2.

διμοιρίτης, leader of a half-file, ii. 2.

διπλασιάζω, to double either the number of soldiers in a given area, or the area by deploying the soldiers, x. 1.

διφαλαγγία, double corps, or wing, theoretically 8192 men, ii. 10.

διχοτομία, point of division, ii. 6.

δορατοφόρος -ον, spear-bearing, of cavalry, i. 3.

δόρυ, spear; ἐπὶ δόρυ, to the right, x. 1, etc.

δρεπανηφόρος -ον, scythe-bearing, of chariots, viii. 1.

εἴλη, squadron of cavalry, vii. 2.

ἑκατοντάρχης = ταξίαρχος, captain of hundred, really 128 men, ii. 8.

ἑκατονταρχία, two platoons of light-armed troops, a company, composed of 128 men, vi. 3.

ἐκπερισπασμός, three-quarter-turn, x. 1 and 8.

ἔκτακτος -η -ον; οἱ ἔκτακτοι, the supernumeraries, attached originally to the τάξις, but later either to the σύνταγμα, ii. 9, or the ἑκατονταρχία of light-armed troops, vi. 3, or the φάλαγξ of light-armed troops, vi. 3.

ἐλεφαντάρχης, commander of sixteen war-elephants, ix. 1.

ἐμπλέκω, to incorporate, of light infantry, man beside man, in the phalanx of hoplites, vi. 1.

ἐναντίος -α -ον; ἀπ' ἐναντίας, on the other hand, i. 2.

ἐνωμοτάρχης, leader of an ἐνωμοτία, ii. 2.

ἐνωμοτία, quarter-file, ii. 2.

ἐξάριθμος -η -ον, outside the normal number, or in addition to it, ii. 9.

ἐξελιγμός, counter-march, x. 13 ff.

ἐξελίσσω, to counter march, x. i; xii. 11.

335

ἐπαγωγή, sequence formation, *i.e.*, when one wing follows the other, both marching in column, x. 1 ; xi. 2 and 4.

ἐπιθηραρχία, a unit of four war-elephants, ix. 1.

ἐπιθήραρχος, a commander of four war-elephants, ix. 1.

ἐπικαθίστημι, to advance to original position, x. 10 ; *cf.* ἐπικατάστασις.

ἐπικάμπιος -ον ; ἐπικάμπιος εἰς τοὐπίσω (sc. φάλαγξ), half-square march backward, xi. 1 ; ἐ. εἰς τὸ πρόσω, the same forward, xi. 1.

ἐπικατάστασις, advance to original position after wheeling, x. 1 and 9 ; *cf.* ἀποκατάστασις.

ἐπικοινωνέω, to be attached to, or stationed upon, i. 3.

ἐπιλαρχία, battalion of cavalry, vii. 11.

ἐπιξεναγία, a division of light-armed troops, 2048 men, vi. 3.

ἐπιξεναγός, commander of an ἐπιξεναγία, vi. 3.

ἐπιστάτης, 2nd, 4th, 6th, etc., man in a file, ii. 3 and 4 ; iv. 2.

ἐπιστροφή, quarter-turn, x. 1, 4, etc. ; wheeling towards (the enemy), attack, vii. 2.

ἐπισυζυγία, unit of eight war-chariots, viii. 1.

ἐπίταγμα, supporting-force, the phalanx of light-armed troops, 8192 men, vi. 3 ;

vii. 10 ; the full force of cavalry, vii. 11.

ἐπίταξις, supporting-position, x. 1 (*cf.* vii. 10).

ἐπιφάνεια, facing - right, or -left, of an army, x. 4 and 5.

ἑτερόστομος -ον ; ἑτερόστομος πορεία, when the wings of an army march in column, with their front-line men on opposite sides, xi. 4.

ἐφιππαρχία, division of cavalry, vii. 11.

ζυγαρχέω, cf. ζυγάρχης, vii. 9.

ζυγάρχης, rank-leader in cavalry, the man at the corner of each rank when in wedge-formation, vii. 9.

ζυγαρχία, a unit of two war-chariots, viii. 1.

ζυγέω, to stand in ranks, of a phalanx, ii. 6 ; of a cavalry squadron, vii. 4 and 5, etc.

ζώαρχος, driver or commander of a war-elephant, ix. 1.

ἡμιλόχιον, half-file, ii. 2.

ἡμιλοχίτης, commander of a ἡμιλόχιον, ii. 2.

ἡμισιάζω, to halve intervals, xii. 11.

θηραρχία, unit of two war-elephants, ix. 1.

θήραρχος, commander of two war-elephants, ix. 1.

θυρεοφόρος -ον, bearing a large, oblong shield, of cavalry, i. 3.

ἰλάρχης, (1) front-man of a cavalry squadron, stationed at the point of the wedge, vii. 2 ; 3, etc. ; (2) commander of eight war-elephants, ix. 1.

ἰππαρχία, two Ταραντιναρχίαι (q.v.) of cavalry, vii. 11.

καταπυκνος -ον ; ἐν καταπύκνῳ στάσει, in compact formation, v. 1.

κεράρχης, (1) commander of a wing, 8192 men, ii. 10 ; (2) commander of thirty-two war-elephants, ix. 1.

κέρας, (1) wing of an army, formerly 2048 men = μεραρχία, later a double-corps, consisting of 8192 men, ii. 10 ; (2) squadron of thirty-two war-chariots, viii. 1.

κλίσις, right- or left-face, x. 1 and 2.

κοιλέμβολος, hollow - wedge, xi. 5.

κοῖλος -η -ον ; κοίλη φάλαγξ, concave formation, xi. 1.

κυρτός -ή -όν ; κυρτὴ φάλαγξ. convex formation, xi. 1.

λοξός -ή -όν ; λοξὴ φάλαγξ, a phalanx in march with extended front, one wing in advance of the other, x. 1 ; xi. 1.

λοχαγός, first man and leader of a file (λόχος), ii. 2, etc.

λόχος, a file, consisting of sixteen men, ii. 1, etc.

μεράρχης, commander of a μεραρχία, ii. 10.

μεραρχία, command of 2048 men, a division, ii. 10 ; iii. 2.

μεταβάλλω, (act.) to cause to about face, xii. 5 ; (mid.) to about face, xii. 3.

μεταβολή, about-face, x. 1 and 3.

μεταγωγή, manœuvring, wheeling, vii. 5.

μετατάττω, to reorganize, ii. 2.

μέτωπον, front line of phalanx, ii. 5 ; iv. 4 ; v. 1 and 2.

μῆκος, first line of a phalanx, ii. 5.

ξεναγία, two battalions of light-armed troops, a regiment of 512 men, vi. 3 [supplied from Aelian, Tactica, xvi. 3].

ὀκταλοχία, a military unit of eight λόχοι, ii. 9.

ὁμόζυγος, comrade-in-rank, ii. 4. Cf. παραστάτης.

ὁμοιόστομος -ον ; πορεία ὁμοιόστομος, when the divisions of an army march in parallel formation, with the front-line men on the same side, xi. 3 ; or in column, with the same disposition, xi. 4.

ὄμφαλος, centre, point of division between the two wings, ii. 6 ; xii. 9.

ὄρθιος -α -ον ; φάλαγξ ὀρθία, the phalanx marching forward in file, or in column, xi. 1 ff.

337

ὀρθός -ή -όν ; εἰς ὀρθὸν ἀποδοῦναι, to face the front originally held, lines front, x. 1 and 12 ; xii. 6, etc.

οὐρά ; ἐπ' οὐράν, about face to the rear from the enemy, x. 3 ; ἀπ' οὐρᾶς, about face from the rear toward the enemy, x. 3.

οὐραγός, (1) the last man in file, file-closer, ii. 2 ; iii. 6, etc. ; (2) the man at the rear corner of a squadron, vii. 2, etc. ; (3) a supernumerary to the τάξις, ii. 9 ; iii. 6 ; or the ἑκατονταρχία, vi. 3.

ὀχηματικός -ή -όν, pertaining to the mounted force of an army, whether cavalry, chariots, or elephants, i. 1 and 3.

παραγωγή, march in line, where the phalanx on the march keeps the original battle-line, x. 1 ; xi. 1 ff.

παραστάτης, comrade-in-rank, ii. 4 ; iv. 2. Cf. ὁμόζυγος.

παράταξις, first line, or front line, of a phalanx, ii. 5.

παρεδρεύω ; ὁ παρεδρεύων, comrade behind in file, iii. 6.

παρεμβολή, insertion, differing from παρένταξις in that soldiers of the same branch are inserted in the battle-line, as hoplites beside hoplites, vi. 1.

παρένθεσις, insertion, general term including both παρεμβολή and παρένταξις, vi. 1.

παρένταξις, insertion, differing from παρεμβολή in that soldiers of different branches of the army, as light-armed troops, are inserted in the phalanx of hoplites, man beside man, vi. 1.

πεντακοσιάρχης, commander of a πεντακοσιαρχία, ii. 10.

πεντακοσιαρχία, command of 512 men, ii. 10 ; iii. 3.

πεντηκονταρχία, two squads of light-armed troops, a platoon, composed of sixty-four men, vi. 3.

περισπασμός, half-turn, x. 1 and 7.

πλάγιος -α -ον ; πλαγία φάλαγξ, an army in march with the front extended, x. 1 ; xi. 1.

πλαγιοφύλαξ, guard on the flank of a wedge-shaped squadron, vii. 2 ; 6, etc.

προαγωνίζομαι, to open battle, vii. 1.

πρόπτωσις, projection of spears before a phalanx, v. 1.

προσένταξις, flank-position, used of light infantry stationed on the wings of the phalanx, vi. 1.

πρόσωπον, front line of phalanx, ii. 5.

πρόταξις, position of the light-armed troops in front of the phalanx, vi. 1.

πρωτολοχία, front line of the phalanx, ii. 5.

πρωτοστάτης, front man in a

file, ii. 3; also 1st, 3rd, 5th, etc., man in a file, *ibid.*, 3 and 4.

πύκνωσις, close order, a compact arrangement used in attack, the men being spaced two cubits from one another, iv. 1 and 3; xii. 4 and 9.

σαλπιγκτής, bugler, ii. 9; vi. 3.

σημειοφόρος, signalman, ii. 9; vi. 3.

Σκύθης, branch of cavalry armed only with bows, i. 3.

στῖφος, two divisions of light-armed troops, a corps, 4096 men, vi. 3.

στίχος, a row of soldiers, used for both ' rank ' and ' file,' ii. 5; as an old designation of ' file,' ii. 2.

στοιχέω, to be in file, of a phalanx, ii. 6; of a cavalry squadron, vii. 4 and 5, etc.

στόμα, front line of phalanx, ii. 5; xi. 1; van of army, xi. 1, etc.

στρατηγός, general, formerly of a corps of 4096 men, but properly commander-in-chief of a phalanx of 16,384 men, ii. 10.

στρατοκῆρυξ, army-herald, ii. 9; vi. 3.

σύζευξις ; κατὰ σύζευξιν, used of the march of an army when the columns are parallel with each other;

opposed to κατ' ἐπαγωγήν, xi. 2.

συζυγία, a unit of four war-chariots, viii. 1.

συλλοχισμός, assembly of the files in parallel formation, constituting the phalanx, ii. 5.

συνασπισμός, formation with locked shields, to meet attack, iii. 6; iv. 3.

συνεδρεύω, to close up, draw together, of troops taking up the compact formation, iii. 6 (but *cf.* crit. note).

συνεπισκέπω, to protect at the same time, of armour protecting both man and horse, i. 3.

σύνταγμα, two companies or a battalion, ii. 8; iii. 6; συνταξιαρχία takes its place in ii. 10; iii. 3 and 4.

συνταγματάρχης, commander of a σύνταγμα, ii. 8.

συνταξιαρχία, battalion, ii. 9; takes the place of σύνταγμα, ii. 10; iii. 3 and 4.

συνωμοτία, a squad of soldiers bound by an oath, an early term for file (λόχος), ii. 2.

σύστασις, four files of light-armed troops, a squad, consisting of thirty-two men, vi. 3.

σύστρεμμα, brigade of light-armed troops, 1024 men, vi. 3.

ταξιαρχία, eight files (λόχοι)

339

of infantry, = τάξις, ii. 10 ; iii. 4.

ταξίαρχος, commander of a company, composed of eight files (λόχοι), ii. 8.

τάξις, a company, eight files (λόχοι) of infantry, ii. 8 and 9.

Ταραντιναρχία, two battalions of cavalry, vii. 11.

Ταραντῖνος -η -ον ; οἱ Ταραντῖνοι, cavalry who fight only at a distance with javelins, i. 3.

τελάρχης, commander of a τέλος = μεραρχης, ii. 10.

τέλος, (1) in infantry, a division, 2048 men = μεραρχία, ii. 10 ; (2) in cavalry, a half-phalanx, vii. 11.

τετράρχης, commander of a τετραρχία, ii. 8.

τετραρχία, four files (λόχοι) of infantry, a platoon, ii. 8 ; iii. 4.

τετράς ; κατὰ τετράδα, on a fourfold division or basis, iii. 1.

τόξευμα, missile of any kind, i. 2.

τοξότης, archer, part of the cavalry, i. 3.

ὑπερβάλλω ; τὸ κέρας ὑπερβαλέσθαι, to outflank on one wing, x. 2 and 18.

ὑπερκεράω = ὑπερβάλλω, x. 18.

ὑπερφαλαγγέω, to outflank on both wings, x. 18.

ὑπηρέτης, aide-de-camp, ii. 9 ; vi. 3.

ὑποβαίνω, to march behind, as one rank of soldiers marches a certain distance behind another, v. 1.

ὑποστολή ; δι' ὑποστολῆς, held back, partly withdrawn, refused, x. 21.

ὑπόταξις, rear - position, of light infantry stationed behind the phalanx, vi. 1.

φαλαγγάρχης, (1) commander of a φαλαγγαρχία, ii. 10 ; (2) commander of a full force of sixty-four war-elephants, ix. 1.

φαλαγγαρχία, corps, 4096 men, ii. 10 ; iii. 2.

φάλαγξ, (1) any branch of the service, i. title ; i. 4 ; (2) specifically, the force of hoplites, consisting of 16,384 men, ii. 10, etc. ; (3) the full force of sixty-four war-chariots, viii. 1.

χιλιάρχης, commander of a χιλιαρχία, ii. 10.

χιλιαρχία, brigade, 1024 men, ii. 10 ; iii. 2 and 3.

ψιλαγία, a command of two ἑκατονταρχίαι, a battalion of light-armed troops, vi. 3 [supplied from Aelian, Tactica, xvi. 3].

PREFACE

In the preparation of the present work Mr. Oldfather is primarily responsible for the introduction, text, and list of rare words. Mr. Titchener rendered assistance in collecting material and collating MSS., and also prepared the first draft of the translation, which has been further revised by Mr. Pease.

WILLIAM A. OLDFATHER
ARTHUR STANLEY PEASE
JOHN B. TITCHENER.

URBANA, ILLINOIS, *Feb. 1,* 1922.

INTRODUCTION

Of Onasander, the author of the present Στρατηγικός
(sc. λόγος), or *The General*, we know from the
biographical article in Suidas that he was a Platonic
philosopher who, in addition to a military work,[1]
composed a commentary upon Plato's *Republic*.[2]

Traces of Platonic philosophy have been sought
in the present work, especially in the admonition
that friends should fight beside friends (Ch. 24),
and in the distinction made between φθόνος and
ζῆλος (Ch. 42. 25). But the essence of the first idea
is as old as Nestor's advice in the *Iliad* (B 362 f.);
it was practised among the Eleans, Italic Greeks,
Cretans, and Boeotians, being characteristic of the
Sacred Band of Thebes, and something similar
may not have been unknown at one time in Sparta,[3]

---

[1] The mss. of Suidas give Τακτικὰ περὶ στρατηγημάτων.
Bernhardi (following Küster) puts a comma after τακτικά,
as though different works were referred to, but it is much
more likely that only one was meant, whether we take the
words περὶ στρατηγημάτων as explanatory of τακτικέ, or
suppose that ἤ has fallen out. In any event the title given
by Suidas is inexact, for the better mss. of Onasander give
Στρατηγικός (the inferior ones Στρατηγικά or Στρατηγική),
which is undoubtedly correct, and is attested also by the
so-called Leo xiv. 112. Suidas exemplifies late usage
which applied τακτικά to any military treatise.

[2] This has left no trace.

[3] The evidence is collected and discussed by Erich Bethe,

hence it can hardly have escaped the attention of military writers. The same topic is treated also in extant literature from before the time of Onasander by Xenophon in his *Symposium*, viii. 32, 34, 35, so that, although Onasander can hardly have been ignorant of the famous passage in Plato (*Symposium*, 178 E ff.), it is hardly necessary to assume that this was the immediate source.

As for the discrimination between φθόνος and ζῆλος there is no real parallel in Plato, whereas an almost exact counterpart exists in Aristotle (*Rhet.* ii. 11. 1), a circumstance which escaped Schwebel.[1] Such definitions, however, were the stock in trade of philosophers,[2] and do not presuppose a specific source unless there is some marked similarity in expression. On the contrary, one would rather be inclined to wonder that, in an ethical study of warfare like the present, a commentator upon Plato's *Republic* should have failed to show at any point some trace of the not infrequent references to war and its basic cause, the character of the good soldier,

---

Rhein. Mus., 1907, lxii: 445 ff. The φίλων ἴλη of the younger Scipio (Appian, *Hisp.* 84) seems to have been composed rather of friends of Scipio, than of mutual friends, so that I cannot agree with Wecklein, *Philol.*, 1876, xxxiv: 413, who compares it with the ἱερὸς λόχος of Thebes. In Magna Graecia so closely connected was paederasty with war that it was even said to have been in origin a military measure. (Suidas *s.v.* Θάμυρις.)

[1] The Pseudo-Platonic "Ὅροι (which Schwebel, following a very dubious tradition, ascribes to Theophrastus) give a somewhat different definition of φθόνος, and of φθόνος only.

[2] Compare the scholium to Aristophanes, *Plutus*, 87, where the definition of the word as given by the philosophers (παρὰ τοῖς φιλοσόφοις) is contrasted with that given by the rhetoricians. The Stoics, of course, had their definition, see Diog. Laert. vii. 111.

the need of constant military exercise, the style of life of the soldier, the professional aspect of successful military preparation, mathematics as a necessary element in an officer's education, proposals looking toward the elimination of certain of the more cruel aspects of warfare, at least between civilized states, and similar topics discussed in that great work. Such silence on the part of Onasander, although not sufficient, perhaps, to cast doubt on the identity of our author with the writer mentioned by Suidas, would more naturally suggest that in *The General* we have a study anterior to a period of preoccupation with Plato.

The only other references to Onasander from antiquity are in Johannes Lydus, *De magistratibus*, i. 47, who names an Ὀνήσανδρος among Greek military writers, and in the *Tactica* of the so-called Leo,[1] xiv. 112, Ὀνήσανδρος δὲ καὶ αὐτὸς στρατηγικὸν συντάξας λόγον. In this connexion some conclusion must be reached about the proper form of the name, which has been much in doubt. The reading of all known MSS. except F and D (see below under 'MSS.' and 'Symbols'), supported by Suidas, is Ὀνόσανδρος and so the majority of editors print the name. On the other hand the earliest

---

[1] This work, long ascribed to Leo VI, is now known to antedate his period, and must go back to Leo III (A.D. 711–741), commonly, but incorrectly, called the Isaurian. This conclusion was first advanced by Zachariae von Lingenthal, *Byz. Zeitschr.*, 1894, iii : 437 ff., and the demonstration completed by K. Schenk, *ibid.*, 1896, vi : 298 f. Of course the Emperor is only to be regarded as the one under whose auspices the work was composed. See also R. Helbing in his review of R. Vari's new edition of the *Tactica*, Budapest, 1917 (unfortunately inaccessible as yet), in *Berl. philol. Wochenschr.*, 1919, 97.

ONASANDER

authorities, Johannes Lydus and the so-called
Leo, of whom the latter must have had access to
better sources than Suidas in this matter, give the
form Ὀνήσανδρος.[1]   Scholars have been divided,
Schwebel (in his commentary), Fabricius, Koraes,
M. Haupt, von Rohden, Jähns, Bechtel (à propos of
an inscription, Bezz. Beitr., 1896, xxi : 236) favouring
Ὀνήσανδρος, while the early editors and translators
uniformly, Haase, Köchly, K. K. Müller, Christ-
Schmid, and works of reference in general employ
Ὀνόσανδρος.   As far as the then available evidence
went it favoured slightly the spelling with η, for all
the MSS. but F go back to but a single source of
the tenth century,[2] the period to which Suidas
belongs, while the Tactica of Leo[3] and the work of
Johannes Lydus are respectively two and four
centuries earlier.   If the literary evidence is about
evenly divided, then one feels inclined to decide
in favour of the form Ὀνήσανδρος, because this,
especially in its Doric form Ὀνάσανδρος, was a

[1] It is worthy of note that the so-called Leo has the
correct form of the title, while the designation in Suidas is
markedly inexact.

[2] See K. Krumbacher, Byzant. Literaturgesch., 2nd ed.,
1897, 638, and the literature there cited.

[3] The author of this work must have had a MS. of
Onasander before him, because he paraphrases a large part
of the present treatise, and since he worked under the
encouragement of the Emperor it is to be supposed that he
had the best available sources.   No doubt the author of the
archetype of the majority of our present codices, in the
tenth century, also had good MS. material to work upon,
but that was two centuries later, and besides this archetype
clearly represents a seriously corrupt and interpolated
vulgate.   The testimony of D, a late interpolated MS., for
Ὀνήσανδρος is worthless.

relatively common name,[1] while Ὀνόσανδρος seems to occur but once, and then, as Bechtel (*loc. cit.*) and others have thought, by a mere stone-cutter's error.[2]

Such was the status of the question until Dr. Rostagno's collation of the Florentinus, which is incomparably the best MS., showed that it had the following subscription :

ὈΝΑϹΆΝΔΡΟΥ ϹΤΡΑΤΗΓΙΚΌϹ :—

Plut. lv. 4 f. 215ᵛ.

a form of the name, which had been known, indeed, before, but because it appeared only in the late MS. B, had been rejected by Köchly with a " *sic !* " I have not, however, hesitated to accept it as the correct form of the name, partly because of the high value of the testimony of the Florentinus, but especially because it affords the best explanation of the other two forms, for Ὀνόσανδρος is an easy corruption of Ὀνάσανδρος, and Ὀνήσανδρος merely the Attic (or Koine) spelling.

With reference to the period in which Onasander lived, it can scarcely be doubted that the Quintus Veranius to whom the present work is dedicated was the consul of A.D. 49 who died while in command in Britain ten years later, so that 59 is the *terminus ante quem* for the composition of the treatise.[3] If

---

[1] Approximately thirty-five instances have been noted, without making an exhaustive search, principally from Rhodes, Eretria, Athens, Laconia, and Ionia.

[2] Ὀνόσανδρος can hardly be derived from ὄνος, whatever one may think of the possibility of such a name among the Greeks, while the stem ὀνόσασθαι, as Bechtel observed, does not seem to appear in Greek nomenclature.

[3] Earlier but baseless conjectures are mentioned by Schwebel, p. [8]. The year 58 might be more appropriately taken, as it is unlikely that Onasander would have dedicated

we are inclined to press a little the author's own characterization of his work as παλαιῶν τε ἡγεμόνων κατὰ τὴν σεβαστὴν εἰρήνην ἀνάθημα (prooem. 4), and see in these words a reference to the time of composition being a moment of universal tranquility, we might accept Zur-Lauben's suggestion (preface, p. 6) that the treatise was composed in the year 58, this being perhaps the only one in the period for which there exists no record of military operations. But the expression employed, while certainly appropriate at a time of complete peace, does not necessarily imply quite so much, and it is better to rest content with a date shortly anterior to A.D. 59.[1]

The treatise consists of forty-two chapters upon various aspects of a commander's duties, notably ethical considerations regarding the character, social status, bearing, behaviour, and attitude of a general towards his troops, the enemy, and his fellow-citizens; the morale of the troops, the effect of particular policies and tactics upon morale, and the like; together with much sound advice about elementary matters. In two respects Onasander differs markedly from other Greek and Roman military writers. He regards everything from the point

his work to Veranius after the latter had gone to Britain in this year. For Veranius see the article in *Prosop. Imp. Rom.* iii. 399 f.

[1] Some slight general confirmation of this approximate dating is supplied by von Rohden (see Bibliography), who finds approximately the same technique regarding the avoidance of hiatus in Onasander and in Ps.-Longinus, for the latter, it is now agreed, belongs to the period of the early empire. Von Rohden's results may, however, need modification, because they are based upon Köchly's text which departs at many places from the best MS. tradition in the matter of elision.

348

of view primarily of the commanding officer, to the question of selecting whom he devotes a long and valuable passage, and he lays uncommon stress upon the *imponderabilia*, especially ethical and religious considerations. There is nothing very philosophic nor technically military in the treatise, which is intended to give merely the broad principles of generalship (στρατηγικαὶ ὑφηγήσεις, prooem. 3), and lays no claim to originality (*ibidem*).[1]

One feels no more inclined to extol the treatise as being " the most learned, concise, and valuable to be found upon the art of war," [2] than to decry it as " useless and pedantic," and the author as one who " talks Greek like a doctor of the Sorbonne," [3] or to regard it as a mere " wilderness of general phrases," whose " useful observations are but grains in the chaff of trivialities." [4] The truth, as often, lies here between extremes : κρατίστη δ' αἵρεσις ἡ τοῦ μέσου, as Onasander himself says (A, 10).

Actual performance falls below the statement in the prooemium that the study has drawn merely

[1] It seems unduly severe for Köchly and Rüstow: 1855, 84 and Max Jähns, 92, to denounce Onasander for lack of originality when he disclaims it himself.
[2] Guilliman writing in 1583, as quoted by Zur-Lauben, preface, p. 9.
[3] The Prince de Ligne, as quoted by Jähns, 94. One's respect for the prince's judgement is seriously qualified, however, by the circumstance that he has the highest admiration for the so-called Leo (*ibid.* 120), ranging him beside Napoleon, and far above a mere Caesar or Frederick the Great, whereas the *Tactics* of Leo are in part a watered paraphrase of Onasander himself, together with extensive extracts from the *Strategica* ascribed to Mauricius, and from other sources.
[4] Köchly and Rüstow: 1855, 85.

upon those arts and practices employed by the Romans in the establishment of their empire, for specifically Roman institutions are regularly neglected even when appropriate, and in only one instance (Ch. 19) is a manœuvre recommended, which, though perhaps not impossible in a Greek phalanx, is certainly suggestive of the Roman maniple tactics. Elsewhere only general principles are proposed which apply to almost any army at any time, or else, although very rarely, if ever, is a custom peculiar to the Greeks described.[1] In particular many of the qualities which Onasander requires of a commander-in-chief, are, *mutatis mutandis*, quite as applicable to-day to higher officers in general, as they were in the reign of Claudius.

The burden of the treatise is really ethics, morale, and the general principles of success in arms. As such, a good deal of it will necessarily sound commonplace, some of it even trivial, for the principles of success in war have often been declared by experts

---

[1] Thus it has been noted that in Ch. 10. 25 ff. the Greek inspection of victims before battle is mentioned, not the Roman augury with the sacred chickens. But the Romans also took auspices before battle, no less than the Greeks, at least during the Republic. In the same chapter (10. 4) exercises for soldiers are mentioned, which are drawn from Xenophon (*Cyrop.* ii. 3. 17 f.). But similar exercises were employed by the Romans (see the article " Exercitus " in Pauly-Wissowa, 1654), and although exercise in throwing clods is not recorded for the Romans, so far as I am aware, Vegetius (ii. 23) especially recommends that soldiers be trained to throw stones, and in a sham battle what better substitute for these could be desired than clods? It is true that the Roman legion is not specifically mentioned, but neither is the Greek, for that matter. The word φάλαγξ could be used of either, but Onasander is writing of armies in general and not of particular forms of organization.

to be very simple, and the difficult matter in war, as in many sports and occupations, is not the principles, but their application. Nevertheless every failure is easily traceable to the neglect of some important principle, and these can hardly be inculcated too often. If a manual expresses the principles of the art clearly and pointedly, one can hardly in fairness demand more of it. Estimates of value regarding a work of this kind will necessarily differ, but when so great a commander as Prinz Moritz von Sachsen, Marshal of France, and author likewise of a classic work on the art of war, *Mes Rêveries*, " declared with pleasure that he owed his first conceptions of the conduct of a commander-in-chief to Onasander " (Zur-Lauben, preface, p. 5), no mere closet philologist, at all events, may deny the possibility that it may prove useful to the professional soldier. The little treatise is merely a plain tale simply told, and it is the better part of criticism to express appreciation of the work that is valuable and well done rather than to strain to find what is useless or inappropriate.

The style of Onasander is straightforward and not ill adapted to the subject matter. Although it is not so fluent and simple as that of Xenophon, whom he seems to have admired and followed,[1] it nevertheless stands comparison with that of Polybius or Plutarch, but only an enthusiast like Zur-Lauben could speak of its " beauté majestueuse, élégance nerveuse, et clarté perçante."

The influence of Onasander in antiquity was con-

[1] He was especially indebted to the *Cyropaedia* and the *Anabasis*. He drew also from Homer, Herodotus, Thucydides, and Polybius among extant authors, but is in no case slavishly dependent upon any particular source that has come down to us.

351

siderable. Most subsequent military writers are indebted to him, notably the so-called Mauricius and Leo, of whom the latter in a large measure paraphrases Onasander, turning him into " wretched Byzantine Greek." [1]   In the Renaissance he enjoyed a remarkable popularity. Translations, beginning with that of Sagundinus in 1493, appeared in rapid succession in Latin, Spanish, German, French, Italian, and English, and such a demand, for these were no mere philological exercises, shows that many a practical soldier took to heart his counsel, and that much of it has passed thereby into the common body of military science. Towards the end of the next century the first Greek text appeared, a fairly good piece of scholarship, by Rigaltius, which held its place until Schwebel's elaborate study, more than a century and a half later. Since that time Onasander has been known to few beside professional philologists, but it may be hoped that others outside the ramparts of scholarship may have their attention drawn to his work by the present unpretentious publication.

A few words seem to be necessary by way of explaining this edition. It would have been much easier to reprint Köchly's text, but inasmuch as only one of the four old and really valuable mss. of Onasander was adequately known (namely the Parisinus 2442), the great Laurentian ms. of the Tacticians had never been really collated, and the Vatican and the Neapolitan mss. never examined at all, it would have been scarcely proper merely to reproduce an old and occasionally imperfect, though in the main most admirable, text. The

[1] Köchly and Rüstow: 1855, 85, note 198.

apparatus aims to give all the MS. readings that have any critical value, or may throw light upon the tradition of the text, and all the valuable emendations of modern scholars, especially those of Köchly. Knowledge of the inferior MSS. and readings of earlier editors have been drawn generally from Köchly, whose work in this respect is most exact and thorough, although we have been able to use the work of Rigaltius from the edition of 1600 in a privately owned copy, as well as Schwebel's edition of 1762, and that of Koraes, 1822, lent by the courtesy of the libraries of Harvard University and Princeton University respectively. Departures from Köchly's text have generally been recorded except in matters of elision (where Köchly nearly always elided with or without MS. authority), and of movable *nu* (which Köchly added somewhat arbitrarily). In these points the best MS. authority (F, and frequently FGH) has been followed. Cases where FGH merely run preposition and substantive together have not been recorded, or where iota subscript (without indication of a different construction) has been omitted, or movable *nu* has been added or left off (except for F), or compound words written as two (unless such a usage is occasionally recognized), or obviously erroneous accents or breathings occur, or where GH have trivial misspellings. The punctuation of FGH has likewise not been recorded, although it has been duly regarded in constructing the text.

The bibliography, which is more complete perhaps than any to be found elsewhere, has been drawn up with especial care, and omits, we trust, no title of substantial value for the criticism of Onasander.

ONASANDER

EDITIONS

Nicolaus Rigaltius: Ὀνοσάνδρου Στρατηγικός. Onosandri Strategicus. Sive de imperatoris institutione. Accessit Οὐρβικίου Ἐπιτήδευμα. Paris, 1598 and 1599. This is the *editio princeps*.[1] It was republished in 1600 at Heidelberg by the Commelin Press with the notes of Portus and Gruterus, and again in 1604 with the notes of Portus, with which edition the more elaborate observations of Gruterus, published separately in the same year, were sometimes bound. See below.

[Henricus Monantholius: Onosandri et Aristotelis Mechanica cum commentariis. Paris, 1599. Fabricius, *Bibl. Graeca*, vol. iv. 339, quotes this entry from a Leyden catalogue, but the title itself is absurd, and the entries in the catalogues of the Brit. Mus. and the Bibl. Nat. under the Monantholius edition of Aristotle do not mention Onasander. We have here probably a cataloguer's error, due possibly to two different works being bound together. The Onasander was probably the edition of Rigaltius.]

---

[1] Max Jähns, *Gesch. der Kriegswiss.* i. 9, note, who mentions an edition of the *Scriptores* (*i.e.*, the *Rei Militaris Scriptores*, Rome, 1487, and frequently thereafter), Rome, 1499, in which the collection is enlarged by the addition of Onasander's treatise, which, however, was again omitted in the edition of Bologna and the subsequent reprints, had no doubt in mind the Latin translation of Sagundinus, *q.v.*, which meets his description in every detail except that it appeared in the edition of Rome, 1494, only, not 1499.

354

Aemilius Portus and Janus Gruterus : Ὀνοσάνδρου
Στρατηγικός. Accedit seorsim in eundem
Onosandrum Jani Gruteri uberior commentarius. Item Aemilii Porti . . . breues . . .
observationes. Ex Officina Commeliniana
[Heidelberg], 1600 ; also the work of Rigaltius
and Portus alone, *ibidem*, 1604. Gruterus'
notes were published also by the same firm
in Varii discursus, sive prolixiores commentarii
ad aliquot insigniora loca Taciti et Onosandri,
Part I, 1604, and Part II, 1605.[1] These
observations of Gruterus seem to have been
bound occasionally with the edition of Rigaltius,
and also with the notes of Portus, but not always,
since the latter combination alone was used by
Schwebel (preface, [6]). On the somewhat
complicated relations of these three works see
Schwebel, *loc. cit.* ; Fabricius, *op. cit.* 338 ;
Haase : 1835, 98. The copy of the edition of
1600 owned by Mr. A. S. Pease, although its
title-page professes to have Gruterus' notes,
does not contain them. The *Notae* of Rigaltius
are dated in both preface and colophon 1598.

Joannes à Chokier de Surlet : Onosandri Strategicus,
sive de imperatoris institutione . . . , without
place or date, but the preface is dated Rome,
1610. This edition is a part of Chokier's
Thesaurus aphorismorum politicorum, Rome, 1611.
It contains the text and translation of Rigaltius.

---

[1] The copy in the Brit. Mus. is described thus : " Another
edition) [*i.e.*, of Rigaltius]. Accessit Urbici inventum, Graece
et Latine : interprete N. Rigaltio, cujus item adjiciuntur
notae ; ut item J. Gruteri discursus varii. . . . In Biblio-
polio Commeliniano : [Heidelberg] 1604, 1600-05."

ONASANDER

Its only value lies in the " political dissertations " added by Chokier. The *Thesaurus* (containing Onasander) was republished at Mainz, 1613 and 1619 (third ed.; Cat. Bibl. Nat.); Frankfurt, 1615; Liége, 1643; Köln, 1649, 1653, and 1687. The editions of Liége and Köln do not contain the Greek text (Cat. Bibl. Nat.).

Nicolaus Schwebelius : Onosandri Strategicus, sive de imperatoris institutione liber, etc., . . . notis perpetuis criticis emendatus. . . . Accedunt duo indices, etc. . . . Nürnberg [1762]. This is commonly bound with the translation of Zur-Lauben, Paris, 1757.

A. Koraes (Korais, Corais, or Coray) : Ὀνησάνδρου Στρατηγικὸς καὶ Τυρταίου τὸ πρῶτον Ἐλεγεῖον, μετὰ τῆς Γαλλικῆς ἑκατέρου μεταφράσεως. Παρέργων Ἑλληνικῆς βιβλιοθήκης τόμος πέμπτος, Paris, 1822. The French translation is that of Zur-Lauben, which Koraes reproduces even when it is based upon readings different from those which he prints.

Arminius Koechly : Ὀνοσάνδρου Στρατηγικός. Onosandri de imperatoris officio liber. Leipzig, 1860. This is the most valuable edition of the text. It completely supplants the earlier editions, using all the critical materials previously collected, and adds new manuscript readings, especially from one of the oldest MSS., Paris. 2442.

INTRODUCTION

TRANSLATIONS

Latin

Nicolaus Sagundinus : Onosander ad Q. Verānium
de optimo imperatore eiusque officio per
Nicolaum Sagundinum (*sic*),[1] e Graeco in
Latinum traductus. Rome, 1494.[2] This publication was in the well-known and frequently
reprinted *Rei militaris scriptores*, which included among others Vegetius, Frontinus,
Modestus, and Aelian. Only the 1494 edition,
however, contains Onasander. This translation
of Onasander was reprinted at Paris, 1504
(colophon) or 1506 (preface) ; at Basel, 1541,
1558, and 1570.[3]

Joachimus Camerarius : Onosandri Graeci autoris
de re militari commentarius in Latinum sermo-
nem conversus. . . . Nürnberg, 1595. This was
an independent work made from a mutilated
MS. It was published after the death of
Camerarius by his sons. Max Jähns, *Gesch.
der Kriegswiss.* 93, is certainly in error in

---

[1] There seems to have been some doubt as to the correct
spelling of the name. The *editio princeps* and the Paris
reprint have *Sagundinus*, the Basel reprints and editors
use the form *Saguntinus*. Fabricius, *Bibl. Gr.* iv. 337, and
Haase, 1835, 99 give some references where the form
Secundinus appears.

[2] So Haase, 1835, 98; Köchly in his edition, p. vii.;
and the catalogues of the Brit. Museum and the Bibl. Nat.
and Hain* 15915. Fabricius, *loc. cit.*, gives 1493.

[3] A Latin translation in MS. exists in the Escurial library,
iii. S. 11 ; also at London, 12 C. XIII, the latter under the
name *Nicolao Secundino*, so that the Escurial translation
is probably the same work ; see Haase, 1835, 99.

357

speaking of this edition as containing also the
Greek text.

Nicolaus Rigaltius. For his translation and reprints
of it, see under *Editions*, Rigaltius, Portus, and
Chokier. The Latin translation by itself was
published at Helmstadt in 1619.[1]

Spanish

Al. de Palencia : Tratado de la perfeçion del
triunfo militar. Printed about 1495, but without
indication of place or date. The translation
was composed in 1459.[2]

Iac. Dieg. Gracian de Aldarete : Onosandro Plá-
tonico de las calidades y partes que ha de tener
un excellente capitan general y de su officio y
cargo. Barcelona, 1567.

German

Anon. : Onexander von den Kriegsshandlungen und
Räthen der hocherfarn guten Hauptleute sampt
iren Zugeordenten. Mainz, 1524 and 1532.[3]

---

[1] It is more than doubtful if the work of Dominicus
Syllenius Graecus, described by Fabricius, *op. cit.*, 339,
under the heading *Versiones*, as being " de vetere et recen-
tiore scientia militari, omnium bellorum genera terrestria
perinde ac naualia, nec non tormentorum rationes complec-
tente. Venet. 1599 ", contains a translation of Onasander.

[2] Max Jähns, *Gesch. der Kriegswiss.*, 93.

[3] Fabricius, *loc. cit.*, gives 1531. This translation is
said to contain a chapter, otherwise unknown, upon the
Athenians, Spartans, and Macedonians. See Zur-Lauben,
quoted by Fabricius, *loc. cit.* ; Jähns, *op. cit.*, 93. It
can hardly fail to be spurious, since any such details would
be alien to the general tenor of the work, as well as opposed
to the express statement of the prooemium.

INTRODUCTION

A. H. Baumgärtner: Onosanders Unterricht eines
Feldherrn, übersetzt und mit Anmerkungen
erläutert; in Vollständige Sammlung aller
Kriegschriftsteller der Griechen. Mannheim,
1777,[1] and separately in 1786. This is said to
be a poor piece of work, based on Schwebel's text.

French

Jehan Charrier: L'art de la guerre composé par
Nicolas Machiavelli; l'éstat aussi et charge
d'un lieutenant général d'armée, par Onosander,
ancien philosophe platonique . . ., Paris, 1546.[2]

Blaise de Vigenère: L'art militaire d'Onosender,
autheur grec, où il traicte de l'office et devoir
d'un bon chef de guerre, etc., Paris, 1605.
The translation seems to have been completed
in 1593, but was not published until after
the author's death (Jähns, op. cit., 93). The
commentary and essays were so extensive as
to make the whole work extremely bulky.[3]
It was by means of this translation that Prinz
Moritz von Sachsen made his acquaintance with
Onasander (Zur-Lauben, preface, 5).

Baron de Zur-Lauben: Le général d'armée, par

---

[1] Jähns, op. cit., 94, gives the place of publication as
Frankfurt and the date as 1779 (on p. 10, Frankenthal
and München). This may have been a different edition
but it is more likely that we have here only a different title-
page.

[2] The catalogue of the Bibl. Nat. indicates that there
were other editions of this translation, but the volume
which would contain them has not yet appeared. The
Brit. Mus. possesses only this edition of 1546.

[3] Max Jähns, op. cit., speaks of 1500 pages, but the Brit.
Mus. cat. records only 734. The book is a quarto.

Onosander. Ouvrage traduit du Grec, etc.
Paris, 1754 and 1757. The reprint of 1757 is
bound with Schwebel's edition of 1762. Another
edition appeared in vol. i. of Zur-Lauben's
Bibliothèque militaire historique et politique, Cos-
mopolis [Paris], 1760. It was also reprinted by
A. Koraes in his edition, Paris, 1822, *q.v.*

Charles Guischardt[1]: Les institutions d'Ónosandre
pour servir a l'instruction d'un général. Tra-
duites du Grec. In his *Mémoires militaires sur
les Grecs et les Romains*, vol. ii, 49-106. The
Hague, 1757,[2] and Lyon, 1760. This translation
was reprinted by Liskenne and Sauvan ; see
below.

[A. Koraes : Paris, 1822. See *Editions*.]

F. C. Liskenne et J. B. B. Sauvan : Bibliothèque
historique et militaire. In eight vols. Paris,
1835-46 ; and 1851 ff. The translation of
Onasander, by Guischardt, is in vol. iii, 405-35.

Italian

Fabio Cotta : Onosandro platonico dell' ottimo
capitano generale e del suo offizio. Tradotto
di Greco in lingua volgare Italiana. Venezia,
1546 and 1548. This work was translated into
English by Peter Whytehorne. It was republished by G. Daelli in *Biblioteca rara*,
Milano, 1863, vol. iv.

[1] Thus Haase: 1835, 98, and the catalogues of the Brit.
Mus. and the Bibl. Nat. ; Guischard, Fabricius, *op. cit.*,
339, Brunet, Graesse ; Guischart, Jähns, *op. cit.*, 93.
[2] Haase, *ibid.*, and the catalogues of the Brit. Mus. and
the Bibl. Nat. give 1758.

INTRODUCTION

English

Peter Whytehorne : Onosandro Platonico, of the
generall captaine and of his office, translated
out of Greke into Italyan by Fabio Cotta, a
Romayne ; and out of Italyan into Englysh by
Peter Whytehorne. London, 1563.

Modern Greek

G. Apostolos Skalasteras : Bucharest, 1832. M.
Konstantiniades (see next item) claims that this
version was not made from the original Greek,
but only from a translation.
Michael Konstantiniades : Ὀνησάνδρου Στρατηγικός,
μεταφρασθεὶς ἐκ τῆς ἀρχαίας εἰς τὴν καθ' ἡμᾶς
Ἑλληνικήν. Athens, 1897.

CRITICISM

Anon.: *Acta litteraria*, vol. i, part I, 22-8 ; *Nova
acta erudita*, 1763, 201-11 ; *ibid.*, 1768, 313-19.
The last two articles are devoted to a critique
of Schwebel's edition. The first is not accessible
to me.
H. Delbrück : *Geschichte der Kriegskunst im Rahmen
der politischen Geschichte.* Berlin, 1921, vol. ii, 200.
Christ - Schmid - Stählin : *Griechische Literaturgeschichte*, 6th ed., München, 1921, vol. ii, 422.
Th. Crenius : *De eruditione comparanda.* Leyden,
1699, 470, 570 ff. Crenius seems to have

added some observations of his own to the work of Naudaeus which he republished. See Schwebel, pref. [10].

J. A. Fabricius: *Bibliotheca Graeca*. Leipzig, 1795, vol. iv, 336-40.

Fr. Haase: " Über die griechischen und lateinischen Kriegsschriftsteller," *Jahrb. für Philol.*, 1835, 14 : 86-118.

De militarium scriptorum Graecorum et Latinorum omnium editione instituenda. Berlin, 1847.

M. Haupt: *Varia* (including a brief note on Onasander). *Hermes*, 1871, 5 : 175. Reprinted in *Opuscula*, 1876, vol. iii, 518 f.

Max Jähns: *Geschichte der Kriegswissenschaften*, etc., München und Leipzig, 1889, vol. i, 5-10 ; 90-94.

Herman Köchly: *Index lectionum in literarum universitate*. Zürich, 1854. A discussion of MSS. of Onasander, principally Bern. 97 and Paris. 2522.

H. Köchly and W. Rüstow: *Griechische Kriegsschriftsteller*, Leipzig, 1855, vol. ii, 1, 84 f.

K. K. Müller: " Ein griechisches Fragment über Kriegswesen," in *Festschrift für L. Urlichs*, Würzburg, 1880, 106-38. On the Laurentian MS. of Onasander.

" Eine griechische Schrift über Seekrieg ", in *Festgabe zur dritten Säcularfeier der Universität Würzburg*, Würzburg, 1882. On the general classification of the MSS.

Gabr. Naudaeus: *Syntagma de studio militari*. Rome, 1637. Republished as *Naudaei bibliographia militaris*, Jena, 1683, and included in Thomas Crenius, *De eruditione comparanda*, Leyden, 1699.

G. Rathgeber: Article " Onosandros," in Ersch

and Grüber's *Encyklopädie der Wissenschaften und Künste*, series III, vol. iv, 9-12.

H. von Rohden: "Quas rationes in hiatu vitando scriptor de sublimitate et Onesander secuti sint," in *Commentationes in honorem F. Bücheleri et H. Useneri. . . .* Bonn, 1873, 68-94.

Cl. Salmasius: *De re militari Romanorum*, Leyden, 1657. Republished in J. G. Graevius: *Thesaurus antiquitatum Romanarum*. For Onasander see vol. x, 1389.

MANUSCRIPTS

The MSS. of Onasander are much more numerous than those of the other Greek military writers, and thus testify to his abiding influence throughout antiquity, but only a few of them, and these mainly copies from existing codices, have ever been collated, and two of the very oldest seem not to have been used at all prior to this edition.[1] As K. K. Müller has observed (*Festgabe, etc.*), the MS. tradition of Greek military authors falls into three main groups, the first of which is composed of the Florentinus LV. 4, s. X, and its descendants (especially A and B, see below); the second, of the Parisinus 2442, s. XI, the Vaticanus Graecus 1104, s. XI, and the

[1] Most of them are listed by Zur-Lauben in the preface to his translation (from Montfaucon, *Bibl. Bibl.*); Haase, *De milit. script. Gr.*; and K. K. Müller, *Festgabe zur dritten Säcularfeier*. Add to those mentioned in these works one at Perugia (Blume, *Bibliotheca librorum MSS. Italica*, in *Supplementum itineris Italici*, Göttingen, 1834, 122), and another at Turin (Fabricius, *Bibl. Graeca*, iv (1795), 337).

Neapolitanus III C 26, s. XI, and their descendants (*e.g.*, M and Vat. 2201 are direct copies of the Vaticanus) or closely related MSS. ; the third, of the Ambrosianus 139 (old no. B 119), s. X (or XI according to an older dating).

The Florentinus is incomparably the best MS. for Onasander, so that the disagreements of other MSS. need be considered only in the relatively few passages where it has obviously suffered from corruption. Mss. A and B are faithful copies of the Florentinus, and Köchly collated these two MSS. himself, so that this branch of the tradition was fairly well known even before the collation of the parent MS. In view of this fact and of the rare critical acumen of Köchly it is but natural that the present edition will be found to differ in only a few places, and generally in points of minor importance (but uniformly along the line of closer adherence to the Florentinus), from the text as constituted by that great scholar.

The second family represents a markedly inferior text, but probably one of wider circulation, and so presumably the vulgate of Leo's time. It is valuable primarily only when the Florentinus is corrupt. I have given, however, in the *apparatus criticus* all the important variations of the three leading MSS. of this family from the printed text, so that the material upon which a judgement must be based may not be withheld from others.

The third group, represented by the Ambrosianus, gives us a text varying so widely from that of the other lines of tradition that both K. K. Müller and the editors of the catalogue of the Ambrosian Library, Drs. Martini and Bassi, regard it as no longer a recension but as a Byzantine paraphrase. I have taken, therefore, no cognizance of it, not, of course, because I am unaware of the value which a close paraphrase like this, and even a much freer one like that of many passages in Leo's *Tactica*, have in attesting the direct MS. tradition, but merely because it has been impossible in the time available, because of the delay and uncertainty of communication with Italy, to secure photographs of the Ambrosianus and present this secondary material in a form suitable for a volume of this series.[1]

To sum up : we have in F an excellent, old, uninterpolated, but not faultless text ; in PGH and most other MSS. a Byzantine vulgate ; in the Ambrosianus 139 a Byzantine paraphrase; in Leo a Byzantine plagiarism.

[1] Similarly, in the case of Leo, it has been impossible to secure from Hungary the new critical edition of the *Tactica* prepared by Dr. R. Vari, and published by the Budapest Academy as long ago as 1917, while any extensive use of this work in the old editions would be unprofitable. It should be noted, however, that Leo agrees occasionally with F against all other MSS., which would suggest that the tradition represented by F and not the vulgate was the basis of his paraphrase, a condition apparently somewhat different from that which Wescher, *Poliorcétique grecque*, p. xxxix, presupposes for the tradition of the military technicians.

ONASANDER

SYMBOLS

I give here, in addition to the symbols for the four great MSS., those used by Köchly for the MSS. from which readings were given by his predecessors. The names Rigaltius, Schwebel, Koraes, and Köchly in the *apparatus* refer to the texts, or notes as the case may be, and those of Sagundinus and Camerarius, to the translations produced respectively by these scholars.

A Parisinus 2522, s. XV, a copy of F. The corrector, A m², is derived from R, or a very closely related MS. (Köchly.)

B Bernensis 97, s. XV-XVI, a copy of F but with some emendations. (Köchly.)

C Morellanus, once in the possession of F. Morellus at Paris. It seems to be descended from F but has many deviations and peculiar readings. (Rigaltius.)

D An inferior sixteenth century MS. (Koraes.)

E In the library at Munich in the eighteenth century; it agrees closely with the late MSS. of Rigaltius. (Schwebel.)

F Florentinus LV. 4, s. X, collated by Prof. Dott. Enrico Rostagno for this edition. The symbol F is used by Köchly for a very few readings from a Florentine MS. (presumably LV. 4) furnished Schwebel by Dom. Mar. Manni. For these the designation " F (*sic*) " is used.

G Vaticanus Graecus 1164, s. XI. See H. Photographs of this MS. were used. Two leaves are missing (for details see *apparatus* on 10. 27 and 35. 3). Some portions, especially of

366

    fol. 11 ʳ, are illegible. For a description see Wescher, *Poliorcétique grecque*, pp. xxiv ff.

H Neapolitanus III C 26, s. XI. H and G agree so closely that they are certainly copies of the same archetype, probably uncial. Photographs of this ms. were used.

K A late and inferior ms. owned by Koraes. (Koraes.)

M " Cod. Mediceus, ex Bibl. Reg. Catharinae ", a direct copy of G. (Rigaltius.)

N A late ms. owned by Joh. Nagel, agreeing generally with the late mss. of Rigaltius. (Schwebel.)

P Parisinus 2442, s. XI, collated for Köchly by Jakob Huntziker. For a description see Wescher, *Poliorcétique grecque*, pp. xxvi f. (Köchly.)

R A late and extensively interpolated ms. of Rigaltius, the probable source of the readings of the second hand of A. (Rigaltius.)

V " Vet. Membranae " or " Vetusta Macrocola," seldom reported upon. (Rigaltius.)

v Vulgate reading of the mss. used by Köchly and his predecessors. With this A m² (although Köchly quotes the latter separately) nearly always agrees, and when it does so is included under that symbol. Because of its age and importance P is cited separately, even if agreeing with v, when specially reported by Köchly.

Ω All mss. or all other mss. (including FGH).

    Note.—The quoted phrases " alii codd. ut vid.", " ceteri codd. ut vid.", etc., are taken from Köchly's *apparatus* (based upon inferences from the earlier editions), unless some other authority is cited.

ΟΝΑΣΑΝΔΡΟΥ[1]

ΣΤΡΑΤΗΓΙΚΟΣ

ΠΡΟΟΙΜΙΟΝ

Ἱππικῶν μὲν λόγων ἢ κυνηγετικῶν ἢ ἁλιευτι-
κῶν τε αὖ καὶ γεωργικῶν συνταγμάτων προσ-
φώνησιν ἡγοῦμαι πρέπειν[2] ἀνθρώποις, οἷς πόθος
ἔχεσθαι τοιῶνδε ἔργων, στρατηγικῆς δὲ περὶ
θεωρίας, ὦ Κόϊντε Οὐηράνιε, Ῥωμαίοις καὶ
μάλιστα Ῥωμαίων τοῖς τὴν συγκλητικὴν ἀριστο-
κρατίαν λελογχόσι[3] καὶ κατὰ τὴν Σεβαστοῦ Καί-
σαρος ἐπιφροσύνην ταῖς[4] τε ὑπάτοις καὶ στρατηγικαῖς ἐξουσίαις κοσμουμένοις[5] διά τε παιδείαν,
ἧς οὐκ ἐπ᾽ ὀλίγον ἔχουσιν ἐμπειρίαν, καὶ προγόνων
2 ἀξίωσιν. ἀνέθηκα δὲ πρώτοις σφίσι[6] τόνδε τὸν
λόγον οὐχ ὡς ἀπείροις[7] στρατηγίας, ἀλλὰ μάλιστα
τῇδε θαρρήσας, ᾗ[8] τὸ μὲν ἀμαθὲς τῆς ψυχῆς καὶ
τὸ[9] παρ᾽ ἄλλῳ κατορθούμενον ἠγνόησεν, τὸ δὲ
ἐν ἐπιστήμῃ τῷ καλῶς ἔχοντι προσεμαρτύρησεν.
3 ὅθεν, εἰ καὶ παρὰ πολλοῖς φανείη νενοημένα τὰ
παρ᾽ ἐμοῦ συντεταγμένα, καὶ κατὰ τοῦτο ἂν
ἡσθείην, ὅτι μὴ μόνον στρατηγικὰς συνεταξάμην

---

[1] F (subscr.) : Ὀνησάνδρου D : Ὀνοσάνδρου Ω. See Introd.
[2] πρέπει GH.   [3] λελογχῶσιν GH.

ONASANDER

THE GENERAL

Prooemium

It is fitting, I believe, to dedicate monographs on horsemanship, or hunting, or fishing, or farming, to men who are devoted to such pursuits, but a treatise on military science, Quintus Veranius, should be dedicated to Romans, and especially to those of the Romans who have attained senatorial dignity, and who through the wisdom of Augustus Caesar have been raised to the power of consul or general, both by reason of their military training (in which they have had no brief experience) and because of the distinction of their ancestors. I have dedicated this treatise primarily to them, not as to men unskilled in generalship, but with especial confidence in this fact, that the ignorant soul is unaware even of that in which another is successful, but knowledge bears additional witness to that which is well done. For this reason, if what I have composed should seem to have been already devised by many others, even then I should be pleased, because I have not only

---

⁴ Koraes : τοῖς vH (G illeg.).   ⁵ Corrected from -νης P.
    ⁶ ENR : φησὶ GHP.   ⁷ ἀπείρης P.
  ⁸ EN : ἡ GHP.   ⁹ Added by Köchly (G illeg.).

ὑφηγήσεις, ἀλλὰ καὶ στρατηγικῆς ἐστοχασάμην
καὶ τῆς ἐν αὐτοῖς φρονήσεως, εὐτυχοίην τ' ἄν, εἰ,
ἃ δὴ Ῥωμαίοις δυνάμει καὶ δι' ἔργων πέπρακται,[1]
ταῦτ' ἐγὼ λόγῳ περιλαβεῖν[2] ἱκανὸς εἶναι παρὰ[3]
τοιούτοις ἀνδράσι δοκιμασθείην.

4   Τὸ δὲ σύνταγμα θαρροῦντί μοι λοιπὸν εἰπεῖν ὡς
στρατηγῶν τε ἀγαθῶν ἄσκησις ἔσται παλαιῶν τε
ἡγεμόνων κατὰ τὴν σεβαστὴν εἰρήνην ἀνάθημα,
εἰσόμεθά τε καὶ εἰ μηδὲν ἄλλο, παρ' ἣν αἰτίαν οἵ τε
πταίσαντες ἐσφάλησαν τῶν στρατηγησάντων, οἵ τε
εὐπραγήσαντες ἐγέρθησαν[4] εἰς δόξαν· μάλιστα δὲ
τὴν Ῥωμαίων ἀρετὴν ἐννοήσομεν, ὡς οὔτε βασιλεὺς
οὔτε πόλις οὔτε ἔθνος μεῖζον ἡγεμονίας ἐκρατύ-
νατο μέγεθος, ἀλλ' οὐδ' εἰς ἴσον ἤλασεν,[5] ὥστε
τοσούτοις βεβαιώσασθαι χρόνοις ἀκίνητον δυνα-
5 στείαν.   οὐ γὰρ τύχῃ μοι δοκοῦσιν ὑπεράραντες
τοὺς τῆς Ἰταλίας ὅρους ἐπὶ πέρατα γῆς ἐκτεῖναι
τὴν σφετέραν ἀρχήν, ἀλλὰ πράξεσι στρατηγικαῖς.
συνεπιλαμβάνεσθαι μὲν γὰρ εὔχεσθαι δεῖ καὶ τὴν
τύχην, οὐ μὴν τὸ παράπαν οἴεσθαι ταύτην κρατεῖν.
6 ἀλλ' ἀνόητοι[6] οἱ καὶ τὰ σφάλματα[7] τῆς τύχης
ἐγκλήματα μόνης ποιούμενοι,[8] οὐ τῆς τῶν στρατη-
γούντων ἀμελείας, καὶ τὰ κατορθώματα ταύτης,[9]
οὐ τῆς ἐμπειρίας τῶν ἡγουμένων· οὔτε γὰρ
ἐπιεικὲς ἀνεπιτίμητον οὕτως ἀπολιπεῖν[10] τὸν πται-
οντα τοῖς ὅλοις, ὡς πάντων αἰτιᾶσθαι τὴν τύχην,
οὔτε δίκαιον ἀμάρτυρον ἐπὶ τοσοῦτον ἐπαίνου τὸν

---

[1] Köchly : πρᾶξαι Ω (πρα///// G : πρᾶξαι H).
[2] GH : περιβαλεῖν v.
[3] Köchly : εἶναι δόξαιμι · εἰ δὴ παρὰ Ω.
[4] ἐγέρθεσαν P : ἠέρθησαν Köchly.   [5] ἤλασαν P.
[6] ἀλλὰ νόητοι (the breathing over the second α changed
to an accent) H : ἀνόητος von Rohden.

compiled precepts of generalship, but have also endeavoured to get at the art of the general and the wisdom that inheres in the precepts. I should be fortunate if I should be considered capable, before such men, of making a summary sketch of what the Romans have already accomplished by their mighty deeds.

It remains for me to say with good courage of my work, that it will be a school for good generals, and an object of delight for retired commanders in these times of holy peace ; and we shall know, if nothing else, for what reason some generals have stumbled and fallen, but others have prospered and been raised to fame ; and we shall consider above all the valour of the Romans, how that neither king, nor state, nor nation has held a greater position of leadership, nor even equalled them in the establishment of a dominion, unshaken through so many years. For it is not by chance, as it seems to me, that they have overrun the boundaries of Italy and extended their sway to the limits of the earth, but by deeds of generalship. For it is necessary to pray to Fortune to do its share, but not to consider that Fortune has entire control. Stupid are those who make disasters chargeable to Fortune alone, rather than to the negligence of commanders, as well as those who attribute successes to her, and not to the skill of the generals. It is neither reasonable simply to dismiss without punishment a general who has met with complete disaster, on the ground that Fortune is responsible for all things, nor is it just to

---

⁷ σφάλμαται G : σφάλμα ται H.   ⁸ ποιούμενας von Rohden.
⁹ With this word F (and its copies A and B) begins.
¹⁰ ἀπολείπειν v.

κατορθοῦντα περιορᾶν, ἐφ' ὅσον ἁπάντων ἀνατιθέναι τῇ τύχῃ τὴν χάριν.

7 Ἐπειδὴ δὲ φύσει πάντες ἄνθρωποι τοῖς μὲν δι' ἐμπειρίας συντετάχθαι δοκοῦσι, κἂν ἀσθενῶς ἀπαγγέλληται,[1] τὸ πιστὸν εἰς ἀλήθειαν ἀπονέμουσιν, τοῖς δὲ ἀπείροις,[2] κἂν ᾖ δυνατὰ[3] πραχθῆναι, διὰ τὸ ἀδοκίμαστον ἀπιστοῦσιν, ἀναγκαῖον ἡγοῦμαι περὶ τῶν ἐν τῷδε τῷ λόγῳ στρατηγημάτων ἠθροισμένων τοσοῦτο[4] προειπεῖν, ὅτι πάντα διὰ πείρας ἔργων ἐλήλυθεν καὶ ὑπὸ ἀνδρῶν τοιούτων, ὧν ἀπόγονον ὑπάρχει Ῥωμαίων ἅπαν τὸ γένει καὶ ἀρετῇ[5] μέχρι τοῦ δεῦρο πρω-
8 τεῦον. οὐθὲν γὰρ ἐσχεδιασμένον ἀπολέμῳ καὶ νεωτέρᾳ γνώμῃ τόδε περιέχει τὸ σύνταγμα, ἀλλὰ πάντα διὰ πράξεων καὶ ἀληθινῶν ἀγώνων κεχωρηκότα μάλιστα μὲν[6] Ῥωμαίοις· ἅ τε γὰρ ποιήσαντες[7] ἐφυλάξαντο[8] παθεῖν καὶ δι' ὧν ἐμηχανή-
9 σαντο[9] δρᾶσαι, πάντα μοι συνείλεκται. καίτοι οὐκ[10] ἠγνόηκα, ὅτι μᾶλλον ἄν τις εἵλετο[11] πάνθ' ἑαυτοῦ καὶ τῆς ἰδίας ἀγχινοίας τὰ στρατηγήματα δοκεῖν εἶναι, πλείονα θηρώμενος ἔπαινον τῶν πιστευσάντων, ἢ ἀπὸ[12] τῆς ἀλλοτρίας ἐπινοίας· ἐγὼ
10 δὲ οὐ παρὰ τοῦτ' ἐλαττοῦσθαι δοκῶ. καθάπερ γάρ,[13] εἴ τις ἐν πολέμοις αὐτὸς στρατευσάμενος[14] συνετάξατο τοιόνδε λόγον, οὐκ ἂν παρὰ τοῦτο ἥττονος ἠξιοῦτο μαρτυρίας, ὅτι μὴ μόνον φυσικῆς

---

[1] ἀπαγγέλληται GH.   [2] ἀπειράτοις GH Koraes.
[3] εἰ δύναται GHv.   [4] τοσοῦτον GHv.
[5] τῷ γένει καὶ ἀρετὴν v : τῷ γένει· καὶ ἀρετὴν GH.
[6] Om. vGH Köchly.
[7] πολεμήσαντες Köchly.   [8] ἐφύλαξαν τὸ P.
[9] ἐμαχήσαντο GH : δίκαιον ἐμαχήσαντο EF(sic)N "aliique codd." (Schwebel) A m[2].

372

leave the successful general so far without recognition
that gratitude for everything is offered to Fortune.

Now since all men naturally give credit for
truthfulness to those who appear to write with
professional experience, even though their style
be feeble, while for inexperienced writers, even
though their teachings are practicable, they feel
distrust on account of their lack of reputation, I
consider it necessary to say in advance, about the
military principles collected in this book, that they
have all been derived from experience of actual deeds,
and, in fact, of exploits performed by those men
from whom has been derived the whole primacy
of the Romans, in race and valour, down to the
present time. For this treatise presents no im-
promptu invention of an unwarlike and youthful
mind, but all the principles are taken from authentic
exploits and battles, especially of the Romans.
For the expedients they used in order to avoid
suffering harm, and the means by which they contrived to inflict it, all this I have collected. Nor have
I failed to perceive that a writer, seeking greater
praise from credulous readers, would prefer to have
it appear that the source of all the military stratagems
he described was himself and his own shrewdness
rather than the sagacity of others. But I do not
think that the latter diminishes one's glory. For if
a general after experience in the field had composed
such a work, it would not be considered of less value
because he introduced and commemorated in his

---

[10] γ' von Rohden.　　　　[11] εἵλατο GHA m².
[12] Köchly: ἀπὸ τῶν πιστευσάντων ἢ τῆς F: ἀπὸ τ. π. ἢ ἀπὸ
τῆς vGH.
[13] Om. v.　　　　[14] αὐτοστρατευσάμενος vGH

ἀγχινοίας ἰδίαν εὕρεσιν εἰσηνέγκατο στρατηγημάτων, ἀλλὰ καὶ τὰ δι' ἄλλων εὖ πραχθέντα
μνήμῃ παραθέμενος εἰς σύνταξιν ἤγαγεν, οὕτως
οὐδ' ἐμαυτὸν οἴομαι τοὐλαττον ἐπαίνων οἴσεσθαι
παρὰ τοῦθ', ὅτι μὴ πάντα τῆς ἐμῆς ὁμολογῶ
συνέσεως εἶναι,[1] τοὐναντίον δὲ προείληφα τόν
τ' ἔπαινον ἀνεπίφθονον ἕξειν καὶ τὴν πίστιν ἀσυ-
κοφάντητον.

I. [Περὶ αἱρέσεως στρατηγοῦ[2]]

Φημὶ τοίνυν αἱρεῖσθαι τὸν στρατηγὸν οὐ κατὰ
γένη κρίνοντας, ὥσπερ τοὺς ἱερέας, οὐδὲ κατ'
οὐσίας, ὡς τοὺς γυμνασιάρχους,[3] ἀλλὰ σώφρονα,
ἐγκρατῆ, νήπτην, λιτόν, διάπονον, νοερόν, ἀφιλάργυρον, μήτε νέον μήτε πρεσβύτερον, ἂν τύχῃ καὶ
πατέρα παίδων, ἱκανὸν λέγειν, ἔνδοξον.

2 [α'][4] σώφρονα μέν, ἵνα μὴ[5] ταῖς φυσικαῖς
ἀνθελκόμενος ἡδοναῖς ἀπολείπῃ τὴν ὑπὲρ τῶν
μεγίστων φροντίδα.

3 [β'] ἐγκρατῆ δέ, ἐπειδὴ[6] τηλικαύτης ἀρχῆς
μέλλει τυγχάνειν· αἱ γὰρ ἀκρατεῖς[7] ὁρμαὶ προσ-
λαβοῦσαι τὴν τοῦ δύνασθαί τι[1] ποιεῖν ἐξουσίαν
ἀκατάσχετοι γίγνονται πρὸς τὰς ἐπιθυμίας.

---

[1] Om. vGH.
[2] Not in FGH. F has no indication of any break between the prooemium and the first chapter, but only after
§ 1 of the chapter. GH have in the body of the text ἀρχὴ
τοῦ στρατηγικοῦ. All the titles date from different periods
subsequent to the original composition; that of Chap. ix,
because of ἄπληκτα, *castra*, must be assigned to Byzantine
times.   [3] γυμνασιάρχας A m² vGH.
[4] These marginal paragraph letters are not in F but they
appear in GH (and apparently most of the later MSS., to

work, not only the personal discoveries of his native wit, but also the brilliant deeds of other generals; in the same way I do not consider that I myself shall win less praise, because I admit that not everything I write springs from my own intelligence. On the contrary, I have chosen the opposite course, that I may have praise without reproach and trust without slander.

I. [*The Choice of a General*]

I believe, then, that we must choose a general, not because of noble birth as priests are chosen, nor because of wealth as the superintendents of the gymnasia, but because he is temperate, self-restrained, vigilant, frugal, hardened to labour, alert, free from avarice, neither too young nor too old, indeed a father of children if possible, a ready speaker, and a man with a good reputation.

The general must be temperate in order that he may not be so distracted by the pleasures of the body as to neglect the consideration of matters of the highest importance.

He must be self-restrained, since he is to be a man of so great authority; for the licentious impulses, when combined with the authority which confers the power of action, become uncontrollable in the gratification of the passions.

---

judge from the silence of Köchly). In F the first line of each subdivision begins with a red letter, and in nearly every instance an interval is left between each pair of subdivisions.

[5] ταῖς φυσικαῖς μὴ vGH.   [6] ἐπεὶ vGH.
[7] ἐγκρατεῖς corr. to ἀκρατεῖς P.

ONASANDER

4 [γ'] νήπτην δ', ὅπως ἐπαγρυπνῇ ταῖς μεγίσταις πράξεσιν· ἐν νυκτὶ γὰρ ὡς τὰ πολλὰ ψυχῆς ἠρεμούσης στρατηγοῦ γνώμη τελειοῦται.

5 [δ'] λιτὸν δέ, ἐπειδὴ κατασκελετεύουσιν[1] αἱ πολυτελεῖς θεραπεῖαι δαπανῶσαι χρόνον ἄπρακτον εἰς τὴν τῶν ἡγουμένων τρυφήν.

6 [ε'] διάπονον δ', ἵνα μὴ πρῶτος τῶν στρατευομένων, ἀλλ' ὕστατος[2] κάμνῃ.

7 [ϛ'] νοερὸν δέ·[3] ὀξὺν γὰρ εἶναι δεῖ τὸν στρατηγὸν ἐπὶ πᾶν ἄττοντα δι' ὠκύτητος ψυχῆς κατὰ τὸν Ὅμηρον

ὡσεὶ πτερὸν ἠὲ νόημα·[4]

πολλάκις γὰρ ἀπρόληπτοι[5] ταραχαὶ προσπεσοῦσαι σχεδιάζειν ἀναγκάζουσι τὸ συμφέρον.

8 [ζ'] ἀφιλάργυρον δέ· ἡ γὰρ[6] ἀφιλαργυρία δοκιμασθήσεται καὶ πρώτη· τοῦ γὰρ ἀδωροδοκήτως καὶ μεγαλοφρόνως προΐστασθαι τῶν πραγμάτων αὕτη[7] παραιτία· πολλοὶ γάρ, κἂν διὰ[3] τὴν ἀνδρίαν ἀσπίσι πολλαῖς καὶ δόρασιν ἀντιβλέψωσιν, περὶ τὸν χρυσὸν ἀμαυροῦνται· δεινὸν γὰρ πολεμίοις ὅπλον τοῦτο καὶ δραστήριον εἰς τὸ νικᾶν.

9 [η'] οὔτε δὲ νέον οὔτε πρεσβύτερον, ἐπειδὴ ὁ μὲν ἄπιστος,[8] ὁ δ' ἀσθενής·[9] οὐδέτερος γὰρ[10] ἀσφαλής, ὁ μὲν νέος, ἵνα μή τι[11] διὰ τὴν ἀλόγιστον πταίσῃ τόλμαν, ὁ δὲ πρεσβύτερος, ἵνα μή τι[12]
10 διὰ τὴν φυσικὴν ἀσθένειαν ἐλλείπῃ.[13] κρατίστη

---

[1] κατασκελετεῦσιν F.
[2] Köchly : ὕστερος FGHEN : ὕστερον P.
[3] Om. F.   [4] ἡ ἐννόημα GH.   [5] ἀπροσδόκητοι vGH.
[6] Schwebel supported by Leo, Tactica, ii. 8 : συμφέρον· (interval) ἡ δ' ἀφιλαργυρία Ω.   [7] αὐτὴ vGH.
[8] Ω def. Koraes : ἀλόγιστος Köchly.

Vigilant, that he may spend wakeful nights over the most important projects ; for at night, as a rule, with the mind at rest, the general perfects his plans.

Frugal, since expensive attendance upon the luxurious tastes of commanders consumes time unprofitably and causes resources to waste away.

Hardened to labour, that he may not be the first but the last of the army to grow weary.

Alert, for the general must be quick, with swiftness of mind darting at every subject—quick, as Homer says, " as a bird, or as thought." [1] For very frequently unexpected disorders arise which may compel him to decide on the spur of the moment what is expedient.

Free from avarice ; for this quality of freedom from avarice will be valued most highly, since it is largely responsible for the incorruptible and large-minded management of affairs. For many who can face the shields and spears of a host with courage are blinded by gold ; but gold is a strong weapon against the enemy and effective for victory.[2]

Neither too young nor too old ; since the young man does not inspire confidence, the old man is feeble, and neither is free from danger, the young man lest he err through reckless daring, the older lest he neglect something through physical weakness. The ideal lies between the two, for physical

[1] *Odyssey*, vii. 36.
[2] The Romans of this period enjoyed among the Greeks a singularly evil reputation for greed ; see especially a striking passage in Diodorus Siculus xxxi. 26.

---

[9] ἐπειδὴ . . . ἀσθενής del. von Rohden.
[10] δὲ Koraes (δ' Köchly): οὐδ' ἕτερος F(GH).
[11] Om. vGH.   [12] B : om. Ω.   [13] ἐλλίπῃ Koraes.

δ' αἵρεσις ἡ¹ τοῦ μέσου· καὶ γὰρ τὸ δυνατὸν ἐν
τῷ μηδέπω² γεγηρακότι καὶ τὸ φρόνιμον ἐν τῷ
μὴ πάνυ νεάζοντι, ὡς οἵτινές γε ἢ³ σώματος
ῥώμην ἄνευ ψυχῆς ἔμφρονος⁴ ἐδοκίμασαν ἢ
ψυχὴν φρόνιμον ἄνευ σωματικῆς ἕξεως, οὐδὲν
ἐπέραναν· ἡ⁵ γὰρ ὑστερήσασα φρόνησις οὐδὲν
ἐνόησε⁶ κρεῖττον, ἡ δ'⁷ ἐλλείπουσα δύναμις οὐδὲν
11 ἐτελείωσεν. ὅ γε μὴν εὐδοκιμῶν οὐ μικρὰ τοὺς
ἑλομένους⁸ ὤνησεν· ὅντινα γὰρ ἄνθρωποι φιλοῦσιν
αὐτομάτῃ⁹ διανοίας ἐμπτώσει, τούτῳ ταχὺ μὲν
ἐπιτάττοντι πείθονται, λέγοντι δ' οὐκ ἀπιστοῦσι,
κινδυνεύοντι δὲ συναγωνίζονται.

12 [θ'] πατέρα δὲ προύκρινα μᾶλλον, οὐδὲ τὸν
ἄπαιδα παραιτούμενος, ἂν¹⁰ ἀγαθὸς ᾖ· ἐάν¹¹ τε
γὰρ ὄντες τύχωσι νήπιοι, ψυχῆς εἰσιν ἰσχυρὰ
φίλτρα περὶ τὴν εὔνοιαν ἐξομηρεύσασθαι δυνάμενα
στρατηγὸν¹² πρὸς πατρίδα, δεινοὶ καὶ ὀξεῖς
μύωπες πατρός, οἷοί τε ἀναστῆσαι θυμὸν ἐπὶ
πολεμίους, ἄν τε τέλειοι, σύμβουλοι καὶ συστρά-
τηγοι¹³ καὶ πιστοὶ τῶν ἀπορρήτων ὑπηρέται
γιγνόμενοι συγκατορθοῦσι τὰ κοινὰ πράγματα.

13 [ι'] λέγειν δ' ἱκανόν· ἔνθεν γὰρ ἡγοῦμαι τὸ
μέγιστον ὠφελείας ἵξεσθαι¹⁴ διὰ στρατεύματος·
ἐάν τε γὰρ ἐκτάττῃ πρὸς μάχην στρατηγός, ἡ τοῦ

---

¹ διαίρεσις τοῦ RP (corr. to δ' ἡ αἵρεσις and so v): δι' αἵρεσις
GH.
² μὴ δέπω GH.   ³ ἢ G.   ⁴ ἐμφρόνως F.
⁵ ἢ vGH.   ⁶ ἐνενόησε GH.
⁷ Köchly: ἡ ἐλλείπουσα Ω.   ⁸ ἐλλομένους GH.
⁹ αὐτομάτει corr. to αὐτομάτῳ P: αὐτομάτῳ v: αὐτομάτη
FGH.   ¹⁰ ἐὰν AB Köchly: ἂν Ω.
¹¹ FC: ἂν vGH.   ¹² Schwebel: στρατηγοῦ Ω.
¹³ AB (συστρατηγοι GH): συσστρατηγοι F: στρατηγοι v.
¹⁴ ἥξεσθαι P: ἥξεσθαι GH.

vigour is found in the man who has not yet grown old, and discretion in the man who is not too young. Those who value physical strength without discretion, or discretion without physical strength, have failed to accomplish anything. For a weak mind can contribute no valuable ideas, nor can strength unsupported bring to completion any activity. Moreover, a man of good reputation is of no slight assistance to those who choose him; for if men have a spontaneous and natural love for their general, they are quick to obey his commands, they do not distrust him, and they coöperate with him in case of danger.

I should prefer our general to be a father, though I would not refuse a childless man, provided he be a good man. For if he happens to have young children, they are potent spells to keep his heart loyal, availing to bind him to the fatherland, a powerful and keen incentive to a father, capable of arousing his heart against the foe. And should his children have reached manhood, they will become advisers and aides, faithful guardians of his secrets, and they will help him to bring the affairs of state to a successful issue.

A ready speaker[1]; for I believe that the greatest benefit can accrue from the work of a general only through this gift. For if a general is drawing up his

---

[1] Thus Homer felt that the great leader must be μύθων τε ῥητῆρ’ ἔμεναι πρηκτῆρά τε ἔργων (*Iliad*, ix. 443), and the harangue before battle was a necessary formality, which a Caesar felt must be delivered even to his tenth legion and in the crisis of the unexpected attack of the Nervii (*Bellum Gallicum*, ii. 21. 1 f.). Compare also Cicero, *Philippica*, iv. 5.

λόγου παρακέλευσις τῶν μὲν δεινῶν ἐποίησε καταφρονεῖν, τῶν δὲ καλῶν ἐπιθυμεῖν, καὶ οὐχ οὕτως
ἀκοαῖς ἐνηχοῦσα σάλπιγξ ἐγείρει ψυχὰς εἰς ἅμιλ-
λαν μάχης, ὡς λόγος εἰς προτροπὴν ἀρετῆς
ἐναγωνίου[1] ῥηθεὶς αἰχμάζουσαν[2] ἀνέστησε πρὸς
τὰ δεινὰ τὴν διάνοιαν, ἄν τέ τι[3] συμβῇ πταῖσμα
περὶ τὸ στρατόπεδον, ἡ τοῦ λόγου παρηγορία τὰς
ψυχὰς ἀνέρρωσε, καὶ πολὺ δὴ χρησιμώτερός ἐστι
στρατηγοῦ λόγος οὐκ ἀδύνατος ὥστε παραμυθεῖσθαι
τὰς ἐν στρατοπέδοις[4] συμφοράς, τῶν ἑπομένων
14 τοῖς τραυματίαις ἰατρῶν· οἱ[5] μὲν γὰρ ἐκείνους
μόνους[6] τοῖς φαρμάκοις θεραπεύουσιν, ὁ δὲ καὶ
τοὺς κάμνοντας εὐθυμοτέρους ἐποίησεν καὶ τοὺς
15 ἐρρωμένους ἀνέστησε·[7] καὶ ὥσπερ τὰ ἀόρατα νο-
σήματα τῶν ὁρωμένων δυσχερεστέραν ἔχει τὴν
θεραπείαν, οὕτως ψυχὰς ἐξ ἀθυμίας ἰάσασθαι
λόγῳ παρηγορήσαντα δυσκολώτερον, ἢ σωμάτων
16 φανερὰν ἐξ ἐπιπολῆς[8] θεραπεῦσαι[9] νόσον. οὐδὲ
χωρὶς στρατηγῶν[10] οὐδὲ μία[11] πόλις ἐκπέμψει
στρατόπεδον, οὐδὲ δίχα τοῦ δύνασθαι λέγειν
αἱρήσεται στρατηγόν.
17 [ια΄] τὸν[12] δὲ ἔνδοξον, ὅτι τοῖς ἀδόξοις ἀσχάλλει
τὸ πλῆθος ὑποταττόμενον· οὐθεὶς[13] γὰρ ἑκὼν
ὑπομένει τὸν αὑτοῦ[14] χείρονα κύριον ἀναδέχεσθαι
18 καὶ ἡγεμόνα. πᾶσα δὲ ἀνάγκη τὸν τοιοῦτον

---

[1] ἐν ἀγῶνι vGH. [2] ἀκμάζουσαν vGH.
[3] Om. vGH. [4] τοῖς στρατ. vGH.
[5] ἰατρῶν μὲν F. [6] μόνοις PR.
[7] Köchly's suggestion that the order might be τοὺς κάμνοντας
ἀνέστησε καὶ τοὺς ἐρρωμένους εὐθυμοτέρους ἐποίησεν perhaps
derives some support from F's forms ἐποίησεν and ἀνέστησε,
but Leo, Tactica. ii. 14, as Köchly himself observed, had
clearly the present order in the text before him.

men before battle, the encouragement of his words makes them despise the danger and covet the honour; and a trumpet-call resounding in the ears does not so effectively awaken the soul to the conflict of battle as a speech that urges to strenuous valour rouses the martial spirit to confront danger. Should some disaster befall the army, an encouraging speech will give the men's souls new strength; and a not unskilful address by the commander is far more useful in counteracting the despondency of an army in the hour of defeat than the physicians who attend to the wounded. For the physicians with their medicines care only for the wounded, whereas the eloquent general not only heartens the disabled but also sets the well on their feet again. Just as hidden diseases are harder to cure than those with external symptoms, so it is more difficult by a consoling speech to cure a heart of its despondency than to minister to an obvious and manifest disease of the body. No city at all will put an army in the field without generals nor choose a general who lacks the ability to make an effective speech.

The general should be a man of good reputation, because the majority of men, when placed under the command of unknown generals, feel uneasy. For no one voluntarily submits to a leader or an officer who is an inferior man to himself. It is absolutely

---

8 ἐπιπολλῆς P : ἐπιστολῆς (in marg. γρ. ἐπιπολλῆς) GH.
9 θεραπεύει GH : θεραπεύειν v.
10 στρατηγοῦ Koraes and Köchly.
11 FGH (though the testimony of GH on such a point is practically worthless): οὐδεμία Köchly.
12 τὸ GH.   13 οὐδεὶς vH (οὐ δεῖς G).
14 αὐτοῦ FGH.

ὄντα καὶ τοσαύτας ἀρετὰς ἔχοντα ψυχῆς,[1] ὅσας εἴρηκα,[2] καὶ ἔνδοξον εἶναι.

19 Φημὶ δὲ μήτε τὸν πλούσιον, ἐὰν ἐκτὸς ᾖ τούτων, αἱρεῖσθαι στρατηγὸν διὰ τὰ χρήματα, μήτε τὸν πένητα, ἐὰν ἀγαθὸς ᾖ, παραιτεῖσθαι διὰ τὴν ἔνδειαν· οὐ μὴν χρή γε τὸν πένητα οὐδὲ τὸν πλούσιον, ἀλλὰ καὶ τὸν πλούσιον καὶ τὸν πένητα·[3] οὐδ' ἕτερον[4] γὰρ οὔθ' αἱρετὸν[5] οὔτ' ἀποδοκιμαστέον διὰ τὴν τύχην, ἀλλ' ἐλεγκτέον[6] διὰ

20 τὸν τρόπον. οὐδὲ[7] πλούσιος ἀγαθὸς ὢν τοσούτῳ[8] διοίσει τοῦ γενναίου πένητος, ὅσον αἱ ἐπάργυροι καὶ κατάχρυσοι πανοπλίαι τῶν καταχάλκων καὶ σιδηρῶν—αἱ μὲν γὰρ[9] τῷ κόσμῳ πλεονεκτοῦσιν, αἱ δ' αὐτῷ[10] τῷ δραστηρίῳ διαγωνίζονται[11]—, εἴ γε μὴ χρηματιστὴς εἴη·[12] τὸν δὲ χρηματιστήν, οὐδ' ἂν πλουσιώτατος ὢν τύχῃ,[13] συμβουλεύσω ποτὲ αἱρεῖσθαι· λέγω δὲ ὀβολοστάτην,[14] μετάβολον, ἔμπορον ἢ τοὺς παραπλήσιόν τι τούτοις πράττοντας· ἀνάγκη γὰρ τοὺς τοιούτους μικροφρόνας εἶναι καὶ περὶ τὸ κέρδος ἐπτοημένους καὶ μεμεριμνημένους[15] περὶ τὸν πορισμὸν τῶν χρημάτων ὅλως μηδὲν[16] ἐσχηκέναι τῶν καλῶν ἐπιτηδευμάτων.

21 Προγόνων δὲ[17] λαμπρὰν[18] ἀξίωσιν ἀγαπᾶν μὲν δεῖ προσοῦσαν, οὐ μὴν ἀποῦσαν ἐπιζητεῖν, οὐδὲ ταύτῃ[19] τινὰς κρίνειν ἀξίους ἢ μὴ[20] τοῦ στρατηγεῖν,

---

[1] τῆς ψυχῆς B Köchly.   [2] εἴρηκε F.
[3] καὶ τὸν πένητα om. F.
[4] FGH Rigaltius Schwebel : οὐδέτερον Köchly.
[5] F : αἱρετέον GH Köchly.   [6] ἐκλεκτέον vGH.
[7] ὁ δὲ FvGH : corr. AB (οὐ δὲ C : οὐκ δὲ R).
[8] τοσοῦτον vGH.   [9] After γὰρ vGH add καί.
[10] After αὐτῷ vGH add μόνῳ.   [11] διαγωνίζωνται GH.
[12] χρηματιστὴ εἴη F, which marks a break at this point.
[13] ἂν τύχῃ F : ἂν τύχει R.

essential, then, that a general be such a man, of such excellent traits of character as I have enumerated, and besides this, that he have a good reputation.

A wealthy man in my opinion must not be chosen general on account of his wealth, if he has not these qualities ; nor must a poor man, provided that he be competent, be rejected on account of his poverty. It is not necessary that the general be rich or poor ; he may be the one or the other. Neither the one nor the other must be chosen nor rejected on account of his fortune in life, but must be tested by the standard of character. Even the wealthy general who is good will surpass the noble but poor general only in the same degree that armour inlaid with gold and silver surpasses that of bronze and iron —the former have the advantage in ornamentation but the latter prove superior in efficiency—provided that he is not a man who deals in money. Were he the richest man in the world, I should not ever advise choosing a man who deals in money. I mean by this expression a usurer, a trader, a merchant, or those who are in a similar business. For these men must have petty minds ; excited over gain and worried about the means of getting money, they have acquired absolutely none of the noble habits of a general.

An illustrious family name we should welcome, if it be present, but if lacking it should not be demanded, nor should we judge men worthy or unworthy of commands simply by this criterion ; but

---

[14] ὀβολογιάτην RG (ὀβ-) H (ὀβ-) P (corr. to ὀβολοστάτην).
[15] μεμορημένους GH.　　[16] ὅλως δὲ μηδὲν GH.
[17] Koraes: τε Ω.　　[18] λαμπρῶν Köchly.
[19] οὐδ' ἐκ ταύτης vGH.　　[20] Köchly: εἰμὴ F: εἶναι vGH.

ἀλλ' ὥσπερ τὰ ζῷα ἀπὸ τῶν ἰδίων πράξεων ἐξε-
τάζομεν, ὅπως εὐγενείας ἔχει, οὕτω χρὴ σκοπεῖν
22 καὶ τὴν τῶν ἀνθρώπων εὐγένειαν. καὶ γὰρ ἀ-
περίοπτον,[1] τί τοῖς ἔμπροσθεν ἐπράχθη καλόν, ἐξετάζειν, οὐ τί ποιήσουσιν οἱ νῦν αἱρεθέντες· ὥσπερ
τῶν πάλαι γεγονότων σῴζειν ἡμᾶς δυναμένων καὶ
τὰ νῦν, καὶ[2] τὰ πρόσθεν τηρησόντων ἐκείνων. ἔτι
δὲ πῶς[2] οὐκ ἀπαίδευτον τοὺς μὲν στρατιώτας
τοῖς ἀριστείοις τιμᾶν, οὐ τοὺς ἐκ πατέρων[3]
λαμπρῶν,[4] ἀλλὰ τοὺς αὐτούς τι γενναῖον ἐργασα-
μένους, τοὺς δὲ στρατηγοὺς διὰ τοὺς προγόνους
αἱρεῖσθαι, κἂν ὦσιν ἄχρηστοι,[5] μὴ διὰ τὴν σφῶν
23 αὐτῶν ἀρετήν, κἂν μὴ γένει λαμπρύνωνται; προσ-
όντων μὲν δὴ τούτων ἐκείνοις εὐτυχὴς ὁ στρατηγός,
ἀπόντων δ' ἐκείνων, κἂν παρῇ ταῦτα, ἄ-
24 πρακτος. ἐλπίσαι δ' ἄν τις τάχα καὶ ἀμείνους
ἔσεσθαι στρατηγοὺς τοὺς οὐκ ἔχοντας ἐνσεμνύ-
νεσθαι προγόνοις· οἱ μὲν γὰρ ἐπὶ πατράσι κυ-
δαινόμενοι, κἂν ἐλλίπωσιν,[6] οἰόμενοι τὴν ἐκ τῶν
πρόσθεν εὔκλειάν σφισι φυλάττεσθαι πολλὰ καὶ
ῥαθυμότερον διοικοῦσιν, οἷς δ' οὐδεμία προϋπ-
άρχει δόξα προγόνων, οὗτοι τὴν ἐκ πατέρων[3]
ἐλάττωσιν ἐθέλοντες[7] ἀναπληρῶσαι τῇ σφετέρᾳ
προθυμίᾳ φιλοκινδυνότερον ἐπὶ τὰς πράξεις ἁμιλ-
25 λῶνται· καὶ καθάπερ οἱ πενέστεροι τῶν εὐπο-
ρωτέρων ταλαιπωρότερον ἐπὶ τὴν τοῦ βίου κτῆσιν
ὥρμηνται τὸ ἐλλεῖπον ἀναπληρῶσαι τῆς τύχης
σπεύδοντες, οὕτως, οἷς μὴ πάρεστι κληρονομου-

---

[1] ἂν περίοπτον F, corr. C: ἀνόητον vGH.
[2] Köchly: καὶ πρόσθεν (τὰ πρόσθεν CRDENA m²): τήρησον
θᾶττον ἐκείνον ὅτε πῶς F: καὶ πρόσθεν. ἐκείνο δὲ πῶς vGH.
[3] FGHR: προγόνων v.   [4] λαμπρούς vGH.

just as we test the pedigrees of animals in the light of the things they actually do, so we should view the pedigrees of men also. For it is dangerous to consider what fine thing a general's ancestors have done, rather than what the generals now chosen will do, as if those long dead could still protect us, and as if they would maintain us in our former possessions. As a matter of fact, is it not sheer stupidity to honour soldiers for valour, not those of famous families but those who have done some noble deed themselves, but on the other hand to select generals, even if they are incompetent, on account of their ancestors and not on account of their own worth, even if their families are unknown? Of course, if a general has birth in addition to these other qualities, he is fortunate, but even if he has a famous name without the other qualities, he is useless. It might perhaps be expected that those men who cannot take pride in their ancestors would become even better generals; for men who glory in their forefathers, even if they are themselves failures, believing that the fame of their family is theirs forever are often too careless as administrators, whereas those who have no ancestral renown to begin with, desiring to make up for the obscurity of their lineage by their own zeal, are more eager to take part in dangerous enterprises. Just as the poor man, eager to supply what fortune omitted, will endure more than the rich man in getting a start to make his fortune, so the man who can avail himself of no inheritance

---

5 FC: χρηστοὶ Ω (including P).   6 ἐλλείπωσιν vGH.
7 FCD: ἐλθόντες vGH.

μένη πατέρων[1] ἀποχρήσασθαι δόξῃ, τὴν ἀρετὴν ἰδιόκτητον οἰκειώσασθαι προαιροῦνται.

II. [Περὶ ἀγαθοῦ στρατηγοῦ διαίρεσις][2]

Ζηλούσθω[3] μὲν δὴ ἡμῖν ὁ στρατηγὸς ὁ ἀγαθὸς[4] εὐγενὴς καὶ[5] πλούσιος, μὴ ἀποδοκιμαζέσθω δὲ πένης μετὰ ἀρετῆς, εἰ καὶ μὴ[6] ἀπὸ λαμπρῶν.

2 αἱρεθεὶς δ' ὁ στρατηγὸς ἔστω χρηστός, εὐπροσήγορος, ἕτοιμος, ἀτάραχος, μὴ οὕτως ἐπιεικὴς ὥστε καταφρονεῖσθαι, μήτε φοβερὸς ὥστε μισεῖσθαι, ἵνα μήτε ταῖς χάρισιν ἐκλύσῃ τὸ στρα-

3 τόπεδον μήτε τοῖς φόβοις ἀλλοτριώσῃ. λοχαγοὺς δὲ καθιστάτω καὶ ταξιάρχους[7] καὶ χιλιάρχους,[8] καὶ εἴ τινων ἄλλων ἡγεμόνων προσδεῖν αὐτῷ δόξαι,[9] τοὺς εὐνουστάτους τῇ πατρίδι, πιστοτάτους,[10] εὐρωστοτάτους, ἔνθεν δ'[11] οὐδὲν ἂν κωλύοι[12] καὶ

4 τοὺς εὐπορωτάτους καὶ τοὺς εὐγενεστάτους· οὐ γάρ, ὡς ὀλίγους αἱρουμένους[13] στρατηγοὺς ἐκ τρόπου δοκιμάσαι ῥᾷον, κἂν ἀπῇ ὁ τῶν χρημάτων[14] μετ' εὐγενείας ὄγκος, οὕτως που καὶ λοχαγῶν καὶ

5 ταξιαρχῶν πλῆθος. ὅθεν τὸ μὲν εὐγενὲς ἐπὶ τούτων προκριτέον εἰς πρόχειρον ἐν ὀξεῖ καιρῷ δοκιμασίαν,[15] τὸ δὲ ἐν εὐπορίᾳ,[16] ἐπειδὴ[17] ἀναλῶσαί τε καὶ δοῦναι στρατιώταις οἱ ἐκ περιουσίας δυνατοί, χορηγία δ' ἀπὸ τῶν ἡγουμένων ὀλίγη πρὸς

[1] FGHR : προγόνων v.
[2] In text GH (v?): om. F : C puts it after § 1 where it really belongs, since § 1 is properly the conclusion of the preceding chapter.   [3] Ζητείσθω Koraes.
[4] F : ἡμῖν στρατηγὸς ὁ ἀγαθὸς GH : στρατηγὸς ἀγαθὸς v : δὴ στρατηγὸς ἡμῖν ἀγαθὸς von Rohden.
[5] Om. Ω.   [6] εἰ μὴ καὶ vGH.   [7] ταξιάρχας GH.
[8] καὶ χιλιάρχους FC : om. vGH.   [9] δόξει vGH.

386

of ancestral glory determines to make his own the
virtue which he himself acquires.

II. [*The Characteristics of a good General*]

So that general is to be praised who is good,
wealthy, and well-born, but the excellent general
who is not wealthy is not to be rejected, even if
of humble family. The general when chosen must
be trustworthy, affable, prompt, calm, not so lenient
as to be despised, nor so severe as to be hated, so
that he may neither through favours loosen the
bonds of discipline, nor estrange the army through
fear. He must appoint as lieutenants, captains,
and colonels, as well as other officers, if it seems
necessary, men who are most loyal to their country,
most faithful, and most vigorous—though there
is nothing to prevent their being of the greatest
wealth and nobility. As the number of generals to
be chosen is small, they may be easily judged
from their characters, even if the dignity of wealth
and birth is lacking; but this is not the case with the
multitude of subordinate officers. And so by off-
hand judgement required at a crucial moment the
nobility have to be preferred, but when there is no
urgency, the wealthy, since those who have abundant
means can spend money on the soldiery and make
them gifts; for a slight expenditure by the officers

---

[10] καὶ πιστοτάτους vGH: πιστοτάτους τε καὶ C.
[11] Om. vGH. [12] κωλύῃ v: κωλύη GH. [13] αἱρουμένοις F.
[14] Köchly: ἀπῆ χρημάτων F: ἀπὸ χρημάτων GH: ἀπὸ (om.
τῶν?) v: ἀπῆ τῶν χ. μετ' or ἀπῆ τῶν χ. ὁ μετ' von Rohden.
[15] καιρὸν δοκιμασίας GH: καιρῷ δοκιμασίας ENRA m².
After δοκιμασίαν an interval in F.
[16] ἀπορίᾳ Rigaltius. [17] ἐπειδή γ' von Rohden.

τοὺς ὑποταττομένους[1] εὐνούστερα παρασκευάζει
τὰ πλήθη· καὶ ἀσφαλεῖς αἱ[2] μειζόνων πίστεις[3]
πραγμάτων τοῖς περὶ πλειόνων κινδυνεύουσιν, εἰ
μή[4] πάνυ τὸ πιστόν, ὡς ἂν εἰ στρατηγοῖ τις,[4]
ἐκ τοῦ τρόπου παρέχοιτο.

III. [Περὶ τοῦ ἔχειν τὸν στρατηγὸν βουλευτάς[5]]

Αἱρείσθω δὲ ἤτοι[6] συνέδρους, οἳ[7] μεθέξουσιν
αὐτῷ πάσης βουλῆς καὶ κοινωνήσουσι γνώμης
αὐτοῦ[8] οἳ[9] τούτου εἴνεκα[10] ἀκολουθήσοντες,[11] ἢ ἐξ
αὐτῶν τῶν ἡγεμόνων τοὺς ἐντιμοτάτους μεταπεμ-
πόμενος συνεδρευέτω, ὡς,[12] ἅ γέ τις ἂν ἐννοήσῃ
μὲν μόνος, ὡς τὰ αὐτοῦ, οὐ βεβαίως[12] οἰκειοῦται.
2 γνώμη γὰρ ἡ μὲν ἀνεπικούρητος μονουμένη πα-
πταίνει[13] περὶ τὴν ἰδίαν εὕρεσιν,[14] ἡ δὲ ὑπὸ τῶν
πέλας ἐπιμαρτυρηθεῖσα πιστοῦται τὸ μὴ σφαλερόν.
3 οὐ μὴν ἀλλὰ μήθ' οὕτως ἄστατος ἔστω τὴν διάνοιαν, ὡς αὐτὸν αὑτῷ[15] πάμπαν ἀπιστεῖν, μήθ'
οὕτως αὐθάδης, ὡς μή τι καὶ παρ' ἄλλῳ τοῦ παρ'
αὑτῷ[16] κρεῖττον οἴεσθαι νοηθῆναι· ἀνάγκη γὰρ
τὸν τοιοῦτον ἢ πᾶσι[17] προσέχοντα καὶ μηδὲν
αὑτῷ[18] πολλὰ καὶ ἀσύμφορα πράττειν, ἢ μηδ'
ὀλίγ' ἄλλων[19] ἀκούοντα, πάντα δ' αὑτοῦ,[20] πολλὰ
καὶ δεινὰ[21] διαμαρτάνειν.[22]

[1] ὑποτεταγμένους vGH.   [2] FC: ἀσφάλεια vGH.
[3] πίστις GH.   [4] F: εἰ πάνυ στρατηγὸς ἐκ vGH.
[5] Om. F which has not even an interval between II and III.
[6] F: δὲ αὖ καὶ vGH.   [7] οἱ καὶ vGH.
[8] αὐτῷ Koraes.   [9] ἢ vGH.   [10] F: ἕνεκα Ω Köchly.
[11] Del. οἱ . . . ἀκολουθήσοντες von Rohden.
[12] Köchly: ὡς ἅ γέ τις ἐννοήσῃ μὲν μόνος τὰ αὐτοῦ βεβαίως F:

388

for the benefit of their men makes the rank and file better disposed; and the pledges of greater rewards can be depended upon when made by those who have more at stake—that is, if the confidence a general ought to inspire is not altogether furnished by his character.

III. [*The General's advisory Council*]

The general should either choose a staff to participate in all his councils and share in his decisions, men who will accompany the army especially for this purpose, or summon as members of his council a selected group of the most respected commanders, since it is not safe that the opinions of one single man, on his sole judgement, should be adopted. For the isolated decision of one man, unsupported by others, can see no farther than his own ingenuity, but that which has the additional testimony of councillors guarantees against mistake. However, the general must neither be so undecided that he entirely distrusts himself, nor so obstinate as not to think that anyone can have a better idea than his own; for such a man, either because he listens to every one else and never to himself, is sure to meet with frequent misfortune, or else, through never listening to others but always to himself, is bound to make many costly mistakes.

ὥστε (ὥστε τε PD) δεῖ ἃ ἐννοῆσαι μὲν μελετᾶν μόνος δὲ οὐ τὰ αὑτοῦ βεβαίως PDGH : von Rohden objects to οὔ.
[13] πταίει vGH.   [14] αἵρεσιν vGH.
[15] Köchly : αὐτὸν αὑτῶ F : αὐτὸς αὑτῷ vGH (αὑτῶ GH).
[16] Köchly : αὑτῶ F : αὐτὸν vGH.   [17] πάση F.
[18] Köchly : αὑτῶ FGH : αὑτῷ v.   [19] Köchly : ὀλίγων Ω.
[20] Koraes : δ' αὑτοῦ FC : δι' αὑτοῦ PGH.
[21] Köchly : om. Ω.   [22] ἁμαρτάνειν vG (ἁμ-) H.

389

IV. [Περὶ τοῦ ὅτι δεῖ τὴν ἀρχὴν τοῦ πολέμου
ἐξ εὐλόγου αἰτίας ἐπάγειν][1]

Τὰς δ' ἀρχὰς τοῦ πολέμου μάλιστά φημι χρῆ-
ναι φρονίμως συνίστασθαι καὶ μετὰ τοῦ δικαίου
πᾶσι φανερὸν γίγνεσθαι πολεμοῦντα· τότε γὰρ καὶ
θεοὶ συναγωνισταὶ τοῖς στρατεύουσιν εὐμενεῖς
καθίστανται,[2] καὶ ἄνθρωποι προθυμότερον ἀντι-
2 τάττονται τοῖς δεινοῖς·[3] εἰδότες γάρ, ὡς οὐκ
ἄρχουσιν ἀλλ' ἀμύνονται,[4] τὰς ψυχὰς ἀσυνει-
δήτους κακῶν ἔχοντες ἐντελῆ[5] τὴν ἀνδρείαν[6] εἰσ-
φέρονται, ὥς, ὅσοι γε νομίζουσι νεμεσήσειν[7] τὸ
θεῖον ἐπὶ τῷ παρὰ τὸ δίκαιον ἐκφέρειν πόλεμον,
αὐτῇ τῇ οἰήσει, κἂν μή τι δεινὸν ἀπὸ τῶν πολεμίων
3 ἀπαντήσειν μέλλῃ,[8] προκατορρωδοῦσιν. διὰ τοῦτο
δεῖ τὸν στρατηγόν, ὧν τε βούλεται τυχεῖν καὶ ὧν
μὴ παραχωρῆσαι, λόγῳ καὶ πρεσβείαις προ-
καλεῖσθαι[9] πρῶτον, ἵν' ἐν τῷ μὴ συγκαταβαίνειν
τοῖς ἀξιουμένοις τοὺς ἐναντίους[10] ἀνάγκη δοκῇ,[11]
καὶ μὴ προαιρέσει τὴν δύναμιν ἐξάγειν πολεμή-
σουσαν,[12] ἐπιμαρτυράμενος[13] τὸ θεῖον, ὡς οὔτε
καταφρονῶν ὧν συμβαίνει τοὺς πολεμοῦντας
πάσχειν, ἀνεμεσήτως ἔπεισιν, οὔτε ἐκ παντὸς
τρόπου τὰ δεινὰ δρᾶσαι προῃρημένος τοὺς πο-
4 λεμίους.[14] εἰδέναι δὲ χρή, καθότι οὐ μόνον οἰκίας

[1] Title om. F.
[2] θεὸς συναγωνιστὴς τοῖς στρατεύμασιν εὐμενὴς καθίσταται vGH
(a Christian interpolation).
[3] ἐναντίοις Köchly.   [4] ἀμύνωνται PGH.
[5] ἐντελεῖ corr. to ἐντελῆ F m²(?): ἐντελεῖ AB.
[6] ἀνδρίαν v.   [7] μὴ νεμεσήσειν vGH.
[8] Koraes: μέλλει Ω.
[9] F (also conj. by Schwebel): προσκαλεῖσθαι vGH.
[10] FCGH: τοὺς ἀξίους τοῖς ἐναντίοις FNPRV.

IV. [*The Necessity of a reasonable Cause for War*]

The causes of war, I believe, should be marshalled with the greatest care; it should be evident to all that one fights on the side of justice. For then the gods also, kindly disposed, become comrades in arms to the soldiers, and men are more eager to take their stand against the foe.[1] For with the knowledge that they are not fighting an aggressive but a defensive war, with consciences free from evil designs, they contribute a courage that is complete; while those who believe an unjust war is displeasing to heaven, because of this very opinion enter the war with fear, even if they are not about to face danger at the hands of the enemy. On this account the general must first announce, by speeches and through embassies, what he wishes to obtain and what he is not willing to concede, in order that it may appear that, because the enemy will not agree to his reasonable demands, it is of necessity, not by his own preference, that he is taking the field. He should call heaven to witness that he is entering upon war without offence, since he has not failed to consider the dangers that fall to the lot of combatants, and is not deliberately seeking, in every possible manner, to ruin the enemy. He should know that not only is a firm foundation

---

[1] Something of a commonplace even in antiquity; for typical expressions see Thucydides ii. 74; Xenophon, *Cyropedia*, i. 5. 13-14; Dionysius of Halicarnassus ii. 72. 30.

---

[11] δοκεῖ v (incl. P) GH.

[12] F (also conj. by Koraes): πολεμοῦσαν vGH.

[13] ἐπιμαρτυρόμενος vGH.

[14] FC: προῃρημένος τοῖς πολεμίοις GH: προῃρημένοις τοῖς πολεμίοις Pv.

καὶ τείχους ἑδραιότερον ὑφίστασθαι δεῖ τὸν θε-
μέλιον, ὡς ἀσθενοῦς γε ὄντος[1] συγκαταρρυησο-
μένων[2] καὶ τῶν ἐποικοδομουμένων, ἀλλὰ καὶ πολέμου τὰς[3] ἀρχὰς δεῖ κατασκευασάμενον ἰσχυ-
ρῶς καὶ κρηπῖδα περιθέμενον ἀσφαλείας,[4] οὕτως ἐξάγειν τὰς δυνάμεις· ὧν γὰρ ἀσθενῆ τὰ πράγ-
ματά ἐστιν, ἐπειδὰν οὗτοι μέγα βάρος ἀναλάβωσιν
5 πολέμου, ταχὺ θλίβονται καὶ ὑστεροῦσιν. ὅθεν,
ὥσπερ ἀγαθὸν κυβερνήτην ἐκ λιμένος ἐξαρτυσά-
μενον τὸ[5] σκάφος καὶ τὰ παρ' αὑτῷ[6] ἅπαντα
ποιήσαντα, τότ' ἐπιτρέπειν[7] χρὴ τῇ τύχῃ, ὡς
αἴσχιστόν γε[8] καὶ σφαλερὸν ὑποδείξαντα πολέμου
κίνησιν, ὥστε καὶ διὰ θαλάττης ἤδη καὶ διὰ γῆς
ἄγειν τὸ στράτευμα, κἄπειτα πρύμναν κρούεσθαι·[9]
6 τῆς μὲν γὰρ ἀνοίας καὶ προπετείας ἕκαστος κατ-
εγέλασεν, τῆς δ' ἀσθενείας κατεφρόνησεν,[10] οἱ δ'
ἐχθροί, οἵτινές ποτ' ἂν ὦσιν, κἂν μὴ πάθωσιν, ὡς
οὐχὶ μὴ βουληθέντας[11] ἀλλ' οὐ δυνηθέντας δια-
θεῖναί τι[12] δικαίως ἐμίσησαν.

V. [Περὶ τοῦ ἐξιλεοῦσθαι πρῶτον ὑπὲρ τῶν ἁμαρ-
τιῶν τὸ θεῖον[13] ὁ στρατηγὸς ἐξάγων εἰς πόλεμον][14]

Ἐξαγέτω δὲ τὰς δυνάμεις ὁ στρατηγὸς καθαρὰς
ἢ οἷς νόμοι[15] ἱεροὶ ἢ οἷς μάντεις ὑφηγοῦνται κα-

---

[1] FENRGH : ὄντας PA m² and "quidam libri" (Schwebel).
[2] A m² GH (v?): συγκαταρτισομένων F.
[3] PGH : τοῦ πολέμου τὰς v : πολεμοῦντας F.
[4] Köchly suggests ἀσφαλῶς.   [5] Om. vGH.
[6] Köchly: αὑτῷ ENR: αὑτῶν vGH: αὑτὸν F : παρ' αὑτῷ
περὶ αὑτὸ von Rohden.
[7] F (and Leo, *Tactica*, xx. 170 ἐπίτρεπε): ἐπιτρέχειν vGH.
[8] τε vGH.

necessary for houses and walls—for if this is weak
the superstructures will also collapse—, but that in
war also it is only after one has prepared a firm
beginning, and has laid a safe foundation, that he
should take the field. For those whose cause is
weak, when they take up the heavy burden of war, are
quickly crushed by it and fail. Just as a careful ship-
captain, after he has given his ship a thorough overhauling and outfitting while in harbour, and has
done everything within his own power, must then
commit his craft to Fortune, so it is most disgraceful
and dangerous for a general, after he has given
intimations of a beginning of war, implying an
immediate advance of his forces by both land and
sea, then to back out. For while every one laughs
at folly and rashness, we despise weakness, and the
enemy — whoever they may be — even if they
experience no harm, have good reason to hate the
would-be invaders, as men who have not lacked the
will, but lacked the ability to put a matter through.

V. [*Propitiation of the divine Power by the General
before leading the Army into Battle*]

Before the general leads out his army he must see
that it is purified, by such rites as either the laws or

9 Ω: κρούσασθαι Köchly, after the emendation in A.
10 κατεφρόνησαν F, followed by an interval, as though a
chapter ended here, with the first letter of μὴ rubricated.
11 βουληθέντες G: βουληθέντα H.   12 Added by Köchly.
13 τὸ θεῖον GH : om. v.
14 Om. F (whole title) : in text GH.
15 ὡς νόμοι PGH : ὡς οἱ νόμοι ENR.

θαρσίοις, πᾶσαν, εἴ τις ἢ δημοσίᾳ[1] κηλὶς ἢ ἰδίου
μολύσματος[2] ἑκάστῳ σύνεστιν, ἀποδιοπομπού-
μενος.

VI. [Περὶ τοῦ ἄγειν ἐν τάξει τὸ στρατόπεδον][3]

Ἀγέτω δὲ τὸ στράτευμα πᾶν ἐν τάξει, κἂν μήπω
μέλλῃ συμβάλλειν, ἀλλὰ διὰ μακρᾶς ὁδοῦ πε-
ραιοῦσθαι καὶ πολλῶν ἡμερῶν ἀνύειν πορείαν, καὶ
ἐν τῇ φιλίᾳ καὶ ἐν τῇ πολεμίᾳ· διὰ μὲν τῆς φιλίας,[4]
ἵνα ἐθίζηται[5] τὰ στρατεύματα μένειν ἐν τάξει
καὶ συμφυλάττειν τοὺς ἰδίους λόχους καὶ ἕπεσθαι
τοῖς ἡγεμόσιν, διὰ δὲ τῆς πολεμίας πρὸς τὰς
ἐξαίφνης ἐπιβουλὰς[6] γιγνομένας, ἵνα μὴ ἐν ὀξεῖ
καιρῷ[7] θορυβούμενοι καὶ[8] ἐπαναθέοντες καὶ ἄλλοι
πρὸς ἄλλους φερόμενοι[8] μηδὲν μὲν ἀνύσωσι φθα-
σθέντες,[9] πολλὰ δὲ καὶ[10] δεινὰ πάθωσιν, ἀλλ᾽ ἅμα
καὶ εἰς πορείαν[11] ὦσιν ἐπιδέξιοι καὶ εἰς μάχην
εὐτρεπεῖς,[12] ἔχοντες καὶ τὸ σύνθημα[13] καὶ ἀλ-
2 λήλους ἐν τάξει βλέποντες.[14] συστέλλειν δὲ πει-
ράσθω τὴν πορείαν[15] τοῦ στρατεύματος, ὡς ἔνι
μάλιστα, πρὸς ὀλίγον, καὶ διὰ τοιούτων, ἂν
δυνατὸν ᾖ, χωρίων ἀγέτω τὰς τάξεις, δι᾽ ὧν οὐκ
ἂν ἐκθλιβόμεναι στεναὶ καὶ οὐκ ἔχουσαι πλάτος
3 ἐκ πλευρᾶς ἐπὶ μήκιστον ἐκταθεῖεν· καὶ γὰρ εὐ-
παθέστεραι[16] γίγνονται[17] πρὸς τὰς αἰφνιδίους τῶν

---

[1] δημοσίᾳ Ω.
[2] Köchly: ἢ (or ἦ F) διαμολύσματος FPGH: διαμόλυσμα R.
[3] Om. F (whole title): in text GH.
[4] FC (καὶ πολεμίᾳ): καὶ ἐν τῇ π. . . . φιλίας om. vPGH.
[5] FCENR: ἐθίζεται PGH: ἐθίζεσθαι v.
[6] ἐπιβολὰς Schwebel.   [7] καιροῦ vGH.
[8] Om. καὶ . . . φερόμενοι CH (added in margin by m¹[?]).
[9] φθάσαντες vGH.

soothsayers direct, and must avert whatever taint
there is in the state or in any citizen, by expiatory
sacrifices.

VI. [On Maintaining Military Formation]

The general must lead his entire army in military
formation, even if he is not on the point of battle,
but is completing a long journey and a march of
many days through either a friendly or a hostile
country; through a friendly country, that the soldiers
may become accustomed to remaining in rank, to
keeping to their own companies, and to following
their own leaders; through a hostile country, to guard
against sudden attacks from ambush, that the soldiers
may not be thrown into disorder at a critical moment,
running against and stumbling over one another,
and so accomplishing nothing but rather suffering
severe loss; they must proceed, prepared at the
same time for marching and for battle, remembering
their watchword and keeping their eyes on their
comrades in the ranks. The general must attempt
to make the marching order of his army as compact
as possible, and should lead his troops through such
a country—so far as he is able—that the ranks may
not be so cramped, being narrow and having no
width, that they cannot be deployed to a considerable
distance laterally. For lines so disposed suffer more

---

[10] Om. H (end of line).　　[11] ἐς πορείαν v: εὐπορείαν GH.
[12] FC: εὐπρεπεῖς vGH.
[13] In GH in marg. περὶ τοῦ ἔχειν σύνθημα τὸν λαόν (which
Rigaltius found in three mss. and which appears also in A m²),
absurd as a chapter heading.
[14] βλέποντας F.　　　　[15] FC: στρατείαν vPGH.
[16] εὐπαθέστερον R: εὐπαθέστεροι v.　　[17] γίγνωνται GH.

πολεμίων ἐπιφανείας αἱ τοιαῦται καὶ ἥκιστα δρα-
στήριοι· ἄν τε γὰρ σφισι κατὰ μέτωπον ὑπαντή-
σωσιν οἱ πολέμιοι πλατύτεροι τεταγμένοι, ῥᾳδίως
αὐτοὺς τρέπονται, καθάπερ οἱ τοὺς ἐπὶ κέρως
ὄντας ἐν ταῖς μάχαις κυκλούμενοι, ἄν τε κατὰ
μέσην τὴν δύναμιν ἐκ πλευρᾶς ἐπιβάλωσι,[1] ταχὺ
διέσπασαν αὐτῶν τὴν πορείαν καὶ διέκοψαν — ἐπι-
στρεψάντων γὰρ αὐτῶν εἰς φάλαγγα πρὸς ἄμυναν
ἀσθενὴς ἡ μάχη γίνεται[2] καὶ οὐκ ἔχουσα βάθος—,
ἐάν[3] τε τοῖς κατόπιν, ἡ[4] κατὰ νώτου μάχη δεινὴ[5]
καὶ προφανῆ τὸν ὄλεθρον ἔχουσα, κἂν ἐπιστρέψαι
δὲ τολμήσωσιν εἰς μέτωπον, ἡ αὐτὴ[6] γίγνεται
μάχη τοῖς ἐν τῇ πρωτοπορείᾳ τεταγμένοις· ταχὺ
4 γὰρ αὐτοὺς περιστήσονται. συμβαίνει δὲ καὶ τὰς
παραβοηθείας δυσχερεῖς καὶ ἀπράκτους γίνεσθαι.[7]
τῶν γὰρ ἀπὸ τῆς οὐραγίας τοῖς εἰς τὴν πρωτο-
πορείαν βουλομένων[8] βοηθεῖν ἢ τῶν πρώτων τοῖς
κατόπιν βραδεῖα ἡ ἄφιξις καὶ οὐ κατὰ καιρὸν[9]
γίγνεται, διὰ πολλῶν, ὧν ὑστεροῦσιν ἢ προηγοῦν-
ται, σταδίων ἰέναι προθυμουμένων.
5 Ἡ δὲ συνεσταλμένη πορεία καὶ τετράγωνος ἡ μὴ
πάνυ[10] παραμήκης εἰς πάντα καιρὸν εὐμεταχείρι-
στός[11] ἐστι καὶ ἀσφαλής. ἔστι δ' ὅτε καὶ[12]
συνέβη τι τοιοῦτον[13] ἐκ τῶν ἐκτεινομένων στρατευμάτων, ὥστε[14] Πανικὰ καὶ πτοίας[15] ἀμφι-

<hr>

[1] F: ἐπιβάλωσιν vGH : ἐπιβάλωσιν Koraes (Köchly).
[2] F: γίγνεται GH Köchly.   [3] ἐὰν . . . ἔχουσα om. R.
[4] ἢ F.
[5] Köchly: δεινὴ μάχη κ. π. τ. ὀ. ἔ. βάθος· κἂν F: δεινὴ
μάχη ὁμοίως κ. π. ποιεῖται τ. ὀ. ὡσαύτως (ὡς αὔτως G, ὡς αὔτως
H) οὐκ ἔχουσα βάθος κἂν vGH. The order δεινὴ μάχη is
defended by von Rohden.   [6] αὐτῇ GH.
[7] FGH: γίγνεσθαι A m² Köchly.   [8] βουλομένοις R.

under sudden attacks of the enemy and are least effective; should the enemy with a more extended front encounter the head of the column, they would easily put it to flight, just as in battle one army, by outflanking an enemy advancing in column formation, routs it. Should the enemy attack the centre of the column from the flank, they would quickly pierce it and cut through—for if the column wheels to meet the enemy, forming a phalanx, even this, lacking depth, will make but a weak resistance—; and, finally, should the enemy attack the rear of the column, the fighting with back to the foe would be dangerous and entail obvious destruction; and even if the soldiers in the column venture to face about and form a new front, the battle would amount to the same thing as the previous attack on the advance guard, *i.e.*, the enemy would quickly surround them. Furthermore, assistance is difficult to give and ineffectual, for when those in the rear desire to give aid to the head of the column, or those at the head to those in the rear, their arrival is delayed and ill-timed, however eager they may be to cover the many stades which separate them from the van or the rear respectively.

A marching formation that is compact and rectangular—not very much longer than its width—is safe and easy to manage for every emergency. A too greatly extended line of march may at times produce panic and apprehension due to uncertainty,

---

⁹ καιρῶν F.   ¹⁰ ἢ μὴ πάνυ C (Capps): ἤπερ ἡ πάνυ vGH.
¹¹ εὐμεταχείριτοσ F.   ¹² Köchly: τι F: om. vGH.
¹³ τοσούτων F.   ¹⁴ Om. vGH.
¹⁵ Köchly: om. AB(F?): πτύας ποιὰς PGH: πανικὰς πτοίας ποιὰς R: πανικὰ καὶ ποίαν τινὰς EN.

δόξους ἐμπίπτειν· ἐνίοτε γὰρ οἱ πρῶτοι κατα-
βεβηκότες ἐξ ὀρεινῶν εἰς ψιλὰ καὶ ἐπίπεδα χωρία[1]
θεασάμενοι τοὺς κατόπιν ἐπικαταβαίνοντας ἔδο-
ξαν εἶναι πολεμίων ἔφοδον, ὥστε μελλῆσαι[2] προσ-
βάλλειν ὡς ἐχθροῖς, τινὰς δὲ καὶ εἰς χεῖρας
ἐλθεῖν ἤδη.

6 Λαμβανέτω δὲ τὴν θεραπείαν καὶ τὰ ὑποζύγια
καὶ τὴν ἀποσκευὴν ἅπασαν ἐν μέσῃ τῇ[3] δυνάμει
καὶ μὴ χωρίς· ἂν δὲ μὴ τὰ κατόπιν ἀσφαλῆ πάνυ
καὶ εἰρηναῖα νομίζῃ, καὶ τὴν οὐραγίαν ἐκ τῶν
ἐρρωμενεστάτων καὶ ἀνδρειοτάτων συνιστάσθω,
μηθὲν[4] διαφέρειν αὐτὴν οἰόμενος πρὸς τὰ συμβαίνοντα τῆς πρωτοπορείας.

7 Προπεμπέτω δὲ ἱππεῖς τοὺς διερευνησομένους
τὰς ὁδούς, καὶ μάλισθ᾽, ὅτ᾽ ἂν ὑλώδεις καὶ περικε-
κλασμένας[5] λόφοις ἐρημίας διεξίῃ· πολλάκις γὰρ
ἐνέδραι πολεμίων ὑποκαθέζονται,[6] καὶ λαθοῦσαι
μὲν ἔστιν ὅτε τὰ ὅλα συνέτριψαν τῶν ἐναντίων
πράγματα, μὴ λαθοῦσαι δὲ διὰ μικρᾶς φροντίδος
φρόνησιν μεγάλην ἐμαρτύρησαν τῷ πολεμίῳ[7]
8 στρατηγῷ. τὴν μὲν γὰρ πεδιάδα καὶ ψιλὴν ἡ
πάντων ὄψις ἱκανὴ προερευνήσασθαι.[8] καὶ γὰρ
κονιορτὸς ἀναφερόμενος[9] μεθ᾽ ἡμέραν[10] ἐμήνυσεν
τὴν τῶν πολεμίων ἔφοδον, καὶ πυρὰ καιόμενα[11]
νύκτωρ ἐπύρσευσεν[12] τὴν ἐγγὺς στρατοπεδείαν.

9 Ἀγέτω δὲ[13] τὰς δυνάμεις, μὴ μέλλων μὲν ἐκ-

---

[1] χωρεῖα GH. [2] μελῆσαι vGH.
[3] δυνάμει . . . οὐραγίαν Köchly (in part after Schwebel
and Koraes): δυνάμει χωρὶς ἂν μὴ τὰ κατόπιν (κατόπιν F) ἀσφαλῆ
πάλιν καὶ εἰρηναῖα νομίζῃ (νομίζη F) εἰ δὲ καὶ μὴ (μὴ καὶ F) τὴν
οὐραγίαν Ω.   [4] F: μηδὲν vGH.
[5] περικεκλεισμένους v: περικεκλεισμένας GH.
[6] FC: ὑπερκαθέζονται GH.

398

for sometimes the leaders, after descending from mountains into treeless and level regions, observing those in the rear still descending, have thought the enemy were attacking, so that they have been on the point of marching against their own men as enemies, and some have even come to blows.

The general must place his medical equipment, pack animals, and all his baggage in the centre of his army, not outside. Should he consider that his rear is not quite secure and undisturbed he should form his rear guard of the most vigorous and courageous soldiers, realizing that, in the light of experience, the rear is no less important than the front.

He must send ahead cavalry as scouts to search the roads, especially when advancing through a wooded country, or a wilderness broken up by ridges. For ambuscades are frequently set by the enemy, and sometimes failure to detect them brings complete disaster to the opposing side, while their discovery, by a slight precaution, attests to the general of the enemy great prudence on the part of his adversary. For in a level and treeless country a general survey is sufficient for a preliminary investigation; for a cloud of dust announces the approach of the enemy by day, and burning fires light up a near-by encampment at night.

If the general is not about to form his line of

---

⁷ F (τῷ πολεμίῳ) πολεμίων vGH : τῷ τῶν πολεμίων Köchly.
⁸ FC : ψιλὴν πάντων ὄψις (ὄψις GH) καὶ μὴ προερευνήσαντός τινος (-νήσαντος τινὸς GH) ἐδήλωσεν vGH.
⁹ FCD : ἀναφαινόμενος vGH.
¹⁰ FC : καθ᾽ ἡμέραν vGH.   ¹¹ FC : πυρακτούμενα vGH.
¹² F : ἐπύρσευσαν A m² GH (v ?) Köchly.   ¹³ δὴ F.

τάξειν εἰς μάχην, ἐὰν[1] ἐπείγηταί τι φθάνειν συν-
τομώτερον, εἰ ἀσφαλὲς εἶναι νομίζοι, καὶ νύκτωρ·
μέλλων δὲ κρίνειν ἅμα[2] τῷ[3] σύνοπτον[4] γενέσθαι
τοῖς πολεμίοις εὐθὺς[5] τὰ πράγματα διὰ μάχης
σχολῇ[6] προΐτω καὶ μὴ πολλὴν ἀνυέτω· πολλάκις[7]
γὰρ πρὸ τῶν κινδύνων ὁ κόπος ἐδαπάνησεν
τὴν ἀκμὴν[8] τῶν σωμάτων.

10 Διοδεύων δὲ συμμαχίδα γῆν παραγγελλέτω
τοῖς στρατεύμασιν ἀπέχεσθαι τῆς χώρας, καὶ μήτ'
ἄγειν τι μήτε[9] φθείρειν· ἀφειδὲς γὰρ πλῆθος
ἅπαν ἐν ὅπλοις, ὅτ' ἂν ἔχῃ τὴν τοῦ δύνασθαί τι
ποιεῖν ἐξουσίαν, καὶ ἡ ἐγγὺς ὄψις ἀγαθῶν[10]
δελεάζει τοὺς ἀλογίστους ἐπὶ πλεονεξίαν· μικραὶ
δὲ προφάσεις[11] ἢ ἀπηλλοτρίωσαν συμμάχους ἢ καὶ
11 παντελῶς[12] ἐξεπολέμωσαν. τὴν δὲ τῶν πολεμίων
φθειρέτω καὶ καιέτω καὶ τεμνέσθω.[13] ζημία γὰρ
χρημάτων καὶ καρπῶν ἔνδεια μειοῖ πόλεμον, ὡς
περιουσία[14] τρέφει. προανατεινέσθω[15] μέντοι πρῶτον,
ὃ μέλλει ποιεῖν· πολλάκις γὰρ ἡ τοῦ μέλλοντος
ἔσεσθαι δεινοῦ[16] προσδοκία συνηνάγκασε, πρὶν ἢ
παθεῖν, ὑποσχέσθαι τι τοὺς κινδυνεύοντας ὧν
πρότερον οὐκ ἐβουλήθησαν[17] ποιεῖν· ἐπειδὰν δ' ἅπαξ
πάθωσιν, ὡς[18] οὐδὲν ἔτι χεῖρον ὀψόμενοι τῶν λοιπῶν
12 καταφρονοῦσιν. εἰ δὲ πολὺν ἐν τῇ πολεμίᾳ μέλλει[19]

---

[1] F : μάχην μεθ' ἡμέραν (μεθημέραν G) ἐὰν δὲ ἐπείγηται vGH.
[2] FC : εὐθὺς ENAm²GH and the mss. of Rigaltius.
[3] τὸ R.   [4] σύνοπτοσ F corr. by AB.
[5] FC : om. ENA m² GH and the mss. of Rigaltius.
[6] σχολὴ GH and the mss. of Rigaltius.
[7] With this word F indicates the beginning of a new
section instead of after σωμάτων below.   [8] ἀγμὴν GH.
[9] μὴ θίγειν (θήγειν GH) τινὸς μηδὲ vGH.
[10] τῶν ἀγαθῶν vGH.

battle, but is hurrying to be the first to arrive at a given point, he should lead his army by night marches also, provided he thinks it safe. But if he intends to decide the issue by battle as soon as he comes in sight of the enemy, he should at once advance slowly and not try to march too far; for in many cases, before the actual fighting, fatigue lessens men's physical fitness.

When passing through the country of an ally, the general must order his troops not to lay hands on the country, nor to pillage or destroy; for every army under arms is ruthless, when it has the opportunity of exercising power, and the close view of desirable objects entices the thoughtless to greediness; while small reasons alienate allies or make them quite hostile. But the country of the enemy he should ruin and burn and ravage, for loss of money and shortage of crops reduce warfare, as abundance nourishes it. But first he should let the enemy know what he intends to do; for often the expectation of impending terror has brought those who have been endangered, before they have suffered at all, to terms which they previously would not have wished to accept; but when they have once suffered a reverse, in the belief that nothing can be worse they are careless of future perils. If he intends to

---

[11] Köchly: ἐπιπλέον ἔξει αἱ μακραὶ δὲ προφάσεις F: ἐπὶ πλεονεξίᾳ· μικρᾷ (μικρὰ GH) δὲ προφάσει vGH.

[12] ἢ (ἢ GH) παντελῶς vGH.

[13] τεμνέτω vGH.   [14] ὥσπερ ἡ οὐσία vGH.

[15] ENP (margin) V (margin) G (margin) H (margin): πρὸσ ἀνατεινέσθω F: προανατιθέσθω P: πρὸὰνατιθέσθω GH.

[16] δεινοῦ ἔσεσθαι vGH.   [17] οὐκ ἠβουλήθησαν vGH.

[18] FC: om. vGH.   [19] ἂν . . . μέλλῃ (μέλλη GH) vGH.

καταστρατοπεδεύειν χρόνον, τοσαῦτα καὶ τοιαῦτα
φθειρέτω[1] τῆς χώρας ὧν αὐτὸς οὐχ ἕξει χρείαν,
ἅττα δὲ ἀναγκαῖα[2] φυλαχθέντα τοῖς φιλίοις[3] ἔσται,
τούτων φειδέσθω.[4]

13 Τῶν δὲ δυνάμεων ἐκπεπληρωμένων μήτ' ἐπὶ τῆς
ἰδιοκτήτου[5] μήτ' ἐπὶ τῆς ὑπηκόου μήτ' ἐπὶ τῆς
συμμαχίδος καθεζόμενος ἐγχρονιζέτω χώρας· τοὺς
γὰρ ἰδίους ἀναλώσει καρποὺς καὶ ζημιώσει πλέον
τοὺς φίλους ἢ τοὺς πολεμίους· μεταγέτω[6] δ' ὡς
θᾶττον, ἐὰν ἀκίνδυνα ᾖ τὰ οἴκοι,[7] τὰς δυνάμεις·
ἐκ γὰρ τῆς πολεμίας, εἰ μὲν εἴη δαψιλὴς καὶ εὐ-
δαίμων, τροφὴν ἕξει καὶ ἄφθονον,[8] εἰ δὲ μή,
τήν γε φιλίαν[9] οὐ λυμανεῖται, πολλὰ δ' ὅμως[10]
καὶ ἀπὸ λυπρᾶς[11] τῆς ἀλλοτρίας ἕξει πλεονεκτήματα.

14 Φροντιζέτω δὲ περί τε ἀγορᾶς καὶ τῆς τῶν
ἐμπόρων καὶ κατὰ γῆν καὶ κατὰ θάλατταν
παραπομπῆς,[12] ἵν' ἀκινδύνου τῆς παρουσίας σφίσιν
οὔσης[13] ἀόκνως παρακομίζωσι[14] τὸν εἰς τὰ ἐπιτήδεια φόρτον.

VII. [Περὶ τοῦ ὅταν[15] διὰ στενῶν μέλλῃ τὸ
στρατόπεδον ἄγειν][16]

Ἐπειδὰν δὲ ἤτοι[17] διὰ στενῶν μέλλῃ[18] ποιεῖσθαι τὴν[19] πάροδον ἢ δι' ὀρεινῆς καὶ δυσβάτου

---

[1] φθειρέσθω v.   [2] ἂν καὶ ἃ F.
[3] FC: φίλοις vGH.   [4] Köchly: φειδέσθαι Ω.
[5] FC: μήτ' ἐπὶ τῆς ἰδιοκτήτου om. vGH : μήτ' ἐπὶ τῆς ὑπηκόου
om. R.
[6] With this word F indicates the beginning of a new
section.
[7] ἀκίνδυνον ἢ οἴκοι vPGH.

encamp for some time in the enemy's country, he must destroy only things of such a number and sort as he himself will not need ; whatever, if preserved, will be of advantage to his friends he should spare.

When the army is recruited to full strength, he must not settle down and stay either in his own country, or in that of a subject nation, or in that of an ally ; for he will consume his own crops, and do more damage to his friends than to his enemies. He should lead out his forces over the frontier as soon as possible, if matters are safe at home; for from the enemy's country, if it is fertile and wealthy, he will have abundant provisions, but if it is not, he will at least not be injuring a friendly country, and he will still derive great gain even from the distress of the hostile country.

He should consider the matter of supplies, and the convoying of his merchants by land and sea, that they may arrive safely at his base of supplies, and that they may without hesitation transport their cargoes of provisions.

VII. [*On Leading an Army through narrow Defiles*]

Whenever the general intends to march through a narrow pass, or to lead his army over mountainous

---

⁸ τρυφὴν . . . ἀφθονίαν vPGH.
⁹ τὴν τελέαν R.   ¹⁰ δι' ὅμως RGH.
¹¹ λαμπρᾶς EFNPRH (λαμπρὰς G) Saguntinus and Camerarius.
¹² ἢ καταθάλατταν ἢ παραπομπῆς F.
¹³ οὕτως P : οὕτω EN.   ¹⁴ παρακομίζουσι PGH.
¹⁵ ὅτε v.   ¹⁶ Title om. by F : in marg. GH.
¹⁷ εἶτε vGH.
¹⁸ Köchly (v ?): μέλλει FGH.   ¹⁹ Added by Koraes.

χώρας ἄγειν τὸν στρατόν,[1] ἀναγκαῖον προεκπέμ-
ποντά τι μέρος τῆς δυνάμεως προκαταλαμβά-
νεσθαι τάς τε ὑπερβολὰς καὶ τὰς τῶν στενῶν
παρόδους, μὴ φθάσαντες οἱ πολέμιοι καὶ καταστάντες ἐπὶ τῶν ἄκρων κωλύσωσι τὴν διεκβολὴν
2 ποιεῖσθαι. τὸ δ' αὐτὸ πεφροντίσθω,[2] κἂν αὐτὸς[3] δεδίῃ πολεμίων εἰσβολήν· οὐ γὰρ δὴ[4]
δρᾶσαι μὲν χρήσιμον, φυλάξασθαι δὲ παθεῖν[5] οὐκ
ἀναγκαῖον, οὐδὲ φθάσαι μὲν αὐτοὺς εἰσβαλόντας[6]
εἰς τὴν πολεμίαν ἐπεῖγον, ἀποκλεῖσαι[7] δὲ[8] τοὺς
ἐναντίους[9] ἐπὶ σφᾶς ἰόντας οὐ προνοητέον.

VIII. [Περὶ τοῦ ποιεῖν χάρακα][10]

Ἐν δὲ δὴ[11] τῇ τῶν ἐχθρῶν καταστρατοπε-
δεύων[12] χάρακα περιβαλέσθω[13] καὶ τάφρον, κἂν[14]
ἐφ' ἡμέραν μέλλῃ τὴν παρεμβολὴν θήσειν· ἀμετα-
νόητος γὰρ ἡ τοιαύτη καὶ ἀσφαλὴς[15] στρατο-
πεδεία διὰ τὰς αἰφνιδίους καὶ ἀπρολήπτους[16]
ἐπιβολάς.[17] καθιστάτω δὲ φύλακας,[18] κἂν μακρὰν εἶναι νομίζῃ τοὺς πολεμίους, ὡς ἐγγὺς ὄντων.[19]
2 ὅποι[20] δ' ἂν μέλλῃ[21] πολυχρόνιον τίθεσθαι τὴν
παρεμβολὴν οὐκ ἀντεπιόντων[22] τῶν πολεμίων,
ἐπὶ[23] τῷ φθείρειν τὴν χώραν ποιούμενος τὴν
μονὴν[24] ἢ καὶ[25] καιροῖς ἐφεδρεύων[26] βελτίοσιν,[27]

---

[1] FGH: στρατηγὸν P and " mss. quidam " Schwebel.
[2] πεφροντίσθω or -εἰσθω F m¹ corr. by m².
[3] FC and perhaps others: om. PGH.
[4] FEN and perhaps others: δεῖ GH (v ?).
[5] μὴ παθεῖν vGH.
[6] F (and conj. by Koraes): εἰσβάλλοντας vGH Köchly.
[7] ἀποκλεῖσθαι Mm²: ἀποκεκλεῖσθαι EN. [8] μὲν F.
[9] πολεμίους vGH. [10] Title om. F: in margin GH.
[11] Om. F. [12] καταστρατοπεδευόντων F.

and difficult country, he must send ahead part of
his force to occupy the mountain-passes and the
defiles, lest the enemy, coming first, make a stand
on the summits and prevent the army from crossing.
This he should observe even if fearing an attack by
the enemy. For naturally it is not advantageous
to take the initiative, without also recognizing the
necessity of taking precautions against injury; nor
is it necessary to outstrip the enemy in making an
invasion into his country, without taking measures
to prevent the enemy from marching against one's
own country.

VIII. [On Making a palisaded Camp]

When encamping in the territory of the enemy,
the general should fortify his camp with a palisade
and a ditch, even if planning to remain in camp but
one day; for on account of sudden and unexpected
attacks, a fortified camp of this sort will be safe
and never regretted. He should place guards, even
if he believes the enemy to be at a great distance,
just as if they were at hand. Whenever the enemy
are not attacking, and he intends to encamp for
some time, either for the purpose of ravaging the
country, or to await a more advantageous time for

13 περιβαλλέσθω vGH.
14 F (and conj. by Koraes): ἂν vGH.   15 ἀσφαλεῖς H.
16 ἀπροσλήπτους C: ἀπροσδοκήτους vGH.
17 F (and conjecture of Schwebel): ἐπιβοιλάς Ω.
18 φυλακάς Koraes and Köchly.   19 FC: ὄντας vGH.
20 ὅπου vGH.   21 R: μέλλοι Ω.
22 οὐ κατεπιόντων P: οὐκατεπιόντων G: οὐ | κάτεπιόντων H:
οὐ κατεπειγόντων EN.
23 ἢ ἐπὶ vGH.   24 νομὴν ENR.   25 FPGH: om. v.
26 ἐφεδρευόντων F.   27 βελτίοσον H.

ἐκλεγέσθω χωρία μὴ ἑλώδη[1] μηδὲ νοτερά·[2] τὰ
γὰρ τοιαῦτα ταῖς ἀναφοραῖς καὶ ταῖς ἀπὸ τῶν
τόπων δυσωδίαις νόσους καὶ λοιμοὺς ἐμβάλλει
στρατεύμασι,[3] καὶ πολλῶν μὲν ἐκάκωσε τὰς
εὐεξίας, πολλοὺς δὲ ἀπώλεσεν, ὥστε μὴ μόνον
ὀλίγον, ἀλλὰ καὶ ἀσθενὲς ἀπολείπεσθαι στράτευμα.[4]

IX. [Περὶ τοῦ συνεχῶς ὑπαλλάσσειν τὰ ἄπληκτα][5]

Χρήσιμον δέ που καὶ σωτήριον στρατοπέδῳ
μηδ᾽ ἐπὶ τῆς αὐτῆς μένειν παρεμβολῆς, ἐὰν μὴ
χειμαδεύῃ καὶ τοῖς σκηνώμασι διὰ τὴν ὥραν τοῦ
καιροῦ πεπολισμένη τυγχάνῃ· αἱ γὰρ[6] τῶν ἀναγκαίων ἐκκρίσεις[7] ἐπὶ τῶν αὐτῶν γιγνόμεναι[8]
χωρίων ἀτμοὺς διεφθορότας ἀναπέμπουσαι συμ-
μεταβάλλουσιν καὶ τὴν τοῦ περιέχοντος ἀέρος
2 χύσιν. ἐν δὲ ταῖς χειμασίαις[9] γυμναζέτω τὰ
στρατόπεδα καὶ πολεμικὰ καὶ σύντροφα[10] ποιείσθω
τοῖς δεινοῖς, μήτ᾽ ἀργεῖν ἐῶν[11] μήτε ῥαθυμεῖν·
ἡ μὲν γὰρ ἀργία τὰ σώματα μαλθακὰ καὶ ἀσθενῆ
κατεσκεύασεν, ἡ δὲ ῥαθυμία τὰς ψυχὰς ἀνάνδρους
καὶ δειλὰς ἐποίησεν· αἱ γὰρ ἡδοναὶ δελεάζουσαι
τῷ καθ᾽ ἡμέραν συνήθει τὰς ἐπιθυμίας διαφθεί-
3 ρουσι καὶ τὸν εὐτολμότατον.[12] ὅθεν οὐ μακρὰν
ἀπάγειν[13] τοὺς ἄνδρας τῶν πόνων· ἐπειδὰν γὰρ
μετὰ χρόνον ἀναγκάζωνται[14] πρὸς τὰ πολεμικὰ
χωρεῖν, οὔθ᾽[15] ἡδέως ἐξίασιν οὔτ᾽ ἐπὶ πολὺ

[1] FEN : ἑλώδη PRGH.
[2] Köchly : μηδὲ (μὴ δὲ FGH) νοσερά· Ω.
[3] τοῖς στρατεύμασιν vGH.   [4] τὸ στράτευμα vGH.
[5] Title om. by F : in margin GH. ἄπληκτον is a Byzantine
word unknown earlier ; see Du Cange and Sophocles.

battle, he must choose a locality that is not marshy, nor damp; for such places by their rising vapours and rank smell bring disease and infection to the army, and both impair the health of many and kill many, so that the soldiers are left few in number and weakened in strength.

IX. [*On continually Changing Camp*]

The general will find it advantageous and healthful for his army not to remain long in the same camp, unless it is winter and the army happens to be in huts on account of the time of year; for the necessary bodily excrement, deposited in the same place, gives off rank vapours and taints all the surrounding air. In winter quarters he should exercise his army and train it to be skilled in war and accustomed to danger, permitting no idleness nor relaxation; for idleness makes the body soft and weak, while relaxation makes the soul cowardly and worthless; since pleasures, capturing the passions by the enticement of daily habit, corrupt even the most courageous man. For this reason the soldiers must never be without occupation. When after some time spent in idleness they are compelled to go against the enemy, they do not go willingly nor

---

⁶ Om. P.
⁷ FCEN: ἐγκρήσεις P: ἐκρήσεις GH: ἐπικρίσεις R.
⁸ γιγνόμενοι F.
⁹ B and Schwebel: χειμαδίαις Ω: τοῖς χειμαδίοις Koraes.
¹⁰ σύστροφα vGH. ¹¹ ἑκόντα R: ἔχων corr. to ἔκων A m².
¹² εὐτολμώτατον P.
¹³ ἐπάγειν ENM (margin): ἐπείγειν PGH. Köchly suggests the addition of δεῖ.
¹⁴ ἀναγκάζονται GH. ¹⁵ οὐχ vGH.

μένουσιν,[1] ἀλλ' ἐκδεδιητημένοι[2] ταχὺ μὲν ὀρρω-
δοῦσι, πρὶν ἢ καὶ πειρᾶσαι τὰ δεινά, ταχὺ δὲ
καὶ[3] πειράσαντες ἀποχωροῦσιν, οὔτ' ἐλπίζειν
οὔτε φέρειν τοὺς κινδύνους δυνάμενοι.

X. α'. [Περὶ τοῦ δεῖν[4] γυμνάζειν τὸν στρατὸν[5]
ἀδείας οὔσης[6]]

Διόπερ ἀγαθοῦ στρατηγοῦ καὶ τὰ χρήσιμα τότε
κατασκευάζειν, ὅτ' οὐκ ἐπείγουσιν αἱ τῶν ἐκ
παρατάξεως ἀγώνων ἀνάγκαι, καὶ τὰ ἄχρηστα διὰ
τὴν τῶν σωμάτων ἄσκησιν ἐπιτάττειν. ἱκανὴ
γὰρ στρατοπέδοις ἄνεσις, κἂν[7] σφόδρα ταλαίπωροι
ὦσιν,[8] ἢ[9] μὴ διὰ τῶν δεινῶν εἰς τὸ ἀληθινὸν ἀγώ-
νισμα πεῖρα.[9] γυμναζέτω δὲ[3] τοιοῖσδέ τισι[10]
τρόποις.

2   Ἐκαττέτω πρῶτον ἀναδοὺς τὰ ὅπλα πᾶσιν, ἵν'
ἐν μελέτῃ[11] σφίσιν ᾖ τὸ μένειν ἐν τάξει, καὶ ταῖς
ὄψεσι καὶ τοῖς ὀνόμασι συνήθεις ἀλλήλοις γιγνόμενοι,[12] τίς ὑπὸ τίνα καὶ ποῦ καὶ μετὰ πόσους,[13]
ὑπ' ὀξὺ[14] παράγγελμα πάντες ὦσιν[15] ἐν τάξει·
καὶ τάς τε ἐκτάσεις καὶ συστολὰς καὶ ἐγκλίσεις
ἐπὶ λαιὰ καὶ δεξιά,[16] καὶ λόχων μεταγωγὰς καὶ
διαστήματα καὶ πυκνώσεις, καὶ τὰς δι' ἀλλήλων
ἀντεξόδους καὶ εἰσόδους, καὶ τὰς κατὰ λόχους

---

[1] μενοῦσιν F.
[2] FEN (and M by conj.): ἐκδεδιτιτημένοι P: ἐκδεδιηττη-
μένοι GH: ἐκδεδιττομένοι R.   [3] Om. vGH.
[4] δεῖ ENRGH.   [5] στρατηγὸν ENR.
[6] Title om. F: in margin GH.
[7] κἂν μὴ Capps.   [8] ταλαιπωρῶσιν von Rohden.
[9] εἰ . . . πείρᾳ ENRA m².
[10] FGH: τοίοις δέ τισι v.   [11] ἐκ μελέτης vGH.

408

do they long stand their ground, but because they have departed from their former habits, they quickly become dismayed, even before making trial of danger, and even if they do make trial, they quickly retreat, being incapable either of feeling hope or of sustaining the stress of battle.

X. (1) [*The Need for Drilling the Army in Time of Peace*]

On this account it is the duty of a good general to prepare what is useful for war, when the necessity of a pitched battle is not pressing. He should also assign unproductive tasks to keep the army in good condition. For it is sufficient relaxation for soldiers, even if they are very weary, to exercise in arms without the dangers involved in a real battle. The general should train his troops in some such manner as the following.

First arming the soldiers, he should draw them up in military formation that they may become practised in maintaining their formation; that they may become familiar with the faces and names of one another; that each soldier may learn by whom he stands and where and after how many. In this way, by one sharp command, the whole army will immediately form ranks. Then he should instruct the army in open and close order; in turning to the left and right; the interchange, taking distance, and closing up of files; the passing and repassing of files through files; the division into files; the

---

[12] γιγνόμεναι καὶ GH : γιγνόμεναι· καὶ P : γίγνωνται a MS. of Scaliger.　　[13] πόσων C.　　[14] ὑπό τι R.
[15] σώσιν GH.　　[16] λαιᾷ καὶ δεξιᾷ V.

διαιρέσεις, καὶ τὰς[1] κατατάξεις καὶ τὴν[2] ἐπὶ
φάλαγγα ἐκτείνουσαν[2] καὶ τὴν ἐπὶ βάθος ὑποστέλλουσαν,[3] καὶ τὴν ἀμφιπρόσωπον μάχην, ὅτ᾽
ἂν οἱ κατ᾽ οὐρὰν ἐπιστρέψαντες πρὸς τοὺς κυ-
κλουμένους μάχωνται,[4] καὶ τὰς ἀνακλήσεις ἐκ-
διδασκέτω.

3 Καθάπερ γὰρ ἐπὶ τῶν μουσικῶν ὀργάνων οἱ
μὲν[5] ἀρχὴν ἔχοντες τοῦ μανθάνειν ἐπιτιθέντες
τοὺς δακτύλους ἐπί τε τὰ τρήματα[6] τῶν αὐλῶν
καὶ διαστήματα τῶν χορδῶν πολλάκις ἄλλον
ἔθεσαν ἐπ᾽ ἄλλην[7] καὶ οὐ κατὰ τὴν ἁρμονικὴν
διάστασιν, εἶτα μόλις ἐπεκτείναντες[8] βραδὺ μὲν
αἴρουσι,[9] τοὺς δακτύλους, βραδὺ δὲ τιθέασιν, οἱ
δ᾽ ἐν μελέτῃ τῆς μουσικῆς ἀνεπιτηδεύτως ἤδη[10] ἐρ-
ρυθμισμένῃ[11] τῇ χειρὶ δι᾽ ὀξύτητος μεταφέρουσιν,
ὅπῃ τε βούλονται παραθλίψαι τῆς ἀναπνοῆς καὶ
ἀνοῖξαι καὶ παραψῆλαι[12] χορδῆς· τοῦτον δήπου
τὸν τρόπον οἱ μὲν ἀσυνήθεις καὶ ἀνάσκητοι τῆς
τάξεως διὰ ταράχου πολλοῦ μόλις ἀλλήλων δια-
μαρτάνοντες ἐγκατατάσσονται[13] πολὺν ἀναλίσκον-
τες χρόνον, οἱ δὲ συγκεκροτημένοι διὰ τάχους,
ὡς εἰπεῖν αὐτόματοι, φέρονται πρὸς τὴν τάξιν
ἐναρμόνιόν τινα καὶ καλὴν ἐκπληροῦντες[14] ὄψιν.

4 Εἶτα διελὼν τὰ στρατεύματα πρὸς ἀλλήλους
ἀσιδήρῳ μάχῃ συναγέτω νάρθηκας ἢ στύρακας
ἀκοντίων ἀναδιδούς, εἰ δέ τινα καὶ βεβωλασμένα

---

[1] Om. vGH.   [2] Om. F.
[3] After ὑποστέλλουσαν vGH add καὶ τὴν ἐπὶ μῆκος ἐκτείνουσαν
(μῆκος GH), obviously a gloss on ἐπὶ φάλαγγα ἐκτείνουσαν
which means the same thing.
[4] μάχονται vGH.   [5] μὲν γὰρ R.
[6] τρήμματα PGH.
[7] RA m[2]: ἐπ᾽ ἄλλη F: ἐπ᾽ ἄλλῃ vGH (ἐπάλλη GH).

arrangement and extension of files to form the phalanx; withdrawing of files for greater depth of the phalanx; battle formation facing in two directions, when the rear guard turns to fight an encircling enemy; and he should instruct them thoroughly in the calls for retreat.

For just as those who begin to learn to play a musical instrument, in placing their fingers on the stops of the pipe or on the strings of the lyre, often set one finger on one and then another on another, without observing the interval that produces harmony, and then, with great effort, extending their fingers, they lift them slowly and slowly place them again; whereas practised players, no longer giving any evidence of care, with disciplined hand swiftly change from one note to another, lightly checking or opening the flow of air at will or lightly plucking the strings; in just this manner men unpractised and inexperienced in military formations, with great confusion and failure to find one another, will only after loss of much time take their places; but those who are well trained in formations quickly—indeed automatically, so to speak—rush to their stations, presenting a harmonious, I may say, and beautiful sight.

Next after dividing the army into two parts he should lead them against each other in a sham battle, armed with staves or the shafts of javelins; if there should be any fields covered with clods, he

---

[8] FC: ἐπεκτείνουσι vGH.   [9] αἴρουσι F.
[10] Deleted by von Rohden.
[11] FCE: ῥερυθμισμένη PGH: ἀρρυθμισμένη R.
[12] παραψίλαι PGH.
[13] ἐγκατάσσονται corr. to ἐγκατατάσσονται G.
[14] FC: ἀποπληροῦντες vGH.

411

πεδία εἴη, βώλους[1] τε κελεύων[2] αἴροντας[3] βάλ-
λειν·[4] ὄντων δὲ καὶ ἱμάντων ταυρείων[5] χρῆσθων[6]
ἐπὶ τὴν μάχην· δείξας δ' αὐτοῖς καὶ λόφους ἢ
βουνοὺς ἢ ὀρθίους τόπους[7] κελευέτω σὺν δρόμῳ
καταλαμβάνεσθαι· ποτὲ δὲ καὶ ἐπιστήσας ἐπὶ
αὐτῶν τινας τῶν στρατιωτῶν καὶ ἀναδοὺς ἃ
μικρῷ πρόσθεν ἔφην ὅπλα, τούτους ἐκβαλοῦντας[8]
ἑτέρους ἐκπεμπέτω· καὶ ἤτοι[9] τοὺς μείναντας[10]
ἐπαινείτω καὶ μὴ ἐκπεσόντας ἢ τοὺς ἐκβαλόντας.[11]
5 ἐκ γὰρ τῆς τοιαύτης ἀσκήσεως καὶ γυμνασίας
ὑγιαίνει μὲν τὸ στράτευμα, πᾶν δ'[12] ὅ τι οὖν
ἥδιον ἐσθίει καὶ πίνει,[13] κἂν λιτὸν ᾖ,[14] πολυτελέ-
στερον οὐθὲν[15] ἐπιζητοῦν· ὁ γὰρ ἀπὸ τῶν πόνων
λιμὸς καὶ τὸ δίψος ἱκανὸν ὄψον ἐστὶν[16] καὶ γλυκὺ
κρᾶμα, καὶ[17] στερρότερά τε τὰ σώματά σφισι[18]
γίγνεται καὶ ἄκμητα,[19] καὶ συνεθίζεται τοῖς μέλλουσι δεινοῖς, ἱδρῶτι καὶ πνεύματι καὶ ἄσθματι[20]
καὶ θάλπεσιν ἀσκιάστοις καὶ κρυμοῖς[21] ὑπαίθροις
ἐγγυμναζόμενα.[22]
6 Παραπλησίως δὲ γυμναζέτω καὶ τὸ ἱππικὸν
ἁμίλλας ποιούμενος[23] καὶ διώγματα καὶ συμ-
πλοκὰς καὶ ἀκροβολισμοὺς ἐν τοῖς ἐπιπέδοις καὶ[24]
περὶ αὐτὰς τὰς ῥίζας τῶν λόφων, ἐφ' ὅσον δυνατόν
ἐστι καὶ τῶν τραχέων ἐπιψαύειν· οὐ γὰρ οἷον

---

[1] καὶ βελόνας (space for nine letters) εἴη βώλους F: βεβολα-
σμένα παιδία εἴη βόλους GH (παιδία PR and βόλους P).
[2] τὲ καὶ λεύων H.   [3] αἴροντας F.   [4] βαλεῖν vGH.
[5] DEKN: καὶ ταυρείων F: ἐκ ταυρείων vGH.   Köchly
suggests ταυρείων καὶ τούτοις.   [6] χρήσθω vGH.
[7] Köchly after Saguntinus: ἢ ὀρθίους βουνοὺς τόπους F:
ἢ ὀρθίους βουνοὺς ἢ τόπους vGH.
[8] ἐκβαλόντας K: ἐκβαλόντας C: ἐκβάλλοντας vGH.
[9] ἢ vGH.   [10] μείνοντας PGH: μένοντας EN.
[11] ἐκβάλλοντας F.   [12] δι' GH.   [13] ἐσθίη καὶ πίνη F.

412

should command them to throw clods ; if they have any leather straps, the soldiers should use them in the battle.[1] Pointing out to the soldiers ridges or hills or steep ascents, he should command them to charge and seize these places ; and sometimes arming the soldiers with the weapons I have just mentioned, he should place some on the hilltops and send the others to dislodge them. He should praise those who stand firm without retreating, and those who succeed in dislodging their opponents. For from such exercise and training the army is kept in good health, eating and drinking everything with heartier appetite, even if the fare is plain, desiring nothing more luxurious. For the hunger and thirst derived from toil are a sufficient relish and a sweet draught, and muscles become harder and untiring ; and trained by sweating, puffing, and panting, and exposed to summer heat and the bitter cold under the open sky, the soldiers become accustomed to future hardships.

In the same way the general should train his cavalry, arranging practice battles, both pursuits and hand-to-hand struggles and skirmishes in the plain and around the base of the hills, as far as it is possible to go in the broken country ;

---

[1] This passage is derived from Xenophon, *Cyropaedia*, ii. 3. 17-18. Compare the Introduction.

---

[14] Koraes: ἂν λιτὸν ἢ FGH : ἀντὶ ληϊτὸν ἢ P : ἀντὶ λιτὸν ἢ EN : ἄντε λιτὸν ἢ R : ἂν τε λιτὸν ᾖ C : ἀντιληϊτὸν ἢ A m². [15] FGH : οὐδὲν v. [16] ποιεῖ vGH. [17] Added by Köchly. [18] σφίσι Ω. [19] ἀγμητὰ PGH : ἀκμητὰ DEN. [20] σώματι καὶ πνεύματι vPGH. [21] κρημνοῖς EN. [22] συγγυμναζόμενα vGH. [23] ποιουμένοις F : ποιούμενον R. [24] Om. vGH.

τε βιάζεσθαι πρὸς ἀνάντη καὶ κατὰ πρανοῦς[1]
ἱππάζεσθαι.[2]

β'. [Περὶ προνομῶν][3]

7 Σωφρονείτω δὲ περὶ τὰς προνομὰς καὶ μὴ ἐφιέτω
ταῖς δυνάμεσιν,[4] ἐπειδὰν εἰς εὐδαίμονα πολεμίων εἰσβάλῃ[5] χώραν, ἀτάκτως φέρεσθαι πρὸς
τὰς ὠφελίας·[6] αἱ γὰρ μέγισται συμφοραὶ κἂν
τοιοῖσδε[7] γίγνονται·[8] πολλάκις γὰρ ἀτάκτοις καὶ
σπόρασι περὶ τὴν λείαν σεσοβημένοις[9] ἐπιπε-
σόντες οἱ πολέμιοι καὶ διὰ τὸ ἀσύντακτον τοῦ
πλήθους καὶ διὰ τὸ βαρεῖς εἶναι[10] τοὺς ἀποχω-
ροῦντας ταῖς ὠφελείαις οὔτε τοῖς ὅπλοις χρῆσθαι
δυναμένους οὔτ'[11] ἀλλήλοις ἐπικουρῆσαι πολλοὺς
8 διέφθειραν. εἰ δέ τινες δίχα τοῦ τὸν στρατηγὸν
κελεῦσαι προνομεύοιεν,[12] οὗτοι κολαζέσθων.[13] αὐτός
γε μὴν[14] ὅτ' ἂν ἐπὶ τὴν λείαν ἐκπέμπῃ,[15] τοῖς
ψιλοῖς καὶ ἀνόπλοις συντασσέτω[16] μαχίμους ἱππεῖς
καὶ πεζούς, οἳ[17] περὶ μὲν τὴν λείαν οὐκ ἀσχο-
λήσονται,[18] μένοντες δὲ ἐν τάξει παραφυλά-
ξουσι[19] τοὺς προνομεύοντας, ἵν' ᾖ σφισιν ἀσφαλὴς
ἡ ἀποχώρησις.[20]

---

[1] πραμνοὺς A m[2].
[2] ἱπτάζεσθαι GH : ὑπτάζεσθαι A m[2].
[3] Title om. FGH : τῶν προνομῶν A.
[4] F puts the break here.
[5] εἰσβάλλῃ GHK (εἰσβάλλη GH).
[6] ὠφελείας GH Köchly (v ?).
[7] τοῖς τοιοῖσδε vGH Köchly : om. C.
[8] γίγνωνται F.
[9] σεσοβημαίνους GH.
[10] διὰ τὸ ἀσύντακτον . . . εἶναι om. R.

for it is not possible to charge uphill nor to ride downhill.

(2) [Foraging Expeditions]

The general should be cautious in the matter of foraging expeditions, and not allow troops, when invading a rich hostile country, to search for plunder in an undisciplined manner ; for the greatest misfortunes befall men acting in this way, since it has often happened that the enemy, falling on men scattered and without order in their eager search for booty, on account of this lack of order and the fact that they were loaded with their booty have killed many as they were retreating, unable to give aid to their comrades or to use their arms. If any men do plundering without the command of the general, they should be punished. When the general himself sends out foraging parties, he should send with the light-armed and unarmed men guards, both horse and foot, who shall have nothing to do with the booty but are to remain in formation and guard the foragers, that the return to camp may be safely accomplished.

---

[11] δυναμένοις οὔτε vGH.
[12] προνομεύειν ἐπιχειρήσωσιν vGH : ἐπιχηρήσουσιν Koraes.
[13] κολαζέσθωσαν vGH.
[14] αὐτὸ γέ μην CR.
[15] πέμπη vGH (πέμπη GH).
[16] FKRGH: ἐνταττέτω v.
[17] οἱ F.
[18] ἀσχολήσωνται Jos. Scaliger reports from an old ms.
[19] παραφυλάξωσι v.
[20] ὑποχώρησις Koraes.

γ΄. [Περὶ κατασκόπων][1]

9 Εἰ δὲ συλλάβοι ποτὲ κατασκόπους, μὴ μιᾷ κε-
χρήσθω γνώμῃ· ἀλλ᾽, ἐὰν μὲν ἀσθενέστερα τὰ ἴδια
ἤπερ[2] τὰ παρὰ τῶν πολεμίων εἶναι νομίζῃ,[3]
κτεινάτω[4] τούτους, ἂν[5] δὲ καὶ ὁπλισμῷ καλῷ
κεχρημένος ᾖ καὶ παρασκευαῖς ἐντελέσι[6] καὶ
δυνάμει πολλῇ καὶ εὐεξίᾳ σωμάτων καὶ πειθηνίῳ
στρατεύματι καὶ ἡγεμόσιν ἀρίστοις καὶ ἐμπειρίᾳ
μεμελετημένῃ, παραλαβὼν τοὺς κατασκόπους καὶ
ἐν κόσμῳ τὴν στρατιὰν[7] ἐπιδειξάμενος οὐκ ἂν
ἁμάρτοι ποτὲ καὶ ἀθώους ἀποπέμψας.[8] τὰ μὲν
γὰρ πλεονεκτήματα τῶν ἀντιπολέμων[9] ἀγγελλόμενα φοβεῖσθαι συνηνάγκασεν, τὰ δ᾽ ἐλαττώματα
θαρρεῖν παρεστήσατο.

δ΄. [Περὶ νυκτοφυλάκων][1]

10 Φύλακας δὲ κατατατέτω καὶ πλείους, ἵν᾽[10] ἐν
μέρει διελόμενοι[11] τὴν τῆς νυκτὸς ὥραν οἱ μὲν
ὑπνοῦν[12] οἱ δὲ γρηγορεῖν[13] αἱρῶνται·[14] οὔτε γὰρ
ἀναγκαστέον οὔθ᾽ ὑπισχνουμένοις πιστευτέον ὅλην
ἀγρυπνήσειν[15] νύκτα τοὺς αὐτούς·[16] εἰκὸς γάρ[17]
ποτε[18] καὶ παρὰ γνώμην ἐνδιδόντων τῶν μελῶν
11 αὐτόματον ὕπνον ἐπελθεῖν. ὀρθοὶ δ᾽ ἑστῶτες
φυλαττόντων.[19] αἱ γὰρ καθέδραι καὶ ἀναπτώσεις

---

[1] Title om. FGH.
[2] τὰ ἴδια ἤπερ om. F: εἰ ENP: ἤπερ GH.
[3] ἴσως παραχρῆμα after νομίζῃ A m[2] in margin.
[4] κτεινάτω R.
[5] ἐὰν v (ἐὰν GH) ἂν F.
[6] ἐντελέσει G: ἐν τελέσι H.
[7] Schwebel: στρατείαν Ω.
[8] ἀποπέμψαι F.
[9] ἀντιπάλων vGH.

416

(3) [*Spies*]

If the general should at any time capture spies, he should not employ any one single method in dealing with them. If he considers that his own army is weaker than that of the enemy, he should kill them, but if he has complete equipment of arms, thorough preparation for war, a powerful army, vigorous and disciplined, excellent officers, all trained by experience, he will make no mistake if, after making the spies examine his army drawn up in battle array, he occasionally even sends them away unharmed; for reported superiority of the enemy necessarily causes fear, but reported inferiority brings courage.

(4) [*Guards by Night*]

The general should appoint guards and a rather large number of them, that, by dividing the night into watches, some may sleep and some stand guard. Men must not be compelled to stand guard the entire night, nor even if they volunteer to do so must they be trusted; for it is only reasonable that sometimes, when the body is tired, sleep will come of its own accord, even against one's will. The guards must remain standing while on duty; for seats and

---

¹⁰ FEN : ἦ PGH : ἦν R.   ¹¹ διελλόμενοι GH.
¹² ὕπνον vGH.   ¹³ ἐγρήγορσιν vGH.
¹⁴ αἱροῦνται "quidam libri mss." (Schwebel).
¹⁵ ἀγρυπνῆσαι vGH.   ¹⁶ τούτοις for τοὺς αὐτοὺς F.
¹⁷ γὰρ ἂν vGH.   ¹⁸ Om. R.
¹⁹ τῶν φυλασσόντων vPGH.

ONASANDER

συνεκλύουσαι[1] τὰ σώματα μαραίνουσιν εἰς ὕπνον,
ἡ δ' ἀνάστασις[2] καὶ ὁ τόνος τῶν σκελῶν[3] ἐγρή-
12 γορσιν ἐντίθησι τῇ διανοίᾳ. καιόντων δ' οἱ
φύλακες πυρὰ[4] πορρωτέρω τῆς στρατοπεδείας·
οὕτως γὰρ τοὺς μὲν προσιόντας[5] διὰ τοῦ φωτὸς
ἐκ πολλοῦ συνόψονται, τοῖς δ' ἐκ τοῦ φωτὸς ἐν
σκότῳ τυγχάνοντες οὐκ ἀθρήσονται, μέχρις ἂν
εἰς χεῖρας ἔλθωσιν.

ε'. [Περὶ λαθραίας ἀναχωρήσεως τοῦ
στρατεύματος][6]

13 Εἰ δὲ βούλοιτό ποτε[7] νύκτωρ ἀναστῆσαι τὸ
στράτευμα λανθάνων τοὺς πολεμίους, ἢ τόπους
προκαταλαβέσθαι προαιρούμενος[8] ἢ τοὺς ὄντας
φεύγων[9] ἢ μηδέπω[10] βουλόμενος[11] εἰς ἀνάγκην
ἐλθεῖν τοῦ μάχεσθαι, πυρὰ πολλὰ καύσας ἀναχω-
ρείτω· βλέποντες μὲν[12] γὰρ οἱ πολέμιοι τὰ φῶτα
δοκοῦσι κατὰ χώραν αὐτὸν μένειν, ἀφωτίστου δὲ
μεταξὺ[12] γενομένης τῆς παρεμβολῆς ὑπόνοιαν
ἀναλαβόντες,[13] ὡς φεύγουσιν, ἐνέδρας[14] τε προεκ-
πέμπουσι καὶ διώκουσιν.

ϛ'. [Περὶ στρατηγῶν κοινολογουμένων τοῖς
τῶν ἐναντίων στρατηγοῖς][6]

14 Ἐὰν δ' ἐπὶ τῶν αὐτῶν μένων εἰς ὄψιν ἔρχηταί
ποτε τῷ τῶν[15] πολεμίων στρατηγῷ,[16] κοινολογη-

---

[1] συλλύουσαι vGH : συλλύονται A m².
[2] δ' ἀνάτασις FG : δὲ ἀνάστασις H.
[3] FGH : τῶν σκελῶν καὶ ὁ τόνος v.
[4] FC (δὲ C) : δὲ τῶν φυλάκων πυρὰ (πρὰ P) vPGH.
[5] Schwebel: ἰόντας C : ὄντας Ω.

418

reclining positions, relaxing the body, are conducive
to sleep, but standing erect and keeping the legs
stretched makes the mind wakeful. The guards
must build fires at some distance from the camp.
Thus because of the light they will see at a distance
men advancing toward the camp, but those who come
from the light will not perceive the guards, who are
in the dark, until they fall into their hands.[1]

(5) [*Secret Retreat of the Army*]

If the general desires to withdraw his army by
night without the knowledge of the enemy, either to
be the first to occupy a certain position or to escape
from the position he is in, or to avoid the present
necessity of battle, he should retreat leaving many
fires burning ; for as long as the enemy see the fires
they believe that the army is remaining in the same
place, but if the camp becomes dark while the
retreat is going on, the enemy will suspect their
flight, send ahead ambushes, and follow in pursuit.

(6) [*Parleys with the Generals of the Enemy*]

But if, while keeping his army in the same spot,
he should come to a conference with the opposing

---

[1] This precept also derives apparently from Xenophon,
Cyropaedia, iii. 3. 25. Compare Thucydides iii. 23. 3-4.

---

[6] Title om. FGH.   [7] παρὰ R.   [8] προαιρουμένους R.
[9] φ (space for five letters) P and "veteres membranae"
(V? Rigaltius).
[10] μὴ δέ πω F : μηδὲ vGH : μὴ καὶ RA m².
[11] FEN : βουλομένοις PGH (v ?).
[12] Om. vGH.   [13] λαβόντες vGH.
[14] ἐνέδρας . . . διώκουσιν om. R.
[15] N : om. τῷ F : om. τῶν Ω.   [16] στρατηγῶν F.

σόμενος, ὡς αὐτὸς εἰπεῖν ἢ ἀκοῦσαί τι βουλόμενος, ἐκλεξάμενος[1] τοὺς κρατίστους καὶ ἀξιο-
πρεπεστάτους τῶν νέων, εὐρώστους καλοὺς μεγά-
λους, ὅπλοις[2] διαπρεπέσι κοσμήσας ἔχων[2] περὶ
αὑτὸν[3] ἀπαντάτω· πολλάκις γὰρ τοιόνδε τὸ
πᾶν ἀπὸ μέρους ὀφθέντος[4] ἠλπίσθη,[5] καὶ οὐκ ἐξ
ὧν ἤκουσεν ὁ στρατηγὸς ἐπείσθη, τί δεῖ ποιεῖν,
ἀλλ' ἐξ ὧν εἶδεν[6] ἐφοβήθη.

ζ'. [Περὶ αὐτομόλων][7]

15 Τῶν δὲ αὐτομόλων εἴ τινες ἢ καιρὸν ἀφικ-
νοῦνται μηνύσοντες ἢ ὥραν ἐπιθέσεως, ἢ ὁδὸν
ἐπαγγέλλονται καθηγήσασθαι[8] καὶ διὰ σκοπῶν[9]
ἀοράτων τοῖς[10] πολεμίοις ἄξειν, δήσας αὐτοὺς
ἀγέτω,[11] τοῦτο ποιῶν σφισι[12] φανερόν, ὡς, ἐὰν μὲν
ἀληθεύσωσι καὶ ἐπὶ σωτηρίᾳ καὶ νίκῃ πάντα
ποιήσωσι τοῦ στρατεύματος, λύσει τέ σφας καὶ
δωρεὰς δώσει καταξίους,[13] ἐὰν δ' ἐξαπατήσωσι
καὶ ψεύσωνται[14] τοῖς σφετέροις ἐγχειρίσαι[15] βουλόμενοι τὸ στράτευμα, παρ' αὐτὸν ἐκεῖνον τὸν
καιρὸν ὄντες[16] ἐν δεσμοῖς ὑπὸ τῶν κινδυνευόντων
κατασφαγήσονται· πίστις γὰρ αὐτομόλου τι μηνύον-
τος αὕτη βεβαιοτάτη, τὸ μὴ αὐτὸν εἶναι τῆς
αὑτοῦ[17] ψυχῆς κύριον, ἀλλὰ τοὺς ὁδηγουμένους.[18]

[1] Om. H.
[2] Köchly suggests καὶ before ὅπλοις and καὶ οὕτως before
ἔχων.
[3] Köchly: αὐτὸν FEMN: αὑτῶν PGH and "quidam mss."
(Schwebel).
[4] Köchly: ὀφθὲν Ω.   [5] ἐλπισθὲν F.   [6] ἴδεν F.
[7] Title om. FGH.   [8] ἢ ὥραν . . . καθηγήσασθαι om. R.
[9] διασκοπῶν F: διὰ σκόπων R: ἴσως τόπων C margin:
στίβων or στενῶν conj. Koraes.
420

general, either to make or to receive some proposal,
he should choose as an escort the strongest and
finest-looking of the younger soldiers, stalwart,
handsome and tall men, equipped with magnificent
armour, and with these about him he should meet
the enemy. For often from the view of a part the
whole is judged to be like it, and a general does not
determine his course of action by what he has heard,
but is terrified by what he has seen.

(7) [Deserters]

If any deserters arrive in camp to tell of a suitable opportunity or hour for attack, or if they
offer to act as guides over a road and assert
that they will lead the army along it, unseen
by the enemy, the general should lead these
deserters with him securely bound, making it plain
to them that, if they are truthful and bring safety
and victory to the army, he will set them free and
present them with fitting rewards, but that if they
attempt to deceive him and wish to betray his army
into the hands of their own friends, at that same
'suitable opportunity' they will be slain in their
bonds by the endangered army. Confidence may
be most safely placed in the word of a deserter,
when he knows that his life is not in his own hands,
but in the hands of those whom he leads.

---

10 Om. R.   11 ἀγέτωι GH.   12 FC: om. vGH.
13 FC: κατ' ἀξίαν v (καταξίαν GH). F indicates a break at
this point.   14 ψεύσονται GH.
15 An old ms. reported by Scaliger: ἐγχειρῆσαι Ω.
16 Om. vGH.   17 Köchly: αὐτοῦ F: ἑαυτοῦ vGH.
18 FC: ἡγουμένους vGH.

η΄. [Περὶ τοῦ ὁρᾶν καὶ τὴν τῶν πολεμίων
παρεμβολήν][1]

16 Ὁράτω δὲ καὶ τὴν τῶν πολεμίων παρεμβολὴν
ἐμπείρως· μήτε γάρ, ἐὰν ἐν[2] ἐπιπέδῳ καὶ κατὰ
κύκλον ἴδῃ[3] κείμενον βραχὺν τὴν περίμετρον
καὶ συνεσταλμένον χάρακα,[4] δοκείτω τοὺς πολεμίους ὀλίγους[5] εἶναι — πᾶς γὰρ κύκλος ἐλάττω
τὴν τοῦ σχήματος ὄψιν ἔχει τῆς ἐξ ἀναλόγου
στερεομετρουμένης θεωρίας, καὶ πλείους δύναται
δέξασθαι τὸ ἐν αὐτῷ[6] περιγραφόμενον εὖρος, ἢ
ἰδὼν ἄν[7] τις ὄψει τεκμήραιτο —, μήτε, ἂν αἱ
πλευραὶ τοῦ χάρακος ἐπὶ μῆκος ἐκτείνωσι[8] καὶ
κατά τι μέρος στεναὶ τυγχάνωσιν ἢ σκολιαὶ καὶ
πολυγώνιοι καὶ ὀξυγώνιοι,[9] πολὺ πλῆθος ἐλπιζέτω·
τῆς[10] μὲν γὰρ στρατοπεδείας ἡ ὄψις μεγάλη
φαίνεται, τοὺς δ᾽ ἐν αὐτῇ περιειλημμένους ἄνδρας
οὐ πάντως πλείονας ἔχει τῶν ἐν κύκλῳ περι-
17 γραφομένων. οἱ δ᾽ ἐπὶ τῶν ὀρῶν καὶ λόφων
χάρακες, ἐὰν μὴ συμφυεῖς[11] ὦσι πάντῃ, μείζους
μὲν ὁρῶνται τῶν ἐν τοῖς ἐπιπέδοις, ἐλάττους
δὲ ἢ κατὰ τὴν ὄψιν ἄνδρας περιέχουσιν· πολλὰ
γὰρ ἀνθρώπων ἐντὸς ἀπολείπεται γυμνὰ μέρη·
τῶν γὰρ τοιούτων τόπων ἀνάγκη πολλὰ μὲν εἶναι
βάραθρα, πολλὰ δὲ κρημνώδη[12] καὶ τραχέα καὶ
ἀκατασκήνωτα, τοῦ δὲ χάρακος πρὸ τῶν ἀνθρώπων
τιθεμένου, τούτου τὸ[13] μῆκος εὐλόγως ἐπεκτεί-
18 νεται.[14] μήτ᾽ οὖν, ἐπειδὰν ἴδῃ βραχὺν[15] καὶ

[1] Title om. FGH.
[2] CEMN: om. FPGH.   [3] ἤδη R.
[4] κειμένην τάχα ἐν περιμέτρῳ καὶ συνεσταλμένῳ χάρακι vGH.
[5] ἐλάττους vGH: om. πολεμίους R.   [6] τὸν ἑαυτῷ F.

(8) [*On the Inspection of the Enemy's Camp*]

The general should skilfully inspect the camp of the enemy. If he sees a circular palisade contracted into a small circumference, lying in a plain, he should not conclude that the enemy are few in number; for every circle appears to contain less than it actually does by the theory of proportionate geometrical contents,[1] and the space enclosed within a circle can hold more men than one would think to see it. If the sides of the palisade happen to be long and close together in certain parts, or crooked with many acute angles, he should not conclude that the camp contains a great number of men; for this type of camp appears large but has no more men within its walls in every case than circular camps have. Palisades on hills and mountains, unless compact in every respect, appear greater than those in plains, but they contain fewer men than the eye judges; for many parts of such camps are bare of men, since there must be many ravines in them and many steep and precipitous banks unsuitable for pitching tents, and as the palisade is built to defend the men, its length must be accordingly greater. The general, therefore, judging merely the position and shape of a camp,

---

[1] The author seems to be using of a plane figure a term properly applicable only to a solid.

[7] Added by Koraes: om. Ω: τις πάντως R may retain a suggestion of it.
[8] ἐκτείνουσι F.   [9] καὶ ὀξυγώνιοι om. vGH.
[10] ἧς F.   [11] συνφυεῖς H.   [12] Om. vGH.
[13] τοῦτο τὸ vGH: του R: τοῦ A m². [14] ἐπεκτείνουσι vGH.
[15] ἐπειδὰν ἴδη βραχὺν F: ἐπεὶ δὰν ἴδη βραχὺ GH: βραχὺ vP.

συνεσταλμένον, καταφρονείτω συλλογιζόμενος καὶ
τὸν τόπον καὶ τὸ σχῆμα, μήτ', ἂν καὶ παραμήκη,
καταπληττέσθω.

19 Ταῦτα μέντοι γιγνώσκων[1] εὐκαίρῳ ποτὲ στρατη-
γίᾳ χρησάσθω. καὶ καταστρατοπεδεύσας ἐν ὀλίγῳ
κατὰ τὸ προειρημένον σχῆμα, καί, εἰ δέοι, καὶ
συνθλίψας τὸ στράτευμα μὴ προαγέτω μήτε[2]
δεικνύτω[3] τοῖς ἀντεστρατοπεδευκόσι,[4] καὶ δὴ
προκαλουμένοις εἰς μάχην μὴ[5] ἐξαγέτω· δοκείτω
20 δὲ καὶ δεδιέναι. πολλάκις γὰρ οἱ πολέμιοι κατα-
φρονήσαντες ὡς ὀλίγων[6] ὄντων τῶν ἐναντίων,
ὄψει καὶ οὐκ ἐμπειρίᾳ[7] στρατηγικῇ τὰ πράγματα
κρίνοντες,[8] ῥᾳθυμότερον ἀνεστράφησαν, ἀφυλάκτως
καὶ ἀτάκτως τῆς ἰδίας προϊόντες[9] παρεμβολῆς, ὡς
οὐ τολμησόντων σφίσι τῶν πολεμίων ἐπεξελεύ-
σεσθαι, ἢ καὶ τῷ χάρακι περιστάντες[10] πολιορκοῦσιν ἀπροσδόκητοι[11] τοῦ μέλλοντος ἐκχυθή-
σεσθαι πλήθους· ἡ δ' ἀνελπιστία τῶν δεινῶν
ἀμελεστέρους ἐποίησε τοὺς στρατιώτας. ἔνθα
δεῖ[12] τὸν καιρὸν ἁρπάσαντα[13] κατὰ πολλὰς ἐκ-
δραμόντα[14] τοῦ χάρακος πυλίδας ἐν τάξει τῶν
ὑποκειμένων ἀνδρείως ἔχεσθαι πραγμάτων.

21 Ὁ δὲ εἰδὼς οὕτως στρατηγεῖν εἴσεται, κἂν
ὑπὸ τῶν πολεμίων ἐν τοῖς αὐτοῖς καταστρατηγη-
ται, καὶ δρᾶσαί τι φρόνιμος ἔσται καὶ φυλάξασθαι
προμηθής· ἐξ ὧν γὰρ αὐτὸς εἴσεται, τί δεῖ ποιεῖν,
ἐκ τούτων ἑτέρου ποιοῦντος γνώσεται, τί χρὴ μὴ

---

[1] γινώσκων F.   [2] εἴτε F: μηδὲ Koraes.
[3] Om. P " alii codices " (Schwebel).

[4] ἀντεστρατοπεδευκόσι (το) F: ἀντιστρατοπεδευκόσι v.
[5] καὶ vGH.   [6] FENRGH: ὀλίγον P " alii codd."
[7] οὐκεμπειρία F: ἐκπειρία H.   [8] κρίναντες K Koraes.

should not be emboldened at the sight of a small contracted camp nor downhearted at the sight of an extended one.

With this knowledge he should make use of opportune strategy. Stationing his army in a small camp, according to the above-mentioned plan, and if necessary, even crowding the soldiers together, he should not lead them from the camp nor show them to the enemy encamped opposite, nor lead them into battle if the enemy challenge, but he should even give the impression that he is afraid. For often the enemy, growing bold in the belief that their opponents are few, judging by sight and not by strategic experience, behave thoughtlessly. They go forth from their camp carelessly and without discipline, believing that their opponents will not dare to come out and attack; or they even surround and blockade the palisade, unaware of the multitude of men about to pour forth upon them; and with no expectation of danger soldiers become heedless. Then, seizing a favourable opportunity, the army must rush forth from the many little gates of the palisade, and in battle array courageously grapple with the task before them.

The general, having this knowledge, will know how to do his part, and even if he is out-generaled in these same matters, will be both wise in action and prudent in devising protection; for from the knowledge that instructs him in what he must do, he will know, when his opponent is trying to do this to him, what he must not himself suffer, since

---

⁹ προϊόντας R.   ¹⁰ FC: om. vGH.
¹¹ ἀπροσδόκητον F.   ¹² δὴ F.   ¹³ ἁρπάσαντας vPGH.
¹⁴ FPGH: ἐκδραμῄντας v.

παθεῖν· αἱ γὰρ ἴδιαι πρὸς τὸ λυπεῖν ἐμπειρίαι καὶ
τὰς τῶν πέλας ἐπινοίας τεκμαίρονται.

θ'. [Περὶ ἀπορρήτων][1]

22 Προάγειν δ' εἰ δέοι[2] νύκτωρ ἢ μεθ' ἡμέραν ἐπί
τι τῶν ἀπορρήτων, ἢ φρούριον[3] ἢ πόλιν ἢ ἄκρα[4]
ἢ παρόδους καταληψόμενον[5] ἤ τι τῶν ἄλλων[6]
δράσοντα,[7] ἃ[8] διὰ τάχους λαθόντα[9] τοὺς πολεμίους,
ἄλλως δ' οὐκ ἔστι πρᾶξαι, μηδενὶ προλεγέτω,
μήτ' ἐπὶ τί μήτε τί ποιήσων ἄγει[10] τὴν στρατιάν,
εἰ μή[11] τισι τῶν ἡγεμόνων ἀναγκαῖον εἶναι νομίζοι
23 προειπεῖν. γενόμενος δ' ἐπ' αὐτῶν τῶν τόπων
ἐγγὺς ὄντος τοῦ παρ' ὃν δρᾶσαί τι δεῖ καιροῦ[12]
διδότω τὸ παράγγελμα καὶ τί δεῖ πράττειν σημαι-
νέτω· ταχὺ δὲ τοῦτο ἔστω[13] καὶ δι' ὀλίγης ὥρας·
ἅμα γὰρ οἱ ἡγεμόνες ἀκούουσι καὶ οἱ ὑποτε-
24 ταγμένοι τούτοις[14] ἴσασιν. ἄφρων δὲ καὶ ἀτελής,
ὅστις ἂν πρὸ τοῦ δέοντος εἰς τὸ πλῆθος ἀνακοινώ-
σηται τὴν πρᾶξιν· οἱ γὰρ πονηροὶ μάλιστα περὶ[15]
τοὺς τοιούτους αὐτομολοῦσι καιρούς, παρ' οὓς
ἐροῦντές τι καὶ[16] μηνύσοντες οἴονται τιμῆς καὶ
δωρεᾶς τεύξεσθαι[17] παρὰ τῶν πολεμίων· οὐκ
ἔστιν δ' ἀφ' οὗ στρατεύματος οὐκ ἀποδιδράσκουσι
πρὸς ἀλλήλους δοῦλοί τε καὶ ἐλεύθεροι κατὰ
πολλὰς προφάσεις, ἃς[18] ἀνάγκη παρέχεσθαι πόλεμον.

---

[1] Title om. FGH.   [2] δὲ ἤδη vGH : δὲ K.
[3] φρουρίων F.   [4] ἄκραν vGH.
[5] καταλειψόμενον H.   [6] ὅλων D.
[7] δράσαντα FPGH (corr. A ?).   [8] Added by Koraes.
[9] λαθεῖν vGH.   [10] FC : ἄγειν vPGH.   [11] εἰ δὲ μή F.

personal experience in inflicting damage warns of
the designs of others.

(9) [*Secret Plans*]

If the general must make a march by night or
by day for some secret purpose, to seize a fortress,
city, height, or pass, or to do anything else that
must be done quickly without the knowledge of the
enemy, which otherwise could not be done at all,
he must tell no one beforehand against what place
or for what purpose he is leading his army, unless
he considers it necessary to warn some of the higher
officers in advance. But when he has reached the spot
and the moment is near at hand when he must act,
he must give his orders and point out what is to be
done. These orders must be quick and brief, for at
the same instant that the leaders receive instructions
their subordinates also know them. Thoughtless
and futile is he who communicates his plan to the
rank and file before it is necessary; for worthless
scoundrels desert to the foe especially at critical
times, when, by revealing and disclosing secrets,
they believe they will receive honour and reward
from the enemy. There is no army in which both
slaves and freemen do not desert to the other side
on the many occasions that war necessarily affords.

---

[12] **Koraes:** ὄντων τὸ παρὸν δρᾶσαι τί δεῖ καιροῦ Ω : ὄντων, παρ᾿
ὃν δρᾶσαί τι δεῖ καιρὸν Schwebel after Scaliger.

[13] **Koraes:** ἔσται Ω.

[14] F: τούτους οἱ ὑποτεταγμένοι PR: τούτοις οἱ ὑ. v: οἱ ὑ.
τούτους GH.

[15] AB Köchly: παρὰ Ω.

[16] καιροὺς· αἱροῦνται ἔτι καὶ F.

[17] τεύξασθαι EN "alii codd." GH.   [18] Om. vGH.

ί'. [Περὶ τῆς πρὸ μάχης ἐπισκέψεως τῶν ἱερῶν][1]

25 Μήτε δὲ εἰς πορείαν ἐξαγέτω τὸ[2] στράτευμα
μήτε πρὸς μάχην ταττέτω, μὴ πρότερον θυσάμενος·
ἀλλ' ἀκολουθούντων αὐτῷ[3] θῦται[4] καὶ μάντεις.
ἄριστον μὲν γὰρ καὶ αὐτὸν ἐμπείρως ἐπι-
σκέπτεσθαι δύνασθαι τὰ ἱερά.[5] ῥᾷστόν γε μὴν
ἐν τάχει μαθεῖν ἐστιν καὶ αὐτὸν αὑτῷ[6] σύμ-
26 βουλον ἀγαθὸν γενέσθαι. γενομένων δὴ καλῶν
τῶν ἱερῶν ἀρχέσθω πάσης πράξεως καὶ καλείτω
τοὺς ἡγεμόνας πάντας ἐπὶ τὴν ὄψιν τῶν ἱερῶν, ἵνα
θεασάμενοι τοῖς ὑποταττομένοις[7] θαρρεῖν λέγοιεν
ἀπαγγέλλοντες,[8] ὡς οἱ θεοὶ κελεύουσι μάχεσθαι·
πάνυ γὰρ ἀναθαρροῦσιν αἱ δυνάμεις, ὅτ' ἂν μετὰ
τῆς τῶν θεῶν γνώμης ἐξιέναι νομίζωσιν ἐπὶ
τοὺς κινδύνους· αὐτοὶ γὰρ ὀπιπεύονται[9] κατ' ἰδίαν
ἕκαστος καὶ σημεῖα καὶ φωνὰς παρατηροῦσιν,
ἡ δ' ὑπὲρ πάντων καλλιέρησις καὶ τοὺς ἰδίᾳ
27 δυσθυμοῦντας[10] ἀνέρρωσεν. ἐὰν δ' ἐπὶ τοὐναντίον τὰ ἱερὰ γένηται,[11] μένειν ἐπὶ τῶν αὐτῶν, κἂν
σφόδρα τι ἐπείγῃ, πᾶν ὑπομένειν τὸ δύσχρηστον
—οὐθὲν γὰρ δύναται παθεῖν χεῖρον, ὧν προμηνύει
τὸ δαιμόνιον—, ὡς, ἄν γέ τι κρεῖττον[12] ἔσεσθαι
μέλλῃ τῶν παρόντων,[13] ἀνάγκη καλλιερεῖν, θύεσθαι
δὲ τῆς αὐτῆς ἡμέρας πολλάκις· ὥρα γὰρ μία καὶ
ἀκαρὴς χρόνος ἢ φθάσαντας ἐλύπησεν[14] ἢ ὑστε-
28 ρήσαντας.[15] καί μοι[16] δοκεῖ τὰς κατ' οὐρανὸν

---

[1] Title and break om. FGH.   [2] Om. F.
[3] αὐτῶν R.   [4] θῦσαι R.
[5] F indicates a break here.
[6] Köchly : αὐτῷ Ω (αὐτῷ GH) : αὐτον αὐτῷ F.
[7] τοὺς ὑποταττομένους vGH : τοὺς ὑποτεταγμένοις D.
[8] ἀπαγέλον . . R.

428

(10) [*Taking the Omens before Battle*]

The general should neither lead his army on a journey, nor marshal it for battle, without first making a sacrifice ; in fact, official sacrificers and diviners should accompany him. It is best that the general himself be able to read the omens intelligently ; it is very easy to learn in a brief time, and thereby become a good counsellor to himself. He should not begin any undertaking until the omens are favourable, and he should summon all his officers to inspect the offerings, that, after seeing, they may tell the soldiers to be of good courage, since the gods command them to fight. Soldiers are far more courageous when they believe they are facing dangers with the good will of the gods ; for they themselves are on the alert, every man, and they watch closely for omens of sight and of sound, and an auspicious sacrifice for the whole army encourages even those who have private misgivings. But if the omens are unfavourable, he must remain in the same place, and if he is hard pressed for time he must patiently submit to every inconvenience—for he can suffer nothing worse than what Fate indicates beforehand, — since, if his condition is going to improve, he must have favourable signs in a sacrifice, and he must sacrifice several times on the same day ; one hour, even one minute, ruins those who start too soon or too late. And it seems to me that the

---

⁹ ὅτι τεύξονται KA m² GH and all Schwebel's MSS.
¹⁰ δυσφημοῦντας vGH (-μούντας H).
¹¹ γίνηται GH : γίγνηται vA m².
¹² From κρεῖτ. to ὁ στρατηγὸς XIII. 1 is missing in G.
¹³ τῶν παρόντων μέλλῃ vH.   ¹⁴ ἑαυτῆς ἐν F.
¹⁵ στερήσαντας R.   ¹⁶ ὑστερήσαντάς μοι F.

ONASANDER

ἀστέρων κινήσεις καὶ ἀνατολὰς καὶ δύσεις καὶ
σχημάτων ἐγκλίσεις[1] τριγώνων καὶ τετραγώνων
καὶ διαμέτρων ἡ θυτικὴ διὰ σπλάγχνων ἀλλοιο-
μόρφῳ θεωρίᾳ προσημαίνειν, ὧν αἱ παρὰ μικρὸν
διαφοραὶ καὶ δυνάμεις καὶ ἀποθειώσεις[2] ἐν ἡμέρᾳ
μιᾷ μᾶλλον δὲ[3] ὥρᾳ καὶ βασιλεῖς ἐποίησαν καὶ
αἰχμαλώτους.

XI. αʹ. [Περὶ τοῦ ὅτι δεῖ τῶν πολεμίων σχημα-
τιζομένων φεύγειν μὴ ἁπλῶς καὶ ὡς ἔτυχεν
ἔχεσθαι τῆς διώξεως][4]

Ἐπειδὴ δὲ πολλάκις θυμένοις ὡς μὲν εἰς μάχην
καλὰ γίγνεται τὰ ἱερά, διὰ δὲ μάχης ὅλον ἐνίοτε
στρατευμάτων ὄλεθρον προσημαίνει, τῶν ἀναγ-
2 καιοτάτων[5] ἡγοῦμαι περὶ[6] τούτου φράσαι. τῆς
γὰρ συμπάσης οἰκουμένης πολλὰς καὶ παντοίας
εἶναι συμβέβηκεν ἰδέας τόπων, ἄδηλον δέ, ἐν
ὁποίοις[7] ἕκαστοι πολεμήσουσιν· καὶ τῆς μὲν
σφῶν[8] αὐτῶν ἐμπειρίαν ἔχουσι[9] χώρας ἄνθρωποι,[10]
3 τὴν δ' ἀλλοτρίαν οὐκ ἴσασι.[11] πολλάκις δ' εἰ[12]
στρατηγὸς ἀκούσας μιᾶς ἡμέρας ὁδὸν ἀπέχειν
τοὺς πολεμίους ἀναστήσας ἄγει τὸν στρατόν,
ἐπειγόμενος διὰ μάχης ἐλθεῖν τοῖς πολεμίοις,[13]
τῶν δ' ὑποχωρούντων ἐπίτηδες καὶ μὴ μενόντων,[14]
ὡς κατορρωδοῦσιν ἕπεται, τῶν δὲ[15] ταὐτὸ[16] τοῦτο
ποιούντων, ἕως[17] ἔλθωσιν εἰς δυσχωρίας καὶ

---

[1] ἐκκλίσεις R : ἐκλίσεις A m[2].
[2] ἀποθεώσεις K : ἀποθέσεις Koraes.   [3] δ' Köchly.
[4] Title om. FP : in margin in HAPRM (and therefore in
G) after the first line of § 4.
[5] ἀναγκαίων vH.   [6] Koraes suggested καὶ before περί.
430

motions of the heavenly bodies, their risings and settings, and their positions—trine, square, and in opposition—are indicated by the art of extispicy, through another form of observation, and that trifling differences in these things have, in a single day, or rather in a single hour, led to power and deification, and have made both kings and captives.

XI. (1) [*Pursuit of an apparently fleeing Enemy must not be careless and haphazard*]

Since frequently the omens from a sacrifice are favourable for battle and yet sometimes foretell the complete destruction of the army through battle, I have considered it of the utmost necessity to say a few words on this point. The topography of the inhabited world differs widely in its various parts, and it is impossible to foresee in what sort of country a war will occur. Every man is well acquainted with his own country but not with foreign countries. Often a general, on hearing that the enemy are but a day's march distant, will call out his troops and lead them forward, hurrying to come to close quarters with the enemy, who, purposely retreating, do not make a stand against him; and so he assumes that they are afraid and pursues them. This continues until they come into a broken country,

---

[7] τοίοις v : ποίοις H.

[8] σαφῶς Rigaltius and " alii codd. ut vid."

[9] ἔχουσιν H.   [10] οἱ ἄνθρωποι A m².

[11] ἴσασιν HA m² (v ?), but F writes ἴσασι πολλάκις without a stop.   [12] δ' ἢ F: corr. A : δὲ v : δὴ H.

[13] FC: ἀναστήσας . . . πολεμίοις om. vH Saguntinus Camerarius.   [14] κενόντων R.   [15] δὴ F.

[16] ταυτὸ F: αὐτὸ vH.   [17] Koraes conj. ἕως ἂν.

περικεκλεισμένους ὄρεσι τόπους, ἐπίκειται μηδὲν
ὑφορώμενος, εἶτα ἐμβαλὼν[1] εἰς τοὺς τόπους
ὑπὸ τῶν πολεμίων ἀπεκλείσθη τῆς εἰσβολῆς,[2]
ᾗ[3] τὸ στράτευμα εἰσῆλθε, καὶ καταλαβόμενοι
τάς τε εἰς τοὔμπροσθεν[4] διόδους καὶ κύκλῳ τὰ
μετέωρα πάντα κατασχόντες, ὥσπερ ἐν ζωγρείῳ[5]
τινὶ συνεπέδησαν μὲν[6] τοὺς πολεμίους,[7] ὁ δὲ
παριὼν[8] μὲν ὑπὸ τῆς ὁρμῆς ἐφέρετο δοκῶν ἐπι-
κεῖσθαι φυγομαχοῦσι τοῖς πολεμίοις, οἷς[9] προσ-
ελθὼν[10] οὐκ ἔγνω, μετὰ δὲ ταῦτα περιβλεψάμενος
τά τε[11] πρόσω καὶ ὀπίσω καὶ παρὰ πλευράν,
καὶ πάντα πλήρη θεασάμενος πολεμίων ἢ συνη-
κοντίσθη μετὰ τοῦ στρατεύματος, ἢ ἀπομάχεσθαι
μὴ δυνάμενος καὶ μὴ παραδιδοὺς λιμῷ διέφθειρεν
πάντας, ἢ παραδοὺς κυρίους ἐποίησε τοὺς πολεμίους
4 τοῦ ὅ τι[12] βούλονται διαθεῖναι. δεῖ τοίνυν τὰς
ὑποχωρήσεις ὑφορᾶσθαι τῶν πολεμίων καὶ μὴ
ἀπειροκάλως ἕπεσθαι καὶ[13] περιβλέπεσθαι δὲ μᾶλλον τοὺς τόπους ἢ τοὺς πολεμίους καὶ δι' ὧν
ἄγει χωρίων[14] ὁρᾶν, ἐπιλογίζεσθαι[15] δ'[16] ὅτι ταύτῃ
πάλιν ὑποστρέψαι δεῖ, καὶ ἤτοι[17] μηδ' εἰσβάλλειν,
ἀλλ' ἀποτρέπεσθαι τῆς πορείας, ἢ εἰσβάλλοντα
προορᾶν καὶ εἰς[18] τὰς ὑπερβολὰς καὶ τοὺς συνάπτον-
τας αὐχένας τῶν ὁρῶν ἀπολείπειν[19] τοὺς παρα-
φυλάττοντας, ἵν' ἀσφαλής[20] σφισιν ἡ ἀνακομιδὴ

[1] βαλὼν F.   [2] Köchly : ταῖς εἰσβολαῖς Ω.
[3] (v ?) Köchly : ἢ FH.
[4] εἰστοὔμπροσθεν F : εἰς τοὔνομα πρόσθεν R.
[5] NRE (margin) Saguntinus : ζωγρωτινὶ F : ζυγώγρῳ P (in
marg. ζωγροῦ) : ζυγώγρῳ H (in marg. ζωγροῦ ? very faint) :
ζωγραφείῳ E (text). Rigaltius also quotes ζωγροῦ from the
margin of " veteris membr." (= V ?).   [6] Om. vH.
[7] F leaves after this word space for three or four letters.

surrounded by mountains on all sides, and the general, unsuspecting, still attacks them ; next, as he marches against their positions, he is cut off by the enemy from the road by which he led his army in. They seize the passes in front of him, and all the heights round about, and thus confine their enemies in a sort of cage. But the general is carried away by his impetuosity, in the belief that he is pursuing a fleeing enemy, without noticing whom he is approaching ; and later, on looking before and behind and on both sides, and seeing all the hillsides full of the enemy, he and his army will be destroyed by javelins, or, unable to fight and unwilling to surrender, he will cause all to die of hunger, or by surrender enable the enemy to dictate whatever terms they wish. Therefore retreats on the part of the enemy should be suspected and not stupidly followed ; the general should observe the country rather than the enemy, and notice through what sort of terrain he is leading his forces ; and he should take into consideration that it is necessary to return by the same road by which he came, and should either refrain from advancing and turn aside from the route, or, if he does advance, he should take precautions, leaving forces to hold the mountain passes and connecting defiles in order that his return may

---

⁸ Köchly: παρὼν Ω (παρῶν H): πρότερον Koraes.
⁹ FCD: ὡς R: ὃς EKN: οἱ H Rigaltius.
¹⁰ FCD: προελθὼν v: προελθῶν H.   ¹¹ τά τε om. vH.
¹² Schwebel: τουτὶ F: τοὺς ὅτι v: τοὺς ὅ τι HR: ἐς ὅτι EN.
¹³ ἔχεσθαι (om. καὶ) vH.
¹⁴ FCH: χῶρον Pv: χῶρον A m²: δι' ὃν ἄγει χῶρον R.
¹⁵ ὑπολογίζεσθαι vH.   ¹⁶ τε Koraes.   ¹⁷ εἴτε vH.
¹⁸ ἢ εἰσβάλλοντα προορᾶν and εἰς om. F: εἰσβάλλοντο A m².
¹⁹ ἀπολίπειν PH.   ²⁰ ἀσφαλεῖς H.

be safe. This advice is given for the purpose both
of outwitting the enemy by these tactics and of not
being outwitted oneself; for though it is a fine thing
to be able in this fashion to ensnare the enemy, yet
it is absolutely essential to avoid being ensnared
oneself.

(2) [*Receiving Messengers*]

The general should receive every man who wishes
to report anything, whether slave or freeman, by
night or day, on the march or in camp, while resting,
in the bath, or at table. For generals who pro-
crastinate and are difficult of access, and who order
their servants to keep out those who come to see
them, naturally either miss many important oppor-
tunities or even through their negligence suffer
complete ruin; for often men bring information at
a critical moment about something that can be
frustrated in the nick of time.[1]

XII. [*Meal-times*]

The general, if encamped opposite the camp of
the enemy, should not be careless of the proper
time at which to serve meals. For if he considers
that it lies with him to lead out his troops to battle

---

[1] Alexander, on being asked how he conquered Greece,
replied, μηδὲν ἀναβαλλόμενος, 'By never putting anything
off' (Schol. A on Homer's *Iliad* ii. 435).

---

[11] FH : φασθῆναι v : φρασθῆναι DR Koraes : πραχθῆναι conj.
Koraes.   [12] Title om. FH.
[13] πολεμίω F : πολεμίων vH Köchly.
[14] ἀριστοποσίας F.   [15] Del. Koraes.

ἡνίκα[1] ἂν ἐθέλῃ,[2] παραγγελλέτω ταῖς δυνάμεσιν
ἀριστοποιεῖσθαι· ἐὰν δὲ εἰς τοσαύτην ἀνάγκην
ἐληλυθὼς τυγχάνῃ διά τινας τόπους ἢ χάρακος
ἀσθένειαν ἤ τινας ἄλλας αἰτίας, ὥστ' ἐπὶ τοῖς πολεμίοις ἀπολελεῖφθαι τὸ[3] ἐξάγειν ὁπότε προαιροῦνται καὶ τὴν ἀνάγκην σφίσιν ἐπιτιθέναι τοῦ
τὰ ὅπλα λαμβάνειν καὶ ἀντιπαρατάττεσθαι, μὴ
ὀκνείτω καὶ ἕωθεν ἀριστοποιεῖσθαι σημαίνειν, μὴ
φθάσωσιν νήστισιν ἐπιθέντες οἱ πολέμιοι τὴν
ἀνάγκην τοῦ μάχεσθαι. καὶ τὸ σύνολον οὐκ ἐν
μικρῷ[4] θετέον οὐδὲ παρορατέον τὴν τῶν τοιούτων
πρόνοιαν· ἐμφαγόντες γὰρ στρατιῶται μετρίως,
ὥστε μὴ πολὺν ἐνφορτίσασθαι[5] τῇ γαστρὶ κόρον,
δυναμικώτεροι πρὸς τὰς μάχας εἰσίν· πολλάκις
καὶ[6] παρὰ τοῦθ' ἡττήθη στρατόπεδα τῆς[7] ἰσχύος
ἐλλειπούσης[8] διὰ τὴν ἔνδειαν, ὅταν μὴ ἐν[9] ὀξεῖ
καιρῷ κρίνηται τὰ τῆς μάχης, ἀλλὰ δι' ἡμέρας
ὅλης λαμβάνῃ[10] τὸ τέλος.

XIII. [Περὶ τοῦ εἶναι τὸν στρατηγὸν εὔθυμον ἐν
ταῖς δυσπραγίαις][11]

῝Οτ' ἂν δέ τις ἐμπέσῃ δυσθυμία στρατεύμασι[12]
καὶ φόβος ἢ συμμαχίας τοῖς πολεμίοις ἀφιγμένης[13]
ἢ προτερήματός σφισι[14] γεγονότος, ὁ[15] στρατηγὸς
τότε δὴ[16] μάλιστα τοῖς στρατιώταις ἱλαρὸς καὶ
γεγηθὼς καὶ ἀκατάπληκτος φαινέσθω.[17] αἱ γὰρ
ὄψεις τῶν ἡγεμόνων συμμετασχηματίζουσι τὰς

---

[1] ἡνίκ' Köchly. [2] θέλῃ v (θέλη H).
[3] Om. vH. [4] FH : σμικρῷ v.
[5] F : ἐνφο τίσαι H : ἐμφορτίσαι v : ἐνφορτῶσαι R.
[6] γὰρ καὶ vH. [7] τὴν R.
[8] ἐλλιπούσης (Schwebel) Koraes. [9] FC : om. vH.

whenever he wishes, he may set a meal hour for his troops at whatever time he wishes. But if he should chance to have come into such extremities, because of the terrain, or the weakness of his camp, or for some other reason, that it is left in the power of the enemy to attack whenever they desire, and to compel his army to seize their arms and draw up for defence, he should not hesitate to order the first meal at sunrise, lest the enemy, by a prior attack, force his men to fight while still hungry. On the whole, this matter must not be considered of slight importance nor should a general neglect to pay attention to it; for soldiers who have eaten moderately, so as not to put too great a load into their stomachs, are more vigorous in battle; armies have often been overpowered for just this reason, their strength failing for lack of food — that is, whenever the decision rests, not on a moment's fighting, but when the battle lasts throughout the entire day.

XIII. [*Courage on the Part of the General when in Adversity*]

Whenever despondency or fear has fallen on an army because the enemy has received reinforcements or gained an advantage, then especially the general should show himself to his soldiers gay, cheerful, and undaunted. For the appearance of the leaders brings about a corresponding change in the minds

---

¹⁰ λαμβάνει vH.   ¹¹ Title om. F: in margin H.
¹² στρατεύματι Köchly.   ¹³ FENRH: ἀφιγμένοις v.
¹⁴ εἴς τι vPH.   ¹⁵ With this word G resumes.
¹⁶ FEN: δεῖ vPH (a lacuna in G but the top of δ and a circumflex accent can be seen).
¹⁷ Koraes: φαίνεσθαι vGH: om. F.

ψυχὰς τῶν ὑποταττομένων,[1] καὶ στρατηγοῦ μὲν
εὐθυμουμένου[2] καὶ ἱλαρὸν βλέποντος[3] ἀναθαρρεῖ
καὶ τὸ[4] στρατόπεδον ὡς οὐδενὸς ὄντος δεινοῦ,[5]
κατεπτηχότος δὲ καὶ λυπουμένου συγκαταπίπτουσι ταῖς διανοίαις ὡς μεγάλου σφίσι κακοῦ
3 προφαινομένου. διὸ χρὴ πλέον τῷ σχήματι τοῦ
προσώπου στρατηγεῖν τὴν τοῦ πλήθους εὐθυμίαν
ἢ τοῖς λόγοις παρηγορεῖν· λόγοις μὲν γὰρ πολλοὶ
καὶ[6] ἠπίστησαν ὡς τοῦ καιροῦ πεπλασμένοις
εἵνεκεν,[7] ὄψιν δὲ θαρσοῦσαν[8] ἀνυπόκριτον εἶναι
νομίζοντες ἐπιστώσαντο τὴν ἀφοβίαν· ἀγαθὴ δὲ[9]
ἡ ἐξ ἀμφοῖν[10] ἐπιστήμη τοῦ τε εἰπεῖν, ἃ[11] δεῖ,
καὶ ὀφθῆναι, ὁποῖον δεῖ.

XIV. α΄. [Πότε δεῖ[12] φόβον ἐμβάλλειν τῷ στρατεύματι τῷ ἰδίῳ τὸν ἀπὸ τῶν ἐναντίων][13]

Καθάπερ γε μὴν ἐν καιρῷ στρατεύματος ἀνα-
θάρσησις[14] ὤνησεν, οὕτως καὶ φόβος ὠφέλησεν.
ὅτ᾽ ἂν γὰρ ῥαθυμῇ στρατόπεδον καὶ ἀπειθέστερον
ᾖ τοῖς ἡγουμένοις, τὸν[15] ἀπὸ τῶν πολεμίων[16]
ὑποσημαίνειν δεῖ[17] κίνδυνον, οὐχ ἥκιστα φοβερο-
ποιοῦντα τὴν ἐκείνων ἐφεδρείαν· οὐ γὰρ δειλοὺς ἔσται[18] ποιεῖν οὕτως, ἀλλὰ ἀσφαλεῖς· ἐν
μὲν γὰρ ταῖς δυσθυμίαις θαρρεῖν ἀναγκαῖον, ἐν
δὲ ταῖς ῥαθυμίαις φοβεῖσθαι· τοὺς μὲν γὰρ
δειλοὺς ἀνδρείους ποιεῖ, τοὺς δὲ θρασεῖς[19] προ-

---

[1] ὑποτεταγμένων vGH.   [2] εὐθύμου vGH.
[3] FENGH: βλέποντες Pv.   [4] FGH: om. v.
[5] ὡς οὐδενὸς ὄντος δεινοῦ om. Camerarius.
[6] καὶ πολλοὶ R m².   [7] ἔνεκεν GH Köchly.
[8] Ω: θάρσους F: θαρροῦσαν Köchly.
[9] δ᾽ Köchly.   [10] ἀμφοῖς A m².

of the subordinates, and if the general is cheerful
and has a joyful look, the army also takes heart,
believing that there is no danger; but should he
have a frightened, worried appearance, the spirits
of the soldiers fall with his, in the belief that
disaster is impending. On this account, the general
must inspire cheerfulness in the army, more by the
strategy of his facial expression than by his words;
for many distrust speeches on the ground that they
have been concocted especially for the occasion,
but believing a confident appearance to be unfeigned
they are fully convinced of his fearlessness; and it
is an excellent thing to understand these two points,
how to say the right word and how to show the
right expression.

XIV. (1) [*When one's own Army must be made to fear
the Enemy*]

Just as the recovery of courage at a crucial
moment benefits an army, so also fear is advantageous. For whenever an army becomes idle and
inclined to disobey its officers, the general should
suggest the danger from the enemy, especially by
representing their reserves to be formidable. It will
not be possible thus to make the soldiers cowardly but
only steady, since in despondency it is necessary
to be of good courage, but in idleness to fear; for
fear makes cowards bold and the rash cautious.

---

[11] ὅτε vGH : Köchly suggests οἷα.   [12] Om. EN.
[13] Title om. F: after ὠφέλησεν GHAP (in text GH).
     [14] ἀναθάρρησις vGH.   [15] τῶν F.
     [16] πολέμων F.   [17] Om. R.
[18] ἐστὶ GHA m².   [19] FKR : θαρσεῖς vGH.

2 μηθεῖς. ἀμφότερα δὲ[1] συμβαίνει στρατοπέδοις,
καὶ οὕτως καταπεπλῆχθαι πολεμίους ὥστε μηδὲν
ἐθέλειν τολμᾶν, καὶ οὕτως καταφρονεῖν[2] ὥστε
μηδὲν φυλάττεσθαι· πρὸς ἑκάτερον δὲ δεῖ τὸν
στρατηγὸν ἡρμόσθαι καὶ εἰδέναι, πότε δεῖ τἀντί-
παλα ταπεινὰ[3] καὶ λόγῳ καὶ σχήματι ποιεῖν,
καὶ πότ' αὐτὰ[4] δεινὰ καὶ φοβερώτερα.

β'. [Περὶ τὸ θαρρύνειν τὸ δεδιὸς στράτευμα][5]

3 Μελλούσης δὲ μάχης, ὅτε ἄδηλον ἔχοντα τὰ
στρατεύματα[6] τὴν κρίσιν τοῦ πολέμου διατετά-
ρακται[7] τῷ φόβῳ, δυνηθείς πῃ λαβεῖν αἰχμαλώτους ὁ στρατηγὸς[8] ἢ ἀπὸ ἐνέδρας ἢ δια-
κροβολισάμενος[9] ἢ καὶ ἀποστατοῦντας τῆς ἰδίας
παρεμβολῆς, εἰ μέν τινας γενναίους[10] τοῖς φρο-
νήμασι καὶ τοῖς σώμασι καταμάθοι, τούτους ἢ
ἀποκτεινάτω παραχρῆμα λαβὼν ἢ δήσας παρα-
δότω τοῖς ἐπὶ ταῦτα τεταγμένοις φυλάττειν κελεύσας,[11] ὅπως μὴ πολλοὶ θεάσωνται τοὺς ἄνδρας,
εἰ δὲ ἀσθενεῖς καὶ ἀγεννεῖς[12] καὶ μικροψύχους, ἔτι
καὶ προαπειλήσας[13] σφίσιν ἐπὶ τῆς ἰδίας σκηνῆς
καὶ προδουλώσας[14] σφῶν[15] τῷ φόβῳ[16] τὰς ψυχὰς
εἰς τὰ πλήθη προαγέτω[17] δακρύοντας καὶ δεο-
μένους, ἅμα λέγων καὶ ἐνδεικνύμενος[18] τοῖς στρα-

---

1 γὰρ vGH.
2 ὥστε μηδὲν ἐθέλειν τολμᾶν καὶ οὕτως καταφρονεῖν om. R.
3 δεῖ τὰ ταπεινὰ vGH (δεῖ τὰ τἀπεινὰ G).
4 Köchly: ποτ' αὖ F: πότ' ἂν τὰ vGH.
5 Title om. F (but a break is indicated) GH (both without
any break); probably composed by Koraes, since Rigaltius
and Schwebel print merely the Latin caption "Militum
animos ex captivorum adspectu excitari posse."
6 ἔχον τὸ στράτευμα vGH.

These two misfortunes happen to armies, to become
so terrified of the enemy that they are unwilling to
attempt any offensive, and so bold that they are unwilling to take any precautionary measures. With
regard to each the general must arrange his plans,
and know when by voice and look he must make the
enemy appear weak, and when more threatening
and formidable.

(2) [Encouraging the frightened Army]

On the eve of battle, when the army, uncertain of
the outcome of the war, is distrustful and fearful, the
general, if he is able, should manage to capture some
prisoners by ambush or skirmishing, or some men
who have strayed from their own camp. If he
learns that they are strong in courage and in body,
he should either kill them on the spot or turn them
over, securely bound, to men assigned to this duty,
with orders to guard them, so that not many of his
own forces may see them; but if they are weak
and cowardly and spiritless, after threatening them
in the privacy of his own tent and enslaving their
minds through fear, he should lead them, weeping
and supplicating, before his army, pointing out to

---

⁷ FDGH : διαπέπρακται " omnes codd." (Schwebel, meaning probably EN and the mss. of Rigaltius [except M]).
⁸ εἰ δυνηθῇ (δυνηθῆ GH, -θεῖ A m²) ἐφόδῳ λαβεῖν ὁ στρατηγὸς
αἰχμαλώτους vGH.   ⁹ δι' ἀκροβολισάμενος F.
¹⁰ FRGH : γενναίοις Rigaltius " ceteri codd. ut vid."
¹¹ FGH : κελεύσας φυλάττειν v.
¹² ἀγενεῖς PGHv(?).   ¹³ προ//////////λήσας G (lacuna).
¹⁴ σφίσιν . . . προδουλώσας om. R.
¹⁵ προδουλω//////////ῶν G (lacuna).   ¹⁶ τοῦ φόβου F.
¹⁷ προσαγέτω vGH.   ¹⁸ FGH : δεικνύμενος vGH.

τιώταις, ὡς ἀγεννεῖς[1] καὶ ταπεινοὶ καὶ οὐδενὸς
ἄξιοι, καὶ ὡς πρὸς τοιούτους ἐστὶν ἄνδρας[2]
αὐτοῖς ἡ μάχη δεδιότας οὕτως τὸν θάνατον, ἀπτομέ-
νους γονάτων καὶ προκυλιομένους τῶν ἑκάστου
4 ποδῶν. ἐπαναθαρρεῖ γὰρ ἐπὶ τούτοις ὁ στρατὸς
ἤδη προκατανενοηκὼς τῶν πολεμίων ὄψεις τε
καὶ πάθη ψυχῆς· ἀεὶ[3] γάρ, ὃ μηδέπω τις ἑώρακεν,
ἐλπίζει[4] μεῖζον γενήσεσθαι[5] τῆς ἀληθείας,[6] ἔτι
καὶ τῷ τοῦ μέλλοντος φόβῳ τὴν ἐλπίδα μετρεῖ
πρὸς τὸ χαλεπώτερον.

XV. [Ὅτι διαφοραὶ πολλαὶ τῶν τάξεων][7]

Τάξις δ' οὐ μία πολέμου,[8] πολλαὶ δὲ καὶ διά-
φοροι καὶ παρὰ τοὺς ὁπλισμοὺς καὶ παρὰ τοὺς
στρατευομένους[9] καὶ παρὰ τοὺς τόπους καὶ παρὰ
τοὺς ἀντιπολέμους,[10] ὧν τὰς διαφορὰς ὁ στρατηγὸς
ἐπ' αὐτῶν εἴσεται τῶν καιρῶν·[11] ἃ δ' ἂν οὐχ[12]
ἥκιστα πολλαῖς ἁρμόζοι[13] παρατάξεσι δίχα τῶν
ἐπ' αὐτῶν τῶν πραγμάτων ἀνάγκην ἐχουσῶν
νοεῖσθαι, ταῦθ' ὡς ἐν κεφαλαίῳ δίειμι.

XVI. [Ὅτι πρὸς τὸ ἀντιπόλεμον καὶ τὸ ἴδιον
συντάξει][14]

Ἱππεῖς μὲν δὴ στρατηγὸς οὐχ οὕτως, ὡς βούλεται, μᾶλλον δ' ὡς ἀναγκάζεται, τάξει· πρὸς

---

[1] ἀγενεῖς PGH.
[2] ἄνδρας ἐστιν Rigaltius Schwebel Koraes.
[3] εἰ vGHKPA m².   [4] ἐλπίζειν K.
[5] Köchly (note): γίγνεσθαι (text): γενέσθαι Koraes: γίνεται
vGH : γε F. Perhaps γεγενῆσθαι.
[6] Schwebel: ταῖς ἀληθείαις Ω.
[7] Title om. F and no break indicated : in margin GH.

his soldiers how base and wretched and worthless they are, and saying that it is against such men that they are to fight, men who are so greatly afraid of death, who cling to the knees and grovel at the feet of every one. The army is emboldened at all this, since they know before the conflict the appearance of the enemy and his state of mind. For what a man has never seen he always expects will be greater than it really is ; so also because of his fear of the future, a man measures his apprehensions by reference to the more grievous outcome.

XV. [*The Difference in Battle Formations*]

Battle formation is not of one but of many and various kinds, with regard to arms and soldiers and terrain and enemies. These differences the general will have to know on the occasions themselves, but what pertains in large part to many formations I shall briefly summarize, without considering the details which, in the actions themselves, must necessarily be understood.

XVI. [*Battle Formation with regard to that of the Enemy*]

The general will arrange his cavalry not as he wishes but rather as he is compelled ; for he will

---

[8] FC Leo, *Tactica*, xx. 182: om. vPGH Saguntinus Camerarius.   [9] F Leo (*l.c.*): στρατευσαμένους vGH.

[10] ἀντιπολεμίους vGH.

[11] FCD: αὐτὸν . . . τὸν καιρὸν vGH.

[12] FGH: ἃ δ' οὐχ v.   [13] ἁρμόζει vGH.

[14] Title om. F : in margin GH : συντάξει Koraes : συντάσσει GH Rigaltius Schwebel.

γὰρ τὸ ἀντιπόλεμον ἱππικὸν καὶ τὸ ἴδιον στήσει. ταττέτω δ' ὡς τὰ πολλὰ κατὰ τὰς ἐκ παρατάξεως μάχας ἐπὶ κέρως,[1] ἵνα καὶ[2] κατὰ πρόσωπον καὶ ἐκ πλαγίων προσβάλλοντες[3] καὶ τόπῳ μείζονι χρώμενοι, μεθ' οὓς[4] οὐκ ἔτ' ἄλλοι τεταγμένοι τυγχάνουσιν, ἔχωσιν ἀποχρῆσθαι τῇ τῆς ἱππικῆς ἐπιστήμῃ.

XVII. [Ὅτι τοὺς ψιλοὺς ἀκοντιστὰς καὶ τοξότας καὶ σφενδονιστὰς[5] πρώτους στήσει τῆς φάλαγγος][6]

Ψιλοὺς δέ, ἀκοντιστὰς καὶ τοξότας[7] καὶ σφενδονήτας,[8] πρώτους πρὸ τῆς φάλαγγος τάξει.[9] κατόπιν μὲν γὰρ ὄντες πλείονα κακὰ διαθήσουσι τοὺς ἰδίους ἢ τοὺς πολεμίους, ἐν μέσοις δ' αὐτοῖς ἄπρακτον ἕξουσι τὴν ἰδίαν ἐμπειρίαν, οὔθ' ὑποχωρεῖν ἀνὰ πόδα δυνάμενοι κατὰ τὴν ἀνάτασιν[10] τῶν ἀκοντίων, οὔτ' ἐξ ἐπιδρομῆς βαλεῖν[11] προηγουμένων ἄλλων καὶ παρὰ ποσὶν ὄντων, οὐδὲ μὴν[12] οἱ σφενδονῆται κυκλόσε τὸν δῖνον[13] ἀποτελεῖν τῆς σφενδόνης παρὰ πλευρὰν ἑστώτων[14] φιλίων[15] ὁπλιτῶν καὶ πρὸς τὸν ῥόμβον ἀντιπταιόντων,[16] οἵ τε τοξόται προϊόντες μὲν τῶν ἄλλων εἰς αὐτὰ τὰ σώματα καὶ κατὰ σκοπὸν ἐκτοξεύουσι τὰ βέλη,[17] μετὰ δὲ τοὺς λόχους ἢ ἐν αὐτοῖς μέσοις[18]

---

[1] ἐκ παρατάξεως . . . ἐπικήρως F.
[2] κατὰ τὰς . . . ἵνα καὶ om. R and Camerarius.
[3] προβάλλοντες v (?)GH.   [4] Om. H.
[5] The ending is too much abbreviated in GH to tell which form is used. See below, § 1.
[6] Title om. F: in margin GH.
[7] καὶ τοξότας om. F.
[8] F (without accent) R: σφενδονιστάς vGH.

444

oppose his own cavalry to that of the enemy. As a rule, in pitched battles he should arrange his cavalry in column formation, in order that attacking both in front and on the flanks and covering a greater amount of space (if no other soldiers are drawn up in their rear), they may thus be able to make use of their skill in cavalry fighting.

XVII. [*Placing the light-armed Troops, Javelin-throwers, Bowmen and Slingers, before the Phalanx*]

The general will assign his light-armed troops—javelin-throwers, bowmen, and slingers—to a position in front of the phalanx, for if placed in the rear they will do more damage to their own army than to the enemy, and if in among the heavy-armed, their peculiar skill will be ineffectual because they will be unable to take a step backwards in throwing their javelins or to charge forward and cast them, as other soldiers are in front of them and at their heels, nor will the slingers be able to execute the whirling of their slings, as their fellow-soldiers stand at their side and, in their turn, are caused to stumble in trying to avoid the whirling slings. If the bowmen are placed in front of the army, they will shoot their arrows at the enemy as at a target; but drawn up behind the ranks or in among the

9 FC : στήσει vGH.   10 ἀνάστασιν F.

11 βάλλειν vGH Köchly.   12 μὲν vGH.

13 Köchly : σφενδονηταὶ κυκλοσε τον δεινὸν F : σφενδονῆται (σφενδονίται GH) κύκλους τῶν λίνων vGH.

14 παραπλευραν ἔστω τῶν F.   15 χιλίων R.

16 Köchly : ἀντιπαιόντων F : ἀντιπιπτόντων vGH.

17 F indicates a break at this point.

18 FPGH : τοῖς μέσοις vGH.

ὄντες εἰς ὕψος[1] τοξεύουσιν,[2] ὥστε πρὸς μὲν τὴν
ἄνω φορὰν τόνον ἔχειν τὸ βέλος, αὖθις δέ, κἂν
κατὰ κεφαλῆς πίπτῃ τῶν πολεμίων, ἐκλελύσθαι
καὶ μὴ πάνυ τι[3] λυπεῖν τοὺς ἐχθρούς.

XVIII. [Περὶ τοῦ ἐν τοῖς τραχέσι τόποις τάττειν
τοὺς ψιλούς][4]

Εἰ δὲ συμβαίνοι[5] γίγνεσθαι[6] τὴν μάχην ἐν
χωρίοις τινὰς μὲν χθαμαλούς τινας δὲ βουνοειδεῖς
ἔχουσι τόπους, τότε δὴ μάλιστα τοὺς ψιλοὺς ἐν
τοῖς τραχέσιν ταττέτω, καὶ δή, κἂν αὐτὸς τὰ
πεδινὰ κατειλημμένος ᾖ, τῶν δὲ πολεμίων μέρη
τινὰ τῆς φάλαγγος ὀχθώδεις[8] διακατέχῃ[9] τόπους,
κατὰ τούτους ἐπαγέτω[10] τοὺς ψιλούς· ῥᾷόν τε γὰρ
βαλόντες[11] ὑποχωροῦσιν ἀπὸ τῶν τραχέων, ῥᾷστά
τε τοῖς ἀνάντεσιν ἐπαναθέουσιν, ἂν[12] ἐλαφροὶ
τυγχάνωσιν.[13]

XIX. [Περὶ τοῦ χωρία ἔχειν τὰς παρατάξεις δι᾿ ὧν
ὀφειλοῦσιν οἱ ψιλοὶ ἐντὸς τῶν κοντῶν[14] εἰσ-
ερχόμενοι ὑποστέλλεσθαι][4]

Ἔστω δὲ διαστήματα[15] κατὰ τὰς τάξεις,[16] ἵν᾿,
ἐπειδὰν ἐκκενώσωσιν[17] ἔτι προαγόντων[18] τῶν πολεμίων τὰ βέλη, πρὶν εἰς χεῖρας ἐλθεῖν τὰς φάλαγ-

[1] ὕψους R.   [2] τοξεύσουσιν F.
[3] FC: πάντη ENPGH Rigaltius "alii codd. ut vid." (but
om. καί).   [4] Title om. F: in margin GH.
[5] συμβαίνει vGH Köchly.   [6] FGH: γίνεσθαι v.
[7] καί RA m².   [8] FGH: ὀχθώδη Pv.
[9] διακατέχει vGH.
[10] ἀπαγέτω GH Rigaltius "ceteri codd. ut vid."

heavy-armed they will shoot high, so that the arrows have impetus only for their upward flight, and afterwards, even if they fall on the heads of the enemy, will have spent their force and cause little distress to the foe.

XVIII. [*Disposition of light-armed Troops in a broken Country*]

If the battle should happen to be in a country that is level in some places but hilly in others, then the light-armed troops should by all means be stationed in the uneven section, and then, if the general himself should have seized the plain and some part of the enemy's phalanx should possess the heights, he should send against them the light-armed troops ; for from the uneven ground they can more easily hurl their weapons and retreat, or they can very easily charge up the slopes, if they are agile.

XIX. [*The Phalanx should leave Intervals for the light-armed Troops to retire through the Ranks*]

There should be intervals within the ranks, so that, when the light-armed troops have discharged their weapons while the enemy is still advancing, before the

---

¹¹ βάλλοντες vGH.   ¹² Om. F.

¹³ FEN : τυγχάνουσιν GH.

¹⁴ κον GH (probably κοντῶν): κτὸν VM (a copy of G):
ἀκοντίων K (and others – Koraes).   ¹⁵ διάστημα vGH.

¹⁶ FCGH : πράξεις PD : παρατάξεις Koraes.

¹⁷ FGH : ἐκκενώσας P (" codd. reliqui omnes " Schwebel).

¹⁸ προαγαγόντων vGH.

γας, ἐπιστρέψαντες ἐν κόσμῳ διεξίωσιν[1] μέσην τὴν φάλαγγα καὶ ἀταράχως ἐπὶ τὴν οὐραγίαν ἀποκομισθῶσιν· οὔτε γὰρ κυκλεύειν αὐτοὺς ἅπαν τὸ στράτευμα καὶ κάμπτειν[2] κατὰ κέρας ἀσφαλές ἐστι[3]—τάχα γάρ που φθάσουσιν[4] αὐτοὺς ἐν τούτῳ συμμίξαντες οἱ πολέμιοι καὶ μέσους ἀπολαβόντες—, οὔτε διὰ τῶν πεπυκνωμένων βιάζεσθαι, καὶ εἰς τὰ ὅπλα ἐμπίπτοντας τάραχον ἐμποιεῖν ταῖς τάξεσιν ἄλλου πρὸς ἄλλον ἐνσείοντος. 2 αἱ δὲ κατὰ κέρας ἔφοδοι τῶν ψιλῶν πλείονα λυμαίνονται τοὺς πολεμίους, ἐκ πλαγίων ἀκοντιζόντων καὶ εἰς τὰ γυμνὰ παραβιαζομένων[5] παίειν. 3 ἡ δὲ τῆς σφενδόνης ἄμυνα χαλεπωτάτη τῶν ἐν τοῖς ψιλοῖς ἐστιν· ὅ τε γὰρ μόλιβδος ὁμόχρους ὢν τῷ ἀέρι λανθάνει φερόμενος, ὥστ' ἀπροοράτως ἀφυλάκτοις[6] τοῖς τῶν πολεμίων ἐμπίπτειν[7] σώμασιν, αὐτῆς τε[8] τῆς ἐμπτώσεως σφοδρᾶς οὔσης καὶ ὑπὸ τοῦ ῥοίζου[9] τριβόμενον τῷ ἀέρι[10] τὸ[11] βέλος ἐκπυρωθὲν ὡς βαθυτάτω δύεται τῆς σαρκός, ὥστε μηδ' ὁρᾶσθαι, ταχὺ δὲ καὶ τὸν ὄγκον ἐπιμύειν.

XX. [Ὅπως δεῖ, ἐὰν ἀπορῇ ψιλῆς συμμαχίας ὁ στρατηγός, οἱ δὲ πολέμιοι εὐπορῶσιν, ἐπιφέρεσθαι αὐτοῖς[12]]

Εἰ δὲ αὐτὸς μὲν ἐνδεὴς εἴη τῆς τῶν ψιλῶν συμμαχίας, οἱ δὲ[13] πολέμιοι ταύτῃ[14] πλεονεκτοῖεν,

---

[1] δείξωσιν GH: δείξωσι v: διεξίωσι Köchly: διήξωσι Koraes.
[2] κατακάμπτειν vGH.   [3] ἐστιν Köchly.
[4] φθάσωσιν vGH.
[5] παραβιαζομένειν P and "quidam mss." (Schwebel).
[6] FCGH: ἀφυλάκτως ἀπροοράτως P Rigaltius A m². : ἀφυλάκτως καὶ ἀπροοράτως EN.   [7] FC: ἐμπίπτει PGHA m².

448

two armies come to close quarters, they may about-face, pass in good order through the centre of the phalanx, and come without confusion to the rear. For it is not safe for them to go around the whole army, encircling the flanks—since the enemy would quickly anticipate them in this manœuvre, coming to close quarters and intercepting them on the way—nor is it safe for them to force their way through the closed ranks, where they would fall over the weapons and cause confusion in the lines, one man stumbling against another. Attacks of the light-armed troops on the flanks cause the enemy greater loss, since they cast their javelins from the side and of necessity strike the body where unprotected. The sling is the most deadly weapon that is used by the light-armed troops, because the lead slug is the same colour as the air and is invisible in its course, so that it falls unexpectedly on the unprotected bodies of the enemy, and not only is the impact itself violent, but also the missile, heated by the friction of its rush through the air,[1] penetrates the flesh very deeply, so that it even becomes invisible and the swelling quickly closes over it.

XX. [*How to attack, without light-armed Troops, an Enemy who has many*]

If the general himself should lack an auxiliary force of light-armed troops while the enemy has a

---

[1] For other testimony as to the heating of the lead *glans* by the rapidity of its flight through the air see Lucretius vi. 306 f. ; Ovid, *Metam.* ii. 727 ff. ; xiv. 825.

---

[8] δὲ GH. [9] ῥύζου GH. [10] ἐν τῷ ἀέρι vGH.
[11] Om. PGH. [12] Title om. F : in margin GH.
[13] μὲν F. [14] ταύτην vGH.

οἱ μὲν[1] πρωτοστάται πυκνοὶ πορευέσθων[2] ἔχοντες ἀνδρομήκεις[3] θυρεούς, ὥστε σκέπειν ὅλα τὰ σώματα τοῖς μήκεσιν,[4] οἱ δὲ μετὰ τούτους καὶ οἱ κατόπιν τούτων ἄχρι τῶν τελευταίων ὑπὲρ[5] κεφαλῆς ἀράμενοι τοὺς θυρεοὺς τέως ἐχόντων, ἄχρι ἂν ἐντὸς γένωνται[6] βέλους· οὕτως γάρ, ὡς εἰπεῖν,[7] κεραμωθέντες οὐθὲν πείσονται[8] 2 δεινὸν ὑπὸ τῶν ἐκηβόλων. εἰ δὲ παρ' ἑκατέροις ἢ τῶν ψιλῶν εἴη βοήθεια, πρῶτοι πρὸ τῆς ἐκ χειρὸς μάχης[9] ἀκροβολιζέσθων[10] τοῖς ἀντιπάλοις, ἢ μετὰ τὴν συμπλοκὴν τῆς φάλαγγος ἐκ πλαγίων ἐπιθέοντες[11] ἀποχρήσθων[12] τοῖς βέλεσιν· συνελαύνονται[13] γὰρ εἰς ὀλίγον καὶ οὐχ ἧττον θορυβοῦνται τοῖς τοιούτοις ἀμυντηρίοις.

XXI. [Περὶ τοῦ μὴ εἰς πολὺ μῆκος ἐκτείνειν τὴν φάλαγγα τὰς κυκλώσεις τῶν ἐναντίων φοβουμένους[14]]

Τὰς δὲ κυκλώσεις φυλάττεσθαι βουλόμενος μήθ' οὕτως ἐπὶ μῆκος ἐκτεινέτω[15] τὴν δύναμιν, ὥστε πάμπαν ἀσθενῆ καὶ ἀβαθῆ ποιῆσαι τὴν φάλαγγα —ταχὺ γάρ που συμβαίνει τοὺς πολεμίους διαρρήξαντας αὐτὴν δίοδον ποιεῖσθαι, καὶ μηκέτι παρὰ κέρας ἐνεργεῖν ταῖς κυκλώσεσιν, ἀλλὰ διεκπεσόντας[16] μέσους κατὰ νώτου γίγνεσθαι τῶν

---

[1] δὲ F.   [2] πορευέσθωσαν vGH.
[3] Köchly : ἐπιμήκεις Ω.   [4] Köchly : ἀνδρομήκεσιν Ω.
[5] ἐπὶ RA m[2].   [6] γίνωνται F.
[7] FC : ὡς εἶπον GH : εἶπον P (om. ὡς).
[8] πήσονται R.   [9] μάχεις H.
[10] ἀκροβολιζέσθωσαν vGH.   [11] FGH : ἐπιθέντες v.
[12] ἀποχρήσθωσαν vGH.

large force of them, the front rank men should advance in close formation, with shields the height of a man, tall enough to protect the whole body, and those who follow and the ones behind them, even to the last rank, should carry their shields above their heads, while they are within bowshot of the enemy. For thus roofed in, so to speak, they will suffer no danger from missiles. But if each army should have a number of light-armed troops, the general should order his own light-armed men to be the first to hurl their weapons against their opponents before the hand-to-hand battle; or after the clash of the phalanx, attacking from the flank, they should make use of their missiles, for thus the enemy will be forced together into a narrow space and will be greatly confused by such tactics.

XXI. [*The Needlessness of Lengthening the Phalanx in Fear of an encircling Movement of the Enemy*]

The general who wishes to guard against an encircling movement of the enemy should not so extend his forces lengthwise as utterly to weaken the phalanx by giving it no depth. For this would result in the enemy somewhere quickly breaking through; and no longer attempting an encircling movement on the flank, but piercing the centre instead, they would take their opponents in the

---

¹³ συνελαύνωνται P Rigaltius and "quidam libri" (Schwebel).
¹⁴ Rigaltius Köchly: φοβουμένοις A: φοβούμενος Schwebel: φοβούμενον Koraes. Title om. F: in margin GH.
¹⁵ ἐκτεινάτω ἐπὶ μῆκος A m². ¹⁶ διαπεσόντας A m².

ἐναντίων· τὸ δὲ¹ αὐτὸ μὴ μόνον φυλαττέσθω
παθεῖν, ἀλλὰ καὶ ζητείτω ποιεῖν, ἐὰν ἀσθενῆ καὶ
λεπτὴν κατανοήσῃ τὴν τῶν πολεμίων² φάλαγγα—,
μήθ' οὕτως ἐπ' οὐρὰν συστελλέτω³ τὴν παράταξιν
εἰς πολὺ βάθος ὑποστέλλων,⁴ ὥστ' ἐκ τοῦ ῥάστου
τοὺς πολεμίους ὑπερκεράσαντας ἐντὸς αὐτὴν λα-
2 βεῖν. ἰσχυροποιείτω μέντοι⁵ γε τὴν οὐραγίαν
καὶ τοὺς παρὰ πλευρὰν τῶν κεράτων μὴ ἔλαττον
τῶν πρωτοστατῶν· οὐχ ἧττον γὰρ⁶ ἀποκωλύου-
σιν οἱ κατ' οὐρὰν τὰς κυκλώσεις τῶν ἐπὶ κέρας
ἐκτεινομένων, ἐὰν ἤτοι⁷ φθάσας ὁ στρατηγὸς
τὸ μέλλον ἁπλώσας τὴν οὐραγίαν καὶ παρὰ τὰ
κέρατα⁸ τῆς φάλαγγος ἀναβιβάσας⁹ ἑκατέρωθεν
παραστήσῃ τοὺς κατόπιν εἰς τὸ πρόσωπον τῶν
πολεμίων, ἢ καὶ παραγγείλῃ τοῖς ἐφθασμένοις
ἤδη κυκλωθῆναι τὰ νῶτα τοῖς τῶν προηγουμένων
νώτοις ἐγκλίνοντας¹⁰ ἀμφίστομον ποιεῖσθαι τὴν
μάχην.

3 Ἀγχίνους μὲν στρατηγός τις πολλοὺς ὁρῶν
τοὺς πολεμίους¹¹ αὐτὸς ἐλάττοσι¹² στρατιώταις
μέλλων¹³ κινδυνεύειν ἐξελέξατο καὶ ἐπετήδευσε
τοιούτων ἐπιτυχεῖν τόπων, ἐν οἷς ἢ¹⁴ παρὰ ποτα-
μίαν ὀφρὺν ταξάμενος ἀπωθεῖται¹⁵ ταύτῃ τὴν
κύκλωσιν τῶν πολεμίων, ἢ παρώρειαν ἐκλεξά-
μενος¹⁶ αὐτοῖς τοῖς ὄρεσιν ἀποκλείσει τοὺς ὑπερ-
κεράσαι¹⁷ βουλομένους, ὀλίγους ἐπιστήσας ἐπὶ τῶν

---

¹ τοῦτο δ' Koraes.
² Koraes and Köchly independently and so the tr. of
Camerarius: πεδίων F : πεζῶν vGH.
³ συστελέτω GH.   ⁴ Köchly : ἀποστέλλων Ω.
⁵ Köchly : μὲν γὰρ Ω.   ⁶ ἧττον μὲν γὰρ vGH.
⁷ ἤδη vGH.   ⁸ Köchly : τὰ παρὰ vH : τὰ παρακέρατα G.
⁹ καὶ παρὰ . . . ἀναβιβάσας om. F.

rear; and this very manœuvre the general should not only guard against but also strive to execute if he discovers that the enemy's phalanx is weak and thin. Nor should he contract his phalanx, drawing it out toward the rear to great depth to such an extent that the enemy would easily outflank and surround it. But he should make his rear and the flanks of the wings as strong as the front ranks. For those in the rear will prevent the phalanx being encircled no less than those who are posted so as to extend the flanks, if the general, anticipating what is to happen, spreads out his rear guard and posting it on either flank of the phalanx opposes his rear to the front of the enemy, or if he commands those who are already encircled to turn their backs to the backs of the front ranks and fight on a double front

A shrewd general who sees that the enemy has many troops when he himself is about to engage with fewer, will select, or rather make it his practice to find, localities where he may prevent an encircling movement of the enemy, either by arranging his army along the bank of a river, or, by choosing a mountainous district, he will use the mountains themselves to block off those who wish to outflank him, placing a few men on the summits to prevent

---

[10] ἐγκλίναντας Koraes Köchly (but the latter probably through a misprint; compare his note).
[11] Köchly: μὲν γὰρ ὅστις πολλοὺς ὁρῶν τ. π. FCv (ὁρων F): μὲν γὰρ ὅστις ὁρῶν τοὺς πολεμίους πολλοὺς GH.
[12] ἐλάττωσιν F.   [13] μέλλον GH.   [14] ὁ R.
[15] Rigaltius (in a note correcting C) Koraes Köchly: ἀποτελεῖται FC: ἀποθεῖται Schwebel (probably a misprint): om. P Rigaltius GH (Köchly's apparatus is partly in error).
[16] ἀπωθεῖται . . . ἐκλεξάμενος om. P Rigaltius GH.
[17] CENA m²: ὑπὲρ κέρας F: ὑπερκεράσας PGH.

ὑψηλῶν τοὺς ἀποκωλύσοντας[1] ὑπὲρ κεφαλὴν
4 ἀναβάντας γίγνεσθαι τοὺς πολεμίους. οὐ μὴν
ἡ στρατηγικὴ φρόνησις ἐνταῦθα συλλαμβάνεται
μόνον, ἀλλὰ καὶ ἡ τύχη· δεῖ γὰρ ἐπιτυχεῖν τοιούτων χωρίων· οὐ γὰρ αὑτῷ[2] γε κατασκευάσασθαι
δυνατὸν τοὺς[3] τόπους· τῶν ὄντων μέντοι τοὺς
ἀμείνους ἐκλέξασθαι καὶ τοὺς συνοίσοντας ἐννοῆσαι
φρονίμου.
5 Πολλάκις δὲ[4] εἰώθασιν οἳ[5] μεγάλη δυνάμει καὶ
πολυάνδρῳ κεχρημένοι μηνοειδὲς σχῆμα ποιήσαντες τῆς παρατάξεως ἐπιέναι, νομίζοντες ὅτι
προσάγονται[6] τοὺς πολεμίους καὶ κατ' ἄνδρα[7]
βουλομένους[8] συνάπτειν, εἶτα κατὰ τὸ ἡμικύκλιον
εἰς ὁδὸν κυρτουμένους ἐναπολήψονται τῷ περι-
έχοντι κόλπῳ,[9] τὰς ἰδίας κεραίας ἐπισυνάπτοντες
6 ἀλλήλαις[10] εἰς κύκλου σχῆμα. πρὸς οὓς ἀντεπακ-
τέον[11] οὐχ ὧδε· τριχῇ δὲ διελὼν τὴν ἰδίαν δύναμιν τῶν[12] μὲν δυεῖν[13] ἑκατέρῳ μέρει κατὰ κέρας
προσβαλλέτω[14] τοῖς πολεμίοις, τῷ[15] δὲ ἑνί, τοῖς
εἰς τὸν μέσον κόλπον τοῦ μηνοειδοῦς ἀντι-
παρατεταγμένοις,[16] ἐναντίος[17] ἑστάτω[18] καὶ μὴ
προαγέτω· ἢ[19] γὰρ μένοντες ἐπὶ τοῦ κυκλοειδοῦς
σχήματος οἱ κατὰ μέσην τὴν[20] φάλαγγα τεταγμένοι
τῶν ἐχθρῶν ἄπρακτοι μηδὲν[21] δρῶντες ἑστήξον-
ται, ἢ προϊόντες εἰς τοὔμπροσθεν, εἰ βούλοιντο
προάγειν φαλαγγηδὸν εἰς εὐθεῖαν ἐκ τοῦ σιγματο-

---

[1] ἀποκωλύσαντας PA m[2].
[2] Köchly: αὑτῷ F: αὑτῷ CEN: αὑτό PGH and "alii."
[3] Om. F.   [4] γὰρ KA m[2].   [5] οἳ γε vGH.
[6] FPGH: προσάξονται v.   [7] FC: κατὰ ἄνδρας vPGH.
[8] βουλομένοις vPGH: βουλόμενοι Koraes: αὐτοὺς should be
added, suggests Köchly.
[9] FGH: κύκλῳ PvA m[2].   [10] ἀλλήλοις vGH.

the enemy from climbing above the heads of the
main army. Not alone does knowledge of military
science play a part in this matter but luck as well;
for it is necessary to have the luck to find such
places; one cannot prepare the terrain for oneself.
To choose the better positions, however, from those
at hand, and to know which will be advantageous,
is the part of the wise general.

It is often the custom of generals who are in
command of a powerful and numerous army to
march to battle in a crescent formation, believing
that their opponents also wish the battle to come
to close quarters, and that they will thus induce
them to fight; then, as their opponents are bent
back into the road at the points of the crescent,
they will intercept them with their enveloping folds,
joining the extremes of their own wings to form a
complete circle. Against troops advancing in this
fashion, one should not likewise adopt the crescent
formation, but dividing his own army into three parts.
the general should send two against the enemy, one
against each wing, but the third division, that which
faces the central hollow of the crescent, should
stand still, opposite the enemy, and not advance.
For if the enemy maintain this crescent formation,
those drawn up in the centre of their army will be
useless, standing still and doing nothing; but if
marching forward they wish to advance in a body,

---

[11] αὐτοὺς τακτέον R: ἀντιτακτέον vGH.
[12] τοῖν vGH: τοῖς PA m[2].   [13] δυοῖν ENR: δοιεῖν GH.
[14] προβαλλέτω F.   [15] τὸ R.
[16] ἀντιπαρατεταγμένος F (corr. B): ἀντιπαραταττομένοις vGH.
[17] ἐναντίως vGH.   [18] ἱστάτω R.   [19] οἱ F.
[20] Om. vGH.   [21] καὶ μηδὲν Koraes.

εἰδοῦς ἁπλούμενοι σχήματος, ἀλλήλους ἐκθλίψουσι[1]
καὶ λύσουσι τὴν τάξιν[2] — τῶν γὰρ ἐπὶ κέρως[3] ἐπὶ
τῆς αὐτῆς μενόντων χώρας[4] καὶ μαχομένων οὐχ
οἷόν τε τὸ ἡμικύκλιον εἰς εὐθεῖαν ἀνελθεῖν[5] —
ἔνθα δὴ τεταραγμένων αὐτῶν καὶ λελυκότων
τὴν τάξιν τῷ τρίτῳ τάγματι[6] καὶ ἐφέδρῳ[7]
προσβαλλέτω[8] τοῖς ἀπὸ τοῦ μέσου κυρτώματος
7 προάγουσιν[9] ἀτάκτους εἰς τοὔμπροσθεν. ἐὰν
δὲ διαμένωσιν[10] ἐπὶ τοῦ κοίλου σχήματος, τοὺς
ψιλοὺς καὶ ἐκηβόλους ἔνθα[11] κατ' ἀντικρὺ ταττέτω·
8 βάλλοντες γὰρ αὐτοὺς πολλὰ λυπήσουσιν. οὐ
μὴν ἀλλὰ καὶ εἰ[12] λοξῇ πάσῃ τῇ ἰδίᾳ φάλαγγι
προσβάλλει[13] κατὰ θάτερον κέρας[14] τῶν πολεμίων,
οὐκ ἂν ἁμάρτοι πρὸς τὴν ἐκ τοῦ μηνοειδοῦς σχήματος κύκλωσιν οὕτως ἀντεπιών· ἐπὶ πολὺ[15] γὰρ
οἱ ἐξ ἐναντίας εἰς χεῖρας ἰέναι πανστρατιᾷ κω-
λυόμενοι κατ' ὀλίγους κερασθήσονται, τῶν ἐπὶ
θατέρου κέρως[16] μόνων μαχομένων, οἳ καὶ πρῶτοι
κατ' ἀνάγκην συμμίξουσι διὰ τὴν λοξὴν ἔφοδον.
9   Οὐκ ἄχρηστον δέ ποτε καὶ ἀντιπαραταξάμενον
ὑπὸ πόδα τῷ στρατεύματι χωρεῖν, ὡς κατα-
πεπληγμένον,[17] ἢ καὶ ἐπιστρέψαντα παραπλησίαν
φυγῇ ποιεῖσθαι τὴν ἐπιχώρησιν[18] ἐν τάξει, εἶτ'
αὖθις μεταβαλόμενον[19] ἀντεπιέναι τοῖς ἐπιοῦσιν·
ἐνίοτε[20] γὰρ ὑπὸ χαρᾶς οἱ πολέμιοι δόξαντες

---

[1] ἐκθλίψουσιν GH.   [2] F marks a break here.
[3] Schwebel : ἐπὶ κέρας Ω (ἐπικέρας FGH).   [4] χορείας F.
[5] Köchly : ἐλθεῖν Ω (ἐλθειν F).   [6] πράγματι A m².
[7] ἐφόδῳ ENR (marg.): ἐφόδρῳ A m².
[8] FC : περιβαλλέτω vPGH.
[9] προσάγουσιν GH Rigaltius "alii codd."
[10] Koraes : δὲ δὴ μένωσιν F : δὲ δὴ μένουσιν vPGH.
[11] ἐνταῦθα vGH.   [12] Om. F.

456

changing from the crescent formation to a straight line, they will be crowded together and will lose their formation—for while the wings are remaining in the same position and fighting, it is impossible for a crescent to return to a straight line. Then when they are confused and their ranks disordered, the opposing general should send the third and reserve division against the men advancing in disorder from the centre of the curve. But if the enemy remain in the crescent position, the general should post his light-armed troops and archers opposite them, who with their missiles will cause heavy loss. However, if he advances with his whole phalanx obliquely against one wing of the enemy, he will make no mistake in attacking in this manner, as far as the encircling movement of the crescent formation is concerned; for the enemy will be prevented for a long time from coming to close quarters with their whole army, and will be thrown into confusion little by little, since only those of one wing will be fighting, that is, those who will necessarily be the first to be engaged because of the oblique attack.

It is sometimes a useful stratagem for an army facing the enemy to retire gradually, as if struck by fear, or to about-face and make a retreat similar to a flight but in order, and then, suddenly turning, to attack their pursuers. For sometimes the enemy, delighted by the belief that their opponents are

---

[13] προσβαλλει F : προσβάλλῃ v (προσβάλλῃ GH) : προσβάλῃ K : προσβάλοι Koraes.   [14] μέρος vGH.
[15] πο πολὺ G.   [16] κέρατος vGH.
[17] καταπεπληγμένων vGH.   [18] ὑποχώρησιν vGH Köchly.
[19] Koraes : μεταβαλλόμενον Ω.   [20] ἐνίους F.

φεύγειν τοὺς ἐναντίους λύσαντες τὰς[1] τάξεις
ἐπικέονται[2] προπηδῶντες ἄλλων ἄλλοι, ἐφ' οὓς
ἀκίνδυνον ἐπιστρέψαντας[3] μάχεσθαι καὶ αὐτῷ τῷ
παρ' ἐλπίδα τοῦ στῆναι θάρσει[4] καταπληξα-
μένους εἰς φυγὴν αὖθις τοὺς πάλαι διώκοντας
τρέπεσθαι.

XXII. [Περὶ τοῦ ἔχειν κεχωρισμένους ἐπιλέκτους
εἰς βοήθειαν τῶν καταπονουμένων. περὶ[5] τοῦ
ἔχειν ἐγκρύμματα][6]

Ἐχέτω δέ που καὶ στρατιώτας λογάδας ἰδίᾳ
τεταγμένους ἀπὸ τῆς φάλαγγος ὥσπερ ἐφέδρους
τοῦ πολέμου πρὸς τὰ καταπονούμενα μέρη τῆς
δυνάμεως, ἵν' ἐξ ἑτοίμου τοὺς ἐπικουρήσοντας[7]
ἐπάγῃ· καὶ ἄλλως οὐκ ὀλίγον ὤνησαν ἀκμῆτες
ἐπελθόντες ἤδη κεκοπιακόσι· τούς τε γὰρ
ταλαιπωρηκότας[8] ἤδη τῶν φίλων ἀνέλαβον
καὶ τοῖς πολεμίοις ἐκλελυμένοις ἀκμάζοντες ἐπ-
2 έθεντο. γίγνοιτο δ' ἄν τι καὶ τούτου[9] χρησι-
μώτερον, ἐκ[10] τῆς παρατάξεως ἀπωτέρω σταδίοις,
ὁπόσοις ἂν ἀποχρῆν αὐτῷ δοκῇ,[11] ἐκπέμψαι[12]
μέρος τι[13] τῆς αὐτοῦ[14] στρατιᾶς[15] ἀπροόρατον τοῖς
πολεμίοις, παραγγείλας[16] σφίσιν, ἐπειδὰν συμ-
βάλῃ[17] τοῖς ἐναντίοις, τότε πυθομένους παρὰ τῶν
σκοπῶν ἀναστάντας[18] ἐπείγεσθαι·[19] καὶ μάλιστα

[1] Om. R.
[2] PGH: ἐπικέωνται F: ἐπικέρονται DENR: ἐπιφέρονται
Koraes: ἐπιχέονται Köchly.   [3] ἐπιστρέψαντα vPGH.
[4] θαρσεῖν vGH.   [5] καὶ περὶ Koraes.
[6] Title om. F (and no indication of a break): in margin
GH. The second sentence is probably a correction of the
first, but it seems to be in all the mss. which have the other
also.   [7] ἐπικουρήσαντας A m[2].

fleeing, break ranks and rush forward, leaping ahead
of one another. There is no danger in turning to
attack these men ; and those who have for some
time been pursuing, terrified by the very unexpectedness of this bold stand, immediately take to
flight.

XXII. [*Holding Reserves for the Assistance of
exhausted Troops. Holding Reserves in Concealment*]

The general should also have somewhere a picked
corps, stationed apart from the phalanx as military
reserves, that he may have them ready to give
assistance to those detachments of his force that
are exhausted. These fresh troops are of not a little
advantage in attacking tired men ; for, besides relieving those of their own men who are worn out, they
attack in their full freshness a wearied enemy. It
would be even more advantageous for the general to
send a certain part of his army some little distance
from the encampment—as far as seems best to him,—
unseen by the enemy, with orders to rise up and
hasten when the battle is begun, which they will
learn from scouts. This is especially to be done

---

8 κεκοπιακότας v (κοπιακότας A m²): κεκοπτακότας GH.
9 τοῦτο vGH.   10 εἰ vGH.
11 δοκῇ αὐτῷ v (δοκῇ αὐτῶ GH).
12 ἐκπέμψῃ v (-η GH): ἐκπέμψας A m²: ἐκπέμψοι Koraes.
13 τὸ F.   14 Koraes: αὐτοῦ Ω.
15 στρατίας GH : στρατείας v.
16 vGH : παραγγεῖλαι F : παραγγεῖλαί τε Köchly.
17 συμβάλλει GH : συμβάλλῃ v.
18 ἀναστάντας F : ἀντιστήσαντας v : ἀναστείσαντας GH :
ἀναστήσοντας A m².
19 ἐπάγεσθαι Schwebel and Köchly.

τοῦτο ποιητέον, ὅταν προσδόκιμος οὖσα συμμαχία
τοῦ καιροῦ καθυστερῇ·[1] δόξαντες γὰρ οἱ πολέμιοι
τούτους ἐκείνους εἶναι καὶ συμμάχους ποθὲν[2]
ἥκειν τοῖς ἐναντίοις, ἴσως ἂν ἔτι καὶ προσιόντων
πρὶν ἢ συμμίξαι τοὺς ἐπιβάλλοντας εἰς φυγὴν
ὁρμήσαιεν,[3] οὐ τοσοῦτον, ὅσον ἐστίν, ἀλλὰ πλεῖον
3 ἐπιέναι πλῆθος νομίζοντες. ἄλλως τε καὶ ἐν
αὐτοῖς τοῖς δεινοῖς ἐπιφάνειαι πολεμίων ἀπειρά-
στων[4] ἐκπλήττουσι τὰς ψυχάς· προλαμβάνουσαι[5]
γάρ τι χεῖρον, οὗ[6] πείσονται,[7] φοβερώτερον ἐκ-
δέχονται τὸ μέλλον.

4 Ἐκπληκτικωτάτη δ᾽, ἣ[8] καὶ δραστικωτάτη[9]
μάλιστα πάντων, ἡ κατὰ νώτου τῶν[10] πολεμίων
αἰφνίδιος ἐπιβολή,[11] εἴ πῃ[12] δυνατὸν γένοιτο προ-
εκπέμψαντι[13] στρατιωτῶν σύνταγμα[14] νύκτωρ ἐκ-
περιελθεῖν κελεῦσαι[15] τοὺς πολεμίους, ἵνα κατόπιν αὐτῶν γένωνται πάντες, ὥστε ἕωθεν ἀναστάντας[16] ἐκ τῆς ἐνέδρας μετὰ τὸ συμμίξαι
πρὸς μάχην τὰ στρατεύματα κατὰ τὴν οὐραγίαν
ἐπιφαίνεσθαι τοῖς πολεμίοις· οὐδὲ γὰρ φεύγουσιν ἂν[17] ἔτι σφίσιν ἐλπὶς ἀπολείποιτο[18] σωτηρίας,
οὐδ᾽ εἰς τοὐπίσω δυναμένοις[19] ἐπιστραφῆναι διὰ
τοὺς ἐξ ἐναντίας μαχομένους, οὐδ᾽ εἰς τὸ πρόσω
φέρεσθαι διὰ τοὺς κατόπιν ἐπικειμένους.[20]

---

[1] καθύστερῇ F: καθυστερεῖ R.
[2] Om. vGH.
[3] FC: ὁρμῆσαι vPG (ὁρμῆσαι H).
[4] Ω (cf. Galen xiv. 679 ed. Lips.): ἀπροοράτων Köchly (with other suggestions): ἀπειράτων Koraes.
[5] ὑπολαμβάνουσαι vGH.
[6] Köchly: οὐ FC (ἡ C in marg.): δ PGH "ceteri codd. ut vid.": ὧν Schwebel.
[7] πήσονται R.
[8] δ᾽ ἢ F: δὲ vGH: δ᾽, ἢ Köchly.

when expected reinforcements come too late for the battle, for the enemy believe that these are the reinforcements arriving from some place or other for their opponents ; then possibly even while these reinforcements are still advancing and before they enter the battle, the enemy will take to flight, judging this force to be, not what it is, but much greater. Besides, the arrival of unfamiliar hostile troops at the very moment of battle lowers the morale ; for anticipating some greater misfortune than they are about to suffer, soldiers regard the future with greater fear.

Most terrible, or rather most effective, of all manœuvres, is a sudden attack against the enemy's rear. For this purpose, if in any manner it should be possible, a detachment of soldiers should be sent ahead by night, with orders for all to march around the enemy in order to come to their rear, so as to start up from ambush early the next morning, after the battle is begun, and to appear suddenly on the enemy's rear. For no hope of safety would remain for them in flight, and they would be unable to turn backwards, since the opposing army would attack, or to go forward, because of the detachment assailing their rear.

⁹ δραστηριωτάτη vGH.   ¹⁰ Om. F.
¹¹ ἐπιβουλή ENR.   ¹² καὶ εἰ vGH.
¹³ προεκπέμψαι τι vGH.   ¹⁴ σύστημα vGH.
¹⁵ κελεύσας F.
¹⁶ ἀναστάντες vGH.
¹⁷ ἐὰν vGH : om. F (at end of line).
¹⁸ ὑπολείποιτο vGH.
¹⁹ δυναμένους PA m².
²⁰ At this point M is said to have a long interpolated passage, which, since it does not appear in M's archetype G, need not concern us.

461

XXIII. [Περὶ τοῦ ἐν τῷ καιρῷ αὐτῷ τῆς μάχης
ἐκφωνεῖν χαρμόσυνα τοῖς ὑπηκόοις· εἰ καὶ[1]
ψευδῆ, ὅμως συμφέρει][2]

Καὶ δή ποτε παριππαζόμενος ἐμβοησάτω τοῖς[3]
φίλοις, εἰ μὲν ἐπὶ τοῦ δεξιοῦ τύχοι[4] κέρως ὤν,[5]
" νικῶσιν ἄνδρες[6] οἱ ἐπὶ τοῦ λαιοῦ τὸ δεξιὸν
κέρας τῶν πολεμίων," εἰ δ' ἐπὶ τοῦ[7] λαιοῦ, νικᾶν
λεγέτω τὸ φίλιον δεξιόν, ἐάν τε καὶ[8] κατ' ἀλήθειαν ᾖ τοῦτο γινόμενον[9] ἐάν[10] τε μή· καὶ γὰρ
δή[11] τὸ ψεῦδος ἀναγκαῖον εἰπεῖν, ὅπου " μέγα
νεῖκος[12] ὄρωρεν.[13] " οἷον βοῆσαι πάλιν αὖ μακρὰν
ἀποστατοῦντος τοῦ[14] τῶν πολεμίων ἡγεμόνος ἢ
ἐπὶ θατέρου κέρως ὄντος ἢ τὰ μέσα[15] συνέχοντος
τῆς φάλαγγος, " τέθνηκεν ὁ τῶν πολεμίων στρατηγὸς " ἢ " βασιλεύς," ἢ ὅστις ἄν ποτε ᾖ.[16]
2 καὶ ταῦτα χρὴ βοᾶν οὕτως, ὥσθ' ἅμα[17] καὶ τοὺς
πολεμίους κατακούειν· οἵ τε γὰρ φίλιοι[18] τοὺς
σφετέρους ἀκούοντες ἐπικυδεστέρους ἀναθαρ-
ροῦσι καὶ διπλάσιοι γίγνονται[19] ταῖς προθυμίαις,
οἵ τε ἐχθροὶ τὰ σφῶν αὐτῶν ἐλαττώματα πυν-
θανόμενοι συγκαταπίπτουσι ταῖς διανοίαις, ὥστ'
ἔστιν ὅτε καὶ εἰς φυγὴν ἅμα τῷ δέξασθαι τοιαύτην
3 φήμην ὁρμᾶν.[20] οὕτως πολλάκις συνήνεγκεν καὶ

---

[1] ὑπακόοις· ὁ μὲν A.
[2] Title om. F and no break indicated: in margin GH.
[3] τὴν R.   [4] τύχῃ v (τύχη GH).   [5] ὤν F.
[6] Köchly : ἄνδρες Ω.
[7] λαιοῦ . . . ἐπὶ τοῦ om. R (A m[2] with the note λείπει ἐν
ἀντιγράφῳ).
[8] κἂν (κἄν F) τε καὶ Ω : ἐάν τε Köchly : κἂν τε Koraes.
[9] ἐάν τε . . . γιγνόμενον om. R.
[10] κἄν GH.   [11] FC : δεῖ PGHv(?).
[12] νῖκος FGH.   [13] ὥρωρεν P (ὤρωρεν GH).

XXIII. [*Announcing favourable News in the Midst of Battle ; even if false it is advantageous*]

Sometimes the general should ride along the lines and call out to his men, if he happens to be on the right wing, " Our left wing is defeating the right wing of the enemy," or if he is on the left he should say that his right wing is conquering, whether this is true or not,[1] for deceit is necessary when " a great strife has arisen." [2] For example, when the leader of the enemy is some distance away either on one wing or holding the centre, he should call out, " The general of the enemy has been killed," or " the king," or whoever it may be. And one should shout this in such a manner that the enemy also may hear ; for his own soldiers, learning that their side is more successful, are encouraged and doubly eager to fight, while the enemy, learning of the misfortunes of their side, lose heart, so that sometimes they start into flight immediately on hearing such a report. In this

[1] There are many instances of such *salubria mendacia* in antiquity ; see especially Herodotus iii. 72 ; Frontinus i. 11. 6 ff. ; ii. 7. 1 ff. Actual instances when one wing was falsely told that the other was victorious are given by Livy ii. 64 ; Frontinus ii. 4. 11 ; Polyaenus i. 35.

[2] Homer, *Iliad* xiii. 122.

[14] Om. R.

[15] Köchly: κέρως ἢ ἐπὶ τὰ μέσα Ω: ἢ ἐπὶ τὰ μέσα ὄντος or ἢ τὰ μέσα ἔχοντος or ἢ τὰ μέσα συνέχοντος Koraes.

[16] ἦν F.   [17] F Saguntinus Camerarius : ὡς θαῦμα υ.

[18] φίλοι R.   [19] γίγνωνται PGH.

[20] FC: ὁρᾶν GH (and probably P and " ceteri codd. ut vid.," though Köchly gives the obviously false reading ὁρμᾶν for them).

τοὺς φιλίους[1] ἅμα τοῖς πολεμίοις ἐξαπατῆσαι, τοῖς μὲν τὰ κρείττω, τοῖς δὲ τὰ χείρω ψευδόμενον.

XXIV. [Περὶ τοῦ οἰκείους[2] πρὸς οἰκείους[2] καὶ γνωρίμους πρὸς γνωρίμους τάττειν][3]

Φρονίμου δὲ στρατηγοῦ καὶ τὸ τάττειν ἀδελφοὺς παρ' ἀδελφοῖς, φίλους παρὰ φίλοις,[4] ἐραστὰς παρὰ παιδικοῖς·[5] ὅταν γὰρ ᾖ τὸ κινδυνεῦον τὸ πλησίον[6] προσφιλέστερον, ἀνάγκη τὸν ἀγαπῶντα φιλοκινδυνότερον ὑπὲρ[7] τοῦ πέλας ἀγωνίζεσθαι· καὶ δή τις αἰδούμενος μὴ ἀποδοῦναι χάριν ὧν εὖ πέπονθεν αἰσχύνεται καταλιπὼν τὸν εὐεργετήσαντα[8] πρῶτος αὐτὸς ἄρξαι[9] φυγῆς.

XXV. [Περὶ τοῦ μὴ δι' ἑαυτοῦ διδόναι τὸν στρατηγὸν[10] τὰ σημεῖα εἴτε τῆς συμβολῆς εἴτε ἄλλης[11] τινὸς πράξεως, ἀλλὰ διὰ τῶν ἡγεμόνων][12]

Πᾶν δὲ παράγγελμα καὶ σύνθημα καὶ παρασύνθημα διδότω διὰ τῶν ἡγεμόνων· ἐπιόντα γὰρ κηρύττειν ἅπασιν ἰδιώτου καὶ ἀπείρου κομιδῇ καθέστηκεν, καὶ χρόνος ἐν τῷ παραγγέλλειν ἀναλίσκεται, καὶ θόρυβος ὁμοῦ πάντων[13] ἀλλήλους ἐρωτώντων·[14] εἶθ' ὁ μὲν προσέθηκέ τι πλεῖον[15] ὧν ὁ στρατηγὸς εἶπεν, ὁ δ' ἀφείλετο τοῦ ῥηθέντος

---

[1] φιλίους vGH.
[2] AENRGH: οἴκους P "et ceteri codd. ut vid."
[3] Title om. F: in margin GH.   [4] φιλίοις F.
[5] FC: ἐραστὰς παρὰ παιδικοῖς om. PGH "ceteri codd. ut vid."
[6] F: τοῦ πλησίον PGH "ceteri codd. ut vid.": πλησίον τὸ Köchly: τῷ πλησίον Koraes.
[7] ὑπὸ F.   [8] ENR Camerarius indicate a break here.
[9] ἄρξασθαι vGH.

464

way it is very often useful to deceive both one's own army and that of the enemy by false news, good for the former, but bad for the latter.

XXIV. [*In the Ranks Friends must be placed by Friends and Acquaintances by Acquaintances*]

It is the part of a wise general to station brothers in rank beside brothers, friends beside friends, and lovers beside their favourites.[1] For whenever that which is in danger near by is more than ordinarily dear the lover necessarily fights more recklessly for the man beside him. And of course one is ashamed not to return a favour that he has received, and is dishonoured if he abandons his benefactor and is the first to flee.

XXV. [*The General must not give the Signal for Battle or any other Action to his Army in Person but through his Officers*]

The general should give every command or watchword or countersign through his officers, for to come and give orders personally to the whole army is the act of an unpractised and inexperienced commander. Time is lost in passing orders down the line, and confusion arises, as all the soldiers question each other at the same time. One man through ignorance adds something to what the general has said and

[1] See the Introduction, p. 343 f.

---

[10] Schwebel: τοῦ στρατοῦ A Rigaltius H (G has lost all but στρα in binding) " alii codd.": τοῦ στρατηγοῦ ENR.

[11] GH: εἴτε ἄλλης om. v (AP?).

[12] ἡμετέρων GH (ἡμετέρ[G). Title om. F and no break indicated: in margin GH. [13] πάντας F.

[14] ἐρωτώντων ἀλλήλους vGH. [15] FGH: πλέον v.

ONASANDER

2 παρὰ τὴν ἄγνοιαν. δεῖ[1] δὲ τοῖς πρώτοις ἡγεμόσιν
εἰπεῖν, ἐκείνους δὲ ἀπαγγεῖλαι τοῖς μετ' αὐτούς,
εἶτα τούτους τοῖς κατόπιν,[2] εἶθ' ἑξῆς ἄχρι τῶν
τελευταίων, τοὺς πρώτους τοῖς[3] ὑπὸ πόδα[4] ση-
μαίνοντας· οὕτως γὰρ ἐν τάχει καὶ μετὰ κόσμου
καὶ μεθ' ἡσυχίας εἴσονται, παραπλησίου[5] τοῦ
παραγγέλματος τοῖς φρυκτωροῦσι γιγνομένου.[6]
3 καὶ γὰρ ἐκείνων, ὅταν ὁ πρῶτος ἄρῃ τὸν φρυκτόν,
ὁ δεύτερος τῷ[7] μετ' αὐτὸν ἐπύρσευσεν, εἶθ'
ὁ τρίτος τῷ τετάρτῳ, καὶ τέταρτος πέμπτῳ,[8] καὶ
πέμπτος ἕκτῳ[9] καὶ καθ' ἕνα πάντες[10] ἀλλήλοις,
ὥστ' ἐν ὀξεῖ διὰ μήκους σταδίων τὸ σημανθὲν
ὑπὸ τοῦ πρώτου πάντας ἐπιγνῶναι.

XXVI. [Περὶ τοῦ μὴ μόνον συνθήματα, ἀλλὰ καὶ
παρασυνθήματα[11] διδόναι][12]

Τὸ δὲ παρασύνθημα μὴ διὰ φωνῆς λεγέσθω,
ἀλλὰ διὰ σώματος γινέσθω, ἢ νεύματι[13] χειρὸς ἢ
ὅπλων[14] συγκρούσει ἢ ἐγκλίσει δορατίου ἢ παρα-
φορᾷ ξίφους, ἵνα μὴ μόνον γενομένης ποτὲ ταραχῆς[15]
πιστεύσωσι τῷ λεγομένῳ συνθήματι—τοῦτο γὰρ
δύνανται καὶ πολέμιοι καταλαβέσθαι πολλάκις
2 ἀκούοντες—, ἀλλὰ καὶ τῷ παρασυνθήματι.[16] χρησι-
μώτατον δέ που τοῦτο καὶ πρὸς τὰς ἑτερογλώσ-
σους συμμαχίας τῶν ἐθνῶν· οὔτε γὰρ λέγειν οὔτε
ξυνιέναι δυνάμενοι[17] φωνῆς ἀλλοτρίας αὐτῷ τῷ παρα-

---

[1] εἰ F.   [2] αὐτοὺς τούτοις κατόπιν F.
[3] τοὺς vGH.   [4] ὑποπόδας F.
[5] παραπλήσιον GH : παραπλήσιον v: παρὰ τοῦ παραπλησίου R.
[6] FGH : γινομένου v.   [7] FP : τὸν vGH.
[8] καὶ τέταρτος πέμπτῳ added by Koraes.
[9] ὁ πέμπτος τῷ ἕκτῳ vGH.

466

another omits something. But one should communicate his orders to his higher officers and they
should repeat them to the officers next below them,
who in turn pass them to their subordinates, and so
on to the lowest, the higher officers in each case
telling the orders to those below them. In this
manner the soldiers will learn the commands quickly
with order and calmness, just as a message is carried
by fire-signals. For after the first signaller uplifts his
fire, the second signals to the next, and the third
to the fourth, and the fifth to the sixth, and one by
one each follows the other, so that in a short time,
over a distance of many stades, the message signalled
by the first is known to all.

XXVI. [On giving both Watchwords and Countersigns]

He should give the countersign not by the voice but
by some gesture, as a wave of the hand, or the clash
of weapons, or dipping a spear, or by a side-wave of
his sword, in order that when confusion arises the
soldiers may not have to trust to the spoken watchword alone—for the enemy hear this so often that
they are able to get it—but also to the countersign.
This is most useful in the case of allies who speak a
different language, for, unable to speak or to understand a foreign tongue, they differentiate between

---

[10] FC : καθ' ἕν (καθὲν G : καθὲν H) ἅπαντες vGH.

[11] GHEN : περὶ συνθημάτων A " ceteri."

[12] Title om. F without indication of break : in margin
GH : before ἵνα μὴ AR.

[13] M (conjecture): νεῦμα F : νεύματος PvGH.

[14] ὅπλου R (well thought of by Köchly but certainly
wrong).

[15] γενομένου ποτὲ ταραχοῦ R.   [16] F indicates a break here.

[17] οὔτ' ἐχόντων λέγειν οὔτε ξυνιέναι δυναμένων R.

συνθήματι κρίνουσι τό τε φίλιον καὶ τὸ[1] πολέμιον. διδόσθω δὲ ταῦτα, κἂν μὴ μάχεσθαι μέλλωσιν,[2] ἐν ταῖς παρεμβολαῖς πρὸς τὰς ἀδήλους ταραχάς.

XXVII. [Περὶ τοῦ μὴ λύειν τὰς τάξεις μήτε ἐν ταῖς διατάξεσι μήτε ἐν ταῖς ὑποχωρήσεσι][3]

Παραγγελλέτω δὲ καὶ τὰς ὑποχωρήσεις ἐν τάξει ποιεῖσθαι καὶ τὰς[4] διώξεις, ἵνα ἧττόν τε σφαλλόμενοι βλάπτωνται[5] μὴ κατ' ἄνδρα σποράδες ἐν ταῖς φυγαῖς ὑποπίπτοντες τοῖς πολεμίοις, πλέονά τε[6] κατορθοῦντες βλάπτωσι κατὰ τάξεις καὶ λόχους ἰσχυρότεροι τοῖς φεύγουσιν ἐπιφαινόμενοι, πρὸς δὲ καὶ ἀσφαλέστεροι· πολλάκις γὰρ ἀτάκτως[7] ἐπιφερομένους οἱ πολέμιοι θεασάμενοι συμφρονήσαντες αὖθις ἐκ μεταβολῆς αὐτῶν καταστάντες εἰς τάξιν παλίντροπον[8] ἐποιήσαντο τὴν δίωξιν· ὅλως δὲ μηδέν σφισιν ἄμεινον εἶναι λεγέτω[9] τοῦ μένειν ἐν τάξει μηδ' ἐπισφαλέστερον τοῦ λύειν.

XXVIII. [Περὶ τοῦ[10] δι' ἐπιμελείας ἔχειν τὸν[11] στρατηγὸν λαμπρὸν ἐκτάττειν τὸ στράτευμα][12]

Μεμελημένον δ' ἔστω τῷ στρατηγῷ[13] λαμπρὸν ἐκτάττειν τὸ στράτευμα τοῖς ὅπλοις, ῥᾳδία[14] δ' ἡ

---

[1] Added by Köchly.   [2] καὶ . . . μέλλουσιν vGH.
[3] AGH: ὑποχωρήσεσιν v Köchly. Title om. F without indication of break : in margin GH.   [4] Om. vGH.
[5] βλάπτονται GH : βλαπτόμενοι σφάλλωνται (σφάλλονται P) P " ceteri codd. ut vid."
[6] πλείονα δὲ vGH : πλείονά τέ Koraes.   [7] ἀταράκτως F.
[8] παλίστροφον GH Rigaltius " ceteri codd. ut vid."
[9] λεγόντων vGH.

468

friends and enemies by this countersign. One should
instruct the army in these signals in camp, even if it
is not about to fight, as a protection against confusion and uncertainty.

XXVII. [*Soldiers should never leave the Ranks whether
in Formation or in Retreat*]

One should command both retreats and pursuits
to be made in formation, so that, if defeated, the
soldiers may suffer less injury, when in their flight
they encounter the enemy, by not being scattered,
man by man, and, if successful, they may inflict
greater injury on the enemy by keeping their ranks
and companies unbroken, appearing stronger to the
fugitives, and moreover being safer themselves. For
often the enemy, observing their opponents advancing without order, by a concerted plan about-face,
form ranks once more and reverse the pursuit. In
a word, the general should say that nothing is more
advantageous to his men than remaining in rank, and
nothing more dangerous than breaking ranks.

XXVIII. [*The General must be attentive to the Splendour
of the Army's Equipment*]

The general should make it a point to draw up his
line of battle resplendent in armour[1]—an easy matter,

---

[1] This was a principle upon which Julius Caesar laid great
emphasis (Suetonius, *Iulius*, 67 ; Polyaenus viii. 23. 20).

[10] τοῦ μὴ δι' PGH Rigaltius " ceteri codd. ut vid.": τοῦ δι'
AENM (by conjecture).
[11] Om. A.   [12] Title om. F : in margin GH.
[13] FCP : τὸν στρατηγὸν GH Rigaltius " ceteri codd. ut vid."
[14] ῥηίδια R.

φροντὶς αὕτη παρακαλέσαντι τὰ ξίφη θήγειν καὶ τὰς κόρυθας καὶ τοὺς θώρακας σμήχειν· δεινότεροι γὰρ οἱ ἐπιόντες φαίνονται λόχοι[1] τοῖς τῶν ὅπλων αἰθύγμασι,[2] καὶ πολλὰ τὰ δι' ὄψεως δείματα[3] προεμπίπτοντα[4] ταῖς ψυχαῖς ταράττει[5] τὸ ἀντι-πόλεμον.

XXIX. [Περὶ τοῦ ἐν τῷ καιρῷ τῆς συμβολῆς ἀλαλάζειν][6]

Ἐπαγέτω δὲ τὸ στράτευμα καὶ σὺν[7] ἀλαλαγμῷ,[8] ποτὲ δὲ καὶ σὺν δρόμῳ· καὶ γὰρ ὄψις[9] καὶ βοὴ καὶ πάταγος[10] ὅπλων ἐξίστησι τὰς τῶν ἐναντίων δια-
2 νοίας. ἀνατεινόντων δὲ κατὰ τὰς ἐφόδους ἀθρόοι, πρὶν εἰς χεῖρας ἐλθεῖν, ὑπὲρ[11] τὰς κεφαλὰς μετέωρα τὰ ξίφη πρὸς[12] τὸν ἥλιον θαμὰ παρεγκλίνοντες.[13] ἐσμηγμέναι γὰρ αἰχμαὶ καὶ λαμπρὰ ξίφη καὶ ἐπάλληλα[14] παραμαρμαίροντα πρὸς ἀνταύγειαν ἡλίου δεινὴν ἀστραπὴν πολέμου προεκπέμπει.[15] καὶ ταυτὶ[16] μὲν εἰ γίγνοιτο[17] καὶ παρὰ τοῖς πο-λεμίοις, ἀντικαταπλήττειν ἀναγκαῖον, εἰ δὲ μή, προεκπλήττειν.
3 Ἐνίοτε δέ[18] ποτε χρήσιμον ἐν καιρῷ μὴ φθάνειν ἐκτάττοντα τὴν δύναμιν, ἀλλὰ τέως ἐντὸς[19] τοῦ χάρακος κατέχειν, ἄχρι[20] ἂν κατοπτεύσῃ τὴν τῶν

---

[1] λόχοις R.   [2] αἰθίγμασι F: ἐθύγμασιν GH.
[3] δείγματα PGH Rigaltius " ceteri codd. ut vid."
[4] προσεμπίπτοντα v (πρὸς ἐμ- GH).   [5] παράττει P.
[6] Title om. F without indication of break: in margin GH: before ἀνατεινόντων AR.
[7] καὶ τὸ στράτευμα σὺν Köchly.
[8] FENRGH: σὺναλαγμῷ Rigaltius " ceteri codd. ut vid."

requiring only a command to sharpen swords and to clean helmets and breast-plates. For the advancing companies appear more dangerous by the gleam of weapons, and the terrible sight brings fear and confusion to the hearts of the enemy.

XXIX. [*Shouting in the Midst of Battle*]

One should send the army into battle shouting, and sometimes on the run, because their appearance and shouts and the clash of arms confound the hearts of the enemy. The dense bands of soldiers should spread out in the attack before coming to close quarters, often waving their swords high above their heads toward the sun. The polished spear-points and flashing swords, shining in thick array and reflecting the light of the sun, send ahead a terrible lightning-flash of war. If the enemy should also do this, it is necessary to frighten them in turn, but if not, one should frighten them first.

It is sometimes advantageous before a critical battle for the general not to be the first to form a line of battle but to wait within the camp for a time

---

9 ὄψεις R.   10 πάταγοι EN : πάγοι PGHA m².
11 FGH : ὑπὸ P Rigaltius "ceteri codd. ut vid."
12 καὶ πρὸς vGH.   13 παρεκκλίνοντα vGH.
14 προσάλληλα vGH.
15 Köchly : προσεκπέμπει F : ἀντιπέμπει vGH.
16 ταυτῇ P : ταύτη v (ταύτῃ GH) : ταῦτα Koraes.
17 γίγνοιτο PGH Rigaltius "alii codd. ut vid.": ἐγίγνοντο ENR.
18 FGH : δή v : δεῖ ποτὲ τὲ χρήσιμον R.
19 FC : ἐγγὺς PGHA m² "cet. codd. ut vid."
20 ἄχρις GH Köchly.

πολεμίων παράταξιν, ὁποία τίς ἐστι καὶ ὡς τέτακται[1] καὶ ἐφ' οἵων ἵσταται χωρίων.

XXX. ["Οτι δεῖ τὸν στρατηγὸν πρὸ τοῦ πολέμου
συλλογίζεσθαι, τίς ὀφειλεῖ[2] ὑπαντῆσαι κατὰ
τὴν συμβολὴν τῷ δεῖνι καὶ τίς τῷ ἄλλῳ[3] καὶ
οὕτως καθεξῆς ἐξετάζειν[4] τοὺς ἰδίους ἄρχοντας[5]
πρὸς τοὺς τῶν ἐναντίων][6]

Εἶτά που τότε[7] συλλογισάμενον, τίνας τίσιν[8]
ἀντιτάττειν χρὴ καὶ τίνα τρόπον, ὥσπερ[9] ἀγαθὸν
ἰατρὸν προκατανοήσαντα[10] νόσον σώματος ἀντεπ-
άγειν τὰ ἀλεξήματα καὶ τὴν δύναμιν ἐκτάττειν,
ὡς ἂν ἄριστ' αὐτῷ δόξαι[11] συμφέρειν· ἀναγκάζονται γὰρ οἱ στρατηγοὶ πολλάκις καὶ[12] πρὸς τοὺς
ὁπλισμοὺς τῶν ἐναντίων καὶ πρὸς τὰ ἔθνη καὶ
πρὸς τὰ ἤθη[13] τὰ ἴδια στρατεύματα κοσμεῖν καὶ
παρατάττειν.

XXXI. [Περὶ τοῦ, ἐὰν οἱ ἐναντίοι προτερεύωσι[14]
τῷ ἱππικῷ, ἐκλέγεσθαι στενοὺς τόπους][15]

Ἱπποκρατούντων δὲ τῶν πολεμίων, ἐὰν ᾖ δυνατόν, ἐπιλεγέσθω[16] χωρία τραχέα καὶ στενὰ καὶ
παρ' ὄρη, ἅ[17] ἥκιστα ἱππάσιμα, ἢ φυγομαχείτω

---

[1] δὲ τέτακται K : διατέτακται Koraes.
[2] φίλος R : ὠφείλει Rigaltius.   [3] Köchly : τῶν ἄλλων Ω.
[4] ἐξισάζειν H(?)M (G has lost the middle of the word in
binding).   [5] ἄρχοντα R.
[6] Title om. F without indication of break : in margin GH
(badly mutilated from trimmed margins in G).
[7] FGH (ποῦ GH): τοῦ πότε PR : τοῦτο ποτὲ Chokier : περὶ
τοῦ πότε EN.

until he observes the battle array of the enemy, its character, arrangement, and position.

XXX. [*The General must decide before Battle who should oppose whom and thus in Order arrange his own Officers against those of the Enemy*]

Next the general must consider which troops to oppose to which of the enemy, and in what manner ; just as a good doctor who foresees an illness of the body, he must bring forward his defences and arrange his forces as it seems to him most advantageous ; for generals are often compelled to equip and marshal their own armies with reference to the armament, nationality, and customs of the enemy

XXXI. [*Narrow Places must be chosen if the Enemy are superior in Cavalry*]

If the enemy are superior in cavalry, the general should choose if possible a locality that is rough and hemmed in, near mountains which are least suitable for riding, or he should avoid battle so far as he

---

8 FGH : τίνα στῆσειν P Rigaltius and all Schwebel's mss.: τίνας δὲ τίσιν Koraes.　　　9 ὥσπερ γὰρ vGH.

10 FGH : καταπρονοήσαντα ENPA m² Rigaltius.

11 δόξῃ v (δόξη GH).

12 καὶ . . . παρατάττειν om. ENR Camerarius.

13 ἔθη vGH.

14 A : προτερεύουσι vG (προτερεύο[H).

15 Title om. F : in margin G (mutilated) H.

16 ἐκλεγέσθω vGH.

17 Köchly : παρδρη ἥκιστα F : παρόρια vGH.

ONASANDER

κατὰ δύναμιν, ἕως ἂν ἐπιτηδείους εὕρῃ τόπους
2 καὶ τοῖς οἰκείοις ἁρμόζοντας πράγμασιν.¹ ἀπο-
λελείφθων² δέ τινες καὶ ἐπὶ τοῦ χάρακος οἱ παρα-
φυλάττοντες τὴν παρεμβολὴν στρατιῶται καὶ πρὸς
τὴν τῆς ἀποσκευῆς³ φυλακήν, ἵνα μὴ κατανοήσας
ὁ στρατηγὸς τῶν πολεμίων ἔρημον ὄντα πέμψῃ
τοὺς ἁρπασομένους τὰ ἐν αὐτῷ καὶ καταληψομέ-
νους τὸ χωρίον.

XXXII. [Περὶ τοῦ μηδὲν παρακεκινδυνευμένον
ποιεῖν τὸν στρατηγόν]⁴

Τοὺς μὲν⁵ γὰρ ἢ τὰ ἴδια καθαιροῦντας⁶ ἐρύματα
στρατηγοὺς ἢ ποταμοὺς διαβαίνοντας ἢ κρη-
μνοὺς καὶ βάραθρα κατόπιν ποιουμένους τῶν
φιλίων,⁷ ἵν' ἢ μένοντες νικῶσιν ἢ βουληθέντες
φεύγειν ἀπόλωνται, οὔτε πάμπαν ἐπαινεῖν οὔτε
ψέγειν ἔχω· πᾶν γὰρ τὸ παρακεκινδυνευμένον
μᾶλλον⁸ τόλμης ἐστὶν ἢ γνώμης καὶ τῇ τύχῃ
2 κεκοινώνηκε πλεῖον⁹ ἢ τῇ κρίσει. ὅπου γὰρ ἢ
νικῶντα δεῖ κρατεῖν ἢ ἡττηθέντα τοῖς ὅλοις¹⁰
ἐσφάλθαι, πῶς ἐνταῦθ' ἄν τις ἤ¹¹ φρονήσει τὸ
νικᾶν ἢ προαιρέσει τὸ¹² ἡττᾶσθαι μαρτυρήσειεν;
3 ἐγὼ δὲ στρατιώταις μὲν ἐκ στρατεύματος φιλο-
τόλμως¹³ κινδυνεύειν ἐπιτρεπτέον¹⁴ εἶναι νομίζω—
καὶ γὰρ δρῶντές τι μεῖζον ὤνησαν καὶ παθόντες
οὐθὲν τοσοῦτον ἐλύπησαν—, στρατεύματι δὲ παντὶ

---

¹ τάγμασιν Köchly. ² ἀπολελείφθωσαν vGH.
³ παρασκευῆς vGH.
⁴ Title om. FAENPR Saguntinus Camerarius: in margin
GH: no break indicated FGH. ⁵ Om. GH.
474

may until he finds an appropriate place, adapted to his own circumstances. A certain number of soldiers must be left behind at the palisade to guard the camp and the baggage in order that the general of the enemy may not discover that the camp is deserted and send men to plunder its contents and seize the place.

XXXII. [*The General must do nothing rash*]

Generals who destroy their own defences or cross rivers or who post their armies with steep cliffs or yawning gulfs in the rear in order that the soldiers may either stand and conquer or in their desire to escape be killed, I am not wholly able to praise nor yet to blame, for everything that is ventured rashly is rather the part of recklessness than of wisdom, and has a greater share of luck than of good judgement. For in a case when one must either win a victory and prevail, or else be defeated and lose everything, in such a case how could anyone attribute victory to foresight or defeat to deliberate choice? But I do believe that certain soldiers of the army must be allowed to run desperate risks— for if they succeed they are of great assistance, but if they fail they do not cause corresponding loss,—

---

[6] μὲν ἄρηται δια καθαιροῦντας F.   [7] φίλων vGH.
[8] Added by Köchly.   [9] πλέον vGH.   [10] ὅπλοις R.
[11] Köchly : πῶς ἐνταῦθά τις ἢ F : πῶς ἐνταῦθα τῇ σῇ (τῇ σῇ GH) vGH : πῶς ἂν ἐνταῦθά τις ἢ Koraes : πῶς ἐνταῦθα τῷ νικᾶν τῇ φρονήσει K.   [12] τοῦ F.   [13] φιλοτίμως vGH.
[14] ἐπιτραπτέον Rigaltius "ceteri codd. ut vid." A m² GH.

ONASANDER

τὴν ἄδηλον ἐκκυβεύειν τύχην[1] οὐ δοκιμάζω.
4 μάλιστα δ' ἁμαρτάνειν οὗτοί μοι δοκοῦσιν,[2] οἵ
τινες ἐν μὲν τῷ[3] νικᾶν ὀλίγα λυπήσειν μέλλοντες
τοὺς πολεμίους, ἐν δὲ τῷ ἡττᾶσθαι μεγάλα βλάψειν
τοὺς φίλους ἀποχρῶνται τοιούτοις στρατηγήμασιν.
5 Εἰ δὲ πρόδηλος μέν σφισιν ὁ ὄλεθρος[4] εἴη, κἂν
μὴ[5] παραβόλοις ἐγχειρήσωσι στρατηγίαις, πρόδηλος δὲ καὶ ἡ τῶν πολεμίων ἡττηθέντων ἀπώλεια,
τότ'[6] οὐκ ἄν μοι δόξειεν ἁμαρτάνειν ἀποφράττων
τὰς φυγὰς τῶν φιλίων.[7] ἄμεινον γὰρ ἐν τῷ τολμᾶν
ἐπ' ἀδήλῳ τῷ[8] τάχα μηδὲ πείσεσθαί τι δεινὸν
ἅμα καὶ δρᾶσαι ζητεῖν, ἢ ἐπὶ προδήλῳ τῷ μηδὲν
δρῶντας ἀπολέσθαι πάντας ἀτόλμως ἡσυχάζειν.[9]
6 ὑποδεικνύτω[10] μέντοι μὴ μόνον ἐν τοῖς τοιούτοις
χωρίοις, ὅπου κατ' ἀλήθειαν οὐκ ἔστι σωτηρία
τοῖς φεύγουσιν, ἀλλὰ καὶ ἐν παντὶ τόπῳ καὶ πάσῃ
μάχῃ διδασκέτω διὰ πλειόνων, ὅτι τοῖς μὲν
φεύγουσι πρόδηλος ὁ[8] ὄλεθρος, ὡς ἂν ἤδη μετ'
ἐξουσίας ἐπικειμένων[11] τῶν πολεμίων μηδενὸς
ἔτι δυναμένου διακωλύειν τοὺς διώκοντας πᾶν[12]
ὃ βούλονται[13] διαθεῖναι[14] τοὺς φεύγοντας, τοῖς
7 δὲ μένουσιν[15] ἄδηλος ὁ θάνατος ἀμυνομένοις. οἵ
τινες γὰρ πεπεισμένοι τυγχάνουσιν ἐν ταῖς παρα-
τάξεσιν,[16] ὡς φεύγοντες μὲν αἰσχρῶς ἀπολοῦνται,
μένοντες δ' εὐκλεῶς τεθνήξονται, καὶ χεῖρον'

[1] τύχειν H.
[2] Köchly: μάλιστα δ' ἂν οὗτοί μοι δοκοῦσιν F: μάλιστα δ' ἂν
οὗτοί (οὗτοί G, οὗτοι H) μοι δοκοῦσιν ἁμαρτάνειν vGH.
[3] τὸ F.
[4] Köchly: σφισιν ὄλεθρος FC: σφισιν (σφίσιν G, σφῖσιν H)
εἴη PGH Rigaltius "ceteri codd. ut vid."
[5] ἄν μοι R.   [6] ἀπώλειά ποτ' F.
[7] φιλίων vGH.   [8] Om. vGH.
[9] ἢ ἐπὶ . . . ἡσυχάζειν om. R Camerarius.
476

yet I cannot countenance gambling with the entire army as the stake. Most of all those generals seem to me to be at fault who make use of stratagems which in the event of victory will cause small loss to the enemy, but in defeat the greatest loss to their own army.

If the destruction of one's army is evident, except through the use of some daring strategy, and if the destruction of the enemy by defeat is also evident, then I do not think a general would be at fault in cutting off the retreat of his own army. For it is better, by showing courage at a time when it is uncertain whether one will perhaps escape a severe defeat himself, to endeavour at the very same time to inflict a defeat, rather than, when it is certain that all will perish if they remain inactive, to keep quiet like cowards. He should not only point this out in those localities where in actual fact there is no safety for fugitives, but also in every locality and every battle he must show by many reasons that death is certain for those who flee, since the enemy would at once press on freely, as soon as no one is able to hinder the pursuit, and could dispose of the fugitives as might suit them; but for men who stand and defend themselves, death is not certain. For the men in the lines who chance to believe that if they flee they will perish shamefully while if they remain in rank they will die a glorious death, and who

---

10 ὑποδείκνυτο R.   11 ἐπικνειμένων R.   12 ἅπαν vGH.
  13 FGH : βούλεται P Rigaltius " ceteri codd. ut vid."
14 διαθῆναι FH.   15 φειγουσιν R.   16 πράξεσιν vGH.

ἀεὶ[1] προσδοκῶσιν ἐκ τοῦ καταλιπεῖν τὴν τάξιν
ἢ ἐκ τοῦ φυλάττειν, ἄριστοι κατὰ τοὺς κινδύνους
8 ἄνδρες ἐξετάζονται. διόπερ ἀγαθὸν μέν, εἰ πάντας οὕτως ἔχειν γνώμης πεῖσαι[2] στρατηγός, εἰ
δὲ μή, ἀλλὰ μέντοι γ᾽[3] ὡς πλείστους· ἢ γὰρ
παντελεῖς περιεποιήσατο[4] νίκας ἢ μικροῖς ἐλαττώμασι[5] περιέπεσε.[6]

9 Τῶν δ᾽ ἐκ προλήψεως καὶ πρὶν ἢ συμβαλεῖν
ἐπινοουμένων στρατηγοῖς[7] αἱ παρ᾽ αὐτὸν τὸν τῆς
μάχης καιρὸν ἐπίνοιαι νίκης καὶ ἀντιστρατηγήσεις[8]
ἔστιν ὅτε καὶ πλείους καὶ θαυμασιώτεραι[9] γίγνονται[10] τοῖς[11] τὴν στρατηγικὴν ἐμπειρίαν ἠσκηκόσιν,
ἃς οὐκ ἔστιν ὑποσημῆναι[12] λόγῳ ἢ[13] προβουλεῦσαι.

10 ὥσπερ γὰρ οἱ κυβερνῆται πρὸς μὲν τὸν πλοῦν ἐκ
λιμένων ἀνάγονται πάντα ἐξηρτυμένοι[14] τὰ κατὰ
τὴν ναῦν, ἐπειδὰν δ᾽ ἐμπέσῃ χειμών, οὐχ ὃ βούλονται ποιοῦσιν, ἀλλ᾽ ὃ ἀναγκάζονται, πολλὰ καὶ[15]
πρὸς τὸν ἀπὸ τῆς τύχης ἐπείγοντα[16] κίνδυνον
εὐτόλμως παραβαλλόμενοι, καὶ οὐ τὴν ἀπὸ τῆς
μελέτης εἰσφερόμενοι[17] μνήμην, ἀλλὰ[18] τὴν ἐκ
τῶν καιρῶν βοήθειαν· οὕτως οἱ στρατηγοὶ τὴν
μὲν δύναμιν[19] ἐκτάξουσιν, ὅπως σφίσι νομίζουσι
συνοίσειν, ἐπειδὰν δ᾽ ὁ τοῦ πολέμου περιστῇ
χειμὼν πολλὰ θραύων καὶ παραλλάττων[20] καὶ

[1] Köchly: χείρονα ἀεὶ vGH : χεῖρον εἰ F.
[2] πεῖσαι F: πείσει vGH.
[3] Köchly (after Camerarius): ἐπεὶ τοῖς γ᾽ F: ἐπεί τοί γε (τοι γε GH) vGH : εἰ δὲ μή, τούς γε πλείστους Koraes.
[4] περιεποιήσαντο F (corr. by a later hand) vGH.
[5] περιεποιήσαντο . . . ἐλαττώμασι om. R.
[6] περιέπεσον vGH : περιέπεσεν Köchly : ἢ γὰρ . . . περιέπεσε om. Camerarius.   [7] τοῖς στρατηγοῖς vGH.
[8] Köchly : ἐπινοίᾳ νῖκαι κἀντιστρατηγήσεις F : ἐπίνοιαι καὶ ἀντιστρατηγήσεις vGH.   [9] θαυμασιώτεροι vGH.

478

constantly anticipate greater dangers from breaking
the ranks than from keeping them, will prove
themselves the best men in the face of danger.
On this account it is a good plan if the general can
win over his whole army to this opinion, or, if not
all, at least as many as possible, for thus he either
gains an absolute victory or meets with but a slight
defeat.

Plans and counter-stratagems for victory that
are originated at the very moment of battle
are sometimes preferable to those which are
conceived and contrived by generals in anticipation
and before the engagement, and they are sometimes more worthy of remark, in the case of those
made by men who are skilled in military science,
though they are things which cannot be reduced
to rules or planned beforehand. For just as
pilots for their voyages, before sailing from the
harbour, fit their ship out with everything that a
ship requires; yet when a storm blows up they do,
not what they wish, but what they must, boldly
staking their fortunes against the driving peril of
chance and calling to their aid no memory of their
past practice but assistance appropriate to the
existing circumstances; just so generals will prepare
their armies as they believe will be best, but when
the storm of war is at hand repeatedly shattering,

---

10 γίγνωνται GH.   11 τοῖς εὖ vGH.
12 ἐπισημᾶναι v: ἐπισημάναι GHA m²: ἐπισημῆναι (?) C.
13 Om. F which also marks a break after προβουλεῦσαι.
14 ἐξηρτήμενοι P: ἐξηρτημένοι GH Rigaltius "ceteri codd.
ut vid."
15 πολλάκις C.   16 ἐπείγονται Rigaltius.
17 ἐπιφερόμενοι vGH.   18 ἀλλὰ καὶ vGH.
19 οἱ μὲν στρατηγοὶ τὴν δύναμιν F.   20 παραλάττων GH.

ποικίλας ἐπάγων περιστάσεις, ἡ τῶν ἀποβαινόντων[1]
ἐν ὀφθαλμοῖς ὄψις ἐπιζητεῖ τὰς ἐκ τῶν καιρῶν
ἐπινοίας, ἃς ἡ ἀνάγκη τῆς τύχης μᾶλλον ἢ ἡ[2]
μνήμη τῆς ἐμπειρίας ὑποβάλλει.

XXXIII. [Περὶ τοῦ μὴ τὸν στρατηγὸν αὐτοχειρὶ
πολεμεῖν][3]

Μαχέσθω δὲ ὁ στρατηγὸς αὐτὸς προμηθέστερον
ἢ[4] τολμηρότερον, ἢ καὶ τὸ παράπαν ἀπεχέσθω
τοῦ[5] τοῖς πολεμίοις εἰς χεῖρας ἰέναι· καὶ γὰρ εἰ
κατὰ[6] τοὺς ἀγῶνας ἀνυπέρβλητον[7] ἀνδρίαν εἰσενέγκαιτο,[8] τοσοῦτον οὐδὲν ὠφελῆσαι δύναται στράτευμα μαχόμενος, ὅσον ἀποθανὼν βλάψαι· στρατηγοῦ γὰρ ἡ[9] γνώμη πλέον ἰσχύει τῆς[9] ῥώμης·
σώματος μὲν γὰρ ἀνδρίᾳ δρᾶσαί τι[10] μέγα καὶ
στρατιώτης δύναται, γνώμης δὲ προμηθείᾳ βου-
2 λεῦσαί τι κρεῖττον[11] οὐκ ἄλλος. ὅνπερ δ' ἂν
τρόπον, εἰ κυβερνήτης ἀφειμένος τῶν οἰάκων, ἃ
δεῖ τοὺς ναύτας[12] ποιεῖν, αὐτὸς πράττοι, κινδυνεύειν ἂν συμβαίη τὸ σκάφος, τούτου, εἰ στρατηγὸς[13] ἀποστὰς τοῦ γνώμῃ τι βουλεύειν ἐπὶ τὰς
τῶν στρατιωτῶν καταβαίνοι χρείας, ἡ τῶν
ὅλων[14] ἀκυβέρνητος ἀμέλεια τὴν ἀναγκαιοτέραν ἄ-
3 πρακτον ποιήσει βοήθειαν. ὅμοιον δὴ κρίνω
τὸν[15] στρατηγὸν ἐμπαραβαλέσθαι[16] τῇ ἑαυτοῦ ψυχῇ[17]

---

[1] FC: ἀπομαινόντων GH: ἀπομενόντων P.
[2] Om. ἡ F.   [3] Title om. F: in margin GH.
[4] ἢ μὴ vGH.   [5] Om. R.   [6] εἰ καὶ κατὰ vGH.
[7] FGH: ὑπέρβλητον P Rigaltius "ceteri codd. ut vid."
[8] εἰσηνέγκατο vGH.   [9] Om. vGH.
[10] ἀνδρίᾳ ἀνδρᾶσαι τί F (ἀνδρείαι δράσαι τὶ G11).
[11] κρειττων Koraes.

overthrowing, and bringing varied conditions, the sight of present circumstances demands expedients based on the exigencies of the moment, which the necessity of chance rather than the memory of experience suggests.

XXXIII. [*The General should not himself enter Battle*]

The general should fight cautiously rather than boldly, or should keep away altogether from a hand-to-hand fight with the enemy. For even if in battle he shows that he is not to be outdone in valour, he can aid his army far less by fighting than he can harm it if he should be killed, since the knowledge of a general is far more important than his physical strength. Even a soldier can perform a great deed by bravery, but no one except the general can by his wisdom plan a greater one. If a ship's captain leaving the helm should himself do what the sailors ought to do, he would endanger his ship ; in the same way, if the general, leaving his function of wise direction, should descend to the duties of a simple soldier, his neglect of the whole situation, due to his lack of governing, will render useless the common soldier's mere routine service. Similar, I think, is the notion which the general gets into his heart

---

[12] FC : ταῖς ναύταις PGH Rigaltius "plerique codd." (Schwebel) : om. ποιεῖν GH.
[13] τοῦτο ποιεῖ στρατηγὸς · εἰ vGH.
[14] Köchly : ἡ τῶν ἀμεινόνων F : ἡ γὰρ τῶν ἀμεινόνων vGH : perhaps ἡ τῶν ἀμεινόνων can stand. [15] τὸ τὸν Koraes.
[16] ἐκπαραβάλλεσθαι K : ἐκπαραβαλλέσθαι GH.
[17] ψυχῇ (ψύχη corr. by marg. gloss misplaced at συμπάσης to ψυχῇ GH) τὸ τῆς vGH : ψυχῇ τοῦτο τῷ τῆς Köchly.

481

ONASANDER

τῷ τῆς συμπάσης, εἰ πείσεταί τι, δυνάμεως
ἀκηδεῖν· εἰ γάρ, ἐν ᾧ τοῦ σύμπαντος ἡ σωτηρία
στρατεύματός ἐστιν, οὗτος οὐδὲν εἰ τεθνήξεται[1]
πεφρόντικε, τὸ πᾶν αἱρεῖται συνδιαφθεῖραι, καὶ
ὀρθῶς δ'[2] ἄν τις αἰτιάσαιτο τοῦτον ὡς ἄπρακτον
4 στρατηγὸν μᾶλλον ἢ ἀνδρεῖον. ὁ μὲν γὰρ πολλὰ
γνώμῃ στρατηγήσας ἀρκεσθήσεται σεμνυνόμενος
ἐπὶ ταῖς ἀπὸ ψυχῆς εὐπραγίαις, ὅστις δ' οὕτως
ἀπειρόκαλός ἐστιν, ὥστ' ἄν,[3] εἰ μὴ διὰ μάχης
εἰς χεῖρας ἔλθοι τοῖς πολεμίοις,[4] οὐδὲν αὑτὸν
ἄξιον εἰργάσθαι[5] νομίζειν, οὐκ ἀνδρεῖος, ἀλλὰ
5 ἄλογος[6] καὶ τολμηρός ἐστιν.[7] ὅθεν ἐπιφαίνειν[8]
μὲν δεῖ[9] τῷ πλήθει τὸ φιλοκίνδυνον, ἵνα τὴν
προθυμίαν ἐκκαλῆται[10] τῶν στρατιωτῶν, ἀγωνίζεσθαι δὲ ἀσφαλέστερον, καὶ τοῦ θανάτου μὲν
καταφρονεῖν, εἴ τι πάσχοι τὸ στράτευμα, μηδ'
αὐτὸν[11] αἱρούμενον ζῆν, σωζομένου δὲ[12] καὶ[13] τὴν
ἰδίαν φυλάττειν ψυχήν· ἤδη γὰρ ἐπικυδέστερα τὰ
τῶν φιλίων[14] ὄντα ποτὲ στρατηγὸς ἀποθανὼν
ἐμείωσεν· οἱ μὲν γὰρ πταίοντες ἐπανεθάρρησαν
τὸ ἀντίπαλον ἀστρατήγητον ἰδόντες, οἱ δ' εὐτυ-
χοῦντες ἐδυσθύμησαν τὸν ἴδιον ἡγεμόνα ζητοῦντες.[7]
6 στρατηγοῦ δ' ἔστι τὸ παριππάζεσθαι ταῖς τάξεσιν, ἐπιφαίνεσθαι τοῖς κινδυνεύουσιν, ἐπαινεῖν
τοὺς ἀνδριζομένους, ἀπειλεῖν τοῖς ἀποδειλιῶσι,
παρακαλεῖν τοὺς μέλλοντας, ἀναπληροῦν τὸ[15] ἐλλεῖπον, ἀντιμετάγειν εἰ δέοι λόχον, ἐπαμύνειν τοῖς

---

[1] τοῦ σύμπαντος . . . τεθνήξεται om. ENPRV Camerarius.
[2] Om. vGH.   [3] ὥστε vGH.
[4] FC: τῶν πολεμίων P Rigaltius Schwebel's mss. GH.
[5] εἴργασται P Rigaltius Schwebel's mss. : ἤργασται GH :
ἤργασται R.
[6] Added by Köchly : καὶ del. Koraes.

when he thus disregards the welfare of his whole
force in the event of accident to himself; for if
he, with whom the safety of the whole army lies,
has no care lest he himself should die, he prefers
that everyone should die with him, and rightly he
would be censured as an unsuccessful rather than
a courageous general. He who has accomplished
many feats of generalship through his wisdom must
be satisfied with the honour for his intellectual
successes, but he who is so stupid that, unless he
comes to close quarters with the enemy, he believes
he has accomplished nothing worthy of mention,
is not brave but thoughtless and foolhardy. Hence
the general must show himself brave before the
army, that he may call forth the zeal of his soldiers,
but he must fight cautiously; he should despise
death if his army is defeated, and not desire to live,
but if his army is preserved he should guard his
personal safety, for sometimes the death of a general
lessens the glory of his army, since the defeated
enemy is encouraged, perceiving that its opponents
are without a general, and the successful army is discouraged, feeling the need of its own general. The
duty of the general is to ride by the ranks on horseback, show himself to those in danger, praise the
brave, threaten the cowardly, encourage the lazy,
fill up gaps, transpose a company if necessary, bring

---

⁷ F indicates a break here.

⁸ ὑποφαίνειν vGH.   ⁹ δή F.

¹⁰ ἐκκαλεῖται P Rigaltius " cet. codd. ut vid." GH.

¹¹ Köchly: μηδὲ αὐτὸν (?) v: μηδεαυτὸν GH: μηδὲ αὐτὸν R:
μήδ' αὐτὸν F.   ¹² αἱ, ξεῖν σώζομεν οὐδέ R.

¹³ FGH Saguntinus Camerarius: om. v.

¹⁴ φίλων vGH.

¹⁵ μέλλοντας ἀναπληροῦν τι RM (conjecture) Camerarius.

κάμνουσι, προορᾶσθαι τὸν καιρόν, τὴν ὥραν, τὸ μέλλον.

XXXIV. [Περὶ τοῦ εὐεργετεῖν κατὰ τὸ μέτρον ἕνα ἕκαστον τῶν ἀνδραγαθούντων[1]]

Ἀνακαλεσάμενος δ᾽ ἐκ τῆς μάχης πρῶτον μὲν ἀποδιδότω τοῖς θεοῖς θυσίας καὶ πομπάς,[2] αἷς ἐκ τοῦ καιροῦ χρῆσθαι[3] πάρεστι, τὰ νομιζόμενα χαριστήρια μετὰ τὴν τοῦ πολέμου παντελῆ νίκην ἐπαγγελλόμενος[4] ἀποδώσειν· ἔπειτα τοὺς μὲν ἀρίστους ἐν τοῖς κινδύνοις ἐξετασθέντας τιμάτω δωρεαῖς καὶ τιμαῖς, αἷς νόμος, τοὺς δὲ κακοὺς
2 φανέντας κολαζέτω.[5] τιμαὶ δ᾽ ἔστωσαν μὲν καὶ αἱ κατὰ τὰ[6] πάτρια καὶ κατὰ[7] τὰ παρ᾽ ἑκά-στοις νόμιμα· στρατηγικαὶ[8] δὲ αὗται· πανοπλίαι,[9] κόσμοι, λαφύρων δόσεις, πεντηκονταρχίαι, ἑκα-τονταρχίαι, λοχαγίαι, τάξεων[10] ἀφηγήσεις, καὶ αἱ[11] ἄλλαι αἱ[12] κατὰ νόμους παρ᾽ ἑκάστοις ἡγεμονίαι· τῶν[13] μὲν ἰδιωτῶν τοῖς ἀνδραγαθήσασιν αἱ ἥττους ἐξουσίαι, τῶν δὲ ἡγεμόνων τοῖς ἀριστεύσασιν[14] αἱ μείζους ἡγεμονίαι· αὗται γὰρ ἀμοιβαί τε[15] μεγαλόψυχοι τοῖς ἤδη τὸ γενναῖον εἰργασμένοις προτροπαί τε ἀναγκαῖαι τοῖς τῶν αὐτῶν ἐπι-

---

[1] τὸν ἀνδραγαθοῦντα GH. Title om. F without indication of break: at τῶν μὲν ἰδιωτῶν § 2 (or a little above GH) Ω: in margin GH.   [2] πομπαῖς F.
[3] C: χρηστὰ Ω.   [4] ἐπαγγειλάμενος vGH.
[5] F indicates a break here.   [6] GEN: om. FvPH.
[7] Köchly: καὶ τὰ παρ᾽ F: καὶ παρ᾽ Ω.
[8] FENR: στρατηγικαῖς P Rigaltius GH "ceteri codd. ut vid."
[9] ENR: πανοπλίας F: πανοπλίαις P Rigaltius GH "ceteri codd. ut vid."   [10] λοχαγίαι τάξεων· F: τάξεως vGH.
[11] Om. vGH.   [12] Del. von Rohden.

aid to the wearied, anticipate the crisis, the hour, and the outcome.

XXXIV. [*Conferring Rewards proportional to the Valour of each*]

On returning from battle, the general should first offer to the gods such sacrifice and festal celebrations as the circumstances permit, promising to offer the customary thank-offerings after complete victory ; then he should honour those soldiers who have faced danger most bravely with the gifts and marks of distinction which are usually given, and he should punish those who have shown themselves cowards. Honours should be bestowed according to tradition and custom in each case. Those bestowed by generals[1] are the following : full equipments of armour, decorations, spoils, and appointments to commands such as over fifties, over hundreds, over companies, over squads, and the other parts of command prescribed by the laws of the country in question. The bravest of the private soldiers should receive the lesser commands, and those of his officers who have distinguished themselves should have the higher commands, since these rewards strengthen the self-esteem of those who have deserved well, and encourage others who desire similar rewards.

[1] Or, reading στρατηγικαὶ δὲ αὗται πανοπλίαι and taking στρατηγικαὶ with πανοπλίαι (Schwebel and Konstantiniades), the meaning is "full equipments of armour for generals." Possibly the words πεντηκονταρχίαι . . . ἑκάστοις ἡγεμονίαι belong after αἱ μείζους ἡγεμονίαι just below.

13 v indicates a break at this point (but not FGH).
14 FCEN: ἀριστεύουσι P: -σιν GH Rigaltius.
15 αἱ ἀμοιβαί τε καὶ vGH.

3 θυμοῦσιν. ὅπου δὲ τιμὴ μὲν ἀποδίδοται τοῖς ἀγαθοῖς, τιμωρία δ' οὐ παραπέμπεται τῶν κακῶν, ἐνταῦθα καλὰς ἐλπίδας ἔχειν ἀνάγκη τὸ στρατόπεδον· οἱ[1] μὲν γὰρ ἐφοβήθησαν ἁμαρτάνειν, 4 οἱ δὲ ἐφιλοτιμήθησαν ἀνδραγαθεῖν. ἔνθα[2] μέντοι χρὴ καὶ νικῶντα μὴ κατ' ἄνδρα μόνον ἀμοιβὰς ἐκτίνειν,[3] ἀλλὰ καὶ τῷ σύμπαντι στρατεύματι τῶν κινδύνων ἐπικαρπίαν[4] ἀποδιδόναι· τὰ γὰρ[5] τῶν πολεμίων ἐπιτρεπέτω τοῖς στρατιώταις διαρπάζειν,[6] εἰ[7] χάρακος ἢ ἀποσκευῆς ἢ φρουρίου κυριεύσειεν, ὁτὲ[8] δὲ καὶ πόλεως, εἰ μή τι μέλλοι περὶ αὐτῆς 5 χρηστότερον βουλεύειν. οὕτως γὰρ ἂν καὶ μάλιστα[9] μήπω τέλος εἰληφότος τοῦ πολέμου συνοίσοι[10] πρὸς τὰ μέλλοντα προθυμότερον ἐπὶ τὰς μάχας αὐτῶν ἐξιόντων, εἰ μὴ νομίζομεν τοὺς μὲν θηρευτικοὺς κύνας δελεάζειν ἀναγκαῖον εἶναι τοῖς κυνηγοῖς αἵματι θηρίων[11] καὶ τοῖς τοῦ συλληφθέντος ζῴου σπλάγχνοις, τοῖς δὲ νικῶσι στρατιώταις τὰ τῶν ἡττημένων[12] εἰς προτροπὴν[13] οὐ μάλα δή τι[14] συμφέρον ἀποδιδόναι.

XXXV. α'. [Ὅτι οὐ[15] χρὴ πάντοτε ἐπιτρέπειν τὰς ἁρπαγάς, καὶ ὅτι τὰ σώματα οὐ χρὴ ἁρπάζειν, ἀλλὰ τὸν στρατηγὸν πιπράσκειν][16]

Τὰς δ' ἁρπαγὰς οὔτ' ἐπὶ πάσης μάχης ἐπιτρεπτέον, οὐδ' αἰεὶ[17] πάντων, ἀλλ' ὧν μέν, ὧν δ'

---

[1] At this point GH indicate a break.
[2] At this point F indicates a break : ἐνταῦθα vGH.
[3] ἐκτεινειν vGH.
[4] FGH : ἐπικαρδίαν P : ἐπὶ καρδίαν ENRV.
[5] Om. vGH, reading ἐπιτρεπέτω δέ.
[6] ἁρπαζειν A in².   [7] ἢ F.

486

Whenever honour is paid to the brave and punishment of the cowardly is not neglected, then an army must have fair expectation; the latter are afraid to be found wanting, the former are ambitious to show prowess. It is not only necessary in victory to distribute rewards to individual men but also to make recompense to the army as a whole for its dangers. The soldiers should be allowed to plunder the possessions of the enemy if they should capture a camp or baggage train or fortress, or sometimes even a city, unless the general intends to put it to a more profitable use. This course will serve well the interests of the future, especially if the war is not ended, since the soldiers will be more eager to enter battle, unless we are to believe that, while huntsmen must entice their dogs with the blood of wild beasts and the entrails of the animal which the dogs have caught, nevertheless it is not at all advantageous to give the possessions of the defeated enemy, as encouragement, to the victorious army.

XXXV. (1) [*Indiscriminate Pillage must not always be permitted; Prisoners must not be regarded as Loot, but must be sold by the General*]

Plundering should not be permitted after every battle nor in the case of all kinds of property, but

---

8 Köchly: ὅτε GH: ὅτι P Rigaltius "alii codd.": ἔτι DERN.   9 βουλεύειν . . . μάλιστα om. F.
10 Koraes: συνοίσει Ω.   11 θηρίου vGH.   12 ἡττωμένων F.
13 προνομήν vGH.   14 Om. vGH.   15 ὅτι οὐ om. V.
16 Title in vGH only: om. Ω: in margin GH.
17 ἐπί vGH: ἀεί Köchly.

487

οὔ, τῶν δὲ σωμάτων ἥκιστα· ταῦτα δὲ πιπράσκειν
2 τὸν στρατηγόν. εἰ δὲ χρημάτων δέοι καὶ δαπάνης
κοινῆς καὶ μεγάλης, καὶ ὅσα ἄγεται καὶ φέρεται
3 πάνθ᾽ ὡς αὐτὸν ἀναπέμπεσθαι κηρυττέτω. γνώῃ[1]
δ᾽ ἂν αὐτὸς ἄριστα πρὸς τοὺς καιρούς, εἰ τὰ[2]
πάντα δέοι λαμβάνειν, εἴτ᾽ ἐκ μέρους, εἴτε μηθὲν
ὧν[3] ἔτυχεν· οὗ γε μὴν ἔστι[4] πολέμου[5] καὶ τοῖς
κοινοῖς εἶναι χρημάτων δαψίλειαν καὶ τοῖς στρατιώταις ἀνεπικώλυτον[6] ὠφέλειαν· ἤδη δὲ καὶ
παρὰ τοὺς[7] τῶν ἡττημένων[8] πλούτους καὶ παρὰ
τὰς τῶν τόπων εὐδαιμονίας αἱ ὠφέλειαί σφισι
δαψιλέστεραι γίγνονται.[9]

β΄. [Περὶ αἰχμαλώτων][10]

4 Τοὺς δὲ αἰχμαλώτους, ἐὰν ὁ πόλεμος ἔτι συν-
εστὼς[11] ᾖ, μὴ κτεινέτω, μάλιστα μὲν τῶν[12] πρὸς
οὓς ἐστιν ὁ πόλεμος, κἂν δοκῇ οἷ, τοὺς συμμάχους[13]
ἀναιρεῖν, ἥκιστα δὲ καὶ τοὺς[14] ἐνδοξοτάτους καὶ
λαμπροὺς παρὰ τοῖς πολεμίοις, ἐνθυμούμενος τὰ
ἄδηλα τῆς τύχης καὶ τὸ παλίντροπον τοῦ δαιμονίου
φιλοῦντος ὡς τὰ πολλὰ νεμεσᾶν, ἵν᾽ εἴ[15] τινων
αὐτοὶ[16] ἢ σωμάτων, ὧν πολὺς πόθος, ἢ φρουρίου

---

[1] γνοίη vGH.   [2] εἴτε vGH.
[3] FGH: om. P Rigaltius " alii codd. ut vid."
[4] Köchly: οὔτε μήν ἐστι F: οὗ (οὐ GH) γέ μην ἐστὶν Rigaltius GH and "codd. ut vid.": μὴν . . . κινδύνοις (Ch. xxxvii. 4) om. G, by loss of one leaf in binding.
[5] πολέμῳ Koraes.
[6] ἐπικωλυτον Rigaltius Schwebel " ceteri codd. ut vid.": ἐπικωλυτὸν H.   [7] παρ᾽ αὐτοὺς F.
[8] ἡττωμένων FH.   [9] γίγνωνται H.
[10] Title om. FHA: without indication of break in FΠ.

only in the case of certain things, and least of all of prisoners, for these should be sold by the general. If he lack money and resources to meet a large public expense, he should order that all the plundered property, including the live-stock, be turned over to him. The general will know what is best according to the circumstances, whether to seize everything or a part or nothing, of that on which he chances; certainly it is not the characteristic of war to cause both abundance of wealth to the community and unlimited gain to the private soldiers; in fact it happens sometimes that the gains of a victorious army are proportionate to the wealth of the vanquished and the prosperity of their territory.

(2) [Prisoners]

Prisoners, if the war is still in progress, the general should not kill—at the very most he may kill, if he thinks best, the allies of those against whom the war is directed, but least of all those who stand in highest repute and position among the enemy, remembering the uncertainties of chance, and the reversals caused by providence, which usually brings retribution. His purpose should be, if his army should capture certain prisoners for whom there is a great desire in their own country, or some strong-

---

[11] FCH: συνεστὸς P: συνετὸς EM (G missing) NV: συνεχῶς R (?). [12] Capps: τοὺς Ω.

[13] δοκήσῃ (δοκήσει H) τοῖς συμμάχοις vH Saguntinus Camerarius: μάλιστα μέν, κἂν δοκῇ αὐτοῖς, πρὸς οὓς ἐστιν ὁ πόλεμος, τοὺς συμμάχους Köchly. [14] καὶ τότε τοὺς Köchly.

[15] Köchly after C: νεμεσᾶν εἴ F: νεμεσᾶν ἢ PH Rigaltius "ceteri codd. ut vid." [16] αὖθις F: αὐτοῖς H.

κρατήσαιειν,[1] ἱκανὰ ἀντικαταλλάγματα[2] δοὺς ἔχῃ[3]
κομίσασθαι τὰ τῶν φιλίων,[4] ἢ τότε γε[5] μὴ
5 βουλομένων ἐνδίκως εἰς ἴσον ἀμύνηται.[6] μετὰ
δὲ τὰ κατορθώματα καὶ τοὺς κινδύνους ἐπιτρε-
πέσθων[7] αὐτοῖς εὐωχίαι τε καὶ κλισίαι καὶ πόνων
ἀνέσεις,[8] ἵν᾽ εἰδότες, οἷον τέλος ἐστὶ τοῦ[9] μαχομένους νικᾶν, ὑπομένωσι τὰ δυσχερῆ πάντα πρὸ
τοῦ νικᾶν.

XXXVI. αʹ. [Περὶ τοῦ θάπτειν τοὺς ἐν πολέμῳ
ἀναιρουμένους][10]

Προνοείσθω δὲ τῆς τῶν νεκρῶν κηδείας, μήτε
καιρὸν μήθ᾽ ὥραν μήτε τόπον[11] μήτε φόβον προ-
φασιζόμενος, ἄν τε τύχῃ νικῶν, ἄν τε ἡττώμενος·
ὁσία[12] μὲν γὰρ καὶ ἡ πρὸς τοὺς ἀποιχομένους
εὐσέβεια, ἀναγκαία δὲ καὶ ἡ πρὸς τοὺς ζῶντας
2 ἀπόδειξις. ἕκαστος γὰρ τῶν στρατιωτῶν ὡς
αὐτὸς ἀμελούμενος, εἰ πεσὼν ἔτυχεν, παρ᾽ ὀφθαλμοῖς ὁρῶν τὴν τύχην καὶ ὑπὲρ τοῦ μέλλοντος
καταμαντευόμενος, ὡς οὐδ᾽ αὐτός, εἰ[13] τεθναίη,
ταφησόμενος ἐπαχθῶς φέρει τὴν ἀτύμβευτον[14]
ὕβριν.

[1] κρατῆσαι PH Rigaltius (κρατῆσαι H).
[2] ἀντικαταλαγματα H.   [3] ἔχει PH·Rigaltius.
[4] φίλων vH.   [5] τό γε vH: τοῦτό γε Koraes.
[6] ἀμίνεται PH.   [7] ἐπιτρεπέσθωσαν vH.
[8] ἀνέσεις R.   [9] τοὺς vH.
[10] Title om. F without sign of break : in margin H without sign of break.
[11] FPH : μήτε τοπον om. v.   [12] ὅση F.
[13] FC: οὐ H Rigaltius "ceteri codd. ut vid.": ὡς δ᾽ αὐτὸς τεθναίη R.   [14] ἀτύμβυτον F.

hold, that he may be able by giving enough in exchange to redeem the property of his friends, or at least then, should the enemy not wish to deal justly with him, that he may protect himself on equal terms. After successful engagements and the dangers of battle, the general should allow feasts and celebrations[1] and holidays, in order that the soldiers, knowing what happens as the result of victory by battle, may patiently undergo all hardships necessary for such victory.

XXXVI. (1) [On the Burial of the Fallen]

The general should take thought for the burial of the dead, offering as a pretext for delay neither occasion nor time nor place nor fear, whether he happen to be victorious or defeated. Now this is both a holy act of reverence toward the dead and also a necessary example for the living. For if the dead are not buried, each soldier believes that no care will be taken of his own body. should he chance to fall, observing what happens before his own eyes, and thereby judging of the future, feeling that he, likewise, if he should die, would fail of burial, waxes indignant at the contemptuous neglect of burial.

---

[1] The exact meaning of κλισίαι is uncertain, although it seems to denote entertainments at which the participants sat or reclined upon couches. Zur-Lauben (followed by Koraes) renders the word by ' spectacles,' Konstantiniades by ' συμπόσια.'

β'. [Περὶ τοῦ ἐπανορθοῦσθαι τὴν ἐλάττωσιν][1]

3 Εἰ δὲ ἡττῶτο,[2] παραμυθησάμενος[3] τοὺς ἀνασωθέντας ἐκ τῆς μάχης[4] ἐφεδρευέτω, καιρὸν[5]
ἔνθα που καὶ μᾶλλον οἰόμενος ἐπανορθώσασθαι
4 τὴν ἐλάττωσιν. εἰώθασι γὰρ ὡς τὰ πολλὰ μετ᾽
εὐπραγίας[6] οἱ στρατιῶται ῥᾳθυμότερον ἐκλύεσθαι
περὶ τὰς φυλακάς· ἡ γὰρ τῶν πέλας καταφρόνησις
ἀμελείας[7] σφίσι γίγνεται αἰτία[8] τῶν οἰκείων,
οὕτως τε πολλάκις τὰ εὐτυχήματα πλεῖον ἔβλαψε
5 τῶν δυστυχημάτων. ὁ μὲν γὰρ πταίσας ἐδι-
δάχθη καὶ φυλάξασθαι[9] τὸ μέλλον, ἐξ ὧν ἔπαθεν,
ὁ δὲ τοῦ δυστυχεῖν[10] ἄπειρος οὐδ᾽,[11] ὡς δεῖ φυλάξαι
6 τὰς εὐπραγίας,[12] ἔμαθεν. εἶτ᾽[13] αὖ νικῶν τὴν[14]
αὐτὴν ἐχέτω[15] προμήθειαν ὑπὲρ τοῦ μὴ παθεῖν[16]
ἀμελῶν, ἢν ἂν εἰς τὸ[17] δρᾶσαί τι[8] τοὺς ἐχθροὺς
ῥᾳθυμοῦντας εἰσενέγκαιτο.[18] φόβος γὰρ εὔκαιρος[19]
ἀσφάλεια προμηθής, ὡς[20] καὶ καταφρόνησις ἄκαι-
ρος[21] εὐεπιβούλευτος τόλμα.

XXXVII. [Περὶ τοῦ ἐν καιρῷ εἰρήνης μὴ
ἀφυλάκτως[22] εἶναι][23]

Ἀνοχὰς δὲ ποιησάμενος μηδ᾽[24] ἐπιτιθέσθω μηδ᾽
αὐτὸς ἀφύλακτος ἔστω· ἀλλὰ τὸ μὲν ἥσυχον

---

[1] Koraes: title om. Ω: without sign of a break FH.
" De cladibus acceptis sarciendis " Rigaltius Schwebel.
[2] ἡττῶτω H : ἡττῶνται v.   [3] παραμυθησόμενος vH.
[4] τοὺς ἐκ τῆς μάχης ἀνασωθέντας vH.
[5] καιρῷ Schwebel: ἐφεδρευέτω τῷ καιρῷ Koraes.
[6] εὐπραγίαις PV A m².
[7] ἀμέλεια v (ἀμελεία H) defended by von Rohden.
[8] Added by Köchly.
[9] φυλάξας PH Rigaltius "alii codd. ut vid.": φυλάξαι EN.

492

(2) [*Encouragement in Defeat*]

If the general be defeated, by encouraging the soldiers who have survived the battle, he should prepare for another bout, thinking that very likely there is at such a time an even better opportunity to retrieve defeat. For, as a rule, soldiers after victory are accustómed to relax their vigilance, for their contempt for their near-by opponents causes carelessness of their own interests, and thus good fortune has often done more harm than misfortune. For he who has suffered a defeat has been taught to guard in future against that from which he has suffered, but he who is inexperienced in misfortune has not even learned that it is necessary to guard his success. On the other hand, if victorious, the general should take the same precautions against suffering harm through negligence which he would use in trying to inflict harm upon the enemy if they were off their guard. Seasonable fear is wise precaution, as ill-timed contempt is recklessness that invites attack.

XXXVII. [*Precautions in Time of Peace*]

After making a truce he should neither make an attack nor himself remain unguarded; he should, on

---

¹⁰ δυστοιχεῖν H.　　　¹¹ οὐχ vH.　　¹³ οὔτ' vH.

¹² φυλάξασθαι τὰς δυσπραγίας Koraes.

¹⁴ ἢ τὴν F.　　¹⁵ ἔχει vH.　　¹⁶ παχεῖν A m².

¹⁷ Koraes: ἢν ἄρ' εἰς τὸ F: ἢν ἄρ' ἐστὸ H: ἄρ' ἐς τὸ Rigaltius Schwebel: ἀρεστὸν R.　　¹⁸ εἰσηνέγκατο vH.　　¹⁹ εὔκαιρως H.

²⁰ Om. v: προμηθῶς καὶ H.　　²¹ ἄκρος R (A m²).

²² ἀφύλακτος ARH (?) Koraes: ἀφύλακτον P.

²³ Title om. F: in margin H.

²⁴ μήτ' (om. ἐπιτιθέσθω μηδ') αὐτὸς H.

ἐχέτω πρὸς τοὺς πολεμίους, ὡς ἐν[1] εἰρήνῃ, τὸ δ'

2 ἀσφαλὲς εἰς τὸ μὴ παθεῖν, ὡς ἐν πολέμῳ. δεῖ γὰρ οὐκ ἀσύνηθκον ἐν σπονδαῖς εἶναι οὔτ'[2] αὐτόν τι φθάνειν ἀσεβὲς δρῶντα, ἀλλ' ὕποπτον,[3] ὡς φυλάττεσθαι τὸ ἀπὸ τῶν[4] πολεμίων ὕπουλον·

3 ἄδηλοι γὰρ αἱ τῶν σπεισαμένων γνῶμαι. καὶ παρὰ σοὶ μὲν ἔστω τὸ βέβαιον τοῦ μὴ ἀδικῆσαι[5] διὰ τὸ εὐσεβές, παρὰ δὲ τοῖς πολεμίοις ὑπονοείσθω τὸ μὴ πιστὸν διὰ τὸ ἀπεχθές·[6] ἀσφαλὴς γὰρ οὗτος[7] καὶ προμηθής, ὃς οὐδὲ βουληθεῖσι τοῖς πολεμίοις ἐπιθέσθαι τὸν τοῦ δύνασθαι παρασπον-

4 δῆσαι καιρὸν ἀπολείπει.[8] οἵτινες δ' ἐπὶ τοῖς θεοῖς[9] ποιοῦνται τὴν ὑπὲρ ὧν ἂν πάθωσιν ἐκδικίαν, εὐσεβὲς[10] μὲν φρονοῦσιν, οὐ μὴν ἀσφαλῆ ποιοῦσιν.[11]

5 κομιδῇ γὰρ ἀνοήτων[12] ἐστὶν ἐλπίδι τοῦ τοὺς[13] παρασπονδήσαντας ἐκτίσειν δίκας ἀπρονοήτους[14] ἔχειν τοὺς περὶ σφῶν κινδύνους,[15] ὥσπερ αὐτοὺς[16] σῴζε-σθαι μέλλοντας ἅμα τῷ[17] τοὺς ἐχθροὺς ἀπόλλυσθαι,[18] ἐξὸν[19] μετὰ τῆς τῶν[20] ἰδίων πραγμάτων ἀσφαλείας[21] πεῖραν λαμβάνειν τῆς τῶν πολεμίων ἀσεβείας· οὕτως γὰρ αὐτοί[22] τε διὰ τὸ προμηθὲς οὐκ ἂν πταίσαιεν ἐπιβουλευθέντες, ἀσεβήσουσί τε οἱ πολέμιοι τῷ ἐπι-χειρῆσαι καὶ δοκεῖν πεποιηκέναι ἄν,[23] εἰ[24] ἐδυνήθησαν.

---

[1] Del. A m².   [2] οὐκ F: οὔτε H: οὐδ' Koraes.

[3] C: αὐτοπτον Ω (αὖτο πτον H).

[4] τῶν ἀπόντων (for τὸ ἀπὸ τῶν) F: τὸ ὑπὸ τῶν R.

[5] FC: ἀδικεῖσθαι ENPH Rigaltius "ceteri codd. ut vid.": ἀδικῆσθαι A m².

[6] FH: ἀπαχθὲς Rigaltius "quidam codd. ut vid."

[7] οὕτως PH Rigaltius "alii codd. ut vid."

[8] F: ἐπιλείποι H Schwebel: ἐπιλείπει Koraes: διαλείποι Rigaltius (no report of other mss.).

[9] FH: τοὺς θεοὺς v.   [10] εὐσεβῆ vH.

[11] Added by Köchly.   [12] FHV (?): ἀνόητόν v.

494

the one hand, make no move against the enemy, as in peace, but, on the other, he should be protected against danger, as in war. He must not break faith in a treaty, nor be the first to commit any sacrilegious act, but he must be suspicious enough to watch for festering deceit on the part of the enemy, for the intentions of those with whom the treaty has been concluded are uncertain. Let your part be a firm resolution not to transgress, because of the sacred nature of the treaty, but suspect a breach of faith on the part of the enemy due to their hostility. That general is wise and cautious who affords the enemy, even when they desire to attack, no opportunity to break their compact. Those who leave to the gods revenge for what they have suffered are piously minded but certainly do not act safely. For it is absolute folly to be careless of the danger to oneself in the hope that treaty-breakers will pay the penalty—as if one would himself be saved as soon as the enemy perish!—when it is possible to make trial of the irreligion of the enemy while at the same time safeguarding one's own interests. With this precaution one will save himself from defeat if plotted against, but the enemy will commit sacrilege both if they attempt a breach of the truce and if they let it be seen that they would have done it if they could.

13 FK: τούτους H "cet. codd. ut vid." Rigaltius Schwebel.
14 ἀπρονοήτους Oldfather : ἀπρονοήτως Ω.
15 τοῦ . . . κινδύνου vH.   16 αὐτὸς R (A m²).
17 τὸ R.   18 ἀπόλυσθαι PH.
19 FH (Leo, Tactica, xvi. 20 ἔξεστιν): ἐξ ὧν v.
20 FR: om. v.   21 ἀσφαλείαις F.
22 αὐτοῖς F: αὐτός R.   23 Added by Oldfather.
24 καὶ εἰ v : καὶ del. Koraes after Leo, Tactica, xvi. 20: om.
τε οἱ πολέμιοι, ἐπιχειρῆσαι, δοκεῖν πεποιηκέναι F.

XXXVIII. α΄. [Περὶ τοῦ τὰς[1] προσαγομένας πόλεις
ἐν ἀδείᾳ ἔχειν καὶ φιλανθρωπίᾳ][2]

Ταῖς δὲ προσχωρούσαις[3] πόλεσιν, εἴ τινες
ἐπιτρέποιεν αὐτὰς[4] ἀρξάμεναι, φιλανθρώπως καὶ
χρηστῶς προσφερέσθω.[5] προσαγάγοιτο[6] γὰρ ἂν
οὕτως καὶ τὰς ἄλλας. ἡ γὰρ ἐλπὶς τοῦ τῶν
αὐτῶν τεύξεσθαι[7] δελεάζουσα προσάγεται[8] τοὺς
2 πολλοὺς αὐτοὺς ἑκόντας[9] ἐγχειρίζειν. ὅστις δὲ
πικρῶς[10] εὐθὺς καὶ πολεμικῶς[11] προσφέρεται κύ-
ριος γενόμενος πόλεως ἢ διαρπάζων ἢ κτείνων ἢ
κατασκάπτων,[12] ἀλλοτριωτέρας διατίθησι τὰς ἄλλας
πόλεις, ὥστε καὶ τὸν πόλεμον αὐτῷ[13] ἐπίπονον
3 καὶ τὴν νίκην δύσελπιν κατασκευάζειν· εἰδότες
γάρ, ὡς ἀπαραίτητόν[14] ἐστιν ἡ τῶν ὑποχειρίων[15]
πρὸς τοῦ κρατήσαντος[16] τιμωρία, πᾶν ὁτιοῦν
ὑπομένουσι καὶ ποιεῖν καὶ πάσχειν ὑπὲρ τοῦ μὴ
4 παραδοῦναι τὰς πόλεις. οὐθὲν γὰρ οὕτως κατα-
σκευάζει γενναίους, ὡς φόβος[17] ὧν μέλλουσι
πείσεσθαι κακῶν[18] εἴξαντες· ἡ γὰρ προσδοκία τῶν
δεινῶν ἐκ τοῦ καθυφεῖσθαι[19] τὰ σφέτερα δεινὴν
5 ἐντίθησι φιλοτιμίαν ἐν τοῖς κινδύνοις. χαλεπαὶ
δὲ[20] αἱ πρὸς τοὺς ἀπεγνωσμένους πεῖραι μάχης·
οὐδὲν γὰρ χρηστότερον ἐλπίζοντες ἐκ τοῦ παρα-
χωρεῖν ὧν πείσονται κινδυνεύοντες αἱροῦνται μετὰ

[1] Om. A.
[2] Title om. F: in margin H without mark of break.
[3] προχωρούσαις A m[2]. [4] αὐτὰς F.
[5] προσφερέσθων F. [6] προσάγοιτο H.
[7] τεύξασθαι vH. [8] προσάγει vH.
[9] C: ἔχοντας (om. αὐτοὺς) F : οὕτως ἔχοντας vH.
[10] πικρὸς vH. [11] πολεμικὸς vH : πολεμικὸς εὐθὺς R.
[12] κατακόπτων v : κατὰ κόμπτων H.
[13] αὐτῶ F : ἐπίπονον αὐτῶ or αὐτῷ v (ἑ. αὐτῶ H).

XXXVIII. (1) [*Treatment of surrendered Cities with Trust and Humanity*]

If any cities should open their gates in surrender early in the war, the general should treat them in a manner both humane and advantageous, for thus he would induce the other cities also to submit. The enticing hope of a similarly fortunate fate leads the majority to surrender voluntarily. But he who acts in a harsh and savage manner, immediately after becoming master of a city, plundering, slaying, and destroying, makes other cities hostile, so that the war becomes laborious for him and victory difficult of attainment. Since they know that the punishment of the conquered by the conqueror is merciless, they are ready to do and suffer anything rather than surrender their cities. For nothing makes men so brave as the fear of what ills they will suffer if they surrender; indeed the expectation of the evils which will ensue from their subjection produces a terrible pertinacity in danger. Moreover, fighting is dangerous against desperate men,[1] who expect from surrender no amelioration of the fate which will be theirs if they continue to fight, and therefore prefer, if they can inflict much harm, also

[1] The idea was well expressed by Vespasian, μὴ συμπλέκεσθαι θανατῶσιν ἀνθρώποις · οὐδὲν γὰρ ἀλκιμώτερον εἶναι τῆς ἀπογνώσεως (Josephus, *Bell. Iud.* iii. 7. 18).

---

[14] ἀπαραίτητός vH.

[15] FH : ὑποχείρων PA m² Rigaltius " ceteri codd. ut vid."

[16] Köchly (but no note): τοὺς κρατήσαντας FH Rigaltius Schwebel Koraes and apparently v.

[17] οὐθὲν . . . φόβος om. R Camerarius.

[18] κακῶς vH.   [19] καθυφέσθαι F.

[20] With χαλεπαὶ δὲ G resumes.

6 τοῦ πολλὰ δρᾶν καὶ πάσχειν. ὅθεν αἱ πολιορκίαι
τοῖς ὧδε[1] στρατηγοῖς ἄφροσι καὶ τεθηριωμένοις[2]
ταλαίπωροι[3] γίγνονται[4] καὶ πολυχρόνιοι, ποτὲ[5]
δὲ καὶ ἀτελεῖς, οὐχ ἥκιστα δὲ σφαλεραί τε[6] καὶ
ἐπικίνδυνοι.

β'. [Πῶς χρηστέον προδόταις][7]

7 Τοῖς δὲ προδόταις τάς τε πίστεις καὶ τὰς ἐπαγ-
γελίας φυλαττέτω, μὴ διὰ τοὺς γεγονότας, ἀλλὰ
διὰ τοὺς ἐσομένους, ἵν᾽ εἰδότες, ὡς ὀφείλεται
σφισι χάρις, ἑλόμενοι[8] τὰ τῶν πολεμίων ἐπὶ τὰς
αὐτὰς εὐεργεσίας τρέπωνται·[9] λαμβάνει γάρ τι
8 μᾶλλον ὁ[10] προδότῃ διδοὺς ἢ χαρίζεται.[11] διὸ
χρὴ προθύμως ἐκτίνειν[12] τὰς ἀμοιβάς· οὐ γὰρ
δικαστὴς τῆς ἀδικηθείσης πόλεώς ἐστιν, ἀλλὰ
στρατηγὸς τῆς ἑαυτοῦ πατρίδος.

XXXIX. α'. [Περὶ τοῦ τὸν στρατηγὸν ἐν γνώσει
εἶναι τῆς τῶν ἄστρων[13] κινήσεως][14]

Πρὸς δὲ τὰς ἐπιθέσεις καὶ τὰς ἐκ προδοσίας[15]
νυκτερινὰς καταλήψεις τῶν πόλεων[16] οὐκ ἄπειρον
εἶναι δεῖ τῆς ὑπεργείου κατὰ τὴν νύκτα φορᾶς τῶν

---

[1] τοιοῖσδε vGH.
[2] FGH: τεθηρωμένοις P Rigaltius "ceteri codd. ut vid.":
τεθειραμένοις R.
[3] FCD: om. vGH.   [4] γίγνωνται GH.
[5] πολὺ GH: πολλοὶ Rigaltius A m²: πολλαὶ Schwebel
Koraes.   [6] Koraes: σφαλερώτεραι καὶ Ω.
[7] Koraes: title om. FAGH without indication of a break
in any one of these мss.: "Fidem proditoribus esse ser-
vandam" Rigaltius Schwebel.

to suffer much. On this account the sieges of such insensate and savage generals become wearisome and long drawn-out, sometimes even fail of accomplishment, and are extremely dangerous and precarious.

(2) [*How to treat Traitors*]

One should keep promises and pledges to traitors, not on account of what they have done but of what others will do, in order that these, knowing that gratitude will be due them, may choose the interests of their country's enemies and turn to the same sort of service. For he who gives to a traitor receives much more than he bestows. On this account it is necessary to pay the reward cheerfully, for the general is not an avenger of the betrayed city but the commander of the army of his own country.

XXXIX. (1) [*On the General's Knowledge of the Courses of the Stars*]

In night attacks and surprises of towns through treason, the general must know the heavenly courses

---

⁸ ἑλομένοις v : ἑλλομένοις GH.   ⁹ τρέπονται PGH.
¹⁰ ἡ R.   ¹¹ χαρίζεσθαι R.   ¹² ἐκτείνειν vGH.
¹³ τῆς ἀστρῴου P : τοῦ ἄστρου Schwebel.
¹⁴ Title om. FENR : in margin but mostly illegible in photographs GH.
¹⁵ FENRGH : προδοσία P : προδοσίᾳ Rigaltius " ceteri codd. ut vid."
¹⁶ Schwebel following Camerarius : τῶν πολέμων F : τῶν πολεμίων PGH " ceteri codd. ut vid." Saguntinus.

ONASANDER

ἀπλανῶν, ἐπεὶ πολλάκις ἀπράκτους ἕξει τὰς ἐπι-
2 βολάς.[1] ἔστιν γὰρ ὅτε συντέτακταί τις τῶν
προδοτῶν τρίτην ἢ τετάρτην ἢ ὁπόστην[2] ἄν τις[3]
εὔκαιρον ὥραν νομίζῃ[4] τῆς νυκτός, ἀνοίξειν τὰς
πύλας ἤ τινας κατασφάξειν τῶν ἐπὶ τῆς πόλεως
ἀντιπραττόντων[5] ἢ φρουρᾷ[6] τῶν ἔνδον πολεμίων
ἐπιθήσεσθαι· κἄπειτα δυεῖν[7] θάτερον συμβέβηκεν, ἤτοι[8] θᾶττον ἢ ἔδει προσπελάσαντα[9] τὸν
τῶν πολεμίων στρατὸν[10] κατάφωρον[11] γενέσθαι,
πρὶν ἢ τοὺς προδότας ἑτοίμους εἶναι, καὶ οὕτως
ἀποκωλυθῆναι τῆς πράξεως, ἢ ὑστερήσαντα[12] τοῖς
μὲν προδόταις αἴτιον γενέσθαι θανάτου φωρα-
θεῖσιν, αὐτὸν δὲ μηδὲν τῶν προκειμένων[13] ἀνύσαι.
3 διόπερ χρὴ καὶ[14] τὴν ὁδὸν τεκμαιρόμενον, ὅθεν[15]
ἐξοδεῦσαι δεῖ, καὶ τῶν[16] σταδίων καὶ τῆς ὥρας[17]
στοχαζόμενον, ὅσον[18] εἰς τὴν[19] πορείαν ἀναλώσει,
καὶ ἀπὸ τῶν ἄστρων ὁρῶντα,[20] πόσον[19] τὸ παρῳχη-
κὸς ἤδη καὶ πόσον τὸ ἀπολειπόμενον μέρος, οὕτως
ἀκριβῶς συλλογισάμενον,[21] ἵνα μήτε φθάσῃ μήτε
βραδύνῃ, πρὸς αὐτὴν ἥκειν τὴν ὥραν τοῦ συν-
τεταγμένου καιροῦ καὶ ἔτι προσιόντα[22] ἀκούεσθαι
καὶ ἐντὸς εἶναι τῶν τειχῶν.

[1] ἐπιβουλὰς GH "libri scripti tantum non omnes"
(Schwebel).
[2] ὁποστὴν F (corr. AB) GH: ὅπως τὴν Rigaltius "ceteri
codd. ut vid."
[3] Om. K Koraes.   [4] νομίζει GH.
[5] FGH: ἀντιπαραταττόντων Rigaltius A m² "ceteri codd.
ut vid."
[6] φρουρὰ R.
[7] FCKGH (κἀπὶ v: καπι δυεῖν GH): κἄπειτα δυοῖν Koraes:
κἀπιδυεῖν Rigaltius: κἀπιδυοῖν EN: κἀπὶ δυοῖν R Schwebel.
[8] εἴτε v (εἴτε GH).
[9] προσπεράς R: πρὸς πύλας suggested by Köchly.
500

of the stars by night, otherwise his plans will often be
of no avail. For instance, some traitor has appointed
the third or the fourth, or whatever hour of the night
he considers most favourable, for opening the gates
or slaying some of the opposing faction in the town
or attacking the hostile garrison within the town;
then one of two things has happened; the general
has reached the camp of the enemy too early and
has been detected before the traitors are ready
and has been thwarted in his attempt, or else
he has arrived too late and has thus been the
cause of the traitors' being detected and put to
death and of his own failure to accomplish any of
his plans. Accordingly he should form an estimate
of the road, deciding at what point he is to set out;
then he must determine the distance and the time
—how much of each he will have to spend on the
journey;—and, finally, he must, from his observation
of the stars, estimate exactly what part of the night
has passed and what part remains, in order that he
may arrive neither too early nor too late; then he
must get there at precisely the appointed time, so
that news of his attack may not reach the enemy
until he is actually inside the fortifications.

---

[10] τῷ . . . στρατηγῷ vGH.
[11] κατάφορον Fm¹ corr. m².
[12] FR: ὑστερήσαντας GH Rigaltius " ceteri codd. ut vid."
[13] προειρημένων R.   [14] FGR: om. v.
[15] ὅσον vGH: ὅσων K Koraes.
[16] καὶ τῶν added by Köchly.
[17] τὴν ὥραν vGH.   [18] ὅσην vGH.
[19] Om. vGH.   [20] ὁρῶν F.
[21] FC: συλλογισάμενος PGH A m² Rigaltius " ceteri codd.
ut vid."
[22] Köchly: προσιόντας Ω.

β'. [Πῶς ἡμέρας αἱρεῖν χρὴ πόλιν][1]

4 Εἰ δ' ἡμέρας ἀναστήσας ἄγοι στράτευμα πόλεις ἐκ προδοσίας ληψόμενος κατὰ τὴν συγκειμένην ὥραν, τοὺς κατὰ τὴν ὁδὸν ὑποπίπτοντας ἅπαντας[2] προαποστέλλων ἱππεῖς συλλαμβανέτω, μή τις τῶν ἐπὶ τῆς χώρας φθάσας ἀποδραμὼν μηνύσῃ τὴν ἔφοδον τῶν πολεμίων, ἀλλ' αἰφνιδίως[3] ἀφυλάκτοις ἡ ἐπιφάνεια γένηται[4] τοῦ στρατεύματος. 5 ἐπελθόντα δ' ἐξαίφνης ἀπροσδοκήτοις χρή, κἂν μὴ[5] κατὰ προδοσίαν μέλλῃ[6] λαμβάνειν, ἀλλ' ἐκ προρρήσεως ἀγωνίζεσθαι διὰ μάχης, μὴ ἀναβάλλεσθαι, ἀλλ' ὡς ὅτι μάλιστα φθάνειν προσβάλλοντα[7] εἴτε φρουρίῳ εἴτε χάρακι εἴτε πόλει, μάλιστα δ' ὅτ' ἂν ὀλίγον εἶναι δοκῇ[8] τὸ φίλιον 6 στράτευμα καὶ τῶν ἐχθρῶν ἐλαττούμενον· αἱ γὰρ[9] ἀπόληπτοι[10] τῶν πολεμίων ἐπιφάνειαι διὰ τὸ παράλογον ἐκπλήττουσι τοὺς ἐναντίους, κἂν ὦσι κρείττους, ἕως,[11] ἄν γε συνθεωρήσωσιν[12] αὐτοὺς[13] καὶ βουλεύσασθαι καὶ ἀναθαρρῆσαι καιρὸν λάβωσι, κατὰ μικρὸν ἀναγκάζονται καταφρονεῖν· οὕτως ἐνίοτε τὰ πρῶτα καὶ ἀρχόμενα φοβερώτερα τῶν 7 χρονιζομένων εἶναι δοκεῖ. διὸ πολλάκις ἤδη τινὲς τῷ παραδόξῳ τῆς ἐπιφανείας καταπληξάμενοι τοὺς ἐναντίους ἢ ταχὺ καὶ ἄκοντας ὑπέταξαν[14] ἢ ποιεῖν ἑκόντας ἠνάγκασαν τὰ προσταττόμενα.

---

[1] Koraes without ms. authority: Saguntinus alone indicates a heading with the words "De urbe interdiu occupanda."   [2] Om. R.
[3] αἰφνιδίοις F : Köchly suggests αἰφνίδιος.
[4] γίγνηται vGH.   [5] κἂν μὴ om. F.   [6] μέλλει GH.

(2) [*How to capture a City by Day*]

If setting out by day, he lead his army to capture at an appointed hour towns that are to be betrayed, he should send horsemen ahead to seize every one met on the road, that no native of the country may run ahead and warn of the approach of their enemy but that the army may appear suddenly to the enemy and catch him off his guard. He must fall unexpectedly on an unsuspecting enemy, even if he is not expecting to seize the towns through treachery but to fight openly after a declaration of war, and he must not hesitate but strive in every way to attack fort or camp or town before his advance is known, especially if he knows that his own army is small and inferior to that of the enemy. For unexpected appearances of an enemy, because they are unforeseen, terrify their opponents, even should the latter be stronger; but at length, if those who have been taken by surprise should observe their own forces or get the chance to plan and renew their courage, they gradually and of necessity come to despise their foes; in this way the beginning of a war sometimes seems more terrible than the latter part. On this account, armies have often so terrified their opponents by the unexpectedness of their appearance that they have either quickly subdued them against their will or else have forced them to agree to comply with their own demands.

---

⁷ προβάλλειν τα Γ : προβάλλοντα P.   ⁸ δοκεῖ GHR.
          ⁹ αἵ γε F.   ¹⁰ ἀπρόσληπτοι vGH.
    ¹¹ ὡς vGH.   ¹² συνθεωρήσουσιν PGH.
    ¹³ Köchly : αὐτοὺς Ω.   ¹⁴ ὑπέταξεν PGH

XL. [Περὶ πολιορκίας][1]

Πολιορκία δὲ στρατιωτῶν[2] ἀνδρίαν[3] ἐπιζητεῖ
καὶ στρατηγικὴν ἐπίνοιαν καὶ μηχανημάτων παρα-
σκευήν· ἀσφαλὴς μέντοι καὶ μὴ ἧττον ἀπρο-
όρατος τῶν πολιορκουμένων ἔστω· τὸ γὰρ ἐπιβουλευόμενον, ὅτ' ἂν οἷ[4] κακοῦ τυγχάνει γινώσκῃ,
2 τηρεῖ μᾶλλον τὸ ἐπιβουλεῦον·[5] ὁ μὲν[6] γὰρ ἔξω
κινδύνου δοκῶν εἶναι πράττει τι τῶν προκειμένων,
ὁπότ' ἂν αὐτῷ[7] δόξῃ,[8] ὁ δ' ἐν αὐτῷ τῷ κινδυνεύειν[9] ὑπάρχων ζητεῖ φθάσας[10] δρᾶσαι,[11] ὁπότ' ἂν
καιρὸν λάβῃ· διὸ χρὴ τὸν πολιορκοῦντα καὶ τάφρῳ
καὶ χάρακι καὶ φυλακαῖς τὸ ἴδιον ἀσφαλίζεσθαι
3 στρατόπεδον. καὶ γὰρ οἱ μὲν πολιορκοῦντες, ὅ
τι ἂν μέλλωσι πράττειν, ὁρῶνται τοῖς ἀπὸ τοῦ
τείχους, οἱ δὲ πολιορκούμενοι πρόβλημα τὸ τεῖχος
ἔχοντες ἀόρατοι πολλάκις ἐκχυθέντες διὰ πυλῶν
ἢ μηχανὰς ἐνέπρησαν ἢ στρατιώτας ἐφόνευσαν ἤ,
ὅ τι κατὰ χεῖράς σφισιν εἴη, τοῦτο ἐποίησαν.

XLI. [Περὶ τοῦ ἔχειν ἐνέδρας τὸν πολιορκοῦντα
πρὸ τῶν πυλῶν][12]

Ἥκιστα δ' ἂν τοῦτο τολμήσαιεν,[13] εἰ παρὰ
πύλαις[14] καὶ πυλίσι μικραῖς λόχους ὁ πολιορκῶν

---

[1] Om. F without indication of break ENRM (G imperfect
here) Camerarius: in margin H (margin of G patched)
without indication of break.
[2] Köchly: στρατηγῶν Ω.   [3] ἀνδρείαν GH.
[4] FGH: εἰ EN: δ, τι R.
[5] ἐπιβουλευόμενον DPG HA m² Rigaltius "ceteri codd. ut
vid.": ἐπιβουλεῦον G m².

XL. [*Sieges*]

A siege demands courage on the part of the soldiers, military science on the part of the general, and equipment of machines of war. The general must take no fewer precautions and be no less observant than the enemy ; for the army attacked, when it knows just what its danger is, guards especially against the army attacking. The army that believes itself out of danger does what work is at hand when it pleases, but that which is in danger strives to surprise its enemy by dealing him a blow whenever it has an opportunity. Hence it is necessary for the besieging general to fortify his camp with trenches, palisades, and guards. For whatever the besiegers intend to do can be seen from the walls ; but the besieged, with the wall as a shield, often without detection pour through the gates and burn the machines or kill the soldiers or do whatever damage comes to their hands.

XLI. [*Ambush laid by the Besieger before the Gates of a Town*]

The besieged would by no means attempt this if the besieging general should post at both large and

⁶ ὁ μὲν om. DPGHA m² Rigaltius "ceteri codd. ut vid."
⁷ αὐτὸ R.   ⁸ δόξει PGH.
⁹ τὸ κινδυνεῦον R.   ¹⁰ Köchly : φθάσαι Ω.
¹¹ FPGH (δράσαι GH): καί τι δράσαι v : ἢ δράσαι K : δράσαί τι Köchly.
¹² Title om. F : without indication of break AENR Saguntinus Camerarius : in margin without break GH.
¹³ τολμήσειν R (τολμήσειεν A m²).
¹⁴ ταῖς πύλαις vGH.

προκαθίσῃ[1] στρατηγὸς τοὺς τὰς αἰφνιδίους ἐκ-
δρομὰς τῶν πολεμίων[2] ἀποκωλύσοντας, ἐπεὶ κἂν
2 πολλάκις λάθοιεν ἐπιθέμενοι τοῖς ἐκτός. χρήσιμοι
δὲ τὰ πολλὰ νύκτωρ τοῖς πολιορκοῦσιν αἱ προσ-
βολαί· τοῖς γὰρ ἔνδον οὐ δυναμένοις ὁρᾶν τὰ
γιγνόμενα[3] διὰ τὸ σκότος δεινότερα δοκεῖ τὰ
πραττόμενα, καὶ τὴν πρόληψιν ἀναγκάζονται χαλε-
πωτέραν ἔχειν τῶν κατὰ ἀλήθειαν ἐνεργουμένων,
ὅθεν ταραχαί τε[4] καὶ θόρυβοι γίγνονται οὐδενὸς[5]
δυναμένου σωφρονεῖν ἐν τοῖς τοιούτοις, ἀλλὰ καὶ
πολλὰ τῶν οὐ δρωμένων ὡς γίγνεται[6] λεγόντων, οὔθ'
ὅπῃ[7] προσβαλοῦσιν[8] εἰδέναι δυναμένων, οὔθ' ὁπόσοι,[9]
οὔθ' ὁποίοις μέρεσι,[10] διαδρομαὶ δὲ δεῦρο κἀκεῖσε
καὶ βοαὶ καὶ θάμβη Πανικὸν ἔχοντα τάραχον.

XLII. α'. [Περὶ τοῦ ὅτι ὁ[11] φόβος ψευδὴς μάντις[12]
ἐστίν][13]

Ὁ γὰρ φόβος ψευδὴς μάντις, ἃ δέδοικε, ταῦτ'
οἰήσεται καὶ γίγνεσθαι, καὶ πᾶν τὸ ἐν νυκτί, κἂν
μικρὸν ᾖ, φοβερώτερον τοῖς πολιορκουμένοις·
οὐδεὶς γάρ, ὃ βλέπει, λέγει διὰ τὸ σκότος, ἀλλὰ
πᾶς, ὃ ἀκούει· καὶ ἑνός που φανέντος ἢ δυεῖν[14] ἐπὶ
τείχους πολεμίων τὸ πᾶν ἤδη στράτευμα τῶν
τειχῶν ἐπιβεβηκέναι δόξαντες ἀπετράπησαν,[15] ἐρή-
μους καταλιπόντες ἐπάλξεις καὶ πύλας.[16]

---

[1] προκαθίσας F.
[2] F: πόλεων PGH—nothing known about other mss.
[3] γινόμενα GH.   [4] Om. vGH.   [5] μηδενὸς von Rohden.
[6] γίνεσθαι (om. ὡς) v: γίγνεσθαι (om. ὡς) GH Koraes.
[7] GH (οὔθ' ὅπη): οὐ τὸ πῆ F: οὔθ' ὅτη P: οὔθ' ὅτι Rigaltius
"alii codd. ut vid."
[8] προσβάλλουσιν P Rigaltius "alii codd. ut vid.": πρὸς
βάλλουσιν GH.

small gates companies of soldiers to prevent sudden sallies, since otherwise the defenders might without warning attack the besiegers. Attacks by night are generally advantageous to the besiegers, since the besieged are unable to see what is happening, on account of the darkness, and everything seems more terrible to them, and they are compelled to regard the attack as more dangerous than it really is. Hence tumult and confusion arise ; no one is able to use sober judgement in such circumstances, but many things that are not happening are said to be happening ; and the besieged is not able to know from what direction the enemy is attacking, nor in what numbers, nor with what forces, and men run hither and thither, while the shouting and consternation cause disorder and panic.

XLII. (1) [*Fear is a false Prophet*]

Fear is a false prophet and believes that what it fears is actually coming to pass. At night every trifling occurrence seems more terrible to the besieged, for on account of the darkness no man tells what he sees but always what he hears. If one or two of the enemy appear somewhere on the walls, the defenders, believing that the whole army has already mounted the walls, turn and flee, leaving the battlements and gates undefended.

---

9 ὡς . . . ὁπόσοι om. R Camerarius : οὔθ' ὁπόσοι om. vGH.
10 Köchly : κλίμασι Fv : κλίμασιν GH : κλήμασι EKN : κλίμαξι Saguntinus.   11 Om. Köchly.   12 μάντης A.
13 Title om. FPVGH : without indication of even a break FGH.   14 δυοῖν v : δοιεῖν GH.
15 ἀνετράπησαν vGH.   16 FC : πόλεις vG : πόλις H.

β'. ["Οτι αὐτὸν χρὴ παράδειγμα τὸν στρατηγὸν
γίγνεσθαι τοῖς στρατιώταις][1]

2 Εἰ δέ τι διὰ χειρὸς ὁ στρατηγὸς ἐξεργάσασθαι
σπεύδοι, μὴ ὀκνείτω[2] πρῶτος αὐτὸς ὀφθῆναι
ποιῶν· οὐ γὰρ οὕτως ταῖς ἀπὸ τῶν κρειττόνων
ἀπειλαῖς ἀναγκαζόμενοί τι ποιοῦσιν, ὡς ταῖς ἀπὸ
τῶν σεμνοτέρων διατροπαῖς· ἰδὼν γάρ[3] τις τὸν
ἡγεμόνα πρῶτον ἐγχειροῦντα καὶ ὅτι δεῖ σπεύδειν
ἔμαθε[4] καὶ μὴ ποιεῖν ἠδέσθη[5] καὶ ἀπειθεῖν ἐφο-
βήθη· καὶ οὐκ ἔθ' ὡς δοῦλον ἐπιταττόμενον
διετέθη τὸ πλῆθος, ἀλλ' ὡς ἐξ ἴσου[6] παρακαλού-
μενον διετράπη.

γ'. [Περὶ πολιορκητηρίων μηχανημάτων][7]

3 Πολλῶν δὲ καὶ ποικίλων ἐκ τῶν μηχανῶν[8]
πολιορκητηρίων χρήσεται κατὰ δύναμιν[9] ὁ στρατηγός. οὐ γὰρ ἐπ' ἐμοὶ τὸ λέγειν,[10] ὅτι δεῖ
κριοὺς ἔχειν[11] ἤ[12] ἐλεπόλεις ἢ σαμβύκας ἢ
πύργους ὑποτρόχους[13] ἢ χελώνας χωστρίδας ἢ
καταπέλτας· τῆς γὰρ τῶν πολεμούντων τύχης
καὶ πλούτου καὶ δυνάμεως ἴδια ταῦτα καὶ τῆς[14]
τῶν ἑπομένων ἀρχιτεκτόνων[15] ἐπινοίας[16] εἰς τὰς

---

[1] Koraes apparently without MS. authority: FGH do not
indicate even a break (the same holds for all the sub-titles
in Ch. xlii.): "Imperator suo exemplo milites provocat"
Rigaltius Schwebel.
[2] FC: μὴ om. vGH: κινείτω vGH: κινεῖτο A m².
[3] δέ vGH.   [4] ἔμασθαι A m².
[5] ἠδέσθαι RA m².   [6] ἐπίσου vGH: ἐπίσον A m².
[7] Koraes (see on sub-title to § 2): "De machinis ad op-
pugnationem" Rigaltius Schwebel.

(2) [*The General must set a good Example to his Soldiers*]

If the general is in haste to finish some enterprise that he has on hand, he should not hesitate to be prominent in the work, for soldiers are not forced to activity so much by the threats of their immediate superiors as by the influence of men of higher rank. For a soldier seeing his officer the first to put his hand to the task not only realizes the need of haste too but also is ashamed not to work, and afraid to disobey orders; and the rank and file no longer feel that they are being treated as slaves under orders but are moved as though urged by one on the same footing as themselves.

(3) [*Siege Engines*]

Of the many and various siege engines the general will make use according as he has opportunity. It is not my part to say that he must use battering rams or 'city-destroyers' or the *sambuca*,[1] or wheeled towers or covered sheds or catapults; all this depends upon the luck, the wealth, and the power of the combatants, and upon the skill of the workmen who accompany the army for the purpose

[1] An arrangement for lowering a bridge from a movable tower to the walls of a city. Its name was derived from its similarity to the triangular four-stringed musical instrument.

---

[8] ὄντων μηχανημάτων vGH.

[9] τοῖς κατὰ δύναμιν vGH.

[10] Om. R.   [11] C: om. FvPGH.   [12] καὶ vGH.

[13] ἢ ὑποτρόχους GHENP "alii codd. ut vid."

[14] FGH: τοῖς Rigaltius "et alii codd. ut vid."

[15] ἀρχιτεκτονιῶν PGH: ἀρχιτεκτονικῶν v.   [16] ἐπινοίαθ' F.

509

ONASANDER

4 ὀργανικὰς κατασκευάς.¹ στρατηγοῦ δ' ἰδίας
ἀγχινοίας ἔργον τοιόνδε² ἂν εἴη, εἰ¹³ βούλοιτο
προσβάλλειν⁴ μηχανάς· καθ' ἓν μὲν ἀποχρήσθω
μέρος τοῖς ἔργοις αὐτοῖς—οὐδὲ γὰρ ἄλλως⁵ ἄν τις
εὐπορήσειεν ἐν⁶ κύκλῳ παντὶ τῷ τείχει περι-
στῆσαι μηχανάς,⁷ εἰ μὴ πάνυ μικρὰ πόλις εἴη—,
εἰς πολλὰ δὲ τάγματα διελὼν τὸ στράτευμα κατὰ
τὰ ἄλλα⁸ τοῦ τείχους μέρη κελευέτω τὰς κλίμακας
προσφέρειν· οὕτως γὰρ εἰς ἀμηχανίαν οἱ πολιορ-
5 κούμενοι πολλὴν ἐμπίπτουσιν· ἄν τε γὰρ ἀμελήσαντες τῶν ἄλλων μερῶν τοῦ τείχους ἐπὶ τὰς
προσβολὰς⁹ τῶν μηχανῶν ἀμύνωσιν, ἅπαντες οἱ
κατὰ τὰς κλίμακας μηδενὸς ἀποκωλύοντος ῥᾳδίως
ἐπιβαίνουσι τῶν τειχῶν, ἄν τε διελόντες σφᾶ·
αὐτοὺς ἐπιβοηθήσωσι¹⁰ κατὰ μέρη, σφοδροτέρας
ἐνεργείας γιγνομένης κατὰ τὰς ἐμβολὰς τῶν
ὀργάνων οἱ καταλειφθέντες¹¹ οὐδὲ¹² μάχεσθαι τούτοις τολμήσαντες¹³ ἀδυνατήσουσι τὸ ἐπιφερόμενον
6 κακὸν ἀποκρούεσθαι. διόπερ καθάπερ¹⁴ ἀγαθὸν
παλαιστὴν¹⁵ προδεικνύειν μὲν καὶ¹⁶ σκιάζειν¹⁷ εἰς
πολλὰ μέρη δεῖ περισπῶντα καὶ ἐπισφάλλοντα¹⁸
δεῦρο κἀκεῖσε¹⁹ πρὸς πολλὰ τοὺς ἀντιπάλους, ἑνὸς
δὲ ζητεῖν ἐγκρατῶς λαβόμενον ἀνατρέψαι²⁰ τὸ πᾶν²¹
σῶμα τῆς πόλεως.

---

¹ F indicates a break here.
² τοιόνδ' Köchly.　　　³ εἴγε vGH.
⁴ προβάλλειν GH A m² Rigaltius and mss. "tantum non omnes" (Schwebel).
⁵ FR: ἄλλος PGH Rigaltius "ceteri codd. ut vid."
⁶ Köchly: εὐπορήσει ἐν F: εὐπορήσειεν GH: εὐπορήσειε v: ἀπορήσειε R.
⁷ περιστῆναι μηχαναῖς GHP "alii codd. ut vid.": περιθεῖναι μηχαναῖς A m²: περιθῆναι μηχαναῖς DENR.
510

of building engines. The task of a general's peculiar skill, if he wishes to employ engines, is to use them at some one locality—for he would not have a sufficient supply of engines to place them in a circle completely about the wall unless the city were very small,— and, dividing his army into many parts, he should [station his engines at certain points and should] command his men to bring forward their ladders against the other parts of the wall, since in this manner the besieged are rendered helpless. For if the besieged disregard the other parts of the wall and only make a defence against the attacks of the engines, all the besiegers who attack with ladders will easily climb over the wall without opposition, but if the defenders divide their forces and send aid to each part as the battle grows more violent through the attack of these engines, those who are left and who do not venture to fight with them will be unable to repel the advancing menace. On this account, just as a good wrestler, the general must make feints and threats at many points, worrying and deceiving his opponents, here and there, at many places, striving, by securing a firm hold upon one part, to overturn the whole structure of the city.

---

[8] Köchly (except that he read τἄλλα): καὶ κατὰ τὰ ἄλλα FC: καὶ τὰ ἄλλα PGH Rigaltius "ceteri codd. ut vid."

[9] προβολὰς FGHR.   [10] ἐπί τι βοηθήσωσι vGH.

[11] καταληφθέντας F.   [12] ὧδε vGH.

[13] Supplied by Köchly, who suggests also θαρροῦντες.

[14] ὡς v: om. PGH.   [15] παλαιστεῖν H.

[16] Om. P.   [17] FCDGH: σκευάζειν v: σκεδάζειν Koraes.

[18] περισφάλλοντα Koraes.   [19] κακεῖσαι GH.

[20] FD: ἀναστρέψαι PGH Rigaltius Schwebel "ceteri codd. ut vid."   [21] FGH: om. v: πᾶν τὸ Koraes.

δ΄. [Πῶς χρὴ διατελεῖν ἐπείγοντα τὰ τῆς
πολιορκίας]¹

7 Εἰ δ᾽ ἐν τάχει σπεύδοι² τις ἐξελεῖν φρούριον ἢ
πόλιν ἢ χάρακα καὶ αὐτῷ κάμνοι ἡ δύναμις³ μηδὲ
μίαν ὥραν ἀποστῆναι βουλομένῳ τῶν ἐρυμάτων,
εἰς τάγματα διελὼν τὸ στράτευμα, ὅσ᾽⁴ ἂν ἱκανὰ
εἶναί οἱ⁵ δοκῇ κατὰ τὴν ἀναλογίαν τοῦ⁶ πλήθους
καὶ κατὰ τὸ μέγεθος τῆς πολιορκουμένης πόλεως,
νυκτὸς ἀρξάμενος εὐθὺς τῷ μὲν πρώτῳ προσβαλ-
λέτω⁷ τάγματι τῷ δευτέρῳ κελεύσας⁸ ἐφεδρεύειν
καὶ ἑτοίμῳ⁹ εἶναι, τῷ δὲ τρίτῳ καὶ τετάρτῳ, καὶ
εἰ τύχοι πέμπτον ὄν, παραγγελλέτω¹⁰ τρέπεσθαι
8 κατὰ κοῖτον· εἶτα, ὅταν τῷ πρώτῳ καταπειράσῃ¹¹
τινὰ χρόνον, τούτους μὲν ἀνακαλεσάμενος ἀποπεμ-
πέτω κοιμησομένους, σημαινέτω δὲ τῷ δευτέρῳ
προϊέναι τοῦ χάρακος, ὁ δὲ τρίτος ταγματάρχης
ἀναστήσας ἐν τούτῳ καθοπλιζέτω τὸ ὑφ᾽ ἑαυτὸν
9 τάγμα· καὶ μετὰ¹² τοὺς δευτέρους τὴν ἴσην ὥραν
τοῖς πρώτοις ἀγωνίζεσθαι¹³ ἄξει¹⁴ τὸ τρίτον, κοι-
μάσθω¹⁵ δὲ τὸ δεύτερον τάγμα,¹⁶ μετὰ τοῦτο δ᾽ αὖ
τὸ¹⁷ τέταρτον, εἶθ᾽ ἑξῆς τὸ πέμπτον, ἐν μέρει τῶν
10 στρατιωτῶν ἀναπαυομένων. ὁμοίως δ᾽ ἐπισυν-
απτούσης τῆς ἡμέρας οἱ πρῶτοι τῇ νυκτὶ προσ-
βαλόντες¹⁸ ἕωθεν πάλιν πρῶτοι¹⁹ προσαγόντων· εἶθ᾽
ὥρας,²⁰ εἰ μὲν ἐξ εἴη τάγματα, δύο κινδυνεύσαντες,
εἰ δὲ πέντε, δυσὶν²¹ ἔτι μικρὸν ἐπιθέντες, εἰ δὲ

¹ See note on title before § 2: "Quomodo oppugnatio
acriter urgendo continuari possit " Rigaltius Schwebel.
² FGH: σπεύδει v.   ³ ἡ δύναμις αὐτῷ κάμνοι von Rohden.
⁴ Koraes, comparing Leo, *Tactica*, xv. 16: ὅτ᾽ Ω.
⁵ ἱκανὰ εἶ | ναίοι F corr. B: om. οἱ vGH.   ⁶ αὐτοῦ A m².
⁷ προβαλλέτω vGH Rigaltius A m² " ceteri codd. ut vid."

(4) [On ending Sieges by vigorous Action]

If a general desire quickly to capture a fort or
city or camp and his force grow weary, while he
wishes not to spare one hour from attacking the
defences, he should split his army into divisions, as
many as he considers sufficient, according to the
number of his men and the extent of the besieged
city, and then he should attack immediately at
nightfall with the first division, ordering the second
to remain near in readiness, but the third and fourth
and fifth, if there chance to be a fifth, he should order
to sleep. Then when the first division has attacked
for some time, he should recall it and send it to its
quarters to sleep, but he should give the signal to
the second division to march out from the camp;
at this point the commander of the third division
should arouse and arm his troops. After the second
division has fought as long a time as the first, he will
lead out his third division and order the second to
rest; after this the fourth, then in order the fifth,
while the soldiers in turn rest from fighting. Thus,
at daybreak, those who attacked first at night should
again attack first at dawn, remaining at the front
two hours, if there are six divisions, but a little
longer if five; three hours if four divisions, and four

---

⁸ κελεῦσαι F.   ⁹ τὸ δεύτερον . . . ἕτοιμον von Rohden.
¹⁰ παραγγελέτω GH.   ¹¹ κατὰ πείρας ἢ F.
¹² μετὰ τὸ vGH.   ¹³ ἀγωνίσασθαι Koraes.
¹⁴ ἕξει F : τάξει von Rohden.
¹⁵ κοιμᾶσθαι vGH.   ¹⁶ Om. FGH.
¹⁷ δ' αὐτὸ F : δὲ αὖ τὸ vGH.   ¹⁸ προσβάλλοντες vGH.
¹⁹ πρῶτοι πάλιν vGH (πρῶτοι GH) : τῇ νυκτὶ . . . πρῶτοι
om. R Camerarius.
²⁰ ὁρᾷς F.   ²¹ δυοῖν v : δοιεῖν GH.

τέτταρα,[1] τρεῖς, εἰ δὲ τρία,[2] τέτταρας,[3] ἀπιόντες ἀριστοποιείσθων,[4] ἑξῆς δ' οἱ μετ' αὐτοὺς καὶ πάλιν οἱ μετὰ τούτους ἄχρι τῶν τελευταίων, ὥστε
11 κύκλον[5] τινὰ περιάγεσθαι. τούτου γὰρ συμβαίνοντος ἀμφότερα ἂν γίγνοιτο· καὶ αἱ[6] προσβολαὶ καὶ νύκτωρ καὶ μεθ' ἡμέραν ἀδιάλειπτοι προσαχθήσονται, καὶ οἱ προσβάλλοντες ἀκμῆτες καὶ νεαροὶ τὰς ἀναπαύσεις ἐν μέρει ποιούμενοι
12 μαχοῦνται. τοὺς μέντοι πολιορκουμένους, μηδ' ἂν πάνυ πολλοὶ τυγχάνωσιν,[7] οἰέσθω τις τὸ αὐτὸ στρατήγημα ἀντεισοίσεσθαι·[8] τὸ γὰρ κινδυνεῦον, οὐδ' ἂν ἐπιτρέπῃ τις, ὕπνῳ χαρίζεσθαι[9] βούλεται· φόβῳ γὰρ τοῦ δεινοῦ, παρ' ὃν ἀναπαύεται χρόνον, ὡς[10] ἁλωσομένης τῆς[11] πόλεως ἐγρήγορε· καὶ τὸ πολιορκούμενον, κἂν[12] ὀλίγον ᾖ τὸ πολιορκοῦν αὐτό, πασσυδὶ[13] προσαμύνει, καὶ πᾶν ὅσον ἐντειχίδιόν ἐστι κεκίνηται, ὅτι καὶ τὸ μέλλον φοβερώτερον, ὡς, εἰ[14] παρὰ μικρὸν ἀμελήσαιεν, ἀπο-
13 λούμενοι πάντες. ὅθεν δὴ[15] πᾶσα ἀνάγκη τρυχομένους αὐτοὺς καὶ μηδὲ μίαν ὥραν ἀνάπαυλαν ἴσχοντας, ἀλλὰ καὶ[16] ἀγρυπνίαις[17] καὶ πόνοις κάμνοντας, εἶτα καὶ πρὸς τὰ[18] μέλλοντα τεταλαιπωρηκότας[19] ἀσθενέστερον τοῖς σφετέροις προσαμύνειν ἢ τοὺς δεησομένους καὶ παραδώσοντας τὴν πόλιν ἐκπέμπειν.

[1] τέτρα GH.   [2] FGH: τρεῖς v.   [3] τέτταρες R.
[4] ἀριστοποιείσθωσαν vGH.
[5] FCR: κύκλῳ vGH (κύκλω GH): κύκλῳ τινὶ Schwebel Koraes.   [6] FGH: om. v.   [7] τυγχάνουσι P: -σιν GH.
[8] τῷ αὐτῷ στρατηγήματι ἀντιτάσσεσθαι vGHA m[2].

hours if three divisions ; on their return they should
receive their rations in order, the first division, then
the second, and so on to the last, like the revolution
of a wheel. With this plan, there are two results :
unceasing attacks by night and day, while the
attackers, taking their turns at rest, will fight
freshly and vigorously. But no one should believe
that the besieged, even if very numerous, could use
this same stratagem, for in danger no one would
wish to enjoy sleep even if it were permitted, since
from fear of peril, during the time at which one is
resting, he lies sleepless, as though the city were on
the point of capture. The besieged, moreover, even
if their assailants are few, defend themselves with
all their strength, and everything within the walls
of the city is in a state of excitement, in even greater
terror of the future, as though if one minute detail
were overlooked, they would all be lost. On this
account there is every reason why men wearied,
without an hour's rest, tired by guard-duty and
labour, and fearful for the future, should defend
themselves more weakly, or should send out
messengers to discuss the surrender of the city.

---

⁹ Om. τὸ γὰρ . . . χαρίζεσθαι H.
¹⁰ Om. F.   ¹¹ Om. vGH.
¹² καὶ PA m².   ¹³ πάσῃ σπουδῇ v (πάσῃ σπουδῇ GH).
¹⁴ ὡσεί R.   ¹⁵ δεῖ PGH Rigaltius " alii codd. ut vid."
¹⁶ καὶ γ' F.   ¹⁷ ἀγρυπνοίαις GH.
¹⁸ Köchly : εἰ καὶ τὰ πρὸς τὰ F : ἢ καὶ πρὸς τὰ vGH (εἶτα
προς τὰ B).
¹⁹ τεταλεπωρηκότας G : -κότάς H.

ε′. [Πῶς χρὴ τὸν στρατηγὸν ἀναπαύεσθαι][1]

14 Αὐτὸς οὖν ὁ στρατηγός, ἴσως φήσει τις,[2] ἐξ
ἀδάμαντος ἢ σιδήρου κεχάλκευται μόνος ἄγρυπνος ἑστὼς[3] ἐπὶ τοῖς αὐτοῖς ἔργοις[4]; οὐ δῆτα·
ἀλλὰ παρ᾽ ὃν ἀναπαύεται χρόνον — οὗτος[5] δ᾽
ὀλίγος[6] ἔστω καὶ σύντομος[7] —, ἕνα τῶν[8] ἐν δόξῃ
πιστοτάτων καὶ ἀνδρειοτάτων ἡγεμόνα[9] τῶν καὶ
τὰ δεύτερα τῆς στρατηγικῆς ἀρχῆς ἐχόντων
ἐπιστησάτω τοῖς ἔργοις.[10]

ϛ′. [Πῶς τὰ δοκοῦντα τῆς πόλεως μέρη ἀνάλωτα
εἶναι πολλάκις εὐάλωτα γίγνεται][11]

15 Ἐνίοτε δὲ τὰ δοκοῦντα μέρη πόλεως[12] εἶναι
κρημνώδη καὶ πέτραις ἀποτόμοις ὠχυρωμένα[13]
τῶν διὰ χειρὸς ἀνεστηκότων τειχῶν[14] ἔδωκε τοῖς
πολιορκοῦσιν ἀφορμὰς μείζονας[15] εἰς τὸ νικᾶν·
εἴωθεν γάρ πως ὡς τὰ πολλὰ τὰ τοιαῦτα[16] τῶν
πόλεων, ὅσα φύσει πιστεύεται τὸ ἐρυμνόν, ἀφυλα-
κτεῖσθαι καὶ ἥκιστα φροντίδι παραγυρυπνεῖσθαι
16 στρατιωτῶν.[17] ἔνθα στρατηγὸς ἀγαθὸς ἐνόησεν
ὃ δεῖ[18] ποιῆσαι, καί τινας τῶν εὐτολμοτάτων[19]
παρακαλέσας ἐπαγγελίαις καὶ τιμαῖς ὀλίγους,[20] οἷς

---

[1] See note on title before § 2: "Quo pacto imperator
quiescere a laboribus aliquando possit" Rigaltius Schwebel.
[2] τίς corr. τινὲς (?) G.   [3] ἔστω vGH.
[4] καὶ μόνος ἄγρυπνος ἔσται ἐπὶ τοσούτοις ἔργοις Koraes.
[5] οὕτως F.   [6] ὁ λόγος RA m².
[7] οὐ . . . σύντομος om. Camerarius.
[8] ἐν αὐτῷ· F: ἕνα τῶν αὐτῷ Köchly suggests.
[9] ἡγεμόνων vGH.   [10] τοῖς ἔργοις ἐνίοτε δὲ κτλ. F.

(5) [*How the General should rest*]

" But has the general himself, then," some one may perhaps say, " been made of adamant or iron to have remained alone without sleep throughout all these deeds ? " Certainly not ; but during the time that he sleeps—and this must be little and cut short— he should hand over the command of the army to one of his most trusted and courageous officers, who is also second only to himself in military rank.

(6) [*Parts of a City seemingly most impregnable are often easy to capture*]

Sometimes those parts of a city that seem pre- cipitous and are fortified by the sheer rocky cliffs, offer the besiegers greater chances for victory than do fortresses erected by human hands, for those places whose fortification relies upon natural strength are wont to be less carefully watched and guarded by soldiers. Then the wise general considers what he must do, and encouraging a few of his bravest soldiers with promise of reward, men who are best

---

[11] See note on title before § 2: " Loca quae obsessi inaccessa existimant obsidentibus saepenumero prodesse," Rigaltius Schwebel.   [12] τῆς πόλεως vGH.

[13] ὀχυρώτερα vGH (ὀχ- GH).

[14] F indicates a break here.   [15] μείζους vGH Köchly.

[16] FC : ποιοῦντα ENPGH Rigaltius " ceteri codd. ut vid."

[17] παραγνυπνεῖσθαι στρατειωτῶν H.

[18] FENR : δὴ GH Rigaltius " ceteri codd. ut vid."

[19] εὐτολμωτάτων GH.

[20] FGH (ὀλ- GH) : ὀλίγαις ENRA m² Camerarius.

ῥᾷον ἀναβαίνειν[1] εἴτε δι' αὐτῆς τῆς δυσχωρίας,[2] εἴτε διὰ κλιμάκων, ἐκράτησε τῆς πράξεως·[3] ὑποκαταβάντες[4] γὰρ ἐντὸς τείχους[5] ἢ πυλίδα διέκοψαν ἢ πύλην ἀνέῳξαν.

ζ'. [Περὶ τῆς ἀπὸ τῶν σαλπίγγων ὠφελείας][6]

17 Μέγα δ' ἂν ὀνήσειε καί τι[7] τοιόνδε συνεπινοηθέν, εἰ καὶ σαλπιγκτὰς οἱ φθάσαντες ἐπιβῆναι τοῦ τείχους ἀνιμήσαιεν·[8] ἀκουσθεῖσα γὰρ πολεμία σάλπιγξ ἀπὸ τειχῶν ἐν νυκτὶ πολλὴν ἔκπληξιν ἐπιφέρει τοῖς πολιορκουμένοις ὡς ἤδη κατὰ κράτος ἑαλωκόσιν, ὥστε τὰς πύλας καὶ τὰς ἐπάλξεις ἀπολιπόντας φεύγειν· ὅθεν δήπου συμβαίνει γίγνεσθαι τοῖς ἔξω στρατιώταις ῥᾳδίαν τήν τε τῶν πυλῶν ἐκκοπὴν καὶ τὴν ἐπὶ τὰ τείχη διὰ τῶν κλιμάκων ἀνάβασιν, οὐδενὸς ἔτι τῶν πολεμίων ἀπείργοντος· οὕτως που δυνατὸν ἑνὶ καὶ ἀνόπλῳ σαλπιγκτῇ[9] πόλιν ἁλῶναι.

η'. [Τί χρὴ ποιεῖν τὸν στρατηγὸν μετὰ τὸ ἑλεῖν τὴν πόλιν][10]

18 Εἰ δὲ δή τινα ἀκμάζουσαν ἔτι[11] πλήθει τε καὶ δυνάμει πόλιν ἐρρωμένως[12] ἑλὼν εἰς φόβον ἢ ὑπόνοιαν ἥκοι, μή ποτε κατὰ τάγματα καὶ

---

[1] FC: ἅμα βαίνειν ENPGH Rigaltius A m².

[2] F Leo, *Tactica*, xv. 20: διά τινος βιαίας ἀναβάσεως (but a little later Leo uses the expression διὰ τῆς δυσχερείας ἐκείνης): δυσχερείας vGH: δυσχερίας A m².

[3] Köchly suggests πάσης πόλεως.

[4] FGH: ὑποβάντες v.   [5] FGH: τοῦ τείχους v.

able to climb up by using either the natural
unevenness of the ground or else ladders, he accom-
plishes his attempt; for descending stealthily within
the walls they break down a postern or open a gate.

(7) [*The Advantage of Trumpets*]

Some such device as this would be of great
assistance—if those who have succeeded in mounting
the walls draw up trumpets after them. For a
hostile trumpet heard at night from the walls brings
great terror to the besieged, as if they had already
been overcome by force, so that abandoning the
gates and fortifications they flee. The result is that
breaking down the gates and mounting the walls
by ladders is easily accomplished by the soldiers on
the outside since no one of the enemy resists any
longer. Thus in some such way it is possible that
one trumpeter, even without arms, can capture a
city.

(8) [*Conduct of a General after the Capture of a City*]

If the general capture by force some city, flourish-
ing in power and in the number of its citizens, and if
he fear or suspect that the inhabitants advancing

---

[6] See note on title before § 2: "Quid valeat tubicinis
opera in expugnatione" Rigaltius Schwebel.

[7] FGH : καί τοι v.

[8] ἀνιμήσαιεν corr. to καθιμήσαιεν (?) by early, perhaps contemporary, hand in F.   [9] σαλπικτῇ GH.

[10] See note on title before § 2: "Quid debeat agere
imperator in urbem expugnatam invadendo" Rigaltius
Schwebel. A break here is indicated in GH.

[11] ἐπὶ v (ἔπι GH)   [12] ἐρρωμένην F.

συστροφὰς ὑπαντιάζοντες ἀμύνωνται[1] τοὺς[2] ἐπ-
εισπίπτοντας[3] ἢ τὰ μετέωρα καταλαμβανόμενοι[4]
καὶ τὰ ἄκρα τῆς πόλεως ἔνθεν ἀντεπίοιεν[5] ἐπὶ
πολὺ κακώσοντες[6] τοὺς πολεμίους, κηρυττέτω
19 τοὺς ἀνόπλους μὴ κτεῖναι. ἕως[7] γὰρ ἕκαστος
ἐλπίζει ληφθεὶς τεθνήξεσθαι, βούλεται φθάνειν
δράσας καὶ πάσχων ἀλλὰ τι[8] καὶ δρᾶν, πολλοί
τε ἤδη πολεμίους εἰσκεχυμένους ἐξήλασαν ἢ καὶ
μὴ[9] δυνηθέντες εἰς ἀκρόπολιν ἐρυμνὴν κατειλή-
θησαν,[10] ἔνθεν αὖθις εἰς πόνον[11] καὶ ταλαιπωρίαν
κατέστησαν[12] τοὺς πολεμίους, ὥστε δευτέραν ἐπ-
αναιρεῖσθαι πολιορκίαν . . .[13] ἢ καὶ πολυχρονιω-
τέραν, ἔστιν δ' ὅτε καὶ ἐπαλγεστέραν μετὰ πολλῆς
20 πείρας κακῶν. εἰ δὲ διαβοηθείη τόδε[14] τὸ κήρυγμα, τάχα μὲν καὶ πάντες, ὡς δὲ πρόδηλον
εἰπεῖν, οἵ γε πλείους τὰ ὅπλα ῥίψουσι· τῶν τε
γὰρ βουλομένων δι' ὀργῆς[15] ἕκαστος εἰς ἄμυναν
ἰέναι δεδιὼς τὸν πέλας, μή ποτε οὐχ ἑαυτῷ[16]
ταῦτα[17] φρονῇ,[18] ῥίπτειν ἀναγκασθήσεται, ὥστε,
κἂν πάντες βούλωνται[19] τὰ ὅπλα φυλάττειν, διὰ
τὴν πρὸς ἀλλήλους ὑπόνοιαν αὐτὸν ἕκαστον δεδιότα,
μὴ μόνος ὡπλισμένος ληφθῇ,[20] σπεύδειν ἀποτι-

---

[1] ἀμύνοιντο vGH : ἀμύνοιτο A m².   [2] τὰς GH : τοῖς A m².
[3] ἐπιπίπτοντας vGH.   [4] καταλαβόμενοι Koraes.
[5] CGH (B): ἀντ' ἐπίοιεν F: ἀντεπίνοιεν P Rigaltius "alii
codd. ut vid.": ἀντεπιτείνοιεν R.
[6] κακώσαντες v (κακώσαντες GH).
[7] Köchly : ὡς F: ὁ ENGH Rigaltius "alii codd. ut vid.":
δ Schwebel Koraes.
[8] ἀλλό τι G: ἄλλό τι HA m²: ἄλλοτι Rigaltius "ceteri
codd. ut vid.": ἄλλο τι Koraes.
[9] Köchly: ἢ μὴ vGH: καὶ μὴ (om. ἢ) F.
[10] FC: κατηλείθησαι GH: κατηυλίσθησαν ENR: κατηλίσθησαν
P Rigaltius "alii codd. ut vid."
520

in companies and crowds may defend themselves against the invaders, or that seizing the heights and the citadel of the town they may advance from there and cause great loss to their opponents, he should command his own soldiers not to slay unarmed men of the enemy. For so long as every man expects to be killed after capture, he wishes first to do some deed of bravery, and even though he suffer, yet to accomplish something, and many inhabitants of towns have driven out enemies even when introduced into the town, or, failing in this, have crowded into the fortified citadel from which they have caused great labour and loss to their adversaries, who must enter into a second . . . and longer siege, one that is sometimes more distressing and attended by great hardships. But if the above-mentioned command should be published, quickly all the inhabitants, or, needless to say, at least the majority, would throw down their arms. For every one who through anger wishes to defend himself, will be compelled to lay down his arms for fear that his neighbour may not be of the same mind, so that even if all should wish to keep their weapons, on account of this suspicion of one another, each one fearing that he alone may be taken with arms on his person,

---

[11] πόσον A m².

[12] Koraes: κατεστήσαντο Ω.

[13] Schwebel noted the lacuna here: καὶ om. K. Koraes suggested that ἢ καὶ be deleted, Köchly suggests οὐχ ἧττονα.

[14] Om. vGH.

[15] εἰς RA m² for δι ὀργῆς.

[16] αὐτῷ v: αὐτῷ GH (ἑαυτῷ F).

[17] ταῦτα Fv: ταυτὰ C: τ' αὐτὰ GH.

[18] Schwebel: φρονεῖ FP "omnes codd. ut vid." (φρονεῖ GH).

[19] βούλονται GH.   [20] ληφθῇ F: λειφθείη vGH.

θέμενον[1] — οἱ γὰρ ὀξεῖς[2] καιροὶ τὴν[3] κοινὴν[4]
γνώμην φανερὰν οὐκ ἐῶσι[5] γίγνεσθαι —, οἵ τε
ἕτοιμοι πρὸς τὸ σῴζεσθαι, μέχρι μὲν οὐδὲν εἰς
ἐλπίδα κεκήρυκται σωτηρίας, εἰ καὶ[6] μὴ γνώμῃ,
ἀλλ᾽[7] ἀνάγκῃ τὸ ἐπιὸν ἀμύνονται κακόν, ἐπειδὰν δὲ μικρὰν ἐλπίδα τοῦ σῴζεσθαι λάβωσιν,
ἱκέται τὸ[8] λοιπὸν ἀντὶ πολεμίων ὑπαντῶσιν.

21 οὕτως τε ὁ μὲν κηρύξας καὶ τοὺς τὰ ὅπλα φυλάττειν βουλομένους ῥίπτειν αὐτὰ ἀναγκάζει[9] στρατιωτῶν δὲ θάνατος ἐν μὲν[3] μάχαις εὐπαραμύθητος[10]
—δοκεῖ γὰρ τοῦ νικᾶν ἕνεκεν γεγονέναι —, ἐν δὲ
νίκαις καὶ καταλήψεσι πόλεων τοῖς νικῶσιν οἴκτι-
στος, ἀφροσύνης τε[11] μᾶλλον[12] ἢ ἀνδρίας[13] μαρ-

22 τύριον[14]· εἰ μέντοι[15] μνησικάκως ἔχοι[16] τοῖς ἡτ-
τημένοις[17] στρατηγός, μὴ παρὰ τούτοις[18] οἴεσθω
τι[19] φέρεσθαι βλάβος,[20] ὅτι τοὺς[21] ἐντυγχάνοντας
μὴ εὐθὺς κτενοῦσι.[22] σχολῇ γὰρ βουλεύσεται
μετὰ τοῦ ἀκινδύνου τὴν ἄμυναν ἀνανταγώνιστον[23]
ἔχων, τί[24] χρὴ διαθεῖναι[25] τοὺς ἑαλωκότας.

[1] Köchly von Rohden: σπευδειν ἀποτιθέμενοι F: σπεύδειν
ἀποτίθεσθαι vGH.

[2] "οἱ γὰρ ὀξεῖς etc.] desunt in LR" Rigaltius. He means
probably οἱ . . . σῴζεσθαι, words which he brackets in the
text. [3] Om. vGH. [4] καινὴν vGH: καὶ τὴν Koraes.

[5] οὐκ ἐῶσι (ἐῶσιν GH) φανερὰν vGH.

[6] κἂν v: κἂν GH for εἰ καί.

[7] Added by Köchly. [8] FGH: om. v.

[9] Köchly: τοὺς ῥίπτειν αὐτὰ βουλομένους φυλάττειν ἀναγκάζει
F: τοὺς τὰ ὅπλα φυλάττειν βουλομένους ῥίπτειν παρασκευάζει
vGH (except βουλομένοις GH).

[10] ἀπαραμύθητος vGH.   [11] Om. KR Koraes.

[12] μάλιστ᾽ R.   [13] ἀνδρείας GH.

hastens to give up his weapons. For a sudden emergency does not give time for the common opinion to become known. And those who are ready to protect their own lives so long as no hope of safety has been announced, strive to avert the imminent danger, if not as they wish, then as they must, but when they perceive a small hope of safety, they become suppliants instead of enemies. Thus this proclamation compels even those who wish to keep their arms to throw them down. The death of soldiers in battle admits of easy consolation, for it seems to have been the price of victory, but in victory and the occupation of cities it is a matter of sorrow to the conquerors, as an evidence of thoughtlessness rather than bravery. If, however, the general is revengeful toward the conquered, he should not think that no harm is done them if his men do not slay on the spot all whom they meet, since at his leisure he will be able to plan in perfect safety his uncontested vengeance and the fate that the conquered must undergo.

---

[14] Koraes : μαρτυρεῖ F : μαρτυρεῖν vGH.
[15] μέν τοι F : γάρ πως v : γάρ τοι GH.   [16] ἔχει vGH.
[17] ἡττωμένοις R.   [18] τοῦτο vGH.   [19] τί F.
[20] βλάβως GH.   [21] τοὺς μὴ F.
[22] κτενοῦσιν Köchly : κτείνουσιν vGH.

[23] ἀμυν ανˌανταγώνιστον F (the correction is probably by the first hand, in Rostagno's opinion): ἄμυναν ἀνανταγώνιστον CP : ἄμυναν ἀνταγώνιστον GH Rigaltius " ceteri codd. ut vid."
[24] ἔχοντι vPA m² GH : ἔχων τί F.
[25] διαθῆναι H : διαθῆναι (?) corr. to διαθεῖναι G.

θ΄. [Τὸν λιμῷ μέλλοντα πόλιν αἱρήσειν τοὺς κατὰ
τὴν χώραν ἀσθενεῖς εἰς αὐτὴν χρὴ πέμπειν][1]

23 Εἰ δὲ τὴν κατὰ κράτος ἀπεγνωκὼς ἐκπόρθησιν
εἰς χρόνιον καταβαίνοι πολιορκίαν οἰόμενος λιμῷ
πιέσας[2] τὴν πόλιν αἱρήσειν, ἅ τινα ἂν ἐπὶ τῆς
χώρας ἔτι[3] καταλάβῃ σώματα, τούτων τὰ μὲν
ἐρρωμένα καὶ ἀκμάζοντα ταῖς ἡλικίαις εἰς ἄμυναν
πολέμου λαβών, ὅ τι περ ἂν αὐτῷ δόξῃ,[4] διαθέσθω,
γύναια δὲ καὶ παιδάρια[5] καὶ ἀσθενεῖς ἀνθρώπους
καὶ γεγηρακότας ἑκὼν[6] εἰς τὴν πόλιν ἀποπεμπέτω·
ταῦτα γὰρ ἄχρηστα μὲν εἰς τὰς πράξεις ἔσται,[7]
τὰς δὲ παρεσκευασμένας[8] τοῖς[9] ἔνδον τροφὰς[10]
θᾶττον συναναλώσει,[11] καὶ πολεμίων μᾶλλον ἢ
φιλίων ἐφέξει[12] τρόπον.[13]

ι΄. [Ὁποῖον εἶναι χρὴ τὸν στρατηγὸν μετὰ
τὴν νίκην][14]

24 Εἰ δέ τῳ[15] πάντα κατὰ δαίμονα καὶ νοῦν
χωρήσειεν, ὥστε τοῖς ὅλοις ἐπιθεῖναι τοῦ πολέμου
πράγμασι τέλος, ἔστω μὴ βαρὺς ἐπὶ ταῖς εὐπραγίαις, ἀλλ᾽ εὔφορτος,[16] μηδὲ τύφον ἀπηνῆ περιφέρων, ἀλλ᾽ εὐμένειαν προσφιλῆ ἔχων· ὁ[17] μὲν[18]

---

[1] See note on title before § 2: "Imbelles captivos remit-
tendos, si fame urbs premenda sit" Rigaltius Schwebel.
[2] Köchly: λιμῷ πιέσαι F: om. πιέσας vGH.
[3] Om. vGH. [4] δόξει GH.
[5] καὶ παιδάρια FPGH: om. v.
[6] ἑλὼν Koraes. [7] Added by Köchly.
[8] εἰς δὲ τὰς παρασκευὰς μόνας F: τὰς παρασκευασμένας: τὰς
παρεσκευασμένας GH Koraes. [9] τοῖς δὲ vGH.
[10] τὰς τροφὰς GH: στροφὰς P Rigaltius "alii codd. ut vid."

(9) [*Necessity of sending Women and Children into a City to capture it by Famine*]

If the general should despair of sacking a city by force and should settle down to a prolonged siege, believing that he will capture the city if he has pressed it hard by famine, he should take prisoners whatever persons are still in the country. Of these, to the men in the prime of life he should assign work on the defences such as seems best to him, but the women and children and feeble men and old people he should send of his own accord into the city. These will be useless in action but will consume more quickly the supplies of the besieged and will serve the purpose of enemies rather than friends.

(10) [*Conduct of the General after Victory*]

If the war should chance to turn out in everything according to the general's desire, so as to put a complete end to the enemy's activity, he should not be overweening in his good fortune, but gracious; he should not show violent stupidity but kindly good-

---

11 συναναλώσει θᾶττον vGH.

12 φίλων ἕξει vGH (ἔξει GH).   13 τόπον Scaliger.

14 See note on title before §2: "Qualis esse debeat imperator parta victoria" Rigaltius Schwebel.

15 αὐτῷ Scaliger.

16 Köchly: ἀλλάφορτος F: ἀλ᾽λἀφυρτος G: ἀλλάφυρτος H: ἀλλ᾽ ἄφυρτος v: ἀλλ᾽ ἄφορτος Koraes.

17 προσφιλῆ· ἐκεῖνος von Rohden.

18 Köchly: ἔχων· ἁμὲν F: ἐκεῖνα (ἐκείνα GH) μὲν vGH.

525

γὰρ φθόνον ἐγέννησε,[1] αὕτη[2] δὲ ζῆλον ἐπεσπάσατο.[3]
25 φθόνος μὲν οὖν ἐστιν ὀδύνη τῶν πρὸς τοὺς[4] πέλας
ἀγαθῶν, ζῆλος δὲ μίμησις τῶν παρ' ἄλλοις[5]
καλῶν, τοσοῦτόν τε[6] διενήνοχεν ἀλλήλων, ὥστε
τὸ μὲν φθονεῖν[7] εὐχὴν εἶναι τοῦ καὶ παρ' ἄλλῳ τι
καλὸν μὴ εἶναι, τὸ δὲ ζηλοῦν ἐπιθυμίαν τῆς τῶν
26 ἴσων κτήσεως. ἀνὴρ οὖν ἀγαθὸς οὐ μόνον
πατρίδος τε καὶ στρατιωτικοῦ πλήθους ἄριστος
ἡγεμών, ἀλλὰ καὶ τῆς περὶ αὐτὸν εἰς αἰεὶ[8] εὐδοξίας
ἀκινδύνου[9] οὐκ ἀνόητος στρατηγός.[10]

[1] ἐγέννησαν v: ἐγένησαν PGH: ἐγέννησεν Köchly von
Rohden.
[2] Köchly (without a note): ταῦτα FGH Rigaltius Schwebel
Koraes v (apparently).
[3] ἐνεσπάσατο G Rigaltius "alii codd. ut vid.": ἐνεσπάστατο
H: ἐσπάσατο RA m²: ἐσπάσαντο K: ἐπεσπάσαντο Koraes.

will; for the former excites envy, the latter causes emulation. Now envy is a pain of mind that successful men cause their neighbours, but emulation is imitation of the good qualities of others; such is the difference between them that envy is the desire that another may not have good fortune, but emulation is the desire to equal the possessions of another. A good man, then, will be not only a brave defender of his fatherland and a competent leader of an army but also for the permanent protection of his own reputation will be a sagacious strategist.

⁴ παρὰ τοῖς Koraes.
⁵ FGH: ἀλλήλοις P Rigaltius "ceteri codd. ut vid."
⁶ τοσοῦτον δέ τε vGH : τοσοῦτον δέ τοι RA m².
⁷ φθονὴν P.　　　⁸ ἀεὶ GH Köchly.
⁹ Deleted by von Rohden.
¹⁰ Subscription ὀνασάνδρου στρατηγικός F (see Introd.).

INDEX

The numbers refer to pages.

529

INDEX

INDEX

Miletus, 171
Military Preparations, work on, 47, 49, 105, 199
mines, 179, 185, 187, 219
Moon, 129
musical instruments, 411
musical intervals, 411
Mytilene, 173

Naxos, 115
needle for mats, 97
nets, 65, 191, 195
Nicocles, 115

omens, 429, 431
Onesander (sic), 207
Oreus, 125
osiers, 153

Paean, 139
palisades, 423, 505
Pallas, 125
panics, 139, 141, 143, 397
papyrus, 159, 167, 217
Parians, 147
Parium, 147
parleys, 419
party-struggles, 31, 59, 67, 69, 91, 93, 113
party-walls, 33
passports, 55
Patro, 207
pedigrees of animals, 385
Peisistratus, 41
Peloponnesian (word), 139
pent-house, 179, 181
Persian(s), 279, 303, 305
physicians, 381, 473
pilots, simile from, 479, 481
pincers, 95
pipe, stops of, 411
pitch, 183, 207
Plataeans, 33
Plots, work on, 65
poison, 205
Polybius, 201, 205
portcullis, 193, 221, 223
Poseidon, 129
Potidaea, 169, 171
priests, choice of, 375
prisoners, treatment of, 441, 489, 525
proclamations, 53, 57, 59
purification of army, 393
Pyrrhus, 201

Pytho, 147

races, torch and horse, 89
ramp, 113, 115
rams, 177, 509
reinforcements, 461
reserves, 459
rest, how the general should, 517
revolution: see party-struggles
rewards, 57
Rhodian, Temenus the, 99
Romans, 369, 371, 373
rush-mats, 97

sacrifices, 395, 429, 431, 485
sacrilege, 495
sails, 65
sambuca, 509
sandals, 157, 215
sawing through the bar, 103
Scythian(s), 249, 279
sheds, covered, 509
ship-houses, 65
ships, overhauling of, 393
shouting in battle, 471
Sicilians, 279
Sicyonians, 153
siege engines, 509
signals, 39, 45, 47, 75, 87, 101, 111, 139, 203, 205, 467
Sinope, 197
slings, 445, 449
smuggling, 149, 211
soothsayers, 53, 395, 429
spies, 113, 417
sponge, 103, 161
staff of the general, 389
stars, knowledge of the, 431, 499, 501
Stratocles, 201
sulphur, 183, 207
Sun, 129
surrendered cities, treatment of, 497
sweeps, 195
Syracuse, 61

tablet, boxwood, 163
Tarentine, 251, 291
tattooing, 171
Temenus, 99, 101
Teos, 97
thank-offerings, 485
theatre, 31, 37, 107
Thebans, 33, 35

531

INDEX